# RECENT ADVANCES ON VIDEO CODING

Edited by **Javier Del Ser**

**Recent Advances on Video Coding**
Edited by Javier Del Ser

**Published by InTech**

Janeza Trdine 9, 51000 Rijeka, Croatia



**Publishing Process Manager** Natalia Reinic

**Technical Editor** Teodora Smiljanic

**Cover Designe**r InTech Design Team

Additional hard copies can be obtained from orders@intechopen.com

Recent Advances on Video Coding, Edited by Javier Del Ser
p. cm.
ISBN 978-953-307-181-7

For EU product safety concerns:
IN TECH d.o.o., Prolaz Marije Krucifikse Kozulić 3, 51000 Rijeka, Croatia,
info@intechopen.com or visit our website at intechopen.com.

# Meet the editor

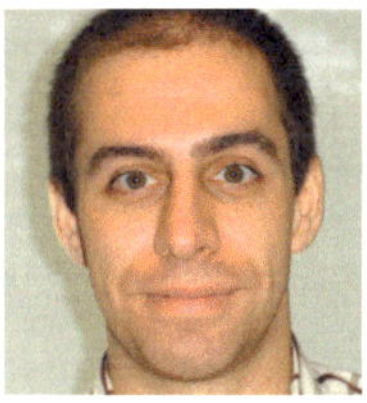

Dr. Javier (Javi) Del Ser was born in Barakaldo (Spain) in 1979. He joined the Faculty of Engineering of the University of the Basque Country (Spain) to study Electrical Engineering, obtaining his combined B.S. and M.S. degree. After finishing this degree, he became a recipient of the Fundacion de Centros Tecnologicos Inaki Goenaga doctoral grant, which allowed him to start working toward his Ph.D. degree CEIT, San Sebastian, in November 2003. In October 2006 he achieved the Ph.D. degree (cum laude) in Electrical Engineering. In addition, he was a teaching assistant at TECNUN (University of Navarra), a visiting scholar at University of Delaware (USA) and an assistant professor and researcher at the University of Mondragon, Spain. Currently he is a senior research scientist and project leader at the Telecom Unit of TECNALIA RESEARCH & INNOVATION, involved in the organization of more than 25 national and international conferences. He is a member of the IEEE Communications, Signal Processing, Computational Intelligence and Information Theory societies.

# Contents

# Preface

In the last decade, video has turned to be one of the most widely transmitted information sources, due to the extraordinary upsurge of new techniques, protocols and communication standards of increased bandwidth, computational performance, resilience and efficiency.

Disruptive technologies, standards, services and applications – as exemplified by on-demand digital video broadcasting, interactive DVB, mobile TV, Bluray® or Youtube® – have undoubtedly benefited from significant advances on aspects belonging to the whole set of OSI layers, ranging from new video semantic models and context-aware video processing, to peer-to-peer information networking and enhanced physical-layer techniques allowing for a better exploitation of the available communication resources.

As a result, this trend has given rise to a plethora of video coding standards such as H.261, H.263, ISO IEC MPEG-1, MPEG-2 and MPEG-4, which has progressively met the video quality requirements (e.g. bit rate, visual quality, error resilience, compression ratios and/or encoding delay) demanded by applications of ever-growing complexity. Research on video coding is foreseen to spread over the following years, in light of recent developments on three-dimensional and multi-view video coding.

Motivated by this flurry of activity at both industry and academia, this book aims at providing the reader with a self-contained review of the latest advances and techniques gravitating on video coding, with a strong emphasis in what relates to architectures, algorithms and implementations. In particular, the contents of this compilation are mainly focused on technical advances in the video coding procedures involved in recently coined video coding standards such as H.264/AVC or H.264/SVC. Readers may also find in this work a useful overview on how video coding can benefit from cross-disciplinary tools (e.g. combinatorial heuristics) to attain significant end-to-end performance improvements.

On this purpose, the book is divided in 5 different yet related sections. First, three introductory chapters to H.264/SVC, H.264/AVC and region of interest video coding are presented to the reader. Next, Section II concentrates on reviewing and analysing different methods for controlling the rate of video encoding schemes, whereas the third section is devoted to novel algorithms and techniques for video coding. Section IV is dedicated to the design and hardware implementation of video coding schemes. Finally, Section V concludes the book by outlining recent research on semantic video coding.

The editor would like to eagerly thank the authors for their contribution to this book, and especially the editorial assistance provided by the INTECH publishing process managers Ms. Natalia Reinic and Ms. Iva Lipovic. Last but not least, the editor's gratitude extends to the anonymous manuscript processing team for their arduous formatting work.

**Javier Del Ser**
Senior Research Scientist
TECNALIA RESEARCH & INNOVATION
48170 Zamudio,
Spain

# Part 1

## Tutorials and Review

# 1

# A Tutorial on H.264/SVC Scalable Video Coding and its Tradeoff between Quality, Coding Efficiency and Performance

Iraide Unanue[1], Iñigo Urteaga[2], Ronaldo Husemann[3], Javier Del Ser[4], Valter Roesler[5], Aitor Rodríguez[6] and Pedro Sánchez[7]
[1,2,4]*TECNALIA RESEARCH & INNOVATION, P. Tecnológico, Zamudio,*
[3,5]*UFRGS - Instituto de Informática. Av. Bento Gonçalves, Porto Alegre,*
[6,7]*IKUSI-Ángel Iglesias, S. A., Paseo Miramón, Donostia-San Sebastian*
[1,2,4,6,7]*Spain*
[3,5]*Brazil*

## 1. Introduction

The evolution of digital video technology and the continuous improvements in communication infrastructure is propelling a great number of interactive multimedia applications, such as real-time video conference, web video streaming and mobile TV, among others. The new possibilities on interactive video usage have created an exigent market of consumers, which demands the best video quality wherever they are and whatever their network support is (Schwarz et al., 2006). On this purpose, the transmitted video must match the receiver's characteristics such as the required bit rate, resolution and frame rate, thus aiming to provide the best quality subject to receiver's and network's limitations. Besides, the same link is often used to transmit to either restricted devices such as small cell phones, or to high-performance equipments, e.g. HDTV workstations. In addition, the stream should adapt to wireless lossy networks (Ohm, 2005). Based on this reasoning, these heterogeneous and non-deterministic networks represent a great problem for traditional video encoders which do not allow for on-the-fly video streaming adaptation.

To circumvent this drawback, the concept of scalability for video coding has been lately proposed as an emergent solution for supporting, in a given network, endpoints with distinct video processing capabilities. The principle of a scalable video encoder is to break the conventional single-stream video in a multi-stream flow, composed by distinct and complementary components, often referred to as *layers* (Huang et al., 2007). Figure 1 illustrates this concept by depicting a transmitter encoding the input video sequence into three complementary layers. Therefore, receivers can select and decode different number of layers – each corresponding to distinct video characteristics – in accordance with the processing constraints of both the network and the device itself.

The layered structure of any scalable video content can be defined as the combination of a base layer and several additional enhancement layers. The base layer corresponds to the lowest supported video performance, whereas the enhancement layers allow for the refinement of

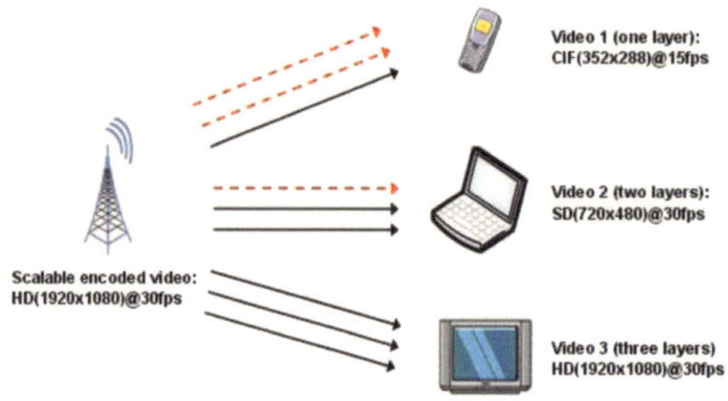


Fig. 1. Adaptation in scalable video encoding.

the aforementioned base layer. The adaptation is based on a combination within the set of selected strategies for the spatial, temporal and quality scalability (Ohm, 2005).
In the last years, several specific scalable video profiles have been included in video codecs such as MPEG-2 (*MPEG-2 Video*, 2000), H.263 (*H.263 ITU-T Rec.*, 2000) and MPEG-4 Visual (*MPEG-4 Visual*, 2004). However, all these solutions present a reduced coding efficiency when compared with non-scalable video profiles (Wien, Schwarz & Oelbaum, 2007). As a consequence, scalable profiles have been scarcely utilized in real applications, whereas widespread solutions have been strictly limited to non-scalable single-layer coding schemes.
In October 2007, the scalable extension of the H.264 codec, also known as H.264/SVC (Scalable Video Coding) (*H.264/SVC*, 2010), was jointly standardized by ITU-T VCEG and ISO MPEG as an amendment of the H.264/AVC (Advanced Video Coding) standard. Among several innovative features, H.264/SVC combines temporal, spatial and quality scalabilities into a single multi-layer stream (Rieckl, 2008).
To exemplify the temporal scalability, Figure 2(a) presents a simple scenario where the base layer consists of one subgroup of frames and the enhancement layer of another. A hypothetical receiver in a slow-bandwidth network would receive only the base layer, hence producing a jerkier video (15 frames per second, hereafter labeled as *fps*) than the other. On the contrary, the second receiver (that would benefit from a network with higher bandwidth) would be able to process and combine both layers, thus yielding a full-frame-rate (30 fps) video and ultimately a smoother video reproduction. Thereafter, Figure 2(b) illustrates an example of spatial scalability, where the inclusion of enhancement layers increases the resolution of the decoded video sample. As shown, the more layers are made available to the receiver, the higher the resolution of the decoded video is. Finally, Figure 2(c) show the concept of quality scalability, where the enhancement layers improve the SNR quality of the received video stream. Once again, the more layers the receiver acquires, the better the user's quality of experience is.
On top of the benefits of the above introduced scalabilities, there are several other advantages furnished by H.264/SVC. One of such remarkable features of H.264/SVC is the support for video bit rate adaptation at NAL (Network Application Layer) packet level, which significantly increases the flexibility of the video encoder. Alternative scalable solutions, however, only support adaptation at the level of slices or entire frames (Huang et al., 2007). Furthermore, H.264/SVC improves the compression efficiency by incorporating an enhanced and innovative mechanism for inter-layer estimation, called ILP (Inter-Layer Prediction). ILP reuses inter-layer motion vectors, intra texture and residue information among subsequent layers (Husemann et al., 2009).

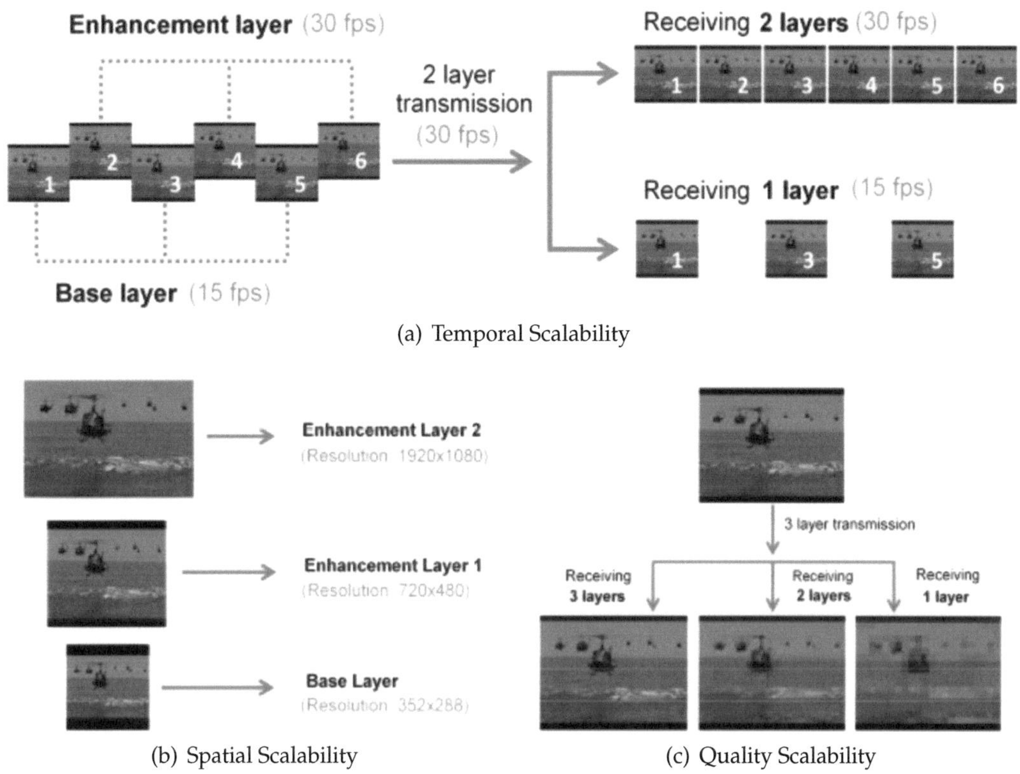


Fig. 2. Illustrative example of scalability approaches in H.264/SVC.

As a consequence of all these aspects, the H.264/SVC standard is currently considered the state-of-the-art of scalable video codecs. As opposed to prior video codecs, H.264/SVC has been designed as a flexible and powerful scalable video codec, which provides – for a given quality level – similar compression ratios at a lower decoding complexity with respect to its non-scalable single-layer counterparts. So as to corroborate this design principle, let us briefly compare H.264/SVC to non-scalable profiles of previous codecs, namely, MPEG-4 Visual (*MPEG-4 Visual*, 2004), H.263 (*H.263 ITU-T Rec.*, 2000) and H.264/AVC (*H.264/AVC*, 2010). Codec performance has been analyzed in terms of both compression efficiency and video quality (focusing on the Peak Signal-to-Noise Ratio PSNR of the luminance component). In this analysis, three different video sequences (further details of these video sequences are included in Section 3) have been encoded, based on equivalent configurations and appropriate bit rates for each one, with the following implementations of the aforementioned codecs: H.263 (*Ffmpeg project*, 2010), MPEG-4 Visual (*Ffmpeg project*, 2010) and H.264/AVC (*JVT reference software*, 2010).

As shown in Figure 3(a), the real encoded file size is different for each codec, even if the same theoretical encoding bit rate has been set. The reason for this dissimilarity lies on the performance of the tested codec implementations, which loosely adjust the encoding process to the specified bit rate. From both Figures 3(a) and 3(b), it is clear that H.264/SVC and H.264/AVC are those codecs generating the lowest file size while achieving similar quality (e.g. 36.61 dB by H.264/AVC and 36.41 dB by H.264/SVC for the CREW video

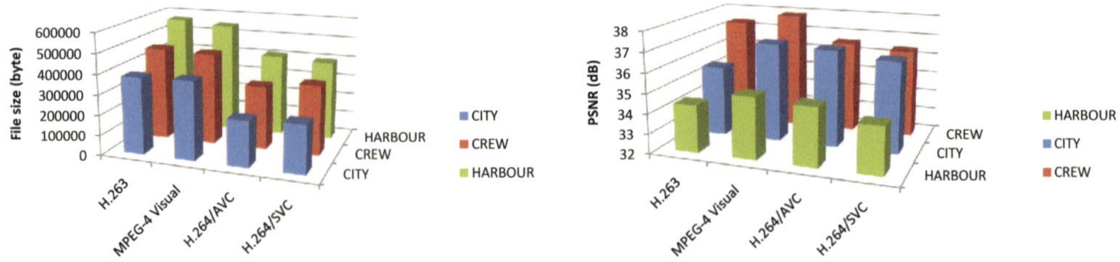


(a) File size

(b) Average PSNR of the Y component

Fig. 3. Performance of different codecs over several video sequences.

sequence). Based on these simulations, it is concluded that H.264/SVC outperforms previous non-scalable approaches, by supporting three types of scalabilities at a high coding efficiency. These results not only evaluate the theoretical behavior of each analyzed codec, but also elucidate the outstanding performance of H.264/SVC with respect to other coding approaches when applied on a given video sample.

In this line of research, this chapter delves into the roots of H.264/SVC by analyzing, through practical experiments, its tradeoff between quality, coding efficiency and performance. First, Section 2 introduces the reader to the details of the H.264/SVC standard by thoroughly describing the functional structure of a H.264/SVC encoder and its supported scalabilities. Next, several applied experiments are provided in Section 3 in order to evaluate the real requirements of a practical H.264/SVC video coding solution. These experiments have all been performed using the official H.264/SVC reference implementation: the JSVM (Joint Scalable Video Model) software (*JSVM reference software*, 2010). Obviously, the scalable nature of this new video coding standard requires a rigorous analysis of its temporal, spatial and quality processing capabilities. Consequently, three scenarios of experiments have been defined to specifically address each type of scalability:

- First, Subsection 3.1 presents the scenario utilized for evaluating the temporal scalability, where the effects of the GOP (Group of Pictures) size parameter and the frame structure are analyzed on practical H.264/SVC encoding procedures. Since the arrangement of the frames within a GOP impacts directly on the performance of the video codec, it is deemed essential to evaluate the advantages and disadvantages of different GOP sizes and structures in the overall encoding and decoding process (Wien, Schwarz & Oelbaum, 2007).
- A second scenario is next included in Subsection 3.2 aimed at evaluating the spatial scalability of H.264/SVC. This subsection analyzes the performance of both video encoder and decoder, emphasizing on distinct relations between screen resolutions of consecutive video layers. Two main algorithms are supported by H.264/SVC: the traditional dyadic solution (only when a resolution ratio of 2:1 among consecutive layer is used) or non-dyadic solution (when any other resolution ratio is possible).
- Subsection 3.3, which comprises the third scenario, analyzes the quality scalability of the H.264/SVC over different configurations. First, the fidelity of the H.264/SVC codec is examined by focusing on the influence of the quantization parameter and the relationship between quality enhancement layers. Besides, the evaluation of the coding efficiency of the H.264/SVC prediction structure between quality layers is also covered. This subsection

concludes by presenting a practical comparison between coarse and medium quality granularity.

Subsequently in Subsection 3.4, other equally-influential features of this scalable codec are scrutinized. On one hand, this final set of experiments investigate the complexity load rendered by different motion-search algorithms and related configurations on practical video encoding procedures. Particularly, the influence in the prediction module of relevant parameters such as the search-window size and the block-search algorithm is evaluated. On the other hand, the benefits of applying distinct deblocking filter types in the encoding and decoding process is examined. Deblocking filters are applied to block-coding based techniques to blocks within slices, looking for the prediction performance improvement by smoothing potentially sharp edges formed between macroblocks (Marpe et al., 2006). Finally, this subsection concludes with the evaluation of the Motion-Compensated Temporal pre-processing Filter (MCTF) included in the H.264/SVC standard.

Based on all the results presented through the chapter, optimized H.264/SVC configurations are suggested in Section 4. These configurations are specifically designed to improve either the efficiency of the encoder or the encoded video quality, which yield significant gains when compared to conventional H.264/SVC solutions. Finally, Section 5 brings up our final considerations.

## 2. Overview of H.264/SVC

The sophisticated architecture of the H.264/SVC standard is particularly designed to increase the codec capabilities while offering a flexible encoder solution that supports three different scalabilities: temporal, spatial and SNR quality (Wien, Cazoulat, Graffunder, Hutter & Amon, 2007). Figure 4 illustrates the structure of a H.264/SVC encoder for a basic two-spatial-layer scalable configuration.

In H.264/SVC, each spatial dependency layer requires its own prediction module in order to perform both motion-compensated prediction and intra prediction within the layer. Besides, there is a SNR refinement module that provides the necessary mechanisms for quality scalability within each layer. The dependency between subsequent spatial layers is managed by the inter-layer prediction module, which can support reusing of motion vectors, intra texture or residual signals from inferior layers so as to improve compression efficiency. Finally, the scalable H.264/SVC bitstream is merged by the so-called multiplex, where different temporal, spatial and SNR levels are simultaneously integrated into a single scalable bitstream.

The following subsections present each scalability type individually, describing their features according to the standardized specifications of the H.264/SVC video codec.

### 2.1 Temporal scalability

The term "temporal scalability" refers to the ability to represent video content with different frame rates by as many bitstream subsets as needed (Figure 2(a)). Encoded video streams can be composed by three distinct type of frames: I (intra), P (predictive) or B (Bi-predictive). I frames only explore the spatial coding within the picture, i.e. compression techniques are applied to information contained only inside the current picture, not using references to any other picture. On the contrary, both P and B frames do have interrelation with different pictures, as they explore directly the dependencies between them. While in P frames inter-picture predictive coding is performed based on (at least) one preceding reference

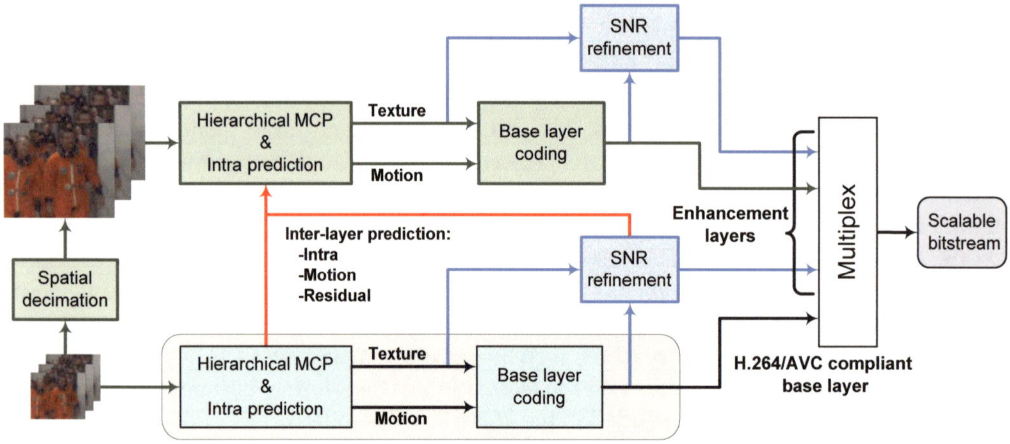


Fig. 4. Block diagram of a H.264/SVC encoder for two spatial layers.

picture, B frames consist of a combination of inter-picture bi-predictive coding (i.e. samples of both previous and posterior reference pictures are considered for the prediction). In addition, the H.264 standard family requires the first frame to be an Instantaneous Decoding Refresh (IDR) access unit, which corresponds to the union of one I frame with several critical non-data related information (e.g. the set of coding parameters). Generally speaking, the GOP structure specifies the arrangement of those frames within an encoded video sequence.

Certainly, the singular dependency and predictive characteristics of each frame type imply divergent coded video stream features. In previous scalable standards (e.g. MPEG-2, H.263 and MPEG-4 Visual), the temporal scalability was basically performed by segmenting layers according to different frame types. For example, a video composed by a traditional *"IBBP"* format (one I frame followed by two B frames and one P frame) could be used to build three temporal layers: base layer ($L_0$) with I frames, first enhancement layer ($L_1$) with P frames and the second enhancement layer ($L_2$) with B frames. This dyadic approach (2:1 decomposition format) has been proven to be functional, although it provides limited bandwidth flexibility (i.e. the total bit rate required by I frames is significantly larger than that of P and B frames (Rieckl, 2008)). By contrast, in H.264/SVC the basis of temporal scalability is found on the GOP structure, since it divides each frame into distinct scalability layers (by jointly combining I, P and B frame types). As for the H.264/SVC codec, the GOP definition can be rephrased as the arrangement of the coded bitstream's frames between two successive pictures of the temporal base layer (Schwarz et al., 2007). It is important to recall that the frames of the temporal base layer do not necessarily need to be an I frame. Actually, only the first picture of a video stream is strictly forced to be coded as an I frame and to be included in the initial IDR access unit.

In order to increase the flexibility of the codec, the H.264/SVC standard defines a distinct structure for temporal prediction, where reference frames for each video sequence are reorganized in a hierarchical tree scheme. This tree scheme improves the distribution of information between consecutive frames and allows for both a dyadic and a non-dyadic temporal scalability. Figure 5(a) exemplifies this hierarchical temporal decomposition for a 2:1 frame rate relation in a four-layer encoded video. In this example, the base layer $L_0$, which is constituted by I or P frames, permits to reconstruct one picture per GOP. The first enhancement layer $L_1$, usually composed by B frames, extracts one additional picture per

GOP in addition to that of $L_0$. The second enhancement layer $L_2$, which is comprised by B frames, further extracts two additional pictures per GOP jointly with those of previous layers. Finally, the third enhancement layer $L_3$ allows recovering eight pictures.

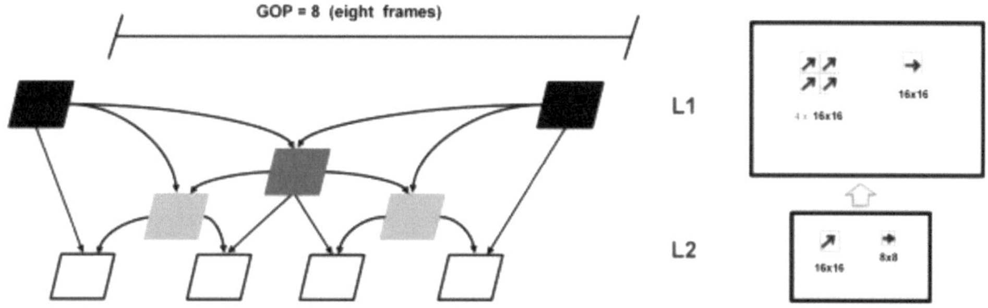


(a) H.264/SVC hierarchical tree structure in a four-layer temporal scalability example.

(b) Motion vector scaling in dyadic spatial scalability.

Fig. 5. Graphical support examples for H.264/SVC temporal and spatial scalabilities.

On top of this, H.264/SVC suggests the inclusion of a pre-processing filter before the motion prediction module, which can improve the data information distribution and eliminate redundancies between consecutive layers. The proposed algorithm is referenced as MCTF. This additional filter, when applied over the original data, performs motion aligned decomposition processing. As a result, the correlation between filtered layers is improved, while the overall complexity of the encoder is increased (Schafer et al., 2005).

### 2.2 Spatial scalability

The spatial scalability is based on representing, through a layered structure, videos with distinct resolutions, i.e. each enhancement layer is responsible for improving the resolution of lower layers (as in Figure 2(b)). The most common configuration (i.e. dyadic) adopts the 2:1 relation between neighbor layers, although H.264/SVC also contemplates non-dyadic ratios (Segall & Sullivan, 2007). This last solution demands the inclusion of a new class of algorithm called Extended Spatial Scalability (ESS) (Huang et al., 2007).

The approaches of previous scalable encoders basically consist of reusing motion prediction information from lower layers in order to reduce the global stream size. Unfortunately, the image quality obtained by this methodology is quite limited. On the contrary, and in order to improve its efficiency, the H.264/SVC encoder introduces a more flexible and complex prediction module called Inter-Layer Prediction (ILP). The main goal of the ILP module is to increase the amount of reused data in the prediction from inferior layers, so that the reduction of redundancies increases the overall efficiency. To this end, three prediction techniques are supported by the ILP module:

- **Inter-Layer Motion Prediction:** the motion vectors from lower layers can be used by superior enhancement layers. In some cases, the motion vectors and their attached information must be rescaled (see Figure 5(b)) so as to adjust the values to the correct equivalents in higher layers (Husemann et al., 2009).
- **Inter-Layer Intra Texture Prediction:** H.264/SVC supports texture prediction for internal blocks within the same reference layer (intra). The intra block predicted in the reference layer can be used for other blocks in superior layers. This module up-samples the

resolution of inferior layer's texture to superior layer resolutions, subsequently calculating the difference between them.

- **Inter-Layer Residual Prediction:** as a consequence of several coding process observations, it has been identified that when two consecutive layers have similar motion information, the inter-layer residues register high correlation. Based on this, in H.264/SVC the inter-layer residual prediction method can be used after the motion compensation process to explore redundancies in the spatial residual domain.

Supplementarily, the H.264/SVC standard supports any resolution, cropping and dimensional aspect relation between two consecutive layers. For instance, a certain layer may use SD resolution (4:3 aspect), while the next layer is characterized by HD resolution (16:9 aspect) (Schafer et al., 2005). The most flexible solution, which does not use a dyadic relation, is called ESS (Extended Spatial Scalability), where any relation between consecutive layers is supported.

### 2.3 SNR scalability

The SNR scalability (or quality scalability) empowers transporting complementary data in different layers in order to produce videos with distinct quality levels. In H.264/SVC, SNR scalability is implemented in the frequency domain (i.e. it is performed over the internal transform module). This scalability type basically hinges on adopting distinct quantization parameters for each layer. The H.264/SVC standard supports three distinct SNR scalability modes (Rieckl, 2008):

- **Coarse Grain Scalability (CGS):** in this strategy (Figure 6(a)), each layer has an independent prediction procedure (all references have the same quality level) in a similar fashion to the SNR scalability of MPEG-2. In fact, the CGS strategy can be regarded as a special case of spatial scalability when consecutive layers have the same resolution (Huang et al., 2007).
- **Medium Grain Scalability (MGS):** the MGS approach (Figure 6(b)) increases efficiency by using a more flexible prediction module, where both types of layer (base and enhancement) can be referenced. However this strategy can induce a drifting effect (i.e. it can introduce a synchronism offset between the encoder and the decoder) if only the base layer is received. To solve this issue, the MGS specification proposes the use of periodic key pictures, which immediately resynchronizes the prediction module.
- **Fine Grain Scalability (FGS):** this version (Figure 6(c)) of the SNR scalability aims at providing a continuous adaptation of the output bit rate in relation to the real network bandwidth. FGS employs an advanced bit-plane technique where different layers are responsible for transporting distinct subsets of bits corresponding to each data information. The scheme allows for data truncation at any arbitrary point in order to support the progressive refinement of transform coefficients. In this type of scalability, only the base layer casts motion prediction techniques.

As a means to understand each SNR scalability granularity mode of H.264/SVC, the internal correlation between layers for a two-layer video stream can be observed in Figure 6. Note that the black frames in Figure 6(b) represent key pictures with periodicity of 4 pictures.

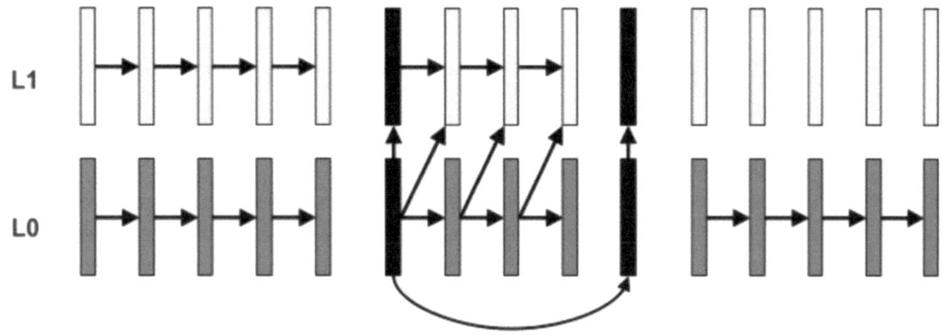


(a) CGS (b) MGS (c) FGS

Fig. 6. H.264/SVC SNR scalability granularity mode for a two-layer example.

## 3. Performance experiments

Heretofore this tutorial has introduced the H.264/SVC video coding standard and its pivotal underlying concepts. This section delves into the description of several experiments evaluating the requirements of a practical H.264/SVC solution. As a consequence of the standardization process of H.264, the different entities involved in it (including the industry members, the ITU-T body and MPEG) formed the so-called Joint Video Team (JVT) which, among various duties, has developed the official H.264/SVC reference code. This reference implementation of the codec, coined as JSVM, undergoes continuous developments so as to track the numerous features of this standard. For the purpose of the experiments later detailed, JSVM version 9.19.4 (*JSVM reference software*, 2010) has been used, which even if not necessarily efficient or optimized, guarantees full compliance with the standard. Since the goal of this section is to provide an overview of the practical characteristics of this scalable codec, it is considered mandatory to tackle every tests from a generic video-sample-agnostic approach. Consequently, experiments have been repeated with different video sequences, thus the performance of the codecs is evaluated over video samples of diverse characteristics: miscellaneous motion patterns, various spatial complexities, shapes, etc.

Specifically, the tested video samples are the conventional CREW, CITY and HARBOUR sequences (*YUV video repository*, 2010). These video sequences cover a wide range of dynamism scales: CREW presents a spatial craft crew walking quickly (i.e. constant object movement); CITY is a 360-degree view of a skyscraper recorded by a slow-motion camera (slow panning motion); finally, HARBOUR shows the filming from a fixed camera in a sailboat race (high dynamism). In addition to the different attributes of each video sequence, diverse resolutions and frame rates have been further considered: 176x144 pixels (QCIF) at 15 fps, 352x288 pixels (CIF) at 30 fps and 704x576 pixels (4CIF) at 60 fps.

For the performance evaluation of the H.264/SVC codec, the following metrics have been used for all the experiments (unless specifically indicated): encoding complexity (measured as the time in seconds required to encode a 10-second video sample), encoding efficiency (defined as the size of the encoded video sequence), decoding complexity (as the number of seconds to decode a 10-second encoded video sequence) and, finally, the objective video-quality resulting from the encoding and decoding process (i.e. the PSNR value of the luma component of the video sequence). The description, results and conclusions of the different experiments provided in the following sections permit to evaluate the key features of H.264/SVC.

### 3.1 Temporal scalability

As explained in Section 2.1, the frame structure imposed on the GOP (Group of Pictures) is essential not only for the temporal scalability offered by this scalable codec, but also for the features of the resulting video stream. In fact, changing the GOP size directly affects the number of temporal layers contained in the encoded bitstream. For example, in a temporal dyadic approach, a video stream encoded with GOP size equal to 16 generates the following five temporal layers: $T_0$ (1 frame per GOP), $T_1$ (2 frames per GOP), $T_2$ (4 frames per GOP), $T_3$ (8 frames per GOP) and $T_4$ (16 frames per GOP). However, encoding the same video with GOP size equal to 8 renders four temporal layers: $T_0$ (1 frame per GOP), $T_1$ (2 frames per GOP), $T_2$ (4 frames per GOP) and $T_3$ (8 frames per GOP). Finally, defining a GOP size of 4 produces only three temporal layers: $T_0$, $T_1$ and $T_2$. Therefore, it may be concluded that the flexibility of a temporal scalable solution (in terms of the number of layers) is directly proportional to the selected GOP size. Nevertheless, increasing the GOP size does have some implicit collateral effects: it influences the overall encoding efficiency, as it imposes a variation in the number of I, P and B frames per GOP.

In order to prove this effect, several experiments have been performed by changing the GOP size parameter while the output bit rate is kept constant. Figure 7 show the obtained results in terms of the quality for the upper and base layer.

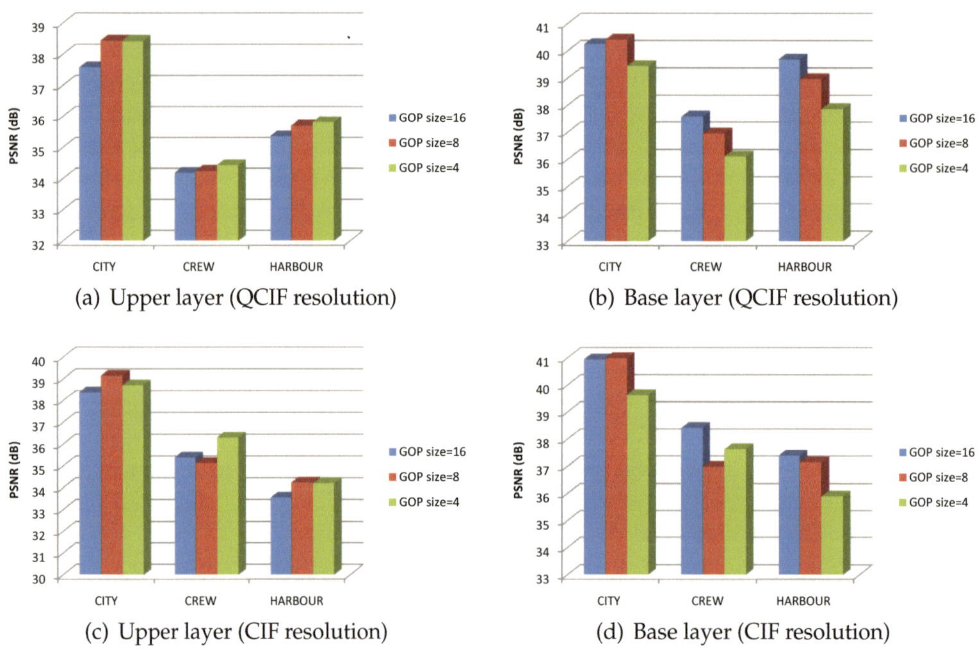


(a) Upper layer (QCIF resolution)

(b) Base layer (QCIF resolution)

(c) Upper layer (CIF resolution)

(d) Base layer (CIF resolution)

Fig. 7. Impact of the GOP size on the H.264/SVC quality for different video sequences.

By taking a closer look at Figures 7(a) and 7(c) the reader may notice that there is no significant quality difference in the final recovered video (i.e. upper layer) when increasing the GOP size. Nevertheless, the behavior of the quality of the base layer lightly varies depending

on both the particularly used video samples and the selected resolutions, as can be seen in Figures 7(b) and 7(d). An increment of the GOP size entails an increment of the quality of the base layer for CREW-QCIF, HARBOUR-QCIF and HARBOUR-CIF video sequences whereas, for instance, such a direct relation in the CREW-CIF video sample is not so evident. This variability in the quality performance can be, in part, induced by the particularities of the scalable prediction module (H.264/SVC ILP). Theoretically speaking, a GOP size increment should imply a quality improvement, as the number of B frames rises while contributing to an efficient encoding.
On the contrary, the complexity of the encoder is clearly influenced by the GOP size parameter, i.e. the increase in the number of layers (and therefore B frames) implies higher requirements for the encoder prediction module. Such an encoding complexity increase (measured in terms of the encoding execution time) is depicted in Figure 8. For instance, an increment around 20% in encoding time is obtained when comparing GOP sizes of 4 and 16 for the CITY video sequence at QCIF resolution.

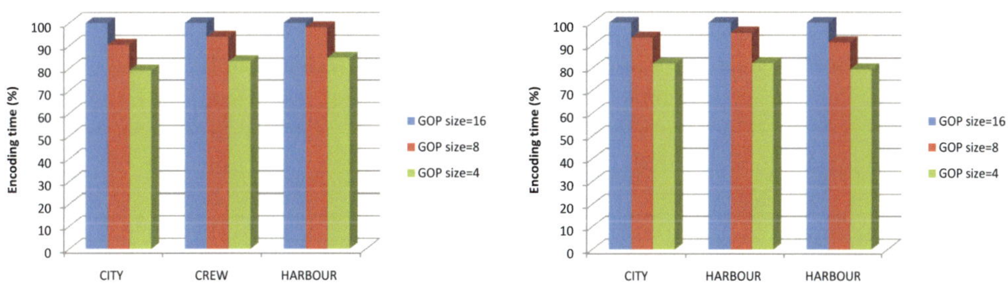


(a) QCIF resolution (b) CIF resolution

Fig. 8. GOP size impact in H.264/SVC encoding time for different video sequences.

It is also interesting to analyze the advantages of using higher GOP sizes for the temporal scalability, as an increment in the GOP size augmentates the number of available temporal layers and ultimately, enhances the flexibility of the video stream. As aforementioned in Section 2.1, three frames types are generally considered to encode a video picture: I, P and B frames. The difference between those frame types mainly resides on the references used by them for the predictive coding. Certainly, the singular dependency and predictive characteristics of each frame type lead to divergent encoded video stream features. Furthermore, the arrangement of the frames within a GOP directly impacts on the codec performance as well. In this context, Figure 9 shows how different GOP structures influences the encoding and decoding complexity, while maintaining a similar video quality. The evaluated GOP structures are:

- ***B***: an initial P frame and 15 consecutive B frames form the GOP structure.
- ***B_I***: the GOP is composed by an initial I frame and 15 consecutive B frames.
- ***B_IDR***: the GOP arrangement corresponds to an initial IDR frame, followed by 15 B frames.
- ***NoB***: only P frames (16) are used in the whole GOP.
- ***NoB_I***: the GOP is composed by an initial I frame, followed by 15 P frames.
- ***NoB_IDR***: an initial IDR frame followed by 15 P frames form the GOP structure.

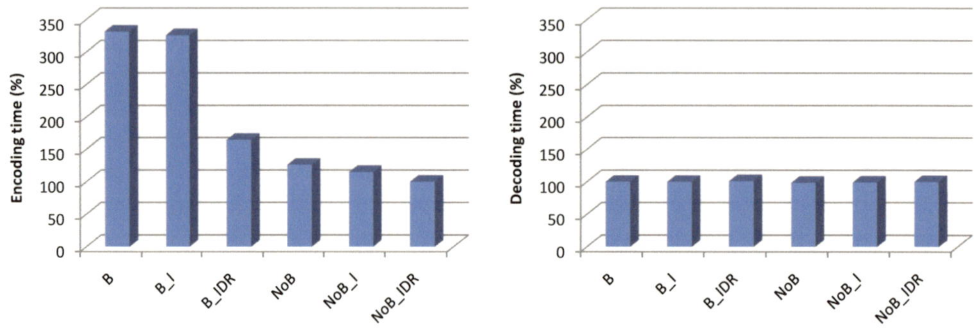


(a) Encoding time (b) Decoding time

Fig. 9. GOP's structure impact in H.264/SVC codec for the HARBOUR video sequence.

This experiment clearly stresses on the influence of B frames within a GOP, since they impose a significant coding complexity increase. However, their inclusion does not provide any comparable advantage, as quality remains almost equal – differences of less than 0.5 dB were obtained in performed experiments – at the cost of a small bit rate variation. Similar results have been observed for other experiments based on different GOP sizes and video sequences, which are not included here for the sake of space. Regarding the influence of I and IDR pictures, further tests indicate that the quality, complexity and bit rate behaviors are similar for both type of frames. Figure 10 supports this claim for different I and IDR inclusion periods (a stream encoded only with P frames has been employed as a reference).

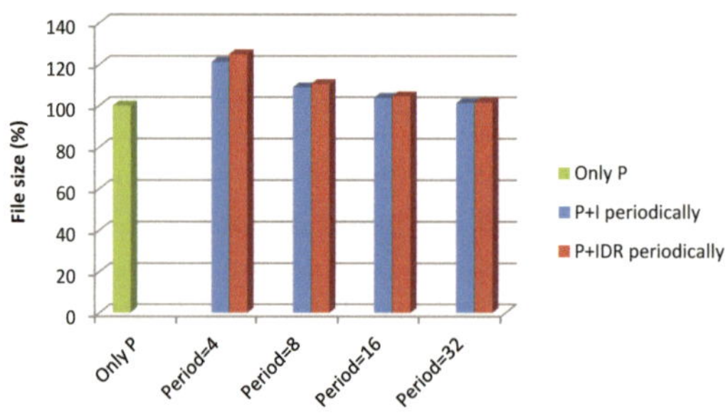


Fig. 10. GOP structure's (I Vs IDR) impact in H.264/SVC codec.

Along with the implications on video bit rate, the determination of the intra-frame frequency also plays an important role when dealing with packet losses in real video streaming applications, which may be due to different phenomena, e.g. congestion, wireless communication losses or handovers (Unanue et al., 2009). As exemplified in Figure 11, video-quality recovery is directly influenced by the GOP structure and particularly, by the reception of an intra-type frame. Due to the intrinsic features of intra-type frames, the sooner an intra-type frame is received, the sooner the video quality is recovered. Based on this rationale and referring to the plotted example, the video quality recovery for H.264/SVC sequences including intra-type frames is much faster (maroon line in Figure 11) than that corresponding to streams without intra-type frames (green line in Figure 11). It is important to remark that with the reception of an intra-type frame, the quality of the received video is almost immediately recovered, whereas the intrinsic dependencies of P and B frames involve a slower quality recovery when facing losses. In other words, due to the use of a predictive encoding structure, a frame loss not only affects the current GOP, but may have impact in preceding and subsequent GOPs as well.

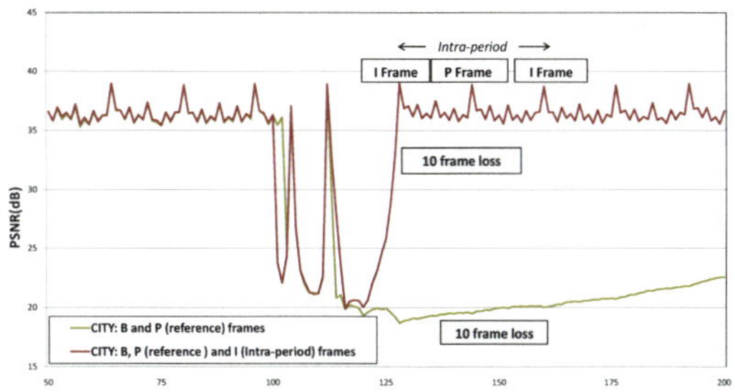


Fig. 11. Frame loss impact on H.264/SVC streams subject to different GOP structures.

Nevertheless, and besides the above proven fact that intra-frames provide faster quality recovery, the speed of video sequence's quality recovery not only depends on the GOP structure, but also on the particular video sequence characteristics. That is, for almost similar frame sequences (e.g. semi-static motion in CITY sequence), the coded P and B frames provide little information with respect to each other. Therefore, in those kinds of motion sequences, it is difficult to recover from the loss of previous frames unless intra-frames are included (Unanue et al., 2009). Consequently, it is deemed crucial to carefully determine the frequency of these type of frames – whether they are I or IDR – which poses a tradeoff between file size and recovery speed: a higher inclusion frequency accelerates the video-quality recovery in lossy environments at a penalty in file size. In summary, granting priority to the bit rate of the stream or to the recovery speed of the video quality is a decision to be taken as a function of the considered scenario. Similarly, the selection between I and IDR frames (or any combination of both) should be also left open to each particular application.

### 3.2 Spatial scalability

With spatial scalability, different layers within the same encoded video stream contain distinct video resolutions. To support this scalability, motion, texture and residual information from previous layers (after rescaling to the new resolution) can be reused at the H.264/SVC encoder. When the relation between layers is 2:1 (i.e. dyadic case), the rescaling algorithm in a H.264/SVC encoder is rather simple, since in this case the operation to rescale a layer reduces to a simple bit-shift operation. However, H.264/SVC also supports any other resolution ratio between subsequent layers (i.e. non-dyadic cases), for which more complex mathematical operations are necessitated.

In order to determine the real requirements of H.264/SVC's spatial scalability encoding, several practical experiments have been performed varying the resolution ratios between layers. In the first case, a QCIF resolution base layer and a CIF resolution enhancement layer (dyadic scenario) were used. In the second experiment, the enhancement layer is adjusted to 240x112 pixels, while keeping the same base layer (non-dyadic scenario). Please note that in order to simplify the comparison, the output bit rate has been adjusted to the same value in both cases.

On one hand, Figure 12(a) depicts the quality comparison for both experiments, where a slightly higher quality for the dyadic scenario can be observed. This phenomenon is explained by noticing that a 2:1 relation does not produce any rescaling distortion, which does not hold

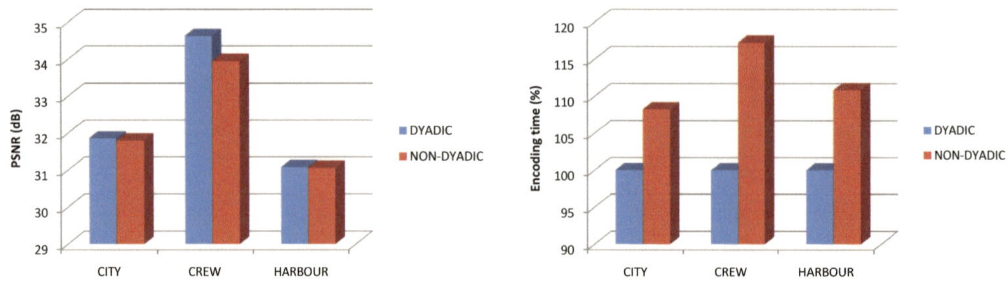


(a) Quality (PSNR) (b) Encoding time

Fig. 12. Spatial scalability evaluation: dyadic and non-dyadic solutions.

for non-integer resolution ratios. On the other hand, when addressing non-dyadic cases the encoder complexity increases significantly, as shown in Figure 12(b). In other words, dyadic configurations can be processed with significant lower encoding time than the non-dyadic ones, e.g. the non-dyadic approach increases the encoding load up to approximately 18% for the CREW video sequence.

### 3.3 SNR scalability

The SNR scalability implicates several techniques in order to create layers of different quality levels within the same encoded bitstream. In this regard, JSVM provides several options to specify the desired quality not only for each particular layer, but also for the overall encoded stream. First, this subsection focuses on the so-called Quantization Parameter (QP), which is directly related to the quantization process of the original video sequence. Then, the specific properties of two of the distinct SNR scalability modes of H.264/SVC are analyzed, namely, CGS and MGS. The FGS mode has not been included in these experiments since, as opposed to CGS and MGS, it does not allow personal configuration of relevant parameters, such as the number of layers or the value of quantization step per layer.

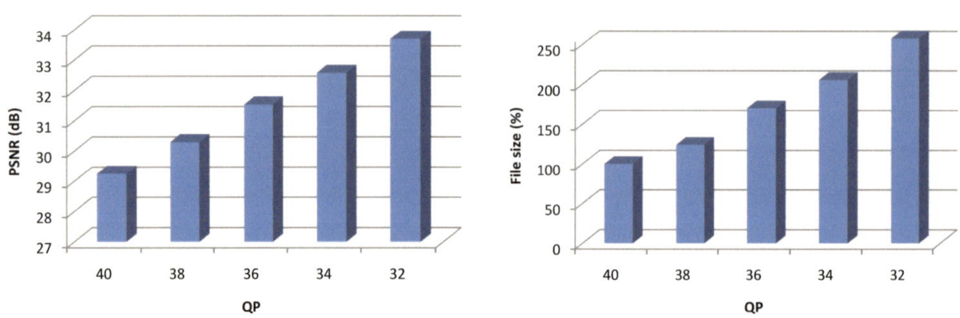


(a) Quality (PSNR) (b) File size

Fig. 13. Evaluation of the SNR scalability: impact of the quantization parameter QP.

In general lower quantization parameter values lead to both better PSNR level and higher bit rate for the encoded video stream. However, during the encoding process, the QP value is not maintained exactly equal for all the frames within the given stream, i.e. it varies slightly depending on the position of each frame within the GOP. The appropriate QP value for each particular scenario or multimedia application should be selected by not only taking into account the desired quality, but also by analyzing the practical impact of the QP on the file size of the encoded bitstream. On one hand, Figure 13 attests the direct relationship between the selected quantization parameter and the resulting video quality and file size. On the other hand, Figure 14 represents the visual quality incurred when assigning different QP values to the encoding process of the CREW video sample.

QP=40 QP=36 QP=32

Fig. 14. Quality for different QP-value based H.264/SVC captured pictures (QCIF resolution).

Once the influence of the QP parameter has been explored, a deeper analysis is performed by evaluating the quality scalability intrinsically provided by H.264/SVC. In the following test two SNR scalable layers are incorporated into the encoded stream (lower quality for the inferior layer, $QP_L$, and better quality for the upper layer, $QP_U$), since with JSVM an independent QP value can be assigned to each scalable layer. One of the basics of H.264/SVC is the ability to benefit from its inter-layer prediction mechanisms so as to perform efficient scalable encoding. However, there is a close dependency between the selected quality scalabilities and the inter-layer prediction into the resulting video stream, as the experiment results included in Figure 15 clearly show.

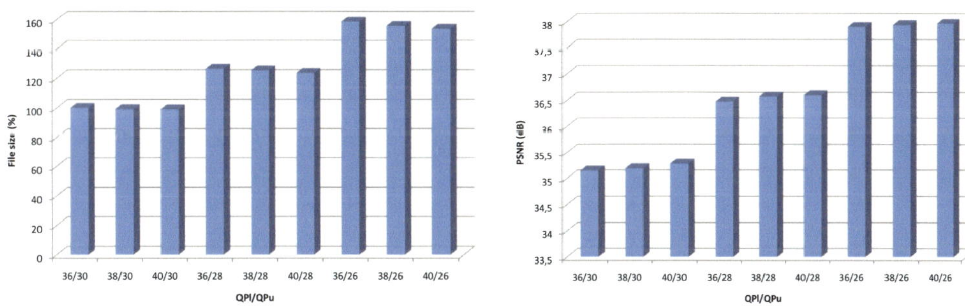


(a) Quality (PSNR) (b) File size

Fig. 15. Evaluation of the dependency between the assigned QP to each SNR scalable layer and the overall quality.

In this example, the quality obtained in the upper layers (defined by $QP_U$) certainly depends on the quality of the lower layers as specified by $QP_L$. Referring to Figure 15(a), even if the same $QP_U$ is set, the resulting video quality is slightly different based on the quality of the underlying lower layer. The reason for this phenomenon gravitates on the inter-layer prediction mechanism: since the enhancement layers progressively refine the quality of lower layers, even when the same $QP_U$ is used, the PSNR achieved by the content roughly depends on the quality of lower layers, which is established by the $QP_L$ parameter.

Additional experiments have been carried out to analyze the specific characteristics of H.264/SVC's distinct SNR scalability modes: CGS and MGS. For both experiments, the same configuration for the quantization parameter has been used: $QP_L$=39 for the base layer, and $QP_U$=33 for the enhancement layer. Besides, and in order to simplify the analysis, both modes have been forced to produce the same output bit rate. The results for these experiments are presented in Figure 16, both for video quality and encoding performance metrics. For all evaluated video sequences, the MGS approach produces better quality results, as evidenced in figures 16(a) and 16(b). This interesting result is due to the improved flexibility of MGS's internal prediction algorithm (as more possible references are supported), which contributes to a reduction of matching errors (i.e. residual data). On the other hand, both scalability modes present similar results in terms of codec's performance (encoding execution time).

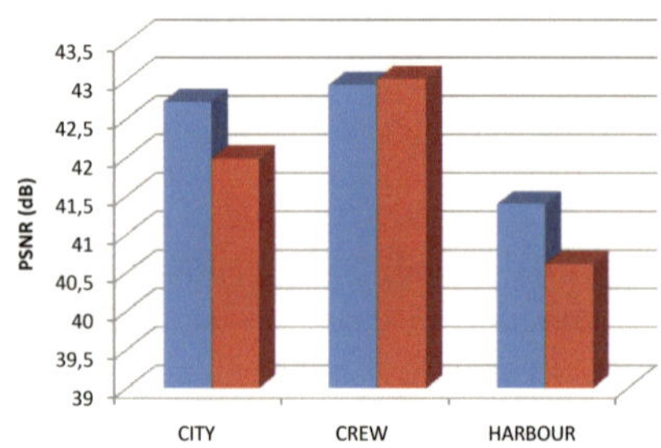


(a) PSNR (QCIF resolution)

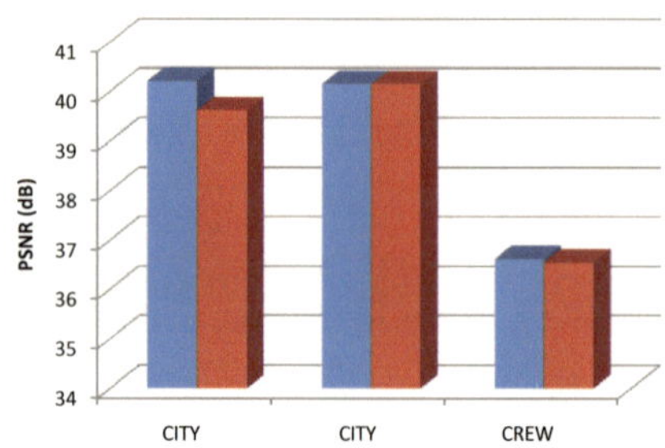


(b) PSNR (CIF resolution)

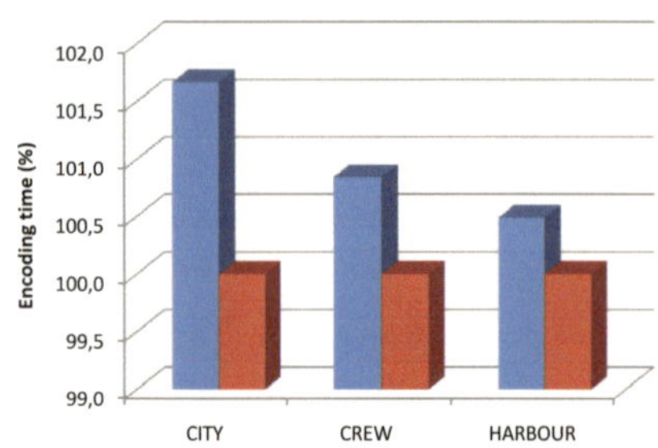


(c) Encoding time (QCIF resolution)

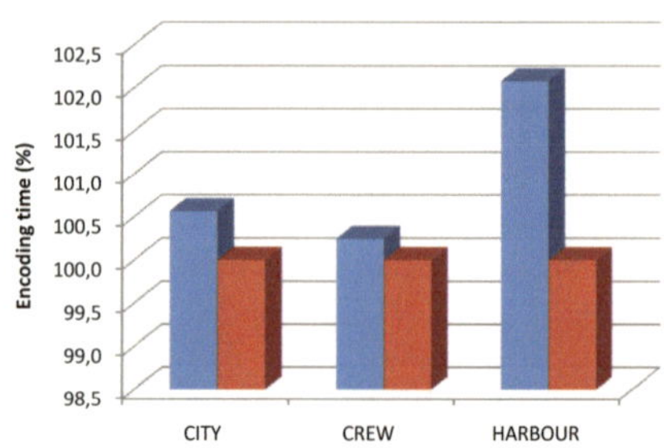


(d) Encoding time (CIF resolution)

Fig. 16. Comparison between MGS and CGS SNR scalable modes for different resolutions.

### 3.4 Additional features

Along with its differentiated temporal, quality and spatial scalabilities, the H.264/SVC standard provides several other innovative features, which are subject to practical experimentation through this subsection.

#### 3.4.1 Prediction module

In general, motion estimation techniques stand for those algorithms that allow determining the vectors that describe the correlation between two adjacent frames in a video sequence. In this context, H.264/SVC allows tuning the searching parameters for its motion estimation algorithm: it is possible to decide whether an exhaustive block-searching algorithm or a speed-optimized approach is to be utilized. Furthermore, the search-range of the chosen

block-search function can also be tweaked. However, the exhaustive block-searching function demands a high computational complexity in the encoding process, while its repercussion on the quality and encoding efficiency is not significant. These claims are buttressed by the results of performed experiments given in Table 1. Notice that these results have been generated by encoding QCIF resolution video sequences, since the encoding complexity increases dramatically for higher resolutions. Since video coding quality is comparable for both search-functions (results not shown due to space constraints), it is highly recommended to select the fast-searching algorithm in practical H.264/SVC encoders due to the derived significant reduction in computational load.
A deeper experimental analysis of the searching algorithm is illustrated in Figure 17, where the influence of the search-range parameter is studied for several CIF resolution video sequences. Experimental results verify that the higher the search-range is, the longer the coding time is. No significant impact has been detected in any other metric.

| **Video sequence** | **Motion-search algorithm** | **Search-range** | **Decoding time** (%) |
|---|---|---|---|
| CITY | Fast | Exhaustive | 100% |
| CITY | Exhaustive | Exhaustive | 6133,20% |
| CREW | Fast | Exhaustive | 100% |
| CREW | Exhaustive | Exhaustive | 3153,25% |
| HARBOUR | Fast | Exhaustive | 100% |
| HARBOUR | Exhaustive | Exhaustive | 6482,42% |

Table 1. Impact of the selected motion-search algorithm in H.264/SVC.

Closely related to the motion compensation, enabling additional 8x8 motion-compensated blocks can notoriously increase the complexity of the encoder. As the experimental results in Figure 18 certify, enabling additional sub-macroblock partitions of 8x8 requires more resources when encoding a given video sequence, whereas it surprisingly has little benefits in the other considered metrics (file size and quality).

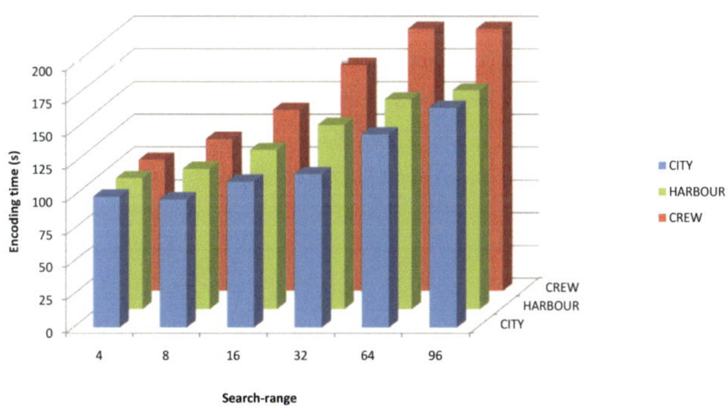


Fig. 17. Search-range parameter impact on H.264/SVC video coding.

Consequently, regarding motion estimation mechanisms in H.264/SVC it is highly recommended to use fast-searching algorithms, small search-ranges, and no additional 8x8 block compensation if the target application requires minimizing the encoder complexity.

### 3.4.2 Deblocking filter

Within this subsection, the benefits of applying distinct deblocking filter approaches in H.264/SVC video coding have been analyzed. Deblocking filters are exploited in block-coding

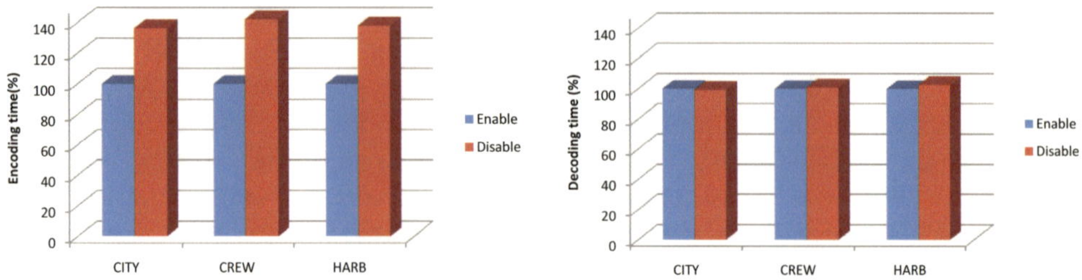


(a) Encoding time (b) Decoding time

Fig. 18. Impact of enabling additional 8x8 sub-macroblock partitions.

techniques by applying them to blocks within frames, which lead to an improved prediction as they smooth potentially sharp edges between macroblocks. The H.264/SVC deblocking filter operates within the motion-compensated prediction loop, embodying an enhanced quality for the end user (Schwarz et al., 2007).

In these experiments the in-loop deblocking filter and the inter-layer deblocking filter included in the H.264/SVC standard are evaluated. To this end, the following cases have been considered in the JSVM reference software: 1) no filter is applied ($LF_0$); 2) filter is applied to all block edges ($LF_1$); 3) two stage filtering where slice boundaries are filtered in the second stage ($LF_2$); and, finally, 4) two-stage deblocking filtering is applied to the luma component (its frame boundaries are filtered in a second stage), but chroma is not filtered ($LF_3$). The assessment of the benefits and drawbacks of each of the aforementioned filtering cases has been done, on top of the metrics used heretofore (i.e. encoding/decoding time, encoding efficiency and PSNR), by resorting to the MSU Blocking Metric (*MSU Video Quality Measurement Tool*, 2010). The MSU Blocking Metric measures the frame-to-frame blocking effect in a given video sequence, by detecting object edges with heuristic methods. A higher value of the MSU Blocking Metric corresponds to a better video quality.

The experiments for the analysis of the in-loop deblocking filter have been performed over different video sequences and configurations combining temporal, spatial and SNR scalable layers. Table 2 shows experiment results for one single spatial layer (QCIF resolution) and two quality layers (a similar behavior has been obtained for other combinations). From these extensive tests an interesting conclusion can be extracted: the performance of the in-loop deblocking filter heavily depends on the specific video sequence and the combination of scalable layers. On one hand, the quality obtained when applying each of the tested filtering techniques diverges substantially and hinges, not only on the dynamics and features of the original video sequence, but also on the specific combination of scalabilities in the H.264/SVC encoding process. On the other hand, the coding and decoding complexity of these filters shows a clear dependency on each input video sequence.

| **Video Sequence** | **$LF_0$** | **$LF_1$** | **$LF_2$** | **$LF_3$** |
|---|---|---|---|---|
| CITY | 1222159 | 1175891 | 1175891 | 1174807 |
| CREW | 1051660 | 1356914 | 1356914 | 1362196 |
| HARBOUR | 1208833 | 1252369 | 1252369 | 1251459 |

Table 2. Impact of selected in-loop deblocking filtering techniques in the performance of H.264/SVC (in terms of average MSU Blocking Metric).

Similarly, the inter-layer deblocking filter has been evaluated over the above mentioned scenarios. The same analysis and procedure has been done and, again, the obtained results have not been conclusive. In this case, the benefit of applying different techniques is not significant and, for the same H.264/SVC encoding configuration, results are tightly coupled to the characteristics of the processed video sequence.
Therefore, the best filtering technique can not be determined beforehand and, for each multimedia application or scenario, a deep analysis needs to be done in order to select the appropriate deblocking filtering technique.

### 3.4.3 Pre-processing filter

To conclude with this practical section, this set of experiments evaluate the practical impact of including an additional pre-processing filter supported by the H.264/SVC standard: the so-called Motion-Compensated Temporal Filtering. This filter has been suggested as an additional solution to improve data similarity between consecutive layers by mainly helping temporal decomposition. Basically, the MCTF scheme consists of a 2-tap filter based on Haar or 5/3 wavelet transforms (Schafer et al., 2005), which must be applied over the original input video, i.e. before any encoder processing.
Within the JSVM reference platform, this filter is an independent software module (labeled as "MCTFPreProcessorStatic"). It receives as input a raw video sequence (in YUV format), generating a filtered output file. In order to integrate this MCTF module into the encoding process, the original video sequences are first filtered and then fed to the JSVM encoder, which is preconfigured to work with the new filtered files. For this experiment, the output bit rate has been adjusted to the same value in order to simplify the comparison.
Results in Figures 19(a) and 19(b) present the obtained video quality with and without MCTF pre-processing filter. It is doubtlessly proven that the filter produces a small improvement in video quality. In order to further quantify the impact of the inclusion of the MCTF filter in the encoding procedure, the filtering time – the delay caused by the "MCTFPreProcessorStatic" – is added to the JSVM encoding time. The comparative results are presented in Figures 19(c) and 19(d) for CIF and 4CIF resolutions, respectively. It is clearly observed therein how enabling MCTF significantly deteriorates the global performance, increasing the total execution time in more than 300% in all cases.

## 4. Recommended configurations for practical integration

The experimental results shown in the previous section highlight the practical influence of several H.264/SVC configuration parameters in the performance of the codec. Therefore, the correct setting of these parameters is critical in order to customize practical scalable solutions. Due to the inherent complexity of the H.264/SVC specification, a plethora of variables must be taken into account so as to tailor each configuration to the particular demands and requisites (objective or subjective) of the scalable application at hand. Even if each particular scenario might present specific requirements, the tradeoff between two opposing metrics must be met in most practical applications: to maximize the video quality (disregarding any computational complexity and processing requirements of the codec), or to minimize the encoding complexity with the minimum associated reduction in quality.
On one hand, and based on the results of previous sections, for those applications where quality is more relevant than computational performance (e.g. video storing), the following recommendations have been concluded: an extensive use of B frames (in order to reduce the

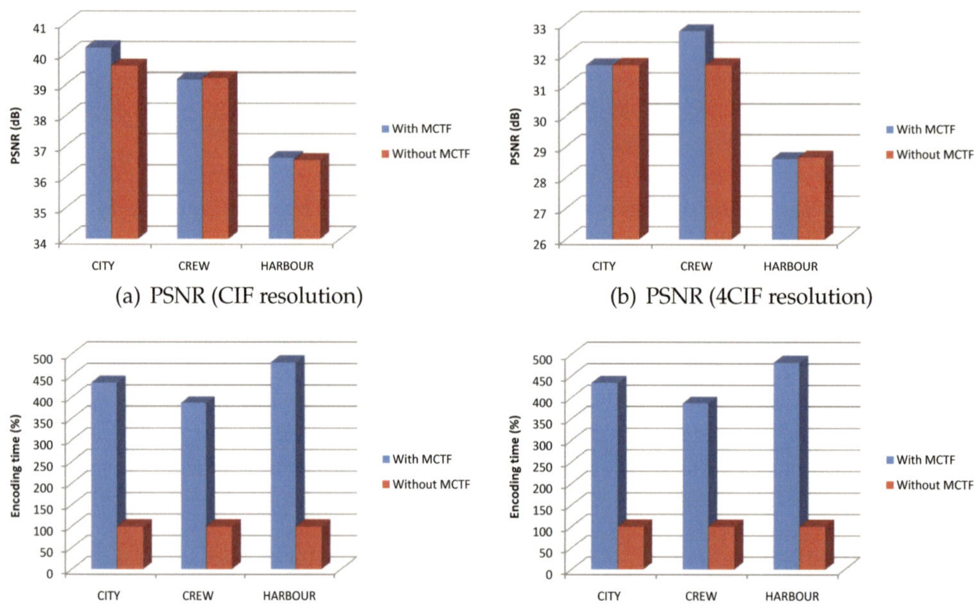


(a) PSNR (CIF resolution)

(b) PSNR (4CIF resolution)

(c) Encoding time (CIF resolution)

(d) Encoding time (4CIF resolution)

Fig. 19. Impact of enabling MCTF pre-processing filter.

bit rate increment due to the quality requirements), the selection of a high search-area size for inter-layer prediction, the adoption of the MGS mode for the SNR scalability and, finally, setting a sufficiently small quantization parameter. On the other hand, for high-performance scalable applications (e.g. IPTV-based solutions), other configuration schemes are more suitable: small GOP values, I and P frame-based GOP structures, high QP values, the use of fast-searching algorithms, disable additional 8x8 motion-compensated blocks and, when possible, the avoidance of non-dyadic spatial scalability ratios. Moreover, and as a general rule for both cases, the inclusion of the MCTF pre-processing filter is deemed unnecessary, since no quality or performance improvement has been obtained in our experiments. The responsibility for selecting advanced techniques as deblocking filters is left on the application, as their performance strongly depends on the specifically processed video sequence.

In order to illustrate this advice, two experimental scenarios have been defined: a high-quality and a high-performance demanding scalable application. In both experiments, a conventional reference configuration is compared to the proposed advanced approaches. This hereafter coined basic-reference configuration consists of the following configured parameters: GOP size equal to 8 in a *"IBBP"* frame pattern, ILP with fast-search mode, search-area equal to 48, CGS mode for SNR scalability, $QP_U$=32 for the upper quality layer, and $QP_L$=38 the lowest quality layer.

### 4.1 High-quality configuration

For this quality-demanding scenario, a hybrid scalable configuration with temporal (4 layers) and SNR (2 layers) scalability has been designed. This high-quality configuration is designed so as to provide a quality improvement with respect to the basic-reference configuration. The key parameters modified for the proposed high-quality configuration are the use of only B frames, an expanded search-area of 92 and MGS mode for providing SNR scalability. Specifically, the QP values determined for this high-quality configuration are $QP_U$=25 and $QP_L$=30. Please recall that these parameters are just particular examples of the general guidelines provided in this chapter, and might need further tweaking in other real scenarios. The practical results obtained from the evaluation of the two suggested configurations (basic-reference and high-quality) for the three video sequences at CIF resolution are shown in Figure 20. Note that, for the sake of fairness in the comparison, the output bit rate of all configurations has been adjusted to the same value (1 Mbps) in order to evaluate only variations in quality and performance. First, it is important to observe the quality improvement obtained in Figure 20(a) when using the suggested high-quality configuration, with gains up to 2.5 dB in some cases. However, a considerable impact in the global computational performance is obtained for this last configuration (Figure 20(b)): the encoding time increases more than five times in some cases.

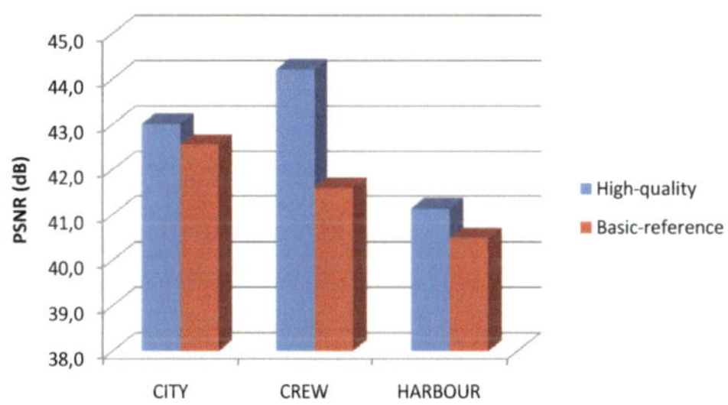


(a) Quality (PSNR)

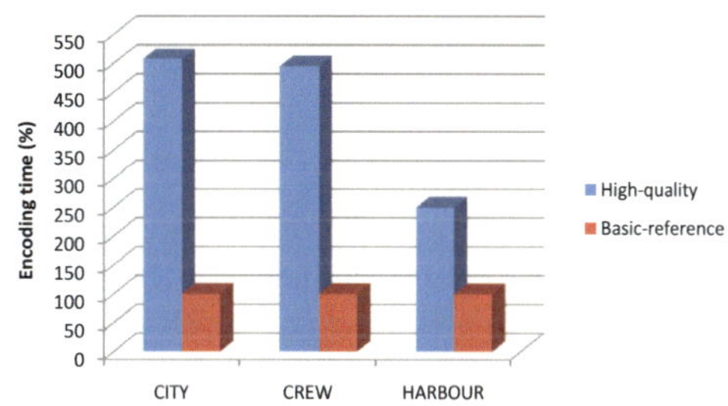


(b) Encoding time

Fig. 20. Comparative between basic-reference and high-quality configurations.

### 4.2 High-performance configuration

For real-time performance-demanding applications such as widespread video conference systems or video surveillance systems, the time spent in encoding a video sequence is critical. In such cases, the computational performance of the codec is considered decisive as long as the quality of the video stream does not degrade dramatically. For these applications a high-performance configuration – aimed at achieving fast execution – is proposed with the following parameters: GOP size equal to 4 with *"IPPP"* structure (one I and three P frames per GOP without including B frames), fast search-mode ILP with search-area reduced to 16, and quantization steps adjusted to $QP_U$=36 and $QP_L$=38. Here again, these specific values are a consequence of the general design guidelines provided throughout this chapter.
When comparing both the basic-reference and the high-performance configurations in terms of quality (Figure 21(a)), observe that the degradation in PSNR varies depending on the encoded video sequence, i.e. the PSNR for the CREW video sequence is almost equal with both configurations, whereas the PSNR for CITY and HARBOUR video sequences decreases approximately down to 1 and 2 dB respectively. However, this drawback finds its counterpart at the noticeable computational performance improvement shown in Figure 21(b), where it is concluded that the encoding time for the high-performance configuration is at least two times faster than the basic-reference solution for all the evaluated video sequences.

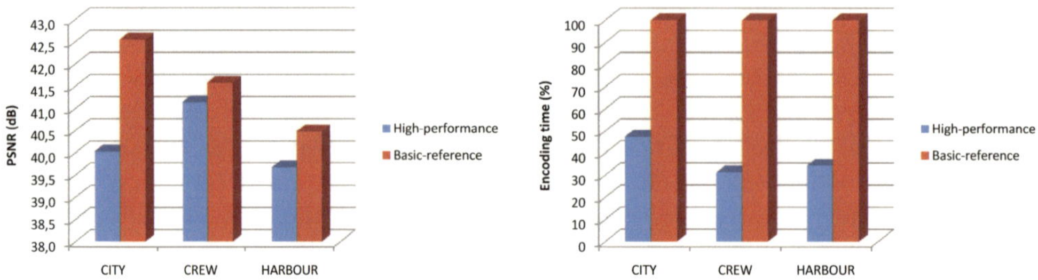


(a) Quality (PSNR) (b) Encoding time

Fig. 21. Comparative between the basic-reference and the high-performance configurations.

## 5. Conclusion

The goal of this tutorial has been to provide an overview of the advances of the H.264/SVC video standard, focusing on both its features and on an experimental analysis of its configuration parameters. H.264/SVC's superiority over other non-scalable approaches is mainly due to its three different scalabilities (temporal, spatial and SNR), which allow for an improved encoding flexibility and efficiency. By combining different scalabilities into a single bitstream it is possible to achieve, in comparison to previous scalable solutions, similar compression ratios with much lower encoding complexity.

After a brief introduction to this scalable standard, the encoding architecture of H.264/SVC and its most important characteristics have been presented in Section 2. The goal of this section has been to discern the most relevant parameters of the H.264/SVC codification, so as to pave the way for later evaluation of their empirical impact on video quality, coding efficiency and performance while considering, at the same time, its scalability levels.

Next, Section 3 has elaborated on the practical performance of H.264/SVC. Several among the numerous parameters to be configured in this standard are highly influential to the overall coding performance. The imprint of the GOP structure has been proven to be crucial in all the considered metrics, not only because it determines the temporal scalability features of the video stream, but also due to its GOP size, the frame type contained therein and their arrangement. Regarding spatial scalability, H.264/SVC's rescaling algorithms have been examined for both the dyadic and the non-dyadic resolution ratios. Finally, as a result of the experiments done on the quantization parameter and the analysis of the supported SNR scalability modes (i.e. CGS and MGS), interesting concluding remarks have been drawn regarding the H.264/SVC's SNR scalability.

Leveraging the insights of all the performed experiments, Section 4 collects the most important conclusions for practical applications of H.264/SVC video coding. From the experiments contained in this chapter, a tradeoff between video quality and coding complexity has been identified. Therefore, for each scenario, the configuration of the H.264/SVC video coding needs to be adjusted, following the guidelines provided in this last section.

All in all, this chapter intends to be an useful wherewithal to help the reader understanding the H.264/SVC standard, as well as a practical design guide for researchers and practitioners for future scalable video applications.

## 6. Acknowledgements

The authors would like to thank several funding resources. On the one hand, TECNALIA's work was supported in part by the Spanish Ministry of Science and Innovation through the CENIT (ref. CEN20071036) and the Torres-Quevedo (refs. PTQ-09-01-00739, PTQ-09-02-01814 and PTQ-09-01-00740) funding programs, while the work of UFRGS was supported by the FINEP (Projects and Studies Financing) program.

## 7. References

*Ffmpeg project* (2010). `http://www.ffmpeg.org/`. Version 0.6.1; accessed online on February-09-2010.

*H.263 ITU-T Rec.* (2000). Video coding for low bit rate communication.

*H.264/AVC* (2010). Information technology - Coding of audio-visual objects - Part 10: Advanced video coding, ISO/IEC 14496-10:2010.

*H.264/SVC* (2010). Ammendment G of Information technology - Coding of audio-visual objects - Part 10: Advanced video coding, ISO/IEC 14496-10:2010.

Huang, H.-S., Peng, W.-H. & Chiang, T. (2007). Advances in the scalable amendment of h.264/avc, *IEEE Communications Magazine* 45(1): 68.

Husemann, R., Roesler, V. & Susin, A. (2009). Introduction of a zonal search strategy for svc inter-layer prediction module, *VLSI-SOC 2009*, Florianopolis, Brazil.

*JSVM reference software* (2010). `http://ip.hhi.de/imagecom_G1/savce/downloads/SVC-Reference-Software.htm`. Version 9.19.4; accessed online on February-09-2010.

*JVT reference software* (2010). `http://iphome.hhi.de/suehring/tml/download/`. Version 17.2; accessed online on February-09-2010.

Marpe, D., Wiegand, T. & Hertz, H. (2006). The h.264/mpeg4 advanced video coding standard and its aplications, *IEEE Communications Magazine* 44(8): 134–143.

*MPEG-2 Video* (2000). Information technology – Generic coding of moving pictures and associated audio information: Video, ISO/IEC 13818-2:2000.

*MPEG-4 Visual* (2004). Information technology - Coding of audio-visual objects - Part 2: Visual, ISO/IEC 14496-2:2004.

*MSU Video Quality Measurement Tool* (2010). `http://compression.ru/video/quality_measure/video_measurement_tool_en.html`. Accessed online on February-09-2010.

Ohm, J.-R. (2005). Advances in scalable video coding, *Proceedings of the IEEE* 86(1): 42–56.

Rieckl, J. (2008). *Scalable video for peer-to-peer streaming*, Master's thesis, University of Wien.

Schafer, R., Schwarz, H., Marpe, D., Schierl, T. & Wiegand, T. (2005). Mctf and scalability extension of h.264/avc and its application to video transmition, storage and surveillance, *Proceedings of the SPIE*, pp. 343–354.

Schwarz, H., Marpe, D. & Wiegand, T. (2006). Overview of the scalable h.264/mpeg4-avc extension, *Proceedings of IEEE International Conference on Image Processing*, pp. 161–164.

Schwarz, H., Marpe, D. & Wiegand, T. (2007). Overview of the scalable video coding extension of the H.264/AVC standard, *IEEE Transactions on Circuits and Systems for Video Technology* 17(9): 1103–1120.

Segall, A. & Sullivan, G. (2007). Spatial scalability within the h.264/avc scalable video coding extension, *IEEE Transactions on Circuits and Systems for Video Technology* 17(9): 1121–1135.

Unanue, I., Del Ser, J., Sanchez, P. & Casasempere, J. (2009). H.264/svc rate-resiliency tradeoff in faulty communications through 802.16e railway networks, *Ultra Modern Telecommunications and Workshops, 2009. ICUMT '09. International Conference on*, pp. 1–6.

Wien, M., Cazoulat, R., Graffunder, A., Hutter, A. & Amon, P. (2007). Real-time system for adaptive video streaming based on svc, *IEEE Transactions on Circuits and Systems for Video Technology* 17(9): 1227–1237.

Wien, M., Schwarz, H. & Oelbaum, T. (2007). Performance analysis of svc, *IEEE Transactions on Circuits and Systems for Video Technology* 17(9): 1194.

*YUV video repository* (2010). `http://www.tnt.uni-hannover.de/`. Accessed online on February-09-2010.

2

# Complexity/Performance Analysis of a H.264/AVC Video Encoder

Hajer Krichene Zrida[1], Ahmed Chiheb Ammari[2],
Mohamed Abid[1] and Abderrazek Jemai[3]
[1]*Sfax University, ENIS Institute, Computer and Embedded Systems CES Laboratory,*
[2]*Carthage University, INSAT Institute, Research Unit in Materials Measurements and Applications (MMA),*
[3]*University of Tunis el Manar, Faculty of Science of Tunis, LIP2 Laboratory, Tunisia*

## 1. Introduction

The evolution of digital video industry is being driven by continuous improvements in processing performance, availability of higher-capacity storage and transmission mechanisms. Getting digital video from its source (a camera or a stored clip) to its destination (a display) involves a chain of components. Key to this chain are the processes of compression and decompression, in which bandwidth-intensive raw digital video is reduced to a manageable size for transmission or storage, then reconstructed for display (Richardson, 2003). The early successes in the digital video industry were underpinned by international standard ISO/IEC 13818 (ISO/IEC, 1995), popularly known as MPEG-2. Anticipation of a need for better compression tools has led to the development of the new generation H.264/AVC video standard. The H.264/AVC is aiming to do what previous standards did in a more efficient, robust and practical way, supporting widespread types of conversational (bidirectional and real-time video telephony, videoconferencing) and no conversational (broadcast, storage and streaming) applications for a wide range of bitrates over wireless and wired transmission networks (Joch et al., 2002).
The H.264/AVC has been designed with the goal of enabling significantly improved compression performance relative to all existing video coding standards (Joch et al., 2002). Such a standard uses advanced compression techniques that in turn, require high computational power (Alvarez et al., 2005). For a H.264 encoder using all the new coding features, more than 50% average bit saving with 1–2 dB PSNR (Peak Signal-to-Noise Ratio) video quality gain are achieved compared to previous video encoding standards (Saponara et al., 2004). However, this comes with a complexity increase of a factor 2 for the decoder and larger than one order of magnitude for the encoder (Saponara et al., 2004).
Implementing a H.264/AVC video encoder represents a big challenge for resource-constrained multimedia systems such as wireless devices or high-volume consumer electronics since this requires very high computational power to achieve real-time encoding. While the basic framework is similar to the motion compensated hybrid scheme of previous video coding standards, additional tools improve the compression efficiency at the expense

of an increased implementation cost. For this, the exploration of the compression efficiency versus implementation cost is needed to provide early feedbacks on the standard bottlenecks and select the optimal use of its coding features.
The objective of this chapter is to perform a high-level performance analysis of a H.264/AVC video encoder to evaluate its compression efficiency versus its implementation complexity and to highlight important properties of the H.264/AVC framework allowing for complexity reduction at the high system level. The complexity analysis focus mainly on computational processing time measures with instruction-level (Kuhn et al., 1998) profiling on a general purpose CISC Pentium processor. Processing time metrics are completed by memory cost measures as this have a dominant impact on the cost-effective realization of multimedia systems for both hardware and software based platforms (Catthoor et al., 2002), (Chimienti et al., 2002).
Actually, when combining the new coding features, the implementation complexity accumulates, while the global compression efficiency becomes saturated (Saponara et al., 2004). To find an optimal balance between the coding efficiency and the implementation cost, a proper use of the AVC tools is needed to maintain the same coding performance as the most complex coding parameters configuration (all tools on) while considerably reducing complexity. In this chapter, we will cover major H.264 encoding tools. Each new tool is typically tested independently comparing the performance and complexity of a complex configuration to the same configuration minus the tool under evaluation. The coding performance is reported in terms of PSNR and bit rate, while the complexity is estimated as the total computational execution time of the application and the maximum memory usage allocated by the source code. Absolute complexity values of the obtained cost-efficient configuration of the H.264 encoder shall confirm the big challenge of its cost-effective implementation using of a well-defined multiprocessor approach to share the encoding time between several embedded processors.
The chapter is organized as follows. The next section provides an overview of the new H.264 technical features. Section 3 defines the adopted experimental environment. The coding performance and complexity of the H.264 major encoding tools are evaluated in section 4. Section 5 shall give the complexity analysis, memory and task level profiling of an obtained cost-efficient configuration. Section 6 discusses some aspects related to previous parallelization studies for an efficient parallel implementation of this standard on a given multiprocessor platform.

## 2. Overview of the H.264/AVC video encoder

An important concept in the design of H.264/AVC is the separation of the standard into two distinct layers: a video coding layer (VCL), which is responsible for generating an efficient representation of the video data; and a network adaptation layer (NAL) (Richardson, 2003) which is responsible for packaging the coded data in an appropriate manner based on the characteristics of the network upon which the data will be used. This chapter is concerned with the VCL layer.

### 2.1 The coding layer block diagram

The block diagram of the video coding layer of a H.264/AVC encoder is presented in figure1. This figure includes a forward path (left to right) and a reconstruction path (right to left) (Richardson, 2003).

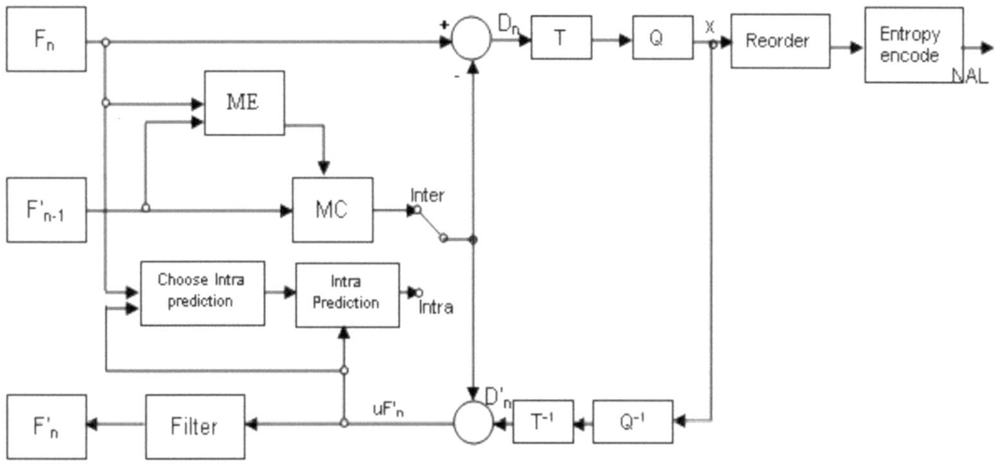


Fig. 1. H.264 / AVC video encoder block diagram

An input frame or field Fn is processed in units of a macro-block (MB). Each MB is encoded in intra or inter mode and, for each block in the MB, a prediction PRED (marked 'P' in figure1) is formed based on reconstructed picture samples. In Intra mode, PRED is formed from spatially neighboring samples in the current slice that have previously been encoded, decoded and reconstructed (uF'n in the figure1 note that unfiltered samples are used to form PRED). The encoding process chooses which and how neighboring samples are used for Intra prediction, which is simultaneously conducted at the encoder and decoder using the transmitted Intra prediction side information (Malvar et al., 2003).

In Inter mode, PRED is formed by motion-compensated prediction from one or multiple reference picture(s) selected from the set of reference pictures. In the figure1, the reference picture is shown as the previous encoded picture F'n-1 but the prediction reference for each MB partition (in inter mode) may be chosen from a selection of past or future pictures (in display order) that have already been encoded, reconstructed and filtered. The prediction PRED is subtracted from the current block to produce a residual difference block Dn that is transformed (using a block transform) and quantized to give X, a set of quantized transform coefficients which are reordered and entropy encoded. The entropy-encoded coefficients, together with side information required to decode each block within the MB (prediction modes, quantization parameter, motion vector information, etc.) form the compressed bit stream which is passed to a Network Abstraction Layer (NAL) for transmission or storage.

As well as encoding and transmitting each block in a MB, the encoder decodes (reconstructs) it to provide a reference for further predictions. The coefficients X are scaled (Q-1) and inverse transformed (T-1) to produce a difference block D'n. The prediction block PRED is added to D'n to create a reconstructed block uF'n a decoded version of the original block (u indicates that it is unfiltered). A filter is applied to reduce the effects of blocking distortion and the reconstructed reference picture is created from a series of blocks F'n.

### 2.2 Main innovations in comparison to previous standards

The basic functional elements of H.264 / AVC presented in figure1 represent a similar set of the generic DPCM/DCT (Richardson, 2003) coding and decoding functions of earlier standards. The H.264 provides higher coding efficiency through added features and functionality that in turn entails additional complexity. Here we present a summary of the most relevant key features for the performance of this standard.

First, the motion compensation model supports the use of multiple reference frames for prediction with a weighted combination of the prediction signals. Also, it introduces variable block-size motion compensation with small block sizes that range from 16x16 up to 7 modes including 16x8, 8x16, 8x8, 8x4, 4x8 and 4x4 pixel blocks. Motion vectors can be specified with higher spatial accuracy with quarter-pixel and eighth-pixel instead of half-pixel accuracy. In order to estimate and compensate fractional-pel displacements, the image signal of the reference image has to be generated on sub-pel positions by interpolation. Pixel interpolation is based on a finite impulse response (FIR) filtering operation: 6 taps for the quarter resolution and 8 taps for the eighth one (Schäfer et al., 2003). A rate-distortion (RD) Lagrangian technique optimizes both motion estimation and coding mode decisions. Moreover, an adaptive deblocking filter is added to reduce visual artifacts produced by the block-based structure of the coding process (Ostermann et al., 2004).

For the intra-frame prediction, in contrast to previous video coding standards where prediction is conducted in the transform domain, prediction in H.264/AVC is always conducted in the spatial domain by referring to neighboring samples of already coded blocks (Schäfer et al., 2003). Two classes of intra coding modes are supported. When using the INTRA-4x4 class, each 4x4 block of the luma component utilizes one of nine prediction modes. Beside DC prediction, the standard supports eight directional prediction modes involving linear combinations of the samples. For the INTRA 16x16 classes, four prediction modes are supported (ISO/IEC, 2003).

The concept of Bipredictive (B) slices is generalized in H.264/AVC. B slices use a similar macroblock partitioning as for the Predicted (P) slices. This includes the Intra 4x4, the intra 16x16 all the inter 16 x16, 16x8, 8x16, 8x8, 8x4, 4x8 and 4x4 modes. B slices are coded in a manner in which some macroblocks may use a weighted average of two distinct motion compensated prediction values, for building the prediction signal. Generally, B slices utilize two distinct reference picture buffers referred as the first and the second reference picture buffer, respectively. Four different types of inter prediction are supported: list0, list1, bi-predictive, and direct prediction. List 0 or List 1 prediction indicates that the prediction signal is formed by motion compensation from a picture of the first respectively the second reference buffer. In the bi-predictive mode, the prediction signal is formed by a weighted average of a motion-compensated list 0 and list 1 prediction signal. The direct prediction mode is inferred from previously transmitted syntax elements and can be either list 0 or list1 prediction or bi-predictive (Schäfer et al., 2003).

For the (T) transform, H.264/AVC employs a purely integer spatial approximation discrete cosine transform (DCT). This transform basically works on 4x4 shapes, as opposed to the conventional floating-point 8x8 DCT specified with rounding error tolerances that is used in earlier standards. The small size helps to reduce blocking and ringing artifacts, while the precise integer specification eliminates any mismatch between the encoder and decoder in the inverse transform (Ostermann et al., 2004). For the quantization (Q) of transform coefficients, H.264/AVC uses scalar quantization. The quantization step size is chosen by a so called quantization parameter QP which supports 52 different quantization parameters. One of 52 quantizers is selected for each macroblock by the Quantization Parameter (QP). The quantizers are arranged so that there is an increase of approximately 12.5% in the quantization step size when incrementing the QP by one (Malvar et al., 2003).

Finally, H.264/AVC specifies two alternative methods of entropy coding: a low-complexity technique based on the usage of context-adaptively switched sets of variable length codes, so-called CAVLC, and the computationally more demanding algorithm of context-based adaptive binary arithmetic coding (CABAC). Both methods represent major improvements in terms of coding efficiency compared to the techniques of statistical coding traditionally used in prior video coding standards (Ostermann et al., 2004).

## 3. Experimental environment

The complexity of the H.264 video encoder application depends on the algorithm, the encoding option tools, the input sequences and the architecture in which it is implemented. For making a complete analysis of the effect of the encoding option parameters on performance and complexity of a H.264 video encoding application, the JM encoder software reference version 10.2 is used with main profile @ level 4 (JM 10.2, 2005). Measurements have been done on a General-Purpose Processor (GPP) platform based on an INTEL Centrino 1.6 GHZ running a Linux operating system.

The encoding option parameters are representative of the standard encoding new tools. For this analysis, each coding tool is tested independently comparing the performance and complexity of a complex configuration to the same configuration minus the tool under evaluation. For the starting complex configuration, a full search algorithm for motion estimation is fixed, P (predicted) and B (Bi predicted) frame weighted prediction is used, motion vectors fractional pixel accuracy is applied with variable block sizes supported (7 motion compensation block types) and multi-frame references fixed to 5. A loop filter and Hadamard transform are used. The Rate-Distortion (R-D) optimization technique with an explicit Lagrangian parameter selection is activated. The input search range is fixed to 32, and the quantization parameter (QP) values is fixed to 28 for I and P slices, 30 for B slices and 29 for B reference slices. For B frame generalization, only one reference is used for list0 and list1. Motion estimation based on the spatial direct and bi-predictive modes is thus activated. The CABAC entropy method is used.

For video streaming and video conferencing applications, we used popular test video sequences in the Common Intermediate Format (CIF, 352 × 288 picture elements) and in the Quarter Common Intermediate Format (QCIF, 176×144 picture elements). 7 test sequences in a 4:2:0 YUV format with different grades of motion characteristics and frame rate (trace.eas, n.d.) are used as given in table1. "Bridge far", "container" and "Mother & Daughter" offer a wide variety of video QCIF content occurring in low-bit-rate applications of tens of Kbps. "Foreman" is a good medium complexity QCIF test sequence for medium bit rate applications of hundreds of Kbps. The CIF version of "Paris" and "Bridge close" are useful test cases for middle-rate applications. Finally, "Mobile" is a high-complexity CIF sequence with lot of movements including rotation and is a good test for high-rate applications of thousands of Kbps.

## 4. H.264/AVC performance and complexity parametric analysis

In this section, the coding performance and complexity of the H.264 major encoding tools are evaluated. The coding performance is reported in terms of PSNR and bit rate output, while the complexity metrics focus mainly on the amount of computing time required to encode a given test sequence on the used GPP platform. As motion estimation is the most important computing part of the encoder, the computing complexity of this module is particularly noted for all the experimented simulations. Processing time metrics are completed by memory cost measures as this have a dominant impact on the cost-effective realization for both hardware and software based platforms.

| Sequence | Format (Pixel) | Frame Rate (Hz) | Frames Coded |
|---|---|---|---|
| Bridge close | CIF (352x288) | 15 | 2000 |
| Mobile | CIF | 25 | 300 |
| Paris | CIF | 15 | 1065 |
| Bridge far | QCIF (176x144) | 15 | 2101 |
| Container | QCIF | 25 | 300 |
| Foreman | QCIF | 25 | 400 |
| Mother & Daughter | QCIF | 25 | 961 |

Table 1. Used test video sequences

### 4.1 Coding structures influence evaluation

The influence of the different H.264 encoding structures, including the classical coding types and the advanced pyramid coding structures is analyzed. In this section, only the first 150 frames of all the test sequences are used. This shall provide the best optimal coding order for the best encoding performance. The used structures are described as follows:

- An I-P-P-P-P… coding and display order using P only coding,
- an I-B-P-B-P… coding order with one non reference B slice,
- an I-B-B-P-B-B-P… coding order with 2 non reference B slices,
- an I0-P4-RB2-B1-B3-P8… coding order with 3 level pyramid using 3 B pictures (3L3B),
- an I0-P6-RB2-RB4-B1-B3-B5-P12… coding order with 3 level pyramid using 5 B pictures (3L5B),
- an I0-P8-RB2-RB4-RB6-B1-B3-B5-B7-P16.. coding order with 3 level pyramid using 7 B pictures (3L7B),
- an I0-P8-RB4-RB2-RB6-B1-B3-B5-B7-P16.. coding order with 4 level pyramid using 7 B pictures (4L7B),
- and an I0-P12-RB6-RB3-B1-B2-B4-B5-RB9-B7-B8-B10-B11-P24… coding order with 4 level pyramid using 11 B pictures (4L11B).

Bit rate output performance results are presented in figure 2 for four selected sequences. This figure indicates clearly that the bit rate output is significantly improved using reference B slices (up to 35% bit rate reduction with one non reference B slice and 15% more bit rate reduction with two non reference B slices for the CIF version of "Bridge-close"). The bit rate output and the PSNR video quality are better using Pyramid structures compared to the classical coding structures (between 5 and 10% bit rate reduction with a light PSNR improvement with 3L3B, and much better with 3L5B and 3L7B). For this, making the use of these pyramid structures is interesting. According to the obtained results, the best structure in term of coding performance is 3Level-7B pyramid. However, compared to 3Level-5B pyramid structure, the 3Level-7B requires more computational time for practical the same performance. Thus, to achieve the best performance with a minimum complexity, the

3Level-5B pyramid is preferred. The 4Level-7B pyramid and the 4Level-11B pyramid don't appear to provide any additional performance compared to the 3Level-5B pyramid as a small performance loss in bit rate is observed.

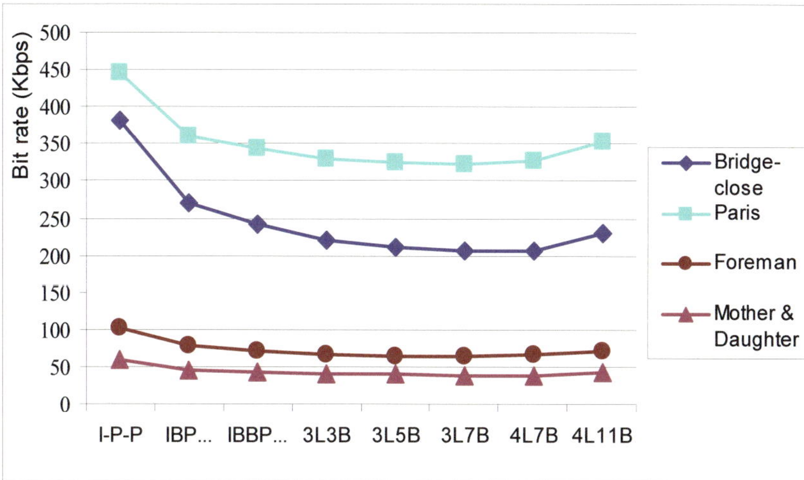


Fig. 2. Bit rate for various coding structures and video format

Given these obtained results, it is clear that the 3Level-5B hierarchical coding order offers the best performance/complexity values. Given this, the 3Level-5B is the adopted structure for the starting complex configuration.

### 4.2 Performance and computing complexity of the reference configuration

Performance and computing complexity of the H.264 complex reference encoder configuration is first estimated for all the test sequences of table 1. Results of this analysis are reported in table 2 as the total processing time, the motion estimation ME time, the bit rate output, and the luminance PSNR values. The PSNR values, given in dB, are representative of the obtained encoding performance. More the PSNR value is high, more the image quality and the encoding performance are better. Given these results, it is obtained that even for the low-bit-rate QCIF "bridge far" sequence, the time required to compute the encoding algorithms on the GPP platform is of 5137.08 second. The associated encoding performance in frames per second is of 0.41 fps. Really, this is too far from a real time video encoding performance of 25 frames per second. As a consequence, an optimal selection of the new coding tools can allow for roughly the same performance as for the complex reference configuration but with a considerable complexity reduction.

### 4.3 Performance and computing complexity of major encoding tools

This section presents a performance and computing complexity analysis of some major encoding tools. The considered tools are the search size, the variable block size, the multiple reference frames, the fractional pixel accuracy, and the bi-prediction motion estimation. The efficiency of the fast motion estimation algorithms, the R-D Lagrange technique, the Hadamard transform and the entropy coding techniques are also evaluated. To find an optimal trade-off between coding efficiency and implementation complexity, the effect of each coding tool is tested separately in comparison with the fixed reference configuration. We will observe varying complexity values at a gain in the obtained video quality and bit-rate output.

| Res. | Sequence | Total time (s) | ME Time (s) | ME Complexity (ME C %) | frames per Seconds (fps) | Bit rate (Kbps) | PSNR-Y (dB) |
|---|---|---|---|---|---|---|---|
| CIF | Bridge-close | 19259,41 | 15670,33 | 81,36 | 0,1 | 106,44 | 35,01 |
| | Mobile | 3027,4 | 2343,04 | 77,39 | 0,1 | 676,08 | 32,82 |
| | Paris | 9479,15 | 7327,81 | 77,3 | 0,11 | 129,54 | 35,28 |
| QCIF | Bridge-far | 5137,08 | 4295,38 | 83,62 | 0,41 | 2,74 | 37,84 |
| | Container | 715,06 | 580,44 | 81,17 | 0,41 | 19,37 | 36,17 |
| | Foreman | 1026,86 | 838,6 | 81,67 | 0,39 | 79,2 | 35,01 |
| | Mother & Daughter | 2145,51 | 1728,42 | 80,56 | 0,45 | 30,32 | 36,3 |

Table 2. Performance/complexity of the reference configuration

#### 4.3.1 Full/Fast full motion estimation

The full Search motion estimation is reported to be the most-consuming part of the entire encoding process (Pascalis et al., 2004). For this, several fast motion estimation algorithms have been proposed (Pascalis et al., 2004), (Chen et al., 2002). In our case, the efficiency of the UMHexagonS fast search algorithm (Chen et al., 2002) is analyzed in comparison with the full search estimation scheme. The obtained results of this analysis are reported in table 3. It is clear from table 3 that using the UMHexagonS search method we got a very slight bit rate and PSNR degradations in comparison with a full search algorithm. But, this comes with up to 45% of computation time complexity reduction. Thus, as the fast full search technique considerably improves the coding complexity without a notable loss in video quality and bit rate for all test sequences, the UMHexagonS will be adopted as a fast motion estimation scheme.

#### 4.3.2 Search range

The influence of the search range (SR) window is evaluated for different SR values. The obtained results are given in table 4 as the total processing time, the bit rate output, and PSNR values. As shown in table 4, an important complexity reduction is obtained using a search range of 8 compared to 16 and 32 values, at a cost of a negligible loss in bit rate and video quality. For consequence and for a cost-efficient configuration, a search range of 8 is chosen.

#### 4.3.3 Variable block sizes

The influence of three block size modes is evaluated. The first mode is with 7 block sizes activated (16x16, 16x8, 8x16, 8x8, 8x4, 4x8, and 4x4), the second is with 4 (16x16, 16x8, 8x16, and 8x8), and the third is with only one 16x16 block size. As presented in table 5, supporting all the seven block sizes increases the computational complexity especially for the motion estimation module, at a gain in the coding efficiency. Compared, with the 4 block size

(16x16, 16x8, 8x16, and 8x8), we got a light video quality degradation with a negligible loss in bit rate (negligible loss for the QCIF version of "bridge far" and less than 2.5% for the CIF version of "mobile"), but with a 10% average complexity reduction. With only one 16x16 block size mode, we got more significant video quality degradation compared to that with four block sizes, but with an encoding time further reduced 10% average. These results confirm that block sizes smaller than 8x8 (i.e. the seven block size mode on) do not provide significant benefits compared with the 4 block size mode. However, with the use of only 16x16 block size, the encoding performance is significantly decreased. For consequence, to reduce the implementation complexity while maintaining the same encoding performance, the 4 block size mode is adopted.

| Resolution | | CIF | | | QCIF | | | |
|---|---|---|---|---|---|---|---|---|
| ME Algo | Seq. | Bridge-close | Mobile | Paris | Bridge-far | Container | Foreman | Mother & Daughter |
| Full Search | ME C (%) | 81,36 | 77,39 | 77,3 | 83,62 | 81,17 | 81,67 | 80,56 |
| | Bit rate | 106,44 | 676,08 | 129,54 | 2,74 | 19,37 | 79,2 | 30,32 |
| | PSNR-Y | 35,01 | 32,82 | 35,28 | 37,84 | 36,17 | 35,01 | 36,3 |
| Fast ME | ΔTEC (%) | -39,43 | -32,33 | -40,16 | -41,66 | -40,03 | -38,53 | -42,92 |
| | ME C (%) | 70,26 | 66,28 | 62,81 | 72,81 | 69,19 | 71,41 | 66,43 |
| | ΔBit rate | -0,03 | 1,43 | 0,8 | -0,01 | 0,08 | 0,08 | -0,04 |
| | ΔPSNR-Y | -0,02 | 0 | -0,02 | -0,03 | 0 | -0,02 | -0,03 |

ΔTotal Encoding Complexity (ΔTEC (%)) = Encoding Complexity (with Fast ME algorithm) - Encoding Complexity (with Full Search). ΔBit rate (Kbps) = Bit rate (with Fast ME algorithm) - bit rate (with Full Search), idem for ΔPSNR-Y

Table 3. Performance and Complexity Results for Full Search and Fast Full Search Algorithms

| Resolution | | CIF | | | QCIF | | | |
|---|---|---|---|---|---|---|---|---|
| Search Range | Seq. | Bridge-close | Mobile | Paris | Bridge-far | Container | Foreman | Mother & Daughter |
| 32 | ME C (%) | 70,26 | 66,28 | 62,81 | 72,81 | 69,19 | 71,41 | 66,43 |
| | Bit rate | 106,41 | 677,51 | 130,34 | 2,73 | 19,45 | 79,28 | 30,28 |
| | PSNR-Y | 34,99 | 32,82 | 35,26 | 37,81 | 36,17 | 34,99 | 36,27 |
| 16 | ΔTEC (%) | -42,68 | -42,58 | -37,46 | -40,63 | -43,09 | -43,61 | -39,68 |
| | ME C (%) | 47,52 | 41,91 | 40,22 | 53,21 | 47,36 | 49,57 | 44,9 |
| | ΔBit rate | 0 | -0,12 | 0,16 | -0,01 | -0,03 | 0,35 | 0 |
| | ΔPSNR-Y | 0,01 | -0,01 | 0 | 0 | 0 | -0,01 | 0,01 |
| 8 | ΔTEC (%) | -23,98 | -19,87 | -19,85 | -28,73 | -23,45 | -24,80 | -20,26 |
| | ME C (%) | 30,72 | 26,38 | 25,78 | 36,4 | 29,81 | 33,42 | 30,94 |
| | ΔBit rate | 0,26 | 1,07 | 0,73 | 0,01 | 0 | 1,81 | 0,08 |
| | ΔPSNR-Y | -0,01 | 0 | 0 | 0 | 0 | 0 | -0,01 |

Table 4. Performance and complexity results for various search sizes

| Resolution | | CIF | | | QCIF | | | |
|---|---|---|---|---|---|---|---|---|
| Block Sizes | Seq. | Bridge-close | Mobile | Paris | Bridge-far | Container | Foreman | Mother & Daughter |
| 7 | ME C (%) | 30,72 | 26,38 | 25,78 | 36,4 | 29,81 | 33,42 | 30,94 |
| | Bit rate | 106,67 | 678,46 | 131,23 | 2,73 | 19,42 | 81,44 | 30,36 |
| | PSNR-Y | 34,99 | 32,81 | 35,26 | 37,81 | 36,17 | 34,98 | 36,27 |
| 4 | ΔTEC (%) | -11,32 | -10,51 | -10,23 | -9,11 | -9,16 | -11,91 | -11,26 |
| | ME C (%) | 27,42 | 22,21 | 22,34 | 33,81 | 26,71 | 29,31 | 26,99 |
| | ΔBit rate | 0,67 | 14,53 | 5,19 | 0 | 0,45 | 1,32 | 0,18 |
| | ΔPSNR-Y | -0,06 | -0,11 | -0,13 | -0,03 | -0,09 | -0,09 | -0,14 |
| 1 | ΔTEC (%) | -11,62 | -14,17 | -11,24 | -13,14 | -12,33 | -13,87 | -12,75 |
| | ME C (%) | 25,67 | 19,11 | 19,98 | 32,8 | 25,14 | 26,73 | 24,58 |
| | ΔBit rate | 2,3 | 58,35 | 15,36 | 0,01 | 2,96 | 9,15 | 2,82 |
| | ΔPSNR-Y | -0,09 | -0,14 | -0,17 | -0,07 | -0,18 | -0,2 | -0,22 |

Block sizes=7, then all seven modes (16x16, 16x8, 8x16, 8x8, 8x4, 4x8, and 4x4) are on.
Block sizes=4, then 16x16, 16x8, 8x16, and 8x8 modes are on.
Block sizes=1 only 16x16 mode is on

Table 5. Performance and complexity results for motion compensation blocks sizes

#### 4.3.4 Multiple reference frames

Results concerning the influence of the multiple reference frame option are reported in table 6. Using this table, we observe for example for the CIF "bridge close" an increase of 43% bit rate for a reference frame number reduction from 5 to 1. This goes also for the QCIF "Foreman" video sequence with a 50% of bit rate increase for also a reference frame reduction from 5 to 1. However, with the use of only 3 reference frames, we observe a slight gain in the computational complexity and less than 5% bit rate increase with a little video quality degradation. Thus, using only 3 reference frames leads to a somewhat computational burden decrease without a noticeable coding efficiency degradation compared to that obtained with 5 reference frames. However, using only one reference frame leads to a sensible loss in coding performance with a slight complexity reduction. Thus, the optimal reference frame number is fixed to 3 for an optimized configuration.

#### 4.3.5 RD-Lagrangian optimization

The R-D optimization is the criterion for selecting the best coding mode. It evaluates the cost of every possible coding mode, considering the balance of the distortion and the number of consumed bits. The obtained mode with the smallest cost will be considered as the best coding mode. As presented in table 7, the R-D Lagrangian technique gives a substantial compression efficiency improvement at a double complexity cost. The encoder without RD optimization is about 2~3 times faster and gives a noticeable loss in bit rate-distortion compared to the case with an RD-Lagrangian technique enabled (an average of 40% in bit rate increase in case of QCIF "bridge far" sequence, as described in table 7). While the considerable computational complexity required by the R-D optimization, it is a very important tool of the JM reference software. As our objective is to obtain comparable performance as for the reference configuration, this option will be maintained.

### 4.3.6 Hadamard transform

A Hadamard transform may be used to improve the error cost functions performance such as the sum of absolute differences (SAD). However, given the obtained results of table 8, activating the Hadamard transform causes a slight complexity increase without any coding efficiency gain. Thus, the Hadamard transform will be disabled for the optimized parameter configuration.

| Resolution | | CIF | | | QCIF | | | |
|---|---|---|---|---|---|---|---|---|
| Reference Frames | Seq. | Bridge-close | Mobile | Paris | Bridge-far | Container | Foreman | Mother & Daughter |
| 5 | ME C (%) | 27,42 | 22,21 | 22,34 | 33,81 | 26,71 | 29,31 | 26,99 |
| | Bit rate | 107,34 | 692,99 | 136,42 | 2,73 | 19,87 | 82,76 | 30,54 |
| | PSNR-Y | 34,93 | 32,7 | 35,13 | 37,78 | 36,08 | 34,89 | 36,13 |
| 3 | ΔTEC (%) | 0,59 | -1,78 | 0,05 | 0,30 | -0,91 | 1,15 | 0,79 |
| | ME C (%) | 27,68 | 22,81 | 22,57 | 33,55 | 27,13 | 30,23 | 27,6 |
| | ΔBit rate | 6,7 | 26,98 | 6,47 | 0 | 0,81 | 2,59 | 1,15 |
| | ΔPSNR-Y | -0,02 | -0,03 | -0,02 | 0 | -0,03 | -0,04 | -0,04 |
| 1 | ΔTEC (%) | 0,19 | 1,80 | 0,68 | -0,43 | -0,21 | 3,89 | 2,53 |
| | ME C (%) | 27,81 | 24,12 | 22,91 | 33,9 | 27,61 | 30,79 | 27,98 |
| | ΔBit rate | 39,5 | 285,65 | 50,9 | -0,08 | 5,27 | 41,43 | 12,44 |
| | ΔPSNR-Y | -0,1 | -0,43 | -0,19 | -0,01 | -0,27 | -0,43 | -0,36 |

Table 6. Performance and complexity results for multiple reference frames

| Resolution | | CIF | | | QCIF | | | |
|---|---|---|---|---|---|---|---|---|
| RD-Lagrange | Seq. | Bridge-close | Mobile | Paris | Bridge-far | Container | Foreman | Mother & Daughter |
| Enabled | ME C (%) | 27,68 | 22,81 | 22,57 | 33,55 | 27,13 | 30,23 | 27,6 |
| | Bit rate | 114,04 | 719,97 | 142,89 | 2,73 | 20,68 | 85,35 | 31,69 |
| | PSNR-Y | 34,91 | 32,67 | 35,11 | 37,78 | 36,05 | 34,85 | 36,09 |
| Disabled | ΔTEC (%) | -61,65 | -68,63 | -66,85 | -53,81 | -59,31 | -59,61 | -60,69 |
| | ME C (%) | 74,28 | 73,26 | 71,26 | 78,43 | 70,66 | 76,48 | 74,68 |
| | ΔBit rate | 23,34 | 152,46 | 13,93 | 1,09 | 2,51 | 14,3 | 5,1 |
| | ΔPSNR-Y | 0,24 | 0,32 | 0,06 | -0,08 | -0,11 | 0,04 | 0,01 |

Table 7. Performance and complexity results for R-D Lagrangian technique

| Resolution | | CIF | | | QCIF | | | |
|---|---|---|---|---|---|---|---|---|
| Hadamard | Seq. | Bridge-close | Mobile | Paris | Bridge-far | Container | Foreman | Mother & Daughter |
| Enabled | ME C (%) | 27,68 | 22,81 | 22,57 | 33,55 | 27,13 | 30,23 | 27,6 |
| | Bit rate | 114,04 | 719,97 | 142,89 | 2,73 | 20,68 | 85,35 | 31,69 |
| | PSNR-Y | 34,91 | 32,67 | 35,11 | 37,78 | 36,05 | 34,85 | 36,09 |
| Disabled | ΔTEC (%) | -3,25 | -2,10 | -1,41 | -3,92 | -2,53 | -2,60 | -2,93 |
| | ME C (%) | 25,29 | 20,6 | 20,47 | 31,38 | 25,09 | 27,65 | 24,89 |
| | ΔBit rate | 0,12 | 1,49 | 0,76 | 0 | 0 | 0,44 | 0,05 |
| | ΔPSNR-Y | -0,01 | -0,04 | -0,05 | 0,01 | -0,03 | -0,06 | -0,07 |

Table 8. Performance and complexity results for Hadamard transform

| Resolution | | CIF | | | QCIF | | | |
|---|---|---|---|---|---|---|---|---|
| | Seq. | Bridge-close | Mobile | Paris | Bridge-far | Container | Foreman | Mother & Daughter |
| With Fractional Pixel Accuracy | ME C (%) | 25,29 | 20,6 | 20,47 | 31,38 | 25,09 | 27,65 | 24,89 |
| | Bit rate | 114,16 | 721,46 | 143,65 | 2,73 | 20,68 | 85,79 | 31,74 |
| | PSNR-Y | 34,9 | 32,63 | 35,06 | 37,79 | 36,02 | 34,79 | 36,02 |
| Without Fractional Pixel Accuracy | ΔTEC (%) | -4,60 | -3,98 | -6,25 | -7,05 | -5,87 | -6,08 | -7,09 |
| | ME C (%) | 21,52 | 16,52 | 16,65 | 26,81 | 20,62 | 22,44 | 20,13 |
| | ΔBit rate | 2,84 | 452,18 | 25,32 | 0,02 | 9,06 | 26,96 | 9,62 |
| | ΔPSNR-Y | -0,14 | -0,45 | -0,12 | -0,05 | 0 | -0,34 | -0,24 |

Table 9. Performance and complexity results for fractional pixel motion compensation accuracy

#### 4.3.7 Fractional pixel motion compensation

According to table 9, disabling the fractional pixel motion compensation accuracy option results in a significant increase of the bit rate output (more than 30% of bit rate increase for the QCIF "foreman" sequence and about 63% for CIF "mobile" sequence), with a light video quality degradation and a 5% average gain in complexity reduction. Thus, in order to maximize the coding performance, the fractional pixel accuracy option should be activated.

#### 4.3.8 Bi-prediction motion estimation

Given results of table 10, disabling the bi-prediction motion estimation tool leads to a 20% average complexity reduction, without any noticeable coding efficiency degradation in terms of bit rate output and PSNR video quality. Thus, the use of bi-prediction motion estimation does not provide any significant improvement in the compression efficiency for all the tested CIF and QCIF sequences. So, the bi-prediction motion estimation option shall be disabled.

### 4.3.9 Entropy coding

Given the results of table 11, it is clear that the CABAC entropy coding method provides noticeable gains in coding efficiency. Typically, it offers, for many sequences, between 5 to 10 percent efficiency gain and larger gains for higher resolution sequences. This comes with noticeable complexity drawbacks. However, The CAVLC entropy method offers much more implementation simplicity and offer about 25% of complexity reduction, with only a slight bit rate increase. Thus, for an optimized complexity configuration, CAVLC entropy coding method will be used.

| Resolution | | CIF | | | QCIF | | | |
|---|---|---|---|---|---|---|---|---|
| Bi-Predict ME | Seq. | Bridge-close | Mobile | Paris | Bridge-far | Container | Foreman | Mother & Daughter |
| Enabled | ME C (%) | 25,29 | 20,6 | 20,47 | 31,38 | 25,09 | 27,65 | 24,89 |
| | Bit rate | 114,16 | 721,46 | 143,65 | 2,73 | 20,68 | 85,79 | 31,74 |
| | PSNR-Y | 34,9 | 32,63 | 35,06 | 37,79 | 36,02 | 34,79 | 36,02 |
| Disabled | ΔTEC (%) | -21,29 | -17,58 | -19,27 | -28,81 | -23,13 | -23,32 | -24,31 |
| | ME C (%) | 6,45 | 6,59 | 5,58 | 7,2 | 6,29 | 8,76 | 7,32 |
| | ΔBit rate | 0,01 | 6,4 | 0,81 | 0 | 0,05 | 1,32 | 0,07 |
| | ΔPSNR-Y | -0,01 | -0,04 | 0 | 0 | 0 | -0,03 | 0 |

Table 10. Performance and complexity results for bi-prediction motion estimation

| Resolution | | CIF | | | QCIF | | | |
|---|---|---|---|---|---|---|---|---|
| Entropy Coding Method | Sequence | Bridge-close | Mobile | Paris | Bridge-far | Container | Foreman | Mother & Daughter |
| CABAC | ME C (%) | 6,68 | 6,74 | 5,75 | 7,39 | 6,33 | 8,89 | 7,33 |
| | Bit rate | 113,95 | 727,49 | 143,5 | 2,51 | 20,92 | 82,88 | 31,11 |
| | PSNR-Y | 34,89 | 32,59 | 35,04 | 37,79 | 35,94 | 34,76 | 36,06 |
| CAVLC | ΔTEC (%) | -24,60 | -24,61 | -26,58 | -21,54 | -26,94 | -23,76 | -24,89 |
| | ME C (%) | 8,66 | 9,28 | 7,62 | 9,46 | 8,29 | 11,66 | 9,56 |
| | ΔBit rate | 8,31 | 37,63 | 6,43 | 0,07 | 1,11 | 5,11 | 2,08 |
| | ΔPSNR-Y | 0,02 | -0,06 | 0,02 | 0,05 | -0,04 | -0,02 | -0,01 |

Table 11. Performance and complexity results for the two entropy coding methods

### 4.4 Memory cost analysis

The data dominance of a video system implies that the memory cost have a dominant impact on the realization efficiency (Denolf et al., 2002). Application specific hardware implementations have to match memory system to the application. An efficient design flow uses this to reduce area and power. Thus, providing for the H.264/AVC a high level analysis of memory cost is essential to identify its resource requirements for hardware and software platforms. For each test sequence and for all the previously reported H.264 configurations, peak memory usage is measured using the "memprof" GNU profiler (memprof, n.d.). The obtained peak memory usage dependencies are reported in table 12. It is obtained that the encoder peak memory usage depends on the video format and linearly on the number of reference frames and the search size. The influence of the other coding tools and the input video characteristics is negligible.

| Search size | QCIF | | | CIF | | |
|---|---|---|---|---|---|---|
| | 1F | 3F | 5F | 1F | 3F | 5F |
| 32 | 5.68 | 10.52 | 15.52 | 10.74 | 18.68 | 26.6 |
| 16 | 2.87 | 5.02 | 7.1 | 7.92 | 12.92 | 18.23 |
| 8 | 2.15 | 3.59 | 4.93 | 7.13 | 11.81 | 16.08 |

Table 12. Memory cost (in Mb) for different video formats, search size and reference frames

## 5. Complexity analysis of the optimized configuration

Given the previous analysis, the optimized configuration is presented as follows. A 3L5B pyramid coding structure, an UMHexagonS fast motion estimation scheme, a search range fixed to 8, 4 variable block sizes, 3 reference frames, R-D Lagrangian optimization activated, Hadamard transform disabled, motion vector fractional pixel accuracy enabled, P and B frames weighted prediction with bi-prediction motion estimation disabled, a QP value fixed to 28, and CAVLC entropy coding technique used.

### 5.1 Performance/computing time complexity

For this final configuration, the encoding performance and computing time complexity are obtained and given in table 13. In comparison with results of table 2, one order of magnitude in complexity reduction has been achieved with less than 10% average bit rate increase for all the CIF and QCIF used video test sequences. However, for this optimized configuration and even for the very low bit rate QCIF "bridge far" sequence, the time required to compute the encoding algorithms on the GPP platform is of 597.87 second. The associated complexity in frames per second is of 3.51 fps. Even with this configuration offering an optimal trade-off between coding efficiency and implementation complexity, we are still very far from a real time performance of 25 frames per second. Implementing this configuration of the encoder represents a big challenge for resource-constrained multimedia systems such as wireless devices or high-volume consumer electronics since this requires very high computational power to achieve real-time encoding.

| Res. | Sequence | Total time (s) | ME Time (s) | ME C (%) | frames per Seconds (fps) | Bit rate (Kbps) | PSNR-Y (dB) |
|---|---|---|---|---|---|---|---|
| CIF | Bridge-close | 2463,25 | 213,42 | 8,66 | 0,81 | 122,26 | 34,91 |
| | Mobile | 488,26 | 45,3 | 9,28 | 0,6 | 765,12 | 32,53 |
| | Paris | 1451,57 | 110,57 | 7,62 | 0,73 | 149,93 | 35,06 |
| QCIF | Bridge-far | 597,87 | 56,54 | 9,46 | 3,51 | 2,58 | 37,84 |
| | Container | 91,71 | 7,6 | 8,29 | 3,22 | 22,03 | 35,9 |
| | Foreman | 130,24 | 15,19 | 11,66 | 3,05 | 87,89 | 34,71 |
| | Mother & Daughter | 289,85 | 27,71 | 9,56 | 3,32 | 33,19 | 36,05 |

Table 13. Performance/computing time complexity of the reference configuration

### 5.2 Memory profiling

For the optimized configuration, the peak memory cost is of 5.02 MB for the QCIF and 12.92 MB for the CIF sequences. Comparisons with MPEG 4 Part2, simple profile with a 16 search size, half pixel resolution and I and P pictures are provided in (Saponara et al., 2004). For the memory usage, MPEG4 requires 2.97 MB for the QCIF and 9.88 for the CIF sequences. This result refers to no optimized MPEG4 source code. Applying platform independent memory optimizations through C level code transformations may be used to get a memory and algorithmic optimized version of the reference code. An example of such optimizations is applied in (Denolf et al., 2000) for an MPEG4 simple profile video decoder and in (Vleeschouwerand et al., 2001) for an encoder. By applying such optimization techniques, an optimized MPEG 4 simple profile is obtained using only 348.2 Kb of memory for CIF sequences (Vleeschouwerand et al., 2001). This represents a memory decrease with a factor of 30.

These memory optimizations can also be applied to our AVC optimized configuration. However, for the AVC case, the number of B frames is not limited to one B between two I/P frames, thus the memory compactation transformations used in (Vleeschouwerand et al., 2001) become invalid. Actually, even with possible optimizations, still around a minimum of few MB would be required, which is a problematic size for a realistic implementation.

Memory profiling of this optimized configuration is shown in figure 3. This figure presents the memory usage distribution over the main modules of the encoder. The "Init_Motion_Search_module" for the motion estimation is the most memory consuming with 67% of the total memory usage.

### 5.3 instruction-level profiling

For the 300 frames QCIF "Container" sequence and using the H.264/AVC encoder with the optimized configuration, we have performed an analysis of dynamic instruction distribution using the "Iprof" GNU profiler (Kuhn, 1999). The obtained results are shown in the following figure 4. It is clear from this figure that the H.264/AVC is dominated by integer operations, most of them are add, sub and shift instructions. Given the lot of data transfer operations, there are more memory instructions (more of 41%) than effective computation ones.

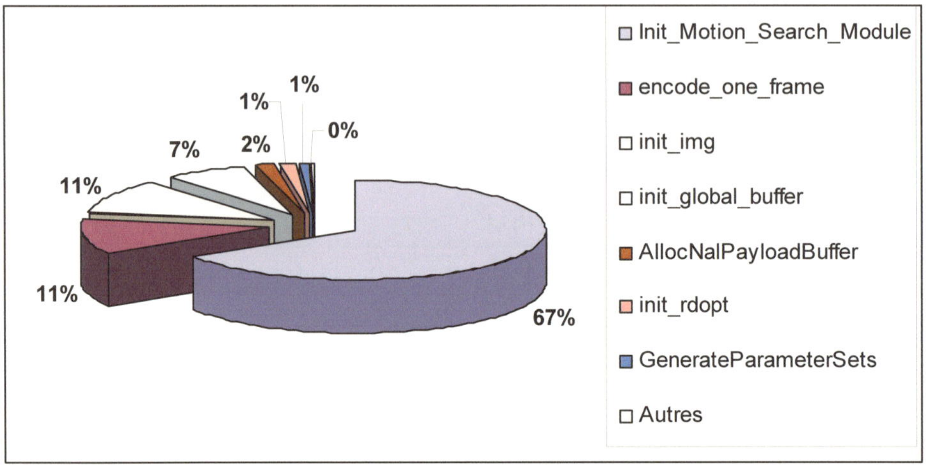


Fig. 3. Memory profiling of the optimized encoder configuration

```
                    iprof 0.4.2
                    ---------
     ... the portable Instruction Level Profiler
         (c) Peter Kuhn, 1996, 1997, 1998
Statistics File: bb.out
Executable File: lencod.exe
File Format:     elf32-i386
Architecture:    x86
Header of bb.out: Basic block profiling finished
on Thu May 10 01:18:21 2007
Number of Basic blocks total: 14556

Instruction Usage Statistics: 0
----------------------------
  0 push              8571320898   (4.77338 %)
  1 mov              73746749854   (41.06965 %)
  2 sub                5059901750 (2.81787 %)
  3 call               2454848755 (1.36711 %)
  4 ret                1199273682 (0.66788 %)
  5 pushl                     256 (0.00000 %)
  6 jmp                 836389570 (0.46579 %)
  7 add              19034677293  (10.60043 %)
  8 xor                 649757875 (0.36185 %)
  9 pop                3207175757 (1.78608 %)
 10 and                 827006618 (0.46056 %)
 11 nop                 255745587 (0.14243 %)
 12 test               2924534178 (1.62868 %)
 13 je                 3407442640 (1.89761 %)
 14 cmpl               6218794987 (3.46325 %)
 ..
Total Instructions used:    179565059320 (100%)
                              = 179565.05932000
Million
```

Fig. 4. Instruction breakdown of the optimized encoder configuration

Taken that the instruction per cycle is given by **IPC=InstCount/(Feq*ExecTime)**, for the used 1.6 GHz clock frequency GPP machine, and with an obtained number of instructions per frame of 598.55 106 (179565.059106 / 300), the obtained IPC is of 0.92. For a higher performance 3.0 GHz GPP machine, the necessary IPC for encoding H.264/AVC in real time should be 4.98. From these results we can note that even with a high frequency 3.0 GHz processor, approximately 5 instructions per cycle have to be executed to achieve H.264 real time encoding QCIF video sequences. Thus, using a single processor to real time encode H.264 bit streams may require a very high performance, high frequency super scalar processor. Such a choice is not suitable for embedded systems that have strict power and cost constraints.

An alternative solution is to use a multiprocessor approach to share the encoding execution time between several embedded processors. The sequential encoder application has to be distributed using a parallel programming model over a multiprocessor architecture. Based on that, we can conclude that it is necessary to explore multiple ways of parallelization apart from SIMD extensions in order to achieve the required performance for real time operation. To find the best scheme for parallel code execution, profiling the execution of the obtained configuration shall identify the major application bottlenecks and the main subcomponents candidate for efficient parallelization.

### 5.4 Execution profiling

Typically, tasks will not need the same amount of processing time. Thus, a computational profiling should be considered to identify the most computationally-expensive tasks and to give a clear picture of the critical code parts candidate for task-level parallelization. After that, complex tasks may also be subdivided further into smaller ones, i.e. each slowest compute node must be split in a set of compute nodes with better execution values.

For this, we have profiled the execution of the 300 frames of QCIF "Container" sequence with the "Gprof" GNU profiler (Graham et al., 1982). The obtained results are reported in the following figure 5 in terms of the CPU time percentage spent in the execution of each module. The obtained profile shows that the motion estimation and compensation (MEC), DCT transform, the entropy coding, the rate-distortion optimization (RDO) intra/inter mode decision, and the intra-prediction modules are the most time-consuming modules. These tasks constitute the major bottlenecks of the encoder.

## 6. Parallelization of the H.264/AVC video encoder

In the previous sections, we motivated the implementation of H.264/AVC encoder application on a multiprocessor platform. Actually, using a single processor to real time encode H.264/AVC bit streams may require a high performance, high frequency super scalar processor. Such a choice is not suitable for systems that have strict power and cost constraints. For such case, it may be probably necessary to use some kind of multiprocessor approach to share the encoding application execution time between several processors.

For the cost-efficient H.264/AVC parameters configuration, the obtained absolute complexity values and profiling analysis results confirmed the big challenge needed for a parallel multiprocessor execution. Parallelization consists in transforming the sequential encoding algorithms into concurrent tasks for execution in a multiprocessor system (Li et al., 2005). The predominant forms of parallelism in such systems are data-level parallelism (DLP) and task-level parallelism (TLP). DLP is perhaps the most commonly used form of parallelism, implemented through vector or SIMD architectures. The benefits of TLP are achieved by

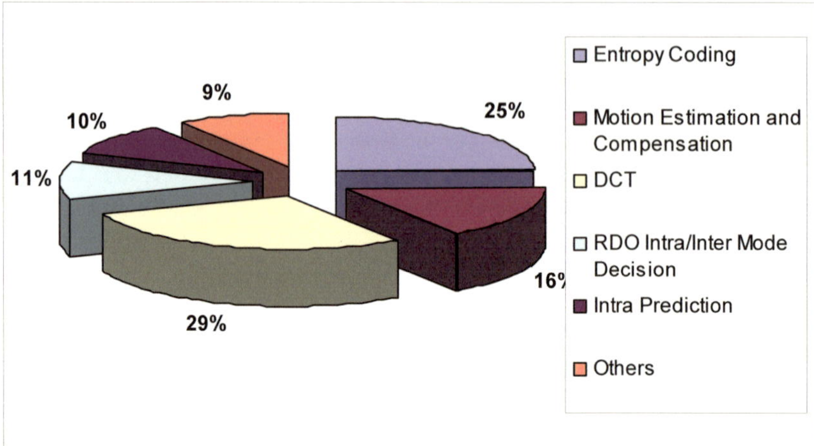


Fig. 5. Computational profile of H.264 video encoding

distributing the workload of a single high performance processor among a number of slower and simpler processor cores. This requires first to split the algorithms into separate tasks that may be executed at the same time, then to establish the necessary inter-task communication using parallel programming model primitives (Youssef et al., 2004). Generally, the parallel task execution is limited by data dependency between tasks. A data dependency means that one task needs the result of another one to be processed therefore limiting ways for parallelization (Pastrnak et al., 2006).

Given this, several multiprocessor and multi-threading encoding systems and parallel implementation methodologies have been proposed and discussed in many previous research studies (Gulati et al., 2005; Chen, 2004; Zhao, 2006; Sun, 2007) to find the best parallel execution scheme of the H.264/AVC video encoder for a chosen multiprocessor platform. Based on the performance results obtained in these previous works, and given our concern with resource constrained devices, we developed in a dedicated work a new high-level independent target-architecture parallelization approach (Krichene Zrida et al., 2009) based on the use of the parallel streaming programming models of computation and the simultaneous exploration of the two predominant concepts of parallelism; the data-level partitioning and the task-level splitting and merging. The goal of this approach is to derive in a structured way a parallel model of the encoder with the best computation and communication workload balance. Based on this parallelization approach (Krichene Zrida et al., 2009), a starting parallel model of the H.264/AVC reference encoder is first proposed. The implementation of this model is performed according to an appropriate programming strategy. According to the communication and computation concurrency properties of the implemented starting model, concurrency optimizations using task-merging and data-partitioning forms of parallelism have been considered. This resulted in an optimized parallel model with the best computation and communication workload balance.

To evaluate the effectiveness of the optimized parallel model, the system-level Sesame/Artemis simulation framework (Coffland et al., 2003) has been used targeting multiple multiprocessor platforms (Krichene Zrida et al., 2010). It has been shown that the encoding performance obtained, in terms of frames per second, are getting linearly better with the number of simulated processors (assumed to be MIPS R3000) as presented in the figure 6.

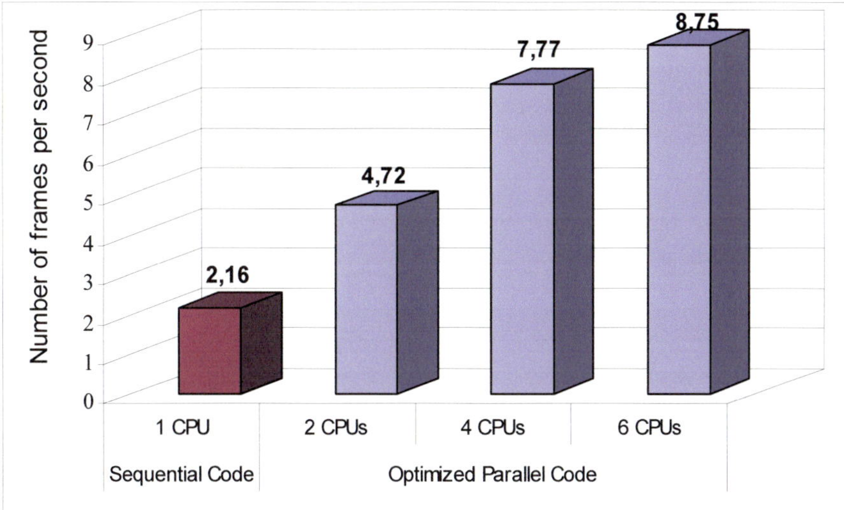


Fig. 6. Sesame/Artemis H.264 encoding performances vs. number of simulated processors

In addition, the encoding performance results of this optimized parallel model have also been compared to those previously obtained using the data-level parallelization approaches proposed in (Zhao, 2006; Sun, 2007). Results of this comparison are given in the table14. This table clearly shows that our solution (Krichene Zrida et al., 2009), based on simultaneous task and data level parallelism, has achieved better performance of the encoding process. Actually, using references (Zhao, 2006; Sun, 2007), data splitting is performed respectively at the Macro-Blocks MBs row and MBs region communication granularity levels. But for our case, a more fine-grain Macro-Block communication granularity level is exploited. Thus, with a more fine grain data amount exchanged by the processors, our proposed approach is more appropriate for use in embedded multiprocessor SoC implementations having limited on-chip memory resources.

| | Number of processors | QCIF YUV frames Encoding simulation time (s) | Number of frames per second (fps) | Speedup | Speedup in (Zhao, 2006) | Speedup in (Sun, 2007) |
|---|---|---|---|---|---|---|
| Sequential H.264 code (JM10.2) | Mono-Processor | — | 2.16 | 1 | 1 | 1 |
| Optimized parallel H.264 model | 2 Processors | 1,6 | 4.72 | 2.19 | — | — |
| | 4 Processors | 1.00 | 7.77 | **3.6** | 3.1 | 3.3 |

Table 14. Obtained Multiprocessor simulation results in comparison to those obtained in (Zhao, 2006; Sun, 2007)

Finally it has been shown, for a four-processor platform with the common bus structure, that the computation cost is much more important than the time spent in reading/writing from/to the shared memory. The communication and computation loads are nearly balanced for all the used components, as shown in the figure 7. These results represent again a solid confirm of the good concurrency properties of the obtained optimized model.

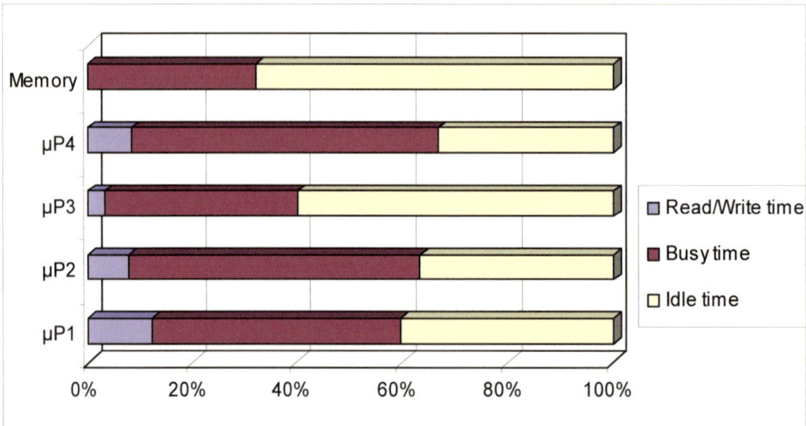


Fig. 7. Reading-Writing/Execution/Idle statistics for the common-bus-based architecture

However given the results of the figure 7, the times being idle are too much important in comparison with those being busy for all the architecture components. This has probably caused a substantial degradation of the final encoding performances. Given the important amount of data communicated between processes for the H.264/AVC encoding process, it is clear that the common memory bus structure constitutes a serious communication bottleneck. Actually, the very important data dependency between processors requires a potential memory access and allocation for the read/write operations. For a common-bus multiprocessor architecture, this causes a saturation of bus and thus a lot of time is spent in waiting to read/write data from/to other component. For further design space exploration and in order to reduce the communication bottleneck observed for the common-bus-based architecture, others inter processors communication structures and topologies need to be evaluated for a better encoding performance.

## 7. Conclusions

The H.264/AVC has been designed with the goal of enabling significantly improved compression performance relative to all existing video coding standards. Implementing a H.264 video encoder represents a big challenge for resource-constrained multimedia systems such as wireless devices or high-volume consumer electronics since this requires very high computational power to achieve real-time encoding. In this chapter, a high-level performance analysis of a H.264 video encoder is first performed to find an optimal balance between the coding efficiency and the implementation cost allowing for a complexity reduction at the high system level.

For an optimal use of the AVC tools, the best configuration parameters are obtained. For this cost-efficient configuration, the absolute complexity values, the memory and task level profiling results confirmed the big challenge needed for its effective implementation. For such implementation, a multiprocessor approach is needed to share the encoding application execution time between several processors for achieving better execution performances and real time encoding.

## 8. References


Richardson, Iain E.G. (2003), H.264 and MPEG-4 *Video Compression: Video Coding for Next-generation Multimedia*, John Wiley & Sons Ltd.

ISO/IEC 13818 (1995), *Information technology: generic coding of moving pictures and associated audio information*, (MPEG-2).

Joch, A., Kossentini, F., & Nasiopoulos, P. (2002). A Performance Analysis of the ITU-T Draft H. 26L Video Coding Standard, *Proceedings of the 12th International Packet Video Workshop*, Pittsburg, Pa, USA, April 2002.

Alvarez, M., Salami, A., Ramirez, A., & Valero, M. (2005), A Performance Characterization of high Definition Digital Video Decoding using H264/AVC, *Proceedings of the IEEE International, Symposium on Workload Characterization*, pp. 24 - 33, 6-8 Oct. 2005.

Saponara, S., Denolf, K., Lafruit, G., Blanch, C. , & Bormans, J. (2004), Performance and Complexity Co-evaluation of the Advanced Video Coding Standard for Cost-Effective multimedia communication, *EURAPIS Journal on Applied Signal Processing*, pp. 220-235, 2004:2.

Kuhn, P. , & Stechele, W. (1998), Complexity analysis of the emerging MPEG-4 standard as a basis for VLSI implementation, *Proceedings of SPIE Visual Communications and Image Processing*, vol. 3309, pp. 498–509, San Jose, Calif, USA, January 1998.

Catthoor, F., Wuytack, S., De Greef, E., Balasa, F., Nachtergaele, L., & Vandecapelle, A. (2002), Data Access and Storage Management for Embedded Programmable Processors, *Kluwer Academic*, Boston, Mass, USA, 2002.

Chimienti, A., Fanucci, L., Locatelli, R., & Saponara, S. (2002), VLSI architecture for a low-power video codec system, *Microelectronics Journal*, vol. 33, no. 5-6, pp. 417–427, 2002.

Schäfer, R., Wiegand, T., Schwarz, H. (2003), The emerging H264/AVC standard, *EBU technical review*, January 2003.

Ostermann, J., Bormans, J., List, P., Marpe, D., Narroschke, M., Pereira, F., Stockhammer, T., & Wedi, T. (2004), Video coding with H.264/AVC: Tools, Performance, and Complexity, *proceedings of the IEEE Circuits and Systems Magazine*, 2004.

ISO/IEC 14496–10:2003, Coding of Audiovisual Objects—Part 10: Advanced Video Coding, 2003, also ITU-T Recommendation H.264 Advanced video coding for generic audiovisual services.

Malvar, H., Hallapuro, A., Karczewicz, M., & Kerofsky, L. (2003), Low-Complexity transform and quantization in H.264/AVC, *proceedings of the IEEE Transactions on Circuits and Systems for Video Technology*, vol. 13, pp. 598–603, July 2003.

H264 Reference Software Version JM 10.2
http://iphome.hhi.de/suehring/tml/. November 2005.

Arizona State University, Video traces for network performance evaluation,
http://trace.eas.asu.edu

Pascalis, P., Pezzoni, L., Mian, G.A., & Bagni, D. (2004), Fast Motion Estimation with size-based predictors' selection hexagon in H264/AVC Encoding, *proceedings of the 12th European Signal Processing Conference*, September 6-10 2004, Vienna, Austria

Chen, Z., & He, Y. (2002), Fast Integer and Fractional Pel Motion Estimation, JVT-E045, *5th Meeting: Geneva*, Switzerland, 9-17 October, 2002.

Denolf, K., Blanch, C., Lafruit, G., & Bormans, J. (2002), initial memory complexity analysis of the AVC codec, *proceedings* of the IEEE Workshop on Signal Processing Systems, pp. 222–227, San Diego, Calif, USA, October 2002. www.gnome.org/projects/memprof/

Denolf, K. et al. (2000), Cost-efficient C-level design of an MPEG-4 video decoder, *proceedings of the IEEE Workshop on Power and Timing Modeling, optimization and Simulation*, pp. 233-242, Goettingen, Germany, September 2000.

Vleeschouwerand, C.D., & Nilsson, T. (2001), Motion estimation for low power video devicrs, *proceedings of the IEEE International Conference on Image Processing*, pp. 953-957, Creece, October 2001.

Kuhn, P. (1999), Complexity Analysis and VLSI Architectures for MPEG-4 Motion Estimation, Kluwer Academic Publishers, 1999.

Graham, S.L., Kessler, P.B., McKusick, M.K. (1982), Gprof: A Call Graph Execution Profiler. *Proceedings of the SIGPLAN '82 Symposium on Compiler Construction.* http://www.gnu.org/software/binutils/manual/gprof-2.9.1/

Li, P., Veeravalli, B., & Kassim, A. (2005), Design and Implementation of Parallel Video Encoding Strategies Using Divisible Load Analysis, *IEEE Transactions on Circuits and Systems for Video Technology*, No. 9, Vol. 15, pp. 1098-1112, September 2005.

Youssef, M., Yoo, S., Sasongko, A., Paviot, Y., & Jerraya, A.A. (2004), Debugging HW/SW interface for MPSOC: Video Encoder System Design Case Study, *proceedings of the 41st Design Automation Conference*, 2004.

Pastrnak, M., de With, P.H.N., Stuijk, S., & van Meerbergen, J. (2006), Parallel Implementation of Arbitrary-Shaped MPEG-4 Decoder for Multiprocessor Systems, *proceedings of the Visual Communications and Image Processing*, pp 60771I-1 - 60771I-10, 2006.

Gulati, A., & Campbell, G. (2005), Efficient mapping of the H.264 encoding algorithm onto multiprocessor DSPs. *proceedings of the SPIE-IS&T Electronic Imaging*, 2005

Chen, Y-K., Tian, X., Ge, S., & Girkar, M. (2004), Towards Efficient Multi-Level Threading of H.264 Encoder on Intel Hyper-Threading Architectures, *Proceedings of the 18th International Parallel and Distributed Processing Symposium*, 2004.

Zhao, Z., Liang, P. (2006), A Highly Efficient Parallel Algorithm for H.264 Video Encoder, *Proceedings of the 31st IEEE International Conference on Acoustics, Speech, and Signal Processing*, 2006.

Sun, Sh., Wang, D., & Chen, S. (2007), A Highly Efficient Parallel Algorithm for H.264 Encoder Based on Macro-Block Region Partition, HPCC 2007, LNCS 4782, pp. 577–585, Berlin Heidelberg 2007.

Krichene Zrida, H., Jemai, A., Ammari, A.C., & Abid, M. (2009), High Level H.264/AVC Video Encoder Parallelization for Multiprocessor Implementation, *Proceedings of the 12th ACM/IEEE Design Automation and Test in Europe conference and exhibition* , Nice-France, 20-24 April 2009.

Coffland. J.E., & Pimentel, A.D. (2003), A Software Framework for Efficient System level Performance Evaluation of Embedded Systems, *Proceedings of the SAC the ACM Symposium on Applied Computing*, Melbourne, Florida, USA, Mar. 2003.

Krichene Zrida, H., Ammari, A.C., Jemai, A., & Abid, M. (2010), High Level Optimized Parallel Specification of a H.264/AVC Video Encoder, *International Journal of Computing and Information Sciences (IJCIS)*, Volume 8, n°3, December 2010.

# 3

# Recent Advances in Region-of-interest Video Coding

Dan Grois and Ofer Hadar
*Ben-Gurion University of the Negev, Beer-Sheva, Israel*

## 1. Introduction

Recently, the content distribution network industry has become exposed to significant changes. The advent of cheaper and more powerful mobile devices having the ability to play, create, and transmit video content and which maximize a number of multimedia content distributions on various mobile networks will place unprecedented demands on networks for high capacity, low-latency, and low-loss communications paths. The reduction of cost of digital video cameras along with development of user-generated video sites (e.g., iTunes™, Google™ Video and YouTube™) have stimulated the new user-generated content sector. Growing premium content coupled with advanced video technologies, such as the Internet TV, will replace in the near future conventional technologies (e.g., cable or satellite TV).

The relatively recent ITU-T H.264/AVC (ISO/IEC MPEG-4 Part 10) video coding standard (Wiegand & Sullivan, 2003), which was officially issued in 2003, has become a challenge for real-time video applications. Compared to others standards, it gains about 50% in bit rate, while providing the same visual quality. In addition to having all the advantages of MPEG-2, H.263 and MPEG-4, the H.264 video coding standard possesses a number of improvements, such as the content-adaptive-based arithmetic codec (CABAC), enhanced transform and quantization, prediction of "Intra" macroblocks (spatial prediction), and others. H.264 is designed for both constant bit rate (CBR) and variable bit rate (VBR) video coding, useful for transmitting video sequences over statistically multiplexed networks (e.g. asynchronous transfer mode (ATM), the Ethernet, or other Internet networks). This video coding standard can also be used at any bit rate range for various applications, varying from wireless video phones to high definition television (HDTV) and digital video broadcasting (DVB). In addition, H.264 provides significantly improved coding efficiency and greater functionality, such as rate scalability, "Intra" prediction and error resilience in comparison with its predecessors, MPEG-2 and H.263. However, H.264/AVC is much more complex in comparison to other coding standards and to achieve maximum quality encoding, high computational resources are required.

Due to the recent technological achievements and trends, the high-definition, highly interactive networked media applications pose challenges to network operators. The variety of end-user devices with different capabilities, ranging from cell phones with small screens and restricted processing power to high-end PCs with high-definition displays, have stimulated significant interest in effective technologies for video adaptation for spatial formats, consuming power and bit rate.

As a result, much of the attention in the field of video adaptation is currently directed to the Scalable Video Coding (SVC), which was standardized in 2007 as an extension of H.264/AVC (Schwarz et al., 2007), since the bit-stream scalability for video is currently a very desirable feature for many multimedia applications.

The need for the scalability arises from the need for spatial formats, bit rates or power (Wiegand & Sullivan, 2003). To fulfill these requirements, it would be beneficial to simultaneously transmit or store video in variety of spatial/temporal resolutions and qualities, leading to the video bit-stream scalability. Major requirements for the Scalable Video Coding are to enable encoding of a high-quality video bitstream that contains one or more subset bitstreams, each of which can be transmitted and decoded to provide video services with lower temporal or spatial resolutions, or to provide reduced reliability, while retaining reconstruction quality that is highly relative to the rate of the subset bitstreams. Therefore, the Scalable Video Coding provides important functionalities, such as the spatial, temporal and SNR (quality) scalability, thereby enabling the power adaptation. In turn, these functionalities lead to enhancements of video transmission and storage applications.

SVC has achieved significant improvements in coding efficiency comparing to the scalable profiles of prior video coding standards. Also, in addition to the temporal, spatial and quality scalabilities, the SVC supports the Region-of-Interest (ROI) scalability. The ROI is a desirable feature in many future scalable video coding applications, such as mobile device applications, which have to be adapted to be displayed on a relatively small screen (thus, a mobile device user may require to extract and track only a predefined Region-of-Interest within the displayed video). At the same time, other users having a larger mobile device screen may wish to extract other ROI(s) to receive greater video stream resolution. Therefore, to fulfill these requirements, it would be beneficial to simultaneously transmit or store a video stream in a variety of Regions-of-Interest (e.g., each Region-of-Interest having different spatial resolution, as illustrated in *Fig. 1*), as well to enable efficiently tracking the predefined Region-of-Interest.

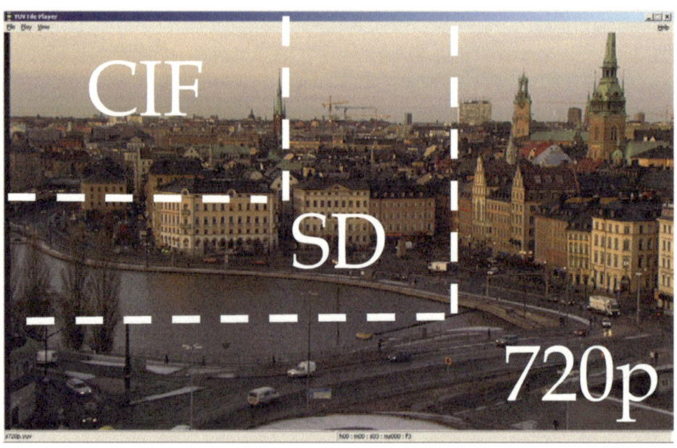


Fig. 1. Defining ROIs with different spatial resolutions (e.g., CIF, SD/4CIF, 720p resolutions) to be provided within a Scalable Video Coding stream.

This chapter is organized as follows: in *Section 2*, the Region-of-Interest (ROI) detection and tracking is described in detail, while presenting the Pixel-Domain approach (*Section 2.1*) and Compressed-Domain approach (*Section 2.2*), and further presenting various models and techniques, such as the Visual Attention model (*Section 2.1.1*), Object Detection (*Section

*2.1.2*), Face Detection (*Section 2.1.3*), Skin Detection (*Section 2.1.4*), etc.; in *Section 3,* the ROI Coding in H.264/SVC Standard is presented, including the ROI Scalability by Performing Cropping (*Section 3.1*) and the ROI Scalability by Using Flexible Macroblock Ordering (FMO) technique (*Section 3.2*); in *Section 4,* the bit-rate control for the ROI coding is presented; and Conclusions are provided in *Section 5.*

## 2. Region-of-interest detection and tracking

In order to successfully perform the ROI coding, it is important to accurately detect, and then correctly track, the desired Region-of-Interest. There are mainly two methods for the ROI detection and tracking: (a) the pixel-domain approach; and (b) the compressed-domain approach. The pixel-domain approach is more accurate compared to the compressed-domain approach, but it requires relatively high computational complexity resources. On the other hand, the compressed-domain approach does not consume many resources since it exploits the encoded information (such as DCT coefficients, motion vectors, macroblock types which are extracted in a compressed bitstream, etc.) (Manerba et al., 2008; Kas & Nicolas, 2009; Hanfeng et al., 2001; Zeng et al., 2005), but it results in a relatively poor performance. Also, for the same reason, the compressed-domain approach has significantly fast processing time and is adaptive to compressed videos. As a result, the compressed-domain approach is applicable mainly for simple scenarios.

Both the pixel-domain and compressed-domain approaches are explained in detail in the following *Sections 2.1 and 2.2.*

### 2.1 Pixel-domain approach

Generally, the main researches on object detection and tracking have been focused on the pixel domain approach since it can provide powerful capability of object tracking by using varyous technologies. The pixel-domain detection can be classified into the following types:

- Region-based methods. According to these methods, the object detection is performed according to ROI features, such as motion distribution and color histogram. The information with regard to the object colors can be especially useful when these colors are distinguishable from the image background or from other objects within the image (Vezhnevets, 2002).
- Feature-based methods (Shokurov et al., 2003). According to these methods, various motion parameters of feature points are calculated (the motion parameters are related to affine transformation information, which in turn contains rotation and 2D translation data).
- Contour-based methods. According to these methods, the shape and position of objects are detected by modeling the contour data (Wang et al., 2002).
- Template-based methods. According to these methods, the objects (such as faces) are detected by using predetermined templates (Schoepflin et al., 2001).

As mentioned above, phe pixel-domain approach is, generally, more accurate than the compressed-domain approach, but has relatively high computational complexity and requires further additional computational resources for decoding compressed video streams. Therefore, the desired ROI can be predicted in a relatively accurate manner by defining various pixel-domain models, such as visual attention models, object detection models, face detection models, etc., as presented in detail in the following *Sub-Sections 2.1.1 to 2.1.4.*

### 2.1.1 Visual attention

The visual attention models refer to the ability of a human user to concentrate his/her attention on a specific region of an image/video. This involves selection of the sensory information by the primary visual cortex in the brain by using a number of characteristic, such as intensity, color, size, orientation in space, and the like (Hu et al., 2008). Actually, the visual attention models simulate the behavior of the Human Visual System (HVS), and in turn enable to detect the Region-of-Interest within the image/video, such as presented in *Fig. 2*.

Fig. 2. An example of concentrating the attention on a specific region of an image.

Several researches have been conducted with this regard in order to achieve better ROI detection performance, and in turn improve the ROI visual presentation quality. Thus, for example (Cheng et al., 2005) presents a framework for automatic video Region-of-Interest determination based on user attention model, while considering the three types of visual attention features, i.e. intensity, color and motion. The contrast-based intensity model is based on the fact that particular color pairs, such as red-green and blue-yellow possess high spatial and chromatic opposition; the same characteristics exist in high deference lighting or intensity pairs. Thus, according to (Cheng et al., 2005), the intensity, red-green color and blue-yellow color constant models should be included into the user attention representation module. Also, when there is more than one ROI within the frame (e.g., a number of football players), then a saliency map is used which shows the ability to characterize the visual attraction of the image/video. The saliency map is divided into $n$ regions, and ROI is declared for each such region, thereby enabling to dynamically and automatically determine ROI for each frame-segment.

Further, (Sun et al., 2010) proposes a visual attention based approach to extract texts from complicated background in camera-based images. First, it applies the simplified visual attention model to highlight the region of interest (ROI) in an input image and to yield a map consisting of the ROIs. Second, an edge map of image containing the edge information of four directions is obtained by Sobel operators; character areas are detected by connected component analysis and merged into candidate text regions. Finally, the map consisting of the ROIs is employed to confirm the candidate text regions.

Further, other visual attention models have been recently proposed to improve the ROI visual presentation quality, such as (Engelke et al., 2009), which discusses two ways of obtaining subjective visual attention data that can be subsequently used to develop visual attention models based on the selective region-of-interest and visual fixation patterns; (Chen et al., 2010) discloses a model of the focus of attention for detecting the attended regions in video sequences by using the similarity between the adjacent frames, establishing the gray histogram, selecting the maximum similarity as predicable model, and finally obtaining a position of the focus of attention in the next fame; (Li et al., 2010) presents a three-stage method that combines the visual attention model with target detection by using the saliency map, covering the region of interest with blocks and measuring the similarity between the blocks and the template; (Kwon et al., 2010) shows a ROI based video preprocessor method that deals with the perceptual quality in a low-bit rate communication environment, further proposing three separated processes: the ROI detection, the image enhancement, and the boundary reduction in order to deliver better video quality at the videoconferencing application for use in a fixed camera and to be compatible as a preprocessor for the conventional video coding standards.

As seen from the above, the visual attention approach has recently become quite popular among researchers, and many improved techniques have been lately presented.

### 2.1.2 Object detection

Automatic object detection is one of the important steps in image processing and computer vision (Bhanu et al., 1997; Lin et al., 2005). The major task of object detection is to locate objects in images and extract the regions containing them (the extracted regions are ROIs). The quality of object detection is highly dependent on the effectiveness of the features used in the detection. Finding or designing appropriate features to capture the characteristics of objects and building the feature-based representation of objects are the key to the success of detection. Usually, it is not easy for human experts to figure out a set of features to characterize complex objects, and sometimes, simple features directly extracted from images may not be effective in object detection.

The ROI detection is especially useful for medical applications (Liu, 2006). Automatic detection of ROI in a complex image or video like endoscopic neurosurgery video, is an important task in many image and video processing applications such as image-guide surgery system, real-time patient monitoring system, and object-based video compression. In telemedical applications, object-based video coding is highly useful because it produces a good perceptual quality in a specified region, i.e., a region of interest (ROI), without requiring an excessive bandwidth. By using a dedicated video encoder, the ROI can be coded with more bits to obtain a much higher quality than that of the non-ROI which is coded with fewer bits.

In the last decade, various object detection techniques have been proposed. For example, (Han et al., 2008) presents a fully automated architecture for object-based ROI detection, based on the principle of discriminant saliency, which defines as salient the image regions of strongest response to a set of features that optimally discriminate the object class of interest from all the others. It consists of two stages, saliency detection and saliency validation. The first detects salient points, the second verifies the consistency of their geometric configuration with that of training examples. Both the saliency detector and the configuration model can be learned from cluttered images downloaded from the web.

Also, (Wang J. M. et al., 2008) describes a simple and novel algorithm for detecting foreground objects in video sequences using just two consecutive frames. The method is divided in three layers: sensory layer, perceptual layer, and memory layer (short-term memory in conceptual layer). In sensory layer, successive images are obtained from one fixed camera, and some early computer vision processing techniques are applied here to extract the image information, which are edges and inconsistent region. In perceptual layer, moving objects are extracted based on the information from the sensory layer, and may request the sensory layer support more detail. The detecting results are stored in the memory layer, and help the perceptual layer to detect the temporal static objects.
In addition, (Jeong, 2006) proposes an objectionable image detection system based on the ROI. The system proposed by (Jeong, 2006) excels in that ROI detection method is specialized in objectionable image detection. In addition, a novel feature consisting of weighted SCD based on ROI and skin color structure descriptor is presented for classifying objectionable image. Using the ROI detection method, (Jeong, 2006) can reduce the noisy information in image and extract more accurate features for classifying objectionable image.
Further, (Lin et al., 2005) uses genetic programming (GP) to synthesize composite operators and composite features from combinations of primitive operations and primitive features for object detection. The motivation for using GP is to overcome the human experts' limitations of focusing only on conventional combinations of primitive image processing operations in the feature synthesis. GP attempts many unconventional combinations that in some cases yield exceptionally good results. Compared to a traditional region-of-interest extraction algorithm, the composite operators learned by GP are more effective and efficient for object detection. Still further, (Kim & Wang, 2009) proposes a method for smoke detection in outdoor video sequences, which contains three steps. The first step is to decide whether the camera is moving or not. While the camera is moving, the authors skip the ensuing steps. Otherwise, the second step is to detect the areas of change in the current input frame against the background image and to locate regions of interest (ROIs) by connected component analysis. In the final step, the authors decide whether the detected ROI is smoke by using the k-temporal information of its color and shape extracted from the ROI.

### 2.1.3 Face detection

The face detection can be regarded as a specific case of object-class detection. In object-class detection, the task is to find the locations and sizes of all objects in an image that belong to a given class (such as pedestrians, cars, and the like). Also, the face detection can be regarded as a more general case of face localization. In face localization, the task is to find the locations and sizes of a known number of faces (usually one). In face detection, one does not have this additional information.
Early face-detection algorithms focused on the detection of frontal human faces, whereas recent face detection method aim to solve the more general and difficult problem of multi-view face detection. The face detection from an image video is considered to be a relatively difficult task due to a plurality of possible visual representations of the same face: the face scale, pose, location, orientation in space, varying lighting conditions, face emotional expression, and many others (e.g., as presented in *Fig. 3*). Therefore, in spite of the recent technological progress, this field still has many challenges and problems to be resolved.

Generally, the challenges associated with face detection can be attributed to the following factors (Yang et al., 2010):

- *Facial expression.* The appearance of faces is directly affected by a person's facial expression.
- *Pose.* The images of a face vary due to the relative camera-face pose (frontal, 45 degree, profile, upside down), and some facial features such as an eye or the nose may become partially or wholly occluded.
- *Occlusion.* Faces may be partially occluded by other objects. In an image with a group of people, some faces may partially occlude other faces.
- *Image orientation.* Face images directly vary for different rotations about the camera's optical axis.
- *Imaging conditions.* When the image is formed, factors such as lighting (spectra, source distribution and intensity) and camera characteristics (sensor response, lenses) affect the appearance of a face.
- *Presence or absence of structural components.* Facial features such as beards, mustaches, and glasses may or may not be present and there is a great deal of variability among these components including shape, color, and size.

Fig. 3. An example of a plurality of possible visual representations of the same face, which has an influence on the accurate face detection. Although the accuracy of face detection systems has dramatically increased during the last decade, such systems still have many challenges and problems to be resolved, such as varying lighting conditions, facial expression, presence or absence of structural components, etc.

During the last decade, many researchers around the world tried to improve the face detection and develop an efficient and accurate detection system. Such for example, (Mustafah et al., 2009) proposes a design of a face detection system for real-time high resolution smart camera, while making an emphasis on the problem of crowd surveillance where the static color camera is used to monitor a wide area of interest, and utilizing a background subtraction method to reduce the Region-of-Interest (ROI) to areas where the moving objects are located. Another work was performed by (Zhang et al., 2009), in which was presented a ROI based H.264 encoder for videophone with a hardware macroblock level face detector. The ROI definition module operates as a face detector in videophone, and it is embedded into the encoder to define the currently processed and encoded ROI macroclocks, while the encoding process is dynamically controlled according to the ROI (the encoding parameters vary according to ROI).

Further, other face detection techniques have been recently proposed to improve the face detection, such as: (Micheloni et al., 2005) presents an integrated surveillance system for the outdoor security; (Qayyum & Javed, 2006) discloses a notch based face detection, tracking and facial feature localization system, which contains two phases: visual guidance and face/non-face classification; and (Sadykhov & Lamovsky, 2008) discloses a method for real-time face detection in 3D space.

### 2.1.4 Skin detection

The successful recognition of the skin ROI simplifies the further processing of such ROI. The main aim of traditional skin ROI detection schemes is to detect skin pixels in images, thereby generating skin areas. According to (Abdullah-Al-Wadud & Oksam, 2007), if ROI detection process misses a skin region or provides regions having lots of holes in it, then the reliability of applications significantly decreases. Therefore, it is important to maintain the efficiency of the human-computer interaction (HCI) based systems. In turn, (Abdullah-Al-Wadud & Oksam, 2007) presents an improved region-of-interest selection method for skin detection applications. This method can be applied in any explicit skin cluster classifier in any color space, while do not requiring any learning or training procedure. The proposed algorithm mainly operates on a grayscale image (DM), but the processing is based on color information. The scalar distance map contains the information of the vector image, thereby making this method relatively simple to implement.

Also, (Yuan & Mu, 2007) presents an ear detection method, which is based on skin-color and contour information, while introducing a modified Continuously Adaptive Mean Shift (CAMSHAFT) algorithm for rough and fast profile tracking. The aim for profile tracking is to locate the main skin-color region, such as the ROI that contains the ear. The CAMSHIFT algorithm is based on a robust non-parameter technique for climbing density gradients to find peak of probability distribution called the mean shift algorithm. The mean shift algorithm operates on probability distribution, so in order to track colored objects in video sequence, the color image data has to be represented as the color distribution first. According to (Yuan & Mu, 2007), the modified CAMSHIFT method is performed as follows:

- Generating the skin-color histogram on training set skin images.
- Setting the initial location of the 2D mean shift search window at a fixed poison in the first frame such as the center of the frame.
- Using the generated skin-color histogram to calculate the skin-color probability distribution of the 2D region centered at the area slightly larger than the mean shift window size.
- Calculating the zeroth moment (area of size) and mean location (the centroid).
- For the next frame, centering the search window at the calculated mean location and setting the window size using a function of the zeroth moment. Then the previous two steps are repeated.

In addition, (Chen et al., 2003) presents a video coding H263 based technique for robust skin-color detection, which is suitable for real time videoconferencing. According to (Chen et al., 2003), the ROIs are automatically selected by a robust skin-color detection which utilizes the Cr and RGB variance instead of the traditional skin color models, such as YCbCr, HSI, etc. The skin color model defined by Cr and RGB variance can choose the skin color region more accurately than other methods. The distortion weight parameter and variance at the macroblock layer are adjusted to control the qualities at different regions. As a result, the quality at the ROI is can significantly improved.

### 2.2 Compressed-domain detection

The conventional compressed domain algorithms exploit motion vectors or DCT coefficients instead of original pixel data as resources in order to reduce computational complexity of object detection and tracking (You, 2010).

In general, the compressed domain algorithms can be categorized as follows: the clustering-based methods and the filtering-based methods.

The clustering-based methods (Benzougar et al., 2001; Babu et al., 2004; Ji & Park, 2000; Jamrozik & Hayes, 2002) attempt to perform grouping and merging all blocks into several regions according to their spatial or temporal similarity. Then, these regions are merged with each other or classified as background or foreground. The most advanced clustering-based method, which handles the H.264/AVC standard, is the region growing approach, in which several seed fragments grow spatially and temporally by merging similar neighboring fragments.

On the other hand, the filtering-based methods (Aggarwal et al., 2006; Zheg et al., 2005; You et al., 2007; You et al., 2009) extract foreground regions by filtering blocks, which are expected to belong to background or by classifying all blocks into foreground and background. Then, the foreground region is split into several object parts through clustering procedure.

### 2.3 Region-of-interest tracking

Object tracking based on video sequence plays an important role in many modern vision applications such as intelligent surveillance, video compression, human-computer interfaces, sports analysis (Haritaoglu et al, 2000). When object is tracked with an active camera, traditional methods such as background subtraction, temporal differencing and optical flow may not work well due to the motion of camera, tremor of camera and the disturbance from background (Xiang, 2009).

Some researchers propose methods of tracking moving target with an active camera, yet most of their algorithms are too computationally complex due to their dependence on accurate mathematical model and motion model, and can't be applied to real-time tracking in presence of fast motion from the object or the active camera, irregular motion and un-calibrated camera. (Xiang, 2009) makes great effort to find a fast, computationally efficient algorithm, which can handle fast motion, and can smoothly follow-up track moving target with an active camera, by proposing a method for real-time follow-up tracking fast moving object with an active camera. (Xiang, 2009) focuses on the color-based Mean Shift algorithm which shows excellent performance both on computationally complexity and robustness.

(Wei & Zhou, 2010) presents a novel algorithm that uses the selective visual attention mechanisms to develop a reliable algorithm for objects tracking that can effectively deal with the relatively big influence by external interference in a-priori approaches. To extract the ROI, it makes use of the "local statistic" of the object. By integrating the image feature with state feature, the synergistic benefits can bring following obvious advantages:

- It doesn't use any a-priori knowledge about blobs and no heuristic assumptions must be provided;
- The computation of the model for a generic blob doesn't take a long processing time.

According to (Wei & Zhou, 2010), during the detection phase, there are some false-alarms in any actual image. To reduce the fictitious targets as much as possible, it needs to identify the extracted ROI, while the tracing target can be defined by the following characteristics:

- *The length of boundary of the tracing target in the ROI.*
- *Aspect ratio.* The length and the width of the target can be expressed by the two orthogonal axes of minimum enclosing rectangle. The radio between them is the aspect ratio.
- *Shape complexity.* The radio between the length of the boundary and the area.

The ROI, whose parameters accord with the above three features, can be considered as the ROI including the real- target.

Further, there are many other recent tracking methods, such as: (Mehmood, 2009) implements kernel tracking of density-based appearance models for real-time object tracking applications; (Wang et al., 2009) discloses a wireless, embedded smart camera system for cooperative object tracking and event detection; (Sun, Z. & Sun, J., 2008) presents an approach for detecting and tracking dynamic objects with complex topology from image sequences based on intensive restraint topology adaptive snake mode; (Wang & Zhu, 2008) presents a sensor platform with multi-modalities, consisting of a dual-panoramic peripheral vision system and a narrow field-of-view hyperspectral fovea; thus, only hyperspectal images in the ROI should be captured; (Liu et al., 2006) presents a new method that addresses several challenges in automatic detection of ROI of neurosurgical video for ROI coding, which is used for neurophysiological intraoperative monitoring (IOM) system. According to (Liu et al., 2006), the method is based on an object tracking technique with multivariate density estimation theory, combined with the shape information of the object, thereby by defining the ROIs for neurosurgical video, this method produces a smooth and convex emphasis region, within which surgical procedures are performed. (Abousleman, 2009) presents an automated region-of-interest-based video coding system for use in ultra-low-bandwidth applications.

## 3. Region-of-interest coding in H.264/SVC standard

Region-of-Interest (ROI) coding is a desirable feature in future applications of Scalable Video Coding (SVC), especially in applications for the wireless networks, which have a limited bandwidth. However, the H.264/AVC standard does not explicitly teach as how to perform the ROI coding.

The ROI coding is supported by various techniques in the H.264/AVC standard (Wiegand & Sullivan, 2003) and the SVC (Schwarz et al., 2007) extensions. Some of these techniques include quantization step size control at the slice and macroblock levels, and are related to the concept of slice grouping, also known as Flexible Macroblock Ordering (FMO). For example, (Lu et al., 2005a) handles the ROI-based fine granular scalability (FGS) coding, in which a user at the decoder side requires to receive better decoded quality ROIs, while the pre-encoded scalable bit-stream is truncated. (Lu et al., 2005a) presents a number of ROI enhancement quality layers to provide fine granular scalability. In addition, (Thang et al., 2005) presents ROI-based spatial scalability scheme, concerning two main issues: overlapped regions between ROIs and providing different ROIs resolutions. However, (Thang et al., 2005) follows the concept of slice grouping of H.264/AVC, considering the following two solutions to improve the coding efficiency: (a) supporting different spatial resolutions for various ROIs by introducing a concept of virtual layers; and (b) enabling to avoid duplicate coding of overlapped regions in multiple ROIs by encoding the overlapped regions such that the corresponding encoded regions can be independently decoded. Further, (Lu et al., 2005b) presents ROI-based coarse granular scalability (CGS), using a

perceptual ROI technique to generate a number of quality profiles, and in turn, to realize the CGS. According to (Lu et al., 2005b), the proposed ROI based compression achieves better perceptual quality and improves coding efficiency. Moreover, (Lampert et al., 2006) relates to extracting the ROIs (i.e., of an original bit-stream by introducing a description-driven content adaptation framework. According to (Lampert et al., 2006), two methods for ROI extraction are implemented: (a) the removal of the non-ROI portions of a bit-stream; and (b) the replacement of coded background with corresponding placeholder slices. In turn, bit-streams that are adapted by this ROI extraction process have a significantly lower bit-rate than their original versions. While this has, in general, a profound impact on the quality of the decoded video sequence, this impact is marginal in case of a fixed camera and static background. This observation may lead to new opportunities in the domain of video surveillance or video conferencing. According to (Lampert et al., 2006), in addition to the bandwidth decrease, the adaptation process has a positive effect on the decoder due to the relatively easy processing of placeholder slices, thereby increasing the decoding speed.
Below we present a novel dynamically adjustable and scalable ROI video coding scheme, enabling to adaptively and efficiently set the desirable ROI location, size, resolution and bit-rate, according to the network bandwidth (especially, if it is a wireless network in which the bandwidth is limited), power constraints of resource-limited systems (such as mobile devices/servers) where the low power consumption is required, and according to end-user resource-limited devices (such as mobile devices, PDAs, and the like), thereby effectively selecting best encoding scenarios suitable for most heterogonous and time-invariant end-user terminals (i.e., different users can be connected each time) and network bandwidths.
In the following *Sections 3.1* and *3.2*, different types of ROI scalability are presented: the ROI scalability by performing cropping and ROI scalability by employing the Flexible Macroblock Ordering (FMO) technique, respectively.

### 3.1 ROI scalability by performing cropping

According to the first method for the ROI video coding, and in order to enable obtaining a high-quality ROI on resource-limited devices (such as mobile devices), we crop the ROI from the original image and use it as a baselayer (or other low enhancement layers, such as Layer 1 or 2), as schematically illustrated in *Fig. 4* below (Grois et al., 2010a).

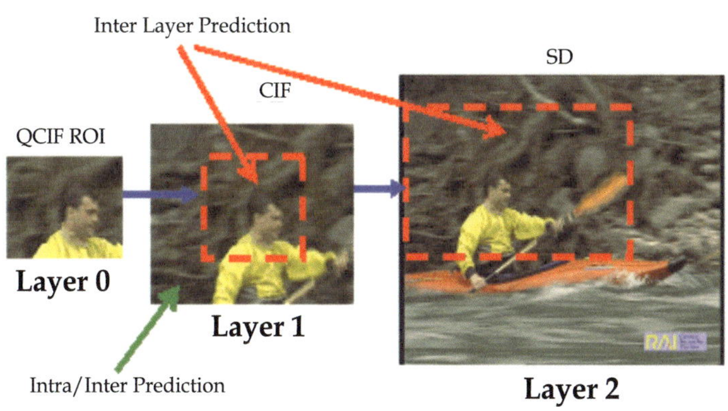


Fig. 4. The example of the ROI dynamic adjustment and scalability (e.g., for mobile devices with different spatial resolutions) by using a cropping method.

Then, we perform an Inter-layer prediction in the similar sections of the image, i.e., in the cropping areas. As a result, for example (*Fig. 4*), by using the Inter-layer prediction for the three-layer (QCIF-CIF-SD) coding (with the similar quantization parameter (QP) settings at each layer), we achieve the significantly low bit-rate overhead. Prior to cropping the image, we determine the location of a cropping area in the successive layer of the image (in Layer 1, and then in Layer 2, as shown on *Fig. 4*). For this, we employ an ESS (Extended Spatial Scalability) method (Shoaib & Anni, 2010). In addition, we define a GOP for the SVC as a group between two I/P frames, or any combination thereof. Thus, as shown for example in *Table 3*, for the "*SOCCER*" video sequence (30 fp/sec; 300 frames; GOP size 16; QPs varying from 22 to 34) we obtain the bit-rate overhead of only 4.7% to 7.9% compared to conventional single layer coding.

*Tables 1* to *3* below present R-D (Rate-Distortion) experimental results for the variable-layer coding with different cropping spatial resolutions, while using the Inter/Intra-layer prediction. As it is clearly seen from these tables, there is significantly low bit-rate overhead, which is especially important for transmitting over limited-bandwidth networks (such as wireless networks). Particularly, the *Tables 1* below presents the R-D (Rate-Distortion) experimental results for the two-layer coding (QCIF-CIF) with the QCIF cropping versus the single layer coding.

| **Quantization Parameters** | **Single layer** | | **QCIF-CIF** | | **Bit-Rate Overhead (%)** |
|---|---|---|---|---|---|
| | **PSRN [dB]** | **Bit-Rate[K/sec]** | **PSNR [dB]** | **Bit-Rate[K/sec]** | |
| 22 | 40.9 | 1636.8 | 40.9 | 1713.5 | 4.5 |
| 26 | 38.6 | 917.2 | 38.6 | 968.8 | 5.3 |
| 30 | 36.5 | 544.0 | 36.5 | 578.1 | 5.9 |
| 34 | 34.4 | 332.9 | 34.4 | 357.5 | 6.9 |

Table 1. Two-layer (QCIF-CIF) spatial scalability coding vs. single layer coding ("*SOCCER*" video sequence, 30 fp/s, 300 frames, GOP size 16).

Also, the *Tables 2* below presents the R-D (Rate-Distortion) experimental results for the two-layer coding (CIF-SD) with the CIF cropping versus the single layer coding.

| **Quantization Parameters** | **Single layer** | | **CIF-SD** | | **Bit-Rate Overhead (%)** |
|---|---|---|---|---|---|
| | **PSRN [dB]** | **Bit-Rate [K/sec]** | **PSNR [dB]** | **Bit-Rate [K/sec]** | |
| 22 | 41.0 | 5663.3 | 40.9 | 5870.7 | 3.5 |
| 26 | 38.8 | 3054.9 | 38.7 | 3190.6 | 4.3 |
| 30 | 36.8 | 1770.2 | 36.7 | 1860.2 | 4.8 |
| 34 | 34.8 | 1071.3 | 34.7 | 1137.0 | 5.8 |

Table 2. Three-layer (CIF-SD) spatial scalability coding vs. single layer coding ("*SOCCER*" video sequence, 30 fp/s, 300 frames, GOP size 16).

Further, the *Tables 3* below presents the R-D (Rate-Distortion) experimental results for the three-layer coding (QCIF-CIF-SD) with the QCIF-CIF cropping versus the single layer coding.

| Quantization Parameters | Single layer | | QCIF-CIF-SD | | Bit-Rate Overhead (%) |
|---|---|---|---|---|---|
| | PSRN [dB] | Bit-Rate [K/sec] | PSNR [dB] | Bit-Rate [K/sec] | |
| 22 | 41.0 | 5663.3 | 41.0 | 5940.6 | 4.7 |
| 26 | 38.8 | 3054.9 | 38.8 | 3248.1 | 6.0 |
| 30 | 36.8 | 1770.2 | 36.8 | 1894.9 | 6.6 |
| 34 | 34.8 | 1071.3 | 34.8 | 1163.6 | 7.9 |

Table 3. Three-layer (QCIF-CIF-SD) spatial scalability coding vs. single layer coding ("*SOCCER*" video sequence, 30 fp/s, 300 frames, GOP size 16).

As was mentioned above, it is clearly seen from the above experimental results that when using the Inter/Intra-layer prediction, the bit-rate overhead is very small and is much less than 10%.

### 3.2 ROI scalability by using flexible macroblock ordering

The second method refers to the ROI dynamic adjustment and scalability (Grois et al., 2010a) by using the FMO (Flexible Macroblock Ordering) in the scalable baseline profile (not for Layer 0, which is similar to the H.264/AVC baseline profile without the FMO).

One of the basic elements of the H.264 video sequence is a slice, which contains a group of macroblocks. Each picture can be subdivided into one or more slices and each slice can be provided with increased importance as the basic spatial segment, which can be encoded independently from its neighbors (the slice coding is one of the techniques used in H.264 for transmission) (Chen et al., 2008; Liu et al., 2005; Ndili & Ogunfunmi, 2006; Kodikara et al., 2006). Usually, slices are provided in a raster scan order with continuously ascending addresses; on the other hand, the FMO is an advanced tool of H.264 that defines the information of slice groups and enables to employ different macroblocks to slice groups of mapping patterns.

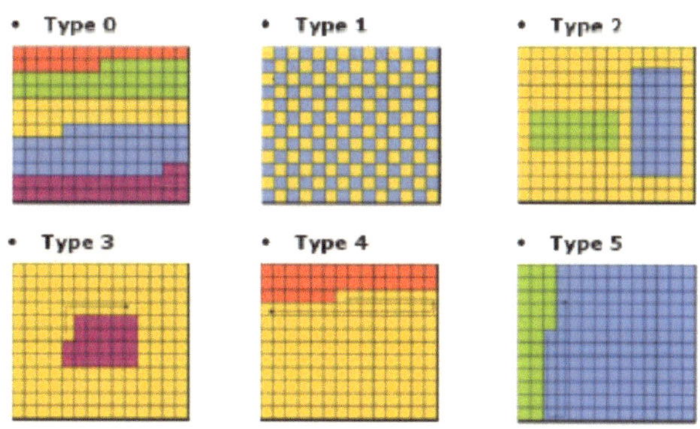


Fig. 5. Six fixed types of the FMO (interleaved, dispersed, foreground, box-out, raster scan and wipe-out), while each color represents a slice group).

Each slice of each picture/frame is independently intra predicted, and the macroblock order within a slice must be in the ascending order. In H.264 standard, FMO consists of seven slice group map types (*Type 0* to *Type 6*), six of them are predefined fixed macroblock mapping types (as illustrated in Fig. 5: interleaved, dispersed, foreground, box-out, raster scan and wipe-out), which can be specified through picture parameter setting (PPS), and the last one is a custom type, which allows the full flexibility of assigning macroblock to any slice group. The ROI can be defined as a separate slice in the FMO *Type 2* which enables defining slices of rectangular regions, and then the whole sequence can be encoded accordingly, while making it possible to define more than one ROI regions (these definitions should be made in the SVC configuration files, according to the JSVM 9.19 reference software manual (JSVM, 2009).

For the Scalable Video Coding, we use the FMO *Type 2* above, where each ROI is represented by a separate rectangular region and is encoded as a separate slice. *Tables 4* presents experimental results for the four layers spatial scalability coding versus six layers coding of the "*SOCCER*" sequence (30 fp/s; 300 frames; GOP size is 16), where four layers are presented by one CIF layer and three SD layers having the CIF-resolution ROI in an upper-left corner of the image. In turn, the six layers are presented by three CIF layers (each layer is a crop from the SD resolution) and three 4CIF/SD layers.

| Quantization Parameters | Four Layers (CIF and three SD layers) | | Six Layers (three CIF layers and three SD layers) | | Bit-Rate Savings (%) |
|---|---|---|---|---|---|
| | PSRN [dB] | Bit-Rate [K/sec] | PSNR [dB] | Bit-Rate [K/sec] | |
| 32 | 36.0 | 2140.1 | 36.0 | 2290.1 | 6.6 |
| 34 | 35.1 | 1549.4 | 35.1 | 1680.1 | 7.8 |
| 36 | 34.0 | 1140.1 | 34.0 | 1279.4 | 10.9 |

Table 4. FMO: Four-layer spatial scalability coding vs. six-layer coding ("*SOCCER*" video sequence, 30 fp/s, 300 frames, GOP size 16).

It should be noted that each of the above three CIF layers (crops extracted from the SD resolution image) can be considered, for example, as a zoom of the image in a upper-left corner, as shown in *Fig. 6* below.

(a) (b)

Fig. 6. (a) the CIF crop (representing Layer 0, i.e. the base-layer) extracted from the SD resolution frame of the "*SOCCER*" sequence; (b) the corresponding HD resolution image, representing Layer 1 of the "*SOCCER*" sequence. The white dashed lines show the zoomed ROI.

Further, *Table 5* presents R-D (Rate-Distortion) experimental results for the HD (High Definition) video sequence "*STOCKHOLM*" (*Fig. 1*, 1280x720, 30 fp/sec, GOP size 8, 160 frames) by using four-layer coding (640x360 layer and three HD layers having two ROIs

(CIF and 4CIF/SD resolutions) in the upper left corner of the image) versus eight-layer coding (two CIF layers (scalable baseline profile without B frames), three 4CIF/SD layers, and three HD layers having different quantization parameters). The quantization parameters vary from 32 to 36 with a step size of 2.

| Quantization Parameters | Four Layers (640x360, and three HD layers) | | Eight Layers (two CIF layers, three SD layers, and three HD layers) | | Bit-Rate Savings (%) |
|---|---|---|---|---|---|
| | PSRN [dB] | Bit-Rate [K/sec] | PSNR [dB] | Bit-Rate [K/sec] | |
| 32 | 34.5 | 2566.2 | 34.5 | 3237.0 | 20.7 |
| 34 | 33.9 | 1730.2 | 33.9 | 2359.1 | 26.7 |
| 36 | 33.3 | 1170.0 | 33.3 | 1759.0 | 33.5 |

Table 5. FMO: Four-layer coding vs. eight-layer coding ("*STOCKHOLM*", 30 fp/s, 96 frames, GOP size 8)

Further, *Table 6* below presents R-D (Rate-Distortion) experimental results for the HD video sequence "*STOCKHOLM*" by using four-layer coding (640x360 layer and three HD layers having two ROIs (CIF and SD resolution, respectively) in the upper-left corner of the image) versus six-layer coding (three CIF and three SD layers).

| Quantization Parameters | Four Layers (640x360, and three HD layers) | | Six Layers (three CIF layers and three SD layers) | | Bit-Rate Savings (%) |
|---|---|---|---|---|---|
| | PSRN [dB] | Bit-Rate [K/sec] | PSNR [dB] | Bit-Rate [K/sec] | |
| 32 | 34.5 | 2566.2 | 34.5 | 3237.0 | 19.3 |
| 34 | 33.9 | 1730.2 | 33.9 | 2359.1 | 29.7 |
| 36 | 33.3 | 1170.0 | 33.3 | 1759.0 | 39.9 |

Table 6. FMO: Four-layer coding vs. six-layer coding ("*STOCKHOLM*", 30 fp/s, 96 frames, GOP size 8)

As it is clearly observed from *Table 4* to *6* above, there are very significant bit-rate savings - up to 39%, when using the FMO techniques.

## 4. Bit-rate control for region-of-interest coding

The bit-rate control is crucial in providing desired compression bit rates for H264/AVC video applications, and especially for the Scalable Video Coding, which is the extension of H264/AVC.

The bit-rate control has been intensively studied in existing single layer coding standards, such as MPEG 2, MPEG 4, and H.264/AVC (Li et al., 2003). According to the existing single layer rate control schemes, the encoder employs the rate control as a way to control varying bit-rate characteristics of the coded bit-stream. Generally, there are two objectives of the bit-rate control for the single layer video coding: one is to meet the bandwidth that is provided by the network, and another is to produce high quality decoded pictures (Li et al., 2007). Thus, the inputs of the bit-rate control scheme are: the given bandwidth; usually, the statistics of video sequence including Mean Squared Error (MSE); and a header of each predefined unit (e.g., a basic unit, macroblock, frame, slice). In turn, the outputs are a quantization parameter (QP) for the quantization process and another QP for the rate-distortion optimization (RDO) process of each basic unit, while these two quantization parameters, in the single layer video coding, are usually equal in order to maximize the coding efficiency.

In the current JSVM reference software (JSVM, 2009) there is no rate control mechanism, besides the base-layer rate control, which do not consider enhancement layers. The target bit-rate for each SVC layer is achieved by coding each layer with a fixed QP, which is determined by a logarithmic search (JSVM, 2009; Liu et al., 2008). Of course, this is very inefficient and much time-consuming. For solving this problem, only a few works have been published during the last years, trying to provide an efficient rate control mechanism for the SVC. However, none of them handles scalable bit-rate control for the Region-of-Interest (ROI) coding. Such, in (Xu et al., 2005) the rate distortion optimization (RDO) involved in the step of encoding temporal subband pictures is only implemented on low-pass subband pictures, and rate control is independently applied to each spatial layer. Furthermore, for the temporal subband pictures obtained from the motion compensation temporal filtering (MCTF), the target bit allocation and quantization parameter selection inside a GOP make a full use of the hierarchical relations inheritance from the MCTF. In addition, (Liu et al., 2008) proposes a switched model to predict the mean absolute difference (MAD) of the residual texture from the available MAD information of the previous frame in the same layer and the same frame in its "base layer". Further, (Anselmo & Alfonso, 2010) describes a constant quality variable bit-rate (VBR) control algorithm for multiple layer coding. According to 0 (Anselmo & Alfonso, 2010), the algorithm allows achieving a target quality by specifying memory capabilities and the bit-rate limitations of the storage device. In the more recent work (Roodaki et al., 2010), the joint optimization of layers in the layered video coding is investigated. The authors show that spatial scalability, like the SNR scalability, does benefit from joint optimization, though not being able to exploit the relation between the quantizer step sizes. However, as mentioned above, there is currently no efficient bit-rate control scheme for the ROI Scalable Video Coding.

Below, we present a method and system for the efficient ROI Scalable Video Coding, according to which we achieve a bit-rate that is very close to the target bit-rate, while being able to define the desirable ROI quality (in term of QP or Peak Signal-To-Noise Ratio (PSNR)) and while adaptively changing the background region quality (the background region excludes the ROI), according to the overall bit-rate.

In order to provide the different visual presentation quality to at least one ROI and to the background (or other less important region of the frame), we divide each frame to at least two slices, while one slice is used for defining the ROI and at least one additional slice is used for defining the background region, for which fewer bits should be allocated. If more than one ROI is used, then the frame is divided on larger number of slices, such that for each ROI we use a separate slice.

The general proposed method for performing the adaptive ROI SVC bit-rate control for each SVC layer is as follows.

a. Compute the number of target bits for the current GOP and after that for each frame (of each SVC layer) within the above GOP by using a Hypothetical Reference Decoder (HRD) ((Ribas-Corbera et al., 2003). The calculation should consider that each SVC layer contains a number of predefined slices (the ROI slice, background slice, etc.), which should be encoded with different QPs.

b. Allocate the remaining bits to all non-coded macroblocks (MBs) for each predefined slice in the current frame of the particular SVC layer.
c. Estimate the MAD (Mean Absolute Difference) for the current macroblock in the current slice by a linear prediction model (Li et al., 2003; Lim et al., 2005) using the actual MAD of the macroblocks in the co-located position of the previous slices (in the previous frames) within the same SVC layer and the MAD of neighbor macroblocks in the current slice.
d. Estimate a set of groups of coding modes (e.g., modes such as Inter-Search16X8, Inter-Search8X16, Inter-Search8X8, Inter-Search8X4, Inter-Search4X8, Inter-Search4X4 modes, and the like) of the current macroblock in the current frame within the above SVC layer by using the actual group of coding modes for the macroblocks in the co-located positions of the previous frame(s) and the actual group of coding modes of neighbor macroblocks in the current frame.
e. Compute the corresponding QPs by using a quadratic model (Chiang & Zhang, 1997; Kaminsky et al., 2008; Grois et al., 2010c).
f. Perform the Rate-Distortion Optimization (RDO) for each MB by using the QPs derived from the above step 5.
g. Adaptively adjust the QPs (increase/decrease the QPs by a predefined quantization step size) according to the current overall bit-rate.

In *Fig. 7* below, is presented a system for performing the proposed adaptive bit-rate control for the Scalable Video Coding (for simplicity, only two layers are shown – Base-Layer (Layer 0), and Enhancement Layer (Layer 1). The system contains the SVC adaptive bit-rate controller, which continuously receives data regarding the current buffer occupancy, actual bit-rate and quantization parameters (Grois et al., 2010b).

The step (f) above can be performed by using a method (Lim et al., 2005; Wiegand et al., 2003) for determining an optimal coding mode for encoding each macroblock. According to method (Lim et al., 2005; Wiegand et al., 2003), the RDO for each macroblock is performed for selecting an optimal coding mode by minimizing the Lagrangian function as follows:

$$J(orig,rec,MODE|\lambda_{MODE}) = D(orig,rec,MODE|QP) + \lambda_{MODE} \cdot R(orig,rec,MODE|QP) \quad (1)$$

where the distortion $D(orig,rec,MODE|QP)$ can be the sum of squared differences (SSD) or the sum of absolute differences (SAD) between the original block ($orig$) and the reconstructed block ($rec$); $QP$ is the macroblock quantization parameter; $MODE$ is a mode selected from the set of available prediction modes; $R(orig,rec,MODE|QP)$ is the number of bits associated with selecting $MODE$; and $\lambda_{MODE}$ is a Lagrangian multiplier for the mode decision (Lim et al., 2005).

According to a buffer occupancy constraint due to the finite reference SVC buffer size, the buffer at each SVC layer should not be full or empty (overloaded or underloaded, respectively). The formulation of the optimal buffer control (for controlling the buffer occupancy for each SVC layer) can be given by:

$$\min_{\{r(i)\}}\{\sum_{i=1}^{N} e(i)\}, \quad \text{subject to } B^{Layer}{}_{\max} \geq B^{Layer}(i) \geq 0 \quad (2)$$

for $i = 1, 2, ..., N$

where $e(i)$ is a distortion for basic unit $i$; $B^{Layer}(i)$ is a buffer size and $B^{Layer}{}_{\max}$ is the maximal buffer size. The state of the buffer occupancy can be defined as:

$$B^{Layer}(i+1) = B^{Layer}(i) + r^{Layer}(i) - r_{out}^{Layer} \tag{3}$$

where $r^{Layer}(i)$ is the buffer input bit-rate with regard to each SVC layer and $r_{out}^{Layer}$ is the output bit-rate of buffer contents.

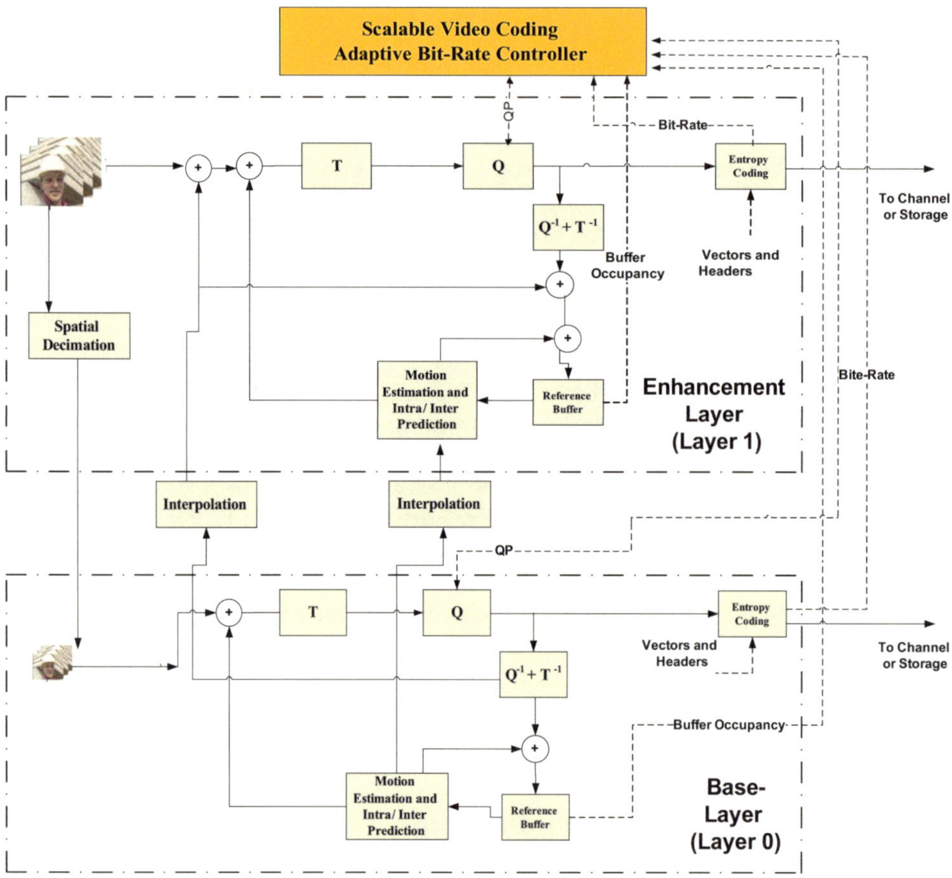


Fig. 7. The system for performing the presented adaptive spatial bit-rate control for the Scalable Video Coding (for simplicity, only two layers - Layer 0 and Layer 1 - are presented).

The optimal buffer control approach is related to the following optimal bit allocation formulation,

$$\min_{\{r(i)\}}\{\sum_{i=1}^{N} e(i)\}\ , \text{subject to } \sum_{i=1}^{n} r^{Layer}(i) \leq R^{Layer} \tag{4}$$

for $i = 1, 2, ..., N$
and is schematically presented in *Fig. 8* below.

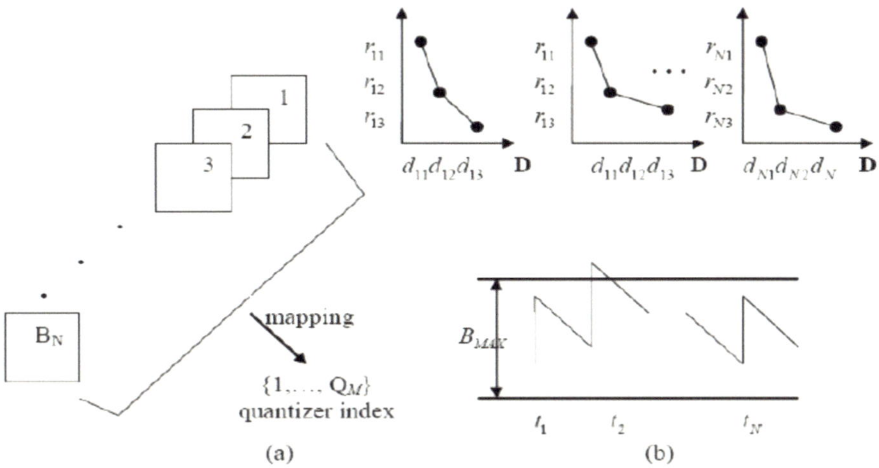


Fig. 8. (a) Each block ($1...B_N$) in the sequence has different R-D characteristics (for a given set of quantizers ($1...Q_M$) for blocks in the sequence, we can obtain R-D (Rate-Distortion) points ($r_{N1}$, $r_{N2}$, $r_{N3}$ *and* $d_{N1}$, $d_{N2}$, $d_N$, etc.) to form composite characteristics); and (b) $R$ at $t_2$ is not a feasible solution to the selected maximum buffer size $B_{MAX}$.

For overcoming the buffer control drawbacks and overcoming buffer size limitations, preventing underflow/overflow of the buffer, and significantly decreasing the buffer delay, the computational complexity (such as a number of CPU clocks) and bits of each basic unit within a video sequence can be dynamically allocated, according to its predicted MAD. In turn, the optimal buffer control problem (2) can be solved by implementing the C-R-D analysis of (Grois et al., 2009) for each SVC layer.

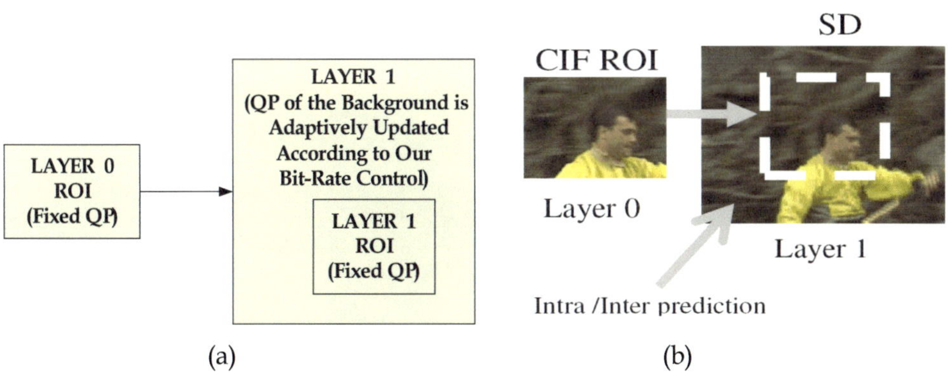


Fig. 9. (a) Defining two or more layers with corresponding QPs. The QP of the background region in Layer 1 is determined adaptively by our bit-rate control; (b) CIF ROI is used as Base Layer (Layer 0), and 4CIF (SD) is used as an Enhancement Layer (Layer 1). The Intra/Inter-prediction is used for reducing the overall bit-rate.

For simplicity, in this section, we show results for the bit-rate control of two layers: Base Layer (Layer 0) and Enhancement Layer (Layer 1), while the ROI region is provided in both Layer 0 and Layer 1, and the background region is provided only in Layer 1, as illustrated in *Fig. 9*. According to the presented adaptive bit-rate control, we preset for each layer different

initial quantization parameters (QPs): e.g., for the whole Layer 0 we can define an initial quantization parameter to be equal to 40, and for the ROI region provided in Layer 1 we can define an initial quantization parameter to be equal to 20; and then the QP of the remaining background region in Layer 1 is determined adaptively by our bit-rate control. In such a way, we can obtain the desired quality of the Region-of-Interest, and as a result, of the remaining background region (or any other less important region) according to the overall network bandwidth (either constant or variable bandwidth).
As a result, by encoding the video sequence with different QPs, we enable obtaining the optimal presentation quality of the predefined ROI region and enable reducing the quality of the background, as presented for example, in *Fig. 10 ("SOCCER"* video sequence, SD resolution).

Fig. 10. The "SOCCER" video sequence (SD 704x576, 25 fp/sec.) containing the ROI region in the upper-left corner.

*Figs. 11* and *12* below illustrate sample frames of the *"PARKRUN"* video sequence, which contains the ROI region - the man with an umbrella. The quantization parameter of the background region can be determined adaptively in order to achieve optimal video presentation quality (as it is clearly seen from *Figs. 11(b)* and *12(b)*, the QP of the background region is much higher than the QP of the ROI region).

(a) (b)

Fig. 11. The "PARKRUN" video sequence containing the ROI region in the middle of the frame - the man with an umbrella (the quantization parameter of the background region can be determined adaptively); (a) the original frame; and (b) the compressed frame with the higher-quality ROI region.

(a) (b)

Fig. 12. The "PARKRUN" video sequence containing the ROI region in the middle of the frame - the man with an umbrella (the quantization parameter of the background region can be determined adaptively); (a) the original frame; and (b) the compressed frame with the higher-quality ROI region.

Further, *Fig. 13* below shows another frame of the *"SHIELDS"* video sequence, which contains the ROI region - man's head and hand pointing to the shields. The quantization parameter of the background region can be determined adaptively according to the adaptive bit-rate control (as it is seen from *Fig. 13(b)*, the QP of the background region is much higher than the QP of the ROI region).

(a) (b)

Fig. 13. The "SHIELDS" video sequence containing the ROI region - man's head and hand pointing to the shields (the quantization parameter of the background region can be determined adaptively); (a) the original frame; and (b) the compressed frame with the higher-quality ROI region.

The following *Table 7* presents experimental results for the bit-rate control operation for various video sequences ("CITY", "CREW", "HARBOR", "ICE", and "SOCCER"), along with the corresponding PSNR and bit-rate values. According to the conducted tests, the QP of Layer 0 is equal to 40, and the QP of the ROI in Layer 1 is equal to 37, while the QP of the background of Layer 1 is determined by our adaptive SVC bit-rate control scheme.

| Video Sequence | Target Bit-Rate for Layer 1 with our Bit-Rate Control | Layers | | | |
|---|---|---|---|---|---|
| | | Actual Bit-Rate: Layer 1 with our Bit-Rate Control (ROI QP=20, the rest by our Rate Control) | | Actual Bit-Rate of Layer 0 with JSVM 9.19 Bit-Rate Control (QP=40) | |
| | Bit-Rate [K/sec] | Bit-Rate [K/sec] | Average PSNR [dB] | Bit-Rate [K/sec] | Average PSNR [dB] |
| CREW | 1600 | 1691.4 | 30.1 | 2195.0 | 35.0 |
| | 1700 | 1691.4 | 30.1 | | |
| SHIELDS | 5000 | 6393.1 | 37.8 | 6969.0 | 38.3 |
| | 6000 | 6399.6 | 38.3 | | |
| PARKRUN | 7000 | 7010.5 | 24.0 | 3435.2 | 28.1 |
| | 7500 | 7140.9 | 24.1 | | |
| | 8000 | 7172.4 | 24.2 | | |
| | 8500 | 8431.8 | 25.1 | | |
| SOCCER | 2300 | 2473.9 | 28.1 | 2105.9 | 34.1 |
| | 2500 | 2478.4 | 28.2 | | |

Table 7. Bit-rate control experimental results for "CREW", "SHIELDS", "PARKRUN", and "SOCCER" video sequences (ROI QP in "Layer 1" is equal to 20; the rest is determined by our bit-rate control).

## 5. Conclusions

In this chapter we have presented a comprehensive overview of recent developments in the area of Region-of-Interest Video Coding, making an emphasis on the ROI Scalable Video Coding field, which has become popular in the last couple of years due to standardization of the SVC in 2007, as an extension of H.264/AVC.

Also, we have presented our efficient novel scalable video coding schemes, enabling to adaptively set the desirable ROI location, size, resolution (e.g., the spatial resolution), ROI visual quality and amount of bits allocated for the ROI, and perform other predefined settings. According to these schemes, we achieve a significantly low bit-rate overhead and very significant savings in bit-rate, thereby enabling to provide an efficient adaptive bit-rate control for the ROI Scalable Video Coding, which was also presented in detail. In turn, the adaptive bit-rate control has enabled us to provide the high-quality video coding for the desired Region-of-Interest, while considering the overall available bandwidth, and other predefined parameters. The performance of the presented schemes was demonstrated and compared with the (Joint Scalable Video Model) JSVM reference software (JSVM 9.19), thereby showing a significant improvement in term of the PSNR values and bit-rate.

## 6. Acknowledgments

This work was supported by the NEGEV consortium, MAGNET Program of the Israeli Chief Scientist, Israeli Ministry of Trade and Industry under Grant 85265610. We thank Igor Medvetsky, Ran Dubin, Aviad Hadarian and Evgeny Kaminsky for their assistance in evaluation and testing.

## 7. References

Abdullah-Al-Wadud, M. & Oksam C. (2007). Region-of-Interest Selection for Skin Detection Based Applications, *Convergence Information Technology, 2007. International Conference on*, vol., no., pp.1999-2004, 21-23 Nov. 2007.

Abousleman, G.P. (2009). Target-tracking-based ultra-low-bit-rate video coding, *Military Communications Conference, 2009. MILCOM 2009. IEEE*, vol., no., pp.1-6, 18-21 Oct. 2009.

Aggarwal, A.; Biswas, S.; Singh, S.; Sural, S. & Majumdar, A. K. (2006). Object Tracking Using Background Subtraction and Motion Estimation in MPEG Videos, *ACCV 2006*, LNCS, vol. 3852, pp. 121-130, Springer, Heidelberg (2006).

Anselmo, T. & Alfonso, D., (2010). Constant Quality Variable Bit-Rate control for SVC, Image Analysis for Multimedia Interactive Services (WIAMIS), 2010 11th International Workshop on, vol., no., pp.1-4, 12-14 April 2010.

Babu, R. V.; Ramakrishnan, K. R. & Srinivasan, S. H. (2004). Video object segmentation: A compressed domain approach, *IEEE Trans. Circuits Syst. Video Technol.*, vol. 14, No. 4, pp. 462–474, April 2004.

Bae T. M.; Thang T. C.; Kim D. Y.; Ro Y. M.; Kang J. W. & Kim J. G. (2006). Multiple region-of-interest support in scalable video coding," ETRI journal 2006, vol. 28, no. 2, pp. 239 - 242.

Benzougar, A.; Bouthemy, P. & Fablet, R. (2001). MRF-based moving object detection from MPEG coded video, *in Proc. IEEE Int. Conf. Image Processing*, 2001, vol. 3, pp 402-405.

Bhanu, B.; Dudgeon, D. E.; Zelnio, E. G.; Rosenfeld, A.; Casasent & D.; Reed, I. S. (1997). Guest Editorial Introduction To The Special Issue On Automatic Target Detection And Recognition, *Image Processing, IEEE Transactions on*, vol.6, no.1, pp.1-6, Jan 1997.

Bing L.; Mingui S.; Qiang L.; Kassam, A.; Ching-Chung Li & Sclabassi, R.J. (2006). Automatic Detection of Region of Interest Based on Object Tracking in Neurosurgical Video, *Engineering in Medicine and Biology Society, 2005. IEEE-EMBS 2005. 27th Annual International Conference of the*, vol., no., pp.6273-6276, 17-18 Jan. 2006.

Chen, M.-J.; Chi, M.-C.; Hsu, C.-T. & Chen, J.-W. (2003). ROI video coding based on H.263+ with robust skin-color detection technique, *Consumer Electronics, 2003. ICCE. 2003 IEEE International Conference on*, vol., no., pp. 44- 45, 17-19 June 2003.

Chen, H.; Han, Z.; Hu, R. & Ruan, R. (2008). Adaptive FMO Selection Strategy for Error Resilient H.264 Coding, *Int. Conf. on Audio, Lang. and Image Proc., ICALIP* 2008, Jul. 7-9, pp. 868-872, Shanghai, China.

Chen, Q.-H.; Xie X.-F.; Guo T.-J.; Shi L. & Wang X.-F (2010). The Study of ROI Detection Based on Visual Attention Mechanism, *Wireless Communications Networking and Mobile Computing (WiCOM), 2010 6th International Conference on*, vol., no., pp.1-4, 23-25 Sept. 2010.

Chiang, T. & Zhang, Y.-Q. (1997). A new rate control scheme using quadratic rate distortion model, *IEEE Trans. Circuit Syst. Video Technol.*, vol. 7, no. 1, pp. 246–250, 1997.

Engelke, U.; Zepernick, H.-J. & Maeder, A. (2009). Visual attention modeling: Region-of-interest versus fixation patterns, *Picture Coding Symposium, 2009. PCS 2009*, vol., no., pp.1-4, 6-8 May 2009.

Grois, D.; Kaminsky, E. & Hadar, O. (2009). Buffer control in H.264/AVC applications by implementing dynamic complexity-rate-distortion analysis, *Broadband Multimedia Systems and Broadcasting, 2009. BMSB '09. IEEE International Symposium on*, pp.1-7, 13-15 May 2009.

Grois, D.; Kaminsky, E. & Hadar, O., (2010). ROI adaptive scalable video coding for limited bandwidth wireless networks, *Wireless Days (WD), 2010 IFIP*, pp.1-5, 20-22 Oct. 2010.

Grois, D.; Kaminsky, E. & Hadar, O. (2010). Adaptive bit-rate control for Region-of-Interest Scalable Video Coding, *Electrical and Electronics Engineers in Israel (IEEEI), 2010 IEEE 26th Convention of*, pp.761-765, 17-20 Nov. 2010.

Grois, D.; Kaminsky, E. & Hadar, O. (2010). Optimization Methods for H.264/AVC Video Coding, The Handbook of MPEG Applications: Standards in Practice, (eds M. C. Angelides and H. Agius), John Wiley & Sons, Ltd, Chichester, UK.

Hanfeng, C.; Yiqiang, Z. & Feihu, Q. (2001). Rapid object tracking on compressed video, in *Proc. 2nd IEEE Pacific Rim Conference on Multimedia*, Oct. 2001, pp.1066-1071.

Haritaoglu, I.; Harwood, D. & Davis, L. S. (2000). $W^4$: real-time surveillance of people and their activities, *Pattern Analysis and Machine Intelligence, IEEE Transactions on*, vol.22, no.8, pp.809-830, Aug 2000.

Hu, Y.; Rajan, D.; Chia, L. (2008). Detection of visual attention regions in images using robust subspace analysis, *Journal of Visual Communication and Image Pepresentation*, 19(3): 199-216, 2008.

Jamrozik, M. L. & Hayes, M. H. (2002). A compressed domain video object segmentation system, *in Proc. IEEE Int. Conf. Image Processing*, 2002, vol. 1, pp.113-116.

Jeong, C. Y.; Han, S. W.; Choi, S. G. & Nam, T. Y., An Objectionable Image Detection System Based on Region of Interest, *Image Processing, 2006 IEEE International Conference on*, vol., no., pp.1477-1480, 8-11 Oct. 2006.

Ji, S. & Park, H. W. (2000). Moving object segmentation in DCT-based compressed video, *Electronic Letters*, Vol. 36, No. 21, October 2000.

JSVM (2009). JSVM Software Manual, Ver. JSVM 9.19 (CVS tag: JSVM_9_19), Nov. 2009.

Kaminsky, E.; Grois, D. & Hadar, O. (2008). Dynamic Computational Complexity and Bit Allocation for Optimizing H.264/AVC Video Compression, *J. Vis. Commun. Image R.*, Elsevier, vol. 19, iss. 1, pp. 56-74, Jan. 2008.

Kas, C. & Nicolas, H. (2009). Compressed domain indexing of scalable H.264/SVC streams," Signal Processing Image Communication (2009), Special Issue on scalable coded media beyond compression, pp. 484-498, 2009.

Kim, D.-K. & Wang, Y.-F. (2009). Smoke Detection in Video, *Computer Science and Information Engineering, 2009 WRI World Congress on*, vol.5, no., pp.759-763, March 31, 2009-April 2, 2009.

Kodikara Arachchi, H.; Fernando, W.A.C.; Panchadcharam, S. & Weerakkody, W.A.R.J. (2006). Unequal Error Protection Technique for ROI Based H.264 Video Coding, *Canadian Conference on Electrical and Computer Engineering*, pp. 2033-2036, Ottawa, 2006.

Kwon, H.; Han, H.; Lee, S.; Choi, W. & Kang, B. (2010). New video enhancement preprocessor using the region-of-interest for the videoconferencing, *Consumer Electronics, IEEE Transactions on*, vol.56, no.4, pp.2644-2651, Nov. 2010.

Lambert, P.; Schrijver, D. D.; Van Deursen, D.; De Neve, W.; Dhondt, Y. & Van de Walle, R. (2006). A Real-Time Content Adaptation Framework for Exploiting ROI Scalability in H.264/AVC, *Advanced Concepts for Intelligent Vision Systems*, pp. 442-453, 2006.

Li, Z.; Pan, F.; Lim, K. P.; Feng, G.; Lin, X. & Rahardja, S. (2003). Adaptive basic unit layer rate control for JVT, in Joint Video Team (JVT) of ISO/IEC MPEG and ITU-T VCEG (ISO/IEC JTC1/SC29/WG11 and ITU-T SG16 Q.6), Doc. JVT-G012, Pattaya, Thailand, Mar. 2003.

Li, Z. G.; Yao, W.; Rahardja, S. & Xie, S. (2007). New Framework for Encoder Optimization of Scalable Video Coding, *2007 IEEE Workshop on Signal Processing Systems*, pp.527-532, 17-19 Oct. 2007.

Li, Z.; Zhang, X.; Zou, F. & Hu, D. (2010). Study of target detection based on top-down visual attention, *Image and Signal Processing (CISP), 2010 3rd International Congress on*, vol.1, no., pp.377-380, 16-18 Oct. 2010.

Lim, K-P.; Sullivan, G. & Wiegand, T. (2005). Text description of joint model reference encoding methods and decoding concealment methods, Study of *ISO/IEC 14496-10 and ISO/IEC 14496-5/ AMD6 and Study of ITU-T Rec. H.264 and ITU-T Rec. H.2.64.2*, in Joint Video Team (JVT) of *ISO/IEC MPEG and ITU-T VCEG*, Busan, Korea, Apr. 2005, Doc. JVT-O079.

Liu, L.; Zhang, S.; Ye, X. & Zhang, Y. (2005). Error resilience schemes of H.264/AVC for 3G conversational video services, *The Fifth International Conference on Computer and Information Technology*, pp. 657- 661, Binghamton, 2005.

Liu, Y.; Li, Z. G. & Soh, Y. C. (2008). Rate Control of H.264/AVC Scalable Extension, *Circuits and Systems for Video Technology, IEEE Transactions on*, vol.18, no.1, pp.116-121, Jan. 2008.

Lu, Z.; Peng, W.-H.; Choi, H.; Thang T. C. & Shengmei, S. (2005). CE8: ROI-based scalable video coding, JVT-O308, Busan, KR, 16-22 April, 2005.

Lu, Z.; Lin, W.; Li, Z.; Pang Lim, K.; Lin, X.; Rahardja, S.; Ping Ong, E. & Yao, S. (2005). Perceptual Region-of-Interest (ROI) based scalable video coding, JVT-O056, Busan, KR, 16-22 April, 2005.

Manerba, F.; Benois-Pineau, J.; Leonardi, R. & Mansencal, B. (2008). Multiple object extraction from compressed video, JASP – *EURASIP Journal on Advances in Signal Processing*, Vol. 2008 (2008), Article ID 231930, 15 pages, doi:10.1155/2008/231930.

Mehmood, M. O. (2009). Study and implementation of color-based object tracking in monocular image sequences, *Research and Development (SCOReD), 2009 IEEE Student Conference on*, vol., no., pp.109-111, 16-18 Nov. 2009.

Micheloni, C.; Salvador, E.; Bigaran, F. & Foresti, G.L. (2005). An integrated surveillance system for outdoor security, *Advanced Video and Signal Based Surveillance, 2005. AVSS 2005. IEEE Conference on*, vol., no., pp. 480- 485, 15-16 Sept. 2005.

Mustafah, Y.M.; Bigdeli, A.; Azman, A.W. & Lovell, B.C. (2009). Face detection system design for real time high resolution smart camera, *Distributed Smart Cameras, 2009. ICDSC 2009. Third ACM/IEEE International Conference on*, vol., no., pp.1-6, Aug. 30 2009-Sept. 2 2009.

Ndili, O. & Ogunfunmi, T. (2006). On the performance of a 3D flexible macroblock ordering for H.264/AVC, *Digest of Technical Papers International Conference on Consumer Electronics*, 2006, pp. 37-38.

Qayyum, U. & Javed, M.Y. (2006). Real time notch based face detection, tracking and facial feature localization, *Emerging Technologies, 2006. ICET '06. International Conference on*, vol., no., pp.70-75, 13-14 Nov. 2006.

Ribas-Corbera, J.; Chou, P. A. & Regunathan, S. L. (2003). A generalized hypothetical reference decoder for H.264/AVC, *IEEE Trans. Circuit Syst. Video Technol.*, vol. 13, pp. 674-686, Jul. 2003.

Roodaki, H.; Rabiee, H. R. & Ghanbari, M. (2010). Rate-distortion optimization of scalable video codecs, *Signal Processing: Image Communication*, vol. 25, iss. 4, Apr. 2010, pp. 276-286.

Sadykhov, R. Kh. & Lamovsky, D. V. (2008). Algorithm for real time faces detection in 3D space, *Computer Science and Information Technology, 2008. IMCSIT 2008. International Multiconference on*, vol., no., pp.727-732, 20-22 Oct. 2008.

Schwarz, H.; Marpe, D. & Wiegand, T. (2007). Overview of the scalable video coding extension of the H.264/AVC standard, *IEEE Trans. Circ. Syst. for Video Technol.*, vol. 17, no. 9, pp. 1103–1120, Sept. 2007.

Schoepflin, T.; Chalana, V.; Haynor, D. R. & Kim, Y. (2001). Video object tracking with a sequential hierarchy of template deformations, *IEEE Trans. Circuits Syst. Video Technol.* 11, pp.1171-1182, 2001.

Shoaib, M. & Anni C. (2010). Efficient residual prediction with error concealment in extended spatial scalability, *Wireless Telecommunications Symposium (WTS)*, 2010, vol., no., pp.1-6, 21-23 Apr. 2010.

Shokurov, A.; Khropov, A. & Ivanov, D. (2003). Feature tracking in images and video," in *International Conference on Computer Graphics between Europe and Asia* (*GraphiCon-2003*), pp.177-179, Sept. 2003.

Sun, Z. & Sun, J. (2008). Tracking of Dynamic Image Sequence Based on Intensive Restraint Topology Adaptive Snake, *Computer Science and Software Engineering, 2008 International Conference on*, vol.6, no., pp.217-220, 12-14 Dec. 2008.

Sun, Q; Lu, Y. & Sun, S. (2010). A Visual Attention Based Approach to Text Extraction, *Pattern Recognition (ICPR), 2010 20th International Conference on*, vol., no., pp.3991-3995, 23-26 Aug. 2010.

Wang, T. & Zhu, Z. (2008). Intelligent multimodal and hyperspectral sensing for real-time moving target tracking, *Applied Imagery Pattern Recognition Workshop, 2008. AIPR '08. 37th IEEE*, vol., no., pp.1-8, 15-17 Oct. 2008.

Thang, T. C.; Bae, T. M.; Jung, Y. J.; Ro, Y. M.; Kim, J.-G.; Choi, H. & Hong, J.-W. (2005). Spatial scalability of multiple ROIs in surveillance video, JVT-O037, Busan, KR, 16-22 April, 2005.

Vezhnevets, M. (2002). Face and facial feature tracking for natural Human-Computer Interface," in *International Conference on Computer Graphics between Europe and Asia (GraphiCon-2002)*, pp.86-90, September 2002.

Wang, J.-M.; Cherng, S.; Fuh, C.-S. & Chen, S.-W. (2008). Foreground Object Detection Using Two Successive Images, *Advanced Video and Signal Based Surveillance, 2008. AVSS '08. IEEE Fifth International Conference on*, vol., no., pp.301-306, 1-3 Sept. 2008.

Wang, H.; Leng, J. & Guo, Z. M. (2002). "Adaptive dynamic contour for real-time object tracking," in Image and Vision Computing New Zealand (IVCNZ2002), December 2002.

Wei, Z. & Zhou, Z. (2010). An adaptive statistical features modeling tracking algorithm based on locally statistical ROI, *Educational and Information Technology (ICEIT), 2010 International Conference on*, vol.1, no., pp.V1-433-V1-437, 17-19 Sept. 2010.

Wiegand, T. & Sullivan, G. (2003). Final draft ITU-T recommendation and final draft international standard of joint video specification (ITU-T Rec. H.264 ISO/IEC 14 496-10 AVC), in Joint Video Team (JVT) of ITU-T SG16/Q15 (VCEG) and ISO/IEC JTC1/SC29/WG1, Annex C, Pattaya, Thailand, Mar. 2003, Doc. JVT-G050.

Wiegand, T.; Schwarz, H.; Joch, A.; Kossentini, F. & Sullivan, G. J. (2003). Rate-constrained coder control and comparison of video coding standards, *IEEE Trans. Circuit Syst. Video Technol.*, vol. 13, iss. 7, pp. 688- 703, Jul. 2003.

Wiegand, T.; Sullivan, G.; Reichel, J.; Schwarz, H. & Wien, M. (2006). Joint draft 8 of SVC amendment, ISO/IEC JTC1/SC29/WG11 and ITU-T SG16 Q.6 9 (JVT-U201), 21st Meeting, Hangzhou, China, Oct. 2006.

Xiang, G. (2009). Real-Time Follow-Up Tracking Fast Moving Object with an Active Camera, *Image and Signal Processing, 2009. CISP '09. 2nd International Congress on*, vol., no., pp.1-4, 17-19 Oct. 2009.

Xu, L.; Ma, S.; Zhao, D. & Gao, W. (2005). Rate control for scalable video model, *Proc. SPIE, Visual Commun. Image Process.*, vol. 5960, pp. 525, 2005.

Yang, M.-H.; Kriegman, D.J. & Ahuja, N. (2002). Detecting faces in images: a survey, *Pattern Analysis and Machine Intelligence, IEEE Transactions on*, vol.24, no.1, pp.34-58, Jan 2002.

You, W.; Sabirin, M. S. H. & Kim, M. (2007). Moving object tracking in H.264/AVC bitstream, *MCAM* 2007, LNCS, vol. 4577, Springer, Heldelberg, 2007, pp.483-492.

You, W.; Houari Sabirin, M. S. & Kim M. (2006). Real-time detection and tracking of multiple objects with partial decoding in H.264/AVC bitstream domain, *Proceedings of SPIE*, N. Kehtarnavaz and M.F. Carlsohn, San Jose, CA, USA: SPIE, 2009, pp. 72440D-72440D-12.

You, W. (2010). Object Detection and Tracking in Compresses Domain. Available from http://knol.google.com/k/wonsang-you/object-detection-and-tracking-in/3e2si9juvje7y/7#.

Youlu, W.; Casares, M. & Velipasalar, S. (2009). Cooperative Object Tracking and Event Detection with Wireless Smart Cameras, *Advanced Video and Signal Based Surveillance, 2009. AVSS '09. Sixth IEEE International Conference on*, vol., no., pp.394-399, 2-4 Sept. 2009.

Yuan, L. & Mu, Z.-C. (2007). Ear Detection Based on Skin-Color and Contour Information, *Machine Learning and Cybernetics, 2007 International Conference on*, vol.4, no., pp.2213-2217, 19-22 Aug. 2007.

# Part 2

## Rate Control in Video Coding

# 4

# Rate Control in Video Coding

Zongze Wu[1], Shengli Xie[1,2], Kexin Zhang[1] and Rong Wu[1]
[1]*School of Electronic and Information Engineering,*
*South China University of Technology*
*NO.381 Wushan Road, Tianhe Area, Guangzhou,*
[2]*Faculty of Automation, Guangdong University of Technology,*
*NO.100 Waihuanxi Road, Guangzhou university City, Panyu Area Guangzhou,*
*China*

## 1. Introduction

Rate control plays an important role in video coding, although it's not a normative tool for any video coding standard. In video communications, rate control must ensure the coded bitstream can be transmitted successfully and make full use of the limited bandwidth. As a consequence, a proper rate control scheme is usually recommended by a standard during the development, e.g. TM5 for MPEG-2, TMN8 and TMN12 for H.263, and VM8 for MPEG-4, etc. H.264/AVC is the newest international video coding standard, and some work on rate control has been done for H.264/AVC too. In the contribution, a rate control scheme based on VM8 is adopted by H.264/AVC test model. In another contribution, an improved rate control scheme for H.264/AVC is provided with rate distortion optimization (RDO) and hypothetical reference decoder (HRD) jointly considered, part of which has also been adopted by H.264/AVC test model.

### 1.1 Function of rate control

Rate control is that the encoder estimates the video bitrate based on the network available bandwidth, ensures the coded bitstream can be transmitted successfully and makes full use of the limited bandwidth. In other words, it is adjusting video output bits according to the channel is fixed or variable transmission rate.

Now the core part of many video coding standards is the motion compensation and the DCT transform coding based on block. The number of the encoder output bits of each frame is changing with the active input image. Therefore, the bitstream has the inherent characteristics of changing. If the coding parameters remain unchanged in the compression process, the bits of the consumption of different frame will be significantly different. Due to the actual network bandwidth and storage medium, if we have nothing to do with the bitstream, the video communication system is likely to go abnormally. Generally, using a buffer makes the output bitstream smooth. The buffer capacity has certain limitation (If buffer is too big, the propagation delay of real-time communication is longer which is difficult to be accepted). In order to prevent buffer "overflow" and "underflow", rate control must be used in encoder.

### 1.2 History of rate control

In recent years, rate control has been the research focus in the field of video coding, many scholars and experts have achieved a lot of research achievements in the video rate control.

The rate control in the video coding was proposed in 1992. The core of TM5 rate control algorithm is, under the situation that buffer is not overflow or overflow, distributing bits and determining the reference value of quantitative parameter by estimating the global complexity of the encoding frame, and adjusting the quantitative parameter by the activity of each block. In 1997, Chen (Chem., Hang.H.M., 1997) proposed a rate control algorithm which adjusting the frame rate adaptively is by the comprehensive consideration of the image contents and buffer state. This algorithm predicts the bitrate and quality of the image by source video model which is deduced according to the rate-distortion theory and used to describe the relationship of the bitrate, distortion and quantization step, and thus decides the number of skip frames. TMN8 infers the predicted formula of the target bitrate according to the experience of entropy model, then refers to the rate-distortion model, then computes the optimum quantization step under the MSE rule by Lagrange optimization. VM8 is based on quadratic R-Q model, and uses the model in different types of image frames to achieve rate control, meanwhile introduces sliding window to adjust the parameters of the model in order to realized multi-scale, different complexity rate control. In 2001, he (Zhihai He, 2001) proposed a ρ domain code rate control algorithm; it establishes the one-to-one correspondents between output rate and the quantification step by the linear relationship of the percentage of the quantified DCT coefficients and the output rate. This algorithm has achieved good results in the standard of JPEG, H.263, MPEG-4 and so on.

The latest video coding H.264 standard in the code control is proposed by Li Zhengguo etc in 2003.The problem with the JM H.264 encoder lies with the fact that the residual signal depends on the choice of coding mode and the choice of coding mode depends on the choice of QP which in turn depends on the residual signal (a chicken and egg type of problem). The adopted solution in the JM encoder is one where the choice of QP is made prior to the coding mode decision using a linear model for predicting the activity of the residual signal of the current basic unit (e.g. frame, slice, macroblock) based on the activity of the residual signal of past (co-located) basic units. Once the residual signal activity is predicted, the same rate model used in VM8 is employed to find a QP which will lead to a bit stream that adheres to the specific bit budget allocation and the buffer restrictions.

In order to get a better effect on rate control, we usually make some melioration based on the joint scalable video model (JSVM). The JSVM provides a rate control scheme, and the JSVM software is the reference software for the Scalable Video Coding (SVC) project of the Joint Video Team (JVT) of the ISO/IEC Moving Pictures Experts Group (MPEG) and the ITU-T Video Coding Experts Group (VCEG). The JSVM Software is still under development and changes frequently.

### 1.3 The key technique in rate control

Because of transmission bandwidth and storage space limitation, video applications for higher compression ratio, nondestructive coding can provide the compression ratio but cannot satisfy the demand of actual video applications, but if we can accept some degree of distortion, high compression ratio is easy to get. Human visual system for high frequency signals change not sensitive information loss, high frequency part does not reduce subjective visual quality. Video coding algorithm of mainstream DCT quantization method is adopted

to eliminate video signals, the visual physiology redundant than lossless higher compression ratio and will not bring the video quality decrease significantly.
When using a lossy coding method, it is related to the difference between the reconstruction images g (x, y) and the original image f (x, y). Generally, the distortion factor D function can form according to need, such as selecting any cost function, absolute square cost function, etc. In the image coding D is computed as:

$$D = E\{[f(x,y) - g(x,y)]^2\}$$

### 1.3.1 Rate distortion model

Beneath the image compression, there is a problem: under the premise of certain bitrate, how to make the distortion of the reconstructed image coding minimum. Essentially, it is the problem of the relationship between encoding rate and the distortion. The rate-distortion theory is to describe the relations of the distortion of coding and encoding speed. Although the rate-distortion theory is not optimal encoder, but it gives the lower compression allows under the condition of the certain information distortion allows. Practical application of many rate-distortion models is built on the basis of experience. For example, in TM5, a simple linear rate-distortion model is introduced. In TMN8 and VM8, a more accurate quadratic R-D model is used, which can reduce rate control error and provide better performance but have relatively higher computational complexity. In a different way, the relation between rate and QP is indirectly represented with the relation between rate and ρ, where ρ is the percent of zero coefficients after quantization; and also, a modified linear R-D model with an offset indication overhead bits is used for rate control on H.261/3/4 in the contributions. Here are some of the common empirical models:

*1. A simple linear rate-distortion model*

$$R(QP) = C_{QP} \times \frac{S}{QP}$$

Where R(QP) is the bits to encode when then quantization step is QP, S is the encoding complexity. $C_{QP}$ is the coefficient of the model.

*2. Second rate distortion model*

Model hypothesizes information source obey Laplace distribution, namely:

$$p(x) = \frac{\alpha}{2} e^{-\alpha|x|}$$

Where x is the value of the information source, and α is a coefficient.
The distortion defined with absolute deviation as:

$$D(x, \bar{x}) = |x - \bar{x}|.$$

So we can get the rate-distortion function:

$$R(D) = \log \frac{1}{\alpha D}$$

The Taylor expansion of R(D) is

$$R(D) = \left(\frac{1}{\alpha D} - 1\right) - \frac{1}{2}\left(\frac{1}{\alpha D} - 1\right)^2 + R_3(D) = -\frac{3}{2} + \frac{2}{\alpha}D^{-1} + \frac{1}{2\alpha^2}D^{-2} + R_3(D)$$

Then we get the R-D model:

$$R_i = \alpha_1 Q_i^{-1} + \alpha_2 Q_i^{-2}$$

Where $\alpha_1$ and $\alpha_2$ are two coefficients.
In order to enhance the accuracy of the R-D model, bring in two parameters MAD and Rh, then:

$$R(Q) - R_h = \frac{X_1 * MAD}{Q} + \frac{X_2 * MAD}{Q^2}$$

Where MAD is the mean absolute difference between the original frame and reconstruction of frame $R_h$ is the number of bits of the header information and information such as the motion vector occupies; $X_1$and $X_2$ are two coefficients.

*3. ρ domain linear model*

He (Zhihai He,2001) found, the proportion of the coefficient after quantification of zero, increases in a monotonic way with the growth of Quantization step. So the original R - D relationship may be allude to R-ρ relationship. The research finds R-ρ meets the relationship as follow:

$$R(\rho) = \theta(1 - \rho)$$

Where θ is a constant.

*4. Logarithmic model*

Provided the source obeys Gaussian distribution which the mean is 0 and the variance is $\sigma^2$, The distortion defined as :$D(x, \bar{x}) = |x - \bar{x}|$. While the rate-distortion function is:

$$R(D) = \begin{cases} \frac{1}{2}\log\frac{\delta^2}{D} & ,0 \le D \le \delta^2 \\ 0 \quad , \quad D > \delta^2 \end{cases}$$

Where R(D) is the average coding bits of every pixel.
Supposed that distortion and the quantification coefficients is linear relationship, namely:

$$D(Q) = m \times Q$$

So get the R - Q model:

$$R(Q) = \alpha + \beta \log\frac{1}{Q}$$

This model is much simpler, used by many documents. But because the image of the DCT coefficients do not accord with Gaussian distribution and D and Q usually is not linear relationship. Therefore, this adaption of the model is so-so.

### 1.3.2 Rate distortion optimization (RDO)

Rate control usually incorporate with rate distortion optimization (RDO), which could brings more coding efficiency for optimized mode decision and bit allocation. In order to reduce the temporal correlations among successive frames, inter-frame coding is widely used, which is usually realized by motion compensation prediction (MCP). With block basis motion estimation, the residual texture and motion vectors associated in the current block need to be coded finally. Obviously, for a given bit rate, over-large motion information or residual information wouldn't give the best coding efficiency, so the trade-off between the motion information and the residual information, on which the motion compensated video coding heavily depends, should be considered. The trade-off is usually achieved by a rate distortion optimization (RDO) that is formulated by minimizing the cost J, shown as follows

$$J = D + \lambda_{opt} R$$

Here the distortion D representing the residual (texture or prediction error) measured as sum absolute distortion (SAD) or mean absolute distortion (MAD), is weighted against the number of bits R associated with the motion information by using the Lagrange multiplier $\lambda_{opt}$. Each $\lambda_{opt}$ corresponds to a bit rate range and a trade-off between the motion information and the residual information. A large $\lambda_{opt}$ works well at a low bit rate while a small $\lambda_{opt}$works well at a high bit rate.

### 1.3.3 The influences of the coding parameters on the code rate control

Any control on encoding bitrate must consider the tradeoff of the quality and efficiency of compression. The bitrate reduce is at the cost of lower quality. In video encoder, we can control output bitrate by adjusting the following four coding parameters:

1. Frame rate, namely frames per second coding. By adjusting the frame rate, make the encoder output rate achieve specified requirements. A control frame rate for video signal is temporal redundancy, rather than spatial redundancy. Usually the quality requirements in a single image are higher, so we cannot decrease rate by reducing the number of each frame coding bits.
2. The coding for some transform coefficients of each image block, for example, transform coefficient as diagonal coefficient (1,1), (2,2), or just to code pixel pieces of low-frequency coefficients. The DC coefficients have a large proportion in the pixel block energy, therefore, in order to maintain certain quality of image they must be encoded. However, AC coefficients can be discarded or encode a part of them to decrease the output bitrate. In the image with a few of details, spatial correlation, this method can get good quality image in low bit rate, but when the image with a lot of details, if we remove much AC coefficient, the image quality will greatly reduce.
3. Quantization parameter (QP). Quantitative parameter has considerable influence on the coding bits of the image block. When the video sequences have acuteness exercise, in order to obtain high temporal video quality, we can reduce spatial video quality to achieve the code rate control with details quantified roughly by increasing the value of each image QP. With the QP increasing, the value of the quantified DCT coefficients decrease, then the zero coefficient will be more, as a result, the output encoding bits become less. On the other hand, if the QP is smaller, the value of the quantified DCT coefficients increase, then the output encoding bits become more. In H.264, we can achieve different levels of the code rate control through the adjustment frame, the Basic Unit or the quantitative parameters.
4. The optimal QP value, through quantitative determination coefficient of smaller, after can be obtained in the run-length coding before the zero coding, quantity higher degree

after compression coding, output bits less. Instead, the small, DCT QP coefficients quantification, the value after the coding bits. In the h.264 encoder, through the adjustment frame, the Basic Unit (Basic Unit) or the quantitative parameters can achieve different levels of the code rate control.

5. Motion detection threshold. Motion detection threshold is used to determine the macroblock of the prediction frames (P) to code or skip. If the threshold improves, the sensitivity of the movement of the encoder reduces, then the number of coding macroblocks decrease, therefore, the bits of P frame needing to code decrease. However, it is at the cost of image motion video quality. On the other hand, if the threshold is lower, the movement sensitivity will improve, so there will be more macroblock needing to code, as a result, the bits will increase. While INTRA or INTER detection threshold is also available for controlling the output bitrate of P frame. More INTRA coded, more the output bits become, and higher the video quality is.

The process of adjusting the coding the four values of the parameters of the code, can effectively control the output video encoder to meet current rate control requirements. However, they also may cause changes in the image quality. At present, most of the code rate control schemes use quantitative parameters control mode to achieve rate control.

## 2. Rate control theory

The video communication system widely use MC-DPCM or DCT video coding algorithm, the stream has the inherent characteristics of variable bit rate. If encoding parameters remain the same during the compression, different number of bits between frames will consume significantly different. As the actual network bandwidth and storage media capacity constraints on the rate of this stream without any constraints on the impact of video communication system is catastrophic and cannot guarantee that the system work.

Now main international video coding standards (i.e., MPEG-1, MPEG-2, MPEG-4, H.261, H.263 and H.264) video images use DCT to eliminate spatial correlation. Image data (image data to be the original frame and the predicted residual error between frames using the temporal prediction) is divided into blocks of such size, and then block by block implemented of the DCT and quantization. Less or does not contain details of the details of the block will have fewer non-zero coefficient, therefore the details of the block produced more non-zero coefficient is greater. Block of varying degrees of redundancy has led to different blocks of the same frame number of bits needed to encode a big difference.

If only intra-frame coding is taken into account, the number of bits consumed by each frame as the scene complexity will vary. Complex scene is much larger than the number of bits needed to simple scenes. In the same scene, the rate changes are usually small. Figure 2.1 (a) shows the varying bit rate of MPEG-2 using intra-prediction coding in which all coding parameters are unchanged. From the figure we can see: in the same scene, the rate has changed little; when the scene change or changes, the rate changes dramatically.

Motion estimation is another cause to the bit rate fluctuations of compressed bit stream. When using temporal motion estimation, the encoded data includes motion vectors and residual coefficients. Motion estimation in MC-DPCM / DCT coding is based on the basis of translational motion model. If the scene contains only small movements or simple linear sports (such as moving the camera lens), block-based motion estimation can be effective to predict the movement. In this case, the motion vector has relatively high share of the number of bits. If the scene contains fast or complex motion (such as rotation, scaling or random movement, etc.), the block-based motion estimation is difficult to predict the actual movement, especially in the scene change or changes, many of the macro block coding frame will be used intra encoding mode, allows a significant residual coding bits by force mouth.

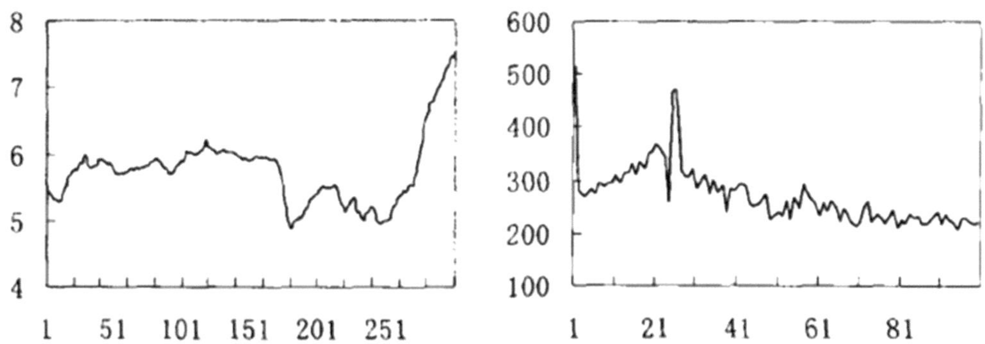


(a) Stefan/MPEG-2 (b) Coatguard/H.263

Fig. 2.1

Figure 2.1 (b) shows the H.263 stream in the frame bits curve. Each frame is the frame from its precursor predicted residual frame using the DCT transform compression. Because there is no prediction reference frame to the first frame, all macro blocks in the first frame are coded in intra mode and therefore consume more bits; the rate of the following frames don't change much, because they are highly related which means containing the same detail and movement. But in the 30-th frame or so, there is a peak value, because the camera lens is dragged here and therefore reduces the efficiency of motion estimation; as a result, most of the macro blocks in these several frames were intra coded, resulting in a rate increase. In the subsequent long period of time, no scene change occurs, rate changes are small.

In video coding, the coding type of frame is another factor that affects the bit rate. I frame uses only intra prediction, so the compression ratio is usually very low. P frame uses inter-frame prediction, and its compression efficiency is usually higher than I frame. B frames can effectively deal with the new target occlusion and scene access issues because of the use of the bi-directional prediction: compared to P frame, the mean of B frame using the two images to compensate obtains higher signal to noise ratio. However, B frames will not be used for prediction and allowing the use of fewer bits encoding the number of coding which will not cause distortion proliferation. In A group of pictures (GOP) of the MPEG-1 and MPEG-2, different types of frame encoding result in a significant difference between the numbers of bit.

Before transmission, all rate fluctuations (including intra-frame, inter-frame and within a GOP) must be effectively controlled, since the actual network bandwidth and storage media capacity is limited. Many of the existing network and storage media are operating in constant bit rate (CBR). Even if they work at a variable bit rate (VBR) model, the maximum stream rate fluctuations will also have the corresponding constraints. So the coded video sequence must be adjusted to meet the network bandwidth and storage media capacity requirements. In addition, the non-binding rate is not conducive to the management of channel bandwidth.

Rate control is a necessary part of an encoder, and has been widely applied in standards including MPEG-2, MPEG-4, H.263, and so on. Rate control belongs to the budget-constrained bit allocation problem whose goal is to determine how many bits to use on different parts of the video sequence and to do so in such a way as to maximize the quality delivered to the end user. A natural way to approach these problems is to consider the R-D trade-offs in the allocation. Therefore, a practical video encoder employs rate control as a way to regulate varying bit rate characteristics of the coded bit stream in order to produce high quality decoded frame at a given target bit rate. In this process, there are two key phrases: 1) to find out a reasonable and accurate R-D model to describe the characteristic of a specific signal source; 2) to allocate every bit unit appropriately in order to minimize to overall distortion.

Rate control in video coding is typical accomplished in three steps:

1. Update the target average bit rate in terms of bps for each short time interval, also referred to as the rate update interval;
2. Determine the coding mode(e.g., I-, P-, or B-frame) and the target bit budget for each frame to be coded in this interval, which is usually based on the target average rate for the interval and the current buffer fullness;
3. Determine the coding mode and QP for each MB in a frame to meet the target rate for this frame.

### 2.1 Bit allocation

We now present a series of generic allocation problem formulations that spell out some of the possible constrains, the encoder will have to meet when performing this parameter selection. It would be trivial to achieve minimal distortion if no constraints on the rate were imposed. We will formulate two classes of closely related problems where the rate constraints are driven by (i) total bit budget (e.g., for storage applications) and (ii) transmission delay (e.g., for video transmission).

**Storage constraints: Budget-constrained allocation**

In this class of problems, the rate is constrained by some restriction on the maximum total number of bits that can be used. This total number of budget $R_T$ has to be distributed among the different coding units with the goal of minimizing some overall distortion metric. The problem can be restated as follows:

Find the optimal quantizer, or operating point, $x(i)$ for each coding unit $i$, such that

$$\sum_{i=1}^{N} r_{ix(i)} \leq R_T \tag{1a}$$

and some metric $f(d_{1x(1)}, d_{2x(2)}, \ldots, d_{Nx(N)})$ is minimized.

Several kinds of metric are mostly used in video coding, such as minimum average distortion (MMSE), minimax approach (MMAX), and lexicographically optimal approach (MLEX).

*Minimum average distortion*

In a MMSE problem, we have that

$$f\left(d_{1x(1)}, d_{2x(2)}, \ldots, d_{Nx(N)}\right) = \sum_{i=1}^{N} d_{ix(i)}.$$

*Minimax approach*
Alternatively, a MMAX approach would be such that

$$f\left(d_{1x(1)}, d_{2x(2)}, \dots, d_{Nx(N)}\right) = max_{i=1}^{N} d_{ix(i)}.$$

*Lexicographically optimal approach*
MLEX approaches have been extensions of the mini-max solution. The MLEX approach compares two solutions by sorting their distortions or their quantization indices. Allocations derived under the MLEX constraint have the interesting property of tending to equalize the distortion or the quantization scale across all coding units.

A more general version of the problem of budget-constrained allocation may arise in situations where there are not only limitations on total rate but also in the rate available for subset of coding units. Assume, for example, that a set of images has to be placed in a storage device that is physically partitioned and that it is impossible for undesirable for performance reasons to split images across one or more devices. In this case, we will have to deal with partial constraints on the set of images assigned to each particular devide, in addition to the overall budget constraint. An optimal allocation that considers only the aggregate storage constraint may result in an invalid distribution between the storage devices.

Consider the case where two storage devices, each one of size $R_T/2$, are used. We will have the following constraint, in addition to the budget constraint of Eq.(1a):

$$\sum_{i=1}^{N_1} r_{ix(i)} \leq R_T/2,$$

Where $N_1$ is the number of coding units that are stored in the first storage device. $N_1$ itself may not be given and may have to be determined.

**Delay-constrained allocation**

Solutions of storage-constrained allocation above cannot encompass situations where the coding units, for example, a series of video frames, are streamed across a link or a network to a receiver. In this situation, each coding unit is subject to a delay constraint; therefore, it has to be available at the decoder by a certain time in order to be played back.

For example, let a coding unit be coded at time $t$ and assume that it will have to be available at the decoder at time $t+\Delta T$, where $\Delta T$ is the end-to-end delay of the system. This imposes a constraint on the rate, which has to be low enough that transmission can be guaranteed within the delay, can be used for each frame. If each coding unit lasts $t_u$ seconds, then the end-to-end delay can be expressed as $\Delta N = \Delta T / t_u$ in coding units. The video encoder will have to ensure that the rate selection for each frame is such that no frames arrive too late at the encoder. Given the delay constraints for each coding unit, the problem can be restated as follows:

Find the optimal set of quantizers x(i) such that (1) each coding unit i encoded at time $t_i$ is received at the decoder before its "deadline" $t_i + \delta_i$, and, (2) a given distortion metric, such as MMSE and MMAX, is minimized.

Note that the problem doesn't impose any constraint on the transmission bandwidth; however, in practical applications we must deal with limited bandwidth and expenditures which rise to meet the incomes.

The complexity of this allocation problem depends on the channel characteristics: we need to know if the channel provides a constant bit rate (CBR) or a variable bit rate (VBR), if the

channel delay is constant, if the channel is reliable, etc. For simplicity, in the followings we assume that $\delta_i = \Delta T$ for all i.
In both CBR and VBR cases, data will be stored in buffers at encoder and decoder. Assume a variable channel rate of *C*(*i*) during the i-th coding unit interval. Then we will have that the encoder buffer state at time I is

$$B(i) = \max(B(i-1) + r_{ix(i)} - C(i), 0),$$

with $B(0) = 0$ being the initial state of the buffer.
Consider the constraints need to be applied to the encoder buffer state. First, the buffer state $B(i)$ cannot grow indefinitely because of the finite physical buffer. If $B_{\max}$ is the physical memory available then we need to guarantee that $B(i) \le B_{\max}$ at all time. Secondly, in order to the delay constraint not to be violated, we need to guarantee that the data corresponding to coding unit $i$ is transmitted before $t_i + \Delta T$; that is, transmission has to be completed during the next $\Delta N$ coding unit intervals.
Then, we can define the effective buffer size $B_{eff}(i)$ as

$$B_{eff}(i) = \sum_{k=i+1}^{i+\Delta N} C(k),$$

Then correct transmission is guaranteed if

$$B(i) \le B_{eff}(i), \forall i.$$

As an example, consider the case where $C(i) = \bar{C} = R_T / N$ is constant. If the system operates with an end-to-end delay $\Delta N$ the buffer can store no more than $\Delta N \cdot C$ bits at time t.
In general, the applicable constraint will be imposed by the smallest of $B_{eff}(i)$ and $B_{\max}$. Assuming that sufficient physical buffer storage is available, the problem becomes:

**Buffer-constrained allocation**

Find the optimal set of quantizers $x(i)$ for each $i$ such that the buffer occupancy

$$B(i) = \max(B(i-1) + r_{ix(i)} - C(i), 0),$$

is such that

$$B(i) \le B_{eff}(i)$$

and some metric $f(d_{1x(1)}, d_{2x(2)}, \dots, d_{Nx(N)})$ is minimized.

### 2.2 Rate distortion optimization

Rate distortion optimization theory, which is derived from information theory, is the theoretical basis for optimization of video coding. Also the rate distortion optimal coding techniques are widely used in every video coding system. First of all, the distortion rate distortion optimization is closely related with the quantization, thus the rate distortion optimization in the quantizer design plays an important role in the design of weighted quantization matrix and adjusting quantified deadzone interval, etc.; rate distortion optimization can also be used to select the macro-block encoding parameters, such as the choosing of the best motion vector and coding mode, etc.

Another important application of rate distortion optimization techniques is to solve the optimization problems of bit allocation, i.e., how to find the optimal solution of numbers of bit distributed among different macro blocks and pictures in order to obtain the minimum total distortion within the total bit budget constraint. And this issue is the goal of rate control. Since the basic unit (macro-block or image) in bit allocation and the distortion is related to each other, which makes the bit allocation problem become more complex. As a result, we often utilize the monotonicity of R-D characteristic or assume independent cases to reduce the complexity of solving the problem.

We first introduce the basic concepts of rate distortion theory, including the definition of rate distortion function and the forms of R-D function about the source of Gaussian distribution and Laplacian distribution. This is because natural images are usually assumed to obey Gaussian distribution, while transformation coefficient is usually assumed to obey the Laplacian distribution. R-D models are generally derived from the typical rate-distortion function based on the foregoing assumptions.

Rate-distortion theory is an important part of information theory and is the theoretical basis of data compression and quantization. "Rate" represents the measure of signal; “distortion” reflects the difference between source signals in current rate and the source. The amount of information is measure by entropy which is defined as:

$$H = -\sum p_i \log p_i$$

For two signals X, Y, the mutual information is defined as:

$$I(X;Y) = H(X) - H(X \mid Y)$$

Rate distortion function reflects the entropy of mutual information between source signals and received signals through the channel transmission or coding distortion. Assume that X to be the source signals, Y to be the signal through channel transmission at the receiver, the rate distortion function is defined as:

$$R(D) = \min_{p(y_j|x_j)} I(X;Y).$$

We can use a curve with convex hull to characterize the relation between R and D, as following Figure 2.2. The convexity of R-D characteristic is essential in the solution of bit allocation.

In video coding, image data is usually assumed to be zero mean and variance as $\sigma^2$ non-memory Gaussian source. Its probability density function is:

$$p(x) = \frac{1}{\sqrt{2\pi\sigma^2}} e^{-\frac{x^2}{2\sigma^2}}.$$

If the mean square error is as a measure of distortion of the standard, then the rate distortion function is:

$$R(D) \geq \frac{1}{2}\log_2 \frac{\sigma^2}{D}, \text{ or } D(R) = 2^{-2R}\sigma^2.$$

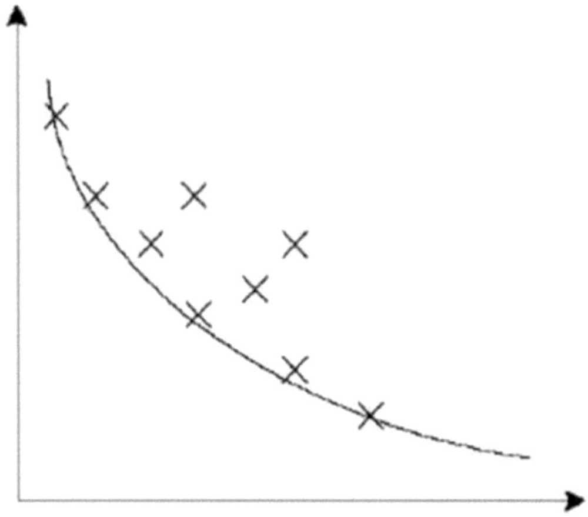

Fig. 2.2 The convexity of R-D characteristic is essential in the solution of bit allocation

In transform coding, DCT transform coefficients are usually simulated with Laplacian distribution. For the Laplacian distribution of rate-distortion function is usually expressed respectively as:

$$D = \frac{2}{\lambda^2} - \frac{Q}{\lambda}(1 + \coth\frac{\lambda Q}{2})e^{-\frac{\lambda Q}{2}},$$

$$R = -\log(1 - e^{-\frac{\lambda Q}{2}}) + e^{-\frac{\lambda Q}{2}} \cdot \log(\frac{2}{1 + e^{-\frac{\lambda Q}{2}}} + \frac{\lambda Q}{2\sinh\frac{\lambda Q}{2}}),$$

where Q is the quantization step size. Note that when the quantization step Q increases, distortion D is close to the source variance $\sigma^2 = \frac{2}{\lambda^2}$.

Bit allocation optimization problem in video coding is given under the constraints of bit rate to find the optimal solution that obtains the best image quality. In order word, it is restated as follow:

$\min\{D\}$, with the constraint that $R \le R_{\max}$

Note that the bit allocation constraints can be either to the entire video sequence bit constrained, minimizing the cost of rate distortion of each image and the final optimal effect of encoded sequence, or to a single frame so that obtains the optimal coding of each macro block. Current methods commonly are used Lagrangian optimization, dynamic programming method and etc.

**Lagrangian optimization**

Consider the case where the rate $R$ and distortion $D$ can be measured independently for each coding unit; i.e., the R-D data for coding unit $i$ can be computed without requiring that other coding units be encoded as well. One example of this scenario is the allocation of bits to different blocks in a DCT image coder where blocks are individually quantized and entropy coded.

Assume that the basic coding units (block or image) are mutually unrelated. Then the distortion and rate are irrelative to the adapted quantization parameter. Suppose the k-th block adapts quantization parameter $Q_k$, then we obtain the corresponding distortion and bit rate of $D_k$ and $R_k$, respectively. To solve the problem, we need to find an optimal set of $Q_k^*$ such that minimizing the total distortion within the constraint of total budget $R$:

$$Q_k^* = (Q_1^*, Q_2^*, \dots, Q_n^*) = \arg \min_{(Q_1, \dots, Q_n)} \sum_{i=1}^{n} D_i(Q_i),$$

with the constraint that $\sum_{i=1}^{n} R_i(Q_i) \le R$.

Lagrangian multiplier can be used to solve this problem. Firstly, we convert it to the optimization without constraints:

$$Q^* = \arg \min_{(Q_1, \dots, Q_n)} \sum_{i=1}^{n} D_i(Q_i) + \lambda \sum_{i=1}^{n} R_i(Q_i).$$

Since the distortions and rates in different units are mutually unrelated, we restate the former equation as:

$$Q_k^* = \arg \min_{Q_k} [D_i(Q_i) + \lambda \cdot R_i(Q_i)]$$

Note that for each coding unit $i$, the point on the R-D characteristic that minimizes $d_{ix(i)} + \lambda \cdot r_{ix(i)}$ is the point at which the line of absolute slope $\lambda$ is tangent to the convex hull of the R-D characteristic. Since $\lambda$ is the same for every coding unit on the sequence, we can refer to this algorithm as a "constant slope optimization".

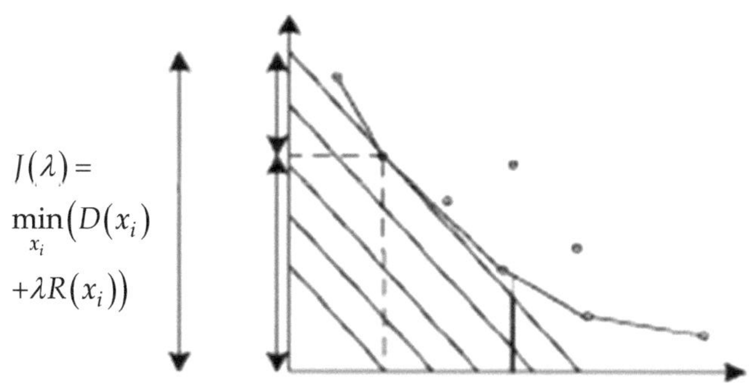


Fig. 2.3

**Dynamic programming**

The foregoing Lagrangian optimization assumes that the basic units are mutually independent, so that minimizing the cost of rate-distortion in each unit results in the optimal solution. However, in the practical encoding process, each unit will have correlations with others because of the introduction of temporal and spatial prediction. As a result, their cost of rate distortion is mutually affected. Dependency exists in this rate-distortion problem can be stated as:

$$Q^* = \arg \min_{(Q_1, \dots, Q_n)} \sum_{i=1}^{n} D_i(Q_1, Q_2, \dots, Q_k),$$

with the constraint that

$$\sum_{i=1}^{n} R_i(Q_1, Q_2, \ldots, Q_k) \leq R .$$

Dependent optimization problems are more complex. We have to calculate the corresponding costs of rate distortion of every combination of quantization parameters, which is quite computationally expensive. Simplified version of this dependency is to assume the quality of encoded picture is better with a good reference than a bad one. Based on this criterion dynamic programming is commonly used to solve this problem.
Dynamic programming is generally used to find the best path, as shown below. Each node corresponds to a current coding mode, and the path between nodes represents the cost of coding. Therefore, the problem of finding an optimal coding solution is equivalent to finding the optimal path. If consider the dependencies between frames or macro blocks, the computational complexity is high. A simplified method is to use greedy method to get the best path at each step, finally get a sub-optimal path.

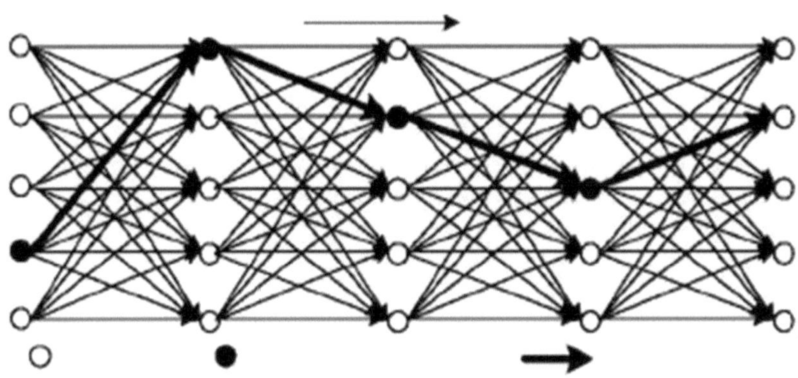

Fig. 2.4

### 2.3 Calculate the quantization parameter

After DCT transformation, the residual signal must be quantized to form the final estimate. Ideally, the choice of quantizer step size $Q$ should be optimized in a rate-distortion sense. Given a quantizer step size $Q$, the quantization of the residual signal (the mapping of the transformed samples to quantization index values) should also be rate-distortion optimized. The choice of the quantizer output level sent for a given input value should balance the needs of rate and distortion. A simple way to do this is to move the decision thresholds of the quantizer somewhat toward lower bit-rate indices . This is the method used in the ITU-T test model. Alternatively, a $D + \lambda R$ decision can be made explicitly to choose the quantization index. However, in modern video coders such as H.263 the bit rate needed to represent a given quantization index depends not only on the index chosen for a particular sample, but on the values of neighboring quantized indices as well (due to the structure of the coefficient index entropy coding method used). The best performance can be obtained by accounting for these interactions. In recent video coder designs, the interactions have become complex, such that a trellis-based quantization technique may be justified.

Transform coefficient bit allocations are optimized quantization of the wavelet coefficients, its purpose is to choose the appropriate quantized index for all transform coefficients, which makes coding coefficients and the number of bits used in coding distortion to achieve a desired balance between, that is the minimum cost. This is one of typical applications using the rate distortion optimization techniques. Quantization is to balance the amount of data encoded with the coding distortion. At the same time it is also closely related with the features of transformation (usually orthogonal transform).

In the latest coding standard H.264 and AVS there is an emergence of new technologies in quantitative transform characteristics. They use integer transform instead of floating-point of the traditional DCT. This modification not only reduces the complexity of transform, but also avoids mismatch caused by floating point calculations. At the same time quantitative and transform normalized combination can be achieved only through multiplication and shift. However, the magnitude of each line in transformation matrix is not necessarily equal, which means to require for normalization in encoder and decoder. If the encoder and decoder implementation with parameter quantization table, more storage space is in need. In AVS, each line of transformation matrix is approximate in magnitude, so there only requires for normalization in encoder, and therefore the size of quantization table in decoder is decreased. As a result, the storage complexity in decoder is reduced. However, this transformation method brings new problems on rate-distortion analysis.

Transform is one of the core technologies in video coding. Through transformation the spatial redundancy between image data can be effectively removed. As DCT transform has excellent property of energy concentration, it is widely applied to various types of coding standards, such as MPEG-2, MPEG-4, H.263, etc.

The algorithm for the rate-constrained mode decision can be modified in order to incorporate macro block quantization step-size changes. For that, the set of macro block modes to choose from can be extended by also including the prediction mode type $INTER+Q$ for each macro block, which permits changing $Q$ by a small amount when sending an $INTER$ macro block. More precisely, for each macro block a mode $M$ can be chosen from the set

$$M \in \{INTRA, SKIP, INTER, INTER+4V, ..., INTER+Q(-4),$$
$$INTER+Q(-2), INTER+Q(+2), INTER+Q(+4)\}$$

where, for example, $INTER+Q(-2)$ stands for the $INTER$ mode being coded with quantizer step size reduced by two relative to the previous macroblock. Hence, the macroblock Q selected by the minimization routine becomes dependent on $\lambda_{MODE}$ Otherwise the algorithm for running the rate-distortion optimized coder remains unchanged.

Figure 2.5 shows the obtained average macro block QUANT gathered when coding the complete sequences Foreman, Mobile-Calendar, Mother-Daughter, and New. The red curve relates to the function

$$\lambda_{MODE} = 0.85 \cdot (QUANT)^2$$

which is an approximation of the functional relationship between the macro block QUANT and the Lagrange parameter $\lambda_{MODE}$ up to QUANT values of 25, and H.263 allows only a choice of $QUANT \in \{1,2,...,31\}$ . Particularly remarkable is the strong dependency between $\lambda_{MODE}$ and QUANT , even for sequences with widely varying content. Note, however, that for a given value of $\lambda_{MODE}$, the chosen QUANT tends to be higher for sequences that require higher amounts of bits (Mobile-Calendar) in comparison to sequences requiring smaller amounts of bits for coding at that particular $\lambda_{MODE}$ (Mother-Daughter)-but these differences are rather small.

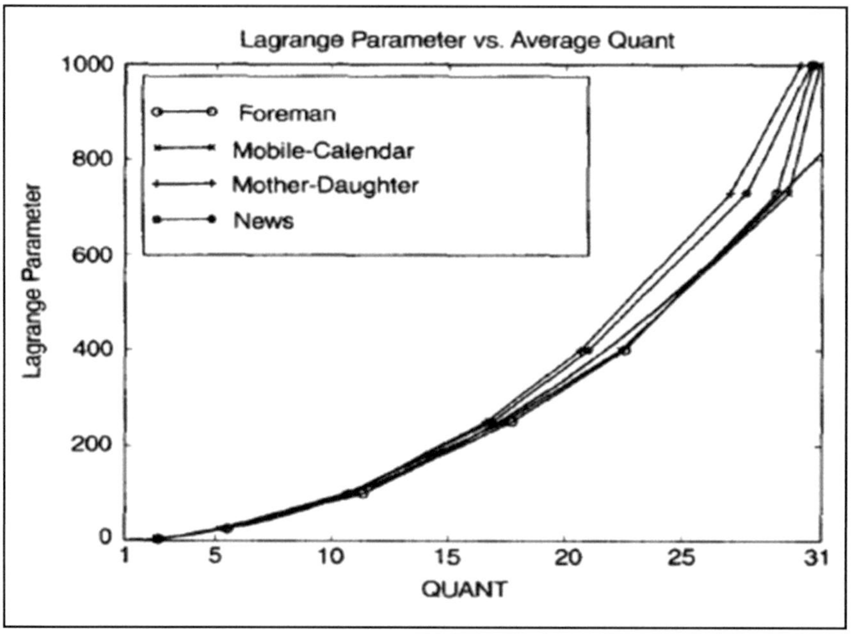


Fig. 2.5 Language parameter $\lambda_{mode}$ VS. average macroblock QUANT

As a further justification of our simple approximation of the relationship between $\lambda_{MODE}$ and Q, let us assume a typical quantization curve high-rate approximation [ 59, 60] as follows

$$R(D) = a\ln(\frac{\sigma^2}{D}),$$

where $a$ is a constant that depends on the source pdf. The minimization of cost function $J = D + \lambda R$ for a given value of $\lambda_{MODE}$ then is accomplished by setting the derivative of $J$ with respect to $D$ equal to zero. This is equivalent to setting the derivative of $R(D)$ with respect to $D$ equal to $\frac{-1}{\lambda_{MODE}}$, which yields

$$\frac{dR(D)}{dD} = -\frac{a}{D} \stackrel{\Delta}{=} \frac{-1}{\lambda_{MODE}}$$

At sufficiently high rates, a reasonably well-behaved source probability distribution can be approximated as a constant within each quantization interval [60]. This leads readily to the typical high bit-rate approximation $D \cong (2 \cdot QUANT)^2 / 12$. The approximations then yield

$$\lambda_{MODE} \cong c \cdot (QUANT)^2$$

where $c = 4/(12a)$. Although our assumptions may not be completely realistic, the derivation reveals at least the qualitative insight that it may be reasonable for the value of the Lagrange parameter $\lambda_{MODE}$ to be proportional to the square of the quantization parameter. As shown above, 0.85 appears to be a reasonable value for use as the constant c. This ties together two of the three optimization parameters, *QUANT* and $\lambda_{MODE}$. For the third, $\lambda_{MOTION}$, we make an adjustment to the relationship to allow use of the SAD measure rather than the SSD measure in that stage of encoding. Experimentally, we have found that an effective method to measure distortion during motion estimation using SAD and to simply adjust $\lambda$ for the lack of the squaring operation in the error computation, as given by

$$\lambda_{MOTION} = \sqrt{\lambda_{MODE}}$$

This strong dependency that we have thus derived between *QUANT*, $\lambda_{MODE}$, and $\lambda_{MOTION}$ offers a simple treatment of each of these quantities as a dependent variable of another. For example, the rate control method may adjust the macro block *QUANT* occasionally so as to control the average bit rate of a video sequence, while treating hand $\lambda_{MODE}$ and $\lambda_{MOTION}$ dependent variables using Eqs. (13) and (17). In the experiments reported herein, we therefore used the approximation (17) with the SAD error measure for motion estimation and the approximation (13) with the SSD error measure for mode decisions.

### 2.4 Buffering mechanism

Video buffer verifier model is an important part of coding standards. According to this buffer model, decoder determines the memory size, decoding delay and other parameters to ensure that neither overflow nor underflow will occur in the decoding process. Encoder buffer model uses this model to impose constraint on the encoded bit stream to ensure the decoding in which case the memory size of the decoder is determined. This process usually requires rate control techniques.

Buffer model can usually be expressed as a ternary parameter model (*R*,*B*,*F*), which is often referred as leaky bucket model. Where R is the rate of data into the buffer zone; it can be either constant or variable. For variable bit rate, rate can be regarded as the general case of a constant rate, which means subparagraph a constant rate. Where R is the peak rate; B is the buffer size; F to buffer the initial saturation. Different kinds of decoders and applications can be expressed by different set of parameters (*R*,*B*,*F*).

A leaky bucket is a direct metaphor for the encoder's output buffer, At frame time, the encoder instantaneously encodes frame $i$ into $b_i$ bits and pours these bits into the leaky bucket. In the constant bit rate (CBR) case, the leaky bucket drains its accumulated bits into the communication channel at a fixed bit rate $R$, and the encoder must add enough bits to the leaky bucket often enough so that the leaky bucket does not underflow in any interval of time. On the other hand, the encoder must not add too many bits to the leaky bucket too frequently, or else the leaky bucket, which has capacity $B$, will overflow. Thus, the leaky bucket, which may begin at an arbitrary initial state $F$ (with $0 \le F \le B$), constrains the encoding sequence $(s_i,b_i)$, $i = 0, 1, 2,...$ Graphically, the encoding sequence, or encoding *schedule*, can be represented by the cumulative number of bits encoded by time, as illustrated in the left half of Figure. Furthermore, the leaky bucket constraint can be represented by the two parallel lines bounding the encoding schedule. The later/lower line represents the schedule on which bits drain from the leaky bucket, and the earlier/upper line represents the capacity constraint of the leaky bucket, that is, an upward shift of the later/lower line by $B$ bits.

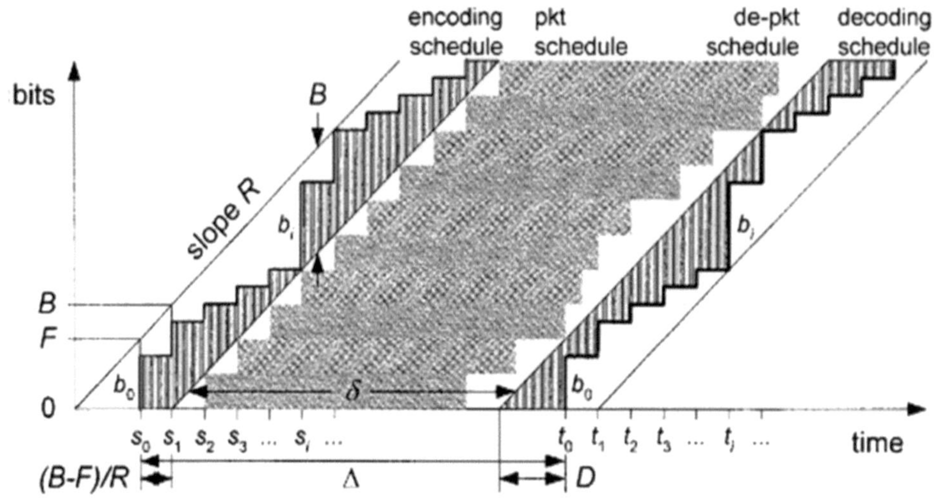


Fig. 2.7 The decoding schedule

Although a leaky bucket is a metaphor for the encoder buffer, it also characterizes the decoder buffer. In the CBR case, after the encoded bits traverse the channel, they enter the decoder buffer at a fixed bit rate R. Then, at frame time $t_i = s_i + \Delta$, where $\Delta$ is a constant end-to-end delay, the decoder instantaneously extracts bits from the decoder buffer and decompresses frame. This decoding schedule is illustrated in the right half of Fig. 2.7. If, after the first bit enters the decoder buffer, the decoder delays at least seconds before decoding the first frame, then the decoding schedule is guaranteed not to underflow the decoder buffer, due to the leaky bucket bounds inherited from the parallel encoding schedule. Furthermore, with delay, if the capacity of the decoder buffer is at least, then the decoding schedule is guaranteed not to overflow the decoder buffer, again due to the leaky bucket bounds inherited from the parallel encoding schedule. In fact, observe that the fullness of the encoder and decoder buffers are complements of each other in the CBR case. Thus, the leaky bucket model determines both the minimum decoder buffer size and the minimum decoder buffer delay using three parameters, R, B, and F, by succinctly summarizing with upper and lower bounds the encoded sequence.

The leaky bucket model can also be used with variable bit rate (VBR) channels, such as packet networks. If the VBR channel has a long-term average bit rate that equals the long-term average bit rate of the encoded sequence, then it is often convenient to continue to use the above CBR leaky bucket bounds. At the decoder, the buffering and the delay due to the leaky bucket can be augmented by additional buffering and delay to accommodate both de-packetization and packet network delivery jitter. Likewise, at the encoder, the buffering and delay can be augmented by additional buffering and delay to accommodate packetization. The additional buffering and delay at both the encoder and decoder are illustrated in Fig. 2.8. The resulting total amount of buffering and delay are sufficient to guarantee continuous media playback without stalling due to decoder buffer underflow and without loss due to decoder buffer overflow. In essence, at the decoder, the leaky bucket provides a deadline by which packets must be available for decoding, or risk being late. Similarly, at the encoder, the leaky bucket provides a deadline by which the encoded bits will be available for packetization.

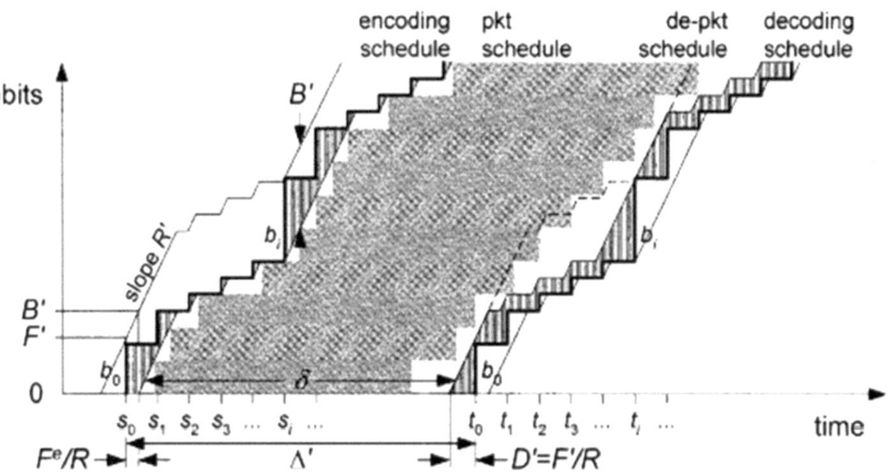


Fig. 2.8

## 3. Rate control in video coding

In the video coding, the module of the rate control adjusts the output bitrate based on the bandwidth and the signal channel and improves the quality of the video. The main purpose of the rate control is to find a rate-distortion model to improve the quality of the compression video in given conditions. The classic rate control algorithms or models mainly are the RM8 (Reference Model 8) in H.264, TM5 (Test Model 5) in MPEG-2, TMN8 (Test Model Near-term 8) in H.263 and VM8 (Verification Model 8).

### 3.1 Several classical rate control schemes

#### 3.1.1 Simulation model 3 (SM3)

Simulation Model 3 (SM3) is the final version of the MPEG-1 simulation model. In SM3, the motion estimation technique uses one forward and/or one backward motion vector per macroblock with half-pixel accuracy. A two-step search scheme which consists of a full-search in the range of +/- 7 pixels with the integer-pixel precision, followed by a search in 8 neighboring half-pixel positions, is used. The decision of the coding mode for each macroblock (whether or not it will use motion compensated prediction and intra/inter coding), the quantizer decision levels, and the rate-control algorithm are all specified.

#### 3.1.2 TM5 (Test model 5)

"Test Model 5" (TM5) is the final test model of MPEG-2. TM5 was defined only for main profile experiments. The motion compensated prediction techniques involve frame, field, dual-prime prediction and have forward and backward motion vectors as in MPEG-1. The dual-prime was kept in main profile but restricted to P-pictures with no intervening B-pictures. Two-step search, which consists of an integer-pixel full-search followed by a half-pixel search, is used for motion estimation. The mode decision (intra/inter coding) is also specified. Main profiles were restricted to only two quantization matrices, the default table specified in MPEG-1and the nonlinear quantizer tables. The traditional zigzag scan is used for inter-coding while the alternate scan is used for intra-coding. The rate-control algorithm in TMN5 consists of three layers operating at the GOP, the picture, and the macroblock levels. A bit-allocation per picture is determined at the GOP layer and updated based on the buffer fullness and the complexity of the pictures. And the rate control model comprises the following three steps:

*1. Target bit allocation*

This step first allocates bits for given Group of Pictures (GOP) based on the target bit rate and the number of frames in the GOP. Then before encoding of each frame, it allocates bits for that frame based on the frame type (I, P or B), the complexity measure, the remaining number of bits in the current GOP.

*2. Rate control*

This is a macroblock level step. Here, a quantization parameter Q is computed for the macroblock j under consideration based on the difference between the allocated bits and the actually generated bits till the encoding of previous macroblock in this picture.

*3. Adaptive quantization*

This step tries to refine the quantization parameter calculated in Step 2 based on the complexity of the macroblock. For this an "activity measure" of the macroblock is found using variance of the four sub-blocks in the macroblock. The adaptation of the quantization parameter is done to prevent abrupt changes in the quantization parameter and to achieve a more uniform picture quality.
To find the spatial activity measure $act_j$ for the macroblock j using its four sub-blocks, following computations are done on the intra (i.e. original) pixel values:

$$act_j = 1 + \min(vblk1, vblk2, vblk3, vblk4)$$

Where $vblk_n$ is the variance of the nth sub-block and is given by:

$$vblk_n = \frac{1}{64}\sum_{k=1}^{64}(P_k^n - P\_mean_n)^2$$

and

$$P\_mean_n = \frac{1}{64}\sum_{k=1}^{64} P_k^n$$

and $P_k$ are the sample values in the nth original 8*8blosk.

### 3.1.3 VM8 (Verification model 8)

There are five steps in the MPEG-4 VM8 rate control algorithm (Fukunaga et al., 1999):

1. *Initialization*
   - α1 and α2 are the first and second order coefficients.
2. *Computation of the target bit rate before encoding*
   - The computation of target bit rate is based on the bits available and the last encoded frame bits. If the last frame is complex and uses excessive bits, more bits should be assigned to this frame. However, there are fewer number of bits left for encoding thus, these bits can be assigned to this frame. A weighed average reflects a compromise of these two factors.

- A lower bound of target bit rate (F/30) is used so that the minimal quality is guaranteed (where F denotes total target bits per second).
- The target bit rate is adjusted according to the buffer status to prevent both overflow and underflow.

3. *Computation of the quantization parameter (Q) before encoding*
   - Q is solved based on the model parameters, a1and a2.
   - Q is clipped between 1 and 31.
   - Q varies within 25% of the previous Q to maintain a variable bit rate (VBR) quality.
4. *Encoding current frame*
5. *After encoding, model parameters are updated based on the encoding results of the current frame.*
   - The rate distortion model is updated based on the encoding results of the current frame. The bits used for the header and the motion vectors are deducted since they are not related to Q.
   - The data points are selected using a window whose size depends on the change in complexity. If the complexity changes significantly, a smaller window with more recent data points is used.
   - The model is again calibrated by rejecting the outlier data points. The rejection criterion is the data point and is discarded when the prediction error is more than one standard deviation.
   - The next frame is skipped if the current buffer status is above 80%.

### 3.1.4 TMN8 (Test model near-term 8)

TMN8 includes two steps: (1) the bit allocation in the frame layer, (2) the adaptive quantization in the macroblock layer

*1. Frame rate control algorithm*

The main work of the frame rate control is calculate the target bits(B) based on the encoding bits of last frame(B′), the encoding rate R, target frame rate (F), the original frame rate (G) , the delaying of the buffer A and threshold of skip frame (M):

$$B = (R/F) - \Delta$$

and

$$\Delta = \begin{cases} W/F & W > AM \\ W - AM & \text{otherwise} \end{cases}$$

and the bits in buffer:

$$w = \max(W + B - R/F, 0).$$

If $W > M$, then the skip frames are needed to leave enough space to store the next symbol to be encoded.

*2. Macroblock rate control algorithm*

The unit that TMN8 works is macroblock, and it uses the information of the encoded macroblock to update the current macroblock information. And TMN8 is based on the R-D model as follow:

$$R(Q) = \begin{cases} \frac{1}{2}\log_2\left(2e^2\frac{\delta^2}{Q^2}\right), & \frac{\delta^2}{Q^2} > \frac{1}{2e} \\ \frac{e}{\ln 2}\cdot\frac{\delta^2}{Q^2}, & \frac{\delta^2}{Q^2} \le \frac{1}{2e} \end{cases}$$

### 3.2 Rate control scheme in MPEG

#### 3.2.1 Rate control scheme in MPFG-2

In MPEG-2, a video sequence is partitioned into units of group of pictures (GOPs) with $N_{GOP}$frames to accommodate random access, and each frame is coded as I-, P-, or B-picture. And there are $M_B$ B-frames between two consecutive anchor frames (i.e., I- or P-frames). B-pictures employ the noncausal temporal prediction, that is bi-directional prediction, and thus use an immediate previous coded anchor picture (I- or P-picture) as the first reference and the immediate following coded anchor picture (I- or P-picture) as the second reference. This causes the difference between encoding order and display order.

Considering the coding performance, $N_{GOP}$ is usually set between 12 and 15 and is set to 2. Fig. 3.2.1 shows the GOP structure in display order and coding type for each frame when $N_{GOP} = 12$ and $M_B = 2$.

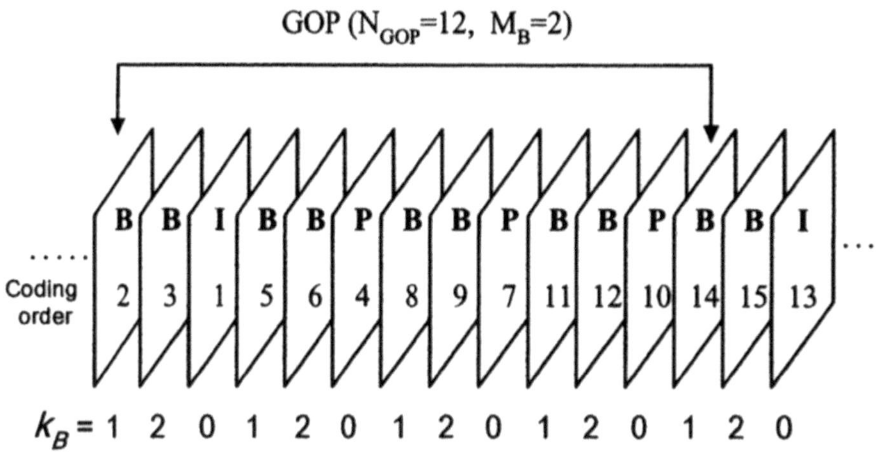


Fig. 3.2.1 GOP structure in display order and picture coding types.

The I-picture removes the spatial redundancy within the present frame, and it is coded independently of other frames. Hence, I-picture is used at the beginning of a GOP, and this picture can also provide the function of periodic re-synchronization to reduce the damages from the transmission errors. P-picture can be coded more efficiently than I-picture because this picture removes not only spatial redundancy but also temporal redundancy from the previous anchor frame by using the forward motion estimation and compensation. B-picture achieves the highest coding efficiency by using the neighboring previous and future anchor frames as references for motion estimation and compensation. Consequently, B-picture results in higher complexity and more delay than P-picture. B-picture is not referred by any other prediction. Therefore, the quality degradation or coding errors in B-picture will not propagate to other frames. In contrast, the quality degradation or coding errors in anchor frames will propagate to other future frames, thus the quality of the anchor frame should be maintained over a certain level.

The rate control model in MPEG-2 is TM5, and the rate control model comprises the following three steps:

1. *Target bit allocation*

This step first allocates bits for given Group of Pictures (GOP) based on the target bit rate and the number of frames in the GOP. Then before encoding of each frame, it allocates bits for that frame based on the frame type (I, P or B), the complexity measure, and the remaining number of bits in the current GOP.

2. *Rate control*

This is a macroblock level step. Here, a quantization parameter Q is computed for the macroblock j under consideration based on the difference between the allocated bits and the actually generated bits till the encoding of previous macroblock in this picture.

3. *Adaptive quantization*

This step tries to refine the quantization parameter calculated in Step 2 based on the complexity of the macroblock. For this an "activity measure" of the macroblock is found using variance of the four sub-blocks in the macroblock. The adaptation of the quantization parameter is done to prevent abrupt changes in the quantization parameter and to achieve a more uniform picture quality.
To find the spatial activity measure $act_j$ for the macroblock j using its four sub-blocks, following computations are done on the intra (i.e . original) pixel values:

$$act_j = 1 + \min(vblk1, vblk2, vblk3, vblk4)$$

Where $vblk_n$ is the variance of the nth sub-block and is given by:

$$vblk_n = \frac{1}{64}\sum_{k=1}^{64}(P_k^n - P\_mean_n)^2$$

and

$$P\_mean_n = \frac{1}{64}\sum_{k=1}^{64} P_k^n$$

and $P_k$ is the sample value in the nth original 8*8blosk.

### 3.2.2 Rate control scheme in MPFG-4

The MPEG group officially initiated an MPEG-4 standardization phase with mandate to standardize algorithms for audio-visual coding in multimedia applications, allowing for interactivity, high compression, universal accessibility and portability of audio and video contents. Target bitrate for the video standard is between 5±64 k bits/s for mobile applications and up to 4 M bits/s for TV/®lm applications. The MPEG-4 video standard will support the decoding of conventional rectangular images and video as well as the decoding of images and video of arbitrary shape. The coding of frame-based video is achieved similar to conventional MPEG-1/2 coding that involves motion prediction/compensation and texture coding. For the content-based functionalities, where the image sequence input may be of arbitrary shaped and location, this approach is extended by also coding shape information.

Shape may be either represented by an 8-bit transparency component or by a binary mask (Fukunaga et al., 1999; Koenen, 1999; Chiariglione, 1997).
According to information theory, two problems are stated: one is source coding (what information should be sent) and the other is channel coding problem (how should it be sent). Rate distortion theory (RDT) is directly related to the source coding problem and that is also related to the lossy image data compression. The key factor in RDT is the rate distortion function (RDF) R(D), which represents the lower bound on the rate: if a certain channel capacity C is given, the RDF can be used to find the necessary minimum average distortion Dave so that the condition for error-free transmission R(Dave) < C is achieved (Schuster et al., 1997). The RDF model shown in Fig. 3.2.2 has been considered as a good choice to represent relations between quantizing distortions and encoder output rates and thus it has been used in wide range. The rate control algorithm based on RDF model (recommended in the MPEG society) has low complexity and yields reasonably good visual quality, however it does not fully exploit the potential of the MPEG standards (MPEG-1, MPEG-2, and MPEG-4).

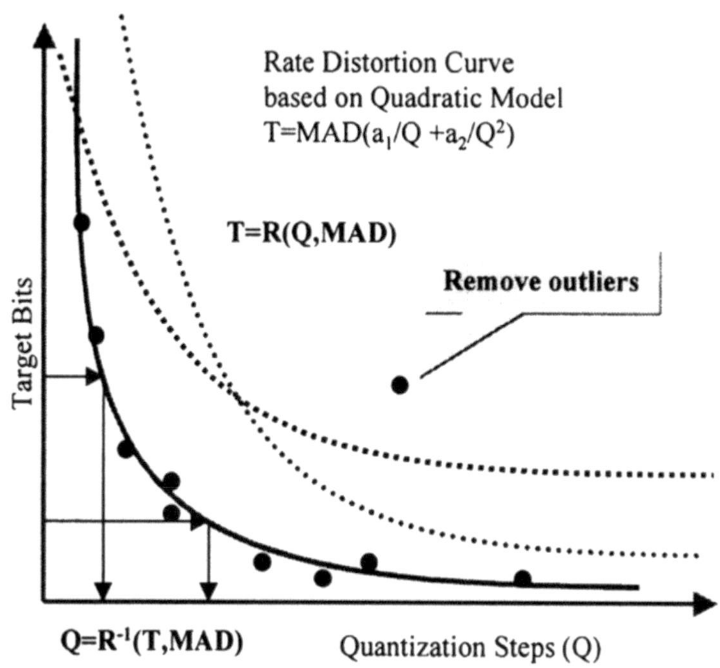


Fig. 3.2.2 Schematic illustration of the mathematical rate distortion function model of MPEG-4

In typical video coding techniques, the choice of quantizer steps at the encoder plays a key role in determining the actually encoded bitrate and the quality of the transmitted video scenes. MPEG specifies only a decoding method and allows much flexibility in encoding methods. Therefore, the picture quality of the reconstructed video sequence is considerably dependent on the rate control strategy at the encoding process. The recommended rate control algorithm in MPEG, to determine the quantizer steps, consists of three steps namely, bit allocation, rate control, and adaptive quantization based on the mathematical model. In bit allocation, past bit usage and quantizer steps are used to estimate the relative complexity of the three kinds of pictures (I, P, and B) and thereby determine the target bit rate for the present picture. In rate control, a reference quantizer step is determined on a macroblock or frame level by evaluating a virtual buffer status and the difference between the target bit rate and the rate that is already consumed till now. In adaptive quantization, regression based on mathematical model is carried out to decide actual quantizer for the present frame or macroblocks. However, updating the regression procedure using mathematical model needs quite an amount of time and the accuracy may not be predictable.

In the MPEG-4 VM rate control algorithm, the quadratic rate distortion model is used to estimate the rate distortion curve to evaluate the target bit rate before performing the actual encoding (Fukunaga et al., 1999):

$$T = R(MAD, Q) = MAD \cdot (a1 \cdot \frac{1}{Q} + a2 \cdot \frac{1}{Q^2})$$

Where, T is denoted as target bits and the mean absolute difference (MAD) is encoding complexity which is sum of absolute difference (SAD) between original image frame and motion compensated reconstructed image frame, and it is already known in the encoding process before rate coding is carried out. And a1 and a2 are the RD modeling parameters that should be updated after finishing encoding process for each image frame.

There are five steps in the MPEG-4 VM8 rate control algorithm (Fukunaga et al., 1999):

1. *Initialization*
   - $\alpha 1$ and $\alpha 2$ are the first and second order coefficients.
2. *Computation of the target bit rate before encoding*
   - The computation of target bit rate is based on the bits available and the last encoded frame bits. If the last frame is complex and uses excessive bits, more bits should be assigned to this frame. However, there are fewer number of bits left for encoding thus, these bits can be assigned to this frame. A weighed average reflects a compromise of these two factors.
   - A lower bound of target bit rate (F/30) is used so that the minimal quality is guaranteed (where F denotes total target bits per second).
   - The target bit rate is adjusted according to the buffer status to prevent both overflow and underflow.
3. *Computation of the quantization parameter (Q) before encoding*
   - Q is solved based on the model parameters, a1and a2.
   - Q is clipped between 1 and 31.
   - Q varies within 25% of the previous Q to maintain a variable bit rate (VBR) quality.
4. *Encoding current frame*
5. *After encoding, model parameters are updated based on the encoding results of the current frame.*
   - The rate distortion model is updated based on the encoding results of the current frame. The bits used for the header and the motion vectors are deducted since they are not related to Q.
   - The data points are selected by using a window
   - Whose size depends on the change in complexity. If the complexity changes significantly, a smaller window with more recent data points is used.
   - The model is again calibrated by rejecting the outlier data points. The rejection criterion is the data point and is discarded when the prediction error is more than one standard deviation.
   - The next frame is skipped if the current buffer status is above 80%.

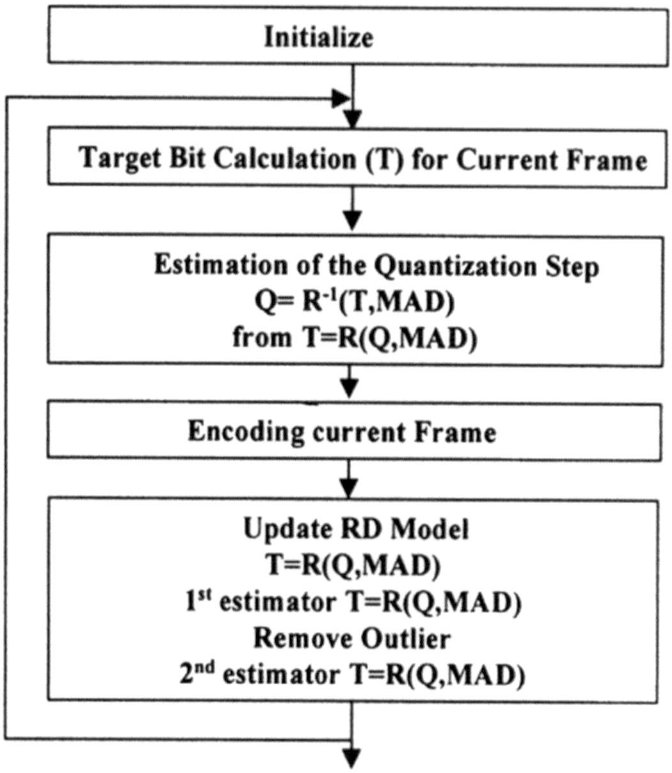


Fig. 3.2.2 Procedure of the MPEG-4 VM rate control algorithm

### 3.3 Rate control scheme in H.26x

#### 3.3.1 Rate control scheme in H.263

The rate control model in H.263 is TMN8. In H.263, the current video frame to be encoded is decomposed into macroblocks of 16_16 pixels per block, and the pixel values for each of the four 8_8 blocks in a macroblock are transformed into a set of coefficients using the DCT. These coefficients are then quantized and encoded with some type of variable-length coding. The number of bits and distortion for a given macroblock depend on the macroblock's quantization parameter used for quantizing the transformed coefficients. In the test model TMN8 for the H.263 standard, the quantization parameter is denoted by QP whose value corresponds to half the quantization step size. The TMN8 rate control uses a frame-layer rate control to select a target number of bits for the current frame and a macroblock-layer rate control to select the values of the quantization step-sizes for the macroblocks. In the following discussions, the following definitions are used:

$B$ : target number of bits for a frame;
$R$ : channel rate in bits per second;
$F$ : frame rate in frames per second;
$W$ : number of bits in the encoder buffer;
$M$ : some maximum value indicating buffer fullness, by default, set R=F;
$W_{prev}$ : previous number of bits in the buffer;
$B`$ : actual number of bits used of encoding the previous frame.

In the frame-layer rate control, a target number of bits for the current frame is determined by

$$B = \frac{R}{F} - \Delta \tag{1}$$

$$\Delta = \begin{cases} W/F, & W > Z, M \\ W - Z \cdot M, & otherwise \end{cases} \tag{2}$$

$$W = max(W_{prev} + B' - R/F,\ \ 0), \tag{3}$$

Where $Z$ = 0:1 by default. The frame target varies depending on the nature of the video frame, the buffer fullness, and the channel throughput. To achieve low delay, the algorithm tries to maintain the buffer fullness at about 10% of the maximum $M$. If $W$ is larger than 10% of the maximum $M$, the frame target $B$ is slightly decreased. Otherwise, $B$ is slightly increased.

The macroblock-layer rate control selects the values of the quantization step-sizes for all the macroblocks in the frame, so that the sum of the bits used in all macroblocks is close to the frame target $B$ in (1). The optimized quantization step size $Q_i^*$ for macroblock i in a frame can be determined by

$$Q_i^* = \sqrt{\frac{AK}{\beta_i - AN_iC} \cdot \frac{\delta_i}{\alpha_i} \sum_{k=i}^{N} \alpha_k \sigma_k}$$

Where,

K : model parameter;

A : number of pixels in a macroblock;

$N_i$ : number of macroblocks that remain to be encoded in the frame;

$\sigma_i$ : standard deviation of the ith macroblock;

$\alpha_i$ : distortion weight of the ith macroblock;

C : overhead rate;

$\beta_i$ : number of bits left for encoding the frame, where $\beta_1$ = B at the initialization stage.

### 3.3.2 Rate control scheme in H.264

H.264 rate control algorithm adopts a linear prediction model of MAD. Meanwhile, according to Fluid Traffic Model, use rate-distortion function to calculate quantization parameter, and then predict the current processing unit MAD.

Rate control can be divided into three levels: GOP level rate control, picture level rate control, the basic unit level rate control. Each level may need to consider the pre-allocation of bits, therefore, how to measure the complexity of each layer is the key. Distribute pre-allocation bits to each level according to the complexity of each level, and then set the quantization parameters. Therefore, complexity and how to set reasonable QP value, is particularly critical.

#### 3.3.2.1 GOP level rate control

GOP level rate control calculates the remaining bits for the rest pictures, and initializes the quantization parameter of the first picture (I or P) in the current GOP. When the $j^{th}$picture in the $i^{th}$GOP is coded, the number of total bits for the restpictures in this GOP is computed as follows,

$$B_i(j) = \begin{cases} \dfrac{R_i(j)}{f} \times N_i - V_i(j) & j = 1 \\ B_i(j-1) + \dfrac{R_i(j) - R_{i-1}(j)}{f} \times (N_i - j + 1) - b_i(j-1) & j = 2,3 \ldots \end{cases} \quad (4)$$

Where $f$ is the predefined frame rate, $N_i$is the size of the$i^{th}$GOP, $R_i$(j), $B_i$(j)and $V_i$(j) are the instant available bit rate, actual generated bits and occupancy of the virtual buffer for the$j^{th}$picture in the $i^{th}$GOP, respectively. For the first picture ($j$ = 1) in a GOP, the number of remaining bits calculated from the upper formula in (4) is the allocated bits for the current GOP in fact. Besides, the instant available bit rate $R_i$(j)can be variable for the different frames or GOPs Considering the VBR case, while in the CBR case, $R_i$(j) is always equal to $R_i$(j − 1) and (4) can be simplified as:

$$B_i(j) = B_i(j-1) - b_i(j-1) \quad (5)$$

Initially, the virtual buffer is filled by the motion bits generated previously in the MCTF, so the occupancy of virtual buffer is initialized as $M_i$(l)which presents the motion bits of the $j^{th}$picture in the $i^{th}$ GOP. Except the first GOP, besides initial motion bits, the virtual buffer's occupancy of the last GOP coded also is considered as upper formula (6) shown. After a picture coded, the $V_i$(j) is updated as bottom formula (6):

$$V_i = \begin{cases} m_i(1) & i = 1 \\ V_{i-1}\left(N_{i-1} + m_i(1)\right) & other \end{cases}$$

$$V_i(j) = V_i(j-1) + b_i(j-1) - \frac{R_i(j-1)}{f} \quad j = 2,3 \ldots N_i \quad (6)$$

Besides bit allocation, the initial quantization parameter decision is also included in the GOP level rate control. For the first GOP, the predefined quantization parameter specified for motion estimation/mode decision in the MCTF is used as the initial quantization parameter for simplicity. For other GOPs, the initial quantization parameter is predicted as follows,

$$QP_i(1) = \frac{sumQP(i-1)}{1 + N_{i-1}^{p}} \quad (7)$$

Where *sumQP(i-1)* is the sum of average QP for all I/P pictures in the *(i-1)*th GOP, and $N_{i-1}^{p}$is the total number of P pictures in the *(i-1 )*the GOP.

**3.3.2.2 Picture level rate control**

Picture level rate control allocates target bits for each picture based on the remaining bits, picture's complexity and virtual buffer's occupancy. Getting the target bits and MAD of current picture, the quantization parameter can be obtained based on the R-D model15. The MAD of a block *A* of size N×N located at *(x, y)* inside the current picture compared to a block *B* located at a displacement of *(vx, vy)* relative to *A* in a previous picture is defined as:

$$MAD(x,y) = \frac{1}{N^2} \sum_{m,n=0}^{N-1} \left| F_i(x+m, y+n) F_i(x + v_x + m, y + v_y + n) \right| \quad (8)$$

Where *Fi* is the current picture and *Fi-t* is a previously coded picture. In our proposed rate control algorithm, the picture level rate control consists of two stages: pre-encoding and post-encoding. In the pre-encoding stage, QP decision for each picture are accomplished with virtual buffer considerations, while in the post-encoding stage, the models updating with the statistical results is implemented.

**3.3.2.1.1 Pre-encoding stage**

In this stage, the quantization parameter of each picture is calculated. Firstly, the target bits are allocated for the current picture, and then the quantization parameter for the current picture can be obtained with the pre-defined rate distortion (R-D) model.
The target bit allocation should both consider the occupancy of virtual buffer and remaining bits for the rest pictures. Firstly, smoothing the occupancy of virtual buffer by regulating bit rate arriving, the target bits allocated for the $j^{th}$ picture in the $i^{th}$ GOP based on instant bit rate and the occupancy of virtual buffer are determined as:

$$\tilde{T}_i(j) = \left(1 - \frac{V_i(j+1) - V_i(j)}{V_i(j)} \times \frac{R_i(j)}{f}\right) \tag{9}$$

Secondly, remaining bit allocation for the $j^{th}$ picture in the $i^{th}$ GOP is computed as:

$$\hat{T}_i^t(j) = \frac{\hat{X}_i^t \times B_i(j)}{\sum_{t=p,b} K_t \times \hat{X}_i^t(j) \times N_{t,r}} \tag{10}$$

Where $N_{p,r}$, and $N_{b,r}$, are the number of the remaining I/P pictures and the number of the remaining B pictures ,respectively, $X_i^t$(j)is the predicted complexity measure for the current coding picture, and *Kp/Kb* is the ratio of I picture's QP and P/B picture's QP regulated with the selected wavelet function in the MCTF1. The complexity measure is the product of target bits and average QP for a picture (basic unit or MB). For pictures with type B, the complexity can be determined beforehand, while for the pictures with type I/P, the complexity only can be predicted from the nearest picture coded previously. After coding a picture in the $i^{th}$ GOP, the actual generated bits and average QP can be obtained, and then, the complexity measure is updated as:

$$X_i(j) = \alpha \times b_i(j-1) \times avgQP_i(j-1) \tag{11}$$

Where *avgQPi(j-1)* is the average of quantization parameters of the previously coded picture, α is a constant and set as 0.9 when next picture is P type otherwise set as 1 in our experiments. Specially, in the SVM, the pictures with type of I or P both are the temporal low sub-band pictures, and also except the first GOP with one I and one P pictures, only one I or P picture is in a GOP, so the complexity of I/P picture in the next GOP shall be predicted from that of I/P picture in the previously coded GOP. In conclusion, the predicted complexity measure is computed as:

$$\hat{X}_i^t(j) = \begin{cases} X_{i-1}(1) & t = i;p, i \neq 1 \\ X_i(1) & t = i;p, \quad i = 1 \\ X_i(j) & t = b \end{cases} \tag{12}$$

Lastly, the parameter of target bits is determined with a weighted combination of $\tilde{T}_I(j)$ and $\hat{T}_\iota(j)$

$$T_i = \beta \times \hat{T}_i(j) + (1-\beta) \times \tilde{T}_i(\mathrm{j}) \tag{13}$$

Where $\beta$ is a constant and set as 0.9 in our experiments. To conform to the virtual buffer requirement, the target bits are further bounded by:

$$T_i(j) = min\{U_i(j), max\{Z_i(j), T_i(j)\}\} \tag{14}$$

Where Zi(j) and Ui(j) are the minimum buffer constraint and maximum buffer constraint for preventing buffer from overflow and underflow. Same as the state-of-the-art hybrid coding, at least a picture needs buffering for decoding successfully. At the same time, the maximum buffer constraint is set as (16) avoiding buffer overflow.

$$U_i(j) = \begin{cases} B_{i-1}(N_{i-1}) + t_{r,1}(1) \times R_i(1) & j = 1 \\ U_i(j-1) + \left(\frac{R_i(j)}{f} - b_i(j)\right) & other \end{cases} \tag{15}$$

$$Z_i(j) = \begin{cases} B_{i-1}(N_{i-1}) + \frac{R_i(j)}{f} & j = 1 \\ Z_i(j-1) + \left(\frac{R_i(j)}{f} - b_i(j)\right) & other \end{cases} \tag{16}$$

Where *tr,1(1)* is the removal time of the first picture from the coded picture buffer.
Getting the target bits for a picture, the QP can be obtained with pre-defined R-D model. After motion estimation and mode selection in the MCTF (pre-mode-decision), the MAD of I/P pictures is still unable to be determined, so it is predicted from the closet picture coded previously by a linear model,

$$\tilde{\delta}(j) = a1 \times \delta_i(j-1) + a2 \tag{17}$$

Where $a1$ and $a2$ are two coefficients with initial values 1 and 0. And then, the quantization parameter corresponding to the target bits is computed as:

$$T_i(j) = c1 \times \frac{\tilde{\delta}_i(j)}{QP_i(j)} + c2 \times \frac{\tilde{\delta}_i(j)}{QP_i^2(j)} - m_{h,i}(j) \tag{18}$$

Where $m_{h,i}$(j) is the total number of header bits and motion vector bits, $c1$and $c2$are two coefficients. Since a drop in peak signal-to-noise ratios (PSNR) among successive pictures will deteriorates the visual quality of the whole sequence, the quantization parameter $QP_i(j)$ is adjusted by:

$$QP_i(1) = \max\{QP_{i-1}(1) - 2, \min\{QP_{i-1}(1) + 2, QP_i(1)\}\} \tag{19}$$

With such modifications, the difference in PSNR is not more than 2 between two successive pictures. And more, considering QP boundary in the SVM, the final quantization parameter is further bounded by 51 and 0. The quantization parameter is then used to perform quantization for each MB in the current picture. Specially, for B pictures, the MAD can be calculated from the current picture except intra block determined in the MCTF. The quantization parameter corresponding to the target bits is then calculated by using the formula (18). But for the intra blocks in B pictures, the MAD can't be obtained, and also is unreasonable predicted from any coded picture; however, only few intra blocks lie in a B picture. When pre-mode-decision is implemented, those intra modes can be recorded.

Therefore, the MAD of the current intra block can be calculated approximately based on the recorded information in the pre-mode-decision stage.

**3.3.2.1.2 Post-encoding stage**

After encoding a picture, the parameters *a1* and *a2* of linear prediction model (17), as well as *c*1 and *c*2 of quadratic R-D model (18) are updated with a linear regression method similar to MPEG-4 Q226,27. Meanwhile, the remaining bits for the rest pictures *Bi(j)* is updated using (5).

**3.3.2.3 Basic unit level rate control**

Basic unit is defined to be a group of continuous MBs. It is used to obtain a trade-off between the overall coding efficiency and the bits fluctuation. The basic unit level rate control is similar to the picture level rate control, including MAD prediction, bit allocation, and quantization parameter decision in basic unit level. In our simulating system, the spatial layers with different resolutions from QCIF (176×144) to 4CIF (704×576) are coded for a same video clip. Generally, the basic unit level rate control is efficient for the large size pictures (>QCIF) from our experience.

Firstly, the MAD of the $l$ th basic unit is calculated in the current coding picture. In case I/P pictures, the predictive $MAD,\tilde{\sigma}_{l,i}(j)$ ,is obtained by model (17) using the actual MAD of co-located basic units in the picture coded previously. In case B pictures, the MAD of current basic unit can be calculated directly. Secondly, determining the target bits for the $l$th basic unit is implemented as follows,

$$\hat{b}_l = T_r \times \frac{\delta^2_{l,i}(l)}{\sum_{n=l}^{Nunit} \tilde{\delta}^2_{n,i}(k)} \tag{20}$$

Where $Tr$ is the remaining bits for the rest basic units in the current picture, and initialized as the picture target bits $Ti(j)$. Thirdly, the quantization parameter $QP_{l,i}(j)$ for the $l$th basic unit of $j$th picture in $i$th GOP is calculated using the quadratic R-D model (18), and then bounded by:

$$QP_{l,i}(j) = max\{QP_{l-1,i}(j) - DQuant, min\{QP_{l,i}(j), QP_{l-1,i}(j) + DQuant\}\} \tag{21}$$

Where DQuant is a constant, and generally is regulated with the quantization parameter. In our experiments, DQuant is 1 if $QP_{l-1,i}(j)$ is greater than 27, otherwise is 2. Meanwhile, to maintain the smoothness of visual quality, (21) is further bounded by

$$QP_{l,i}(j) = \max\{0, Q\bar{P}_i(j-L-1) - 6, \min\{51, Q\bar{P}_i(j-L-1) + 6, QP_{l,i}(j)\}\} \tag{22}$$

Specially, for the first basic unit in the current picture, the QP can be derived from average QP of all basic units in the previously coded picture,

$$QP_i(j) = \alpha \times \frac{sumQP_i(j-1)}{N_{unit}} \tag{23}$$

Where $N_{unit}$ is the number of basic unit in this picture, $\alpha$ is a constant as provided in (11). When the number of remaining bits is less than 0, the QP is set as:

$$QP_{l,i}(j) = QP_{l-1,i}(j) + DQuant \tag{24}$$

Similarly, the QP is further bounded by (20) to maintain the smoothness of perceptual quality. Lastly, the QP is used to perform RDO for all MBs in the current basic unit. After coding a basic unit, the number of remaining bits, the coefficients of linear prediction model (17) and quadratic R-D model (18) are updated.

## 4. Development of rate control method

### 4.1 The development of rate control

The video compression technology has more than 30 years of development history. However, it hadn't made great success and got a wide range of applications until CCJTT approved H. 261 standard in 1988. With the development of the video compression, the MPEG-1, MPEG-2, H.263, MPEG-4 and H.264 and so on had been proposed as the standards of the video compression. Rate control is one of the key technologies of the standards, has a great effect on the systems of the video compression.

In1990, the H.261 has been proposed, and the rate control model is RM8 (Reference Model 8). It proposed a simple algorithm to control rate, but the result is not very well. In 1994, the Moving Picture Experts Group proposed the MPEG-2, and its rate control model is TM5 (Test Model 5). MPEG-2 didn't propose the concrete realization method, but it proposed and integrated the algorithm of rate control in TM5. The rate control concluded 3 steps: target bit allocation, rate control and adaptive quantization. However, this model didn't take the problems into consideration, which was caused by dealing with scene switch. As a result, the quality of different macroblock in the same frame was different and the reference QP had a big difference with the actual QP in the algorithm. In order to control the bitrate more effective, MPEG-4 adopted VM8 (Verification Model 8) to realize rate control in 1998. The thought that there is a strong connection between the neighboring frames and the R-D relation of the coded frames which can be used to predict the encoding frames was used by VM8, and it worked well in the video with low movement. However, when there were many scene switches and changes in the video, the efficiency of the algorithm decreased. At the same year, The H.263 had been proposed, and the TMN8 (Test Model Near-Term 8) was used in the rate control. TMN8 has two steps: the bits allocation in the frame layer and the adaptive quantization in the macroblock layer. Compared to the VM8, TMN8 can realize the rate control more accurately, thereby maintaining the stability of the buffer. However, the TMN8 didn't adjust the dynamic quantization parameter to each macroblock, especially can't realize rate control effectively under the condition of the scene switch.

The latest video coding H.264 standard was proposed in 2003, and the rate control method is different from the previous approaches in that the QP values are chosen prior to the prediction taking place. More specifically, the existence in the H.264 standard of a number of coding modes for each MB - multiple inter and intra modes - and the use of rate distortion optimization in the JM encoder for selecting one makes the application of typical rate control strategies quite problematic. Most of the previously mentioned rate control methods rely on a rate model and a distortion model for choosing an optimal quantiser for each macroblock or frame, given a measure of the variance of the residual signal (the prediction difference signal) and a specific bit budget allocation. The rate model is used to predict the number of bits output after coding a macroblock or frame with a specific quantiser and the distortion model is used to predict the distortion associated with each quantiser. Lagrangian optimisation can then be employed to choose the best QP in a rate distortion sense. The problem with the JM H.264 encoder lies with the fact that the residual signal depends on the choice of coding mode and the choice of coding mode depends on the choice of QP which in turn depends on the residual signal (a chicken and egg type of problem). The adopted solution in the JM encoder is one where the choice of QP is made prior to the coding mode decision using a linear model for predicting the activity of the residual signal of the current basic unit (e.g. frame, slice, macroblock) based on the activity of the residual signal of past (co-located) basic units. Though the rate control in H.264 works well in the rate control, there are some aspects to make rate control more effectively and accurately which are worth studying.

### 4.2 The direction of the development

In the video compression, rate control plays an important role. Because the video quality of the output is related to the bitrate, in order to get a better quality in the video, the output bitrate will be higher. But because of the limited bandwidth or the capacity of the storage, it is required to keep the output bitrate in a certain range to meet the limited of the bandwidth or the capacity of the storage and get as better video quality as possible. So the strategy of the rate control is one of the key success factors of the video encoding.

The purpose of the rate control is getting a better video quality in the limited bandwidth or storage. In order to achieve the goal, the rate control usually has two steps: the allocation of the resources and the calculation of the QP. The allocation of the resources researches the rate control from the angle of from top to bottom, stresses the reasonable allocation of the coding resources among the different frames (the rate control of single sequence) or different sequences (the rate control of the joint sequences); the calculation if the QP researches the rate control in the angle of from bottom to top, chooses the coding mode within the limited of the coding resources based on the rate distortion model and the RDO (rate distortion optimization) in order to make the actual rate and the target rate consistent.

The current video compression standards only make strict restrictive provisions for the streaming grammar, streaming multiplexing and decoding process and so on which are relevant to the compatibility. However, they don't make strict restrictive provisions for the aspects such as motion estimation and rate control and so on which have an important influence on the coding, but have little effect on the compatibility. As a result, they provide a large space to developers, manufacturers and research workers to improve the quality of the coding.

The fundamental tenet of the design of the rate control is determining the appropriate coding parameters to obtain optimal decoding video quality under the limited bandwidth. Though there are many effective rate control schemes nowadays, the requirements on the quality of the video images are higher and higher. As a result, the methods of the rate control should get further developments and improvements. We think the future rate control technology in the following respects will get further development.

*1. The more accurate rate distortion model*

The key problem of the rate control is to estimate or model the rate-distortion model of the video encoder, there are some rate distortion models put forward in the existing documents, but these models are usually assumed source obey Gaussian distribution or Laplace distribution, and when the actual video does not satisfy assumptions, the accuracy of the model will be affected and the quality of the algorithms will decrease. Furthermore, the application scope of some models is very small, because they are usually only for the fixed encoder and not accurate for the rest encoder. Therefore, it is necessary to propose more accurate rate distortion models which are suitable for various video encoders and can reflect the features of the actual video sequences rate-distortion accurately.

*2. The more reasonable control strategy to buffer*

In order to prevent buffer overflow or underflow, the consideration in many documents is making the occupancy degree of the buffer is about 50% when each frame has been coded. The rate control in MPEG-4 keeps the capacity of the buffer not less than 10% and more than 90% by skipping the frame in the stage of the bit allocation to each frame when the occupancy degree of the buffer is more than 80% after the previous frame has been coded. However, the bits of I frame are more than the bits of P or B frame several times, so setting the occupy degree to a fixed value is not a scientific approach. If it can adjust the buffer occupancy degree to a more reasonable value adaptively based on the situation of the encoder, it not only can deal with the buffer overflow, but also can avoid the skip frames where possible.

*3. The processing of the scene switch*

In the real-time video applications, the complexity of the video sequences is changing. In order to adapt to the scene switch, the method of adjusting the size of GOP dynamically and the method of testing the scene switch have been proposed to give special treatment to the pictures with scene switch. But these methods are usually not accurate, and the computations are complex. Therefore, putting forward a more accurate detection method and the reasonable allocation method to the scene switch pictures is a meaningful work.

*4. The rate control algorithm based on the wavelet video encoder*

The wavelet encoder has some advantages: (a). providing a better compromise of R-D; (b). providing a satisfactory subjective image quality; (c). having the character that the interception bits at any point won't cause serious distortion; (d). there is no need to consider the quantification parameters and just only to allocate reasonable bits to each frame. The rate control methods based on the wavelet are simpler than the methods based on DCT, and can be adjusted more easily. The rate control researches relative to the MPEG are very few now, but with the application of the wavelet transform in the video coding and video information transmission, the direction will become a hotspot.

*5. The rate control algorithm based on the video object*

Since MPEG-4 based on video object proposed, many scholars have researched the rate control based on video object and have put forward some effective rate control algorithms. But most of these algorithms are just the continuation of the methods based on the signal video object and not very accurate. The solution to allocate reasonable bits based on video object, the information of shape and motion vector plays an important role in the quality of the decoding pictures. With the wide application of video information based on video object, the rate control algorithm based on video object will get a good development.

*6. The fine granularity scalable rate control allocation algorithm*

The initial goal of the video coding is achieving the optimal decoding quality at the given bitrate, because of the increase in Internet video services in recent years, the goal of the video coding is not just to pursue the best video quality and pay more and more attention to the scalability. Nowadays, it has appeared many effective fine granularity scalable rate control algorithms, and many scholars have been working to improve and develop fine granularity scalable encoding technology. How to design a scalable rate control algorithm adapted to various fine granularity, how to allocate bits to basic and strengthen layers; how to allocate bits in the strengthen layers, which can achieve scalable requirements and can obtain more satisfactory video effect. These are the important problems to solve in the further researchers.

*7. The rate control algorithm in the real-time communication of low bitrate*

The main challenge in the design of multimedia applications in communications network is how to transmit the smallest multimedia streaming to users. The real-time communication applications such as video conference, online ordering require the rate control scheme with low latency and low complexity. The methods based on the optimization of Lagrange have existed in the documents, but they are of high complexity. Simplifying the complexity of the methods to make them meet the requirements of the real-time communication applications has high theoretic and commercial value.

In addition, some of the rate control methods are based on the content of the pictures and the visual characteristic. Compared to the rate-distortion scheme, they are relative simple and easy to realize, but they are not very accurate and need to continue to improve.

## 5. Acknowledgement

this chapter is supported by the National Basic Research Program of China (973 Program, No. 2010CB731800), Key Program of National Natural Science Foundation of China (No.U0835003, 60804051), the Fundamental Research Funds for the Central Universities of SCUT (2009ZM0207), the Doctoral Fund of Ministry of Education of China (200805611074)

## 6. Reference

A. H. Compressed video communication. Jozadak. Beijing: science press. 2004

Asbun E, Salama P. Delp E J. A rate-distortion approach towavelet-based encoding of predictive error frames [A]. In: Proceedings of the 2000 IEEE International Conference on ImageProcessing [C], Vancouver, British Columbia, Canada, 2000: lO～13.

Atul Puri, Xuemin Chen, Ajay Luthra. Video Coding Using the H.264/MPEG-4 AVC Compression standard. Signal Processing: Image Communication.

Chem. Hang. H.M. Source model for transform video coder and its application-partll: variable frame rate coding. IEEE Trans. Circuit and Syst. Video Technol. 1997, 7(2):299-311

Chiang T., Zhang Y Q. A new rate control scheme using quadratic rate distortion model [J]. IEEE Transactions on Circuits and Systems for Video Technology. 1997, 7(1):246-250.

Choi J, Park D. A stable feedback control of the buffer state using the controlled langrange muhiplier method [J]. IEEE Transactions on Image Processing.1994, 3:546-558

Dins W, Liu B. Rate control of MPEG video coding and recordins by rate quantization modeling [J]. IEEE Transactions on Circuits and Systems for Video Technology, 1996, 6(1):12-20.

Farin D, Mache N, P.H.N. de With. A software-based high quality MPEG-2 encoder employing scene change detection and adaptive quantization [J]. IEEE Transactions on Consumer Electronics, 2002, 48(4): 2174-2193

G. Sullivan, T. Wiegand, Keng-Pang Lim, "Joint Model Reference Encoding Methods and Decoding Concealment Methods", JVT-1049, September 2003

Hung-Ju Lee, Ya-Qin Zhang. Scalable Rate Control for MPEG-4 Video. IEEE Trans. Circuits 64 and Systems for Video Technology2000, 10(6): 878-894

ISO/IEC JTC1/SC2/WG11, "MPEG Video Simulation Model Three (SM3)," MPEG 90/041, July 1990.

ISO/IEC JTC1/SC29/WG11/Doc.N3093. MPEG-4 video verification model version 15.0. Dec. 1999.

ISO/IECJTCl/SC29/WG11.MPEG99/M5552. An all FGS Solution for Hybrid Temporal-SNR Sealability[S]

ISO/IEC/IECJTC/29/WG11.MPEG2000/M6475,Motion-compensation Based Fine-granuhr Scalability (MC-FGS) [S]

ISO/IEC JTC/SC29/WGl 1.MPEG 97/M1931. Joint rate control for multiple video objects based on quadratic rate-distortion model[s].

ISO/IEC J'rcI/SC29/WGll. MPEG97/M2554.Multiple.VO rate control and B-VO rate control[s]

ISO/IEC 14496-2/PDAM4, Coding of Audio-Visual Objects, Part-2 Visual, Amendment4: Streaming Video Pmfile[S]

Jay Kuo C C., Leou J J. A newrate control scheme for H.263 video transmission [J]. Singal

J. Ribas-Conklin, S. Lei. Rate control in DCT video coding for low-delay communication. IEEE Trans. Circuit Syst. Video Technol. Feb 1999, 9(1):172-185

Kondi L P, Melnikov G, Katsaggeles A K. Joint optimal coding of texture and shape [A]. In: Proceedings of IEEE International Conference on Image Processing[C], Thessaloniki, Greece, 2001, 3:94-97.

Lain E., G. Richardson. H.264 and MPEG-4 Video Compression Video Coding for Next Generation Multimedia. UK. John Wiley&Sons Ltd. 2003

Lee J., Dickinson B. W. Joint optimization of frame type selection and bit allocation for MPEG video encoders [A]. In: Proceedinss of International Conference on Image Processing 1994[c], Austin TX, USA, 1994: 962-966.

Li Wei-ping. Overview of fine granularity scalability in MPEG-4 video standard [J]. IEEE Transactions on Circuits and Systems for Video Technology. 2001, 11(3):301-317.

Lin D W, Wang M. H., Chen J. J. Optimal delayed·coding of video sequences subject to a buffer-size constraint [A]. In: Proceedings of SPIE Visual Communication and Image Processing 1993[C], Cambridge. MA, USA, 1993: 223-234

Lin L J., Ortega A., Jay Kuo C C. Rate control using spline- interpolated R.D characteristics [A]. In: Proceedings of Visual Communications and Image Processing 1996[c], Orlando. FL, 1996:11I-122.

Liu Hong-mei, Xiao Zi-mei, Liang Fan, et al. Resoaroh on rate scalable wavelet video coding algorithm [J]. Journal of Software, 2002, 13(4):664-668.

Liu Jiu·fen., Huang Da. ren. A rate control method based on wavelet transform [J]. Journal of Zhejiang University (Sciences Edition), 2001, 28(01):14—18

M. Van der Schaar, Radha H. Adaptive motion. Compensation Fine-Granular-Scalability (AMC-FGS) for wireless video [J]. IEEE Transactions on Circuits and Systems for Video Technology, 2002, 12(6): 360-371

MPEG 93/457, Document AVC-491, April 1993.

MPEG-1 AND MPEG-2 Video Standards By Supavadee Aramvith and Ming-Ting Sun

Processing: Image Communication, 2002, 17(7):537-557 ISO/IEC JTC1/SC29/WG11, "Test Model 5",

Proposed draft of adaptive rate control. JVT H017. 8`s Meeting: Geneva, 20-26. May, 2003
Ramchandron K., Ortega A., Vetterli M. Bit allocation for dependent quantization with applications to muhire solution and MPEG video coders C [J]. IEEE Transactions on Image Processing, 1994, 3:533-545
Ribas-Corbera J., Lei S. Rate control in DCT video coding for lowdelay communications [J]. IEEE Transactions on Circuits and Systems for Video Technology, 1999, 9(1): 172-i85
Ronda J, Eckert M, et al. Rate control and bit allocation for MPEG-4. IEEE Trans. Circuit Syst. Video Technol. 1999, 9(8): 1243-1258
Sethuraman S, Krishnamurthy R.Model based multi-pass macroblock-level rate control for visually improved video coding [A]. In: Proceedings of Workshop and Exhibition on MPEG-4 [c], San Jose, California, USA, 2001: 59-62
Shi Cui-zu. Yu Song·yu. Wang Jia. Rate allocation for MPEG-4 FGS video streaming [J]. Computer Simulation, 2004, 21(6): 46-55.
Tao B, Peterson H A, Dickinson B W. A rate. quantiration model for MPEG encoders [A]. In: Proceedings of International Conference on Image Processing 1997 [c], Santa Barbara, CA USA, 1997:338~341.
T. Chiang and Y.-Q. Zhang, "A new rate control scheme using quadratic rate-distortion modelling", IEEE Trans. on Circ. and Syst. for Video Tech., Feb. 1997.
Vetro A, Sun H, Wang Y. Joint shape and texture rate control for MPEG-4 encoders [A]. In: Proceedings of IEEE International Conference on CireuRs and Systems[C], Montery, USA. 1998:285-288.
Wang Hut-bai, Zhang Chun Tian. A buffer control strategy based on importance of the image eontents [J]. Journal of China Institute of Communications, 2000, 21(8): 21-26
Wang O, Wu F, Li S P, et al. Fine-granularity spatially scalable video coding [A]. In: proceedings of IEEE International Conference on Acoustics, Speech and Signal Processing (ICASSP)[C], Salt Lake City, 2001,3:1801 1804
Wang Qi, Zhan Li, Wu Feng, et al. A rate allocation scheme for progressive fine granular scalable video coding [J]. Acts Electronica Sinica. 2002, 30(2):205-209.
Wang L. Rate control for MPEG video coding [J]. Signal Processing: Image Communication, 2000. 15:493-511
Watson A B, Yang G Y, Solomon J A, et al. Visibility of wavelet quantization noise [J]. IEEE Transactions on Image Processing, 1997, 6(8):1168-1175.
Wu F., Li S., Zhang Y. Q. A framework for efficient progressive fine granularity scalable video coding [J]. IEEE Transactions on Circuits and Systems for Video Technology, 2001. 11(3):332-344.
Wu S W., Gersho A. Rate constrained optimal block-adaptive coding for digital tape recording of HDTV [J]. IEEE Transactions on Circuits and Systems for Video Technology. 1991, 1(1):100-112
Yang K H, Jacquin A, Jayant N S. A normalized rate-distortion model for H.263 compatible codecs and its application to quantisor selection [A]. In: Proceedings of International Conference on Image Processing 1997 [C], Santa Barbara, CA, USA, 1997: 41-44.
Yeo B, Liu B. Rapid scene analysis on compressed video [J]. IEEE Transactions on Circuits and Systems for Video Technology, 1995, 5(6):533-544

Yoneyama A., Nakajima Y., Yanagihara H., et al. MPEG encoding algorithm with scene adaptive dynamic GOP structure[A]. In: Proceedings of Ostermann J.Multimedia Signal Processing---1999 IEEE 3" Workshop on [c], Copenhagen: IEEE Pres. 1999: 297-302

Zhao X. J., He Y. W., Yang S. Q., et al. Rate allocation ofequal image quality for MPEG-4 FGS video streaming [EB/OL]. http://amp.ece.cmu.edu/packetvide02002/papers/32-uwsghuasts.poe 2002.

Zhengguo Li, Feng Pan, Keng Pang Lim, Xiao Lin, Susanto Rahardja, "Adaptive Rate Control for H.264", ICIP 2004.

Zhihai He, Yong Kwan Kim, et al. Low-Delay Rate Control for DCT Video Coding via ρ-Domain Source Modeling. IEEE Trans. Circuits and Systems for Video Technology, 2001, 11(8): 928-940

Zhihai He, Sanjit K, et al. A Unified Rate-Distortion Analysis Framework for Transform Coding. IEEE Trans. Circuits and Systems for Video Technology, 2001, 11(12): 1221-1236.

Zhengguo Li, Feng Pan, Keng Pang Lim, et al. Adaptive Basic Unit Layer Rate Control for JVT JVT 6012. 7a' Meeting: Pattaya II, Thailand. March, 2003

# 5

# Rate-Distortion Analysis for H.264/AVC Video Statistics

Luis Teixeira
*Research Center for Science and Technology in Art (CITAR), School of Arts, Portuguese Catholics University, INESC PORTO – Instituto Nacional de Engenharia de Sistemas e Computadores Portugal*

## 1. Introduction

MPEG standards family specify the decoding process and the bit-stream syntaxes allowing research towards the optimizations of the encoding process regarding coding performance improvement and complexity reduction. The purpose of a video encoder for broadcast or storage is to generate the optimal perceptual video quality, or the minimized distortion, under a certain constraint such as storage space or channel bandwidth. In particular, by minimizing the distortion D, the video encoder should optimally compute a set of optimal quantisers to control the output bit-rate for each coding unit to satisfy the allocated bit budget.

There are two main approaches to solve the optimal bit allocation problem: Lagrange optimization (Everett, 1963; Ramchandran et al., 1994) and dynamic programming (DP) (Bellman, 2003). The optimal bit allocation was first addressed in (Huang & Schultheiss, 1963) where the Lagrange multiplier approach for R-D analysis in transform coding was used. Further improvements have been reported in (Shoham & Gersho, 1988) for source quantization and coding. However, the Lagrange multiplier method suffer from problems, such as having negative bits and real numbers (Schuster & Katsaggelos, 1997a) and the computational complexity is very high due to the need to determine R-D characteristics of current and future video frames. DP is employed to achieve the minimum overall distortion through a tree or trellis with known quantisers and their R-D characteristics (Forney, 1973; Ortega, 1996; Ramchandran et al., 1994).

The total of the required bits and coding distortion depend on the quantization step-size. The rate or distortion versus quantization parameter (Q) curve can be produce by encoding for all the possible quantisers to obtain the bit-rate and the quantization error. In order to know how to select a quantization parameter under a specific constraint, e.g., the target bit-budget or distortion, it is importance to model or estimate the coding bit rate in terms of the quantization parameter, namely rate-quantization (R-Q) functions. Together with distortion-quantization (D-Q) functions, R-Q functions characterize the rate-distortion (R-D) behaviour of video encoding, which is the key to obtain an optimum bit allocation. Many R-Q and D-Q functions have been reported in previous studies (Chiang & Zhang, 1997; Ding & Liu, 1996; Hang & J.J. Chen, 1997; ISO/IEC, 1993; ISO/IEC, 1997; ITU-T, 1997; Lin & Ortega, 1998;

Ortega, 1996; Ribas-Corbera & Lei, 1999; Sullivan & Wiegand, 1998; Yin & Boyce, 2004). Some of these schemes were adopted in standard-compliant video coders, such as TM-5 (ISO/IEC, 1993), the test model for MPEG-2, TMN-8 (ITU-T, 1997), the test model for H.263, and VM-8 (ISO/IEC, 1997), the verification model for MPEG-4.

Usually rate control algorithms accept as an assumption that video source statistics are stationary. In this case, video source statistics correspond to some form of probability model such as Gaussian (Hang & J.J. Chen, 1997) or Laplacian (Chiang & Zhang, 1997) and R-D models based on the R-D theory, the theoretical foundation of rate control, can be obtained (Berger, 1971; Chiang & Zhang, 1997; Ribas-Corbera & Lei, 1999).

A video coding algorithm focus on the trade-off between the distortion and bit rate, where usually to a decreasing distortion corresponds an increasing rate and vice-versa. In R-D theory, the R-D function allows to estimate the lower bound for the rate at a given distortion. However, this value may not be possible to obtain in practical video encoders implementations. Operational R-D (ORD) theory applies to lossy data compression with finite number of possible R-D pairs (Schuster & Katsaggelos, 1997a).

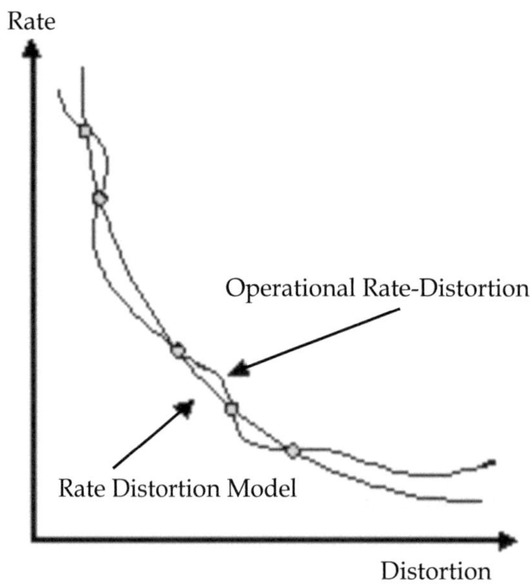


Fig. 1. Operational rate-distortion and rate-distortion model curves.

The ORD function presents the convex curve of the specific compression scheme such that the optimal solution of rate control, i.e., optimal quantiser achieving minimum distortion at given bit rate, can be obtained (Schuster& Katsaggelos, 1997a) (Figure 1). Efficiency problems in many practical video coding applications may occur due to high computational complexity in this approach (Z. Chen & Ngan, 2007). Therefore, in numerous systems, model-based rate control schemes have been adopted (Chiang & Zhang, 1997; Ding& Liu, 1996; Vetro et al., 1999; Z. Chen & Ngan, 2005a; Zhang et al., 2005). R-D models can be obtained based on the statistical properties of video signal and R-D theory (Chiang & Zhang, 1997; Hang & J.J. Chen, 1997; Ribas-Corbera & Lei, 1999), or on empirical observation and benefiting from various regression techniques (Ding& Liu, 1996; Kim, 2003; Lin & Ortega, 1998; Z. Chen & Ngan, 2004; Z. Chen & Ngan, 2005b).

Some rate control schemes incorporate spatio-temporal correlations to improve the accuracy of R-D models, by using statistical regress analysis for dynamical model parameters update. Representative of this approach is the MPEG-4 Q2 (Chiang & Zhang, 1997), and the linear MAD models (Lee et al., 2000), where model parameters are updated by linear regression method from previous coded parameters. H.264/AVC JM rate-control algorithm also uses a quadratic rate model. In addition, the H.264/AVC rate-control solves "chicken-and-egg" dilemma as the Lagrange multiplier is modelled as a function of quantization parameter (Wiegand & Girod, 2001). Rate-quantization relationship can be used to compute the quantization parameter. Nevertheless, the model-based rate functions frequently depend on the complexity of the coding unit that is obtained after the rate-constrained motion estimation and mode decision with the Lagrange multiplier. The JM algorithm of H.264/AVC proposes a linear prediction model to solve this problem by estimating the mean of absolute difference (MAD) from the previously coded units. Then the quadratic model can estimate the quantization parameter. However, rate-distortion re-analysis can be further investigated based on the coding characteristics of the H.264/AVC for improving the coding performance (Kamaci et al., 2005; Ma et al., 2005) particularly in the case of joint video coding and the use of different distortion metrics.

We may find in the literature extensive studies regarding optimizing a video encoder encoder with R-D considerations include mode decision (Chan & Siu, 2001; Chung & Chang, 2003), motion estimation (Pur et al., 1987; Rhee et al., 2001; Wiegand et al., 2003b), optimal bit allocation and rate control in video coding field (H.-Y.C. Tourapis & A.M. Tourapis, 2003; He & Mitra, 2002; J.J. Chen & Lin 1996; Ortega, 1996; Ramchandran et al., 1994; Ribas-Corbera & Neuhoff, 1998; Schuster& Katsaggelos, 1997b; Sullivan & Wiegand, 1997; Wiegand et al., 2003a, 2003c; Zhang et al., 2003).

In summary, to optimize a video encoder, the rate-distortion optimization techniques play a very important role. R-D models are functions that predict the expected distortion at a given bit rate. This is very important for joint video coding applications that attempt to optimized quality, e.g. minimize distortion, in environments where the channel conditions vary dynamically or the number of broadcast programs varies through time. Thus in this section we propose to present and evaluate several R-D models.

At the same time, we propose also to study the bit rate variability as a function of the video quality (Seeling et al., 2004, 2007). This type of analyse is typical of a communication network perspective. By re-analyzing the characteristics of the bit-rate and the data in the transform domain, a simple rate estimation function can be obtained that will allow support the allocating of video bandwidth within different video programmes.

## 2. Rate control in international standards

Although the MPEG video coding standard recommended a general coding methodology and syntax for the creation of a legitimate MPEG bitstream, there are many areas of research left open regarding how to generate high-quality MPEG bitstreams. This allows the designers of MPEG encoder great flexibility in developing and implementing their own MPEG specific algorithms. To optimise the performance-of an MPEG encoder system, it is important to study research areas such as motion estimation, coding mode decisions, and rate control.

The main goal of rate control is to manage the process of bit allocation within a video sequence and thus the quality of the encoded bitstream. Regarding rate control, encoders can operate at Constant Bit Rate (CBR) or in Variable Bit Rate (VBR). In CBR, the video encoder maintains the average bit rate constant. The encoder output has a buffer and its occupancy is controlled dynamically by adjusting the quantization scale, denote as q in MPEG coders. Likewise, the quality of the video sequence varies due to the variations in the scene complexity. VBR reduces the variation in the picture quality by allocating more bits to complex images. A common use of VBR is Open-Loop Variable Bit Rate (OL-VBR), where the quantization scale is constant for all the images of the video sequence. Another VBR scheme is Constant Quality - Variable Bit Rate (CQ-VBR) which aims to maintain an objective video quality constant.

The rate control algorithms usually adjust the coded bit stream according different constraints, such as buffer over- or underflow prevention, variable and/or low bandwidth constraints resulting from limited storage size or communication bandwidth (Ortega, 1996). In order to accomplish this goal rate control schemes are responsible to adjust the quantization parameters.

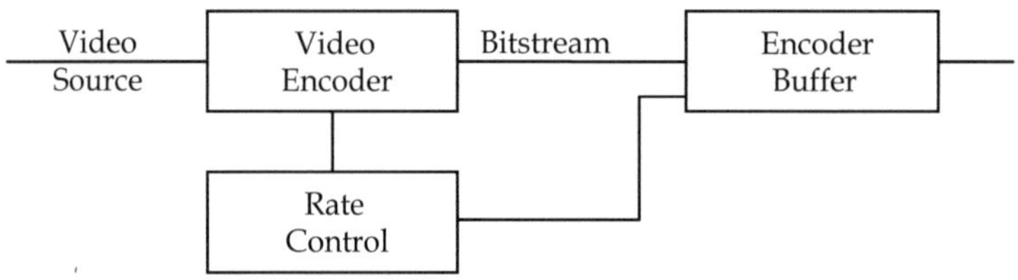


Fig. 2. Rate control in video coding system.

A generic bit rate control is composed the following steps: given an input video signal and a desired bit rate, constant or variable, what should be the encoder settings to maintain the picture quality as high and constant as possible. In MPEG encoding, a quantization scale controls the trade-off between picture quality and the bit rate. This parameter is used to compute the step size of the uniform quantisers used for the different AC DCT coefficients (ISO/IEC, 1993). For each macroblock, a quantiser, q, is selected. It is named "adaptive quantization" to the process for adjusting the value of q between macroblocks within an image frame. There are several schemes for doing the adaptive quantization. For example, in MPEG-2 Test Model 5 (TM5) (ISO/IEC, 1993), a non-linear mapping based on the block variance is used to adapt the q's. Besides the quantization scale, the quantization coarseness is also dependent of the quantization matrix. In MPEG-1, the quantization matrix can be altered in each sequence while in MPEG-2 on a picture basis. It sets the relative coarseness of quantization for each coefficient.

As MPEG does not specify how to control the bit rate, different approaches can be found in the literature (ISO/IEC, 1993; Keesman et al., 1995; Ramchandran et al., 1993). Two approaches have been used: 'feed forward bit rate control' and 'feed backward bit rate control'. In the first approach, after performing a pre-analysis, the optimum settings are compute. This process will increase the computational complexity and time needed while yielding better results. In the second approach, there is limited knowledge of the sequence complexity. Bits are allocated on a picture basis and spatially uniform distributed throughout the image. Thus, too many bits may be spent at the beginning of the picture while the end of the picture may present a higher degree of complexity. The 'feed backward bit rate control' is suitable for real time applications and 'feed forward bit rate control' for applications where the quality is the main goal and time is not a constraint.

## 3. Rate control in H.264/AVC

Existing studies indicate that H.264/AVC brings major improvement in coding performance in relation to prior coding standards (Wiegand et al., 2003a). H.264/AVC presents many new features, which represent huge challenges to the operative encoder control such as how to allocate the bandwidth between the texture coding and the overhead coding.

A major contributor to the high coding efficiency of H.264/AVC compared with previous video compression standards is the rate and distortion (R-D) optimized motion estimation and mode decision (also referred to as RDO) with various intra and inter prediction modes and multiple reference frames. Nevertheless, these innovations increase the rate control process complexity due to the inter-dependency between the RDO and rate control. Only after the end of intra/inters prediction, the rate control scheme can access the exact coding characteristics. This information is necessary for the computation of the quantization parameter. Such a dilemma prevents the rate control scheme from directly accessing the coding characteristic in advance. The dilemma of selecting which parameter should be first determine is sometimes referred in the literature as to the "chicken and egg" dilemma (Li et al., 2003c, 2004; Wu et al., 2005).

To avoid this dilemma, in JVT-D030 a two-pass scheme was proposed, where in each pass a TM-5-alike method was used (Ma et al., 2002). This approach uses an extremely simplified R-D function, which fails to achieve accurate and robust rate control and due to the two-pass increase the level of complexity. Because of these drawbacks, JVT-G012 (Li et al., 2003a) was proposed and accepted as the standardized rate control scheme for H.264/AVC. In JVT-G012, a linear MAD model predicts the coding complexity, and a MPEG-4 Q2 function employed to estimate the quantization parameter (Li et al., 2003a).

First step occurs at GOP level. This step estimates the bits available for the remaining frames in the GOP. In addition, it initializes the QP of instantaneous decoding refresh (IDR) frame. In the following step, rate control algorithm operates at Picture level: an estimation of the target bits for the current basic unit is determined. A basic unit is a group of macroblocks and its size can vary from one macroblock up to the entire picture. The target bits estimation should be allocate so that a similar number of bits are allocate for every picture and the target buffer level is preserve.

The next step is, based on the number of bits used to encode the previous basic units, to estimate the necessary bits to encode the header. The target texture is obtained by subtracting the header estimation to the total target bits estimate. After that, this value is converted to a target QP value using a quadratic model that correlates the QP with the texture bits. The quadratic model needs an estimation of the MAD of the motion-compensated or intra prediction error of the current basic unit's. Consequently, the rate control model requires an additional linear MAD model that, from the previous basic unit MAD, allows the computation of the current basic unit MAD. In summary, the Picture level process consist in computing the quantization step Qstep using a quadratic model and then performing a R-D optimization (RDO) (Wiegand et al., 2003a) for each MB in the frame.

The MAD of the current stored picture, , is predicted by a linear regression method similar to that of MPEG-4 Q2 after coding each picture or each basic unit (1) using the actual MAD of the previous stored picture, $\sigma_i(j-1-L)$

$$\tilde{\sigma}_i(j) = a_1 \times \sigma_i(j-1-L) + a_2 \qquad (1)$$

where a1 and a2 are the model parameters (first-order and second-order coefficients). The initial value of a1 and a2 are set to one and zero, respectively (Lim et al., 2007). The quantization step corresponding to the target bits is computed by the equation (2)

$$T_i(j) = c_1 \times \frac{\tilde{\sigma}_i(j)}{Q_{step,i}(j)} + c_2 \times \frac{\tilde{\sigma}_i(j)}{Q^2_{step,i}(j)} - m_{h,i}(j) \tag{2}$$

where $m_{h,i}(j)$ is the total number of header bits and motion vector bits, $c_1$ and $c_2$ are two coefficients. The corresponding quantization parameter QPi(j) is computed by using the relationship between the quantization step and the quantization parameter of AVC (Lim et al., 2007). Final step consists in updating the quadratic QP/bits linear model and the MAD model. This process repeats for each basic unit until the complete video sequence has been encoded.

In this section, it was introduce the basis of rate control architecture in JM H.264/AVC (Lim et al., 2007). More detail information is available at (Li et al., 2003b , 2003c , 2004; Lim et al., 2007; Ma et al., 2002). Other solutions can be found in the literature. For example, Zhihai He (He, 2001) has proposed a new model that achieves a good performance for H.263 and MPEG4-2 (ISO/IEC 14496-2) codecs. The parameter $\rho$ represents the percentage of zeros among the quantized transform coefficients. He found a linear relationship between the value $\rho$ and the real bit rate because the percentage of zeros plays an important role in determining the final bit rate

## 4. Test video sequences

Selecting a representative set of video sequences is a crucial step in evaluating and analysing the performance of R-D models. A homogeneous set of video sequences may generate biased comparison results, because some models may perform especially well under certain sequences. Two key features are used to characterize video sequences: spatial complexity and temporal complexity. Usually, spatial complexity is measured by averaging all neighbourhood differences in the same frame while temporal complexity is measured by averaging neighbourhood differences between adjacent frames (Adjeroh & Lee, 2004).

The set of test video sequences is composed by twelve CIF video sequences, with the duration of 10 seconds that are known as test video sequences (ITU-T, 2005).

It were included sequences with low spatial and temporal complexity (low complexity sequences) up to sequences with high spatial and temporal complexity (high complexity sequences). Sequences that have either high spatial or temporal complexity but nor both the designated them as medium-complexity sequences. It follows a brief description of the sequences.

In seven video sequences, the position of the camera is fixed: Akiyo (aki), Deadline (dea), Hall (hal), Mother and Daughter (mad), News (new), Paris (par) and Silence (sil). In the Akiyo sequence, the camera is focus on a human subject with a synthetic background (a female anchor reading the news). The movements are very limited, mainly head movements in front of a fixed camera. In Deadline, Mother and Daughter and Paris sequences, the camera is still fixed but there are more movements of the bodies and heads. These are typical videoconferencing content. In the News sequence two reporters, a male and a female anchor, reading the news in front of a fixed camera in a newsroom while in the background, two dancers execute movements. Hall sequence is an example of a video supervision, with stationary camera and two moving persons: one people entering from the left with a briefcase and then leaving the hall. In the middle of the sequence, a second person enters the hall from the right and then grabs a monitor. In the Silence sequence, one can observe a fast moving subject executing deaf gesture language.

(a) Akiyo (b) Coastguard (c) Deadlined (d) Flower Garden

(e) Football (f) Foreman (g) Hall (h) Mobile & Calendar

(i) News (j) Paris (k) Silence (l) Mother & Daughter

Fig. 3. Video test sequences

The Foreman sequence (for) contain the head of a person talking and geometric shapes. Fast camera movement and content motion with a pan to a construction site at the end characterize this sequence. The main characteristics of the Flower Garden sequence (flg) is the slow and steady camera panning over landscape over landscape; the spatial and the colour detail. Coastguard sequence (cgd) was shot as a pan from left to right movement in the first third and a pan from left to right in the rest of the sequence. The camera movement follows the movements of two boats (the first from right to left and the second movement from left to right). The Mobile and Calendar (mcl) sequence is characterized by the slow panning and zooming of the camera, complex motion; high spatial and colour detail. Fast and complex motion movements of the camera and contents and the level of detail characterize the Football sequence (fot). This is a very diverse set of video sequences

## 5. Experimental setup

Simulations were performed with the JM reference software, the official MPEG and ITU reference implementation, for the H.264/AVC Main profile (ITU-T, 2005). Source code was compiled with Microsoft Visual C++:

| GOP Pattern | IntraPeriod | Number of B Frames | Pattern |
|---|---|---|---|
| IBBP_GOP1 | 10 | 2 | IBBPBBPBBPBBPBBPBBPBBPBBPBBPBB |
| IBBP_GOP2 | 4 | 2 | IBBPBBPBBPBB |
| IPPP_GOP1 | 4 | 0 | IPPP |
| IPPP_GOP2 | 10 | 0 | IPPPPPPPPP |

Table 1. Evaluated GOP Patterns

Four different type of GOP patterns were used (Table 1). A typical GOP pattern (IBBP_GOP2), an "extend" B frame version of the typical GOP pattern, and two GOP patterns without Interpolated images.
Additionally, each video test sequence was encoded in two modes: Open-loop (fixed QP with values ranging from 10 up to 42) and Constant Bit Rate (Fixed Rate - 64kbps, 128kbps, 256kbps, 384kbps, 512kbps, 640kbps, 768kbps, 1024kbps, 1536kbps, 2048kbps. The goal was to obtain sufficient data to obtain R-D curves.
Typical quality metrics include Peak signal-to-noise ratio (PSNR) and the Mean Square Error (MSE), Sum of Squared Differences (SSD), Mean Absolute Difference (MAD), and Sum of Absolute Differences (SAD).

$$PSNR = 10\log_{10}\frac{255^2}{MSE} \tag{3}$$

$$MSE = \frac{1}{HW}SSD \tag{4}$$

$$SSD = \sum_{x=0}^{H-1}\sum_{y=0}^{W-1}\left(p(x,y) - \hat{p}(x,y)\right)^2 \tag{5}$$

$$MAD = \frac{1}{HW}SAD \tag{6}$$

$$SAD = \sum_{x=0}^{H-1}\sum_{y=0}^{W-1}\left|p(x,y) - \hat{p}(x,y)\right| \tag{7}$$

where H and W are the height and the width of the image frame, and p(x, y) and $\hat{p}(x,y)$ represent the "original" and the reconstructed image frame pixels at (x, y).
Complementary with the study of rate-distortion performance it is propose to include an analysis of the bit rate variability as a function of the video quality. This is an important topic when considering multimedia traffic. The bit rate variability is usually characterized by the Coefficient of Variation (CoV) of the frame sizes (in bits), whereby the CoV is defined as the standard deviation of the frame sizes normalized by their mean $\overline{X}$ (Seeling et al., 2004, 2007)

$$CoV = \frac{\sigma}{\overline{X}} \tag{8}$$

where $\overline{X}$ is mean size (in bits)

$$\bar{X} = \frac{1}{M}\sum_{m=1}^{M} X_m \tag{9}$$

and the variance $\sigma^2$ (square of the standard deviation) of the frame sizes being defined as

$$\sigma^2 = \frac{1}{(M-1)}\sum_{m=1}^{M}\left(X_m - \bar{X}\right)^2 \tag{10}$$

## 6. Experimental results and discussion

This section presents experimental results: Rate-Distortion analysis and bit rate variability analysis as a function of the video quality.

### 6.1 R-D models

The RD graphs obtained for the video sequences Akiyo, Foreman and Football, in open loop, are show in Figure 4 (bit-rate axe is in logarithm scale). One can observe that a proportional relation exists between Bit-rate and Picture Quality and that quality depend on the video nature: for the same bit-rate, low complexity sequences present higher values of quality and vice-versa. This behaviour occurs in all the different GOP patterns. Figure 5

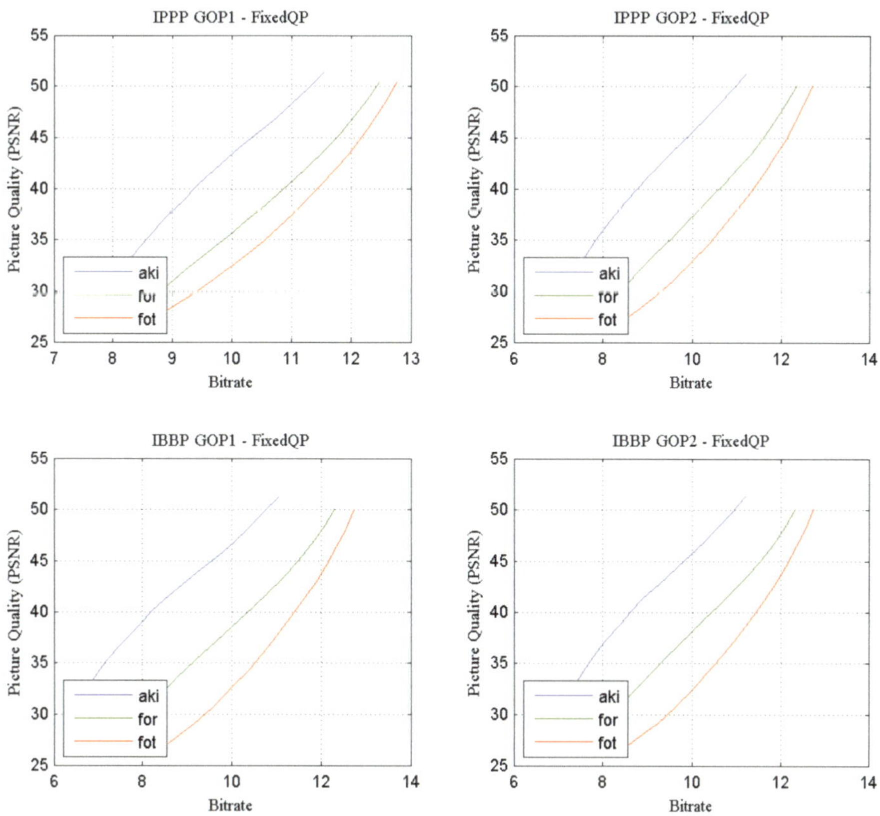


Fig. 4. Rate-distortion curve (Akiyo, Foreman, Football; FixeQP)

present graphic representation for RD data in Constant Bit Rate for the same three video sequences using JM rate control. In this case a relation between bit rate and quality can be observed.

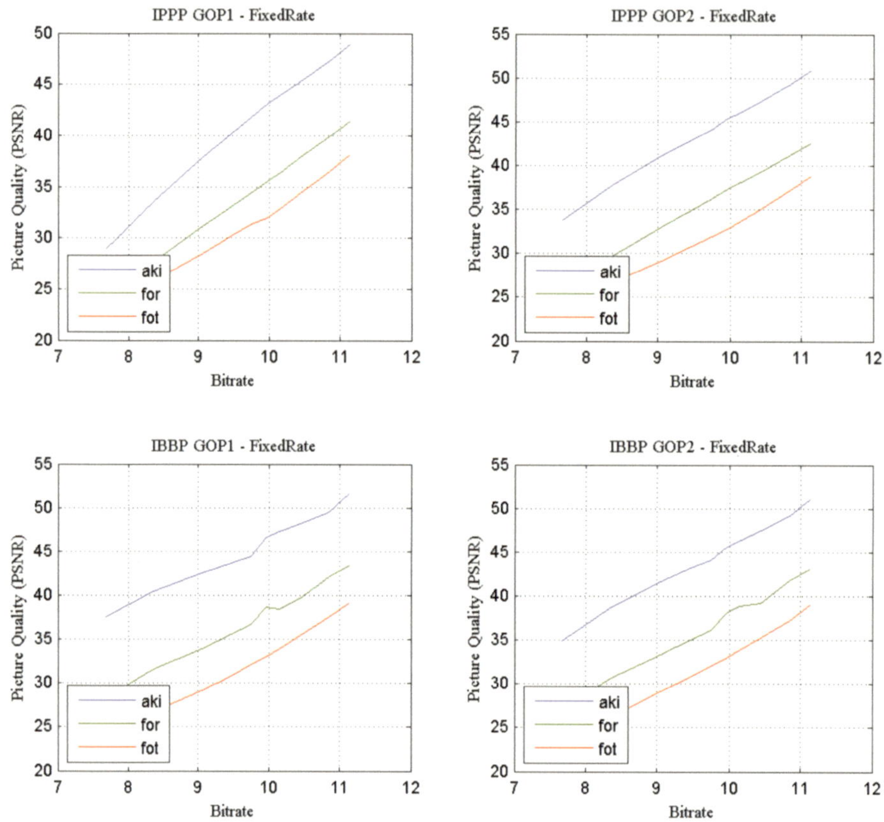


Fig. 5. Rate-distortion curve (Akiyo, Foreman, Football; FixeRate)

Frequently data can be noisy in its nature. Thus recognizing the trends in the data is important (Vardeman, 1994). One of the available methods for data analysis and identify existing trends in physical systems is curve fitting. The concept of curve fitting is rather simple: to use a simple function to describe a trend by minimizing the error between the selected function to fit and a set of data (Vardeman, 1994). The principle of least squares is applied to the fitting of a line to (x, y) data. Representative work for estimate the quantization step size has been most direct towards developing all kinds of rate-quantization (R-Q) models like polynomial (including linear and quadratic) (Chiang & Zhang, 1997; Lin & Ortega, 1998; Ronda et al., 1999; Yan & Liou, 1997), spline ( Lin et al., 1996), logarithmic (Ding& Liu, 1996; Hang & J.J. Chen, 1997), power (Ding& Liu, 1996), etc. Yang et al. (Kyeong Ho Yang at al, 1997) proposed a more complex model that combines a logarithmic and a quadratic model. Most of the models only consider the rate function, and often implicitly assume that the distortion is a linear function of the quantization scale. This work has been extended to include D(QP) implementing several methods in order to compare their results. In fact, the goal is to model the quality versus quantization step

relationship and then to evaluate the different approaches to quality metric. It is presume that there is an inverse relationship between quality and distortion.
Before fitting data into a function that models the relationship between two measured quantities, it is a normal procedure to determine if a relationship exists between these quantities. It was decide to use the correlation method to confirm the degree of probability that a relationship exists between two measured quantities (Vardeman, 1994). In the case of no correlation between the two quantities, then there is no tendency for the values of one quantity to increase or decrease with the values of the second quantity. To evaluate the quality of the fit, it is used the sample correlation that represents the normalized measure of the strength of linear relationship between variables (Vardeman, 1994):

$$r = \frac{x^T y}{\sqrt{(x^T x)(y^T y)}} \tag{11}$$

$$r = \frac{\sum (x_i - \bar{x})(y_i - \bar{y})}{\sqrt{\sum (x_i - \bar{x})^2 (y_i - \bar{y})^2}} = \frac{\sum x_i y_i - \frac{(\sum x_i)(\sum y_i)}{n}}{\sqrt{\left(\sum x_i^2 - \frac{(\sum x_i)^2}{n}\right)\left(\sum y_i^2 - \frac{(\sum y_i)^2}{n}\right)}} \tag{12}$$

where r is a matrix of correlation coefficients (Vardeman, 1994). The sample correlation always lies in the interval from -1 to 1. A value of r near of positive one or negative one, it is interpreted as indicating a relatively strong relationship and r near zero is inferred as indicating a lack of relationship. The sign of r indicates whether y tends to increase or decrease with increase x.

| | IBBP-GOP1 | | | IBBP-GOP2 | | |
|---|---|---|---|---|---|---|
| Sequence | I Type | P Type | B Type | I Type | P Type | B Type |
| Aki | 0.8380 | 0.8470 | 0,9016 | 0,8645 | 0,8447 | 0,9034 |
| Cgd | 0.9210 | 0.9136 | 0,9595 | 0,9180 | 0,9139 | 0,9609 |
| Dea | 0.8853 | 0.8909 | 0,9303 | 0,8943 | 0,8878 | 0,9318 |
| Flg | 0.9137 | 0.9035 | 0,9349 | 0,9147 | 0,8962 | 0,9342 |
| For | 0.8964 | 0.8881 | 0,9197 | 0,8968 | 0,8836 | 0,9197 |
| Fot | 0.9588 | 0.9557 | 0,9691 | 0,9567 | 0,9550 | 0,9695 |
| Hal | 0.8154 | 0.7972 | 0,8589 | 0,8003 | 0,7936 | 0,8628 |
| Mad | 0.8797 | 0.8666 | 0,9124 | 0,8653 | 0,8645 | 0,9129 |
| New | 0.9554 | 0.9081 | 0,9511 | 0,9091 | 0,9128 | 0,9524 |
| Par | 0.9455 | 0.9435 | 0,9638 | 0,9461 | 0,9434 | 0,9651 |
| Sil | 0.9451 | 0.9412 | 0,9567 | 0,9419 | 0,9421 | 0,9576 |
| Mcl | 0.9356 | 0.9272 | 0,9470 | 0,9329 | 0,9250 | 0.9488 |

Table 2. Correlation coefficients between Bits Frames and Quality Metric (PSNR) for different H.264/AVC video sequences (IBBP-GOP1 and IBBP-GOP2).

| | IPPP - GOP1 | | IPPP - GOP2 | |
|---|---|---|---|---|
| Sequence | I Type | P Type | I Type | P Type |
| Aki | 0.8962 | 0.9170 | 0.9107 | 0.9065 |
| Cgd | 0.9608 | 0.9617 | 0.9615 | 0.9609 |
| Dea | 0.9304 | 0.9406 | 0.9354 | 0.9348 |
| Flg | 0.9555 | 0.9586 | 0.9567 | 0.9572 |
| For | 0.9268 | 0.9333 | 0.9326 | 0.9289 |
| Fot | 0.9659 | 0.9686 | 0.9649 | 0.9665 |
| Hal | 0.8540 | 0.8848 | 0.8598 | 0.8646 |
| Mad | 0.9019 | 0.9200 | 0.9225 | 0.9121 |
| New | 0.9353 | 0.9492 | 0.9526 | 0.9391 |
| Par | 0.9609 | 0.9668 | 0.9627 | 0.9630 |
| Sil | 0.9605 | 0.9662 | 0.9613 | 0.9621 |
| Mcl | 0.9584 | 0.9715 | 0.9615 | 0.9636 |

Table 3. Correlation coefficients between Bits Frames and Quality Metric (PSNR) for different H.264/AVC video sequences (IPPP-GOP1 and IPPP-GOP2).

Equation (12) was computed for all the twelve sequences, and results were obtained according the different Picture Type and GOP pattern (Table 2 and Table 3). Thus, it was assess the hypothesis of a relationship between PSNR and Rate. Results are very high, for all the video sequences and GOP patterns, near positive one, pointing clearly to a strong positive linear relationship evident. Next step is thus to select what curve fitting functions should be assessed. Due to its simplicity, the first selected is one of the most commonly used techniques: the fitting of a straight line to a set of bivariate data generating a linear equation such as (13) (Vardeman, 1994):

$$\text{Linear} \quad y = \beta_0 + \beta_1 x \tag{13}$$

A natural generalization of equation (13) is the polynomial equation (14)

$$\text{Polynomial} \quad y = \beta_0 + \beta_1 x + \beta_2 x^2 + \ldots + \beta_k x^k \tag{14}$$

The goal is thus to minimize the function of k + 1 variables.

$$\begin{aligned} S(\beta_0, \beta_1, \beta_2, \ldots, \beta_k) &= \sum_{i=1}^{n} (y_i - \hat{y}_i)^2 \\ &= \sum_{i=1}^{n} \left( y_i - \left( \beta_0 + \beta_1 x_i + \beta_2 x_i^2 + \ldots + \beta_k x_i^k \right) \right)^2 \end{aligned} \tag{15}$$

by selecting the coefficients $\beta_0, \beta_1, \beta_2, \ldots, \beta_k$ (Vardeman, 1994). Upon setting the partial derivatives of S($\beta_0, \beta_1, \beta_2, \ldots, \beta_k$) equal to zero and doing some simplifications, one obtains the normal equations for this least squares problem:

$$\begin{aligned} & n\beta_0 + \left(\sum x_i\right)\beta_1 + \left(\sum x_i^2\right)\beta_2 + \ldots + \left(\sum x_i^k\right)\beta_k = \sum y_i \\ & \left(\sum x_i\right)\beta_0 + \left(\sum x_i^2\right)\beta_1 + \left(\sum x_i^3\right)\beta_2 + \ldots + \left(\sum x_i^{k+1}\right)\beta_k = \sum x_i y_i \\ & \left(\sum x_i^k\right)\beta_0 + \left(\sum x_i^{k+1}\right)\beta_1 + \left(\sum x_i^{k+2}\right)\beta_2 + \ldots + \left(\sum x_i^{2k}\right)\beta_k = \sum x_i^k y_i \end{aligned} \tag{16}$$

Solving the system of k+1 linear equations presented in Equation 16 it is typically possible to obtained a single set of values S($b_0, b_1, b_2, ..., b_k$) that minimize S($\beta_0, \beta_1, \beta_2, ..., \beta_k$). Polynomials are often used when a simple empirical model is required. One of the most uses polynomial models is the quadratic model (Equation 17):

$$\text{Quadratic} \quad y = \beta_0 + \beta_1 x + \beta_2 x^2 \tag{17}$$

To compare with the solution available in the literature it was decide to extend the models and thus include the logarithmic (18), the exponential (19), the power (20) and the linear with nonpolynomial model (LNP) (21).

$$\text{Logarithmic} \quad y = \beta_0 + \log x \tag{18}$$

$$\text{Exponential} \quad y = \beta_0 e^{\beta_1 x} \tag{19}$$

$$\text{Power} \quad y = \beta_0 + \beta_1 x^{\beta_2} \tag{20}$$

$$\text{Linear with nonpolynomial} \quad y = \beta_0 + \beta_1 e^{-x} + \beta_2 x e^{-x} \tag{21}$$

After selecting these six models, it was computed the average absolute error when trying to model the relation between bit-rate and quantization parameter (QP), PSNR and quantization parameter, and bit-rate and PSNR regarding the picture type using each of the six models for all the GOP patterns.

```
for each method do
    square error R(QP)(Picture Type) = 0;
    square error D(QP)(Picture Type) = 0;
    for each frame in the sequence do
        for each QP do
            Extract Statistics [Bits, PSNR, Picture Type];
        endfor
        Estimate the parameters of the model for R(QP) (Picture Type);
        Compute the square error R for each D value (Picture Type);
        Update the accumulative squared error R(Picture Type);
        Estimate the parameters of the model for D(QP) (Picture Type);
        Compute the square error D for each D value (Picture Type);
        Update the accumulative squared error D(Picture Type);
        Estimate the parameters of the model for R(D) (Picture Type);
        Compute the square error R for each D value(Picture Type);
        Update the accumulative squared error R_D(Picture Type);
    endfor
endfor
```

Fig. 6. Pseudo code for R-D model fitting.

It was implemented the procedure described in Figure 6. Results are presented in Table 4, Table 5, and Table 6 for the twelve video sequences.

| Fit Method | IPPP GOP1 | | IPPP GOP2 | | IBBP GOP1 | | | IBBP GOP2 | | |
|---|---|---|---|---|---|---|---|---|---|---|
| | I Type | P Type | I Type | P Type | I Type | P Type | B Type | I Type | P Type | B Type |
| Linear fit | 1285 | 1110 | 2114 | 807 | 4290 | 1166 | 965 | 2453 | 1264 | 1051 |
| Quadratic fit | 231 | 154 | 361 | 128 | 1002 | 328 | 196 | 614 | 363 | 200 |
| Exponential fit | 542 | 505 | 864 | 358 | 1584 | 410 | 396 | 872 | 442 | 436 |
| Logarithmic fit | 996 | 762 | 1603 | 590 | 3329 | 980 | 740 | 1976 | 1065 | 782 |
| Power Regression | 1023 | 1045 | 1712 | 712 | 3255 | 747 | 780 | 1725 | 778 | 880 |
| LNP fit | 1606 | 2344 | 2998 | 1389 | 6326 | 802 | 1377 | 2830 | 856 | 1760 |

Table 4. Mean Absolute Error for Rate-QP curve fitting.

| Fit Method | IPPP GOP1 | | IPPP GOP2 | | IBBP GOP1 | | | IBBP GOP2 | | |
|---|---|---|---|---|---|---|---|---|---|---|
| | I Type | P Type | I Type | P Type | I Type | P Type | B Type | I Type | P Type | B Type |
| Linear fit | 0.05 | 0.03 | 0.08 | 0.03 | 0.18 | 0.06 | 0.04 | 0.11 | 0.06 | 0.04 |
| Quadratic fit | 0.02 | 0.01 | 0.03 | 0.01 | 0.06 | 0.02 | 0.01 | 0.04 | 0.02 | 0.01 |
| Exponential fit | 0.05 | 0.03 | 0.08 | 0.03 | 0.15 | 0.05 | 0.03 | 0.10 | 0.06 | 0.04 |
| Logarithmic fit | 0.08 | 0.04 | 0.12 | 0.04 | 0.20 | 0.07 | 0.05 | 0.13 | 0.08 | 0.05 |
| Power Regression | 0.14 | 0.08 | 0.22 | 0.07 | 0.35 | 0.12 | 0.08 | 0.22 | 0.13 | 0.08 |
| LNP fit | 0.77 | 0.45 | 1.23 | 0.41 | 2.10 | 0.70 | 0.47 | 1.31 | 0.76 | 0.47 |

Table 5. Mean Absolute Error for PSNR-QP curve fitting.

| Fit Method | IPPP GOP1 | | IPPP GOP2 | | IBBP GOP1 | | | IBBP GOP2 | | |
|---|---|---|---|---|---|---|---|---|---|---|
| | I Type | P Type | I Type | P Type | I Type | P Type | BI Type | I Type | P Type | B Type |
| Linear fit | 9789 | 13947 | 10153 | 11387 | 11411 | 9470 | 11659 | 10344 | 9421 | 12543 |
| Quadratic fit | 1548 | 1845 | 1576 | 1652 | 2045 | 1976 | 1914 | 1908 | 2013 | 1970 |
| Exponential fit | 6954 | 11853 | 7034 | 8854 | 9265 | 6966 | 9087 | 8261 | 6726 | 10193 |
| Logarithmic fit | 11497 | 17611 | 12097 | 13859 | 13586 | 10704 | 13852 | 12030 | 10613 | 15178 |
| Power Regression | 4541 | 7258 | 4312 | 5525 | 5788 | 4655 | 5934 | 5321 | 4616 | 6574 |
| LNP fit | 25074 | 50461 | 27787 | 35324 | 33094 | 19738 | 32635 | 26451 | 19489 | 38917 |

Table 6. Mean Absolute Error for Rate-PSNR curve fitting.

From the results, several observations can be produce. First, the linear with nonpolynomial model is the least accurate while the quadratic approach is the most accurate overall. The second observation is that the accuracy of all models varies with the level of complexity of the video source data. Results improve for low complexity video sequences while decrease for sequence with higher complexity. Third observation, GOP pattern has impact on the average of the absolute error for the different type of pictures. For most of the models, the average absolute error (excluding linear with nonpolynomial model) is rather small.

| Sequence | Fit Method | Rate-QP | | PSNR-QP | | Rate - PSNR | |
|---|---|---|---|---|---|---|---|
| | | I Type | P Type | I Type | P Type | I Type | P Type |
| Akiyo | Linear fit | 237 | 406 | 0.03 | 0.02 | 2128 | 6295 |
| | Quadratic fit | 65 | 62 | 0.01 | 0.01 | 635 | 1175 |
| | Exponential fit | 79 | 46 | 0.07 | 0.04 | 761 | 718 |
| | Logarithmic fit | 185 | 269 | 0.11 | 0.07 | 2369 | 7386 |
| | Power Regression | 91 | 211 | 0.16 | 0.10 | 1024 | 1751 |
| | LNP fit | 329 | 856 | 0.75 | 0.44 | 5755 | 22485 |
| Foreman | Linear fit | 1052 | 1076 | 0.05 | 0.03 | 8368 | 13411 |
| | Quadratic fit | 288 | 209 | 0.01 | 0.01 | 1917 | 2238 |
| | Exponential fit | 320 | 449 | 0.05 | 0.03 | 2658 | 10807 |
| | Logarithmic fit | 866 | 780 | 0.08 | 0.04 | 9314 | 16117 |
| | Power Regression | 317 | 831 | 0.12 | 0.07 | 3151 | 7614 |
| | LNP fit | 930 | 1872 | 0.70 | 0.41 | 19274 | 44875 |
| Football | Linear fit | 1864 | 1393 | 0.07 | 0.04 | 13364 | 15256 |
| | Quadratic fit | 324 | 194 | 0.02 | 0.01 | 1931 | 2186 |
| | Exponential fit | 394 | 377 | 0.04 | 0.02 | 8330 | 15092 |
| | Logarithmic fit | 1370 | 981 | 0.05 | 0.03 | 15922 | 19000 |
| | Power Regression | 1191 | 1007 | 0.10 | 0.05 | 4711 | 9574 |
| | LNP fit | 2831 | 2481 | 0.68 | 0.39 | 38402 | 55186 |

Table 7. Absolute error for Rate-QP, PSNR-QP and Rate-PSNR curve fitting (IPPP GOP1)

Considering individual video sequence results, they can be analysed according model fit, picture type, and GOP pattern for the different rate-distortion-quantization models.
Regarding Rate-QP, quadratic approach is the best solution in most of the cases (for IPPP GOP1 and IPPP GOP2 quadratic approach is the best solution for 9 video sequences regarding pictures type Intra and 10 video sequences for pictures type P and for the remaining video sequences the best solution is the exponential fit and power regression). Worst results of quadratic approach take place with IBBP GOP1 and IBBP GOP2 patterns (regarding picture type I, P and B, quadratic approach present the best results in 11, 6 and 8 video sequences for IBBP GOP1 and 10, 6 and 10 for IBBP GOP2). Besides quadratic approach, exponential fit and power regression also present good results, particularly in GOP patterns containing B images and for low to medium spatial and temporal complexity where motion estimation is most effective. In these cases, quadratic approach is usually the second best approach. Finally, quadratic is also the best approach for modelling Rate-PSNR (11 of 12 video sequences for IPPP GOP1 for both I and P frame types; 10 and 11 of 12 video sequences regarding respectively Intra and P frames for IPPP GOP2; 10, 11 and 10 for I, P and B frames regarding IBBP GOP1 and 10, 9 and 10 for I, P and B frames regarding IBBP GOP2). In this case, also exponential and power regression presents good results. Thus, quadratic approach is a good solution particularly for GOP sequences without B frames. For quality versus quantization parameter global results from different models are very good. In

| Sequence | Fit Method | Rate-QP | | PSNR-QP | | Rate - PSNR | |
|---|---|---|---|---|---|---|---|
| | | I Type | P Type | I Type | P Type | I Type | P Type |
| Akiyo | Linear fit | 462 | 228 | 0.03 | 0.01 | 2620 | 3879 |
| | Quadratic fit | 108 | 43 | 0.02 | 0.01 | 671 | 828 |
| | Exponential fit | 111 | 39 | 0.10 | 0.04 | 627 | 687 |
| | Logarithmic fit | 339 | 157 | 0.17 | 0.06 | 2985 | 4504 |
| | Power Regression | 212 | 112 | 0.25 | 0.09 | 974 | 1252 |
| | LNP fit | 791 | 451 | 1.18 | 0.40 | 8110 | 13199 |
| Foreman | Linear fit | 1776 | 717 | 0.09 | 0.03 | 8771 | 10188 |
| | Quadratic fit | 460 | 169 | 0.02 | 0.01 | 1804 | 2044 |
| | Exponential fit | 434 | 277 | 0.07 | 0.02 | 2585 | 6455 |
| | Logarithmic fit | 1444 | 550 | 0.11 | 0.04 | 9857 | 11844 |
| | Power Regression | 542 | 450 | 0.19 | 0.06 | 2680 | 5056 |
| | LNP fit | 1707 | 1045 | 1.11 | 0.37 | 21255 | 29684 |
| Football | Linear fit | 3043 | 1068 | 0.11 | 0.04 | 13687 | 13833 |
| | Quadratic fit | 532 | 179 | 0.03 | 0.01 | 2111 | 2059 |
| | Exponential fit | 664 | 250 | 0.07 | 0.02 | 8938 | 10504 |
| | Logarithmic fit | 2212 | 774 | 0.09 | 0.03 | 16452 | 16704 |
| | Power Regression | 1974 | 711 | 0.16 | 0.05 | 5008 | 6378 |
| | LNP fit | 4872 | 1722 | 1.09 | 0.36 | 40679 | 43617 |

Table 8. Absolute error for Rate-QP, PSNR-QP and Rate-PSNR curve fitting (IPPP GOP2).

| Sequence | Fit Method | Rate-QP | | | PSNR-QP | | | Rate - PSNR | | |
|---|---|---|---|---|---|---|---|---|---|---|
| | | I Type | P Type | B Type | I Type | P Type | B Type | I Type | P Type | B Type |
| Akiyo | Linear fit | 1063 | 115 | 221 | 0.05 | 0.02 | 0.01 | 3554 | 1101 | 3211 |
| | Quadratic fit | 190 | 46 | 51 | 0.04 | 0.02 | 0.01 | 787 | 467 | 821 |
| | Exponential fit | 218 | 56 | 44 | 0.17 | 0.06 | 0.04 | 689 | 561 | 694 |
| | Logarithmic fit | 707 | 99 | 163 | 0.28 | 0.10 | 0.07 | 4164 | 1173 | 3649 |
| | Power Regression | 605 | 37 | 96 | 0.42 | 0.14 | 0.10 | 1134 | 683 | 1129 |
| | LNP fit | 2269 | 65 | 368 | 2.04 | 0.68 | 0.46 | 12646 | 2065 | 9806 |
| Foreman | Linear fit | 2736 | 726 | 767 | 0.14 | 0.04 | 0.03 | 8112 | 6506 | 9608 |
| | Quadratic fit | 894 | 312 | 209 | 0.06 | 0.02 | 0.01 | 2140 | 2286 | 2200 |
| | Exponential fit | 1123 | 389 | 286 | 0.11 | 0.05 | 0.03 | 2798 | 2561 | 5044 |
| | Logarithmic fit | 2175 | 634 | 605 | 0.19 | 0.08 | 0.04 | 9144 | 7028 | 10961 |
| | Power Regression | 1132 | 265 | 428 | 0.32 | 0.12 | 0.07 | 3557 | 3533 | 4228 |
| | LNP fit | 3396 | 414 | 970 | 1.92 | 0.66 | 0.43 | 22550 | 12363 | 25987 |
| Football | Linear fit | 5893 | 1564 | 1368 | 0.21 | 0.07 | 0.05 | 14309 | 12830 | 15554 |
| | Quadratic fit | 1038 | 289 | 241 | 0.07 | 0.03 | 0.02 | 2248 | 2243 | 2346 |
| | Exponential fit | 1779 | 558 | 369 | 0.12 | 0.04 | 0.03 | 12625 | 8303 | 11469 |
| | Logarithmic fit | 4261 | 1179 | 991 | 0.15 | 0.06 | 0.04 | 17668 | 15125 | 18796 |
| | Power Regression | 4411 | 1254 | 962 | 0.28 | 0.10 | 0.06 | 7311 | 4577 | 6842 |
| | LNP fit | 9912 | 2162 | 2207 | 1.95 | 0.67 | 0.43 | 45468 | 33470 | 47853 |

Table 9. Absolute error for Rate-QP, PSNR-QP and Rate-PSNR curve fitting (IBBP GOP1).

this case, linear fit results are very interesting as although they are not among the best approaches, the error is rather small, particularly for low complex video sequences. These results indicate that aggregate video results might be represented by the following equations:

$$R = \beta_0 + \beta_1 QP + \beta_2 QP^2 \tag{22}$$

$$PSNR = \beta_0' + \beta_1' \times QP + \beta_2' \times QP^2 \tag{23}$$

$$R = \beta_0'' + \beta_1'' \times PSNR + \beta_2'' \times PSNR^2 \tag{24}$$

| Sequence | Fit Method | Rate-QP | | | PSNR-QP | | | Rate - PSNR | | |
|---|---|---|---|---|---|---|---|---|---|---|
| | | I Type | P Type | B Type | I Type | P Type | B Type | I Type | P Type | B Type |
| Akiyo | Linear fit | 467 | 120 | 296 | 0.04 | 0.03 | 0.02 | 2452 | 1056 | 4331 |
| | Quadratic fit | 109 | 49 | 58 | 0.03 | 0.02 | 0.01 | 644 | 447 | 939 |
| | Exponential fit | 118 | 59 | 48 | 0.12 | 0.07 | 0.04 | 606 | 547 | 740 |
| | Logarithmic fit | 328 | 104 | 206 | 0.19 | 0.12 | 0.07 | 2835 | 1124 | 5009 |
| | Power Regression | 247 | 38 | 142 | 0.27 | 0.16 | 0.10 | 897 | 664 | 1358 |
| | LNP fit | 915 | 67 | 568 | 1.29 | 0.75 | 0.46 | 8218 | 1961 | 14468 |
| Foreman | Linear fit | 1559 | 768 | 861 | 0.08 | 0.04 | 0.03 | 7387 | 6307 | 10540 |
| | Quadratic fit | 565 | 331 | 206 | 0.04 | 0.02 | 0.01 | 2144 | 2255 | 2173 |
| | Exponential fit | 677 | 430 | 342 | 0.09 | 0.05 | 0.03 | 2361 | 2753 | 6879 |
| | Logarithmic fit | 1297 | 671 | 652 | 0.15 | 0.09 | 0.05 | 8159 | 6801 | 12310 |
| | Power Regression | 544 | 296 | 575 | 0.23 | 0.14 | 0.08 | 3318 | 3672 | 5214 |
| | LNP fit | 1517 | 431 | 1315 | 1.24 | 0.72 | 0.44 | 17604 | 11880 | 31947 |
| Football | Linear fit | 3228 | 1714 | 1428 | 0.12 | 0.07 | 0.05 | 13308 | 12846 | 15837 |
| | Quadratic fit | 547 | 328 | 237 | 0.04 | 0.03 | 0.02 | 2263 | 2280 | 2469 |
| | Exponential fit | 1047 | 609 | 398 | 0.08 | 0.05 | 0.03 | 10027 | 8032 | 12944 |
| | Logarithmic fit | 2368 | 1295 | 1024 | 0.11 | 0.06 | 0.04 | 16052 | 15114 | 19319 |
| | Power Regression | 2510 | 1357 | 1031 | 0.20 | 0.11 | 0.06 | 5714 | 4359 | 7924 |
| | LNP fit | 5049 | 2352 | 2398 | 1.27 | 0.73 | 0.44 | 38424 | 33451 | 51582 |

Table 10. Absolute error for Rate-QP, PSNR-QP and Rate-PSNR curve fitting (IBBP GOP2)

## 7. Rate variability as a function of the video quality.

A second important issue for joint video coding broadcasting is the Rate Variability-Distortion (VD). Two sub-sets have been consider from the initial set of twelve video sequences: a first sub-set with camera movement, medium to high spatial detail and temporal complexity (sequences Foreman, Football, Coastguard, Flower Garden, and Mobile and Calendar), and a second sub-set with fixed camera and low to medium spatial detail and motion activity (Akiyo, Deadline, Hall, Mother and Daughter, News, Paris, and Silence).
Results are presented in Figure 7, Figure 8, Figure 9, and Figure 10. In the left side it can be observe the results from the first sub-set and in the right the charts for the second sub-set. Simulations results are from open-loop coding setup.

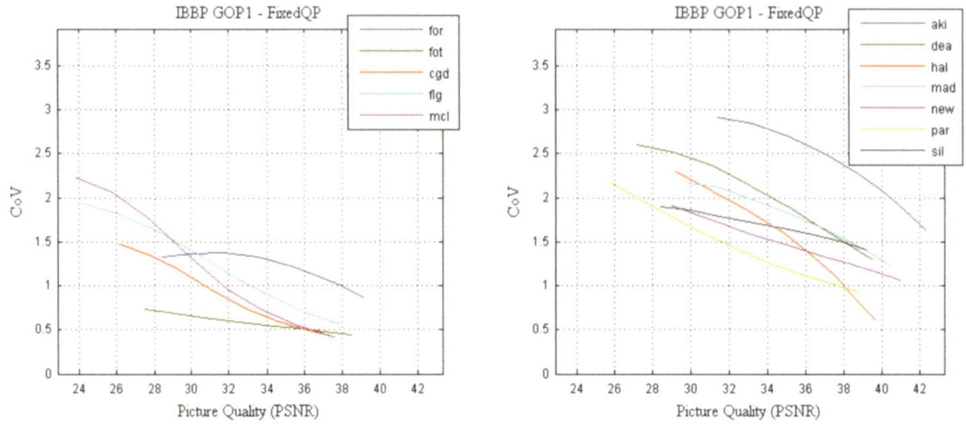


Fig. 7. Rate Variability-distortion (VD) Curve (PSNR; IBBP GOP1).

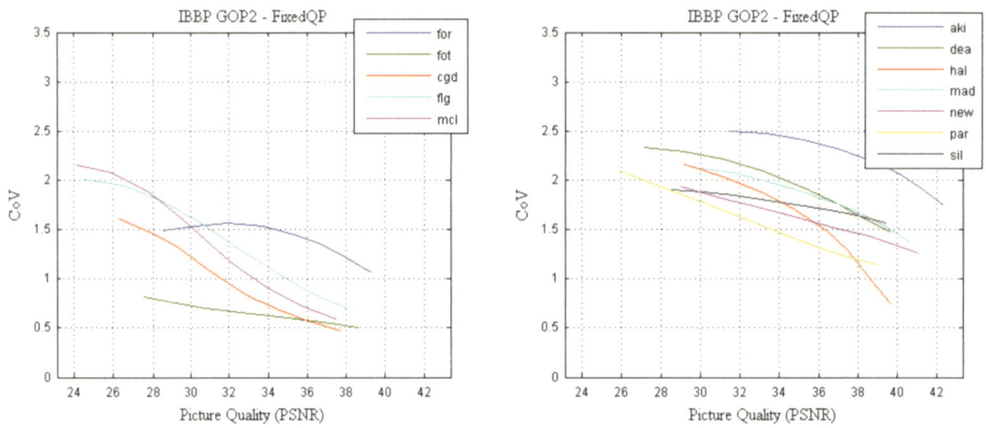


Fig. 8. Rate Variability-distortion (VD) Curve (PSNR; IBBP GOP2).

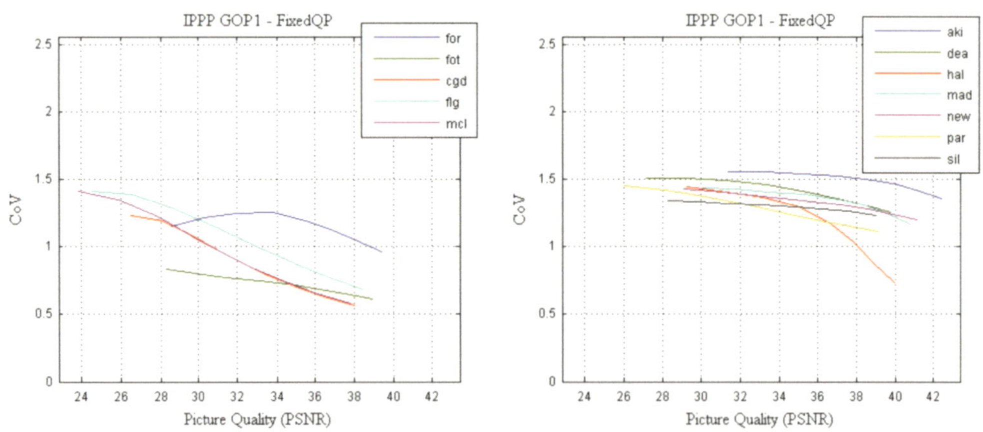


Fig. 9. Rate Variability-distortion (VD) Curve (PSNR; IPPP GOP1).

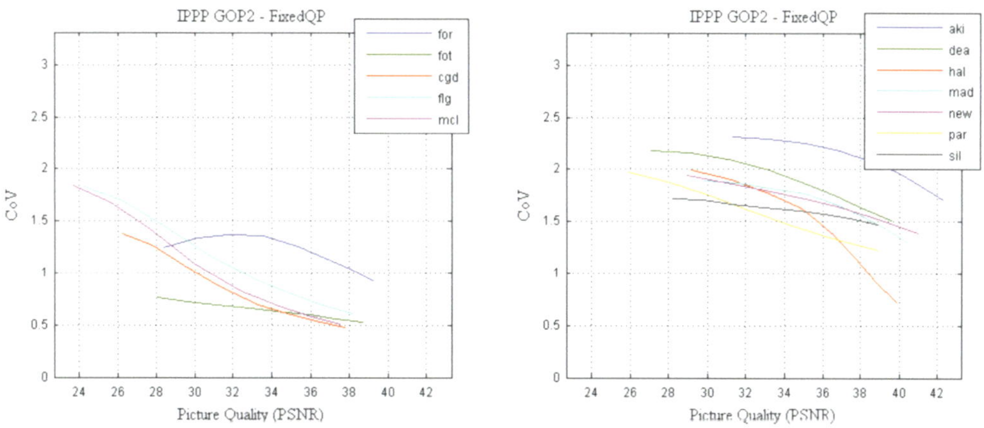


Fig. 10. Rate Variability-distortion (VD) Curve (PSNR; IPPP GOP2).

For high spatial complexity and motion activity sequences, variability is significantly lower than the sub-set of sequences with lower spatial and temporal complexity. At the same time, GOP patterns with B frames present higher values of variability regarding GOP patterns without B frames. As frames of type I show lower compression ratio compared to Predicted and Interpolated frames type, the combination of the different types of frames results in the observed higher bit-rate variability.

As the GOP size increases, the amplitude variation regarding the variability increases. This effect is stronger with the video sub-set of lower spatial and temporal complexity sequences. In these cases, motion estimation is very effective resulting in higher compression ratios for P and B pictures comparing to the bits budget of a typical Intra image. B frames, in general, present a small reduction of the variability in sequences with higher complexity. The amplitude of this variation increases while the sequence complexity decreases.

## 8. Acknowledgment

This work has been supported by "Fundação para a Ciência e Tecnologia" and "Programa Operacional Ciência e Inovação 2010" (POCI 2010), co-funded by the Portuguese Government and European Union by FEDER Program.

## 9. References

Adjeroh, D.A. & Lee, M.C. (2004). Scene-adaptive transform domain video partitioning, *IEEE Transaction on Multimedia*, Vol. 6. No 1 (February 2004), pp 58-69, ISSN 1520-9210.

Bellman, R.E. (2003). *Dynamic Programming*, Princeton University Press, Dover paperback edition (2003), ISBN 0486428095.

Berger, T. (1971). Rate Distortion Theory, Prentice-Hall, Inc., ISBN 0137531036, Englewood Cliffs, NJ.

Chan, Y.-L & Siu, W.-C. (2001). An efficient search strategy for block motion estimation using image features, IEEE Transactions on Image Processing, Vol 10, No 8 (August 2001), pp 1223-1238, ISSN 1057-7149.

Chen, J.J. & Lin, D.W. (1996). Optimal bit allocation for video coding under multiple constraints, *Proceedings of the IEEE International Conference Image Processing 1996*, Vol. 3, pp 403 - 406, ISBN 0-7803-3259-8, Lausanne, Switzerland, Sep 16-19, 1996.

Chen, Z. & Ngan, K. N. (2004). Linear rate-distortion models for MPEG-4 shape coding, *IEEE Transactions on Circuits and Systems for Video Technology*, Vol. 14, No 6 (June 2004), pp 869–873, ISSN 1051-8215.

Chen, Z. & Ngan, K. N. (2005b). Rate-distortion analysis for MPEG-4 binary shape coding, Proceedings of IEEE International Symposium on Intelligent Signal Processing and Communications Systems, pp 801 - 804, ISBN 0-7803-9266-3, Hong Kong, December 13-16, 2005.

Chen, Z. & Ngan, K. N. (2005a). Joint texture-shape optimization for MPEG-4 multiple video objects, *IEEE Transactions on Circuits and Systems for Video Technology*, Vol. 15, No 2 (September 2005). pp 1170–1174, ISSN 1051-8215.

Chen, Z. & Ngan, K. N. (2007). Recent advances in rate control for video coding, Signal Processing: Image Communication, Vol 22, No 1 (January 2007), pp 19-38, ISSN 0923-5965.

Chiang, T. & Zhang, Y.-Q. (1997). A new rate control scheme using quadratic rate distortion model, *IEEE Transactions on Circuits and Systems for Video Technology*, Vol. 7, No 1 (January 1997), pp 246-250, ISSN 1051-8215.

Chung, K.-L. & Chang, L-.C (2003). A new predictive search area approach for fast block motion estimation, *IEEE Transactions on Image Processing*, Vol. 12, No 6 (June 2003), pp 648-652, ISSN 1057-7149.

Ding, W. & Liu, B. (1996). Rate control of MPEG video coding and recording by rate-quantization modeling, *IEEE Transactions on Circuits and Systems for Video Technology*, Vol. 6, No 1 (January 1996), pp 12-20, ISSN 1051-8215.

Everett, H. (1963). Generalized Lagrange multiplier method for solving problems of optimum allocation of resource, in Operations Research, Vol 11, N0. 3, pp 399–417, ISSN 0030-364X.

Forney, G. D. (1973). The Viterbi algorithm, Proceedings of the IEEE , Vol 61, No 3, pp 268–278, ISSN 0018-9219.

Kim, H.M. (2003). Adaptive rate control using nonlinear regression, *IEEE Transactions on Circuits and Systems for Video Technology*, Vol. 13, No 5 (May 2003), pp 432-439, ISSN 1051-8215.

Hang, H. M. & Chen, J.J. (1997). Source model for transform video coder and its application - part I: fundamental theory, *IEEE Transactions on Circuits and Systems for Video Technology*, Vol. 7, No 2 (April 1997), pp 287-298, ISSN 1051-8215.

He, Z. & Mitra, S. K. (2002). Optimum bit allocation and accurate rate control for video coding via-domain source modelling, *IEEE Transactions on Circuits and Systems for Video Technology*, Vol. 12, No 10 (Octobre 2002), pp 840–849, ISSN 1051-8215.

He, Z. (2001). rho-Domain Rate-Distortion Analysis and Rate Control for Visual Coding and Communication, PhD Dissertation, University of California, Santa Barbara, June 2001.

Huang, J. J. Y. & Schultheiss, P.M. (1963). Block quantization of correlated Gaussian random variables, IEEE Transaction on Communications Systems, Vol 11, N 3, pp 289–296, ISSN 0096-1965.

ISO/IEC (1997). Text of ISO/IEC 14496-2 MPEG-4 Video VM-Version 8.0, ISO/IEC JTC1/SC29/WG11 Coding of Moving Pictures and Associated Audio MPEG 97/W1796, Stochholm, Sweden, July 1997.

ISO/IEC, JTC1/SC29/WG11 (1993). MPEG Video Test Model 5 (TM-5), document MPEG93/457, April 1993.

ITU-T (2005). Rec. H.264.2 : Reference software for advanced video coding, 2005.

ITU-T, SG16 (1997). Video Codec Test Model, near-term, Version 8 (TMN8), Document Q15-A-59, Portland, USA, June 1997.

Kamaci, N.; Altunbasak, Y. & Mersereau, R. M. (2005). Frame bit allocation for the H.264/AVC video coder via Cauchy-density-based rate and distortion models, *IEEE Transactions on Circuits and Systems for Video Technology*, Vol. 15, No 5 (August 2005), pp 994–1006, ISSN 1051-8215.

Keesman, G.; Shah, I. & Klein-Gunnewiek, R. (1995). Bit-rate control for MPEG encoders, Signal Processing: Image Communication, Vol 6, No 6 (February 1995), pp 545-560, ISSN 0923-5965.

Lee, H. J.; Chiang, T. & Zhang, Y. Q. (2000). Scalable rate control for MPEG-4 video, *IEEE Transactions on Circuits and Systems for Video Technology*, Vol. 10, No 6 (September 2000), pp 878-894, ISSN 1051-8215.

Li, Z. G.; Pan, F.; Lim, K. P.; Feng, G. ; Lin, X. & Rahardja, S. (2003a). Adaptive basic unit layer rate control for JVT, Joint Video Team of ISO/IEC MPEG and ITU-T VCEG, document JVT-G012r1, March 2003.

Li, Z. G.; Gao, W.; Pan, F.; Ma, S. ; Lin, K. P. ; Feng, G.; Lin, X.; Rahardja, S.; Lu, H. & Lu, Y. (2003b). Adaptive Rate Control with HRD Consideration, document JVT-H014, 8th meeting, Geneva, May 2003.

Li, Z. G.; Pan, F.; Lim, K.P.; Feng, G.N. ; Lin, X. ; Rahardja, S. & Wu, D.J. (2003c). Adaptive frame layer rate control for H.264, Proceedings. 2003 International Conference on Multimedia and Expo, 2003, Vol 1, pp 581-584, ISBN 0-7803-7965-9, July 6-9, 2003.

Li, Z. G.; Pan, F.; Lim, K.P.; Lin, X. & Rahardja, S. (2004). Adaptive rate control for H.264, 2004 International Conference on Image Processing, pp 745-748, ISBN 0-7803-8554-3, October 24-27, 2004.

Lim, K. P ; Sullivan, G. & Wiegand, T. (2007). Text Description of Joint Model Reference Encoding Methods and Decoding Concealment Methods, Joint Video Team of ISO/IEC MPEG and ITU-T VCEG, document JVT-W057, San Jose, April 2007.

Lin, L. J. & Ortega, A. (1998). Bit-rate control using piecewise approximated rate-distortion characteristics, *IEEE Transactions on Circuits and Systems for Video Technology*, Vol. 8, No 4 (August 1998), pp 446-459, ISSN 1051-8215.

Lin, L. J.; Ortega, A. & Kuo, C.-C.J.(1996). Rate control using spline-interpolated R-D characteristics, SPIE Visual Communication Image Processing, Cambridge Visual Communication Image Processing, Cambridge, Orlando, FL, 1996, pp. 111-122.

Ma, S.; Gao, W & Lu, Y. (2002). Rate Control on JVT Standard, Joint Video Team (JVT) of ISO/IEC MPEG & ITU-T VCEG (ISO/IEC JTC1/SC29/WG11 and ITU-T SG16 Q.6), document JVT-D030, 4th Meeting: Klagenfurt, Austria, July 22-26, 2002.

Ma, S.; Gao, W. & Lu, Y. (2005). Rate-distortion analysis for H.264/AVC video coding and its application to rate control, *IEEE Transactions on Circuits and Systems for Video Technology*, Vol. 15, No 12 (December 2005), pp 1533-1544, ISSN 1051-8215.

Ortega, A. (1996). Optimal bit allocation under multiple rate constraints, Proceedings of the Data Compression Conference, pp 349–358, ISBN 0-8186-7358-3, Snowbird, UT, USA, 31 Mar - 01 April, 1996.

Puri, A.; Hang, H.-M. & Schilling, D. L. (1987). Interframe coding with variable block-size motion compensation, *Proceedings of IEEE Global Telecomm. Conf. (GLOBECOM)*, pp 65-69, 1987.

Ramchandran, K.; Ortega, A. & Vetterli, M. (1993). Bit allocation for dependent quantization with applications to MPEG video codec, 1993 IEEE International Conference on Acoustics, Speech, and Signal Processing, pp. 381-385, ISBN 0-7803-7402-9, Minneapolis, April 27-30, 1993.

Ramchandran, K.; Ortega, A. & Vetterli, M. (1994). Bit allocation for dependent quantization with applications to multiresolution and MPEG video coders, IEEE Transactions on Image Processing, Vol.3, No.5, pp.533-545, ISSN 1057-7149.

Rhee, I.; Martin, G. R. ; Muthukrishnan, S. & Packwood, R. A. (2001). Quadtree-structured variable-size block-matching motion estimation with minimal error, *IEEE Transactions on Circuits and Systems for Video Technology*, Vol. 10, No 2 (February 2001), pp 42-50, ISSN 1051-8215.

Ribas-Corbera, J. & Lei, S. (1999). Rate control in DCT video coding for low-delay communications, *IEEE Transactions on Circuits and Systems for Video Technology*, Vol. 9, No 1 (February 1999), pp 172-185, ISSN 1051-8215.

Ribas-Corbera, J. & Neuhoff, David L. (1998). Optimizing block size in motion compensated video coding, *Journal of Electronic Imaging*, Vol. 7, No 1 (January 1998), pp.155-165, ISSN 1017-9909.

Ronda, J. I.; Eckert, M.; Jaureguizar, F. & Garcia, N. (1999). Rate control and bit allocation for MPEG-4, *IEEE Transactions on Circuits and Systems for Video Technology*, Vol. 9, No 12 (December 1999), pp 1243–1258, ISSN 1051-8215.

Schuster, G. M. & Katsaggelos, A.K. (1997a). *Rate Distortion based Video Compression*, Kluwer Academic Publishers, ISBN 978-1-4419-5172-4, Norwell, MA.

Schuster, G. M. & Katsaggelos, A.K. (1997b). A video compression scheme with optimal bit allocation among segmentation motion and residual error, *IEEE Transactions on Image Processing*, Vol 6, No 11 (November 1997), pp 1487–1502, ISSN 1057-7149.

Seeling, P.; Fitzek, F. H. P. & Reisslein, M. (2007). Video Traces for Network Performance Evaluation - A Comprehensive Overview and Guide on Video Traces and Their Utilization in Networking Research, Springer Verlag, 272 pages, ISBN 978-1-4020-5565-2, 2007.

Seeling, P.; Reisslein, M. & Kulapala, B. (2004). Network Performance Evaluation with Frame Size and Quality Traces of Single-Layer and Two-Layer Video: A Tutorial,

*IEEE Communications Surveys & Tutorials*, Vol. 6, No. 3 (Third Quarter 2004), pp 58-78, ISSN 1553-877X.

Shoham, Y. & Gersho, A. (1988). Efficient bit allocation for an arbitrary set of quantizers, *IEEE Transaction in Acoustics, Speech and Signal Processing*, Vol. 36, pages 1445–1453, ISSN 1053-587X.

Sullivan, G. J. & Wiegand, T. (1998). Rate-distortion optimization for video compression, *IEEE Signal Processing Magazine*, Vol. 15, No. 6 (November 1998), pp 74–90, ISSN 1053-5888.

Sullivan, G.J. & Wiegand, T. (1997). A theory for the optimal bit allocation between displacement vector field and displaced frame difference, *IEEE Journal on Selected Areas in Communications*, Vol 15, No 9 (December 1997), pp 1739–1751, ISSN 0733-8716.

Tourapis, H.-Y.C. & Tourapis, A.M. (2003). Fast motion estimation within the H.264 codec, *Proceedings. 2003 International Conference on ICME '03*, Vol 3, pp 517-520, ISBN 0-7803-7965-9, July 6-9, 2003.

Vardeman, S. (1994). Statistics for Engineering Problem Solving, PWS Publishing Company, ISBN 0-534-92871-4, boston, USA.

Vetro, A. ; Sun, H. & Wang. Y. (1999). MPEG-4 rate control for multiple video objects, *IEEE Transactions on Circuits and Systems for Video Technology*, Vol. 9, No 2 (February 1999), pp 186–199, ISSN 1051-8215.

Wiegand, T. & Girod, B. (2001). Lagrange multiplier selection in hybrid video coder control, *Proceedings of 2001 International Conference on Image Processing*, pp 542–545, ISBN 0-7803-6725-1, 07 Oct 2001-10 Oct 2001.

Wiegand, T.; Schwarz, H.; Joch, A.; Kossentini, F. & Sullivan, G. J. (2003a). Rate-Constrained Coder Control and Comparison of Video Coding Standards, *IEEE Transactions on Circuits and Systems for Video Technology*, Vol. 13, No 7 (July 2003), pp 688-703, ISSN 1051-8215.

Wiegand, T.; Sullivan, G. J. & Luthran, A. (2003b). Draft ITU-T Recommendation H.264 and Final Draft International Standard 14496-10 Advanced Video Coding, Joint Video Team of ISO/IEC JTC1/SC29/WG11 and ITU-T SG16/Q.6, document JVT-G050rl; Geneva, Switzerland, May 2003

Wiegand, T.; Sullivan, G. J.; Bjontegaard, G. & Luthra, A. (2003c). Overview of the H.264/AVC video coding standard, *IEEE Transactions on Circuits and Systems for Video Technology*, Vol. 13, No 7 (July 2003), pp 560-576, ISSN 1051-8215.

Wu, Y.; Shouxun, L. & Zhang (2005). Optimum Bit Allocation and Rate Control for H.264/AVC, Joint Video Team (JVT) of ISO/IEC MPEG & ITU-T VCEG (ISO/IEC JTC1/SC29/WG11 and ITU-T SG16 Q.6), document JVT- O016, 15th Meeting, Busan, KR, April 16-22, 2005.

Yan, A. Y. K. & Liou, M. L. (1997). Adaptive predictive rate control algorithm for MPEG videos by rate quantization method, *Proceedings on Picture Coding Symposium*, pp 619-624, Berlin, Germany, September 1997.

Yin, P. & Boyce, J. (2004). A new rate control scheme for H.264 video coding, Proceedings of ICIP '04. 2004 International Conference on Image Processing, pp 449-452, ISBN 0-7803-8554-3, October 24-27, 2004.

Zhang, J. ; He, Y. ; Yang, S. & Zhong, Y. (2003). Performance and complexity joint optimization for H.264 video coding, *Proceedings on IEEE International Symposium Circuits and Systems 2003 (ISCAS'03)*, pp 888-891, ISBN 0-7803-7761-3, May 25-28 , 2003.

Zhang, Z.; Liu, G. ; Li, H. & Li, Y. (2005). A novel PDE-based rate distortion model for rate control, *IEEE Transactions on Circuits and Systems for Video Technology*, Vol. 15, No (2005), pp 1354–1364, ISSN 1051-8215.

# 6

# Rate Control for Low Delay Video Communication of H.264 Standard

Chou-Chen Wang and Chi-Wei Tung
*I-Shou University*
*Taiwan*

## 1. Introduction

The demand for multimedia services is increasing rapidly in the last years. Therefore, efficient video compression has become a very important research for the multimedia communication. H.264 is the state-of-the-art digital video coding recommendation, which is also known as H.264/MPEG-4 Advanced Video Coding (H.264/AVC) (ITU-T, 2003). The standard is a joint collaborative effort between the ISO/IEC Moving Picture Experts Group (MPEG) and the ITU-T Video Coding Experts Group (VCEG). The team responsible for the development and evolution of the standard is known as the Joint Video Team (JVT) and officially the standard is known as H.264 by the ITU-T and MPEG-4 Part 10 by ISO/IEC. The H.264 standard can achieve much higher coding efficiency than the previous standards such as MPEG-1/2/4 (LeGall, 1991; ISO/IEC, 1994 & ISO/IEC, 1999) and H.261/H.263 (CCITT, 1990 and ITU-T, 2003). In addition to coding efficiency, the rate control also plays a key role in a video encoder for multimedia services, especially for real-time communication such as video streaming, video conference and video surveillance. The number of bits required for encoding a video sequence varies with time to provide consistent visual quality because complexity of each frame generally differs from the other frames in the input sequence. Therefore, a rate control scheme which meets a constrained channel rate by controlling the number of generated bits is necessary in an encoder. Nowadays, real-time video streaming scenarios requiring very low end-to-end delay are getting more and more popular. However, it is very difficult to adjust the encoding parameters directly to obtain fixed bits for every encoded frame in the constant bit rate channel. Therefore, it is necessary that the buffer to regulate the bit stream before transmission. With a good rate control technique, it should adjust the output rate to prevent the buffer from overflow and underflow. If the buffer suffers from overflow and underflow, it will cause frames skipping and wastage of channel resource, respectively. Furthermore, the size of buffer is usually very small to achieve low end-to-end delay requirement for real-time communication. It causes the buffer overflowing and underflow easier. So, the low delay video communication requires more accurate bit allocation and encoder parameter adjustment to achieve a suitable rate control.

There are two parts that should be considered when designing a rate control scheme. One is about the bit allocation for each basic unit according to its complexity. The other is the adjustment of the encoder parameter, *i.e.*, quantization parameter (QP) to encode each basic unit to match target bits. Rate control scheme have been widely studied in video standards, such as TM5 for MPEG-2 (ISO/IEC, 1993), TMN8 for H.263 (ITU-T, 1997), and VM-8 for

MPEG-4 (ISO/IEC, 1997). Figure 1 shows the rate control scheme for MPEG-2, H.263 and MPEG-4 using rate-distortion (R-D) model. The amount of encoding bits of the current basic units (macroblock: MB) is predicted from the recent encoded basic units. The encoder shown in Fig. 1 can obtain the motion vectors (MV) using motion estimator (ME) and calculate the statistical data of the residual frame with actual mean absolute difference (MAD) after motion compensation (MC). And then, the rate controller can adjust the quantization parameter (QP) according to the rate-quantization (R-Q) model.

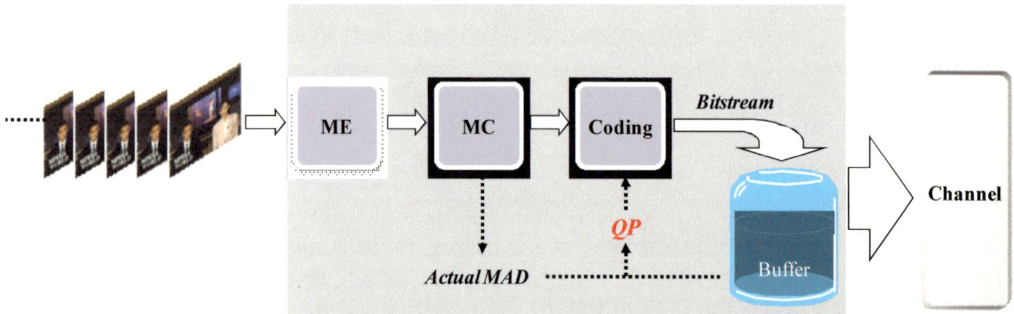


Fig. 1. Rate control scheme for MPEG-2, H.263 and MPEG-4

Compared with these previous standards, there is an additional problem for rate control in H.264 as shown in Fig. 2. The problem is due to that the H.264 encoder determines motion information by using the rate-distortion optimization (RDO) calculations. Before performing RDO for each MB, the quantization parameter should be defined by using MAD of MB. However, the statistical MAD of MB is only available after performing RDO. This is typical chicken and egg dilemma. Therefore, the rate control scheme is more difficult in H.264 (Li, et al., 2003).

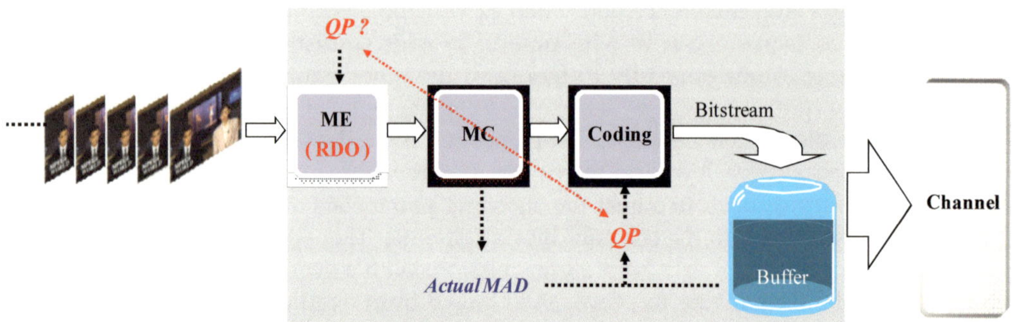


Fig. 2. The problem of QP dilemma for rate control scheme in H.264

In order to solve the QP dilemma problem caused by RDO, one rate control scheme was proposed in JVT-G012 (Li, et al., 2003) and was adopted by the JVT in the H.264 reference model JM 12.1 (JVT). JVT-G012 utilizes the method of temporal MAD prediction and R-Q quadratic model to achieve rate control. However, there are three problems existing in this scheme.

1. *Inaccurate initial quantization parameter*: For real time video applications, an improper initial QP maybe lead to the buffer overflowing and underflow seriously the front frames. It will affect continuity, quality and the demand of low delay directly.

2. *Inaccurate overhead bit prediction*: Due to a much more complex motion compensation strategy adopted by inter/intra coding mode in the H.264, the bits of overhead may highly fluctuate at the differential modes. Therefore, it is inaccuracy to predict overhead bit rate by using an average overhead bits in the JVT-G012.
3. *Inaccurate MAD prediction*: If the high motion or scene changes in the video sequences, the temporal correlation is reduced in the presence of such sudden changes. Therefore, only using the temporal MAD prediction model in the JVT-G012 is poorly in this status.

In this chapter, we will introduce a new rate control scheme for low delay H.264 video communication. A fast and best selection of initial QP is first proposed in the GOP layer rate control (Armstrong, et al. 2006 and Wang, 2008). Then, an improved MAD prediction model and overhead bits prediction method is adopted in the MB layer rate control. The simulation results show that the proposed scheme gives an average PSNRY gain of about 0.55 dB and 0.58 dB when compared with JVT-G012 and the method proposed in (Jiang & Lin, 2006), respectively. In addition, the proposed scheme improves the number of frame skipped and reduces the quality deviations of the initial frames by choosing the best initial QP.

## 2. Improved rate control in H.264

### 2.1 Efficient selection of initial QP

In JVT-G012, the I frame and the first P frame of the GOP are coded by initial QP. Therefore, the initial QP has a great effect in the front frames. The bad selection of initial QP may highly exceed buffer budgets so that the encoder attempting to salvage the over-spend bits in later frames. It leads to decrease rapidly the quality in later frames and even frame skipped. Therefore, according to channel bandwidth and complexity of encoded sequence to choose the best quantization parameter is a very important issue to be overcome. To increase the accuracy of selection, (Armstrong et al. 2006) proposed a selection of initial QP based on binary search scheme. As we know that the optimal QP setting can be obtained by full search for all QP indexes. To reduce the cost time of the full search, they use the binary search algorithm (BSA) to obtain the initial QP. For an example, assuming the bit-rate at QP=1 is 1,040 kbps and QP=51 is 20 kbps, the following example shown in Fig. 3 demonstrates the binary search for a desired target rate of 128 kbps on the first frame of a sequence. The QP=47 is determined as an initial QP to meet the channel bandwidth. The BSA can achieve the selection of QP with 6 processes, while a full search would require 51 processes. By using BSA, we can decrease the huge processing time rapidly.

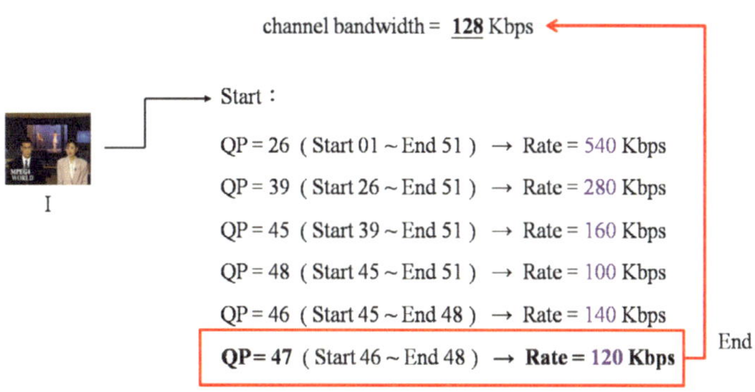


Fig. 3. Example of BSA for a desired target rate of 128 kbps.

However, the time of the search processes is still expended too much for each intra frame of a sequence (or on the first intra frame of each sequence in a group). To further speed up the best decision of initial QP, we propose a fast intra mode decision (FIMD) method to combine the BSA. In our previous research (Wang et al, 2006), we have proposed a fast intra mode selection algorithm for H.264 standard that take advantage of the correlation between MBs/blocks. Since H.264 is a block-based coding scheme, the frame is encoded block by block in a raster scan order, *i.e.*, from the left to right and top to bottom. For a luma MB in an I-slice, RDO exhaustively searches the combinations of the predefined 13 intra modes to produce the best mode for this MB. Figure 4 shows part of the RDO intra-mode map of an I-frame (News video sequence) conducted by the JM 12.1 (JVT) with RDO procedure. Each point (location) in the two intra-mode maps corresponds to a luma Intra_16×16 MB and a luma Intra_4×4 block, respectively. Since MBs/blocks are highly correlated, many MBs/blocks in I-frame correspond to the same modes. In other words, many points in the map have same mode, as shown in Fig. 4.

| | | | | | | | | | | |
|---|---|---|---|---|---|---|---|---|---|---|
| 2 | 1 | 1 | 2 | 1 | 1 | 1 | 1 | 1 | 1 | 1 |
| 0 | 3 | 0 | 2 | 2 | 1 | 3 | 1 | 2 | 1 | 1 |
| 0 | 0 | 0 | 2 | 3 | 2 | 1 | 1 | 0 | 2 | 1 |
| 0 | 0 | 0 | 2 | 1 | 2 | 2 | 2 | 3 | 0 | 3 |
| 0 | 1 | 0 | 3 | 2 | 1 | 2 | 0 | 0 | 0 | 0 |
| 0 | 2 | 0 | 3 | 3 | 1 | 1 | 1 | 0 | 2 | 3 |
| 0 | 0 | 2 | 1 | 2 | 3 | 3 | 1 | 1 | 3 | 3 |
| 0 | 2 | 2 | 1 | 1 | 1 | 3 | 3 | 2 | 3 | 3 |
| 2 | 2 | 3 | 2 | 0 | 2 | 0 | 0 | 3 | 1 | 0 |

(a)

| | | | | | | | | | | | | | | | | | | | | | | | |
|---|---|---|---|---|---|---|---|---|---|---|---|---|---|---|---|---|---|---|---|---|---|---|---|
| 2 | 1 | 1 | 1 | 1 | 1 | 1 | 1 | 2 | 1 | 2 | 1 | 8 | 1 | 1 | 1 | 1 | 1 | 1 | 1 | 1 | 1 | 1 | 1 |
| 0 | 0 | 4 | 5 | 6 | 6 | 1 | 0 | 0 | 8 | 0 | 7 | 4 | 4 | 4 | 0 | 0 | 1 | 1 | 1 | 1 | 1 | 1 | 0 |
| 0 | 4 | 4 | 4 | 4 | 4 | 6 | 0 | 0 | 0 | 0 | 0 | 4 | 4 | 4 | 5 | 0 | 1 | 1 | 1 | 5 | 0 | 1 | 2 |
| 0 | 0 | 2 | 4 | 6 | 6 | 8 | 0 | 0 | 7 | 0 | 0 | 6 | 5 | 4 | 4 | 0 | 0 | 0 | 0 | 1 | 1 | 1 | 1 |
| 2 | 2 | 2 | 2 | 2 | 2 | 2 | 0 | 0 | 0 | 0 | 0 | 0 | 5 | 7 | 4 | 0 | 0 | 1 | 1 | 1 | 1 | 1 | 1 |
| 2 | 2 | 2 | 2 | 2 | 2 | 0 | 0 | 0 | 0 | 0 | 0 | 0 | 0 | 5 | 3 | 0 | 6 | 1 | 1 | 1 | 1 | 1 | 1 |
| 2 | 2 | 2 | 2 | 2 | 2 | 1 | 0 | 0 | 0 | 0 | 3 | 1 | 0 | 0 | 0 | 0 | 0 | 0 | 0 | 0 | 1 | 1 | 1 |
| 2 | 2 | 2 | 2 | 2 | 2 | 1 | 0 | 0 | 0 | 0 | 0 | 0 | 3 | 0 | 0 | 0 | 5 | 1 | 4 | 0 | 0 | 0 | 0 |
| 0 | 2 | 2 | 2 | 2 | 2 | 2 | 2 | 0 | 0 | 0 | 0 | 4 | 0 | 1 | 0 | 0 | 0 | 7 | 4 | 0 | 1 | 1 | 1 |
| 0 | 0 | 1 | 1 | 2 | 2 | 2 | 2 | 0 | 0 | 0 | 0 | 6 | 6 | 6 | 0 | 0 | 0 | 0 | 5 | 5 | 1 | 1 | 1 |
| 0 | 1 | 1 | 1 | 2 | 2 | 2 | 2 | 0 | 0 | 0 | 0 | 1 | 1 | 6 | 1 | 0 | 0 | 0 | 1 | 3 | 4 | 1 | 0 |
| 0 | 0 | 0 | 0 | 2 | 2 | 2 | 2 | 0 | 0 | 0 | 0 | 1 | 1 | 1 | 0 | 0 | 3 | 4 | 0 | 5 | 1 | 1 | 1 |
| 2 | 2 | 2 | 2 | 2 | 2 | 2 | 2 | 0 | 0 | 0 | 7 | 1 | 1 | 0 | 0 | 0 | 0 | 6 | 2 | 1 | 1 | 6 | 3 |
| 2 | 2 | 2 | 2 | 2 | 2 | 2 | 2 | 0 | 0 | 0 | 0 | 6 | 1 | 1 | 0 | 0 | 0 | 0 | 0 | 0 | 0 | 8 | 4 |
| 2 | 2 | 2 | 2 | 2 | 2 | 2 | 2 | 0 | 0 | 0 | 2 | 1 | 1 | 1 | 8 | 0 | 0 | 3 | 8 | 0 | 7 | 0 | 0 |
| 2 | 2 | 2 | 2 | 2 | 2 | 2 | 2 | 0 | 0 | 0 | 0 | 0 | 0 | 8 | 0 | 0 | 3 | 0 | 4 | 0 | 0 | 0 | 0 |
| 0 | 0 | 0 | 0 | 1 | 1 | 1 | 0 | 0 | 0 | 0 | 0 | 0 | 8 | 8 | 8 | 0 | 5 | 1 | 4 | 0 | 1 | 1 | 0 |
| 0 | 1 | 0 | 1 | 2 | 1 | 1 | 0 | 0 | 0 | 0 | 8 | 8 | 8 | 8 | 8 | 0 | 0 | 8 | 7 | 8 | 1 | 1 | 8 |
| 0 | 0 | 0 | 0 | 1 | 1 | 8 | 8 | 0 | 0 | 0 | 3 | 3 | 3 | 7 | 0 | 0 | 0 | 0 | 0 | 1 | 1 | 1 | 1 |
| 2 | 1 | 8 | 8 | 3 | 8 | 8 | 8 | 0 | 5 | 0 | 0 | 0 | 0 | 0 | 0 | 0 | 3 | 8 | 7 | 1 | 1 | 1 | 1 |

(b)

Fig. 4. RDO intra-mode map for an I-frame (a) luma Intra_16×16 (b) luma Intra_4×4

According to the observation of intra prediction modes (including luma Intra_4×4 and luma Intra_16×16) of any MB and those of its four neighboring blocks from different real video sequences, we find that there are a high mode correlation exists in intra mode map of H.264. We exploit the interblock correlation in the intra mode domain to early terminate the RDO calculations. Four modes of neighboring coded macroblocks/blocks shown in Fig. 5 are

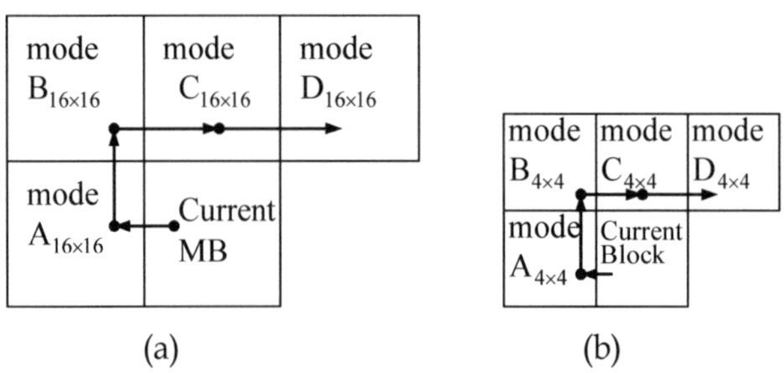


Fig. 5. Four causal neighboring modes of the current block (a) 16×16 MB (b) 4 ×4 block

considered as the good candidate intra modes of the current block in I frame, and we can use the threshold combination to achieve early detection. A detailed description of the method is available in (Wang et al, 2006). In order to evaluate the performance, we use the News in QCIF (176×144) format and 15 Hz frame rate as testing sequence. We compare the results using different methods in terms of PSNR and bitrate. Figure 6 demonstrates the performance of the proposed decision of initial QP is almost the same as BSA under 24 kbps for channel rate. In addition, from the Table 1, we can find that the decision time of initial QP using the proposed method is obviously less than the BSA. The simulation results show that the proposed method achieves an average 62% computational saving compared to BSA method.

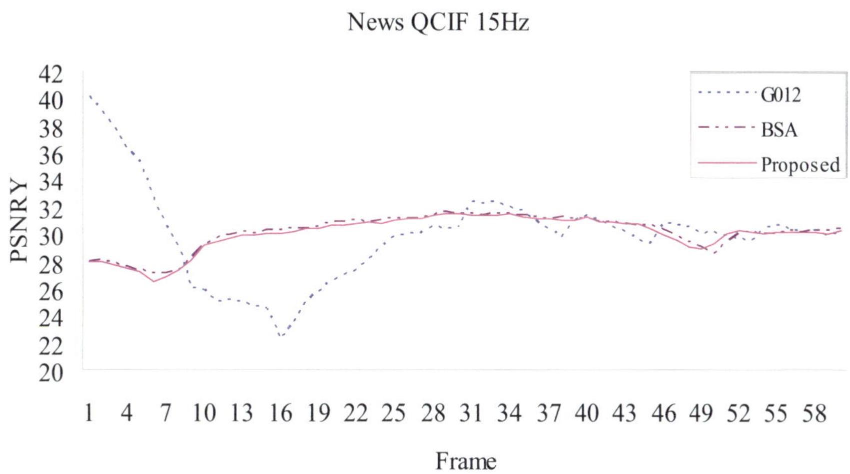


(a) PSNRY vs. Frame

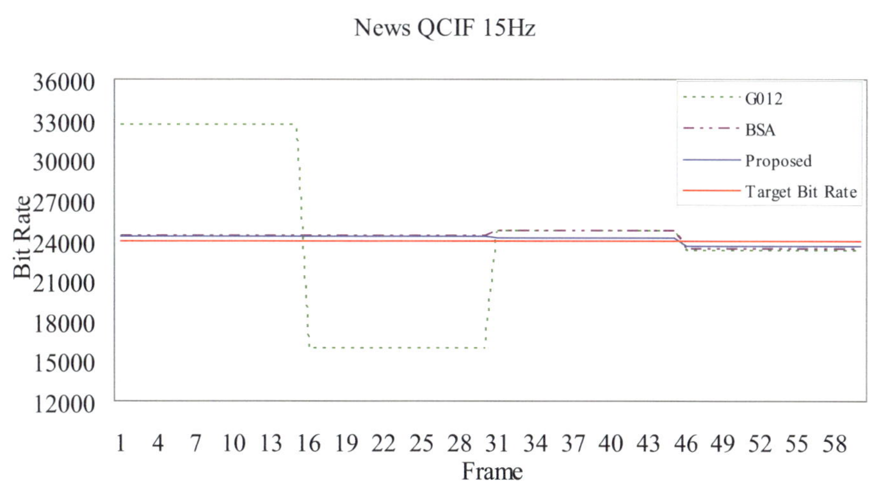


(b) Bitrate vs. Frame

Fig. 6. Comparisons of the PSNRY(dB) and bitrate for initial QP by different methods

| Method \ Sequence | News | Forman | Bus |
|---|---|---|---|
| Full Search | 44.3 | 42.2 | 49.7 |
| BSA | 3.3 | 3.3 | 3.4 |
| Proposed | 1.2 | 1.1 | 1.2 |

Table 1. Comparisons of processing times (seconds) for initial QP using various sequences

### 2.2 Improved overhead bit rate prediction

The overall bitstream generated by the source code is mainly comprised of texture bits and overhead bits. And texture bits are used to recode MB's residua after motion compensation. The overhead bits are used for differential coding and the overhead bits are used to record importance information such as the MB mode, the motion vector and the QP. The overhead bit prediction of rate control schemes in previous standards (including MPEG-1/2/4 and H.261/H.263) usually adopt the average overhead bits to predict, and update it with the average overhead bit rate after coding a MB or a frame. As we know that a more complex motion compensation adopted by the H.264 will lead to the overhead bits fluctuate at the differential mode.Unfortunately, the JVT-G012 rate control scheme follows that way and it produces large prediction error.

From (Yuan, et al., 2006), we can observe that the overhead bit rate is usually close among spatially and temporally adjacent MBs. Figure 7 shows the correlation of overhead bits count for two successive P frames by the Forman sequence in QCIF format, 15 Hz and initial QP=32. A further experiment is conducted to justify the temporal correlation and the typical experiment results are shown in Fig. 8. The experiment is simulated by searching for minimum difference of overhead bits count between the current MB and all of MBs in the previous P frame with a distance to the same position of the current MB not exceeding the searching radius.

| | | | | | | | | | | |
|---|---|---|---|---|---|---|---|---|---|---|
| 47 | 10 | 10 | 22 | 14 | 3 | 49 | 20 | 8 | 13 | 44 |
| 28 | 9 | 11 | 9 | 3 | 3 | 2 | 56 | 2 | 3 | 2 |
| 1 | 2 | 4 | 10 | **25** | 38 | 11 | 44 | 45 | 2 | 8 |
| 0 | 1 | 10 | 30 | 31 | 12 | 27 | 36 | 82 | 8 | 8 |
| 9 | 10 | 2 | 15 | 42 | 19 | 37 | 77 | 19 | 18 | 8 |
| 5 | 12 | 2 | 31 | 12 | 19 | 29 | 71 | 15 | 3 | 43 |
| 2 | 2 | 8 | 24 | 10 | 9 | 6 | 58 | 15 | 13 | 18 |
| 1 | **0** | 4 | 4 | 14 | 8 | 11 | 7 | 3 | **1** | 11 |
| 1 | 0 | 14 | 21 | 28 | 10 | 23 | 27 | 8 | 14 | 12 |

(*j-1*)th frame

| | | | | | | | | | | |
|---|---|---|---|---|---|---|---|---|---|---|
| 42 | 24 | 4 | 10 | 20 | 7 | 12 | 77 | 3 | 24 | 5 |
| 6 | 22 | 3 | 22 | 10 | 3 | 2 | 75 | 6 | 29 | 3 |
| 13 | 17 | 2 | 14 | **26** | 24 | 18 | 32 | 19 | 65 | 7 |
| 11 | 12 | 3 | 56 | 70 | 13 | 15 | 23 | 61 | 20 | 2 |
| 15 | 19 | 2 | 31 | 62 | 31 | 49 | 21 | 39 | 18 | 3 |
| 6 | 3 | 9 | 21 | 20 | 12 | 12 | 23 | 19 | 20 | 2 |
| 1 | 1 | 2 | 27 | 89 | 30 | 6 | 8 | 32 | 16 | 14 |
| 1 | **0** | 1 | 12 | 93 | 9 | 37 | 24 | 4 | **2** | 14 |
| 0 | 1 | 15 | 17 | 41 | 12 | 27 | 67 | 48 | 15 | 9 |

*j*th frame

Fig. 7. Temporal correlation of overhead bits count for two successive P frames

From the Fig. 8, we can observe that the relation between the MB percentage and the difference of overhead bits count in the different searching radius. When the searching radius is increasing, the probability of the similar overhead bits count and the searching complexity are also increasing at the same time. Furthermore, if the searching radius is other than 0, we will get confused with the choice among more than one MB. In order to simplify the problem, (Yuan, et al., 2006) predict the overhead bits count of not yet coded MB directly by that at the co-located position in the previous P frame. However the accuracy of prediction is limited by using their method. In addition, we can also find when the radius more than two, the cumulated probability distribution (CDF) of the overhead bit rate correlation is almost the same. So, we select the searching radius equal to 2 (R=2) to achieve a trade-off between the accuracy of prediction and the searching complexity. In order to overcome the confusion with the choice among more than one MB, we will make use of the rough motion compensation information of MB to determine the overhead bit rate prediction in the searching radius. The rough MAD will be explained in the subsection 2.3 explicitly.

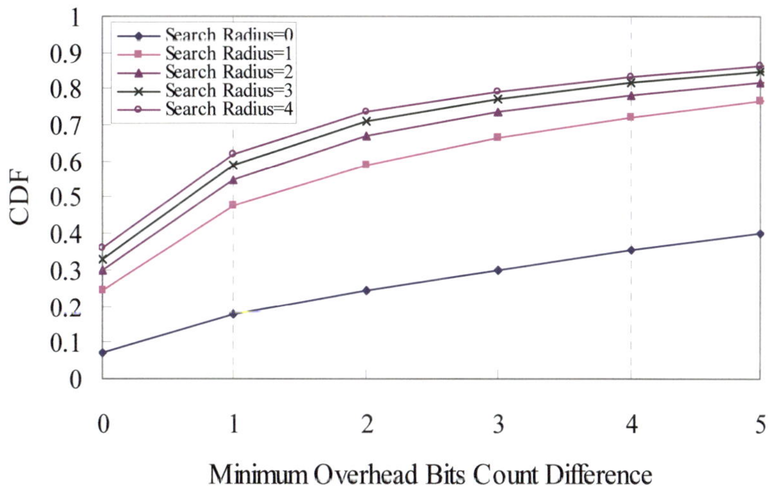


Fig. 8. The CDF of temporal correlation of overhead bits count

### 2.3 Improved MAD prediction

Because RDO in H.264 needs QP parameter before encoding, bit rate controller can't get MAD information of the current MB. To solve the QP dilemma caused by RDO in H.264, a simple linear model is proposed in the JVT-G012 to predict the MAD of not yet coded MB. The prediction model using the temporal information is then given by

$$MAD_{cur,temp}[i] = a_1 \times MAD_{pre}[i] + a_2 \quad (1)$$

where $MAD_{cur,temp}[i]$ denotes the temporal predicted MAD of the current $i$th MB, $MAD_{pre}[i]$ denotes the actual MAD of the co-located MB in the previous frame, $a_1$ and $a_2$ are two coefficients of prediction model. The initial value of $a_1$ and $a_2$ are set to 1 and 0, respectively. They would be updated after coding each MB.

The accuracy of prediction model using the previous temporal information is poorly when MAD changes abruptly due to high motion or scene changes. Thus, the prediction model is unable to predict the current changes, and is less sensitive to input data fluctuations. This situation will lead to error of prediction and error propagation by linear regression model. Therefore, it is desirable to collect more information that is helpful to predict MAD before RDO. In the procedure of H.264 encoding, the RDO module select the best mode by calculating the rate-distortion cost (RDcost) for 9 modes including INTRA16×16, INTRA 4×4, INTER16×16, INTER 16×8, INTER 8×16, INTER 8×8, INTER 8×4, INTER 4×8 and INTER 4×4. Let $MAD_{rough}$ be a rough measure for evaluating the difference between the current original frame and the previous reconstructed frame. To get the additional information, Liu *et al.* build the $MAD_{rough}$ after rough motion determination only with the INTRA16×16 and INTER 16×16 modes. (Liu, et al., 2007) has shown that the $MAD_{rough}$ is highly related to $MAD_{actual}$. A detailed description of the experimental results regarding the relationship between $MAD_{rough}$ and $MAD_{actual}$ is available in (Liu, et al., 2007). Therefore, the prediction model is helpful to improve the accuracy of prediction, especially for abrupt changes. The spatial linear prediction model is determined by

$$MAD_{cur,spat}[i] = b_1 \times MAD_{rough}[i] + b_2 \tag{2}$$

where $MAD_{cur,spat}[i]$ denotes the spatial MAD of the current MB, $MAD_{rough}[i]$ represents the rough MAD of the current MB, $b_1$ and $b_2$ are two coefficients of prediction model. They would be updated after coding each MB.

To combine the temporal prediction model with the spatial prediction model so that we can obtain more accurate MAD prediction. Therefore, we introduce two similarity measures as indicators to switch temporal and spatial prediction models

$$E_{temp}[i] = \sum_{n=i-S}^{i} \left| MAD_{cur,temp}[n] - MAD_{actual}[n] \right| \tag{3}$$

$$E_{spat}[i] = \sum_{n=i-S}^{i} \left| MAD_{cur,spat}[n] - MAD_{actual}[n] \right| \tag{4}$$

where $S$ is the number of MAD samples used to measure $E$. When the measure $E_{spat}$ is greater than $E_{temp}$, the MAD of current MB could be predicted by the temporal prediction model. On the other hand, it could be predicted by the spatial prediction model if $E_{temp}$ is greater than $E_{spat}$. Therefore, in addition to the temporal prediction model, we can also use the spatial prediction model to predict current MB. Due to the fluctuation of $MAD_{rough}$ roughly reflects the fluctuation of $MAD_{actual}$ (Liu, et al., 2007), we adopt the characteristics to determine the optimal position $(v_x, v_y)$ of MB in the searching radius $(R = 2)$ for the temporal and spatial prediction model. Therefore, the optimal position is obtained when the difference of MAD between $MAD_{rough}$ and $MAD_{actual}$ around the searching radius is the minimum value.

Figure 9 shows the proposed searching procedure to find the optimal position of predicted MB. We further use the MB in the position $(v_x, v_y)$ to substitute for the co-located MB adopted in JVT-G012 to predict MAD of the current MB. Therefore, the equations (1) and (2) are rewritten as the following:

$$MAD_{cur,temp}[i] = a_1 \times MAD_{pre,temp,\min}(v_x, v_y) + a_2 \tag{5}$$

$$MAD_{cur,spat}[i] = b_1 \times MAD_{pre,spat,\min}(v_x, v_y) + b_2 \tag{6}$$

where $MAD_{pre,\min}(v_x, v_y)$ denotes the actual MAD of the position $(v_x, v_y)$ in the temporal or spatial frame. In addition, the same technique as MAD prediction is also employed to the prediction of overhead bit rate. They are formulated as the following:

$$H_{i,temp} = MAD_{rough}[i] - MAD_{actual}[i-1]_{-2\le R\le 2,\min} \tag{7}$$

$$H_{i,spat} = MAD_{pred,spat}[i] - MAD_{actual}[i]_{-2\le R\le 2,\min} \tag{8}$$

where $H_{i,temp}$ denotes the temporal prediction and the spatial prediction of overhead bit rate of the $i$th MB in the previous P frame, and $H_{i,spat}$ denotes the spatial prediction of overhead bit rate of the MB in the current P frame.

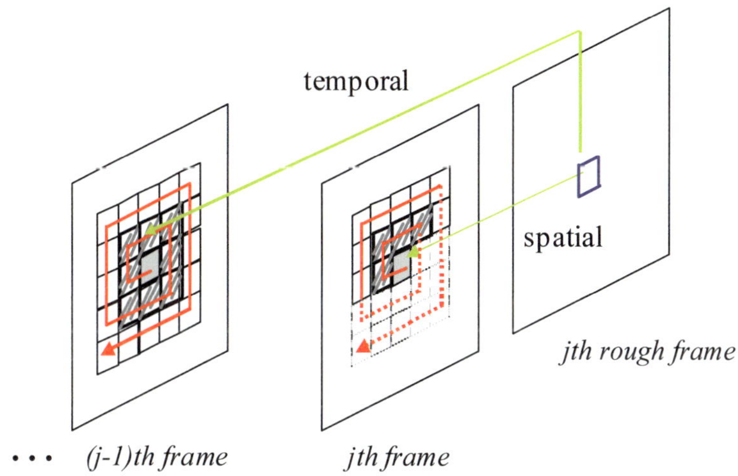


Fig. 9. The proposed searching procedure

## 3. Rate control for low delay video communication

The proposed rate control scheme is composed of three layers: group of picture (GOP) layer rate control, frame layer rate control and MB layer rate control. In the GOP layer, we have to select the best initial QP in each GOP and compute the total number of remaining bits for all non-coded frames. The frame layer rate control determines the target bits for each P frame. The MB layer rate control mainly determines the QP for each MB so that the sum of MB bits count is close to the target bits of frame. Figure 10 shows the flowchart of our proposed rate control scheme.

### 3.1 GOP layer rate control

In low delay applications, the typical format of a GOP used is IPPP…P. In this layer, we first compute the initial QP using our proposed method described in Section 2.1, and then compute the total number of remaining bits for all non-coded frames in the GOP as follows:

$$T_{r,GOP}[j] = \begin{cases} \dfrac{u}{F} \times N_{GOP} & j = 1 \\ T_{r,GOP}[j-1] - A[j-1] & 2 \le j \le N_{GOP} \end{cases} \tag{9}$$

where $T_{r,GOP}[j]$ denotes the remaining bits of the jth frame that not yet coded in the GOP, $u$ denotes the channel bandwidth, $F$ denotes the frame rate, $N_{GOP}$ denotes the total number of frames in the GOP, and the $A[j\text{-}1]$ denotes the actually generated bits in the $(j\text{-}1)$th frame.

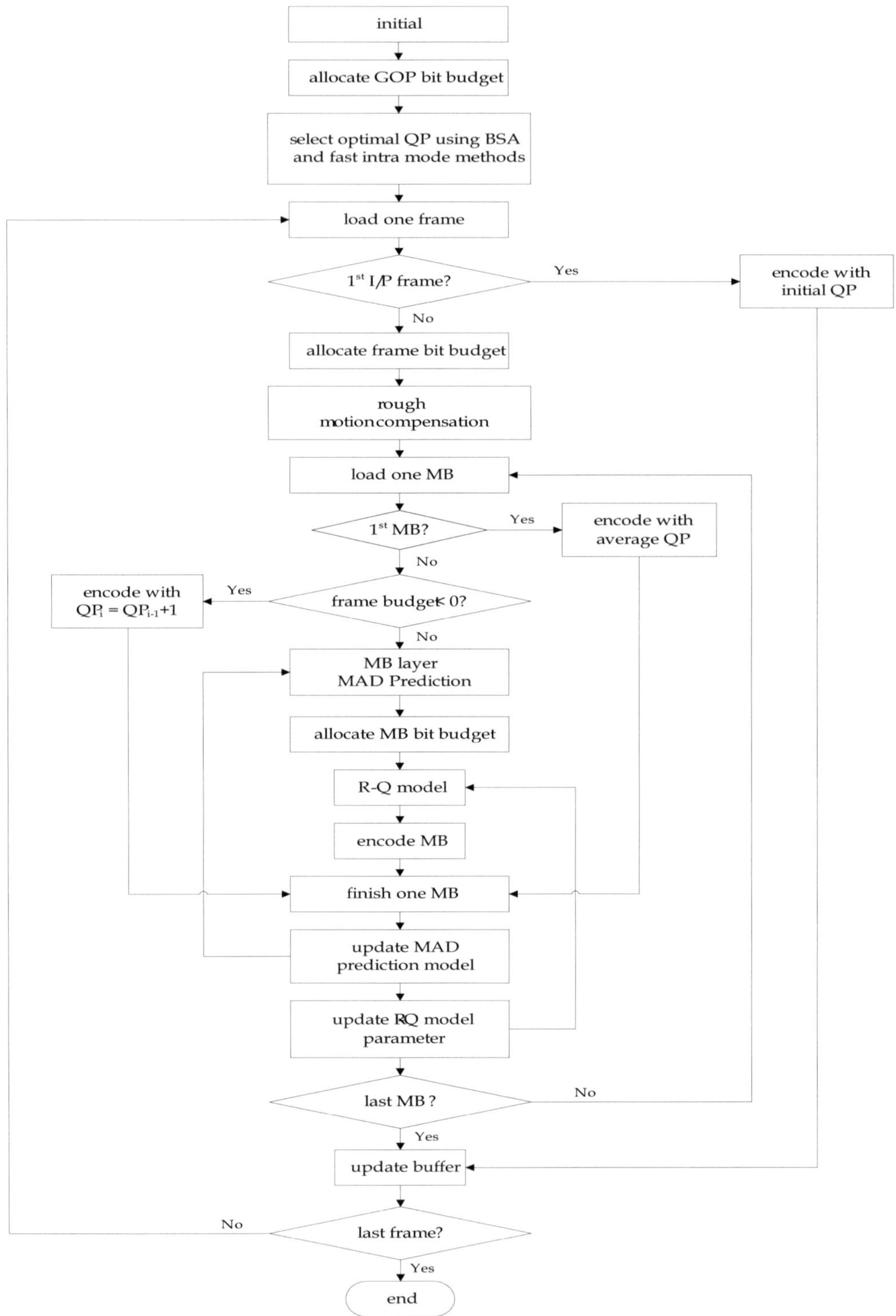


Fig. 10. The flowchart of proposed rate control scheme

### 3.2 Frame layer rate control

The layer mainly allocates the target bits for each frame. It can be calculated from

$$T_{frame}[j] = \beta \times f_1[j] + [1-\beta] \times f_2[j] \tag{10}$$

where $T_{frame}$ $[j]$ is the target sum bits to encode the $j$th frame, $\beta$ is a constant and is set 0.75 in JVT-G012. In addition, the two parameters of $f_1$ and $f_2$ are expressed as follows:

$$f_1[j] = \frac{T_{r,GOP}[j]}{N_{r,p}} \tag{11}$$

$$f_2[j] = \left(\frac{u}{F}\right) + \gamma \times (Tbl[j] - B_c[j]) \tag{12}$$

where $f_1$ represents the number of remaining bits for remaining frames. $f_2$ is estimated from the previous actual buffer occupancy $B_c$, target buffer level $Tbl$, frame rate and the channel bandwidth. The details of these parameters are referred in JVT-G012.

Finally, the target bits of frame $T_{frame}$ $[i]$ is used to avoide overflow and underflow with the hypothetical reference decoder (HRD) which has been defined in H.264. So, the target bit of frame is bounded as follows:

$$\begin{cases} T_{frame}[i] = \max\{ L_{bound} \text{ , } T_{frame}[i]\} \\ T_{frame}[i] = \min\{ U_{bound} \text{ , } T_{frame}[i]\} \end{cases} \tag{13}$$

where $L_{bound}$ and $U_{bound}$ denote the lower and upper boundary, respectively.

### 3.3 MB layer rate control

The MB layer rate control is the detail section to achieve more accurate output rate. If the basic unit is set as one frame, the MB layer rate control is skipped and using the frame layer predicted QP to encode all MBs within the frame. In other words, if the basic unit is set as one MB, the MB layer is to compute QP for each MB. For low delay applications with a small buffer size, the MB layer rate control is demanded generally to avoid buffer overflow and underflow accurately. The MB layer rate control can be described as follows.

**Step 1.** Check whether $i$th MB is the first MB in the current frame. If it is true, calculate the average value of QP for all MBs in the previous frame, then go to step 8. Otherwise go to step 2.

**Step 2.** Update the budget of the current frame as follows:

$$T_{budget}[i] = \begin{cases} T_{frame}[i] & i = 0 \\ T_{frame}[i-1] - R_{MB}[i-1] & otherwise \end{cases} \tag{14}$$

where $T_{budget}[i]$ denotes the number of remaining bits in the current frame after coding $(i\text{-}1)th$ MB, and $R_{MB}[i]$ denotes the actual bits after coding.

**Step 3.** Check whether $T_{budget}$ is not enough. If $T_{budget}$ is smaller than zero, go to step 7. Otherwise go to step 4.

**Step 4.** Predict the MAD of current MB using the two improved prediction model described in Section 2.3.

**Step 5.** Predict the overhead bits of current MB using our method described in Section 2.2 and Section 2.3, and compute the texture bits for the current MB as follows:

$$R_{text} = \frac{f_{rb}}{N_{rb}} - R_{header} \tag{15}$$

where $R_{text}$ denotes the texture bits, $R_{header}$ denotes overhead bits that is predicted by ours method. $f_{rb}$ and $N_{rb}$ denote the number of remaining bits for all non-coded MB in the current frame and the number of non-coded MB, respectively.

**Step 6.** Determine the quantization step of current MB using the quadratic Rate-Quantization
(R-Q) model. Then go to step 8.

$$R_{text} = X_1 \times \frac{MAD_{cur}}{Q_{step}} + X_2 \times \frac{MAD_{cur}}{Q_{step}^2} \tag{16}$$

where $X_1$ and $X_2$ are coefficients of R-Q model, $MAD_{cur}$ denotes $MAD_{pre,temp}$ or $MAD_{pre,spat}$ described in Section 2.3.

**Step 7.** Due to the budget of frame is overspent early, the QP value is increased by 1 to reduce the output rate, that is

$$QP_i = QP_{i-1} + 1 \tag{17}$$

where $QP_i$ denotes the QP of the $i$th MB.

**Step 8.** Actual encoding of the current MB. The QP is applied to perform RDO for the current MB.

**Step 9.** Update the R-D model and two MAD prediction models. After encoding each MB, the encoder should update the parameters of R-Q model and MAD prediction model using the linear regression method.

**Step 10.** Check whether $i$th MB is the last MB in current frame. If it is true, go to step 12. Otherwise go to step 11.

**Step 11.** Set $i = i+1$, then repeat step 1 to step 10.

**Step 12.** Finish the MB layer rate control.

## 4. Experimental results

### 4.1 Simulation setup

In this section, we discuss the experimental model used to simulate the proposed low delay H.264 video communication scheme, the performance metrics to evaluate performance of different methods, and the parameters and methods to encode the video for comparison. We evaluate eight video sequences including Foreman, Bus, Highway, Coastguard, News, Stefan, Mobile and Akiyo. Each sequence consists of 100 frames at QCIF format. For the real-time applications, all the sequences are intra-coded for the first frame (I-frame) and the remaining frames (P-frames) are inter-coded. In addition, the initial QP is set as 38 for JVT-G012 and the rate control presented by (Jiang & Lin, 2006), the channel bandwidth is set as 24 kbps, the symbol mode is CAVLC for low-delay, and RDO is enabled. To evaluate and compare the performance of the different methods, we have implemented our proposed rate control scheme with JVT reference software JM 12.1 (JVT) serving as a test benchmark. For a fair comparison, the JVT-G012 and (Jiang & Lin, 2006) are also implemented based on JM 12.1 (JVT), respectively.

### 4.2 Performance metrics

To analyze the performance of the decoded video sequences, we use the average peak signal-to-noise ratio for luma (PSNRY) of all frames over all realizations to evaluate the objective video quality, because it is the most widely used objective video quality metric. PSNRY is defined by

$$PSNRY = 10\log\frac{255^2}{MSE} \quad \text{dB} \tag{18}$$

where $MSE$ is the mean square error between the original pixel and the decoded pixel.
The video quality is evaluated in terms of PSNRY, buffer fullness and skipped frames. In this work, the size of buffer is set as $u/F\times 1.25$ for low delay applications. The buffer overflow threshold is set as 80% of the buffer size, which it is $u/F$. If the current buffer fullness exceeds 80% of the encoder buffer size, the encoder will skip encoding the next frame until the buffer fullness is lower than 80% of the encoder buffer size. When frame skipping occurs, the decoder displays the previous encode frame in place of the skipped one. Therefore, the previous frame is used in the PSNRY calculation.

### 4.3 Performance evaluation

To evaluate the performance of the proposed rate control scheme for low delay video communication, we compare the JVT-G012 and the coding scheme in (Jiang & Lin, 2006). All other parameters are selected the same among these schemes.
The comparisons of PSNRYs and buffer fullness by adopting the proposed scheme, JVT-G012 and (Jiang & Lin, 2006) are shown in Fig. 11 and Fig. 12, respectively. Figs. 11(a)-(h) shows frame by frame PSNRYs for various sequences, and Figs. 12(a)-(h) shows the number of bits in the buffer at each frame. From Fig. 11, we can find that our proposed scheme can improve the PSNRY significantly for most frames in these sequences. In addition, our proposed scheme can achieve much fewer skipped frames for sequences with high motion than the other two schemes. The improvements in PSNRY and skipped frames are very high for scene change video such as "Mobile". Despite the first frame has higher PSNRY quality for JVT-G012, the buffer fullness above the buffer threshold at the same time as shown in Fig. 12. Therefore, the number of frame skipped is increased for initial frames. The proposed scheme improves the number of frame skipped and reduces the quality deviations of the initial frames by choosing the best initial QP. Thus, it can supply user with a stable and constant viewing experience. In addition, the proposed scheme also improves the accuracy of prediction method to increase the reconstructed quality. From the experimental results, the best initial QP can improve the buffer fullness of initial frames efficiently. It is found from Figs. 12(a)-(h) that our proposed scheme achieves much steadier buffer fullness when compared to that of JVT-G012 and (Jiang & Lin, 2006). This implies that our proposed scheme produces stable buffer delay so that it is suit for real-time video communication. In Figs. 12(a)-(h), if the curve of buffer fullness falls below zero, it yields a buffer underflow problem. In such case, stuffing bits should be inserted into bit stream. Although underflow does not affect motion continuity, it wastes channel bandwidth.

On the other hand, since the bit allocation of each basic unit is not further considered in our rate control scheme, we still use the method of JVT-G012 to allocate the target bits for frame layer and MB layer. Therefore, the improvement of buffer control is limited when compared with JVT-G012. From the analysis of the experimental results, the proposed rate control scheme indeed can achieve better improvements than those of the JVT-G012 and the (Jiang & Lin, 2006) in low delay video communication.
The experimental results are further reported in Table 2. and Table 3. From the two tables we can find that the proposed scheme gives an average PSNRY gain of about 0.55 dB and 0.58 dB when compared with JVT-G012 and (Jiang & Lin, 2006), respectively. In addition, the proposed scheme improves the number of frame skipped and reduces the quality deviations of the initial frames. To compare with all test sequences, the proposed rate control scheme achieves more accurate rate control, especially for high motion sequences. For all sequences, the proposed method can reduce the number of skipped frames with the best reconstructed video quality.

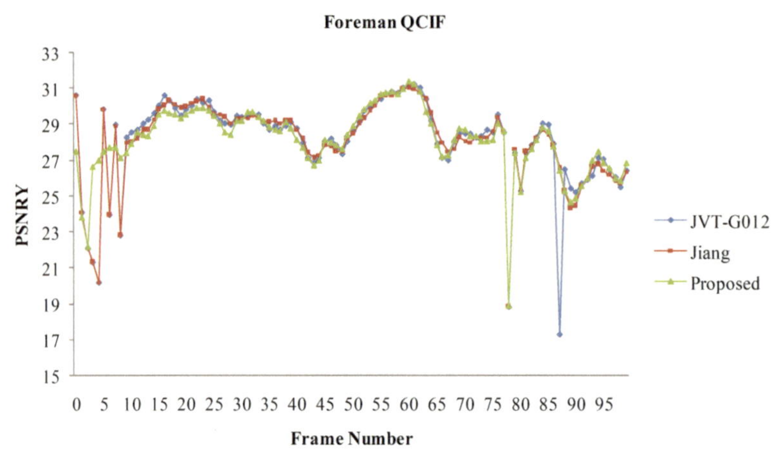


(a)

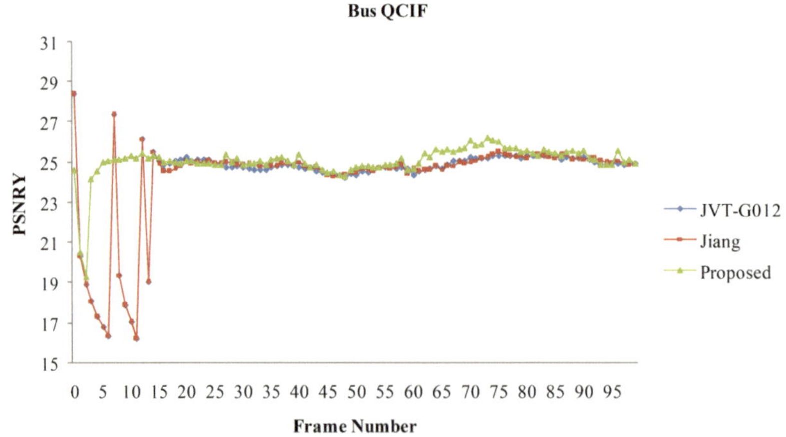


(b)

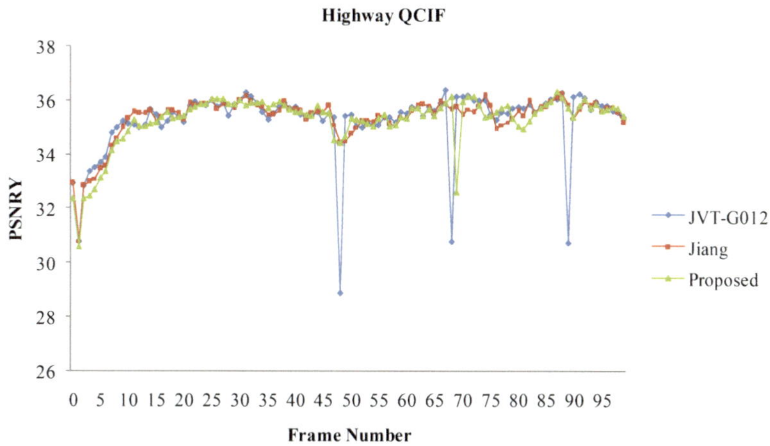
Highway QCIF
PSNRY
38
36
34
32
30
28
26
0 5 10 15 20 25 30 35 40 45 50 55 60 65 70 75 80 85 90 95
Frame Number
JVT-G012
Jiang
Proposed

(c)

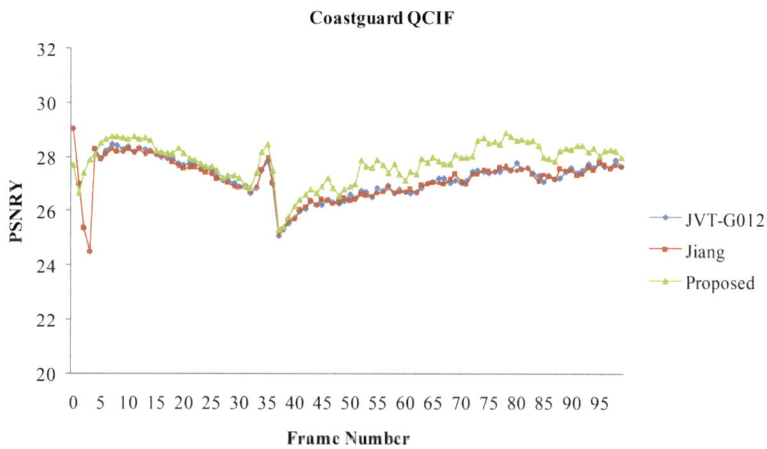
Coastguard QCIF
PSNRY
32
30
28
26
24
22
20
0 5 10 15 20 25 30 35 40 45 50 55 60 65 70 75 80 85 90 95
Frame Number
JVT-G012
Jiang
Proposed

(d)

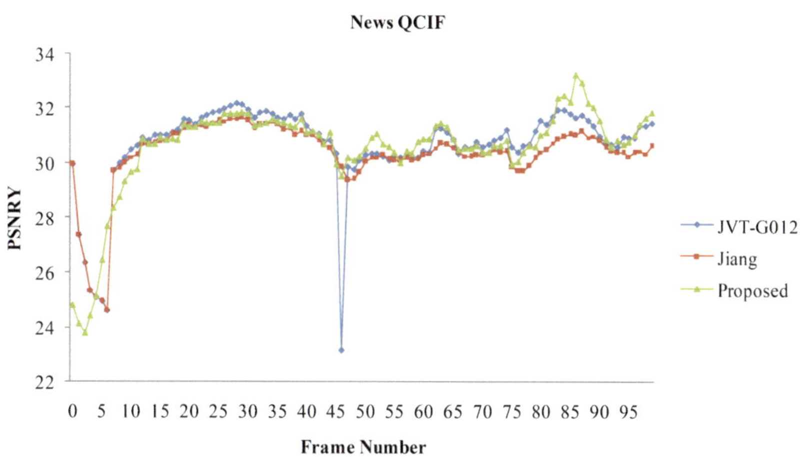
News QCIF
PSNRY
34
32
30
28
26
24
22
0 5 10 15 20 25 30 35 40 45 50 55 60 65 70 75 80 85 90 95
Frame Number
JVT-G012
Jiang
Proposed

(e)

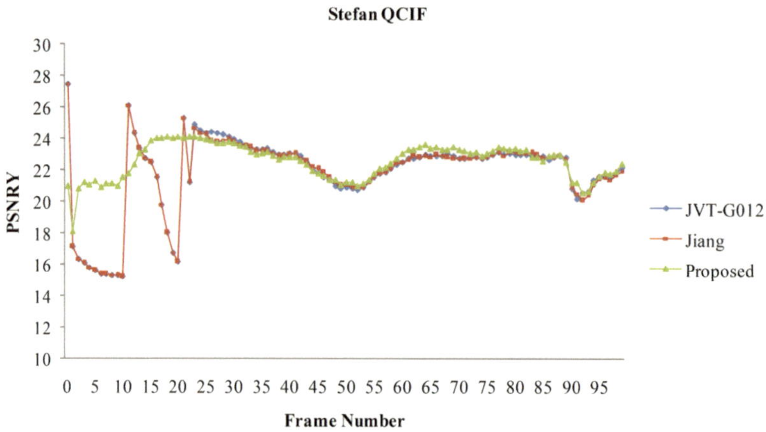


(f)

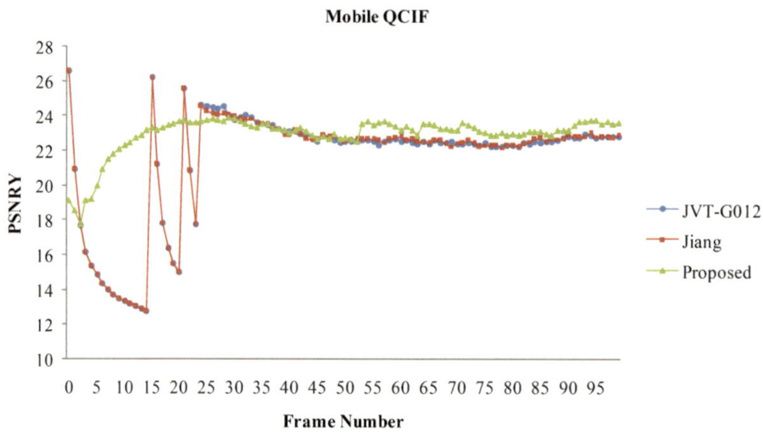


(g)

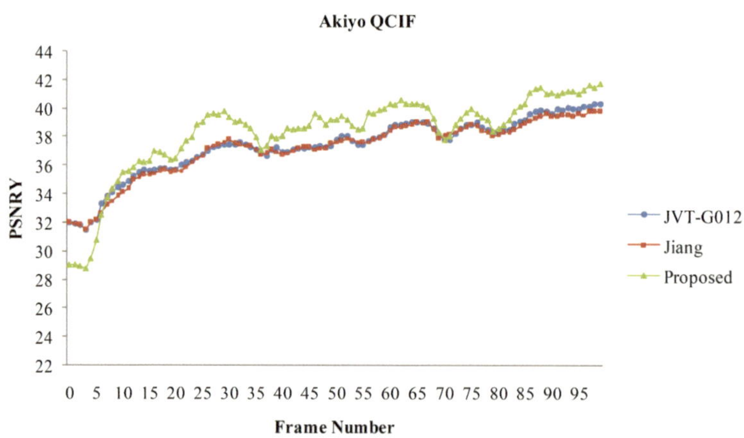


(h)

Fig. 11. Comparisons of PSNRYs for the proposed scheme, JVT-G012 and (Jiang & Lin, 2006)

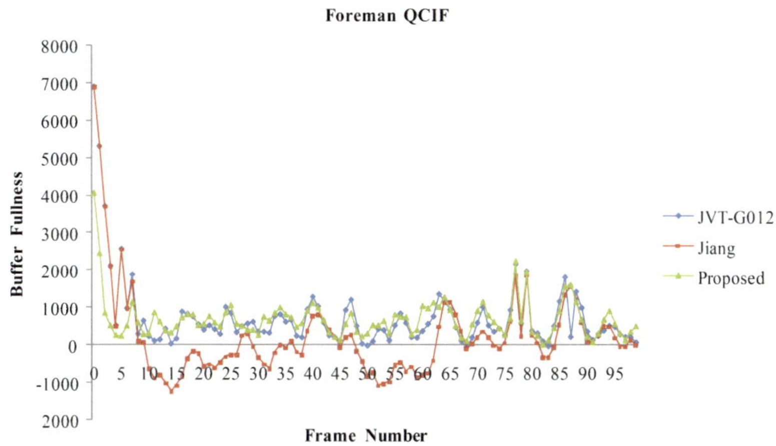
Foreman QCIF
8000
7000
6000
5000
4000
3000
2000
1000
0
-1000
2000
Buffer Fullness
0 5 10 15 20 25 30 35 40 45 50 55 60 65 70 75 80 85 90 95
Frame Number
JVT-G012
Jiang
Proposed

(a)

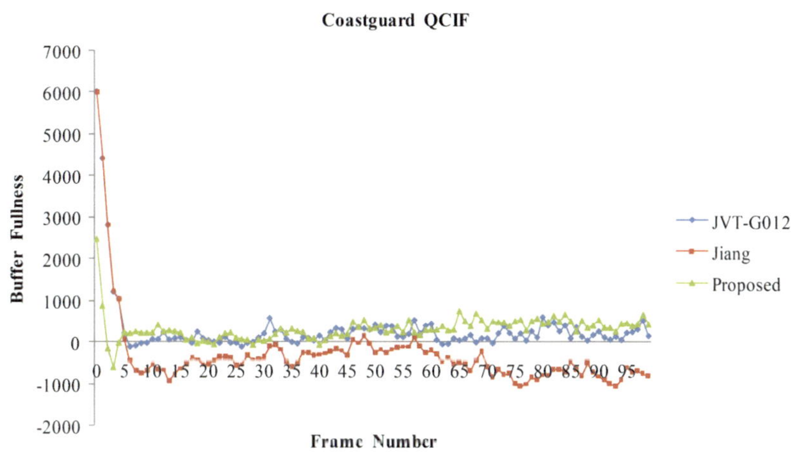
Coastguard QCIF
7000
6000
5000
4000
3000
2000
1000
0
-1000
-2000
Buffer Fullness
0 5 10 15 20 25 30 35 40 45 50 55 60 65 70 75 80 85 90 95
Frame Number
JVT-G012
Jiang
Proposed

(b)

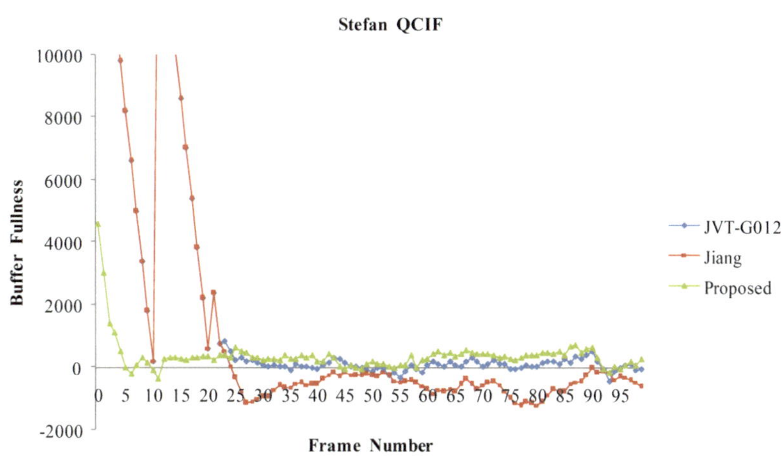
Stefan QCIF
10000
8000
6000
4000
2000
0
-2000
Buffer Fullness
0 5 10 15 20 25 30 35 40 45 50 55 60 65 70 75 80 85 90 95
Frame Number
JVT-G012
Jiang
Proposed

(c)

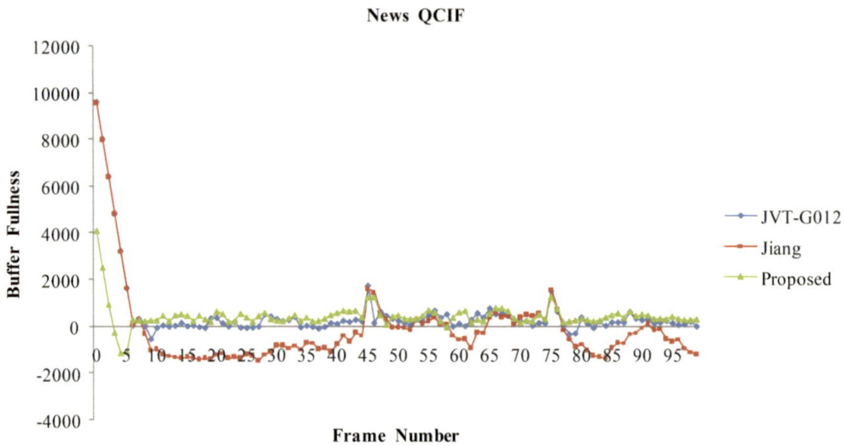
News QCIF
Buffer Fullness
Frame Number
JVT-G012
Jiang
Proposed

(d)

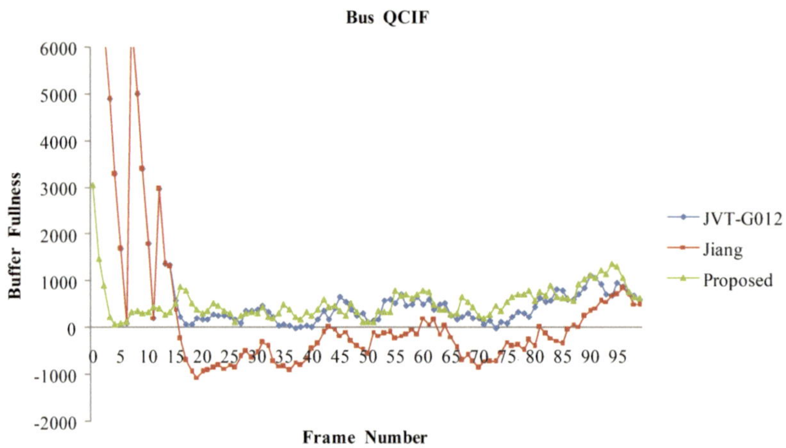
Bus QCIF
Buffer Fullness
Frame Number
JVT-G012
Jiang
Proposed

(e)

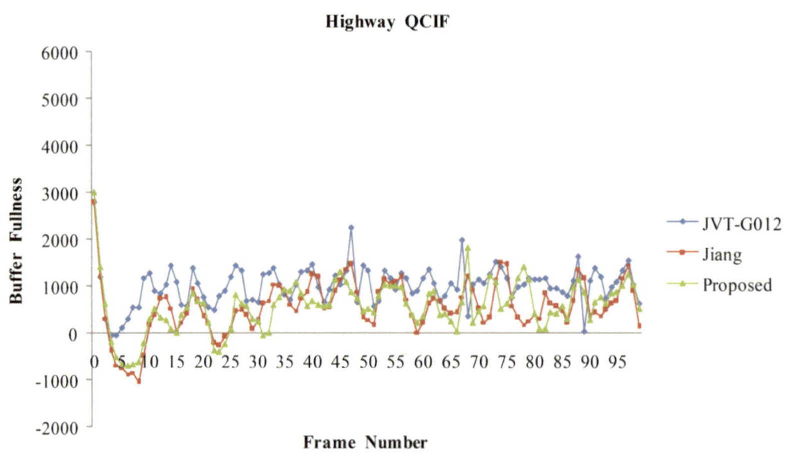
Highway QCIF
Buffer Fullness
Frame Number
JVT-G012
Jiang
Proposed

(f)

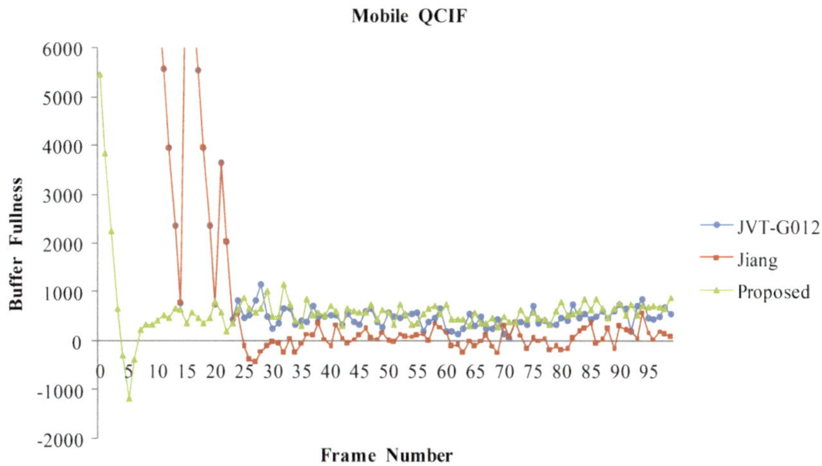


(g)

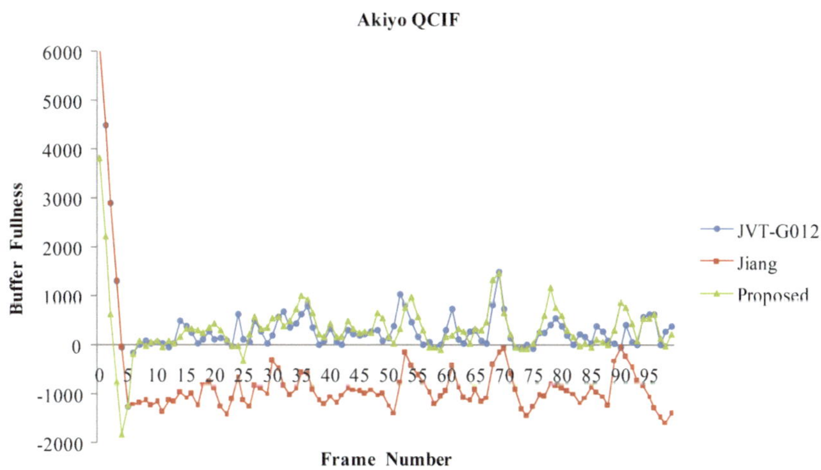


(h)

Fig. 12. Comparisons of buffer fullness for the proposed scheme, JVT-G012 and (Jiang & Lin, 2006)

## 5. Conclusion

In this chapter, we proposed a more efficient rate control scheme for low delay H.264 video coding. A fast and best selection of initial QP is first proposed in the GOP layer rate control. Then, an improved MAD prediction model and overhead bits prediction method is adopted in the MB layer rate control. For low-bandwidth transmission channel applications, the simulation results show that the proposed rate control scheme is more efficient than JVT-G012 and (Jiang & Lin, 2006) for low-delay applications. In addition, the proposed scheme improves the number of frame skipped and reduces the quality deviations of the initial frames by choosing the best initial QP.

| Sequences ( QCIF ) | No. of skipped frames | | | Average PSNRY ( dB ) | | | Bitrate (kbps) | |
|---|---|---|---|---|---|---|---|---|
| | G012 | Proposed | Gain | G012 | Proposed | Gain | G012 | Proposed |
| Foreman | 9 | 4 | 5 | 28.07 | 28.16 | + 0.09 | 24.02 | 24.03 |
| Bus | 11 | 2 | 9 | 24.23 | 25.04 | + 0.81 | 24.11 | 24.11 |
| Highway | 4 | 2 | 2 | 35.28 | 35.29 | + 0.01 | 24.05 | 24.08 |
| Coastguard | 3 | 1 | 2 | 27.19 | 27.80 | + 0.61 | 24.02 | 24.03 |
| News | 7 | 2 | 5 | 30.51 | 30.57 | + 0.06 | 24.00 | 23.98 |
| Stefan | 20 | 1 | 19 | 21.80 | 22.56 | + 0.76 | 24.00 | 24.00 |
| Mobile | 21 | 2 | 19 | 21.45 | 22.95 | + 1.50 | 24.06 | 24.05 |
| Akiyo | 3 | 2 | 1 | 37.35 | 38.30 | + 0.95 | 24.00 | 24.00 |

Table 2. Comparisons of the number of skipped frames, average PSNRY and bitrate between the proposed scheme and JVT-G012

| Sequences ( QCIF ) | No. of skipped frames | | | Average PSNRY ( dB ) | | | Bit rate (kbps) | |
|---|---|---|---|---|---|---|---|---|
| | Jiang | Proposed | Gain | Jiang | Proposed | Gain | G012 | Proposed |
| Foreman | 8 | 4 | 4 | 28.09 | 28.16 | + 0.07 | 24.01 | 24.03 |
| Bus | 11 | 2 | 9 | 24.21 | 25.04 | + 0.83 | 24.08 | 24.11 |
| Highway | 1 | 2 | 1 | 35.36 | 35.29 | - 0.07 | 24.02 | 24.08 |
| Coastguard | 3 | 1 | 2 | 27.17 | 27.80 | + 0.63 | 24.00 | 24.03 |
| News | 6 | 2 | 1 | 30.32 | 30.57 | + 0.25 | 23.95 | 23.98 |
| Stefan | 20 | 1 | 19 | 21.77 | 22.56 | + 0.79 | 23.98 | 24.00 |
| Mobile | 21 | 2 | 19 | 21.46 | 22.95 | + 1.49 | 24.04 | 24.05 |
| Akiyo | 3 | 2 | 1 | 37.19 | 38.30 | + 1.11 | 24.00 | 24.00 |

Table 3. Comparisons of the number of skipped frames, average PSNRY and bitrate between the proposed scheme and (Jiang & Lin, 2006)

## 6. References

ITU-T (2003), Rec. H.264 and ISO/IEC 14496-10 AVC, JVT-G050, March 2003.

ITU-T (1997), Video Codec Test Model, ITU-T/SG15, TMN8, Portland, OR, June1997.

ISO/IEC (1993), Test Model Editing Committee, MPEG-2, Test Model 5, Doc. ISO/IEC, JTC1/SC29 WG11/93-225, April 1993.

ISO/IEC (1997), Coding of Moving Pictures and Associated Audio MPEG 97/W1796, Text of ISO/IEC 14496-2 MPEG-4 Video VM-Version 8.0, ISO/IEC JTC1/SC29/WG11, Video Group, Stockholm, Sweden, July 1997.

CCITT (1990), Rec. H.261—Video codec for audiovisual services at p×64 Kbits/s, CCITT SG XV, COM XV-R37-E, 1990

ITU-T (1996), Rec. H.263—*Video coding for low bit rate communication*, ITU-T Rec. H.263, March 1996

LeGall, D. (1991), MPEG: A video compression standard for multimedia applications, *Communications of ACM*, Vol. 34, No. 4, pp. 46-58, Apr. 1991

ISO/IEC (1994), Information technology - Generic coding of moving pictures and associated audio information - Part 2: Video, ISO/IEC FDIS 13818-2, MPEG-2 1994

ISO/IEC (1999), Information technology - Coding of Audio-Visual Objects - Part 2: Visual, ISO/IEC 14496-2, MPEG-4 1999

Jiang, M. & Ling, N. (2006). Low-delay rate control for real-time H.264/AVC video coding, *IEEE Transactions on Multimedia*, Vol. 8, No. 3, (June 2006), pp.467-477, March 2006.

Li, Z. G.; Pan, F.; Lim, K. P.; Feng, G. N.; Lin, X. & Rahardaj, S. (2003). Adaptive basic unit layer rate control for JVT, *Joint Video Team of ISO/IEC JTC1/SC29/WG11 and ITU-T SG16/Q.6 Doc. JVT-G012*, Pattaya, Thailand, March 2003.

JVT H.264/AVC Reference Software version JM 12.1, http://iphome.hhi.de/suehring /tml/download/jm12.zip.

Armstrong, A.; Beesley, S. & Grecos, C. (2006). Selection of initial quantization parameter for rate controlled H.264 video coding, *Research in Microelectronics and Electronics*, pp. 249 252, June 2006.

Wang, C. C.; Chen, T. S. & Tung, W. C. (2006). Fast intra-mode decision in H.264 using interblock correlation, *IEEE International Conference on Image Processing* (ICIP 2006), pp.1345-1349, Atlanta, USA, October 2006.

Wang, H. & Kwong, S. (2008). Rate-distortion optimization of rate control for H.264 with adaptive initial quantization parameter determination, *IEEE Transactions on Circuits and Systems for Video Technology*, Vol. 18, No. 1, pp.140-144, January 2008.

Yuan, W.; Lin, S.; Zhang, Y. & Luo, H. (2006). Optimum bit allocation and rate control for H.264/AVC, *IEEE Transactions on Circuits and Systems for Video Technology*, Vol. 16, No. 6, pp.705-715, June 2006.

Gu, Y. & Song, B. C. (2009). An intra-frame rate control algorithm for ultralow delay H.264/AVC, *IEEE Transactions on Circuits and Systems for Video Technology*, Vol. 19, No. 5, pp.747-752, May 2009.

Liu, Y.; Li, Z. G. & Soh, Y. C. (2008). Rate control of H.264/AVC scalable extension, *IEEE Transactions on Circuits and Systems for Video Technology*, Vol. 18, No. 1, pp.116-121, January 2008.

Liu, Y.; Li, Z. G. & Soh, Y. C. (2007). A novel rate control scheme for low delay video communication of H.264/AVC standard, *IEEE Transactions on Circuits and Systems for Video Technology*, Vol. 17, No. 1, pp.68-78, January 2007.

Lee, H. J.; Chiang, T. & Zhang, Y. (2000). Scalable rate control for MPEG-4 video, *IEEE Transactions on Circuits and Systems for Video Technology*, Vol. 10, No. 6, pp.878-894, September 2000.

# Part 3

# Novel Algorithms and Techniques for Video Coding

# 7

# Effective Video Encoding in Lossless and Near-lossless Modes

Grzegorz Ulacha
*West Pomeranian University of Technology,*
*Faculty of Computer Science and Information Technology*
*Poland*

## 1. Introduction

The main goal of the research is to develop an algorithm appropriate for hardware realization of a lossless and near-lossless video sequences. The importance of compression is unquestionable in contemporary digital video signal processing systems, with an extensive requirement on a high storage and bandwidth imposed on data storage and transmission. For example, a 60 minutes long uncompressed movie with the TV PAL quality (i.e., 25 frames per second, 720x576 pixels) requires 104.28 GB hard disk space and 9.89 Mpixels/s of bandwidth in the 4:4:4 profile. One of the major requirements for the system is its work in the real-time. This is caused by one of the primary applications of the lossless video compression, i.e., edition of television programs, movies etc. (Andriani et al., 2004). In this situation it is not recommended to use lossy compression methods, such as MPEG2, MPEG4 etc.

Other important applications of the lossless video sequence compression is a storage of medical 2D and 3D images (in general, multi-planar 3D objects) (Xie et al., 2007), as well as astronomical images, and satellite photos compression (photographs of the Earth, Mars and other celestial bodies made by satellites and spaceships should be sent and stored in a lossless form) (Chen et al., 2004; CCSDS, 2007). A novel kind of application is the slow motion video technique for recording from scientific experiments up to dozen of thousands frames per second (fps). For example, recording of one second long video sequence (lumination signal, 8 bit/pixel) using 1000 fps and the SD (720×576 pixel) resolution needs 3955 MB of memory. Nowadays video cameras in the slow motion mode stores the images without any compression and the time of the recording is limited with the volume of the storage card in the device. Recording and archiving files of a larger size becomes an important issue that may be solved by introducing fast, hardware-based, parallel compression realization, e.g., in the near-lossless mode (see Section 3). In combination with the matrix of the effective SSD discs, it may lead to the increase of the functionality of the scientific site using the slow-motion camera.

## 2. Lossless static images and video sequences compression

This section presents the basic features and the motivation of the choice of the prediction blending technique. There are also described the blocks for contextual removing the constant coefficient and for adaptive arithmetic encoding. The proposed method is compared, in terms of effectiveness, with other techniques known from literature.

### 2.1 Existing solutions in the field of lossless image compression

The CALIC method, up to today perceived as one of the most efficient techniques, was presented in 1996 (Wu & Memon, 1996). In that time this method was too computational complex, especially in comparison with the LOCO-I, whose modification has become the JPEG-LS standard (Weinberger et al., 2000). Among the algorithms with high implementation complexity three methods are worth to be mentioned: the TMW method (Meyer & Tischer, 1997) and its further extension, $TMW^{LEGO}$ (Meyer & Tischer, 2001b), WAVE-WLS (Ye, 2002) and MRP 0.5 (Matsuda et al., 2005). An encoding of a single image with any of these methods required a few hours in the time of their proposals (a dozen of minutes using the most efficient contemporary processor). Apart from the mentioned above methods utilizing predictive modelling, there are lossless versions of wavelet codecs used for encoding (e.g. JPEG-2000 (Marcellin et al., 2000)). However, the obtained results are inferior in comparison with the best predictive methods.

In (Andriani et al., 2004), it was presented an analysis of lossles video sequences compression, where methods LOPT-3D, GLICBAWLS-3D, JPEG-LS and JPEG-2000 have been compared. Based on the complexity analysis for the real-time applications, it was proposed to encode each video sequence frame independently with a reduced version of the JPEG-2000 standard (Andriani et al., 2004). It allows us to compress in the visually lossless mode (i.e., with low loss, unvisible for humans). Such the proposals as GLICBAWLS-3D, LOPT-3D (and its extension to the LPOSTC method (Andriani et al., 2005) belong to the solutions of high efficiency, but are too demanding in terms of computational complexity to be applied as real-time implementations.

Having looked for a solution being a compromise between efficiency and complexity, we decided to apply the blending predictors method, which is characterized with the highest flexibility (Seemann & Tisher, 1997a).

### 2.2 Subpredictor blending method

In the case of using contemporary compression methods, two stages must be devised: data modeling, and then compression with one of the efficient entropy method, among whom the most effective are arithmetic and Huffman encoding (Sayood, 2002). Data modeling in such cases aims at reducing maximum possible mutual information between neighboring pixels.

In modeling stage, an $r$-th order linear predictor computes an estimated value $\hat{x}$ of the $n$-th pixel taking into account values of the previously $r$ neighboring pixels. Then, only the estimation errors is encoded, i.e., the difference between the actual and the predicted values (rounded up to the closest integer), which is usually small values close to zero:

$$e = P(0) - \hat{x} \, . \tag{1}$$

The obtained error values of the prediction are considerably lower than the initial values of the variance. Moreover, their distribution resembles the Laplace one. Both these features result in decreasing the value of unconditional entropy.

From the hardware realization point of view, one of the most important factor is time proportion between encoding and decoding. Time symmetric methods are of similar computational complexity of encoder and decoder. It is the reason why we resigned from the methods for selecting an individual static predictor (or a set of such the predictors) based on the criteria of minimizing a minimum mean square error, MMSE (Sayood, 2002; Wu & Memon, 1996) (which requires introducing delays and solving sets of linear equations using floating numbers), and other methods needed an introductory preparation of modeling and compression parameters.

The works of G. Deng (Deng & Ye, 1999, 2003; Ye et al., 2000) show high efficiency of the blending prediction method. Having a given set a simple, constant predictors (named further subpredictors), one may conclude that the unconditional entropy (0-order) value obtained by an encoding with each of these subpredictors individually are far from being efficient; however, using even 7 simple subpredictors together leads to significant decrease of the entropy value (Seemann & Tisher, 1997a) in the majority of benchmark images. It is the main motivation of our interest in this approach. Another benefit of this method is the possibility of performing a number of computation in parallel for a single pixel. In order to evaluate our results and compare them with other authors' and choose the most appropriate set of subpredictors, we made usage of the fact that every author of algorithms utilizing methods of subpredictors blending has presented his own set of subpredictors. Taking into account the problems of implementation complexity, it was usually simple constant subpredictors of the range form 1 to 3. In case of the predictors of range 1, it was proposed to use the closest, neighbour pixels $P(i)$, where $i$ is the index of the neighbour pixels (see Fig. 1). To these simplest subpredictors, there were added also constant predictors, such as planar (known also as Plane or JPEG4), Pirsh, etc.

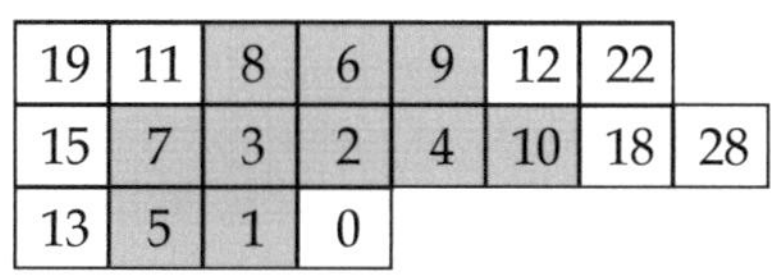


Fig. 1. Numbering of the neighboring pixels

In this section we present the proposed flow for modeling and lossless image and video sequences compression, named Blend-V. This method uses 14 subpredictors: $x_1 = \text{GAP}_+$ (Wang & Zhang, 2004) (an improved version of the non-linear prediction used in the CALIC algorithm, which is a modification of $\text{GAP}_+$ described in (Wu & Memon, 1996), in our previous research, we also analysed a $\text{MED}_+$ modification from (Jiang & Grecos, 2002), but later we concluded that better results are obtained when this subpredictor is excluded), $x_2 = \text{GradWest} = 2P(1) - P(5)$, $x_3 = \text{GradNorth} = 2P(2) - P(6)$, $x_4 = \text{Plane} = P(1) + P(2) - P(3)$, $x_5 = \text{Plane2} = P(1) - P(2) + P(4)$ (Seemann, et al. 1997b), $x_6 = P(1)$, $x_7 = P(2)$, $x_8 = P(3)$, $x_9 = P(4)$, $x_{10} = P(5)$, $x_{11} = P(10)$, $x_{12} = P(18)$, $x_{13} = P(28)$, $x_{14} = P_{j-1}(0)$, where $P(i)$ denotes the pixel with index $i$ from the closest neighborhood - see Fig. 1, and $P_{j-1}(0)$ denotes the pixel from the previous frame of the same coordinates that the currently encoded pixel, $P(0)$. Each of these proposals is suitable for encoding without any delay, they do not require any preliminary calculations referring to data from the entire image. Due to the encoding order (the consecutive rows are encoded top-down, and each of them left-right), both encoder and decoder have an access to the pixels placed above and on the left on the pixel being encoded (decoded). It is then required and access to the 3 previous rows (the row currently encoded and the two previous ones). In the proposed technique, we assigned numbers to neighbor pixels according to the Euclidean metric. The assignment of the numbers with the same distance is performed clock-wise.

A prediction error, $e_i(0) = P(0) - x_i$, is associated with each subpredictor $x_i$. A significance of a particular subpredictor is inversely proportional to prediction errors obtained in the closest neighborhood. The problem to be solved was the fact, that for the analyzed images the optimal neighborhood (common for all subpredictors) were situated in the whole analyzed range of $k$, i.e., from 3 to 30. Seemann and Tisher (Seemann & Tisher, 1997a) have proposed $k = 3$, Deng in his works has used $k = 4$ (Deng & Ye, 1999, 2003; Ye et al., 2000). As a result of our works, for a set of 45 various benchmark images, the best average results have been obtained for $k = 10$. The total error value, $E_i$, of the neighborhood associated with an $i$-th subpredictor is calculated with formula:

$$E_i = 1 + 2(e_i^2(1) + e_i^2(2)) + \sum_{j=3}^{k} e_i^2(j) . \tag{2}$$

where $e_i(j)$ denotes the value of the prediction error obtained with the $i$-th subpredictor in the neighborhood with relative number $j$. To ensure that the value of the subpredictor weight, $w_i$, belongs to range 0 to $\alpha_i$, it is necessary to determine it with the following equation:

$$w_i = \frac{\alpha_i}{E_i} . \tag{3}$$

setting the importance parameter $\alpha_i = 1$ for each subpredictor but Plane2, for which $\alpha_i = 1.5$, and $\alpha_i = 2$ for the GradNorth and GradWest subpredictor. Taking into consideration a set of $m$ subpredictors, we may determine its positive prediction coefficients, $a_i$, using their normalization (i.e., a sum of all the coefficients is to be equal to 1):

$$a_i = \frac{w_i}{\sum_{j=1}^{m} w_j} . \tag{4}$$

Finally, the estimated value is computed in the following way:

$$\hat{x} = \sum_{i=1}^{m} a_i \cdot \hat{x}_i . \tag{5}$$

### 2.3 Context-based error correction

Some particular properties of coded pixel neighborhoods may induce (transient, but long lasting) DC components in prediction errors associated with contexts. Each context is characterised with the individual properties of the closest neighbourhood of the pixels being encoded, taking into account mutual dependences existing between subsequent pixels, and often also their variance value. Context-based error correction methods consist in using occurrence number and cumulated error for each context for correcting current prediction error (Wu & Memon, 1996). Therefore, in our method the next stage is bias cancelation, i.e., usage of an adaptive method to remove the constant component $C_{(i)}$, which determines the error correction of the prediction associated with the appropriate context of the index $i$. This method is used in both the CALIC and JPEG-LS algorithms. In our algorithm we use 1024 contexts and the arithmetic average from the results of these two methods:

$$\dot{x} = \hat{x} + \frac{\mathbf{C}_{\mathrm{CALIC}(i)} + \mathbf{C}_{\mathrm{JPEG\text{-}LS}(i)}}{2}. \tag{6}$$

Then, only the estimation errors is encoded, i.e., the difference between the actual and the predicted values (rounded up to the closest integer):

$$e = P(0) - \dot{x} . \tag{7}$$

The simplest method of calculating the number of context is to determine the weighted average of $n$ constant subpredictors:

$$\overline{x} = \frac{102}{1024}\left(3\cdot(P(1)+P(2)) + \sum_{j=3}^{6} P(j)\right), \tag{8}$$

e.g., for $n = 8$, the following subpredictors are utilised: $P(1)$, $P(2)$, $P(3)$, $P(4)$, $P(5)$, $P(6)$, GradNorth and GradWest. Next, the value of each of them is compared with the weighted average. If the value of the $i$-th subpredictor is higher than the average, bit flag $z_i$ is set to 1, otherwise it is set to 0. From these flags, an $n$-bit number $z_{n-1}...z_3z_2z_1z_0$ is assembled. This number is the number of the context. In case of $n = 8$ we obtain number of the contexts equal to 256. Moreover, it is possible to determine the measure of the deviation from the average, measuring the variance level of these $n$ subpredictors. This value can be quantized into $Q$ partitions, which results in $Q\cdot 2^n = 1024$ contexts. The variance level (multiplied by 8) can be determined with the formula:

$$\sigma^2 = (\overline{x} - \mathrm{GradNorth})^2 + (\overline{x} - \mathrm{GradWest})^2 + \sum_{j=1}^{6}(\overline{x} - P(j))^2 . \tag{9}$$

To obtain the split into 4 quantisation levels, it was determined experimentally 3 thresholds of $\sigma^2$ values equal to 400, 2500, 8000, respectively. More details on the update component $C_{(i)}$ are described in (Ulacha & Stasiński, 2008).

### 2.4 Adaptive arithmetic encoder

In the developed system, an adaptive encoder of prediction errors has been designed as a separate module. Two main assumptions are the encoding without delays (i.e., in the real-time) and no feed-back between the modeling and the encoding/decoding blocks.

As we encode absolute values of the prediction errors, the distribution is close to the Laplace one. The initial distribution, i.e., the instance vector $n_e(i)$ of value $i$ (the values of the absolute values of the prediction errors), can be treated as its approximation utilizing the simplified formula (Meyer & Tischer, 2001a):

$$n_e(i) = \left\lfloor A \cdot 0.8^i \right\rfloor + 1 . \tag{10}$$

Good results are obtained for $A = 10$. After reading and encoding each subsequent value of $|e|$, it is necessary to actualise the instance vector by increasing the $|e|$ index by 1.

Additionally, one can introduce the forgetting effect, which may lead to decreasign the weights of the instances which have appeared rarelier (or have not appeared at all) among the recently encoded values in comparison with the earlier encoding stage (Gallager, 1978). It is the reason why the total number of encoded values (or, more precisely, the counter value) is increased by 1 after every encoded number $|e|$.
The adaptive encoder is capable of adjusting to the distribution in long-term, but it is possible to use also the presence of short-term dependences between subsequently encoded data utilizing the closest neighbourhood of the two-dimensional error prediction signal. The properties of the neighbouring prediction errors (without considering the knowledge of the properties of the pixels neighbourhood) are capable of determining with better precision the distribution type of the currently encoded value $|e_n|$. Consequently, it is possible to design a context-based arithmetic encoder including $K$ probability distributions (instead of one), associated with the context numbers from 0 to $K - 1$. Theoretically, one can assume the increase of compression efficiency with the growing number of contexts, but the problem of too slow adaptiveness of their distribution may appear. The adaptativeness of the distribution construction requires fast stabilisation of the target characteristics of each from the $K$ distributions, so a certain trade-off between the number of contexts and the time of their adaptiveness has to be made. One often use 8 (Wu & Memon, 1996), 16, or even 20 contexts (Deng & Ye, 1999).
The errors, $e$, are compressed using a contextual, adaptive arithmetic encoder. We use seven universal and two 16-contextual adaptive arithmetic encoders ($K = 16$). In order to increase the adaptation speed of the distributions associated with the contextes, the quantisation of $|e|$ values is often applied. It is possible thanks to scaling down the number range from 0 to 255 to a lower range, e.g., from 0 to 17. This idea is applied in numerous encoding methods, e.g., in the JPEG standard. The first 16-contextual encoder compresses the absolute value of the error, $|e|$, quantized according to rule $\mathbf{T}(k) \leq |e| < \mathbf{T}(k+1)$, where $\mathbf{T} = \{0, 1, 2, 3, 4, 5, 6, 7, 8, 10, 12, 14, 16, 20, 24, 32, 64, 128\}$. The value of $k$ is send to the arithmetic encoder. The quantization error, $e_q = |e| - \mathbf{T}(k)$, is treated as $\mathbf{q}(k)$-bit number, where $\mathbf{q}(k)$ is the $k$-th value from vector $\mathbf{q} = \{0, 0, 0, 0, 0, 0, 0, 0, 1, 1, 1, 1, 2, 2, 3, 5, 6, 7\}$. If $\mathbf{q}(k) > 0$, the value of $e_q$ is encoded using one of the 7 universal adaptive arithmetic encoders (with index $\mathbf{q}(k)$).
Due to the symmetry of the prediction error distribution, it is more convenient to encode their absolute values $|e|$, which results in faster adaptation of the distribution of each context of the arithmetic encoder. The second contextual encoder encodes the sign bit of the $e$ value. Both these encoders use context switching based on the error level from the closest neighborhood, which allows us to determine the individual probability distribution type (one of the 16 contexts) for the currently encoded pixel. More details on the selection of the context number are described in (Ulacha & Dziurzański, 2008).

### 2.5 Experimental results

In Table 1, it is presented a comparison of the bitrates of the method proposed in this paper, Blend-V (the intraframe mode), with a few software-based, but fast and effective methods known from literature: JPEG-LS (Strutz, 2002), HBB (Seemann, et al. 1997b), CALIC (Ye et al., 2000), P13 (Deng & Ye, 1999). Among the compared methods there is also a bit slower, but effective method LAT-RLMS (Marusic & Deng, 2002), which shows the high efficiency of the proposed method, which is characterized with the lowest bitrate. The experiment has been performed for the set of 9 grayscale benchmark images of the resolution equal to

720×576 pixels. Relatively few proposals of hardware realizations of the lossless compression systems for video sequences have been presented. The system proposed in (Drost & Bourbakis, 2001) is one of the solutions well-known from literature. For example, for that proposal the bit average for the Lenna image of the 512×512 pixel size in 8-bit grayscale is equal to 4.609 bit/pixel. Applying our system, we are obtaining the average 4.006 bit/pixel, which is about 13 % efficiency improvement.

| Images | JPEG-LS | HBB | CALIC | P13 | LAT- RLMS | Blend-V |
|---|---|---|---|---|---|---|
| **Balloon** | 2.889 | 2.80 | 2.78 | 2.74 | 2.75 | 2.746 |
| **Barb** | 4.690 | 4.28 | 4.31 | 4.29 | 4.15 | 4.172 |
| **Barb2** | 4.684 | 4.48 | 4.46 | 4.47 | 4.45 | 4.441 |
| **Board** | 3.674 | 3.54 | 3.51 | 3.48 | 3.48 | 3.465 |
| **Boats** | 3.930 | 3.80 | 3.78 | 3.75 | 3.74 | 3.716 |
| **Girl** | 3.922 | 3.74 | 3.72 | 3.67 | 3.68 | 3.640 |
| **Gold** | 4.475 | 4.37 | 4.35 | 4.33 | 4.34 | 4.323 |
| **Hotel** | 4.378 | 4.27 | 4.18 | 4.19 | 4.21 | 4.189 |
| **Zelda** | 3.884 | 3.72 | 3.69 | 3.68 | 3.61 | 3.673 |
| **Average** | 4.058 | 3.889 | 3.864 | 3.844 | 3.823 | 3.818 |

Table 1. Average bitrates for standard benchmark images

## 3. Near-lossless mode and color mode

In order to obtain higher compression ratio, it is possible to use an irreversible encoding. There exist a large number of lossy compression methods based on discrete cosines transform, DCT (e.g. JPEG), or wavelet transform (e.g. JPEG-2000) (Sayood, 2002). These methods allows us to adjust the compression level, but their basic implementations do not offer the capabilities of selecting the maximal possible error. This possibility is offered by the *near-lossless* mode, where it is possible to determine the highest acceptable value of the difference module, $d$, between the original and the decoded images. This mode is usually based on the predictive encoding, where the set of prediction error, $e$, is quantized in the following way (Carotti et al., 2004):

$$\bar{e} = \begin{cases} \left\lfloor \dfrac{e+d}{2d+1} \right\rfloor, & \text{for } e \ge 0 \\ \left\lfloor \dfrac{e-d}{2d+1} \right\rfloor, & \text{for } e < 0 \end{cases}, \tag{11}$$

and the original color value can be restored with the accuracy ± $d$. When $d = 0$, we obtain the lossless mode.

The near-lossless method may be used for medical images compression, where experts should determine the error tolerance $d$ that does not influence the diagnosis of the medical images of the given type (that compression kind is sometimes referred to as visually lossless (Andriani et al., 2004)), and in the situation when there is recording of video sequences with very large number of frames and only a slight error level can be acceptable. Often used quality measure, PSNR, is treated as not utterly capable of considering human visual perception. The quality measure Mean Structural SIMilarity Index (MSSIM), developed in (Wang Z. et al., 2004), takes into consideration the comparison of the structural features of the source and the encoded images, as well as the features connected with luminance and contrast. This measure is a value ranged from -1 to 1; the higher value, the higher the images resemblance.

| Blend-V | | | | | JPEG2000 | | | |
|---|---|---|---|---|---|---|---|---|
| *d* | **bitrate** | **PSNR** | **MSSIM** | | *d* | **bitrate** | **PSNR** | **MSSIM** |
| 1 | 2.49144 | 49.89429 | 0.99473 | | 7 | 2.49145 | 45.09458 | 0.98501 |
| 2 | 1.85465 | 45.15079 | 0.98462 | | 8 | 1.85480 | 43.15705 | 0.97573 |
| 3 | 1.46825 | 42.26534 | 0.97124 | | 11 | 1.46783 | 41.74485 | 0.96705 |
| 4 | 1.19771 | 40.26459 | 0.95682 | | 12 | 1.20132 | 40.74678 | 0.95868 |
| 5 | 0.99264 | 38.75684 | 0.94257 | | 17 | 0.99277 | 39.81996 | 0.95150 |
| 6 | 0.84358 | 37.51494 | 0.92906 | | 17 | 0.84363 | 39.10160 | 0.94507 |
| 7 | 0.72745 | 36.45099 | 0.91631 | | 24 | 0.72781 | 38.60727 | 0.93805 |
| 8 | 0.64068 | 35.47136 | 0.90388 | | 27 | 0.64258 | 38.06484 | 0.93290 |
| 9 | 0.57260 | 34.61310 | 0.89212 | | 27 | 0.57275 | 37.49548 | 0.92723 |
| 10 | 0.51554 | 33.86520 | 0.88133 | | 29 | 0.51157 | 37.12479 | 0.92410 |

Table 2. Comparison of Blend-V in the near-lossless mode with JPEG2000 using the Lennagrey image

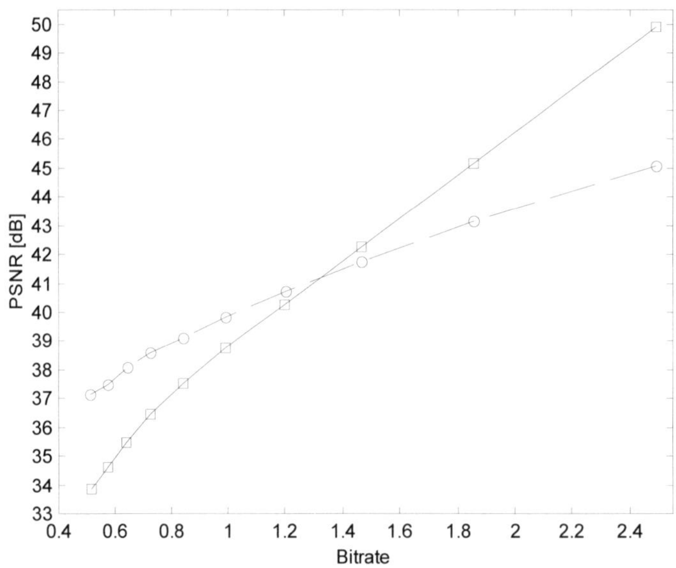


Fig. 2. Comparison of the PSNR of the Lennagrey image with respect to the average bitrate for JPEG2000 (the dashed line) and the Blend-V method in the near-lossless mode with $d \leq 10$ (the solid line)

In Fig. 2 and 3, there is a comparison of PSNR and MSSIM, respectively, between Blend-V and JPEG2000. For majority of the benchmark images the values of PSNR and MSSIM obtained with the Blend-V method with $d \leq 3$ is higher than with the JPEG2000 standard. It is worth stressing that for the wavelet method it is impossible to define the maximal error value $d$ a priori. Under the same average bitrate, the maximum error $d$ is considerably higher in the case of JPEG2000 (see Table 2). Considering the average bitrate and better values of PSNR and MSSIM, Blend-V should be the method of choice when the average bitrate is higher than 1.5 bit per pixel.

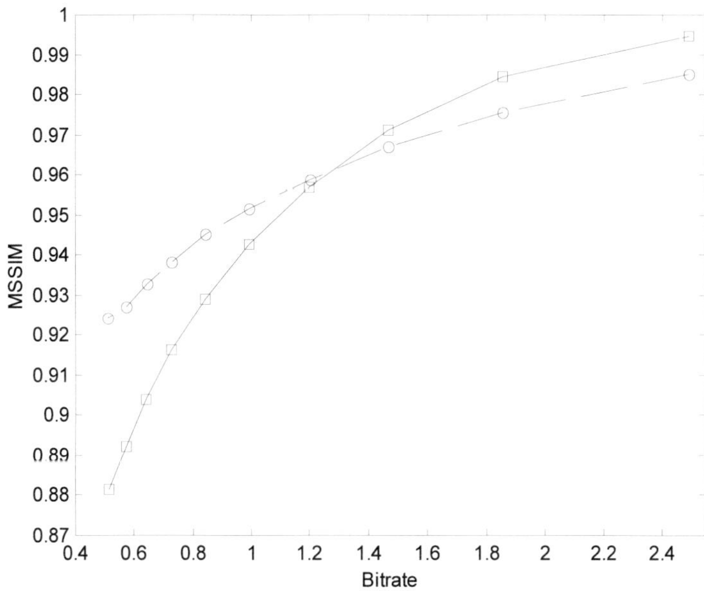


Fig. 3. Comparison of the MSSIM of the Lennagrey image with respect to the average bitrate for JPEG2000 (the dashed line) and the Blend-V method in the near-lossless mode with $d \leq 10$ (the solid line)

Table 3 includes the experimental results of grayscale images for $d = \{2, 10\}$. It is compared the proposed Blend-V method (in the intraframe mode) with two other techniques, known from literature: LOCO-I (Weinberger et al., 2000) and TMW (Meyer & Tischer, 1997). The obtained results show the high efficiency of the Blend-V method not only in the lossless mode, but also in the near-lossless one, where it turns out to be competitive even with TMW, one of the most efficient techniques, but characterized with high computational complexity.

In the case of encoding color images in Blend-V in the lossless mode, the $YD_bD_r$ transform, known from the JPEG2000 standard, is used. This transformation also requires only the addition, subtraction, and bit shifting operation. The equations for this transformation are as follows:

$$\begin{aligned} Y &= \left\lfloor \frac{R+2G+B}{4} \right\rfloor \\ D_b &= B - G \\ D_r &= R - G \end{aligned} \quad . \qquad (12)$$

| Image | $d = 2$ | | | $d = 10$ | | |
|---|---|---|---|---|---|---|
| | **LOCO-I v.0.90N** | **TMW (mode 3)** | **Blend-V** | **LOCO-I v.0.90N** | **TMW (mode 4)** | **Blend-V** |
| **Balloon** | 1.242 | 0.90 | 0.905 | 0.49 | 0.32 | 0.198 |
| **Boats** | 1.902 | 1.65 | 1.646 | 0.78 | 0.66 | 0.546 |
| **Gold** | 2.333 | 2.19 | 2.166 | 0.99 | 0.81 | 0.710 |
| **Airplane** | 1.84 | 1.64 | 1.660 | 0.72 | 0.57 | 0.517 |
| **Baboon** | 3.72 | 3.49 | 3.481 | 1.91 | 1.68 | 1.656 |
| **Lennagrey** | 2.09 | 1.83 | 1.855 | 0.93 | 0.55 | 0.516 |
| **Peppers** | 2.29 | 2.09 | 2.096 | 0.93 | 0.64 | 0.558 |
| **Shapes** | 0.79 | 0.75 | 0.709 | 0.47 | 0.58 | 0.320 |
| **Bridge256** | 3.49 | 3.38 | 3.325 | 1.73 | 1.63 | 1.570 |
| **Camera256** | 2.28 | 2.08 | 2.024 | 0.96 | 0.90 | 0.795 |
| **Couple256** | 1.82 | 1.60 | 1.606 | 0.86 | 0.70 | 0.559 |
| **Average** | 2.163 | 1.964 | 1.952 | 0.979 | 0.822 | 0.722 |

Table 3. Average bitrates in the near-lossless mode with error value $d = \{2, 10\}$

The reverse transform is of the following form:

$$\begin{aligned} G &= Y - \left\lfloor \frac{D_b + D_r}{4} \right\rfloor \\ B &= D_b + G \\ R &= D_r + G \end{aligned} \quad . \tag{13}$$

However, in the near-lossless mode, there is no color transformation. In Table 4, it is presented an efficiency comparison between the proposed Blend-V method with the hardware compression realization system Enhanced Lossless Image Compression (ELIC) from GEMAC (Dittrich, 2005). In table, there is the compression ratio measurement of five color images in the lossless ($d = 0$) and near-lossless mode.

| Image | **Blend-V** $d = 0$ | **ELIC** $d = 0$ | **Blend-V** $d = 1$ | **ELIC** $d = 1$ | **Blend-V** $d = 2$ | **ELIC** $d = 2$ | **Blend-V** $d = 4$ | **ELIC** $d = 4$ | **Blend-V** $d = 8$ | **ELIC** $d = 8$ |
|---|---|---|---|---|---|---|---|---|---|---|
| **lena** | 1.869 | 1.33 | 2.884 | 1.95 | 3.788 | 2.40 | 5.634 | 3.14 | 10.364 | 4.34 |
| **monarch** | 2.741 | 1.84 | 3.841 | 2.76 | 5.298 | 3.34 | 8.383 | 4.20 | 13.515 | 5.68 |
| **peppers** | 2.502 | 1.69 | 3.560 | 2.57 | 4.826 | 3.18 | 7.530 | 4.03 | 14.432 | 5.44 |
| **sail** | 2.322 | 1.50 | 2.444 | 2.16 | 3.072 | 2.58 | 4.187 | 3.16 | 6.233 | 4.03 |
| **tulips** | 2.472 | 1.63 | 3.420 | 2.44 | 4.519 | 2.97 | 6.572 | 3.77 | 10.716 | 4.89 |
| **Average** | 2.381 | 1.598 | 3.230 | 2.376 | 4.300 | 2.894 | 6.461 | 3.660 | 11.052 | 4.876 |

Table 4. Compression ratio of color images in the near-lossless mode with error value $d = \{0, 1, 2, 4, 8\}$

## 4. Video sequence encoding

Although there exist a few non-linear editing systems (NLEs) offering lossless video compression, some of them do not work in real-time, whereas others split video data in long sequences and are not capable of decoding the n-th frame in a sequence without decompressing of $n$-1 previous frames (Ohanian, 1998). These requirements are covered in the proposed approach. The basic rule of a lossless video sequences compression is exploiting both the spatial dependencies (the intraframe mode - in the currently encoded image) and the temporal dependencies (the interframe mode), taking into account the neighboring frames of the sequence. The most popular is encoding of so-called Group of Pictures (GoPs), where the first frame is encoded in the intraframe mode, and the remaining $N$ - 1 frames - in the interframe mode. This technique facilitates a quick access to any video sequences fragment with the accuracy up to $N$ frames. When the whole sequence is encoded in the interframe mode, the correct reconstruction of the last frame is possible only after decoding all the previous frames.

According to (Andriani et al., 2005), only a low number of the papers about lossless video compression is available. Consequently, it is difficult to make some comparison in a solid way. Thus the efficiency of the proposed method has been earlier assessed mainly in the intraframe mode.

In this section, we present the further compression efficiency improvement thanks to the interframe mode introduction.

Among lossy video sequence compression methods, the most popular technique for finding the dependencies between the neighboring frames is to split the image into square blocks (usually 8×8 pixels), for which individual movement vectors are determined, and then the information about shifting according to the previous frame is added to each encoded block. This technique used for a lossless encoding is presented in (Matsuda et al., 2004), but this method is characterized with rather high computational complexity. In (Carotti et al., 2004), it is described a method for expecting a value of the current pixel based on the pixel from the previous frame, whose coordinates are calculated using the movement vector computed from the two previous frames, whereas five reference frames are used in (Maeda et al., 2006).

Each of these methods requires an extra computational expenditure due to the determining the movement vectors. Moreover, one has to consider also a quite complex mechanism for detecting a scene change, which should activate an entrance into the intraframe mode while encoding the first frame from each new scene (Yang & Faryar, 2000). In (Andriani & Calvagno, 2007), the authors resigned from the movement compensation obtaining quite promising results at the scene changes due to rather computationally complex technique named Octopus.

In our proposal, there is also no movement vector analysis; the encoding is performed with the usage of 13 subpredictors operating in the intraframe mode and one referring to the previous frame. As the predictor of the interframe mode, it is used a value of the pixel $P_{j-1}(0)$ from the previous frame of the coordinates the same as in the encoded pixel, $P_j(0)$. The blending prediction method automatically reduces the negative impact of the interframe mode predictor in the situation of the scene change. It is worth stressing that the usage of a simple predictor, which does not take into consideration the movement vector, leads to surprisingly good results. It results from the fact that in numerous situations big image fragments are stable (usually a background of the stage). On the basis of the analysis of the video sequences set, a compromise value of the importance of the interframe predictor is $\alpha = 6$. The influence of the number of frames forming the GoP, $N$, on the average bitrate of the sequence for the $Y$ component is presented in Fig. 4.

In Table 5, it is presented an example of the compression efficiency comparison between the proposed system, denoted here as Blend-V, with the results of the JPEG-LS and CPC encoders (Yang & Faryar, 2000). The results consider 30 frames of the *Y* luminance signal of the Salesman sequence. The experiment has been conducted for both the lossless and near-lossless modes with parameter $d = \{1, 2, 3, 4\}$. The measurement of the Blend-V method is taken in the intraframe mode ($N = 1$), and form the interframe mode with parameters $N = 10$ and $N_{max} = 30$, where $N_{max}$ denotes that in the whole sequence only the first frame is to be encoded in the intrafame mode.

When designing a hardware module it is necessary to determine the trade-off between the compression and the module efficiency so that it can operate in real-time. Considering the dependencies between frames during decoding, we have decided to introduce a pipeline of length $N = 10$ for encoding/decoding separate frames in an image group. Larger value of *N* does not improve the efficiency significantly, whereas higher number of pipeline stages would result in further increase of hardware resource utilization and a more difficult access to any fragment of a decoded sequence.

| *d* | **JPEG-LS** | **CPC** | **Blend-V intraframe** | **Blend-V N = 10** | **Blend-V $N_{max}$** |
|---|---|---|---|---|---|
| 0 | 4.377 | 3.760 | 4.102 | 3.686 | 3.656 |
| 1 | 2.872 | 2.321 | 2.623 | 2.225 | 2.197 |
| 2 | 2.243 | 1.765 | 2.011 | 1.647 | 1.620 |
| 3 | 1.868 | 1.453 | 1.644 | 1.309 | 1.286 |
| 4 | 1.617 | 1.252 | 1.393 | 1.071 | 1.048 |

Table 5. Average bitrates for the Salesman video sequence (30 frames, 352x288 resolution) for various maximal error parameter, *d*, using the near-lossless mode

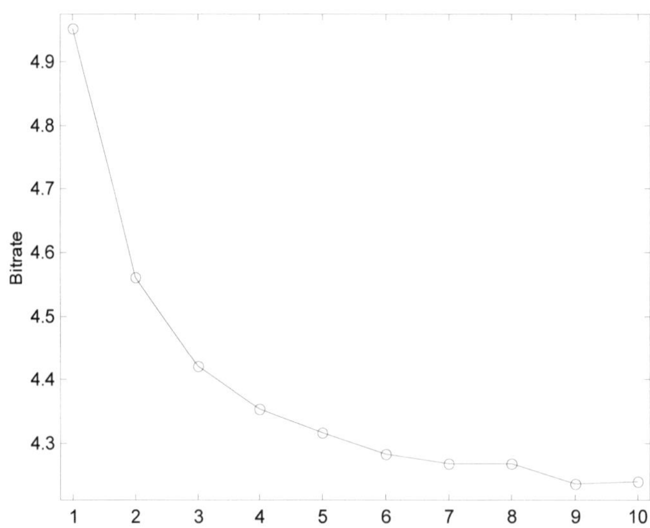


Fig. 4. Average bitrate of the Tennis video sequence with respect to the number of frames, *N*, in GoP

## 5. System-level hardware model

One of disadvantages of the prediction-based methods is a sequential image decoding that makes it impossible to perform computation in parallel (i.e., simultaneously decode more than one pixel). This property is caused with maintaining the principle of causality, where to decode pixel $P(0)$ it is required to have the value of its predecessor $P(1)$ (in general, values of the pixels situated directly on the left side and the rows above the $P(0)$ pixel).

In order to confirm the benefits of hardware realization of the proposed technique, we prepared its system level model; the individual stages of the algorithm are implemented as an MPSoC cores connected with a regular 2D mesh. As the communication infrastructure we utilize the Network on Chip (NoC) paradigm where the cores follow the GALS (Globally Asynchronous, Locally Synchronous) synchronization scheme, i.e., each core is equipped with its individual clock and the clocks communicate each other in the asynchronous manner. Besides, each core is equipped with a router for determining the next hop port for the data to be sent. We decided to use the wormhole routing scheme, where data is sent in packages split into smaller portion of equal length, flits (flow control digits). The first flit of each package is used by the routers to select the route; the remaining packages follows the same path. For more details about our technique, the reader is referred to (Ulacha & Dziurzański, 2009).

We decomposed the algorithm in the following way. The subpredictor values are computed by separate cores in the parallel mode. Having computed these values, each core sends the obtained data to the core realizing the blending procedure. Then the data is transmitted into the core realizing arithmetic encoding.

As in the mesh architecture each core (except the boundary ones) is connected with its four neighbours only, it is crucial to map the functionalities into cores in a meticulous way so that the cores sending each other vast amount of data are located close to each other. Since in our case the amount of cores is relatively low, we managed to check all the possible permutation of the cores with regards to their NoC node mappings and determined the mappings leading to the lowest traffic in the network. After choosing the NoC router architecture, the routing type and the core mapping into mesh nodes, we could start with preparing a system-level model.

The model has been written in the SystemC language at the bus cycle accurate (BCA) level of abstraction and tested with CoCentric® System Studio by Synopsys™ [1]. According to the simulation, the system operates in real-time, confirming our assumptions described in section 1.

## 6. Conclusions

In this paper, a motivation for lossless and near-lossless compression of images and video sequences has been provided. The state of the art of modern compression methods considering their implementation complexity has been described. A technique for blending predictors as an new effective modeling method, which in combination with an adaptive arithmetic encoder allows us to obtain high compression ratio of video sequences. The proposed method leads also to high efficiency in the near-lossless mode.

The Blend-V benefits from various aspects connected with its hardware realization in a novel architecture based on Network on Chip (NoC) (Ulacha & Dziurzański, 2008).

[1] Synopsys and the Synopsys product names described herein are trademarks of Synopsys, Inc.

## 7. Acknowledgment

The research work presented in this chapter was sponsored by Polish Ministry of Science and Higher Education (years 2011-2014).
The software described in this chapter is furnished under a license from Synopsys International Limited.

## 8. References

Andriani, S.; Calvagno, G.; Erseghe, T.; Mian, G.A.; Durigon, M.; Rinaldo, R.; Knee, M.; Walland, P. & Koppetz, M. (2004). Comparison of lossy to lossless compression techniques for digital cinema, *Proc. International Conference on Image Processing*, pp.513-516, ISBN 0-7803-8554-3

Andriani, S.; Calvagno, G. & Mian, G.A. (2005). Lossless Video Compression using a Spatio-Temporal Optimal Predictor, *Proc. 13th European Signal Processing Conference*, on CD.

Andriani, S. & Calvagno, G. (2007). Lossless Compression of Colour Video Sequence using Optimal Prediction Theory - Octopus, *Proc. Data Compression Conference*, pp. 375-375, ISBN 0-7695-2791-4

Carotti, E.S.G.; De Martin, J.C. & Meo, A.R. (2004). Backward-Adaptive Lossless Compression of Video Sequences, *Proc. IEEE International Conference on Acoustics, Speech, and Signal Processing*, Vol.4, pp. 3417-3420, ISBN 0-7803-7402-9

Chen, X.; Canagarajah, C.; N., Vitulli, R. & Nunez-Yanez, J. L. (2008). Lossless Compression for Space Imagery in a Dynamically Reconfigurable Architecture, *Proc. International Workshop on Applied Reconfigurable Computing*, LNCS Vol.4943, pp. 336-341, DOI 10.1007/978-3-540-78610-8_38

Deng, G. & Ye, H. (1999). Lossless image compression using adaptive predictor combination, symbol mapping and context filtering, *Proc. IEEE 1999 International Conference on Image Processing*, Vol.4, pp. 63-67, ISBN 0-7803-5467-2

Deng, G. & Ye, H. (2003). A general framework for the second-level adaptive prediction, *Proc. IEEE International Conference on Acoustics, Speech, and Signal Processing*, Vol.3, pp. 237-240.

Dittrich, C. (2005). FPGAs for lossless image/video and universal data compression, *ECE Magazine*, Vol.4, pp. 42-44.

Drost G. W. & Bourbakis N. G. (2001). A hybrid system for real-time lossless image compression, *Microprocessors and Microsystems*, Vol.25, No.1, pp. 19-31, DOI 10.1016/S0141-9331(00)00102-2

Gallager R. G. (1978). Variations on a theme by Huffman, *IEEE Transactions on Information Theory*, Vol.24, No.6, pp. 668-674, ISSN: 0018-9448

Jiang, J. & Grecos, C. (2002). Towards an improvement on prediction accuracy in JPEG-LS, *Optical Engineering, SPIE*, Vol.41, No.2, pp. 335-341, ISSN 0091-3286

Maeda, H.; Minezawa, A.; Matsuda, I. & Itoh, S. (2006). Lossless Video Coding Using Multi-Frame MC and 3D Bi-Prediction Optimized for Each Frame, *Proc. 14th European Signal Processing Conference*, on CD.

Marcellin, M.; Gormish, M.; Bilgin, A. & Boliek, M. (2000). An Overview of JPEG-2000. *Proc. Data Compression Conference*, pp. 523-541.

Marusic, S. & Deng, G. (2002). Adaptive prediction for lossless image compression, *Signal Processing: Image Communications*, Vol.17, pp. 363-372, DOI 10.1016/S0923-5965(02)00006-1

Matsuda, I.; Shiodera, T. & Itoh, S. (2004). Lossless Video Coding Using Variable Block-Size MC and 3D Prediction Optimized for Each Frame, *Proc. European Signal Processing Conference*, pp. 1967-1970, ISSN 0913-5685

Matsuda, I.; Ozaki, N.; Umezu, Y. & Itoh S. (2005). Lossless coding using Variable Blok-Size adaptive prediction optimized for each image, *Proc. 13th European Signal Processing Conference*, on CD.

Meyer, B. & Tischer, P. (1997). TMW – a new method for lossless image compression, *Proc. International Picture Coding Symposium*, pp. 533-538, Berlin, Germany.

Meyer B. & Tischer P. (2001a). Glicbawls, Grey Level Image Compression by Adaptive Weighted Least Squares, *Proc. of Data Compression Conference*, p. 503, ISBN 0-7695-1031-0

Meyer, B. & Tischer, P. (2001b). TMWLego - An Object Oriented Image Modelling Framework, *Proc. Data Compression Conference*, p. 504, ISBN 0-7695-1031-0

Ohanian T. (1998). *Digital Nonlinear Editing: Editing Film and Video on the Desktop*, Focal Press, ISBN 978-0240802251

Sayood, K. (2002). *Introduction to Data Compression*, 2nd ed., Morgan Kaufmann Publishers, ISBN 978-1558605589

Seemann, T. & Tisher, P. (1997a). *Generalized locally adaptive DPCM*, Department of Computer Science Technical Report CS97/301, pp. 1-15, Monash University, Australia.

Seemann, T.; Tisher, P. & Meyer, B. (1997b). History-Based Blending of Image Sub-Predictors, *Proc. Picture Coding Symposium*, pp. 147-151.

Strutz, T. (2002). Context-Based Adaptive Linear Prediction for Lossless Image Coding, *Proc. 4th International ITG Conference on Source and Channel Coding*, pp. 105-109.

Ulacha, G. & Stasiński, R. (2008). Predictor Blending for Real-Time Lossless Coding System, *50th International Symposium ELMAR'08*, pp. 61-64, 10-13 September 2008, Zadar, Croatia.

Ulacha, G. & Dziurzański, P. (2008). Blending-prediction-based approach for lossless image compression, *Proc. 1st International Conference on Information Technology*, pp. 471-474.

Ulacha, G. & Dziurzański, P. (2009). Lossless and near-lossless image compression scheme utilizing blending-prediction-based approach, *Proc. International Conference on Computer Vision and Graphics*, LNCS Vol.5337, pp. 208-217, ISSN 0302-9743

Wang, H. & Zhang, D. (2004). A linear edge model and its application in lossless image coding, *Signal Processing: Image Communication*, Vol.19, pp. 955-958, DOI 10.1016/j.image.2004.04.006

Wang, Z.; Bovik, A. C.; Sheikh, H. R. & Simoncelli, E. P. (2004). Image Quality Assessment: From Error Visibility to Structural Similarity, *IEEE Transactions on Image Processing*, Vol.13, No.4, pp. 600-612, DOI 10.1109/TIP.2003.819861

Weinberger, M. J.; Seroussi, G. & Sapiro, G. (2000). LOCO-I: Lossless Image Compression Algorithm: Principles and Standardization into JPEG-LS, *IEEE Trans. on Image Processing*, Vol.9, No.8, pp. 1309-1324, ISSN 1057-7149

Wu, X. & Memon, N. D. (1996). CALIC – A Context Based Adaptive Lossless Image Coding Scheme, *IEEE Trans. on Communications*, Vol.45, pp. 437-444, ISSN 0916-8516

Xie, X.; Li, G.L. & Wang, Z.H. (2007). A Near-Lossless Image Compression Algorithm Suitable for Hardware Design in Wireless Endoscopy System, *EURASIP Journal on Advances in Signal Processing*, (2007) pp. 48-61, DOI 10.1155/2007/82160

Yang, K. H. & Faryar, A. F. (2000). A contex-based predictive coder for lossless and near-lossless compression of video, *Proc. International Conference on Image Processing*, Vol.1, pp. 144-147, ISBN 978-1-4244-7994-8

Ye, H. (2002). *A study on lossless compression of greyscale images*, Ph. D thesis, Department of Electronic Engineering, La Trobe University.

Ye, H.; Deng, G. & Devlin, J. C. (2000). Adaptive linear prediction for lossless coding of greyscale images, *Proc. IEEE International Conference on Image Processing*, on CD.

CCSDS (2007). *Lossless Data Compression. Recommendation for Space Data System Standards, CCSDS 120.1-G-1* Green Book, 1.

# 8

# Novel Video Coder Using Multiwavelets

Sudhakar Radhakrishnan
*Professor and Head, Department of ECE,*
*Dr. Mahalingam College of Engineering and Technology,*
*India*

## 1. Introduction

Information has become one of the most valuable assets in the modern era. Recent technology has introduced the paradigm of digital information and its associated benefits and drawbacks. A thousand pictures require a very large amount of storage. While the advancement of computer storage technology continues at a rapid pace a means of reducing the storage requirements of an image and video is still needed in most situations. Thus, the science of digital image and video compression has emerged. For example, one of the formats defined for High Definition Television (HDTV) (Ben Waggoner 2002) broadcasting is 1920 pixels horizontally by 1080 lines vertically, at 30 frames per second. If these numbers are multiplied together with 8 bits for each of the three primary colors, the total data rate required would be 1.5 GB/sec approximately. So compression is highly necessary. This storage capacity seems to be more impressive when it is realized that the intent is to deliver very high quality video to the end user with as few visible artifacts as possible. Current methods of video compression such as Moving Pictures Experts Group (MPEG) standard (Peter Symes 2000, Keith Jack 1996) can provide good performance in terms of retaining video quality while reducing the storage requirements. But even the popular standards like MPEG have limitations.

Research in new and better methods of image and video compression is ongoing, and recent results suggest that some newer techniques may provide much greater performance. This motivates to go for video compression. An extension of image compression algorithms based on multiwavelets and making them suitable for video (as video contains sequence of still pictures) is essential. This chapter gives a summary of the new multiwavelet decomposition algorithm along with quantization techniques and illustrates their potential for inclusion in new video compression applications and standards (Sudhakar et al., 2009, Sudhakar & Jayaraman 2007, Sudhakar & Jayaraman 2008). Video coding for telecommunication applications has evolved through the development of the ISO/IEC MPEG-1, MPEG-2 and ITU-T H.261, H.262 and H.263 video coding standards (and later enhancements of H.263 known as H.263+ and H.263++), (Iain E.G. Richardson 2002) and has diversified from ISDN and T1/E1 service to embrace PSTN, mobile wireless networks, and LAN/Internet network delivery.

## 2. Significance of the present work

Multiwavelets (Cheung, K.W & Po L.M, 1997.; Chui, C.K. & Lian J., 1996) are beginning only now to approach the maturity of development of their scalar counterparts Wavelets and DCT (Xiong et al., 1999.; Devore et al 1992; Gilbert Strang & Truong Nguyen 1996) A few papers that have tested the image compression properties of multiwavelets suggest that multiwavelets (Cotronei et al 2000; Shen 1997; Strela et al 1999; Gilbert Strang & Strela 1994; Michael & Amy E. Bell 2001 and Michael, B.M 1999) can sometimes perform as well as or better than scalar wavelets and DCT. But to date, no researchers have pursued this more thoroughly with the intention of determining whether multiwavelets might be a better choice for video compression than scalar wavelets and DCT. In this chapter, evaluations of the performance of state-of-the-art multiwavelet methods for compression of general classes of videos have been presented. The videos taken for comparison include 'Football', 'Dancer', 'Claire', 'Foreman', 'Trevor' and 'Miss America'. This chapter presents the following new results:

- An efficient algorithm is presented for motion estimation with half pixel accuracy using fast approach algorithms. A comparison between the popularly used block matching algorithm (Diamond search algorithm) (Shan Zhu & Kai-Kuang Ma 2000) and the new Kite cross diamond algorithm (Chi-Wai Lam et al 2004) is provided.
- A comparison between the best known multiwavelets and the best known scalar wavelets is made. Both quantitative and qualitative measures of performance are examined for several videos.
- A novel video encoder combining the advantages of multiwavelets, Kite Cross Diamond Search algorithm and the novel scheme is also provided.

## 3. Proposed video coder

This section deals with proposed video coder and the new concepts which matches with the existing standards. The proposed novel encoder is shown in Figure 1. The new schemes used in this video coder are highlighted first and are explained in the subsequent sections.

- In Intra frame coding the following new schemes are introduced.
  - Multiwavelet transform is used for coding the frames (I-frames)
  - 'SPIHT', 'SPECK', 'Novel scheme' is used for coding of multiwavelet coefficients
- In Inter frame coding the following new schemes are introduced.
  - Fast algorithms for motion estimation
  - Half pixel accuracy motion estimation
  - Predictive coding of motion vectors
  - Multiple reference frame motion compensation

### 3.1 Intra frame coding

Removing the spatial redundancy within a frame is called as intraframe coding. Normally I-frames are coded in this way. This is achieved using transform. There are many transforms like 'DCT', 'DWT', and Multiwavelet transform. As it is obvious that 'DCT' introduces blocking artifacts, normally 'DWT' is used in JPEG 2000 (Skodras, A.N et al 2000). As demonstrated in the papers (Sudhakar et al., 2009; Sudhakar & Jayaraman 2007; Sudhakar & Jayaraman 2008), that multiwavelet transform supersedes wavelets in still image compression, in this proposed coder multiwavelet based transform is extended for video also. The simple reason is that video is a set of still frames arranged in a regular order. Before applying the multiwavelet transform to the input images or residuals, the image is to be preprocessed. The prefilter (Strela, V., 1996; Strela, V., 1998) is chosen corresponding to the filters chosen for applying multiwavelet transforms (Strela, V & Walden A.T., 1998; Strela V et al., 1999). Similarly, the post processing is to be done at the receiver side.

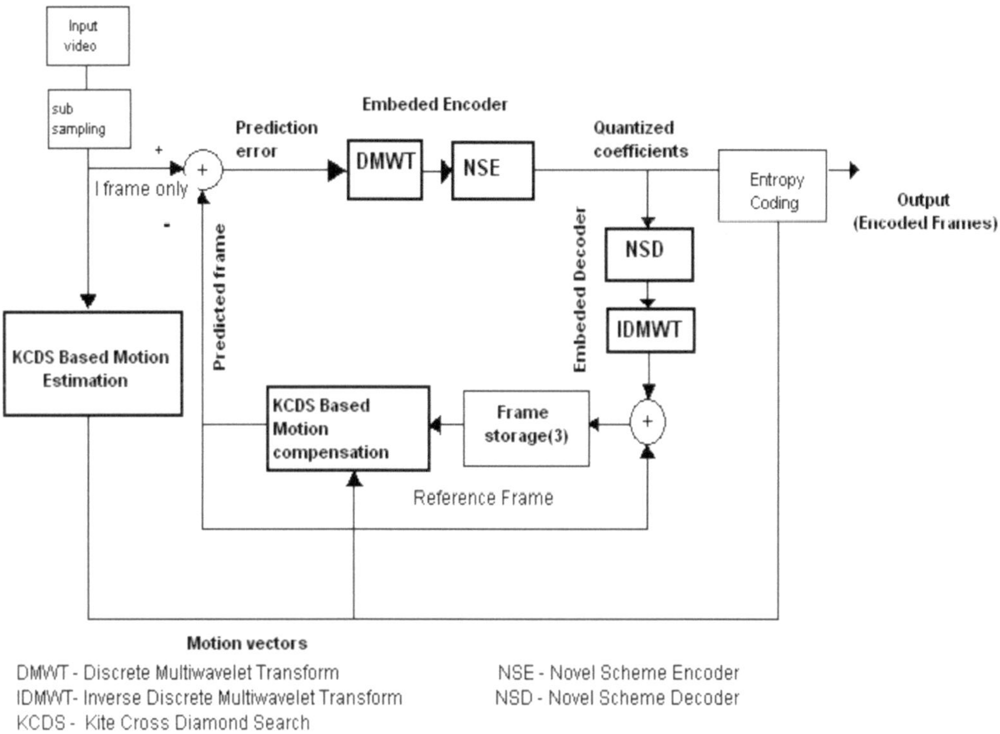


Fig. 1. Block diagram of the Proposed Novel encoder

### 3.1.1 Coding of multiwavelet coefficients

The coding and quantization of the multiwavelet coefficients could be done by SPIHT or SPECK algorithm. The coding of the multiwavelet coefficients using SPIHT and SPECK (Said A & Pearlman 1996; Pearlman et al. 2004) are explained and completely available in the papers (Sudhakar et al., 2009; Sudhakar & Jayaraman 2007; Sudhakar & Jayaraman 2008). Compression is the result of quantization. In this work different multiwavelets (Sudhakar, R.; & Jayaraman, S., 2008) are used and their performances are studied. SPIHT performs better for high bit rate but produces poor quality at low bit rates. SPECK performs well at low bit rates but results in poor compression. So a novel scheme is introduced. In this coder the 'Y' and 'U' components are coded using 'SPIHT' and the 'V' component is coded using 'SPECK' at 75% of the rates used in 'SPIHT'. The very first frame or every twelfth frame of video sequences is coded as I-frame. Every other frame is coded as P-frame. If the mean square error between the predicted frame and the actual frame is greater than the threshold then the current frame is coded as the I-frame. The 'bpp' settings of SPIHT encoder for residual are set to very less rate compared to the I-frame rate.

#### 3.1.2 Entropy coding
The purpose of the entropy coding algorithm (Lei and Sun 1991), is to represent frequently occurring (run, level) pairs with a short code and less frequently occurring pairs with a longer code. In this way, the run-level data may be compressed into a small number of bits. Huffman coding and arithmetic coding are used widely for entropy coding of image and video data. In this chapter Huffman coding is used as the entropy coding.

### 3.2 Inter frame coding
The temporal redundancy between the successive frames is removed by interframe prediction. This is achieved by Motion estimation and compensation. An efficient fast motion estimation algorithm to predict the current frame from the previous reference frames is used. Here the motion estimation is done up to half pixel accuracy. The detailed explanations are given in the subsequent sections

#### 3.2.1 Fast motion estimation algortihm
Full search (FS) block motion estimation matches all possible points within a search area in the reference (target) frame to find the block with the minimum block distortion measure (BDM). Thus this algorithm gives the best possible results. However, a full search algorithm accounts for about two-thirds of the total computational power and it is very intensive computationally. Due to the high requirement of intensive computation for the full search algorithm many fast motion algorithms (Peter Symes 2000) have been proposed over the last two decades to give a faster estimation with similar block distortion compared to the full search method. The most well known fast Block Motion Algorithms (BMA) are the three-step search (TSS) (Li et al 1994; Koga et al 1981), the new three-step search (NTSS), the four-step search (4SS) (Po Ma 1996) and the diamond search (DS) (Shan Zhu and Kai-Kuang Ma 2000). Diamond search is more popular among the existing standards. The main aim of these fast search algorithms is to reduce the number of search points in the search window and hence the computations. This is completely evident from the Table. 1. The motion field for a block of a real world image sequence is gentle, smooth usually and varies slowly. One of the most important assumptions of all fast motion estimation algorithm is 'error surface is monotonic' i.e. BDM is the least at the center or the global minima of the search area and it increases monotonically as the checking point moves away from the global minima.

| Video | FS | TSS | NTSS | 4SS | DS | KCDS |
|---|---|---|---|---|---|---|
| **Trevor** | 202.1 | 23.2 | 20.67 | 18.65 | 16.25 | 12.67 |
| **Dancer** | 202.1 | 23.24 | 21.38 | 18.80 | 16.84 | 12.89 |
| **Foot ball** | 202.1 | 23.06 | 17.65 | 16.69 | 13.67 | 7.73 |
| **Miss America** | 202.1 | 23.46 | 19.99 | 18.319 | 16.36 | 9.54 |
| **Claire** | 202.1 | 23.22 | 15.924 | 16.19 | 12.4 | 5.23 |

Table 1. Average Searching Points for different fast searching Algorithms

Many fast motion estimation algorithms is based on the centre biased motion vector distribution. But this assumption may not hold for videos with very fast motions. Kite Cross Diamond Search (KCDS) algorithm (Chi-Wai Lam et al 2004) which is based on the cross centre biased distribution characteristics is employed in this chapter.

### 3.2.2 Half pixel accuracy motion estimation

Fractional pixel motion estimation is employed in modern coding standards in which the displacement of an object between two frames in videos is not an integer no of pixels. Here motion vectors are used. These vectors point to candidate blocks that are placed at half pixel locations. It is advantageous to place a candidate block at fractional location. This gives better matching properties than at an integer location. Further it helps to reduce the degree of error between origilnal and predicted image. Interpolating linearly or bilinearly the nearest pixels at integer locations, it is possible to obtain the pixel values in the fractional locations. But the demerit here is that the computational overhead increases.
Hence it becomes necessary to save the computation overhead. Conventional encoders can be used for this purpose. The process of motion estimation in this conventional encoder is dealt in two steps.

1. Criteria minimum is found at integer location.
2. Interpolation of candidate block correponding to the eight nearest half pixel displacement motion vectors as shown in fig. 2

Interpolation is done to the best integer and motion vector is refined into sbupixel by computing the criterain between the current block and its eight half pixel candidate block. Real time encoder finds this process too difficult to be implemented because of its complexity in computation, hence much faster methods have been investigated in the literature (Lee and Chen 1997).

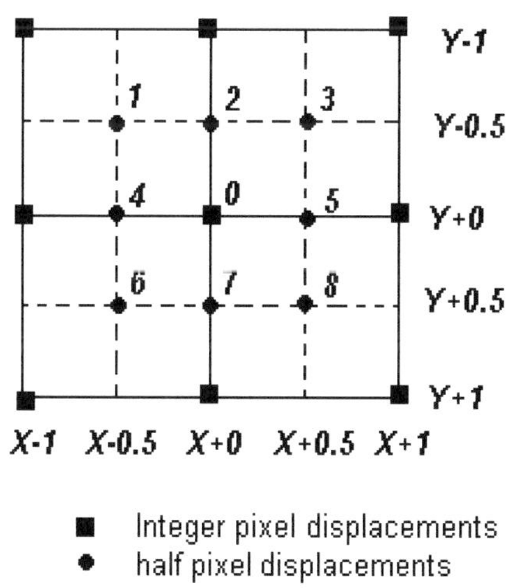


Fig. 2. Integer and half pixel displacements

### 3.2.3 Predictive coding of motion vectors

The motion vectors are predicted from the previously coded motion vectors (Lee et al 2000) so as to reduce the number of bits required to code them. Variable bit rate coding is used to encode the difference. Based on the previously found motion vectors, a predicted vector MVp is formed, which depends on the motion compensation partition size and its availability of nearby vectors. The Motion Vector Difference (MVD) between current and predicted vector is encoded and transmitted. Variable bit length coding is used for encoding the difference. Short codes are used code the most frequenly occuring motion vector. Figure 3 shows the actual motion vectors and the difference between the predicted one and the actual motion vectors.

| | | | |
|---|---|---|---|
| 1.5 | 1.0 | -0.5 | -1.5 |
| 1.0 | 1.5 | 2.0 | 1.5 |
| 0.5 | -0.5 | -0.5 | -1.0 |
| -0.5 | -0.5 | -1.0 | -1.5 |

(a)

| | | | |
|---|---|---|---|
| 1.5 | 0.5 | 1.5 | 1.0 |
| 0.5 | -0.5 | -0.5 | 0.5 |
| 0.5 | 1.0 | 0.0 | 0.5 |
| 1.0 | 0.0 | 0.5 | 0.5 |

(b)

Fig. 3. (a) Actual motion vectors (b) Difference between the predicted and actual motion vectors

Now the difference is encoded as:

- First bit represents the sign of the difference; negative difference is represented by 1 and positive as 0.
- Next to the sign bit is M ones followed by one zero; M is the absolute value of difference.
- Last bit represent the decimal value; 0.5 is represented as 1 and 0.0 is represented as 0

For example, -1.0 and 0.5 are coded as

-1.0 → 1100
0.5 → 001

## 4. Block diagram of the proposed decoder system

The block diagram of the proposed decoder is shown in the figure 4. Here every step is a reverse process to the encoder except the motion prediction. By using the reference frames and the decoded motion vectors a new frame is reconstructed by motion compensation method.

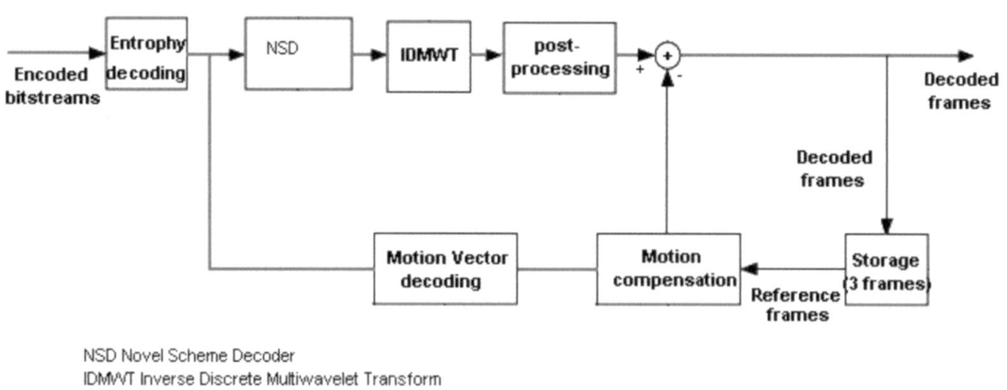


Fig. 4. Block diagram of the proposed decoder system

## 5. Results and discussion

This section has four sub sections. Section 5.1 deals with "SPIHT results" and it gives the information about the performance of SPIHT due to the variation of I rate and P rate. Several comparisons are made here like comparison between 'DS' and 'KCDS' and also between Wavelet and Multiwavelet. Section 5.2 discusses the results between 'SPECK' and 'Novel scheme'. This section also features the performance of 'SPECK' for different videos and the comparison among SPIHT, SPECK and Novel scheme. Novel scheme is one in which the 'Y' and 'U' components are coded with 'SPIHT' but 'V' component is coded using SPECK at 75% of rate used in 'SPIHT'. Summary of the results is provided in section 5.3. Section 5.4 deals with reconstructed frames illustrating the Comparison of 'SPIHT', 'SPECK' and 'Novel scheme'. In this work, two sets of video sequences are used. First set is CIF (352 × 288) which includes "Dancer", "Football" video sequences. The other set is QCIF (176 × 144) with the video sequences, "Claire", "Foreman", "Trevor" and "Miss America". The videos used are listed in the Table 2 and their visuals are shown in Figure 5, followed by some description about them.

| Name | Frame Size |
|---|---|
| Claire | 144 × 176 |
| Foreman | 144 × 176 |
| Trevor | 144 × 176 |
| Miss America | 144 × 176 |
| Dancer | 288 × 352 |
| Football | 288 × 352 |

Table 2. List of test videos

The 'Claire' and 'Miss America' videos have very small motions with still background and contain the motion of only one object. The 'foreman' has large motion and variable background due to camera motion. 'Trevor' video has random motions involving different objects. The 'Dancer' video has moving background and contains the slow motions of two objects. The 'football' video has a very large motion without moving background in the opposite direction. It also contains the motion of many objects moving with different velocities.

The parameters used here are PSNR and Compression ratio. The video format used is "YUV". Each component i.e. 'Y', 'U', 'V' are processed separately and hence the peak signal value is 255. The average of these 3 values will give the average PSNR for a particular frame. When many frames are considered the average PSNR for all the frames is used as the performance factor.

The PSNR in dB for an M × N Video frame for each component is calculated as

$$PSNR = 10 \log \left( \frac{255^2}{MSE} \right) dB \tag{1}$$

where the mean square error (MSE) is defined as

$$MSE = \frac{1}{MN} \sum_{m=0}^{N-1} \sum_{n=0}^{N-1} \mid x(m,n) - \hat{x}(m,n)|^2 \tag{2}$$

Compression ratio (CR) is calculated as CR = M × N × 3 × 8 × No of Frames / No of bits after coding. M × N is the size of the frame

(a) (b) (c) (d)

(f) (e)

Fig. 5. Test videos (a) 'Claire', (b) 'Foreman', (c)'Trevor', (d) 'Miss America' , (e)'Dancer' and (f)'Football'

The other conventions used are the 'I' rate and 'P' rate. 'I' rate is the rate at which the reference or intra frame is coded and 'P' rate is the rate at which the residue is coded. Residue is the difference between the reference frame and the predicted frame. Both have the unit of bpp (bits per pixel). Similarly, the default search algorithm is 'KCDS', and default transform is Multiwavelet. In the case of discrepancy, these conventions can be assumed as default. The multiwavelet filters (Sudhakar, R.; & Jayaraman, S., 2008) used in this work are symmetric / anti symmetric multifilter ("Sa4"), Chui-Lian orthogonal multifilter ("Cl"), "GHM" pair of multifilters, and Cardinal 2-balanced orthogonal multifilter ("Cardbal2"). The corresponding prefilters used are "Sa4ap", "Clap", "Ghmmap", and "Id" respectively. The scalar wavelet filter taken for comparison are Haar wavelet ("Haar"), Daubechies 4 coefficient scalar filter ("Db4") and Daubechies 8 coefficient scalar filter ("La8").

### 5.1 'SPIHT' results

The results are observed with 'I' rate = 0.9 and 'P' rate = 0.05.

### 5.1.1 'Claire' video

Here "Cardbal2" performs well in terms of Average PSNR and "Cl" produces higher compression ratio. In terms of search algorithm, 'KCDS' and 'DS' almost perform equally in terms of average PSNR with 'KCDS' gives better compression ratio.

| Wavelet | Average PSNR (dB) | CR |
|---|---|---|
| Haar | 38.49 | 73.34 |
| Db4 | 39.51 | 72.12 |
| La8 | 39.7 | 72.32 |

Table 3. Comparison of average 'PSNR', 'CR' for different Wavelets in 'Claire' video (84 Frames) using 'KCDS'

| Multiwavelet | Average PSNR (dB) | | CR | |
|---|---|---|---|---|
| | KCDS | DS | KCDS | DS |
| Sa4 | 38.99 | 38.98 | 81.61 | 78.95 |
| Cl | 39.11 | 39.14 | 82.47 | 79.41 |
| GHM | 39.21 | 39.21 | 72.64 | 70.56 |
| Cardbal2 | 39.59 | 39.58 | 71.35 | 69.46 |

Table 4. Comparison of average 'PSNR', 'CR' for different multiwavelets in 'Claire' video (84 Frames)

### 5.1.2 'Foreman' video

Here "GHM" multifilter performs better in terms of average PSNR and "Cl" in terms of compression ratio. "Sa4" performs better as well. In all the cases 'KCDS' performs marginally better than 'DS'.

| Wavelet | Average PSNR (dB) | CR |
|---|---|---|
| Haar | 35.87 | 67.57 |
| Db4 | 36.1 | 66.36 |
| La8 | 36.31 | 66.19 |

Table 5. Comparison of average 'PSNR', 'CR' for different Wavelets in 'Foreman' video (84 Frames) using 'KCDS'

| Multiwavelet | Average PSNR (dB) | | CR | |
|---|---|---|---|---|
| | KCDS | DS | KCDS | DS |
| Sa4 | 35.87 | 35.85 | 73.39 | 69.14 |
| Cl | 35.71 | 35.68 | 73.71 | 69.68 |
| GHM | 36.21 | 36.17 | 65.05 | 62.21 |
| Cardbal2 | 36.12 | 36.08 | 67.03 | 63.69 |

Table 6. Comparison of average 'PSNR', 'CR' for different multiwavelets in 'Foreman' video (84 Frames)

### 5.1.3 'Dancer' video

Here in terms of multiwavelet "cardbal2" performs better in terms of average PSNR and "Cl" in terms of compression ratio. Here also, "Sa4" performs better. 'DS' performs marginally better than KCDS in terms of average PSNR and 'KCDS' perform better in terms of compression ratio.

| Wavelet | Average PSNR (dB) | CR |
|---|---|---|
| Haar | 38.1 | 53.69 |
| Db4 | 38.63 | 53.27 |
| La8 | 38.76 | 52.95 |

Table 7. Comparison of average 'PSNR', 'CR' for different Wavelets in 'Dancer' video (84 Frames) using 'KCDS'

| Multiwavelet | Average PSNR (dB) | | CR | |
|---|---|---|---|---|
| | KCDS | DS | KCDS | DS |
| Sa4 | 37.82 | 37.82 | 56.27 | 55.67 |
| Cl | 37.65 | 37.69 | 56.55 | 55.86 |
| GHM | 37.76 | 37.84 | 51.99 | 51.38 |
| Cardbal2 | 38.08 | 38.11 | 51.56 | 51.04 |

Table 8. Comparison of average 'PSNR', 'CR' for different Multiwavelets in 'Dancer' video (84 Frames)

### 5.1.4 'Football' video

Here in terms of multiwavelet "cardbal2" performs better in terms of average 'PSNR' and "Cl" in terms of compression ratio. But overall "Sa4" performs better. In all the cases KCDS performs marginally better than DS.

| Wavelet | Average PSNR (dB) | CR |
|---|---|---|
| Haar | 32.02 | 43.29 |
| Db4 | 32.47 | 42.94 |
| La8 | 32.31 | 44.31 |

Table 9. Comparison of average 'PSNR', 'CR' for different Wavelets in 'Football' video (84 Frames) using 'KCDS'

| Multiwavelet | Average PSNR (dB) | | CR | |
|---|---|---|---|---|
| | KCDS | DS | KCDS | DS |
| Sa4 | 32.43 | 32.41 | 46.69 | 46.67 |
| Cl | 31.88 | 30.57 | 48.32 | 48.29 |
| GHM | 32.49 | 31.87 | 42.88 | 41.98 |
| Cardbal2 | 32.53 | 32.50 | 43.15 | 43.10 |

Table 10. Comparison of average 'PSNR', 'CR' for different multiwavelets in 'Football' video (84 Frames)

### 5.1.5 'Trevor' video

Here "Cardbal2" performs better in terms of average 'PSNR' and "Cl" in terms of compression ratio. But overall "Sa4" performs better. In all the cases 'KCDS' performs marginally better than DS.

| Wavelet | Average PSNR (dB) | CR |
|---|---|---|
| Haar | 34.8 | 70.2 |
| Db4 | 35.33 | 68.48 |
| La8 | 35.53 | 68.17 |

Table 11. Comparison of average 'PSNR', 'CR' for different Wavelets in 'Trevor' video (84 Frames) using 'KCDS'

| Multiwavelet | Average PSNR(dB) | | CR | |
|---|---|---|---|---|
| | KCDS | DS | KCDS | DS |
| Sa4 | 36.46 | 36.44 | 77.02 | 75.39 |
| Cl | 36.08 | 36.04 | 78.61 | 76.71 |
| GHM | 36.58 | 36.55 | 69.36 | 68.11 |
| Cardbal2 | 36.61 | 36.58 | 68.96 | 67.74 |

Table 12. Comparison of average 'PSNR', 'CR' for different multiwavelets in 'Trevor' video (84 Frames)

### 5.1.6 'Miss America' video

Here "Cardbal2" performs better in terms of average 'PSNR' and "Sa4" in terms of compression ratio.

| Wavelet | Average PSNR (dB) | CR |
|---|---|---|
| Haar | 39.14 | 67.82 |
| Db4 | 39.65 | 67.53 |
| La8 | 39.77 | 67.51 |

Table 13. Comparison of average PSNR, CR for different Wavelets in 'Miss America' video (84 Frames) using 'KCDS'

| Multiwavelet | Average PSNR(dB) | | CR | |
|---|---|---|---|---|
| | KCDS | DS | KCDS | DS |
| Sa4 | 38.81 | 37.44 | 76.37 | 75.39 |
| Cl | 38.75 | 37.45 | 75.21 | 75.11 |
| GHM | 38.36 | 37.54 | 70.02 | 69.01 |
| Cardbal2 | 39.37 | 37.62 | 67.31 | 66.32 |

Table 14. Comparison of average 'PSNR', CR' for different multiwavelets in a 'Miss America' video (84 Frames)

| Video | Wavelet/ Multiwavelet | Average PSNR (dB) for a 'I' rate of | | | |
|---|---|---|---|---|---|
| | | 0.6 | 0.8 | 0.9 | 1 |
| Miss America | Sa4 | 35.78 | 37.96 | 38.59 | 39.37 |
| | Cl | 35.69 | 37.88 | 38.49 | 39.37 |
| | La8 | 36.56 | 38.49 | 39.44 | 39.83 |
| Trevor | Sa4 | 33.18 | 35.72 | 36.67 | 37.39 |
| | Cl | 32.88 | 35.36 | 36.29 | 37.1 |
| | La8 | 33.21 | 36.31 | 37.09 | 37.65 |

Table 15. Average PSNR values for different 'I' rates with a constant 'P' rate of 0.05 bpp; 96 frames

| Video | Wavelet/ Multiwavelet | CR (for a 'I' rate of) | | | |
|---|---|---|---|---|---|
| | | 0.6 | 0.8 | 0.9 | 1 |
| Miss America | Sa4 | 96.04 | 83.01 | 77.41 | 71.53 |
| | Cl | 96.74 | 83.02 | 77.39 | 71.68 |
| | La8 | 85.74 | 73.86 | 68.24 | 63.76 |
| Trevor | Sa4 | 101.71 | 87.66 | 80.92 | 74.84 |
| | Cl | 102.35 | 89.13 | 82.38 | 75.98 |
| | La8 | 91.02 | 78.35 | 72.55 | 67.35 |

Table 16. CR values for different 'I' rates with a constant 'P' rate of 0.05 bpp; 96 frames

The results available in Tables 15 and 16 show the variation of I rate with constant 'P' rate, for two different videos 'Miss America' (slow motion) and 'Trevor' (Fast and Random motion). Irrespective of the videos, the PSNR values show an improvement as 'I' rate increases, with the reduction of compression ratio. The Compression ratio (roughly 5 to 10) is increased in the case of multiwavelets compared to wavelets, irrespective of the videos.

| Video | Wavelet/ Multiwavelet | Average PSNR (For a 'P' rate of) | | | |
|---|---|---|---|---|---|
| | | 0.01 | 0.05 | 0.07 | 0.1 |
| Miss America | Sa4 | 38.33 | 38.59 | 38.7 | 38.93 |
| | Cl | 38.22 | 38.49 | 38.62 | 38.86 |
| | La8 | 39.21 | 39.44 | 39.6 | 39.79 |
| Trevor | Sa4 | 36.4 | 36.67 | 36.77 | 36.96 |
| | Cl | 36.04 | 36.29 | 36.4 | 36.57 |
| | La8 | 36.81 | 37.08 | 37.24 | 37.46 |

Table 17. Average PSNR values for the variation of 'P' rate with a constant 'I' rate of 0.9 bpp; 96 frames

The results available in tables 17 and 18 show the variation of 'P' rate with constant 'I' rate, for two different videos 'Miss America' (slow motion) and 'Trevor'(Fast and Random motion). The PSNR is increased with the increase in P rate with a little variation, at the same time compression ratio is increased in a larger way.

| Video | Wavelet/ Multiwavelet | Compression Ratio (for a 'P' rate of) | | | |
|---|---|---|---|---|---|
| | | 0.01 | 0.05 | 0.07 | 0.1 |
| Miss America | Sa4 | 81.42 | 77.4 | 74.43 | 69.81 |
| | Cl | 81.23 | 77.39 | 74.32 | 69.59 |
| | La8 | 71.28 | 68.24 | 65.93 | 60.78 |
| Trevor | Sa4 | 86.32 | 80.92 | 77.48 | 71.93 |
| | Cl | 87.52 | 82.38 | 79.02 | 73.38 |
| | La8 | 76.49 | 72.54 | 69.71 | 65.39 |

Table 18. 'CR' values for the variation of 'P' rate with a constant 'I' rate of 0.9 bpp; 96 frames

### 5.2 'SPECK' and 'Novel scheme' results

#### 5.2.1 'SPECK' results

From the above tables it is evident that "Sa4" multiwavelet performs better. Hence the following results are achieved with "Sa4" as the reference. KCDS is used as a prediction technique. From the results available in Table 19, 'SPECK' performs well for all the videos with less compression ratio compared to 'SPIHT' results shown in the previous section. On comparing the results available in table 20, SPECK performs better than SPIHT for all the videos at low bit rate (0.4 bpp) whereas SPIHT performs better than SPECK at a bit rate of 1.0 bpp.

| Videos | Average PSNR (dB) | CR |
|---|---|---|
| Claire | 40.07 | 54.48 |
| Trevor | 34.79 | 53.95 |
| Foreman | 36.44 | 53.20 |
| Miss America | 39.49 | 52.79 |

Table 19. Performance of 'SPECK' for different videos with 'I' rate of 0.9bpp and 'P' rate of 0.07bpp; 84 frames

| Videos | Average PSNR for SPECK | Average PSNR for SPIHT |
|---|---|---|
| 'I' rate=1bpp and 'p' rate=0.01bpp | | |
| Claire | 40.56 | 41.1 |
| Trevor | 34.8 | 36.99 |
| Miss America | 41.04 | 41.29 |
| Foreman | 38.67 | 38.3 |
| Dancer | 38.49 | 44.47 |
| 'I' rate=1bpp and 'p' rate=0.01bpp | | |
| Claire | 36.13 | 30.07 |
| Trevor | 31.48 | 26.53 |
| Miss America | 36.64 | 32.03 |
| Foreman | 34.54 | 27.54 |
| Dancer | 36.82 | 29.6 |

Table 20. Comparison between 'SPIHT' and 'SPECK' for different 'I' rates

#### 5.2.2 'Novel scheme' results

The results of the 'Novel scheme' explained previously are available in table 21. The multiwavelet chosen is "Sa4". It is shown that the novel scheme performs well for all the videos both in terms of 'PSNR' and 'CR'.

| Videos | Average PSNR (dB) | CR |
|---|---|---|
| Claire | 39.67 | 75.79 |
| Trevor | 35.32 | 72.67 |
| Foreman | 36.11 | 68.82 |
| Miss America | 38.72 | 71.22 |

Table 21. Performance of 'Novel scheme' for different videos with 'I' rate of 0.9bpp 'P' rate of 0.07bpp; 84 frames

### 5.3 Summary of results

#### 5.3.1 Comparison between 'DS' and 'KCDS'

As mentioned previously "Sa4" multiwavelet performs well, and all the comparisons are with respect to "Sa4" alone. From the results available in table 22, 'KCDS' performs better than 'DS' both in terms of Average PSNR and compression ratio.

| Videos | Average PSNR | | CR | |
|---|---|---|---|---|
| | KCDS | DS | KCDS | DS |
| Claire | 38.99 | 38.98 | 81.61 | 78.95 |
| Trevor | 36.46 | 36.44 | 77.02 | 75.39 |
| Foreman | 35.87 | 35.87 | 73.39 | 69.14 |
| Dancer | 37.82 | 37.82 | 56.27 | 55.67 |

Table 22. Comparison between 'DS' and 'KCDS using 'SPIHT' for different videos with 'I' rate of 0.9bpp; 'P' rate of 0.05bpp; 84 frames

| Videos | Average PSNR(dB) | | Compression Ratio | | Execution time (Secs) | |
|---|---|---|---|---|---|---|
| | KCDS | DS | KCDS | DS | KCDS | DS |
| Claire | 38.84 | 38.81 | 79.07 | 76.45 | 189 | 201 |
| Foreman | 35.39 | 35.39 | 71.24 | 67.17 | 200 | 211 |
| Trevor | 33.53 | 33.54 | 75.34 | 74.14 | 194 | 202 |
| Dancer | 37.52 | 37.59 | 56.27 | 55.52 | 2796 | 2892 |
| Football | 32.24 | 31.62 | 46.72 | 49.74 | 3640 | 3365 |

Table 23. Comparison between 'DS' and 'KCDS' in 'Novel scheme' for different videos with 'I' rate of 0.8bpp; 'P' rate of 0.08bpp; 84 frames

From the results shown in table 23, it is completely evident that for all the videos 'KCDS' and 'DS' performs equally in terms of PSNR with 'KCDS' resulting in higher compression ratio. For the same PSNR, 'KCDS' is faster than 'DS'. In Football video 'KCDS' produces better PSNR and hence it takes more time than 'DS'.

| Videos | Average PSNR (dB) | | CR | |
|---|---|---|---|---|
| | Sa4 | La8 | Sa4 | La8 |
| Claire | 38.99 | 39.88 | 81.61 | 79.5 |
| Trevor | 36.46 | 36.94 | 77.02 | 69.4 |
| Foreman | 35.87 | 36.52 | 73.39 | 66.86 |
| Dancer | 37.82 | 38.27 | 56.27 | 51.36 |

Table 24. Comparison between wavelet and multiwavelet using 'SPIHT' with 'P' rate of 0.05bpp; 'I' rate of 0.9bpp; 84 frames (KCDS)

| Videos | Average PSNR (dB) for SPECK; I-rate:0.8bpp; P-rate:0.08bpp | | Average PSNR (dB) for Novel Scheme I-rate:0.8bpp; P-rate:0.08bpp | |
|---|---|---|---|---|
| | **La8** | **Sa4** | **La8** | **Sa4** |
| Claire | 37.42 | 39.95 | 37.95 | 38.84 |
| Foreman | 32.54 | 36.18 | 33.19 | 35.39 |
| Trevor | 29.07 | 33.34 | 31.98 | 33.53 |
| Dancer | 34.39 | 37.22 | 36.33 | 37.52 |
| Football | 31.85 | 32.76 | 31.67 | 32.24 |
| | **CR for SPECK I-rate:0.8bpp; P-rate:0.08bpp** | | **CR for Novel Scheme; I-rate:0.8bpp; P-rate:0.08bpp** | |
| | **La8** | **Sa4** | **La8** | **Sa4** |
| Claire | 57.29 | 57.41 | 73.99 | 79.07 |
| Foreman | 56.72 | 56.67 | 67.32 | 71.24 |
| Trevor | 57.53 | 57.55 | 71.53 | 75.34 |
| Dancer | 48.45 | 48.84 | 54.09 | 56.27 |
| Football | 43.34 | 43.38 | 44.63 | 46.72 |
| | **Execution time(Secs) for SPECK I-rate:0.8bpp; P-rate:0.08bpp** | | **Execution time(Secs) for Novel Scheme I-rate:0.8bpp; P-rate:0.08bpp** | |
| | **La8** | **Sa4** | **La8** | **Sa4** |
| Claire | 441 | **185** | 443 | **189** |
| Foreman | 444 | **198** | 456 | **200** |
| Trevor | 448 | **198** | 453 | **194** |
| Dancer | 3314 | **2332** | 3838 | **2796** |
| Football | 3672 | **2735** | 4743 | **3640** |

Table 25. Comparison of wavelet and multiwavelet using 'SPECK' and 'Novel scheme' with respect to average PSNR,CR and execution time; 84 frames

### 5.3.2 Comparison between wavelet and multiwavelet

The performance of wavelets and multiwavelets using "SPIHT", for different videos are displayed in table 24. Here, 'La8' performs better for all videos in terms of average PSNR and 'Sa4' in terms of compression ratio. Hence the conclusion is that irrespective of the videos selected, multiwavelet gives good Compression ratio with nearing average PSNR as that of wavelets.

### 5.3.3 Comparison between wavelet and multiwavelet in 'SPECK' and 'Novel scheme'

From the results available in table 25, multiwavelet performs better than wavelets in both 'SPECK' and 'Novel scheme' for all the videos in terms of PSNR, CR, and Execution time.

### 5.3.4 Comparison between 'SPIHT', 'SPECK' and 'Novel scheme'

The results available in table 26, are taken with I rate of 0.8 and 'P' rate of 0.08. The first 84 frames are considered for all the videos. In general 'SPECK' performs better in terms of average PSNR and execution time but with poor compression ratio for all the videos. Novel scheme is found to be a close competitor with better compression ratio. 'SPIHT' yields high compression ratio but it is very slow. Novel scheme matches 'SPIHT' closely and it is also faster than 'SPIHT'. In overall comparison, 'Novel Scheme' performs better than 'SPIHT' and 'SPECK'.

| Videos | Average PSNR (dB) for SPIHT | Average PSNR (dB) for SPECK | Average PSNR (dB) for Novel Scheme |
|---|---|---|---|
| Claire | 37.85 | 39.95 | 38.84 |
| Foreman | 34.68 | 36.18 | 35.39 |
| Trevor | 34.12 | 33.34 | 33.53 |
| Dancer | 37.44 | 37.22 | 37.52 |
| Football | 31.85 | 32.76 | 32.24 |
| | | | |
| | **CR for SPIHT** | **CR for SPECK** | **CR for Novel Scheme** |
| Claire | 85.41 | 57.41 | 79.07 |
| Foreman | 76.26 | 56.67 | 71.24 |
| Trevor | 79.83 | 57.55 | 75.34 |
| Dancer | 59.62 | 48.84 | 56.27 |
| Football | 49.36 | 43.38 | 46.72 |
| | | | |
| **Videos** | **Execution time (Secs) for SPIHT** | **Execution time (Secs) for SPECK** | **Execution time (Secs) for Novel Scheme** |
| Claire | 205 | 185 | 189 |
| Foreman | 211 | 198 | 200 |
| Trevor | 208 | 198 | 194 |
| Dancer | 3162 | 2332 | 2796 |
| Football | 4128 | 2735 | 3640 |

Table 26. Comparison of 'SPIHT', 'SPECK' and 'Novel Scheme' for different videos based on average PSNR,CR and execution time; 84 frames

### 5.4 Reconstructed frames illustrating the comparison of 'SPIHT', 'SPECK' and 'Novel scheme'

The Figures 6(a)-(c) show the reconstructed frames (1, 9 and 13) for 'Miss America' using 'SPIHT'. The Figures 7(a)-(c) show the reconstructed frames (1, 9 and 13) for 'Miss America' using 'SPECK' and Figures 8 (a)-(c) show the reconstructed frames (1, 9 and 13) for the 'Novel Scheme'.

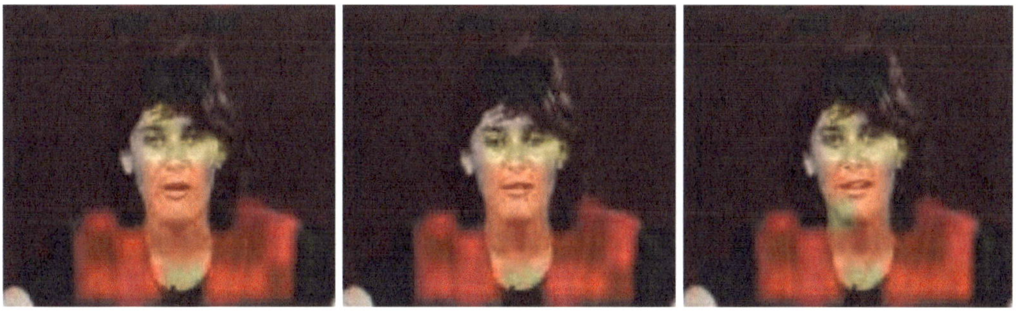

(a) (b) (c)

Fig. 6. Reconstructed frames in 'Miss America' using 'SPIHT' at 'I' rate =0.4bpp and 'P' rate of 0.04bpp (a) 1st frame (b) 9th frame (c) 13th frame

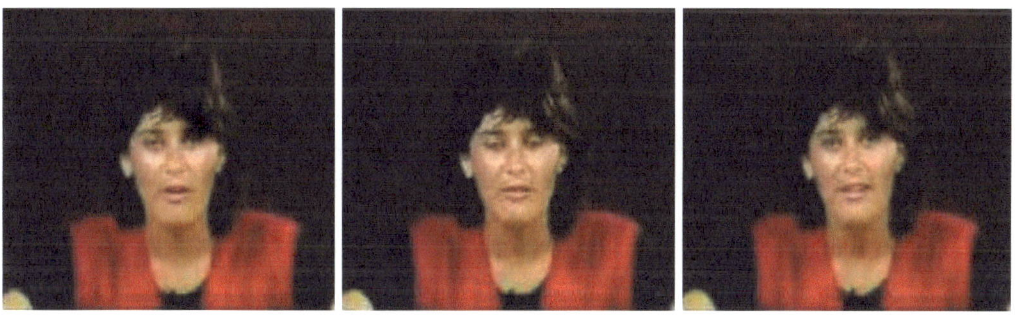

(a) (b) (c)

Fig. 7. Reconstructed frames in 'Miss America' using 'SPECK' at 'I' rate =0.4bpp and 'P' rate of 0.04bpp (a) 1st frame (b) 9th frame (c) 13th frame

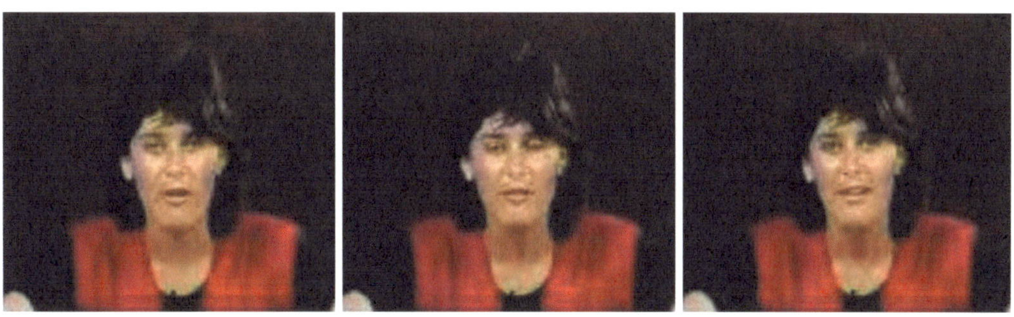

(a) (b) (c)

Fig. 8. Reconstructed frames in 'Miss America' using 'Novel Scheme' at 'I' rate =0.4 bpp and 'P' rate of 0.04 bpp (a) 1st frame (b) 9th frame (c) 13th frame

## 6. Conclusion

The above results lead to the following conclusions based on block matching Algorithms, Transforms, and quantization schemes,as listed below. Based on the block matching algorithm for motion estimation, kite cross diamond search (KCDS) based video compression is faster and gives better quality compared to diamond search (DS).The numerical results elucidate the above fact. The video compression based on wavelets is better for high bit rates (above 0.8 bpp) in terms of average PSNR but it is slow and also results in less compression. But at low bit rate, Multiwavelet performs extremely better than wavelets in terms of average PSNR, compression ratio, and speed. Based on quantization scheme SPIHT based video compression is good for high bit rates but fails for low bit rates where SPECK performs well but with low compression ratio. The proposed novel scheme performs well both at low and high bit rates. Addressing individual multiwavelets, the 'Sa4' and 'Cl' multifilters tend to perform better for all type of videos. Since the Novel scheme employs both SPIHT and SPECK quantization schemes, the merits of both quantization schemes are added to give very good results in terms of PSNR, CR, execution time, and thus, it is found to be a close competitor between the two quantization schemes taken individually. Hence, multiwavelet based coder will give efficient storage space because of higher amount of compression ratio. The lower value in PSNR at high bit rates can be improved by the introduction of better prediction schemes that exploits the statistical nature of every video.

## 7. Acknowledgment

The author wishes to express his deep sense of gratitude and thanks to his mentor Dr. Jayaraman Subramanian, Professor, Electrical and Electronics Engineering Department at BITS Pilani, Dubai Campus who has made this work possible with his persistent help, continued drive and timely motivation. The author is very much grateful to his mother Mrs. Santha Radhakrishnan, his wife Mrs.Vinitha Mohan, his son Master Hemesh S.V. and other family members for their constant encouragement to carry out the project in time.Last but not the least the author submit his thanks for the management where is currently working.

## 8. References

[1] Ben Waggoner (2002), *Compression for Great Digital Video,* CMP Books, ISBN 1-57820-111-x, California.

[2] Cheung, K.W. & Po L.M. (1997), *Preprocessing for Discrete Multiwavelet Transform of Two-Dimensional Signals,* ICIP, Vol.2, pp. 350-353.

[3] Chi-Wai Lam.; Lai-Man Po & Chun-Ho Cheung (2004), *A novel kite-cross-diamond search algorithm for fast block matching motion estimation,* International symposium on Circuits and Systems, ISBN:0-7803-8251-X Vol.3, pp. 729-732 May,2004

[4] Chui, C.K.; & Lian J. (1996), *A study on orthonormal multiwavelets,* Appl. Numer. Math., Vol.20, pp.273-298.

[5] Cotronei, M.; Lazzaro, D.; Montefusco, L.B. & Puccio, L. (2000), *Image Compression through Embedded Multiwavelet Transform Coding,* IEEE Trans. Image Processing, Vol. 9, No. 2, pp.184-189.

[6] Devore, R.A.; Jawerth, B & Lucier, B.J. (1992), *Image compression through wavelet transform coding*, IEEE Trans. Information Theory, Special issue on Multiresolution signal Analysis, Vol.38, No.2, pp.719-746.

[7] Gilbert Strang. & Strela, V.; (1994), *Orthogonal multiwavelets with vanishing moments*, J. Optical Engg., Vol.33, pp.2104-2107.

[8] Gilbert Strang. & Truong Nguyen (1996) *Wavelets and Filter Banks*, 1st Edn. Wellesley-Cambridge Press, Wellesley MA.

[9] Iain E.G. Richardson (2002), *Video CODEC Design*, John Wiley and Sons, New Jersey.

[10] Keith Jack (1996), *Video Demystified*, LLH Technology Publishing, Eagle Rock, Virginia.

[11] Koga, T.; Iinuma, K.; Hirano, A.; Iyima, Y.; & Ishi-guro, T. (1981), *Motion-compensated inter-frame coding for video conferencing*, in Proc.of National Telecommunication Conference, New Orleans, LA pp.G5.3.1-G5.3.5.

[12] Lee, C.H. & Chen L.H. (1997), *A Fast Motion Estimation Algorithm Based on the Block Sum Pyramid*, IEEE Trans. Image Processing, Vol. 6, No. 11, pp.1587-1591.

[13] Lee K.H.; Choi J.H.; Lee Bub-Ki.; & Kim Duk-Gyoo (2000), *Fast two-step half pixel accuracy motion vector prediction*, Electronic letters, IET digital library, Vol. 36, No. 7, pp. 625-627.

[14] Lei, S.M. & Sun, M.T. (1991), *An entropy coding system for digital HDTV applications*, IEEE Trans. Circuits and Systems for Video Technology, Vol.1, No.1, pp.147-154.

[15] Li, R.; Zeng B. & Liou M.L. (1994), *A new three-step search algorithm for block motion estimation*, IEEE Trans. Circuits Systems for Video Technology, Vol. 4,No.4, pp.438-442.

[16] Michael, B.M. (1999), *Application of Multiwavelets to image compression*. MSc. thesis, Virginia Polytechnic Institute and State University.

[17] Michael, B.M. & Amy, E. Bell (2001), *New Image Compression Techniques using Multiwavelets and Multiwavelet Packets*, IEEE Transactions on Image Processing, Vol. 10, No. 4, pp. 500-511.

[18] Pearlman, W.A.; Islam, A.; Nagaraj N. & Said, A. (2004), *Efficient, Low-Complexity Image Coding with a Set-Partitioning Embedded Block Coder*, IEEE Trans. Circuits Systems Video Technol., Vol. 14, No.11, pp. 1219-1235.

[19] Peter Symes (2000), *Video Compression Demystified*, McGraw-Hill Professional Publishing, New York.

[20] Po, L.M. and Ma, W.C. (1996), *A novel four-step search algorithm for fast block estimation*, IEEE Trans. Circuits Systems Video Technol., Vol. 6, No.3, pp. 313-317.

[21] Said, A. & Pearlman W.A. (1996), *A new, fast, and efficient image codec based on set partitioning in hierarchical trees*, IEEE Trans. Circuits Systems Video Technol., Vol. 6, No.3, pp. 243-250.

[22] Shan Zhu.; & Kai-Kuang Ma (2000), *A new diamond search algorithm for fast block matching motion estimation*, IEEE Trans. Image Processing, Vol. 9, No.2, pp 287-290.

[23] Shen K. (1997), *'A Study of Real Time and Rate Scalable Image and Video Compression*, PhD thesis, School of Electrical and Computer Engineering, Purdue University.

[24] Skodras, A.N.; Christopoulos, C.A.; & Ebrahimi T. (2000), *JPEG 2000: The upcoming still image compression standard*, Proc. of the 11th Portugese Conference on Pattern recognition, pp.359-366.

[25] Strela, V. (1996), *Multiwavelets: Theory and Applications*, PhD thesis, Massachusetts Institute of Technology.

[26] Strela, V. (1998), *A note on construction of biorthogonal multi-scaling functions in wavelets, multiwavelets and their applications,* Contemporary Mathematics, American Mathematical Society, Vol.216, pp.149-157.

[27] Strela, V. & Walden A.T. (1998), *Orthogonal and biorthogonal multiwavelets for signal denoising and image compression.* Proc. SPIE, Vol.3391, pp.96-107.

[28] Strela V.; Heller P.N.; Strang G.; Topiwala P.; & Heil, C. (1999), *The application of multiwavelet filter banks to image processing.* IEEE Trans. Image Processing, Vol.8, No.4, pp.548-563.

[29] Xiong, Z.; Ramchandran, K.; Orchard, M.T.; and Zhang Y. (1999), *A comparative study of DCT- and wavelet based image coding,* IEEE Trans. Circuits Systems Video Technol., Vol. 9, No.5.pp.692-695.

[30] Sudhakar, R.; Guruprasad, S. & Karthick, V.(2009), *Wavelet Based Video Encoder Using KCDS,* International Arab journal of Information Technology, Vol. 6, No.3, pp 245-249.

[31] Sudhakar, R. & Jayaraman, S. (2008*), Implemetation of a novel efficient Multiwavelet based Video coding algorithm,* International Arab journal of Information Technology, Vol. 5, No.1, pp 52-60.

[32] Sudhakar R. & Jayaraman S(2007), *A New video coder using multiwavelets* Proceedings of the International conference on Signal Processing communication and Networking (ICSCN-2007), pp.259-264, 22-24 February 2007,Madras Institute of Technology, Chennai, India.

[33] Sudhakar, R. & Jayaraman, S. (2008*), Novel image compression using multiwavelets with SPECK algorithm,* International Arab journal of Information Technology, Vol. 5, No.1, pp 45-51.

# 9

# Adaptive Entropy Coder Design Based on the Statistics of Lossless Video Signal

Jin Heo and Yo-Sung Ho
*Gwangju Institute of Science and Technology (GIST)*
*261 Cheomdan-gwagiro, Buk-gu, Gwangju 500-712,*
*Republic of Korea*

## 1. Introduction

H.264/AVC is the latest international video coding standard. It is currently the most powerful and state-of-the-art standard; thus, it can provide enhanced coding efficiency for a wide range of video applications, including video telephony, video conferencing, TV, storage, streaming video, digital cinema, and many others (Luthra et al., 2003; Sullivan & Wiegand, 2005; Wiegand et al., 2003). To date, since H.264/AVC has been developed by mainly focusing on lossy coding, its algorithms have reached a quite mature stage for lossy video compression.

Lossless compression has long been recognized as another important option for application areas that require high quality such as source distribution, digital document, digital cinema, and medical imaging. Recently, as the number of services and popularity for higher quality video representation are expanding, the interest and importance for lossless or near lossless video coding is also increasing (Brunello et al., 2003). However, since the majority of research pertaining to the H.264/AVC standard has focused on lossy video coding, it does not provide good coding performance for lossless video coding.

In order to provide improved functionality for lossless coding, the H.264/AVC standard first included a *pulse-code modulation* (PCM) macroblock coding mode, and then a transform-bypass lossless coding mode (Joint video Team of the International Telecommunications Union-Telecommunication and the International Organization for Standardization/International Electrotechnical Commission [JVT of ITU-T and ISO/IEC], 2002) that employed two main coding processes: prediction and entropy coding which were not previously used in the PCM macroblock coding mode in the fidelity range extensions (FRExt) (JVT of ITU-T and ISO/IEC, 2004; Sullivan et al., 2004). However, since the algorithms for lossless coding are not efficient, more efficient coding techniques for prediction and entropy coding are still required.

Recently, instead of developing a block-based intra prediction, new intra prediction methods, referred to as sample-wise *differential pulse-code modulation* (DPCM) (JVT of ITU-T and ISO/IEC, 2005; Lee et al., 2006) were introduced for lossless coding. As a result, they have been shown to provide better compression performance.

Two entropy coding methods: *context-based adaptive variable length coding* (CAVLC) (JVT of ITU-T and ISO/IEC, 2002; Richardson, 2003) and *context-based adaptive binary arithmetic coding* (CABAC) (Marpe et al., 2003) in the H.264/AVC standard were originally developed

for lossy video coding; they were designed by taking into consideration the typically observed statistical properties of residual data, i.e., the quantized transform coefficients. However, in lossless coding, residual data are just prediction residuals without transform and quantization (Malvar et al., 2003). Thus, the statistical characteristics of residual data from lossy and lossless coding are quite different. As such, the use of conventional entropy coding methods in H.264/AVC is inappropriate for lossless video coding. Nevertheless, most researches into lossless coding in the H.264/AVC standard have focused on improving its prediction ability, rather than on the development of entropy coders (Heo et al., 2010).
Therefore, in this chapter, we have tried to improve coding performance of entropy coders in H.264/AVC for lossless intra coding. After we analyzed the statistical differences of residual data between lossy and lossless coding, we explained an improved CAVLC and CABAC methods for lossless intra coding based on the observed statistical characteristics of lossless coding. Note that our research goal is to improved coding performance of CAVLC and CABAC, which can then be easily applied to H.264/AVC lossless intra coding by modifying the semantics and decoding processes without requiring any other syntax elements in the H.264/AVC standard.

## 2. Overview of entropy coding methods in the H.264/AVC standard

In this section, we review two entropy coding methods: CAVLC and CABAC in H.264/AVC. The entropy coders are employed to encode residual data; zigzag scanned the quantized transform coefficients, for a 4×4 sub-block. Fig. 1 illustrates the zigzag scan order for the 4×4 sub-block.

| | | | |
|---|---|---|---|
| 3 | 7 | -1 | -2 |
| 9 | 7 | 2 | 0 |
| 8 | -3 | -5 | -1 |
| 2 | -2 | 1 | 0 |

Residual data in the sub-block

| | | | |
|---|---|---|---|
| 1 | 2 | 6 | 7 |
| 3 | 5 | 8 | 13 |
| 4 | 9 | 12 | 14 |
| 10 | 11 | 15 | 16 |

Zigzag scan order for the sub-block

| Scanning Position | | 1 | 2 | 3 | 4 | 5 | 6 | 7 | 8 | 9 | 10 | 11 | 12 | 13 | 14 | 15 | 16 |
|---|---|---|---|---|---|---|---|---|---|---|---|---|---|---|---|---|---|
| Coefficient Level | Absolute Value | 3 | 7 | 9 | 8 | 7 | 1 | 2 | 2 | 3 | 2 | 2 | 5 | 0 | 1 | 1 | 0 |
| | Sign | + | + | + | + | + | - | - | + | - | + | - | - | | - | + | |

Reordered residual data according to scan order

Fig. 1. Zigzag scan order for the sub-block

### 2.1 Overview of CAVLC

The encoding structure of CAVLC for a 4×4 sub-block is depicted in Fig. 2. First, both the number of non-zero coefficients and the number of trailing ones are encoded using a combined codeword (*coeff_token*). Second, the sign of each trailing one is encoded using a 1-bit codeword in reverse order (*trailing_ones_sign_flag*). Third, the absolute value of the level of each remaining non-zero coefficient is encoded in reverse order using one of the seven predefined *Lev-VLC* tables and the sign information is encoded (*level*). Fourth, the number of all zeros before the last non-zero coefficient is encoded (*total_zeros*). Last, the number of consecutive zeros preceding each non-zero coefficient is encoded in reverse order (*run_before*).

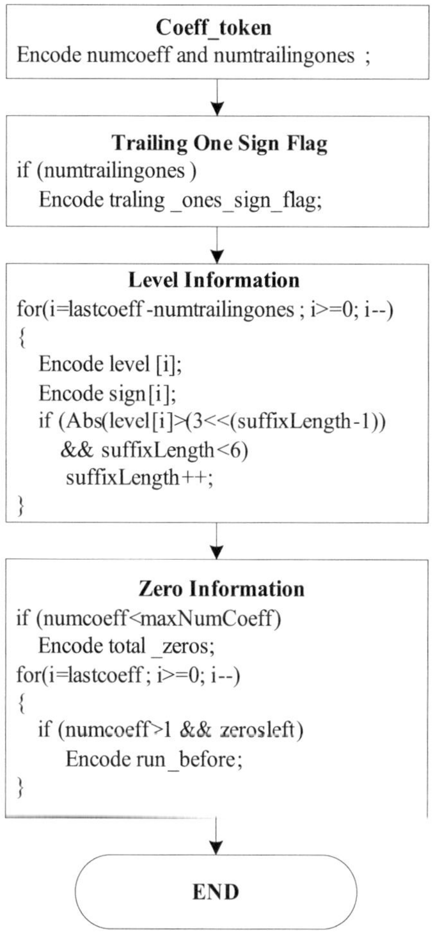


Fig. 2. Encoding structure of CAVLC for residual data coding

More details of each coding step are described below.

**Step 1.** Encode the number of non-zero coefficients (*numcoeff*) and the number of trailing ones (*numtrailingones*).

A trailing one is one of up to three consecutive non-zero coefficient at the end of the scan of non-zero coefficients having an absolute value equal to 1. If there are more than three trailing ones, only the last three are treated as trailing ones, with any others being coded as normal coefficients.

The four VLC tables used for encoding *coeff_token* are comprised of three variable-length code tables (*Num-VLC0*, *Num-VLC1*, and *Num-VLC2*) and one fixed-length code table (*FLC*). The choice of VLC table depends on the number of non-zero coefficients in the previously coded upper and left sub-blocks. If both the upper and left sub-blocks are available, $N = round(N_U + N_L)/2$. If only the upper sub-block is available, $N=N_U$; if only the left sub-block is available, $N=N_L$. If neither is available, $N$ is set to zero. Where $N$ is the number of predicted non-zero coefficients in the current sub-block, and $N_U$ and $N_L$ represent the number of non-zero coefficients in the upper and left previously encoded sub-blocks, respectively. Thus, based on the parameter $N$, an appropriate VLC table for the current sub-block is selected from Table 1.

| *N* | Table for *coeff_token* |
|---|---|
| 0, 1 | *Num-VLC0* |
| 2, 3 | *Num-VLC1* |
| 4, 5, 6, 7 | *Num-VLC2* |
| 8 or above | *FLC* |

Table 1. Choice of VLC table

**Step 2.** Encode the sign of each trailing one.
The trailing one sign flag indicates the sign information of a trailing one coefficient; the sign information is simply encoded by a 1-bit codeword in reverse order. If the sign information is positive (+), *trailing_ones_sign_flag* is equal to zero. Conversely, if the sign information is negative (-), *trailing_ones_sign_flag* is equal to one.

**Step 3.** Encode the levels.
The level (sign and magnitude) of each remaining non-zero coefficient in the sub-block is encoded in reverse order, starting from the highest frequency and working back toward the DC coefficient. Each absolute level value is encoded by a selected *Lev-VLC* table from among seven *Lev-VLC* tables (Table 2), with selection of the *Lev-VLC* table dependent on the magnitude of each recently encoded level. The choice of *Lev-VLC* table is adapted as follows:

1. If (*numcoeff* > 10 && *numtrailingones* ==3)
   Initialize *Lev-VLC1*.
   Otherwise
   Initialize *Lev-VLC0*.
2. Encode the absolute value of the last scanned coefficient.
3. Encode the sign of the last scanned coefficient.
4. If the magnitude of the current encoded coefficient is larger than a predefined threshold in Table 2, increment the *Lev-VLC* table.

| *Lev-VLC table* | Threshold to increment *Lev-VLC table* |
|---|---|
| *Lev-VLC0* | 0 |
| *Lev-VLC1* | 3 |
| *Lev-VLC2* | 6 |
| *Lev-VLC3* | 12 |
| *Lev-VLC4* | 24 |
| *Lev-VLC5* | 48 |
| *Lev-VLC6* | > 48 |

Table 2. Thresholds for determining whether to increment *Lev-VLC* table

**Step 4.** Encode the total number of zeros.
After the encoding process for level information, zeros remain. CAVLC encodes the syntax element, *total_zeros* which represents the number of zero coefficients located before the last non-zero coefficient.

**Step 5.** Encode each run of zeros.
After encoding *total_zeros*, the position of each zero coefficient is encoded. The syntax element *run_before* indicates the number of consecutive zero coefficients between the non-zero coefficients and is encoded with *zerosleft* in reverse order. Note that *zerosleft* indicates the number of zeros that has not yet been encoded. The syntax element *run_before* is encoded for each non-zero coefficient, with two exceptions:

1. If there are no *zerosleft* to encode, processing can be stopped.
2. Processing can be stopped to encode *run_before* for the final (lowest frequency) non-zero coefficient.

## 2.2 Overview of CABAC

### 2.2.1 CABAC framework

The encoding process of CABAC consists of four coding steps: binarization, context modeling, binary arithmetic coding, and probability update. The block diagram for encoding a single syntax element in CABAC is depicted in Fig. 3.

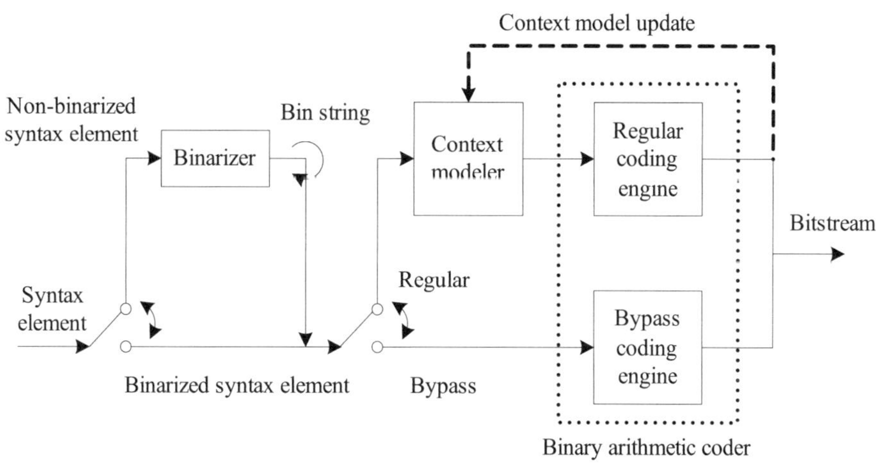


Fig. 3. CABAC encoder framework

In the first step, a given non-binary valued syntax element is uniquely mapped to a binary sequence (*bin string*); when the binary valued syntax element is given, the first step is bypassed. In the regular coding mode, each binary value (*bin*) of the binary sequence enters the context modeling stage, where a probability model is selected based on the previously encoded syntax elements. Then, the arithmetic coding engine encodes each binary value with its associated probability model. Finally, the selected context model is updated according to the actual coded binary value. Alternatively, in the bypass coding mode, each binary value is directly encoded via the bypass coding engine without using an explicitly assigned model.

### 2.2.2 CABAC for residual data coding

Fig. 4 illustrates the CABAC encoding structure for a 4×4 sub-block of the quantized transform coefficients. First, the coded block flag is transmitted for the given sub-block unless the coded block pattern or the macroblock mode indicates that the specific sub-block has no non-zero coefficient. If the coded block flag is zero, no further information is transmitted for the current sub-block; otherwise, the significance map and level information are sequentially encoded. More details of each coding step are described below.

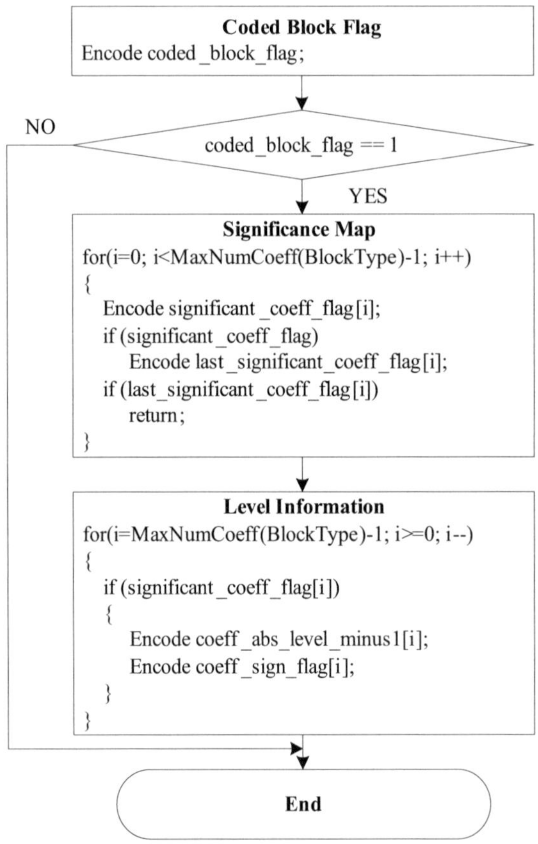


Fig. 4. Encoding structure of CABAC for residual data coding.

**Step 1.** Encode coded block flag.

For each 4×4 sub-block, a 1-bit symbol *coded_block_flag* is transmitted to indicate that a sub-block has significant coefficients. If *coded_block_flag* is zero, no further information is transmitted and the coded block flag coding process is terminated for the current sub-block. However, if *coded_block_flag* is one, the significance map and level information coding processes are continued.

**Step 2.** Encode significance map.

If *coded_block_flag* indicates that a sub-block has significant coefficients, a binary-valued significance map is encoded. For each coefficient, a 1-bit syntax element *significant_coeff_flag* is encoded in scanning order. If *significant_coeff_flag* is one, i.e., if a non-zero coefficient exists at this scanning position, a further 1-bit syntax element *last_significant_coeff_flag* is encoded. This syntax element states whether the current significant coefficient is the last coefficient inside the sub-block or not. Note that *significant_coeff_flag* and *last_significant_coeff_flag* for the last scanning position of a sub-block are not encoded.

**Step 3.** Encode level information.
After the encoded significance map determines the locations of all significant coefficients inside a sub-block, the values of the significant coefficients are encoded by using two syntax elements: *coeff_abs_level_minus1* and *coeff_sign_flag*. The syntax element *coeff_sign_flag* is encoded by a 1-bit symbol, whereas the *Unary/0$^{th}$ order Exponential Golomb* (UEG0) binarization method is used to encode the values of *coeff_abs_level_minus1* representing the absolute value of the level minus 1. The values of the significant coefficients are encoded in reverse scanning order.

## 3. Analysis of the statistical characteristics of residual data in lossless coding

In lossy coding, residual data represent the quantized transform coefficients. The statistical characteristics of residual data in lossy coding are as follows. In a given sub-block, the probability of a non-zero coefficient existing is likely to decrease as the scanning position increases. Moreover, the absolute value of a non-zero coefficient tends to decrease as the scanning position increases. Hence, the occurrence probability of a trailing one is relatively high.

In lossless coding, however, residual data do not represent the quantized transform coefficients, but rather the differential pixel values between the original and predicted pixel values. Therefore, the statistical characteristics of residual data in lossless coding are as follows. First, the probability of a non-zero pixel existing is independent of the scanning position, and the number of non-zero pixels is generally large, compared to the number of non-zero coefficients in lossy coding. Second, the absolute value of a non-zero pixel does not decrease as the scanning position increases and is independent of the scanning position. Finally, the occurrence probability of a trailing one is not so high.

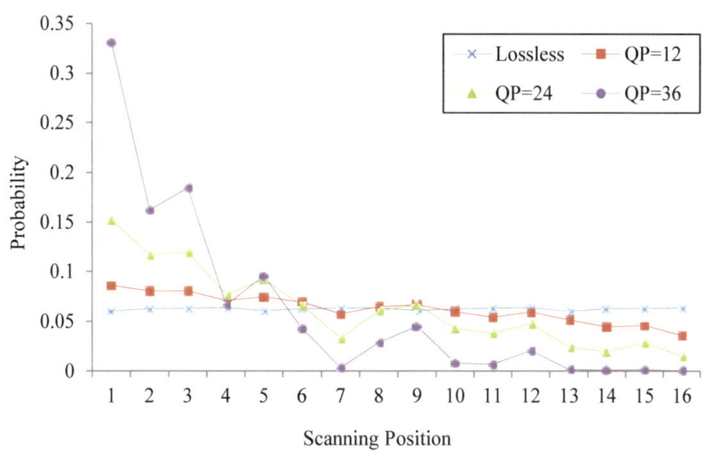


Fig. 5. Probability distribution of non-zero coefficients according to the scanning position.

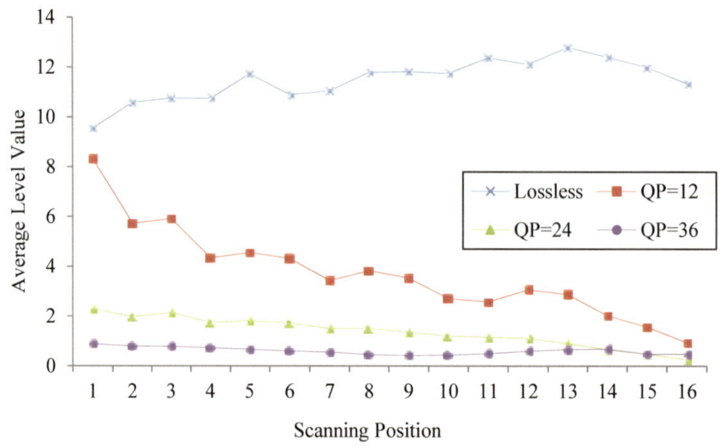


Fig. 6. Distribution of average absolute value according to the scanning position.

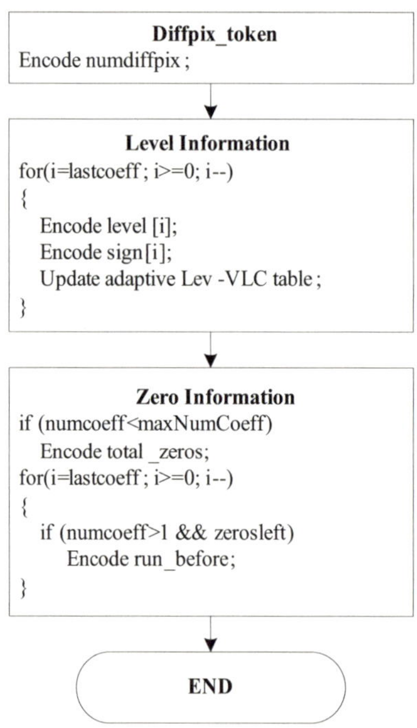


Fig. 7. Encoding structure of the proposed CAVLC for differential pixel value coding.

Figs. 5 and 6 represent the probability distribution of non-zero coefficients existing and the distribution of average absolute value according to the scanning position, respectively. As expected, significant differences can be seen in the statistics between the residual data of lossy and lossless coding.

Therefore, based on the above statistical characteristics of residual data in lossless coding, we propose more efficient CAVLC and CABAC methods for lossless compression in H.264/AVC by modifying the relevant coding parts of each entropy coder.

## 4. Improved CAVLC

In this section, we introduce an improved CAVLC for lossless intra coding. In Fig. 7, we depict the encoding structure of the proposed method for encoding the differential pixel value in lossless coding. The encoding procedure of the proposed CAVLC method can be summarized in the following steps:

**Step 1.** Encode the total number of non-zero differential pixels (*diffpix_token*).
**Step 2.** Encode the level (sign and magnitude) of all non-zero differential pixels (*level*).
**Step 3.** Encode the number of all zeros before the last non-zero differential pixel (*total_zeros*).
**Step 4.** Encode the number of consecutive zeros preceding each non-zero differential pixel (*run_before*).

Further details of these coding methods are described in the following subsections.

### 4.1 Coding the number of non-zero differential pixels

Table 3 represents the occurrence probability distribution of trailing ones according to the quantization parameter (QP). Since, in lossless coding, the occurrence probability of trailing ones turns out to be relatively lower than that in lossy coding, the trailing one does not need to be treated as a special case of encoding. Therefore, in this step, we encode the total number of non-zero differential pixels (*numdiffpix*) but do not consider the number of trailing ones (*numtrailingones*). Since the trailing ones are treated as normal coefficients, they are encoded in the level coding step, which thereby enabled the removal of Step 2, a coding stage of the sign information for each trailing one.

| Sequence | QP | | | |
|---|---|---|---|---|
| | 0 (Lossless) | 12 | 24 | 36 |
| News | 0.3719 | 0.8161 | 0.8825 | 0.9458 |
| Foreman | 0.2598 | 0.7947 | 0.9117 | 0.9585 |
| Mobile | 0.2107 | 0.6962 | 0.8566 | 0.9268 |
| Tempete | 0.2274 | 0.7842 | 0.8861 | 0.9449 |
| City_corr | 0.2100 | 0.8140 | 0.8914 | 0.9507 |
| Crowdrun | 0.1813 | 0.7673 | 0.9240 | 0.9478 |

Table 3. Occurrence probability distribution of trailing ones according to the QP

In CAVLC, the corresponding VLC table is selected based on the predicted *numcoeff*; further details have already been explained in Section 2.1. Note that if the predicted *numcoeff* is larger than seven, the fixed length code (*FLC*) table is selected, as described in Table 1. In lossless coding, the *FLC* table is most often selected because *numdiffpix* is generally larger than seven, as shown in Table 4. From extensive experiments on lossless intra coding with various test sequences, we observed that the *FLC* table was selected about 95% of the time. Hence, we could remove three VLC tables (*Num-VLC0* to *Num-VLC2*) in this step. Since only the *FLC* table is used, we do not need to consider the process for predicting *numcoeff*.
The *FLC* table consists of 4 bits for *numcoeff* and 2 bits for *numtrailingones* in lossy coding; since *numtrailingones* does not need to be considered in lossless coding; only 4 bits for *numdiffpix* remain. However, instead of using the *FLC* table, which uniformly assigns 4 bits

for all *numdiffpix*s, we designed a simple but effective VLC table according to the statistical characteristics of *numdiffpix* in lossless coding.

| Sequence | QP | | | |
|---|---|---|---|---|
| | 0 (Lossless) | 12 | 24 | 36 |
| News | 12.5791 | 6.3077 | 3.3553 | 1.5448 |
| Foreman | 13.7457 | 7.8073 | 3.3253 | 1.0017 |
| Mobile | 14.6338 | 10.9796 | 6.6945 | 2.4879 |
| Tempete | 13.9684 | 9.0754 | 4.9113 | 1.6940 |
| City_corr | 14.4775 | 6.5353 | 3.3869 | 0.9449 |
| Crowdrun | 14.9614 | 10.4297 | 4.0696 | 1.3231 |

Table 4. Average number of non-zero coefficients in a sub-block

Fig. 8 shows the cumulative probability distribution of the number of non-zero coefficients in the sub-block. A significant difference can be seen in the statistical characteristics of the number of non-zero coefficients between lossy and lossless coding. In lossless coding, the probability of the number of non-zero differential pixels turns out to be very low when the number of non-zero differential pixels is small (the number of non-zero differential pixels < 10). However, the probability of the number of non-zero differential pixels drastically increases as the number of non-zero differential pixels increases, especially the number of non-zero differential pixels from 13 to 16.

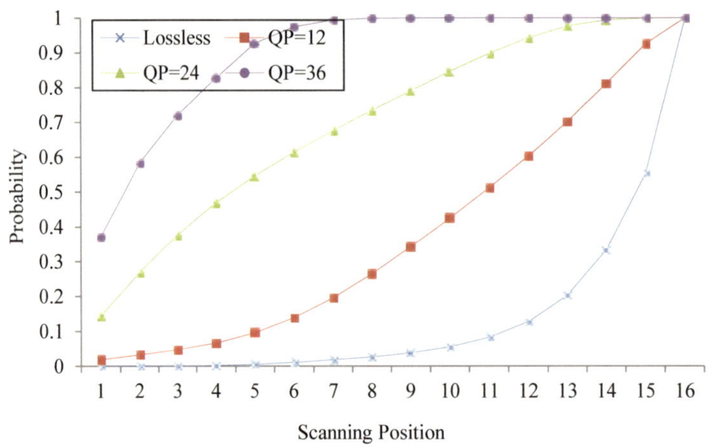


Fig. 8. Cumulative probability distribution of the number of non-zero coefficients.

In our proposed VLC table, first, we assign 4-bit and 2-bit codewords to *numdiffpix* from 1 to 12 and 13 to 16, respectively. In order to enhance coding performance, we assign the different length of codeword to *numdiffpix* from 1 to 12 according to the statistical characteristics of *numdiffpix* instead of assigning 4-bit codewords uniformly. Thus, we use the phased-in code (Salomon, 2007) which is a slight extension of fixed length code (*FLC*). The phased-in code consists of codewords with two different lengths. Therefore, we assign 4-bit and 3-bit codewords to *numdiffpix* from 1 to 9 and 10 to 12, respectively. In order to avoid ambiguity at the decoder, we inserted a check bit into the prefix of each codeword; details regarding the codewords are further described in Table 5.

| *numdiffpix* | Codeword | | |
|---|---|---|---|
| | Check bit | Bits for *numdiffpix* | Codeword length |
| 1 | 1 | 1110 | 5 |
| 2 | 1 | 1101 | 5 |
| 3 | 1 | 1100 | 5 |
| 4 | 1 | 1011 | 5 |
| 5 | 1 | 1010 | 5 |
| 6 | 1 | 1001 | 5 |
| 7 | 1 | 1000 | 5 |
| 8 | 1 | 0111 | 5 |
| 9 | 1 | 0110 | 5 |
| 10 | 1 | 010 | 4 |
| 11 | 1 | 001 | 4 |
| 12 | 1 | 000 | 4 |
| 13 | 0 | 00 | 3 |
| 14 | 0 | 01 | 3 |
| 15 | 0 | 10 | 3 |
| 16 | 0 | 11 | 3 |

Table 5. Codeword table for *numdiffpix*

### 4.2 Level coding

In level coding, the absolute value of each non-zero coefficient (*abs_level*) is adaptively encoded by a selected *Lev-VLC* table from the seven predefined *Lev-VLC* tables (*Lev-VLC0* to *Lev-VLC6*) in reverse scanning order. Each *Lev-VLC* table is designed to encode efficiently in a specified range of *abs_level*, as described in Table 2. As previously mentioned, selection of the *Lev-VLC* table for level coding in CAVLC is based on the expectation that *abs_level* is likely to increase at low frequencies. Hence, selection of the *Lev-VLC* table number monotonically increases according to the previously encoded *abs_level*.

However, the absolute value of the differential pixel (*abs_diff_pixel*) in lossless coding is independent of the scanning position, as shown in Fig. 6. Therefore, we designed an adaptive method for *Lev-VLC* table selection that can decrease or increase according to the previously encoded *abs_diff_pixel*.

In lossy coding, CAVLC typically determines the smallest *Lev-VLC* table in the range of possible *Lev-VLC* tables based on the assumption that the next *abs_level* to be coded is going to be larger. However, in lossless coding, the next *abs_diff_pixel* does not necessarily increase at lower frequencies—we cannot assume that the next *abs_diff_pixel* is larger than the current *abs_diff_pixel*. Therefore, the *Lev-VLC* table for each *abs_diff_pixel* should be selected by considering the previously encoded *abs_diff_pixels* because we cannot predict whether or not the next *abs_diff_pixel* will increase.

In order to determine the most appropriate *Lev-VLC* table, we assign a weighting value to the previously encoded *abs_diff_pixels*. The basic idea for this concept is that the *Lev-VLC* table for the next *abs_diff_pixel* can be determined using the weighted sum of the previously encoded *abs_diff_pixels*. The decision procedure for determining the *Lev-VLC* table is described as follows.

$$T(abs\_diff\_pixel_i) = \frac{1}{a_i + 1}\{a_i \cdot avg_i + abs\_diff\_pixel_i\}, \tag{1}$$

$$a_i = \begin{cases} 0, & i = lastdiffpix \\ 1, & i = lastdiffpix - 1,\ lastdiffpix - 2, \\ 2, & \text{otherwise} \end{cases} \tag{2}$$

$$avg_i = \frac{1}{(lastdiffpix - i + 1)}\left\{\sum_{k=lastdiffpix}^{i} abs\_diff\_pixel_k\right\}, \tag{3}$$

where $a_i$ and $abs\_diff\_pixel_i$ are the weighting coefficient and *abs_diff_pixel* value, respectively, where both values are related to the current scanning position *i*. In addition, $T(abs\_diff\_pixel_i)$ and *lastdiffpix* represent the threshold value for selecting the corresponding *Lev-VLC* table used to encode the next *abs_diff_pixel* ($(i\text{-}1)^{th}$ *abs_diff_pixel*) and the scanning position number of the last non-zero differential pixel, respectively. Note that *abs_diff_pixel* is encoded in reverse order. In Table 6, we represent the *Lev-VLC* table for level coding according to $T(abs\_diff\_pixel_i)$. From extensive experiments on lossless intra coding using various test sequences, we could determine these optimal threshold values.

| *Lev-VLC* table | $T(abs\_diff\_pixel_i)$ |
|---|---|
| *Lev-VLC0* | 0 |
| *Lev-VLC1* | 2 |
| *Lev-VLC2* | 4 |
| *Lev-VLC3* | 9 |
| *Lev-VLC4* | 19 |
| *Lev-VLC5* | 39 |
| *Lev-VLC6* | > 39 |

Table 6. New thresholds for determining the *Lev-VLC* table

In Fig. 6, we can note that the last scanned absolute values are quite different between lossy and lossless coding. In level coding, encoding starts with *Lev-VLC0* or *Lev-VLC1* because the last scanned *abs_level* represents the highest frequency coefficient in lossy coding, and it is likely to be small. However, in lossless coding, the last scanned *abs_diff_pixel* is not small enough to use either *Lev-VLC0* or *Lev-VLC1*. Table 7 represents the average absolute value of the last scanned level for the sub-blocks. In Table 7, the last scanned *abs_diff_pixel* in lossless coding is larger than the last scanned *abs_level* in lossy coding. The average absolute value of the last scanned differential pixel in the sub-blocks is approximately 10.09 in lossless coding. Based on this value, we adjusted the initial *Lev-VLC* table for level coding. The modified *Lev-VLC* table selection method is follows.

1. Level coding starts with *Lev-VLC4*.
2. Encode the absolute value of the last scanned differential pixel.
3. Encode the sign of the last scanned differential pixel.
4. Update the *Lev-VLC* table by considering the previously encoded *abs_diff_pixel*s and new threshold for each *Lev-VLC* table.

| Sequence | QP | | | |
|---|---|---|---|---|
| | 0 (Lossless) | 12 | 24 | 36 |
| News | 9.9371 | 2.5228 | 2.0837 | 1.9113 |
| Foreman | 9.2097 | 2.2939 | 1.8902 | 1.8881 |
| Mobile | 16.3748 | 3.0935 | 2.1962 | 1.7870 |
| Tempete | 11.5824 | 2.6421 | 1.9960 | 1.7655 |
| City_corr | 6.9376 | 1.2654 | 1.1340 | 1.0572 |
| Crowdrun | 8.8483 | 1.3609 | 1.0906 | 1.0611 |

Table 7. Average absolute value of the last non-zero coefficient for the sub-blocks

## 5. Improved CABAC

In this section, we describe an improved CABAC for lossless intra coding. In Fig. 9, we depict the encoding structure of the proposed method for encoding the differential pixel value in lossless coding. The encoding procedure of the proposed CABAC can be summarized in the following steps:

**Step 1.** Encode whether the current sub-block contains non-zero pixel values (*coded_block_flag*)

**Step 2.** Encode whether the differential pixel value at each scanning position is non-zero to the last scanning position (*significant_diff_pixel_flag*).

**Step 3.** Encode the absolute value of a differential pixel value minus 1 with modified binarization method (*abs_diff_pixel_minus1*).

**Step 4.** Encode the sign of a differential pixel value (*diff_pixel_sign_flag*).

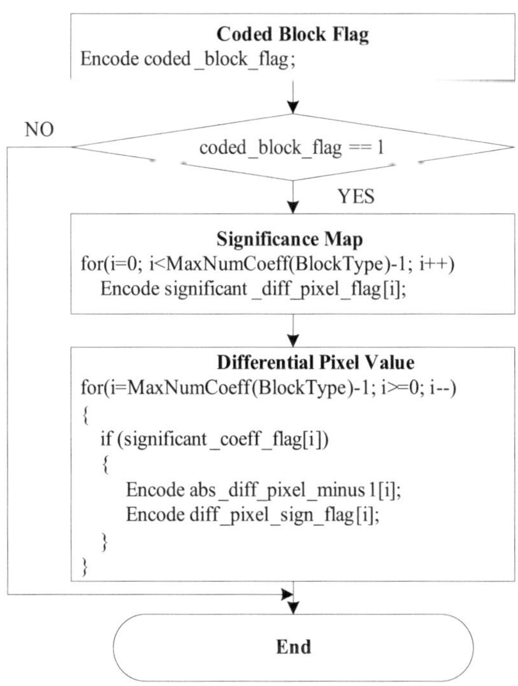


Fig. 9. Encoding structure of the proposed CABAC for differential pixel value coding.

Further details of these coding methods are described in the following subsections.

### 5.1 Significance map coding

In lossy coding, the occurrence probability of a non-zero coefficient is likely to decrease as the scanning position increases because residual data are the quantized transform coefficients. Therefore, the significant coefficient tends to be located at earlier scanning positions. In this case, *last_significant_coeff_flag* plays an important role in the early termination of significance map coding.

However, in lossless coding, since neither transform nor quantization is performed, the occurrence probability of a non-zero differential pixel is independent of the scanning position, as shown in Fig. 5. Thus, the last non-zero differential pixel is terminated at the end of the scanning position, as shown in Table 8. In this case, it is meaningless to encode *last_significant_coeff_flag* to indicate the position of the last significant differential pixel. Therefore, we remove the *last_significant_coeff_flag* coding process and directly encode *significant_diff_pixel_flag*s at all scanning positions from 1 to 16 in the proposed significance map coding.

| Sequence | QP | | | |
|---|---|---|---|---|
| | 0 (Lossless) | 12 | 24 | 36 |
| News | 14.5484 | 9.8368 | 6.6348 | 4.0463 |
| Foreman | 14.7669 | 12.5503 | 6.9935 | 2.8340 |
| Mobile | 14.7906 | 12.8480 | 10.4510 | 6.2891 |
| Tempete | 14.7868 | 12.4645 | 9.0398 | 3.8092 |
| City_corr | 14.7806 | 10.4116 | 5.6708 | 2.3080 |
| Crowdrun | 14.8204 | 13.6042 | 6.6730 | 2.6177 |

Table 8. Average location of the last non-zero coefficient in a sub-block

Fig. 10 represents an example of significance map coding for CABAC in lossy coding when the scanning position of the last significant coefficient is 14; the gray shaded *significant_coeff_flag* and *last_significant_coeff_flag* are encoded in significance map coding. Note that both *significant_coeff_flag* and *last_significant_coeff_flag* for the last scanning position of a sub-block are never encoded.

| Scanning position | 1 | 2 | 3 | 4 | 5 | 6 | 7 | 8 | 9 | 10 | 11 | 12 | 13 | 14 | 15 | 16 |
|---|---|---|---|---|---|---|---|---|---|---|---|---|---|---|---|---|
| Transform coefficient level | 9 | 0 | -5 | 3 | 0 | -7 | 4 | 0 | 8 | -11 | -6 | 0 | 3 | 1 | 0 | 0 |
| significant_coeff_flag | 1 | 0 | 1 | 1 | 0 | 1 | 1 | 0 | 1 | 1 | 1 | 0 | 1 | 1 | | |
| last_significant_coeff_flag | 0 | | 0 | 0 | | 0 | 0 | | 0 | 0 | 0 | | 0 | 1 | | |

Fig. 10. Example of significance map coding in lossy coding.

However, since we removed the *last_significant_coeff_flag* coding process in lossless coding, *significant_diff_pixel_flag* is unconditionally encoded up to the last scanning position. Fig. 11 presents an example of significance map coding in lossless coding. All gray shaded *significant_diff_pixel_flag*s are encoded in the proposed significance map coding.

| Scanning position | 1 | 2 | 3 | 4 | 5 | 6 | 7 | 8 | 9 | 10 | 11 | 12 | 13 | 14 | 15 | 16 |
|---|---|---|---|---|---|---|---|---|---|---|---|---|---|---|---|---|
| Differential pixel value | 9 | 0 | -5 | 3 | 0 | -7 | 4 | 0 | 8 | -11 | -6 | 0 | 3 | 1 | 0 | 0 |
| significant_diff_pixel_flag | 1 | 0 | 1 | 1 | 0 | 1 | 1 | 0 | 1 | 1 | 1 | 0 | 1 | 1 | 0 | 0 |

Fig. 11. Example of significance map coding in lossless coding.

### 5.2 Binarization for differential pixel value

For the absolute value of the quantized transform coefficient (*abs_level*) in lossy coding, the *Unary/kth order Exponential Golomb* (UEGk) binarization method is applied. The design of the UEGk binarization method is motivated by the fact that the unary code is the simplest prefix-free code in terms of implementation cost and it permits the fast adaptation of individual symbol probabilities in the subsequent context modeling stage. These observations are only accurate for small *abs_levels*; however, for larger *abs_levels*, adaptive modeling has limited functionality. Therefore, these observations have led to the idea of concatenating an adapted truncated unary (TU) code as a prefix and a static Exp-Golomb code (Teuhola, 1978) as a suffix.

The UEGk binarization of *abs_level* has a cutoff value $S = 14$ for the TU prefix and the order $k = 0$ for the Exp-Golomb (EG0) suffix. Previously, Golomb codes have been proven to be optimal prefix-free codes for geometrically distributed sources (Gallager & Voorhis, 1975). Moreover, EG0 is the optimal code for a *probability density function* (pdf) as follows:

$$p(x) = 1/2 \cdot (x+1)^{-2} \ \ with \ x \geq 0 \tag{4}$$

The statistical properties of the absolute value of the differential pixel (*abs_diff_pixel*) in lossless coding are quite different from those of *abs_level* in lossy coding. In lossy coding, the statistical distribution of *abs_level* is highly skewed on small values. However, in lossless coding, the statistical distribution of *abs_diff_pixel* is quite wide; note the large variation and wide tails, shown in Fig. 12. Moreover, we can also observe that the TU code is a fairly good model for the statistical distribution of *abs_level* in lossy coding; whereas, it is not appropriate for the statistical distribution of *abs_diff_pixel* in lossless coding. Therefore, as UEG0 binarization was originally designed for lossy coding, it is not appropriate for lossless coding.

In order to efficiently encode *abs_diff_pixel* in lossless coding, we adjusted the cutoff value $S$ of the TU prefix in UEG0 binarization. In Fig. 12, the optimal pdf curve for the TU code and the statistical distribution curve for *abs_diff_pixel* in lossless coding intersect at an absolute value of 5. Moreover, as the absolute value increases, the statistical difference between the TU code and *abs_diff_pixel* in lossless coding becomes larger. Therefore, we determined a new cutoff value $S = 5$ for the TU prefix in the proposed binarization method.

In order to provide a good prefix-free code for lossless coding, we also determined an appropriate parameter $k$ for the EGk code. The prefix of the EGk codeword consists of a unary code corresponding to the value $l(x) = \lfloor \log_2(x/2^k + 1) \rfloor$. The suffix is then computed as the binary representation of $x + 2^k(1 - 2^{l(x)})$ using $k + l(x)$ significant bits. Consequently, for EGk binarization, the number of symbols having the same code length of $k + 2l(x) + 1$ grows geometrically. Then, by inverting Shannon's relationship between the ideal code length and the symbol probability, we can find each pdf corresponding to an EGk having an optimal code according to a parameter $k$.

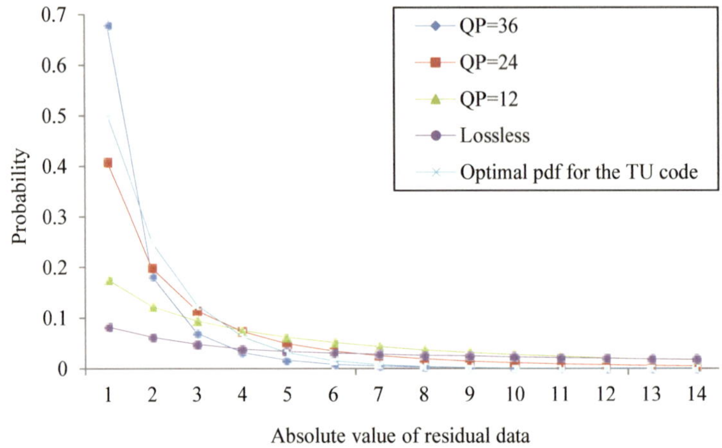


Fig. 12. Probability distribution of the absolute value of residual data and the optimal pdf of the TU code.

$$p_k(x) = 1/2^{k+1} \cdot (x/2^k + 1)^{-2} \ with \ x \geq 0 \tag{5}$$

where $p_k(x)$ is the optimal pdf corresponding to the EGk code for a parameter $k$. This implies that for an appropriately chosen parameter $k$, the EGk code represents a fairly good prefix-free code for tails of typically observed pdfs.
Fig. 13 represents the probability distribution of $p_k(x)$ for $k$ = 0, 1, 2, and 3 and the occurrence probability distribution of *abs_diff_pixel* from 6 to 20, where *abs_diff_pixel*s up to 5 are specified by the TU code. In the figure, the probability distribution of $p_k(x)$ for $k$ = 3 is well matched to the occurrence probability distribution of *abs_diff_pixel*. This result implies that the EG3 code represents a fairly good approximation of the ideal prefix-free code for encoding *abs_diff_pixel* in lossless coding.

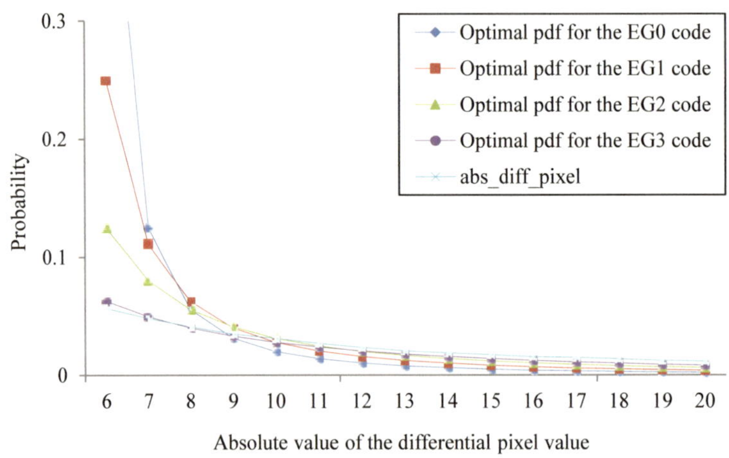


Fig. 13. Probability distribution of the optimal pdf corresponding to the EGk code for $k$ = 0, 1, 2, and 3 and the probability distribution of the absolute value of the differential pixel.

Based on these observations, we designed an efficient binarization algorithm to encode *abs_diff_pixel* in lossless coding. In the proposed algorithm, UEGk binarization of *abs_diff_pixel* is specified by the cutoff value $S = 5$ for the TU prefix and the order $k = 3$ for the EGk suffix. Table 9 shows the proposed UEG3 binarization for *abs_diff_pixel*.

| *abs_diff_pixel* | Bin string | | | | | | | | | | | |
|---|---|---|---|---|---|---|---|---|---|---|---|---|
| | TU prefix | | | | | EG3 suffix | | | | | | |
| 1 | 0 | | | | | | | | | | | |
| 2 | 1 | 0 | | | | | | | | | | |
| 3 | 1 | 1 | 0 | | | | | | | | | |
| 4 | 1 | 1 | 1 | 0 | | | | | | | | |
| 5 | 1 | 1 | 1 | 1 | 0 | | | | | | | |
| 6 | 1 | 1 | 1 | 1 | 1 | 0 | 0 | 0 | 0 | | | |
| 7 | 1 | 1 | 1 | 1 | 1 | 0 | 0 | 0 | 1 | | | |
| 8 | 1 | 1 | 1 | 1 | 1 | 0 | 0 | 1 | 0 | | | |
| 9 | 1 | 1 | 1 | 1 | 1 | 0 | 0 | 1 | 1 | | | |
| 10 | 1 | 1 | 1 | 1 | 1 | 0 | 1 | 0 | 0 | | | |
| 11 | 1 | 1 | 1 | 1 | 1 | 0 | 1 | 0 | 1 | | | |
| 12 | 1 | 1 | 1 | 1 | 1 | 0 | 1 | 1 | 0 | | | |
| 13 | 1 | 1 | 1 | 1 | 1 | 0 | 1 | 1 | 1 | | | |
| 14 | 1 | 1 | 1 | 1 | 1 | 1 | 0 | 0 | 0 | 0 | 0 | |
| 15 | 1 | 1 | 1 | 1 | 1 | 1 | 0 | 0 | 0 | 0 | 1 | |
| ... | ... | | | | | ... | | | | | | |
| Bin index | 1 | 2 | 3 | 4 | 5 | 6 | 7 | 8 | 9 | 10 | 11 | ... |

Table 9. Proposed UEG3 binarization for encoding the absolute value of the differential pixel

## 6. Experimental results and analysis

In this chapter, we introduced the improved CAVLC and CABAC methods for lossless intra coding. In order to verify coding efficiency of the proposed methods, we performed experiments on several test sequences of YUV 4:2:0 and 8 bits per pixel format with QCIF, CIF, and HD resolutions. We implemented our proposed methods in the H.264/AVC reference software version JM13.2 (Fraunhofer Institute for Telecommunications Heinrich Hertz Institute, 2011). Table 10 shows the encoding parameters for the reference software.

| Parameter | CAVLC | CABAC |
|---|---|---|
| *ProfileIDC* | 244 (High 4:4:4) | |
| *IntraPeriod* | 1 (only intra coding) | |
| *QPISlice* | 0 (lossless) | |
| *QPPrimeYZeroTransformBypassFlag* | 1 | |
| *SymbolMode* | 0 | 1 |

Table 10. Encoding parameters

In order to evaluate coding performance for the proposed CAVLC and CABAC methods, we consider two sections based on the following settings in each method.

| Entropy coder | Method | Description |
|---|---|---|
| CAVLC | *Method I* | Modify *numdiffpix* coding |
| | *Method II* | Method I + modify level coding |
| CABAC | *Method III* | Modify significance map coding |
| | *Method IV* | Method III + modify binarization |

Table 11. Each two coding variations in the proposed CAVLC and CABAC methods

Note that these proposed methods were applied to H.264/AVC lossless intra coding by modifying the semantics and decoding processes, without adding any syntax elements to the H.264/AVC standard. The proposed method was implemented on top of the previous sample-wise DPCM prediction method, and it further enhanced coding efficiency for lossless intra coding in H.264/AVC.
To verify efficiency of the proposed methods, we performed two kinds of experiments. In the first experiment, we compared coding perforamcne of the origianl CAVLC and proposed CAVLC methods and then coding performance of the original CABAC and proposed CABAC methods in Tables 12 and 13, respectively. In the second experiment, we encoded only one frame (first frame) for each test sequence using our proposed methods (*Method II* and *Method IV*) and a well-known lossless coding techniques, lossless joint photographic experts group (JPEG-LS) (Sayood, 2006; Weinberger et al., 2000) used as a comparison for coding performance of our proposed methods.

| Sequence | Size (bits) | Method | Total bits (bits) | Bit saving (%) |
|---|---|---|---|---|
| News (QCIF, 176×144) 100 frames | 30412800 | H.264/AVC CAVLC | 13319592 | 0 |
| | | *Method I* | 12772832 | 4.105 |
| | | *Method II* | 12260784 | 7.949 |
| Foreman (QCIF, 176×144) 100 frames | 30412800 | H.264/AVC CAVLC | 14151096 | 0 |
| | | *Method I* | 13595488 | 3.926 |
| | | *Method II* | 12960664 | 8.412 |
| Mobile (CIF, 352×288) 100 frames | 121651200 | H.264/AVC CAVLC | 72406600 | 0 |
| | | *Method I* | 70186288 | 3.066 |
| | | *Method II* | 62959352 | 13.047 |
| Tempete (CIF, 352×288) 100 frames | 121651200 | H.264/AVC CAVLC | 65508056 | 0 |
| | | *Method I* | 63271688 | 3.414 |
| | | *Method II* | 58310688 | 10.987 |
| City_corr (HD, 1280×720) 100 frames | 1105920000 | H.264/AVC CAVLC | 517138472 | 0 |
| | | *Method I* | 497092864 | 3.876 |
| | | *Method II* | 478721808 | 7.429 |
| Crwodrun (HD, 1920×1080) 100 frames | 2488320000 | H.264/AVC CAVLC | 1177553944 | 0 |
| | | *Method I* | 1131495264 | 3.911 |
| | | *Method II* | 1080073896 | 8.278 |
| Average | | H.264/AVC CAVLC | | 0 |
| | | *Method I* | | **3.716** |
| | | *Method II* | | **9.350** |

Table 12. Comparison of bit savings for H.264/AVC CAVLC and the proposed CAVLC

Comparisons were made in terms of bit-rate percentage differences (Tables 12 and 13) and compression ratio differences (Table 14) with respect to the origianl entropy coding methods in H.264/AVC and JPEG-LS, respectively. These changes were calculated as follows:

$$\Delta Saving\ Bits(\%) = \frac{Bitrate_{H.264/AVC} - Bitrate_{Method}}{Bitrate_{H.264/AVC}} \times 100 \tag{6}$$

$$Compression\ Ratio = \frac{Original\ image\ size}{Bitrate_{Method}} \tag{7}$$

| Sequence | Size (bits) | Method | Total bits (bits) | Bit saving (%) |
|---|---|---|---|---|
| News (QCIF, 176×144) 100 frames | 30412800 | H.264/AVC CABAC | 13941080 | 0 |
| | | *Method III* | 12563136 | 9.884 |
| | | *Method IV* | 11760776 | 15.639 |
| Foreman (QCIF, 176×144) 100 frames | 30412800 | H.264/AVC CABAC | 14344176 | 0 |
| | | *Method III* | 12857928 | 10.361 |
| | | *Method IV* | 12572368 | 12.352 |
| Mobile (CIF, 352×288) 100 frames | 121651200 | H.264/AVC CABAC | 91371512 | 0 |
| | | *Method III* | 85034984 | 6.935 |
| | | *Method IV* | 68152408 | 25.412 |
| Tempete (CIF, 352×288) 100 frames | 121651200 | H.264/AVC CABAC | 79063136 | 0 |
| | | *Method III* | 72756080 | 7.977 |
| | | *Method IV* | 60830560 | 23.061 |
| City_corr (HD, 1280×720) 100 frames | 1105920000 | H.264/AVC CABAC | 565080864 | 0 |
| | | *Method III* | 507403880 | 10.207 |
| | | *Method IV* | 470393024 | 16.757 |
| Crowdrun (HD, 1920×1080) 100 frames | 2488320000 | H.264/AVC CABAC | 1250235376 | 0 |
| | | *Method III* | 1120777696 | 10.355 |
| | | *Method IV* | 1047171240 | 16.242 |
| Average | | H.264/AVC CABAC | | 0 |
| | | *Method III* | | **9.287** |
| | | *Method IV* | | **18.244** |

Table 13. Comparison of bit savings for H.264/AVC CABAC and the proposed CABAC

In Tables 12 and 13, we confirmed that the proposed CAVLC and CABAC methods provided better coding performance compared to the conventioanl CAVLC and CABAC methods—by approximately 9% and 18% bit savings, respectively. Table 14 presents the experimental results comparing a well-known lossless coding techniques, JPEG-LS, in terms of lossless intra coding, which again shows that the proposed methods displayed better coding performance compared to JPEG-LS in lossless coding.

Lossless compression techniques, such as JPEG-LS and H.264/AVC lossless mode consist of two independent coding parts; prediction based on modeling and entropy coding of prediction residuals. In JPEG-LS, a simple predictive coding model called *differential pulse-code modulation* (DPCM) is employed. This is a model in which predictions of the sample values are estimated from the neighboring samples that are previously coded in the image.

Most predictors take the average of the samples immediately above and to the left of the target sample. In H.264/AVC, a similar DPCM is employed to predict the original pixel value, but it employs rate-distortion optimization (RDO) (Sullivan & Wiegand, 1998) method to find the best prediction. Hence, H.264/AVC requires the additional coding bits to send the prediction mode but it can reduce more coding bits in the residual coding. However, when the residual data is entered into the entropy coding part, JPEG-LS provides better coding performance than H.264/AVC lossless mode because H.264/AVC still employs CAVLC or CABAC which are mainly designed for discrete cosine transform(DCT)-based lossy coding. As a result, JPEG-LS and H.264/AVC lossless mode provide quite similar coding performance. Since, in this chapter, we have proposed the improved CAVLC and CABAC methods for lossless intra coding, coding performance of the H.264/AVC lossless mode based on the proposed methods is better than that of JPEG-LS, as shown in Table 14.

| Sequence | Method | Compression ratio |
|---|---|---|
| News (QCIF, 176×144) 1 frame | JPEG-LS | 2.0872 |
| | *Method II* | **2.4660** |
| | *Method IV* | **2.5948** |
| Foreman (QCIF, 176×144) 1 frame | JPEG-LS | 1.8179 |
| | *Method II* | **2.3554** |
| | *Method IV* | **2.4528** |
| Mobile (CIF, 352×288) 1 frame | JPEG-LS | 1.4865 |
| | *Method II* | **1.9515** |
| | *Method IV* | **1.7992** |
| Tempete (CIF, 352×288) 1 frame | JPEG-LS | 1.6556 |
| | *Method II* | **2.0813** |
| | *Method IV* | **2.0013** |
| City_corr (HD, 1280×720) 1 frame | JPEG-LS | 1.9079 |
| | *Method II* | **2.2809** |
| | *Method IV* | **2.3248** |
| Crwodrun (HD, 1920×1080) 1 frame | JPEG-LS | 1.6802 |
| | *Method II* | **2.1745** |
| | *Method IV* | **2.1628** |
| Average | JPEG-LS | 1.7726 |
| | *Method II* | **2.2183** |
| | *Method IV* | **2.2226** |

Table 14. Comparison of compression ratio for JPEG-LS, *Method II*, and *Method IV*

Let us now give some information on why we do not address lossless inter coding and why it is outside the scope of our work. Since transform and quantization are not used in lossless video coding, the statistical properties of residual data highly depend on prediction. In general, since video sequences contain more redundancy in time than in space, the accuracy of inter prediction is better than that of intra prediction. Thus, there are significant statistical differences in residual data between lossless intra and lossless inter coding. In other words, for lossless intra prediction, the distribution of the amplitude of residual data is quite wide; in contrast, for lossless inter prediction, the distribution of the amplitude of residual data is skewed on small values. Finally, it is not easy to determine the best entropy coding method that can generally be used for lossless video coding (for both intra and inter coding). Therefore, in this chapter, we focused on the improvement of an appropriate entropy coder for lossless intra coding—though there could be a future work focused on improving upon current entropy coders for lossless video coding.

In terms of scanning patterns for lossy coding, coding performance can change according to various scanning patterns because residual data are the quantized transform coefficients, and the statistical distribution of these coefficients is highly skewed on small values, as depicted in Figs. 5, 6, and 12. Hence, if we can determine an appropriate scanning pattern, we can enhance coding performance by arranging the quantized transform coefficients according to their amplitudes. However, in lossless coding, the statistical distribution of residual data is quite wide; the figures also show that large variations and wide tails are independent of the scanning position. Therefore, theoretically, there is no scanning order that can provide better coding efficiency than that obtained here; we subsequently confirmed this fact by performing extensive experiments using various scanning patterns, including experiments using a zigzag scanning order. Finally, determining the optimum scanning pattern that can be generally accepted for lossless coding is rather difficult. However, a future work may be based on this topic.

## 7. Conclusion

In this chapter, we proposed the improved *context-based adaptive variable length coding* (CAVLC) and *context-based adaptive binary arithmetic coding* (CABAC) methods for lossless intra coding. Considering the statistical differences in residual data between lossy and lossless coding, we designed each new entropy coder by modifying the corresponding encoding parts of each conventional entropy coder based on the observed statistical characteristics of residual data in lossless coding. Experimental results show that the proposed CAVLC and CABAC methods provided approximately 9% and 18% bit savings, compared to the original CAVLC and CABAC methods in the H.264/AVC FRExt high profile, respectively.

## 8. Acknowledgment

This research was supported by the MKE(The Ministry of Knowledge Economy), Korea, under the ITRC(Information Technology Research Center) support program supervised by the NIPA(National IT Industry Promotion Agency). (NIPA-2011-(C1090-1111-0003)).

## 9. References

Bjontegaard G. & Lillevold K. (2002). Context-Adaptive VLC (CVLC) Coding of Coefficients. *Document of Joint Video Team of ISO/IEC JTC1/SC29/WG11 and ITU-T Q.6/SG16*, Fairfax, Virginia, USA, May 6-10, 2002

Brunello D., Calvagno G., Mian G. A., & Rinaldo R. (2003). Lossless Compression of Video Using Temporal Information. *IEEE Transactions on Image Processing*, Vol.12, No.2, (February 2003), pp. 132-139, ISSN 1057-7149

Fraunhofer Institute for Telecommunications Heinrich Hertz Institute. Joint Video Team, *H.264/AVC Reference Software Version 13.2* [Online], January 2011, Available from: http://iphome/hhi.de/shehring/tml/download/old_jm/jm13.2.zip

Gallager R. G. & Van Voorhis D. C. (1975). Optimal source codes for geometrically distributed integer alphabets. *IEEE Transactions on Information Theory*, Vol.21, No.2, (March 1975), pp. 228–230, ISSN 0018-9448

Heo J., Kim S.H., & Ho. Y.S. (2010). Improved CAVLC for H.264/AVC Lossless Intra Coding. *IEEE Transactions on Circuits and Systems for Video Technology*, Vol.20, No.2, (February 2010), pp. 213–222, ISSN 1051-8215

Lee Y.-L., Han K.-H., & Lim S.-C. (2005). Lossless Intra Coding for Improved 4:4:4 Coding in H.264/MPEG-4 AVC. *Document of Joint Video Team of ISO/IEC JTC1/SC29/WG11 and ITU-T Q.6/SG16*, Poznan, Poland, July 24-29, 2005

Lee Y.-L., Han K.-H., & Sullivan G. (2006). Improved lossless intra coding for H.264/MPEG-4 AVC. *IEEE Transactions on Image Processing*, Vol.15, No.9, (September 2006), pp. 2610–2615, ISSN 1057-7149

Luthra A., Sullivan G., & Wiegand T. (2003). Introduction to the special issue on the H.264/AVC video coding standard. *IEEE Transactions on Circuits and Systems for Video Technology*, Vol.13, No.7, (July 2003), pp. 557–559, ISSN 1051-8215

Malvar H., Hallapuro A., Karczewicz M., & Kerofsky L. (2003). Low-Complexity transform and quantization in H.264/AVC. *IEEE Transactions on Circuits and Systems for Video Technology*, Vol.13, No.7, (July 2003), pp. 598–603, ISSN 1051-8215

Marpe D., Schwarz H., & Wiegand T. (2003). Context-based adaptive binary arithmetic coding in the H.264/AVC video compression. *IEEE Transactions on Circuits and Systems for Video Technology*, Vol.13, No.7, (July 2003), pp. 620–636, ISSN 1051-8215

Richardson I. E. G. (2003). *H.264 and MPEG-4 video compression*. New York: Wiley, ISBN 0-470-84837-5, England

Salomon D. (2007). *Variable-length Codes for Data Compression*. Springer, ISBN 978-1-84628-958-3, England

Sayood K. (2006). *Introduction to Data Compression*, CA: Morgan Kaufmann, ISBN 978-0-12-620862-7, USA

Sullivan G. & Wiegand T. (1998). Rate-distortion optimization for video compression. *IEEE Signal Processing Magazine*, Vol. 15, (Nov. 1998), pp. 74-90, ISSN 1053-5888

Sullivan G., McMahon T., Wiegand T., Marpe D., & Luthra A. (2004). Draft Text of H.264/AVC Fidelity Range Extensions Amendment. *Document of Joint Video Team of ISO/IEC JTC1/SC29/WG11 and ITU-T Q.6/SG16*, Redmond, WA, USA, July 17-23, 2004

Sullivan G., Topiwala P., & Luthra A. (2004). The H.264/AVC advanced video coding standard: Overview and introduction to the fidelity range extensions. *Proceedings of SPIE Conference, Special Session on Advances in the New Emerging Standard: H.264/AVC*, ISBN 978-1-59593-695-0, Denver, Colorado, USA, August 2004

Sullivan G. & Wiegand T. (2005). Video compression–from concepts to the H.264/AVC standard. *Proceedings of the IEEE*, Vol.93, No.1, (January 2005), pp. 18–31, ISSN 0018-9219

Sun S. (2002). Intra Lossless Coding and QP Range Selection. *Document of Joint Video Team of ISO/IEC JTC1/SC29/WG11 and ITU-T Q.6/SG16*, Fairfax, Virginia, USA, May 6-10, 2002

Teuhola J. (1978). A compression method for clustered bit-vectors. *Information Processing Letters*, Vol.7, (October 1978), pp. 308–311, ISSN 0020-0190

Weinberger M. J., Seroussi G., & Sapiro G. (2000). The LOCO-I lossless image compression algorithm: Principles and standardization into JPEG-LS. *IEEE Transactions on Image Processing*, Vol.9, No.8, (August 2000), pp. 1309–1324, ISSN 1057-7149

Wiegand T., Sullivan G., Bjøntegaard G., & Luthra A. (2003). Overview of the H.264/AVC video coding standard. *IEEE Transactions on Circuits and Systems for Video Technology*, Vol.13, Vo.7, (July 2003), pp. 560–576, ISSN 1051-8215

10

# Scheduling and Resource Allocation for SVC Streaming over OFDM Downlink Systems

Xin Ji[1], Jianwei Huang[2], Mung Chiang[3], Gauthier Lafruit[4] and Francky Catthoor[5]

[1,5]*IMEC/University of Leuven*

[2]*the Department of Information Engineering,The Chinese University of Hong Kong*

[3]*the Department of Electrical Engineering, Princeton University*

[4]*IMEC*

[1,4,5]*Belgium*

[2]*Hong Kong*

[3]*NJ, USA*

## 1. Introduction

The demand of video transmission over wireless networks exhibits an ever growing trend. However, content distribution and resource allocation are typically studied and optimized separately, which leads to suboptimal network performance. This problem becomes more prominent in wireless networks, where the available network resource is highly dynamic and typically limited in terms of supporting high quality multimedia applications. This makes it challenging to achieve efficient multi-user video streaming over wireless channels.

In this chapter, we consider the problem of multi-user video streaming over Orthogonal Frequency Division Multiplexing (OFDM) networks, where videos are coded in Scalable Video Coding (SVC) format. OFDM is a promising technology for future broadband wireless networks, due to many of its advantages such as robustness against intersymbol interference and the usage of lower complexity equalization at the receiver. It is suitable for supporting high spectrum efficiency communications, and thus is chosen as the core technology for a number of wireless data systems such as IEEE 802.16 (WiMAX), IEEE 802.11a/g (Wireless LANs), and IEEE 802.20 (Mobile Broadband Wireless Access) (34). The resource allocation in OFDM is done in the dimension of power, frequency, and time, and thus is very flexible. SVC, on the other hand, is one of the most promising technologies to enable high coding performance and flexibility (29). It has the attractive capabilities of reconstructing lower resolution or lower quality signals from partially received bitstreams, and hence provides flexible solutions for transmission over heterogeneous networks and allows easy adaptation to various storage devices and terminals. In this chapter, we focus on designing efficient multi-user video streaming protocols that fully exploit the resource allocation flexibility in OFDM and performance scalabilities in SVC.

Most of the previous work on downlink resource allocation in OFDM system focused on elastic data transmissions, where users do not have stringent deadline constraints (e.g., (5; 8; 19; 35; 41)). In (35), the goal was to minimize the total transmit power given users' target bit rates. In (41), the authors investigated the downlink throughput maximization problem with dynamic sub-carrier allocation and fixed power allocation. (19) also considered maximizing the sum-rate without any minimum bit-rate target. In (8), the authors proposed Best Sub-carrier Allocation (BSA) for voice and data users that utilizes the feedback of the radio channel quality and sorts users to choose sub-carrier based on their radio channel feedback. Moreover, (5; 19; 41) considered suboptimal heuristics that use a constant power per sub-carrier. However, due to the deadline requirement feature of real-time video applications, these solutions may not be optimal for delivering multi-user, delay-constrained, real-time streaming video applications.

Video transmission over OFDM channels has been studied recently (15; 36). However, neither of these results considered power allocation, which is critical to wireless multimedia data transmission. For multi-user video streaming over wireless networks, it has been shown that the system performance can be significantly improved by taking the video contents into explicit consideration. In (10), sub-carriers and power are allocated based on rate-distortion model. In (31), video distortion is minimized by considering power and sub-carrier constraints in OFDM systems. Neither (10) nor (31) explicitly took the delay constraint into account.

SVC standard brings various scalabilities (e.g. temporal, spatial, and quality) through adaptation of the bit stream, thus is particularly relevant in heterogeneous network contexts. One niche area of the application of SVC is the transmission over wireless networks. There have been several research results reporting SVC transmission over wireless networks. Most of them focused on exploiting the scalable feature of SVC to provide QoS quarantee for the end users ((6; 28), and the references therein). In (11), the layered bitstream of SVC is exploited in conjunction with a specific congestion control algorithm for distributing video to subscriber stations of an 802.16 system. In (9), the rate distortion model proposed for H.264/AVC is extended to include the effect of random packet loss on the scalable video layers of SVC and the resulting overall video distortion. Reference (32) focused on maximizing the number of admitted users in the communication system by giving different priorities to different video subflows according to their importance. None of the aforementioned solutions for SVC transmission over wireless networks considered power control. An unequal power allocation scheme was proposed in (3) for the transmission of SVC packets over WiMAX communications channels. In (26), a distortion-based gradient scheduling algorithm was proposed. However, they did not consider the influence of video latency on resource allocation.

The main contribution of this chapter is to provide a framework for efficient multi-user SVC video streaming over OFDM wireless channels. The objective is to maximize the average PSNR of all video users under a total downlink transmission power constraint. The basis of our approach is the stochastic subgradient-based scheduling framework presented in ((2; 16; 30)). In previous work (13), an efficient downlink OFDM resource allocation algorithm for *elastic data* traffic has been successfully designed, which is provably optimal for long term utility maximization subject to stochastic channel variations of wireless networks. In this chapter, we generalize such framework to real-time video streaming by further considering dynamically adjusted priority weights based on the current video contents, deadline requirements, and the previous transmission results. The following steps are involved in the proposed joint optimization:

1. Unlike conventional wireless streaming approach, where video data is transmitted indifferently with the achievable rate, we divide the video data into subflows based on the contribution of distortion decrease and the delay requirements of individual video frames.

As discussed in Section 3, this allows the most important video data get transmitted with more priorities and avoid the waste of the network resources.

2. Based on the existing gradient related approach, the rate-distortion weighted transmission scheduling strategy is established in Section 4.3. Our proposed solution involves calculating the weights of the current subflows according to their rate-distortion properties, playback deadline requirements and the previous transmission results.
3. The inherent prioritization brought from the aforementioned weight definition is however conflict with the so-called deadline approaching effect. In Section 4.4, we proposed to deliberately add a product term to the weight calculation which increases when the deadline approaches. This allows the weights of the subflows with low rate-distortion ratio being gracefully increased when their playback deadline approach. We propose a family of algorithms and identify the best tradeoff between meeting deadlines and maximizing the overall video quality.

The resulting algorithms not only fully utilize the temporal and quality scalabilities of the SVC scheme, but also thoroughly explore the time, frequency and multi-user diversities of the OFDM system. Simulations show that the proposed algorithms are better than the content-blind and delay-blind approaches, and the improvement becomes quite significant (e.g., PSNR improvement of as high as 6 dB) in a congested network.
The remainder of this chapter is organized as follows. Section 2 introduces the OFDM network model. Section 3 describes the SVC scheme. Section 4 describes the problem formulation and the proposed algorithms. In Section 5, we examine the performance of our proposed solutions through simulations. Concluding remarks are given in Section 6.

## 2. OFDM model of the wireless transmission

The OFDM network model considered here is similar as in (13). Different video bitstreams are transmitted from the base station to a set $\mathcal{I} = \{1, \ldots, I\}$ of mobile users in an OFDM cell. Time is divided into TDM time-slots that contain an integer number of OFDM symbols. The entire frequency band is divided into a set $\mathcal{J} = \{1, \ldots, J\}$ of tones (carriers). The rate achieved by user $i$ at time $t$, $r_{i,t}$, depends on the resource (tone and power) allocation and the channel gains. In each time-slot, the scheduling and resource allocation decision can be viewed as selecting a rate vector $\boldsymbol{r}_t = (r_{1,t}, \ldots, r_{I,t})$ from the current feasible rate region $\mathcal{R}(\boldsymbol{e}_t) \subseteq \mathbb{R}_+^K$, where $\boldsymbol{e}_t$ indicates the time-varying channel state information available at the scheduler at time $t$. For presentation simplicity, we omit the time index $t$ in the following.
For each tone $j \in \mathcal{J}$ and user $i \in \mathcal{I}$, let $e_{ij}$ be the received signal-to-noise ratio (SNR) per unit power. We denote the power allocated to user $i$ on tone $j$ as $p_{ij}$ and the fraction of time that tone allocated to user $i$ as $x_{ij}$. The total power allocation must satisfy $\sum_{i,j} p_{ij} \leq P$, i.e., the total downlink power constraint at the base station. The total allocation for each tone $j$ must satisfy $\sum_i x_{ij} \leq 1$. For a given allocation with perfect channel estimation, user $i$'s feasible rate on tone $j$ is $r_{ij} = x_{ij} B \log(1 + \frac{p_{ij} e_{ij}}{x_{ij}})$, which corresponds to the Shannon capacity of a Gaussian noise channel with bandwidth $x_{ij}B$ and received SNR $p_{ij}e_{ij}/x_{ij}$.[1] This SNR arises since the active transmission power that user $i$ transmits on tone $j$ is $p_{ij}/x_{ij}$ when only a fraction $x_{ij}$ of the tone is allocated. Without loss of generality we set bandwidth $B = 1$ in the following analysis.
In practical OFDM networks, imperfect carrier synchronization and channel estimation may result in "self-noise" (e.g. (20; 22)). With self-noise, user $i$'s feasible rate on tone $j$ becomes

[1] To better model the achievable rates in a practical system we can re-normalize $e_{ij}$ by $\gamma e_{ij}$, where $\gamma \in [0, 1]$ represents the system's "gap" from capacity.

$$r_{ij} = x_{ij} \log(1 + \frac{p_{ij}\tilde{e}_{ij}}{x_{ij} + \beta p_{ij}\tilde{e}_{ij}}),$$

where $\beta << 1$ is the self-noise coefficient. Under these assumptions, we have

$$\mathcal{R}(\boldsymbol{e}) = \left\{ \boldsymbol{r} : r_i = \sum_j x_{ij} \log\left(1 + \frac{p_{ij}\tilde{e}_{ij}}{x_{ij}+\beta p_{ij}\tilde{e}_{ij}}\right), \forall i \in \mathcal{I}, \sum_{i,j} p_{ij} \leq P, \sum_i x_{ij} \leq 1 \ \forall j \in \mathcal{J}, (\boldsymbol{x}, \boldsymbol{p}) \in \mathcal{X} \right\}, \tag{1}$$

where $\mathcal{X} := \prod_{j=1}^{N} \mathcal{X}_j$, and for all $j \in \mathcal{J}$,

$$\mathcal{X}_j := \left\{ (\boldsymbol{x}^j, \boldsymbol{p}^j) \geq \boldsymbol{0} : x_{ij} \leq 1, p_{ij} \leq \frac{x_{ij}\tilde{s}_{ij}}{\tilde{e}_{ij}}, \ \forall i \in \mathcal{I}, \forall j \in \mathcal{J} \right\}, \tag{2}$$

with $\boldsymbol{x}^j := (x_{ij}, \forall i \in \mathcal{I})$ and $\boldsymbol{p}^j := (p_{ij}, \forall i \in \mathcal{I})$. Here, $\tilde{s}_{ij} = \frac{\Gamma_{ij}}{1-\Gamma_{ij}\beta}$, where $\Gamma_{ij} < 1/\beta$ is a maximum SNR constraint on tone $j$ for user $i$, e.g., to model a constraint on the maximum rate per tone due to a limitation on the available modulation and coding schemes. [2]

We assume that $\tilde{e}_{ij}$ is known by the scheduler for all $i$ and $j$ as is $\beta$ (equivalently, the estimation error variance). In a frequency division duplex (FDD) system, this knowledge can be acquired by having the base station transmit pilot signals, from which the users can estimate their channel gains and feedback to the base station. In a time division duplex (TDD) system, these gains can also be acquired by having the users transmit uplink pilots; the base station can then exploit reciprocity to measure the channel gains. In both cases, this feedback information would need to be provided within the channel's coherence time.

## 3. SVC Scheme of video coding

SVC is an extension of the H.264/MPEG4-AVC video coding standard (33) and provides three different scalabilities: spatial, temporal, and quality. An overview of the features and applications of SVC can be found in (29). In this chapter, we focus on how to exploit the temporal and quality salabilities by adaptive scheduling and resource allocation.[3]

In SVC, the video frames are usually divided into groups, or called groups of pictures (GOPs). The typical SVC GOP structure is shown in Fig. 1, where we assume that one GOP consists of 4 frames. The video frames are further encoded into different temporal and quality layers. One box in Fig. 1 represents the data belonging to one specific temporal layer and one specific quality layer. For the purpose of video distortion calculation, we regard a box as the smallest decodable data unit and call it a "packet". All the packets in one column represent one frame. For example, frame $L_1$ consists of three packets: $L_{10}$, $L_{11}$, and $L_{12}$.

The packets at the same horizontal level belong to the same quality layer. The *quality scalability* refers to the fact that a video decoder can reconstruct video sequences without receiving all quality layers. After receiving the base layer, the decoder can already provide a video with some reasonable quality. The video quality can be improved if one or more enhancement quality layers are received before the required playback deadline of the corresponding video frames. In Fig. 1, the dashed arrows depict the enhancement layers order for each video frame.

---

[2] Another important practical constraint is that each subchannel can be allocated to at most one user, i.e., $x_{ij} \in [0, 1]$. For simplicity, we do not consider such constraint in this chapter. Interested readers are referred to (13) for related detailed discussions.

[3] The spatial scalability is related to downsampling of the video frames, and its effect is difficult to measure in terms of PSNR. We will consider it in the future work.

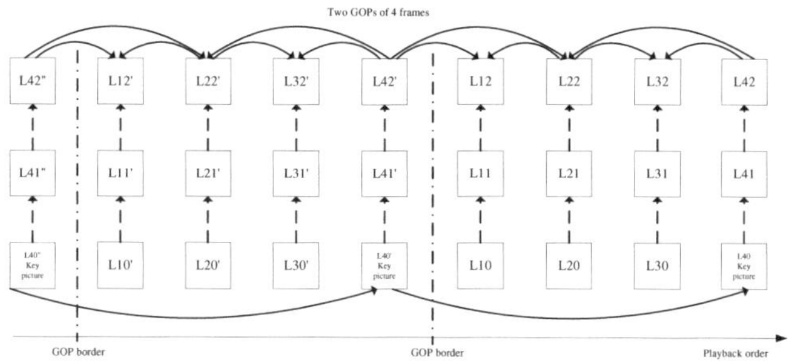


Fig. 1. GOP structure of SVC.

The packets at the same vertical level (i.e., in the same frame) belong to the same temporal layer, and different frames may belong to the same temporal layer. The *temporal scalability* is based on a temporal decomposition using hierarchical B pictures scheme. In Fig. 1, the solid arrows depict the motion predictions for each frame. For example, only after receiving packets $L'_{40}$ and $L_{40}$ (together with all the base layer of video frames they depend on), packet $L_{20}$ becomes decodable at the receiver. Notice that the temporal and quality salabilities are not independent. For example, packet $L_{21}$ can only be decoded if the packets from its lower level quality layer (i.e., $L_{20}$) and previous temporal layer (i.e., $L'_{41}$ and $L_{41}$) are all received.
The quality and temporal scalabilities provide the possibility of adapting the video transmission to different network environments. It is clear that different packets in a GOP have different priorities. Some packets need to be received first in order to make other packets useful (i.e., decodable at the receiver), and this may not follow their own playback order. Also, the sizes of the packets at different quality and temporal layers are typically different. Because this, the compressed SVC video bitstream exhibits a Variable Bit Rate (VBR) nature. It is thus useful to calculate the required rate for delivering the video data with same priority, and use that to facilitate the scheduling and resource allocation decisions.
Let's assume the GOP size is $g$. The total number of temporal levels within a GOP is $\log_2 g$ then. Also we use $P^{t,q,k}$ to denote the packet that belongs to frame $k$, quality layer $q$, and temporal level $t$ in the current GOP. Here $1 \leq k \leq g$, $1 \leq t \leq \log_2 g$, and $0 \leq q \leq Q$. Normally we have $Q \leq 3$ (29). We group the packets with the same deadline as one *subflow* in a way similar as that proposed in (32). For example, in Figure 1, suppose all the packets that are necessary for decoding frame $L_1$ to be one subflow. This subflow consists of packet $L_{40}$, $L_{41}$, $L_{42}$ (and all the packets of former key pictures they depend on, i.e. $L'_{40}$, $L'_{41}$, $L'_{42}$; $L''_{40}$, $L''_{41}$, $L''_{42}$ ... etc. ), $L_{20}$, $L_{21}$, $L_{22}$, $L_{10}$, $L_{11}$, $L_{12}$. Different from the subflow concept in (32), here we also differentiate different quality layers within the same subflow. Among the packets inside this subflow, $L_{40}$ (and the corresponding dependent packets from former GOPs), $L_{20}$, $L_{10}$ belong to the base layer of the current subflow. Other packets belong to the enhancement layers 1 and 2, respectively. This allows us to accurately capture the rate requirements of different packets within one GOP.

## 4. Scheduling and resource allocation algorithms

### 4.1 Gradient-based scheduling framework

Consider a media server that is connected to the base station through a high bandwidth backbone network. Each of the $K$ mobile users in the OFDM cell requests a separate video sequence to be streamed from the media server. We assume that the backbone network is lossless and has high bandwidth, thus the transmission delay from the media server to the OFDM base station is negligible. For each user, only one GOP of the requested sequence will be buffered at the base station at any given time.[4] If the subflow cannot be fully received by the mobile user before its playback deadline, the frames within the partially received subflow may not be able to be decoded at the receiver. Our objective is to design a scheduling and resource allocation algorithm that achieves the maximum overall network streaming quality in the long run, under time varying channel conditions and variable rate video contents.

Our starting point is the stochastic gradient-based scheduling framework presented in (2; 16; 30). In this framework, each user $i$ is assigned a utility function $U_i(W_{i,t})$ depending on their average throughput $W_{i,t}$ up to time $t$, which is used to quantify fairness between users. During each scheduling epoch $t$, the system objective is to choose a rate vector $\boldsymbol{r}_t$ in $\mathcal{R}(\boldsymbol{e}_t)$ that maximizes a (dynamic) weighted sum of the users' rates, where the weights are determined by the gradient of the sum utility across all users. Hence, the scheduling and resource allocation decision is to obtain

$$\max_{\boldsymbol{r}_t \in \mathcal{R}(\boldsymbol{e}_t)} \sum_{i \in \mathcal{I}} \frac{\partial U_i(W_{i,t})}{\partial W_{i,t}} r_{i,t}. \tag{3}$$

The above policy has been shown to yield utility maximizing solutions under time-varying rate region (2; 16; 30), i.e., maximizing $\sum_{i \in \mathcal{I}} U_i(W_{i,t})$. The main advantage of this policy is its greedy nature, i.e., the optimization at time $t$ does not require any rate region information of other time slots (past or future). We notice that Problem (3) needs to be solved for each time slot.

In (13), we proposed an efficient algorithm to solve Problem (3) for an OFDM downlink system with elastic data transmission. Next in Section 4.2 we will briefly review the proposed algorithm in (13). Then in Section 4.3 we will explain the special challenges introduced by the real-time streaming applications and discuss how the algorithm in (13) can be generalized to our case.

### 4.2 Weighted rate maximization algorithm under fixed weights

Consider a given time slot $t$, where we define $w_{i,t} = \partial U_i(W_{i,t})/\partial W_{i,t}$. According to (1), Problem (3) can be stated as follows,

$$\begin{aligned} \max_{(\boldsymbol{x},\boldsymbol{p}) \in \mathcal{X}} V(\boldsymbol{x},\boldsymbol{p}) &:= \sum_i w_i \sum_j x_{ij} \log\left(1 + \tfrac{p_{ij}\tilde{e}_{ij}}{x_{ij} + \beta p_{ij}\tilde{e}_{ij}}\right) \\ \text{subject to:} \quad & \sum_{i,j} p_{ij} \le P, \text{ and } \sum_i x_{ij} \le 1, \ \forall j \in \mathcal{N}. \end{aligned} \tag{4}$$

Here we omit time index $t$ for simplicity. We can solve this problem via a dual decomposition method (4) with complexity $O(NK)$.

First consider the Lagrangian,

$$L(\boldsymbol{x},\boldsymbol{p},\lambda,\boldsymbol{\mu}) := \lambda P + \sum_{j=1}^{N} L_j(\boldsymbol{x}^j,\boldsymbol{p}^j,\lambda,\mu_j), \tag{5}$$

where

$$L_j(\boldsymbol{x}^j,\boldsymbol{p}^j,\lambda,\mu_j) := \mu_j + \sum_{i=1}^{K} w_i x_{ij} \log\left(1 + \frac{p_{ij}\tilde{e}_{ij}}{x_{ij} + \beta p_{ij}\tilde{e}_{ij}}\right) - \mu_j \sum_{i=1}^{K} x_{ij} - \lambda \sum_{i=1}^{K} p_{ij}, \tag{6}$$

[4] If there is enough memory at the base station, we can buffer more than one GOP per user, which does not change the analysis.

and $\boldsymbol{\mu} = (\mu_j)_{j=1}^N$. The corresponding dual function is

$$L(\lambda, \boldsymbol{\mu}) := \max_{(\boldsymbol{p},\boldsymbol{x})\in\mathcal{X}} L(\boldsymbol{x}, \boldsymbol{p}, \lambda, \boldsymbol{\mu}) = \lambda P + \sum_{j=1}^{N} \max_{(\boldsymbol{p}^j,\boldsymbol{x}^j)\in\mathcal{X}_j} L_j(\boldsymbol{x}^j, \boldsymbol{p}^j, \lambda, \mu_j).$$

Since Problem (4) is convex and satisfies Slater's condition, there is no duality gap and so $V^* := \min_{\lambda\geq 0,\boldsymbol{\mu}\geq\mathbf{0}} L(\lambda, \boldsymbol{\mu})$ is the optimal objective value (4).
First, we show that the dual function can be calculated in closed form. Define[5]

$$q(\beta, z) := \begin{cases} z, & \text{if } \beta = 0, \\ \left(\frac{2\beta+1}{2\beta(\beta+1)}\right)\left(\sqrt{1 + \frac{4\beta(\beta+1)}{(2\beta+1)^2}z} - 1\right), & \text{if } \beta > 0, \end{cases}$$

$$h\left(\beta, \omega, \tilde{s}_{ij}\right) := \log\left(1 + \frac{q\left(\beta,(\omega-1)^+\right)\wedge\tilde{s}_{ij}}{1+\beta\left(q\left(\beta,(\omega-1)^+\right)\wedge\tilde{s}_{ij}\right)}\right) - \frac{1}{\omega}\left(q\left(\beta,(\omega-1)^+\right)\wedge\tilde{s}_{ij}\right).$$

and $\mu_{ij}(\lambda) := w_i h\left(\beta, \frac{w_i\tilde{e}_{ij}}{\lambda}, \tilde{s}_{ij}\right)$. Then the dual function is

$$L(\lambda, \boldsymbol{\mu}) := \lambda P + \sum_{j=1}^{N} L_j(\lambda, \mu_j), \tag{7}$$

where $L_j(\lambda, \mu_j) := L_j(\boldsymbol{x}^{j,*}, \boldsymbol{p}^{j,*}, \lambda, \mu_j) = \sum_i \left(\mu_{ij}(\lambda) - \mu_j\right)^+ + \mu_j$.
Second, we can further simplify the dual function by optimizing over $\boldsymbol{\mu}$, i.e.,

$$L(\lambda) := \min_{\boldsymbol{\mu}\geq\mathbf{0}} L(\lambda, \boldsymbol{\mu}) = \lambda P + \sum_j \mu_j^*(\lambda), \tag{8}$$

where for every tone $j$, the minimizing value of $\mu_j^*$ is achieved by $\mu_j^*(\lambda) = \max_i \mu_{ij}(\lambda)$
Since $L(\lambda)$ is the minimum of a convex function over a convex set, it is a convex function of $\lambda$ and can be solved numerically. The overall dual-based algorithm involves evaluating $L(\lambda)$ for a fixed value of $\lambda$ as an inner loop, and a one-dimensional search over $\lambda$ as an outer loop. The outer loop has a constant complexity that is independent of $J$ and $I$[6]. The inner loop has a complexity of $O(JI)$ due to searching for the maximum of $I$ metrics on each of the $J$ tones. Thus the total complexity of this stage is $O(JI)$. Details of the algorithm can be found in (13).

### 4.3 Dynamic weight calculation for streaming applications

The algorithm presented in Section 4.2 solves the weighted rate maximization problem under fixed weights. For elastic data applications, the weights are calculated as the gradients of the utility functions. This weight calculation method, however, is not suitable for real-time video streaming application since the stringent delay constraints are not explicitly considered. This motivates us to design a different weight calculation method in this chapter, which will be based on the required rates to deliver the current subflow and the corresponding distortion decrease.
Without loss of generality, assume that the current time slot starts at $t = 0$. For user $i$'s current unfinished subflow at the base station, its length is $l_i$ bits and the playback deadline is $t_i > 0$.

---

[5] Here $(x)^+ = \max(x, 0)$ and $x \wedge y = \min(x, y)$.

[6] The computational complexity of a bi-section search is $O(\log(1/\epsilon))$, where $\epsilon$ is the relative error bound target for the search.

In order to meet the deadline, the subflow needs to be transmitted at an average rate of

$$\hat{r}_i = \frac{l_i}{t_i}. \tag{9}$$

Note that this may not be the actual rate that user $i$ gets, which depends on the resource allocation decisions.

Denote the distortion of the corresponding frame is $D_{ic}$ if the current subflow can be successfully received before the required playback deadline. Video distortion can be regarded as the negative function of user's utility. The *distortion decrease* depends on how much distortion is at time $t = 0$. This can be calculated as follows:

1. If some of the base layer packets within the current subflow have not been received by the users at time $t = 0$, then the receiver will use the last decodable frames to substitute the desired frames and achieves distortion $D_{il}(> D_{ic})$ at time $t = 0$. In this case, successfully delivering the current subflow on time can lead to distortion decrease of

$$\Delta D_i = D_{il} - D_{ic}. \tag{10}$$

2. If up to $q$ quality layer packets within the current subflow have been fully received at time $t = 0$, where $q$ is less than the maximum number of quality layer available, then the receiver can construct the video frames based on the received quality layers and achieves a distortion $D_{iq}(> D_{ic})$. In this case, successfully delivering the current subflow on time can lead to distortion decrease of

$$\Delta D_i = D_{il} - D_{iq}. \tag{11}$$

Similar as the utility gradient for elastic data traffic, here we can calculate the speed of distortion decrease (i.e., priority weight) in the current time slot as follows:

$$w_{i,t} = \frac{\Delta D_i}{\hat{r}_i} = \frac{\Delta D_i}{l_i} t_i. \tag{12}$$

By taking the users' video contents and deadlines into explicit consideration, we connect the distortion (i.e., utility) with the rate requirement of the video bitstreams.

Nevertheless, using the weight definition of (12) and solving Problem (3) may not lead to good overall video quality. This is due to the "approaching deadline effect". Assume user $i$'s unfinished subflow length $l_i$ is fixed, and so is the possible distortion decrease $\Delta D_i$. If the deadline is approaching, i.e., $t_i$ becomes smaller, priority weight calculated based on (12) actually decreases. This is because for a given amount of data, delivering it within a shorter amount of time requires a larger transmission rate, which leads to a smaller distortion decrease per unit rate. This is counter-intuitive, however, since we would expect that a user with approaching deadline will have higher priority. As a result, weighted rate maximization based on (12) will give users in good channels extra advantage.

For users with the same weight, a user in good channel condition requires less resource to achieve the same transmission rate and thus is favorable. Once a user's current subflow is transmitted completely, the next new subflow has a longer deadline (i.e., a larger $t_i$), which leads to a higher priority weight and more resource allocation. This means that users in worse channels will seldom have chances to transmit and will face a lot of deadline violations. Simulation results in Section 5 also confirm this problem.

To tackle this problem, we next propose a framework to explicitly consider the effect of approaching deadline, which can enforce the deadline to be satisfied with high probability while still achieving an overall good video quality.

### 4.4 Mitigating the approaching deadline effect

We propose to explicitly add a product term to the weight calculation. This term is a decreasing function of $t_i$, i.e., it increases when the deadline approaches. This enforces the system to allocate more resources to "urgent" users and reduce deadline violations. The new priority weight can be calculated as:

$$w_{i,t} = \frac{\Delta D_i}{\hat{r}_i} \Gamma(t_i). \tag{13}$$

where the delay function $\Gamma$ decreases with $t_i$. One choice that achieves the best overall performance in our simulation is to have

$$\Gamma(t_i) = \frac{1}{(t_i)^2}.$$

We will give more examples of function $\Gamma$ in Section 5.

### 4.5 Proposed algorithms

The proposed joint scheduling and resource allocation algorithm for video streaming is given in Algorithm 1, which describes how the scheduling (i.e., which users to transmit) and resource allocation (how much rate each active user gets). For each time slot $t$, there are three key steps in the algorithm:

1. The priority weight of each user is calculated based on its previous transmission results and the deadline of the current subflow.
2. The base station performs the scheduling and resource allocation based on users' priority weights using the algorithm in Section 4.2.
3. Each user transmits the packets based on the allocated resource.

According to the way that the subflow is defined in Section 3, each user transmits the packets in the base quality layer first (from all temporal layers), and then the packets from enhancement quality layers. The video quality degradation is mainly due to two reasons: (i) some packets are discarded at the scheduler before transmission since their deadlines have already passed, or (ii) some packets are discarded at the receiver because they are not decodable due to lack of necessary dependent packets.[7] It is clear that all three steps converge, thus we know that Algorithm 1 converges.
The computational complexity of the proposed algorithm comes from three parts:

1. Merging the remaining packets with the next subflow. The worst case complexity of this step is $O(g(Q+1))$, where $g$ is the GOP size and $Q$ is the maximum number of the quality layers. Since this needs to be done by each user, the overall complexity is $O(Ig(Q+1))$, where $I$ is the total number of users.
2. Calculating the priority weight $w_{i,t}$ according to(13). For a video frame, the distortion of different quality layers can be pre-calculated before streaming. Only if the base layer of a subflow is not successfully received during the transmission, the distortion decrease needs

[7] We assume that the transmitter chooses the appropriate modulation and coding schemes to match the channel conditions of each user such that there is no data corruption during the transmission.

```
initialization t = 0;
repeat
    t = t + 1;
    forall the user i do
        repeat
            check the deadline of the current subflow;
            if the deadline has passed then
                discard those packets not useful for decoding future packets;
                merge the remaining packets with the next subflow, which becomes
                the "current" subflow;
            end
            Calculate the priority weight w_{i,t} according to (13)
        until the deadline of the current subflow has not passed;
    end
    Solve weighted rate maximization problem (4) using the algorithm described in
    Section 4.2, and each user i is allocated transmission rate r_{i,t};
    forall the user i do
        continue to transmit the current subflow with rate r_{i,t};
        if the current subflow is transmitted successfully before the end of the time slot then
            obtain the next subflow from the media server;
            transmit with rate r_{i,t};
        end
    end
until no more video to be streamed;
```

**Algorithm 1:** Joint Scheduling and Resource Allocation Algorithm for Multi-user Video Streaming

to be recalculated between the different frames. Since this rarely happens in practice (as verified by our simulations), the complexity comes from this part is negligible.

3. Solving the weighted rate maximization problem (4), which has complexity $O(IJ)$, where $J$ is the total number of subchannels.

The overall complexity of the algorithm for each time slot $t$ is then $O(I(J + g(Q+1))$.

## 5. Simulation study

### 5.1 Simulation setup

We perform extensive simulations to show the performance gain of our proposed delay-aware scheduling and resource allocation algorithm with different delay functions.

The video sequences used in the experiments are encoded according in H.264 extended SVC standard (using JVT reference software, JSVM 8.12 [5]) at variable bit rates with an average PSNR of 35dB for each sequences. Four sequences ("Harbor", "City", "Foreman", "Mobile and calendar") are used to represent video with dramatically different levels of motion activities. The rate and the quality of the different sequences are shown in Table 1. All the sequences are coded at CIF resolution ($352 \times 288$, 4:2:0) and 30 frames per second. A GOP size of 8 is used. The first frame is encoded as I frame and all the key pictures of each GOP were encoded as P frames.

| Sequence | Bitrate | Average PSNR |
|---|---|---|
| Mobile | 2019 kbps | 35.17 dB |
| Foreman | 449.2 kbps | 35.16 dB |
| City | 585.8 kbps | 35.98 dB |
| Harbour | 1599.7 kbps | 35.32 dB |

Table 1. Encoding rates and average PSNRs of different sequences

For the wireless system, we perform simulation based on a realistic OFDM simulator with realistic industry measurements and assumptions commonly found in IEEE 802.16 standards (17). We simulate a single OFDM cell with a total transmission power of $P = 6$W at the base station. The channel gains $e_{ij}$ are the products of a fixed location-based term for each user $i$ and a frequency-selective fast fading term. The location-based components were picked using an empirically obtained distribution for many users in a large system. The fast-fading term was generated using a block-fading model based upon the Doppler frequency (for the block-length in time) and a standard reference mobile delay-spread model (for variation in frequency). For a user's fast-fading term, each multi-path component was held fixed for 2*m*sec (i.e., a fading block length), which corresponds to a 250MHz Doppler frequency. The delay-spread is 1$\mu$sec. The users' channel conditions are averaged over the applicable channelization scheme and fed back to the scheduler at the base station. All video users are randomly selected from the users with an average channel normalized SNR of at least 20dB. This makes sure that it is possible to support the minimum quality of the video streaming.
We considered a system bandwidth of 5MHz consisting of 512 OFDM tones, which are grouped into 64 subchannels (8 tones per subchannel). The symbol duration is 100$\mu$sec with a cyclic prefix of 10$\mu$sec. This roughly corresponds to 20 OFDM symbols per fading block (i.e., 2*m*sec). This is one of the allowed configurations in the IEEE 802.16 standards (17). The resource allocation is done once per fading block. For each video sequence, we report results that are averaged over 5 randomly generated channel realizations with a length of 10 seconds each (which corresponds to $10^5$ OFDM symbols).

### 5.2 Different weight definitions

We simulate the algorithm with different counter-deadline approaching effect functions $\Gamma$ when calculating the weights $w_{i,t}$ in (13). To illustrate the effectiveness of our proposed algorithm, we also compared with rate maximization algorithm and the algorithm proposed in (26). In total, we simulate seven algorithms. The first two algorithms are benchmark algorithms, and the last five algorithms are our proposed ones with different levels of emphasis on deadline violation avoidance. We will show that algorithm $W_{\Gamma 2}$ achieves the best performance among all proposed ones.

- $W_1$ (benchmark 1: content-blind approach): $w_{i,t} = 1$ for all $i$ and $t$. This is the rate maximization algorithm, which is "content-blind" but widely accepted in data-oriented wireless communication systems (e.g., (13)). On top of this, we use the packet dropping policy for SVC proposed in (24).
- $W_2$ (benchmark 2: deadline-blind approach): the weights in this approach are defined according to (26). Instead of grouping packets into subflows, the schedular will transmit every packet following the order of Method II proposed in (27), which has been proven to achieve similar results as the optimal one. Though special care has been taken to

force every new GOP data to be buffered either after the current GOP's deadline is expired or until all the current GOPs of each user have been transmitted, compared to our subflow scheme (which explicitly consider the deadline of each frame), it is considered as a "deadline-blind" benchmark.

- $W_{rd}$: $\Gamma(t_i - t_c) = 1$. This algorithm takes users' contents into consideration but does not explicit address the deadline approaching effect and thus is "deadline-blind".
- $W_{\Gamma 1}$: $\Gamma(t_i - t_c) = 1/(t_i - t_c)$.
- $W_{\Gamma 2}$: $\Gamma(t_i - t_c) = 1/(t_i - t_c)^2$.
- $W_{\Gamma 3}$: $\Gamma(t_i - t_c) = 1/(t_i - t_c)^3$.
- $W_{\Gamma 4}$: $\Gamma(t_i - t_c) = 1/(t_i - t_c)^4$.

Table 2 shows average PSNR achieved by four users requesting four different video clips with the same starting time. The initial playback deadline is set to be 200ms (25).

| Sequence | $W_1$ | $W_2$ | $W_{rd}$ | $W_{\Gamma 1}$ | $W_{\Gamma 2}$ | $W_{\Gamma 3}$ | $W_{\Gamma 4}$ |
|---|---|---|---|---|---|---|---|
| Mobile | 28.5316 | 26.7014 | 18.6482 | 20.6136 | 28.0960 | 27.6642 | 27.4646 |
| Foreman | 29.0880 | 30.7430 | 27.2240 | 30.6424 | 33.5992 | 33.2444 | 33.0476 |
| City | 34.2552 | 31.0290 | 33.5274 | 34.1902 | 34.0882 | 33.8188 | 33.6754 |
| Harbour | 23.5310 | 26.9150 | 20.1732 | 21.6224 | 26.1610 | 26.0774 | 25.9670 |
| *Average* | 28.8514 | 28.8470 | 24.8932 | 26.7672 | 30.4862 | 30.2012 | 30.0388 |

Table 2. Average PSNR for 4 users with 200ms initial playback deadline

As we can see, the weighted gradient based scheduling reflects the rate-distortion properties of different video contents. Under $W_1$ algorithm, the qualities of Mobile and Foreman are similar, although they have very different rate-distortion properties. This is because $W_1$ simply maximizes the rate without considering the resulting video quality. Instead, by allocating network resource according to the users' video rate-distortion properties, the weighted scheduling and resource allocation schemes can dynamically adjust the resource allocation based on video contents. Since the benchmark algorithm $W_2$ does not dynamically organize the video packet into different subflow or change the weights according to the run-time transmission results, it achieves inferior results compared to our proposed algorithms ($W_{\Gamma 2}$ to $W_{\Gamma 4}$).

Compared to the benchmark $W_1$ and $W_2$ algorithms, the $W_{rd}$ algorithm actually decreases the average video quality among different users. This is due to the deadline approaching effect explained in Section 4.3. Once we take care of this effect by properly chosen $\Gamma$ functions in $W_{\Gamma 1}$ to $W_{\Gamma 4}$, the average PSNR among users is improved over the simple total rate maximization scheme ($W_1$) by 1.1 dB to 1.6 dB. Results of $W_{\Gamma 2}$ reaches the best average PSNR value, while $W_{\Gamma 3}$ and $W_{\Gamma 4}$ tend to decrease the average PSNR value compared with $W_{\Gamma 2}$ since they put too much emphasis on not violating the deadlines.

Figures 2, 3, 4 and 5 show the PSNR values of the first 200 frames achieved by four users requesting different four video clips concurrently under a particular channel realization. The initial playback deadline is set to be 400ms. In these figures, the results of weight definition $W_1$, $W_2$ and our best approach $W_{\Gamma 2}$ are compared.

From the figures, we see that compared to algorithm $W_{\Gamma 2}$, algorithm $W_1$ only considers rate maximization and hence user 2 and user 4's video qualities are sacrificed. Some of the frames' PSNR value of user 1 and user 3 may be higher than those of our proposed algorithm, however without significant performance improvement compared to the video quality of the proposed ones. This proves that our proposed rate-distortion related gradient based scheme is more efficient.

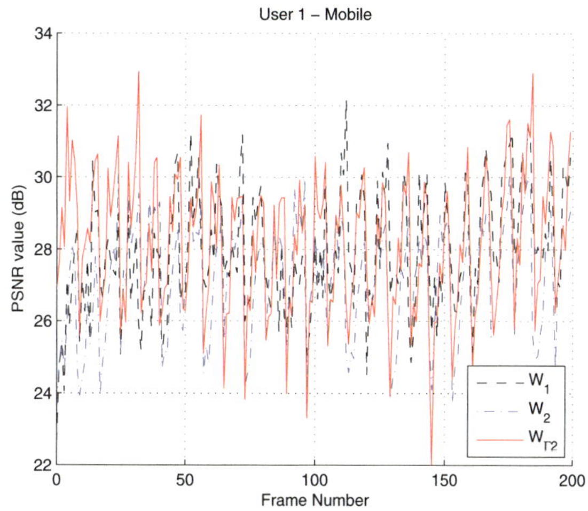


Fig. 2. Frame PSNR of User 1 - Mobile.

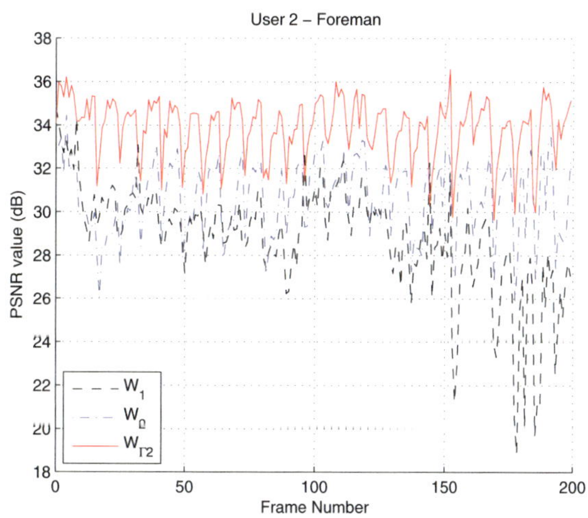


Fig. 3. Frame PSNR of User 2 - Foreman.

### 5.3 Effect of different initial playback deadlines

We now study the impact of different initial playback deadlines in Figure 6. The initial playback deadline means the delay between the time when the user requests the video and the time when the video starts to play at the receiver. According to the user satisfactory study in (25), we test various initial playback deadlines between 200ms to 800ms. Four users request the different video sequences from the server simultaneously. Other parameters are the same as in Section 5.1. We can see that $W_{\Gamma 2}$ always reaches the highest average PSNR value under different deadlines.

### 5.4 Synchronous and asynchronous requirements' influence

So far we have only considered the cases of synchronously deadlines, i.e., all users start requesting the video streaming applications at the same time. In reality, it is more common

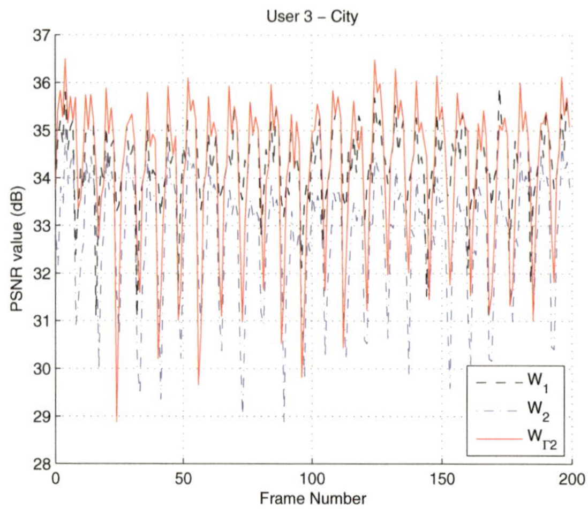


Fig. 4. Frame PSNR of User 3 - City.

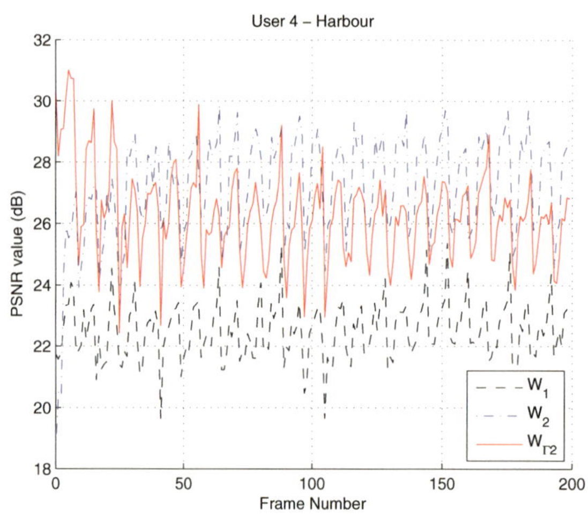


Fig. 5. Frame PSNR of User 4 - Harbour.

that different users request video clips at different time, which we call *a*synchronous deadlines cases. In Figure 7, we compare the results of these cases for four users. In the asynchronous deadline cases, four users randomly start to request the different video sequences from the server within the first initial playback deadline. We again observe that the $W_{\Gamma 2}$ algorithm always performs the best.

**5.5 Different user content and congestion range's influence**

Figure 8 shows the results of eight users requesting video sequences concurrently. Each of the 4 video sequences is requested by 2 users. Synchronous and asynchronous cases are both shown here. For the asynchronous cases, users randomly request the video sequence within one playback deadline. The other setups are the same as in Section 5.2.

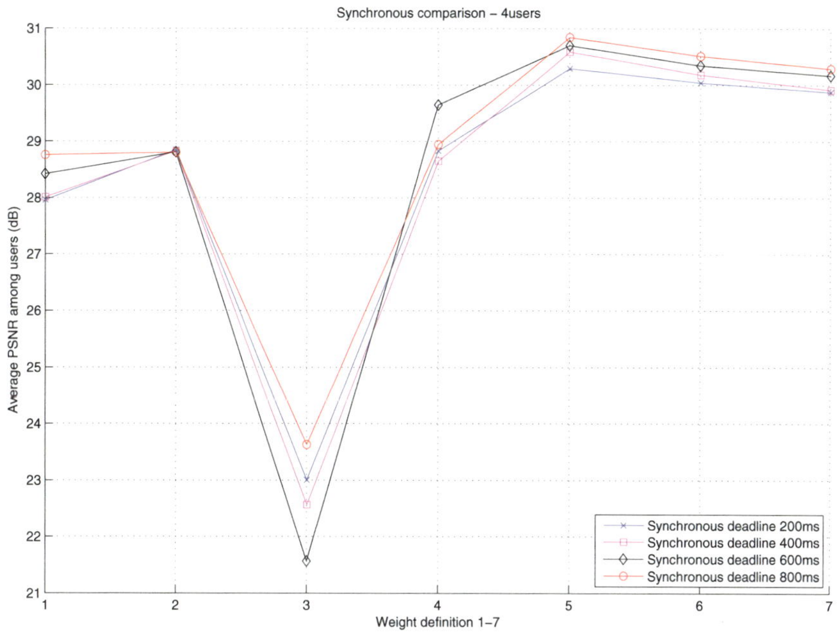


Fig. 6. Synchronous deadlines for 4 users. Horizontal axis represent different algorithms: 1 - $W_1$; 2 - $W_2$; 3 - $W_{rd}$; 4 - $W_{\Gamma 1}$; 5 - $W_{\Gamma 2}$; 6 - $W_{\Gamma 3}$; 7 - $W_{\Gamma 4}$;

The effectiveness of our proposed algorithms is more obvious compared to the rate maximization algorithm $W_1$ in heavily congested network case. For asynchronous cases with playback deadline of 800ms, algorithm $W_{\Gamma 2}$ achieves as high as 6dB improvement in users' average PSNR value. In the asynchronous cases, the advantage of porposed alogirthm is not so obvious as compared to algorithm $W_2$. This is because, the congestion of network is so heavy that "GOP control" is almost as effective as the deadline approaching control. Besides, little can be exploited by dynamically adapting weights according to the video rate-distortion properties.

### 5.6 Fairness analysis

Motived by the Jain's fairness index (18), we propose the following index to evaluate the fairness of video qualities achieved by different algorithms:

$$VideoQualityFairness = \frac{(\sum_i PSNR_i)^2}{n \sum_i (PSNR_i)^2} \quad (14)$$

The fairness index ranges from $1/n$ (worst case) to 1 (best case). For each algorithm, we show the fairness index of different simulation settings in Tables 3, 4, 5 and 6. In all cases, Algorithm $W_2$ always achieves the highest fairness index. However, Table 2 shows that it achieves so by sacrificing the video quality. All of our five proposed algorithms achieve a fairness index of more than 0.98 most of the time. We also find that $W_{rd}$ always has the worst fairness property, which means this algorithm does not consider the fairness but only emphasizes on the rate-distortion property. In fact, both considering the deadline approaching effect and

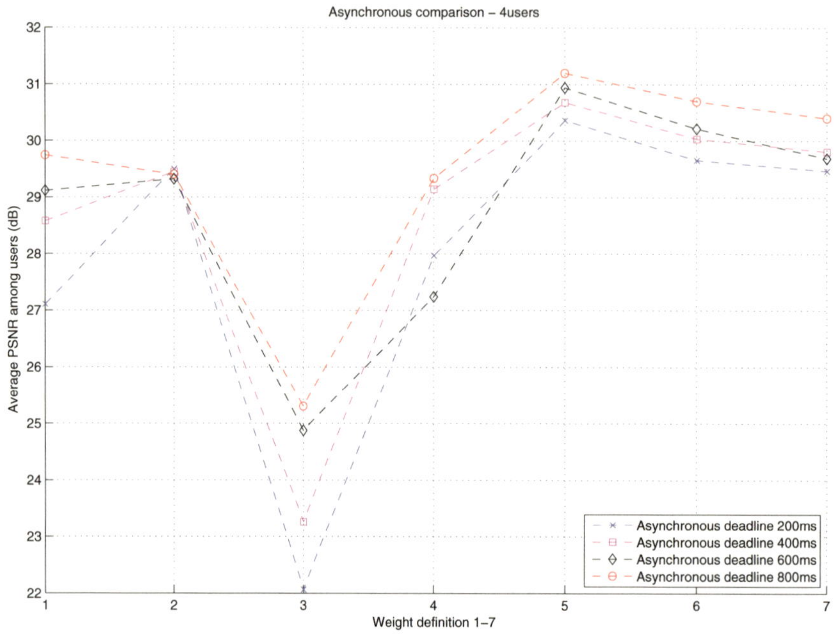


Fig. 7. Asynchronous deadlines for 4 users. Horizontal axis represent different algorithms: 1 - $W_1$; 2 - $W_2$; 3 - $W_{rd}$; 4 - $W_{\Gamma 1}$; 5 - $W_{\Gamma 2}$; 6 - $W_{\Gamma 3}$; 7 - $W_{\Gamma 4}$;

using "GOP control" can improve fairness. The "GOP control" benchmark algorithm ($W_2$) pursues absolute fairness, thus decreases the overall video quality.

| Weight | Channel 1 | Channel 2 | Channel 3 | Channel 4 | Channel 5 |
|---|---|---|---|---|---|
| $W_1$ | 0.9848 | 0.9354 | 0.986 | 0.941 | 0.9426 |
| $W_2$ | 0.995 | 0.9953 | 0.9962 | 0.9898 | 0.9942 |
| $W_{rd}$ | 0.9423 | 0.9328 | 0.8281 | 0.9314 | 0.9341 |
| $W_{\Gamma 1}$ | 0.9799 | 0.9162 | 0.9287 | 0.9544 | 0.9335 |
| $W_{\Gamma 2}$ | 0.9856 | 0.9845 | 0.9868 | 0.9806 | 0.9818 |
| $W_{\Gamma 3}$ | 0.9873 | 0.9855 | 0.9877 | 0.9797 | 0.982 |
| $W_{\Gamma 4}$ | 0.9869 | 0.9848 | 0.988 | 0.9794 | 0.9821 |

Table 3. 4 users with synchronous initial playback deadline of 200ms

## 6. Conclusion

Traditionally the content distribution and network resource allocation are designed separately. Although working well in the wireline communication settings, this approach could be far from optimal for wireless communication networks, where the available network resource changes rapidly in time. In this chapter, we apply a joint design approach to solve the challenging problem of multi-user video streaming over wireless channels. We focused on the SVC coding schemes and the OFDM schemes, which are among the most promising technologies for video coding and wireless communications, respectively.

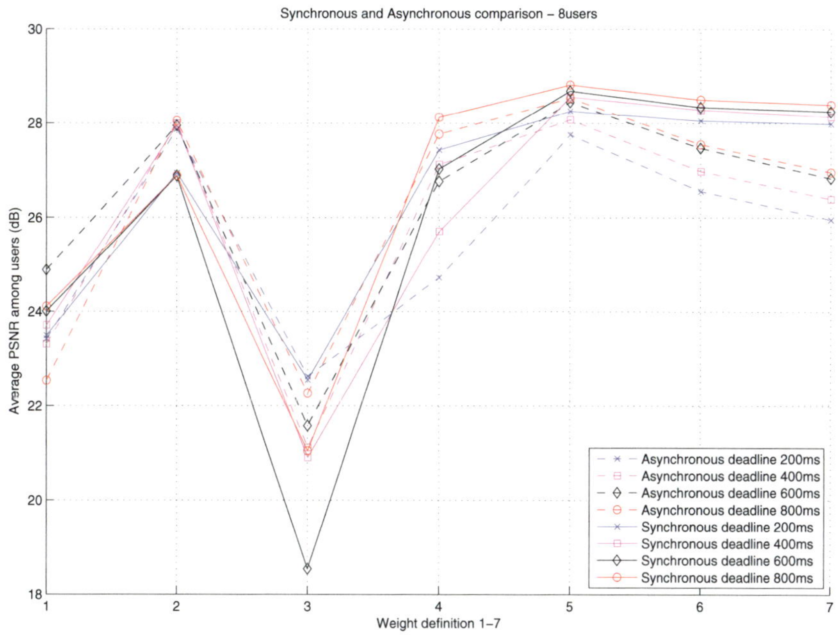


Fig. 8. Synchronous and Asynchronous deadlines for 8 users: 1 - $W_1$; 2 - $W_2$; 3 - $W_{rd}$; 4 - $W_{\Gamma 1}$; 5 - $W_{\Gamma 2}$; 6 - $W_{\Gamma 3}$; 7 - $W_{\Gamma 4}$;

| Weight | Channel 1 | Channel 2 | Channel 3 | Channel 4 | Channel 5 |
|---|---|---|---|---|---|
| $W_1$ | 0.9656 | 0.8883 | 0.9139 | 0.9342 | 0.9088 |
| $W_2$ | 0.9938 | 0.9949 | 0.9888 | 0.9931 | 0.9951 |
| $W_{rd}$ | 0.971 | 0.8965 | 0.9292 | 0.9373 | 0.947 |
| $W_{\Gamma 1}$ | 0.9806 | 0.9804 | 0.9747 | 0.9751 | 0.9816 |
| $W_{\Gamma 2}$ | 0.9839 | 0.9832 | 0.9773 | 0.9777 | 0.9861 |
| $W_{\Gamma 3}$ | 0.9836 | 0.9836 | 0.9774 | 0.978 | 0.9859 |
| $W_{\Gamma 4}$ | 0.9841 | 0.9829 | 0.9767 | 0.9779 | 0.9845 |

Table 4. 8 users with synchronous initial playback deadline of 200ms

| Weight | Channel 1 | Channel 2 | Channel 3 | Channel 4 | Channel 5 |
|---|---|---|---|---|---|
| $W_1$ | 0.9851 | 0.9172 | 0.9805 | 0.8884 | 0.9428 |
| $W_2$ | 0.9945 | 0.9947 | 0.9963 | 0.9793 | 0.9936 |
| $W_{rd}$ | 0.8701 | 0.9534 | 0.8264 | 0.8208 | 0.941 |
| $W_{\Gamma 1}$ | 0.9725 | 0.9817 | 0.95 | 0.8494 | 0.9754 |
| $W_{\Gamma 2}$ | 0.9851 | 0.9846 | 0.9869 | 0.9813 | 0.9824 |
| $W_{\Gamma 3}$ | 0.9831 | 0.9805 | 0.9861 | 0.9804 | 0.9823 |
| $W_{\Gamma 4}$ | 0.9834 | 0.9778 | 0.9867 | 0.9811 | 0.9823 |

Table 5. 4 users with asynchronous initial playback deadline of 200ms

| Weight | Channel 1 | Channel 2 | Channel 3 | Channel 4 | Channel 5 |
|---|---|---|---|---|---|
| $W_1$ | 0.9863 | 0.9414 | 0.9799 | 0.9417 | 0.9429 |
| $W_1$ | 0.9949 | 0.9956 | 0.9956 | 0.9897 | 0.9936 |
| $W_{rd}$ | 0.9437 | 0.9247 | 0.9436 | 0.9329 | 0.8332 |
| $W_{\Gamma 1}$ | 0.9803 | 0.8958 | 0.9826 | 0.9763 | 0.9254 |
| $W_{\Gamma 2}$ | 0.9853 | 0.9834 | 0.9893 | 0.982 | 0.9832 |
| $W_{\Gamma 2}$ | 0.9861 | 0.9852 | 0.9893 | 0.9812 | 0.9823 |
| $W_{\Gamma 2}$ | 0.9865 | 0.9847 | 0.9893 | 0.9818 | 0.9843 |

Table 6. 4 users with synchronous initial playback deadline of 800ms

Building on the gradient-based scheduling framework in our previous work, we proposed a family of algorithms that explicitly calculate the users' priority weights based on the video contents, deadline requirements, and previous transmission results, and then optimize the resource allocation taking various wireless practical constraints into consideration. We first divide the video data into subflows based on their contribution of distortion decrease and the delay requirements of individual video frames. Then we propose to calculate the weights of the current subflows according to their rate-distortion properties, playback deadline requirements and the previous transmission results. To tackle the deadline approaching effect, we also propose to explicitly add to the weight calculation a product term which increases when the deadline approaches.
Simulation results show that our algorithms always outperform the rate maximization (content-blind) scheme and the pure gradient-based (deadline-blind) scheme. Besides improving the average video quality, the proposed algorithms also lead to a fair allocation. Finally, the performance of the algorithms are consistent under both synchronous or asynchronous deadlines.

## 7. References


[1] R. Agrawal and V. Subramanian, "Optimality of certain channel aware scheduling policies," in *Proc. of 2002 Allerton Conference*, 2002.
[2] R. Agrawal and V. Subramanian, "Optimality of certain channel aware scheduling policies," *Proc. of 2002 Allerton Conference on Communication, Control and Computing*, 2002.
[3] Z. Ahmad, S. Worrall and A. Kondoz, "Unequal power allocation for scalable video transmission over WiMAX", *IEEE International Conference on Multimedia and Expo, ICME'08*, pp. 517-520, Hannover, Germany, 2008.
[4] D. Bertsekas, *Nonlinear Programming*, 2nd ed. Belmont, Massachusetts: Athena Scientific, 1999.
[5] T. Chee, C. C. Lim, and J. Choi, "Adaptive Power Allocation with User Prioritization for Downlink Orthogonal Frequency Division Multiple Access Systems," in *Proc. of 9th IEEE International Conf. on Communication Systems*, pp. 210-214, Sept. 2004.
[6] Hsing-Lung Chen, Po-Ching Lee and Shu-Hua Hu, "Improving Scalable Video Transmission over IEEE 802.11e through a Cross-Layer Architecture," *The Fourth International Conference on Wireless and Mobile Communications*, pp. 241-246, 2008.
[7] P. Chou and Z. Miao, "Rate-Distortion Optimized Streaming of Packetized Media," *IEEE Trans. Multimedia*, vol. 8, no. 2, pp. 390–404, 2006.
[8] N. Damji, T. Le-Ngoc, "Dynamic Downlink OFDM Resource Allocation with Interference Mitigation and Macro Diversity for Multimedia Services in Wireless Cellular Systems", WCNC 2005

[9] Y. P. Fallah, H. Mansour, S. Khan, P. Nasiopoulos and H. M. Alnuweiri, "A Link Adaptation Scheme for Efficient Transmission of H.264 Scalable Video Over Multirate WLANs", *Circuits and Systems for Video Technology, IEEE Transactions on*, Volume: 18, Issue: 7, pp. 875-887, July 2008.

[10] Hojin Ha, Changhoon Yim and Young Yong Kim, "Distortion Management Scheme for Multiuser Video Transmission in OFDM Systems", *5th IEEE Consumer Communications and Networking Conference, CCNC'08*, pp. 795-799, Jan. 2008.

[11] O. Hillestad, A. Perkis, V. Genc, S. Murphy and J. Murphy, "Adaptive H.264/MPEG-4 SVC video over IEEE 802.16 broadband wireless networks," *Packet Video 2007*, pp. 26-35, Lausanne, Switzerland, Nov. 2007.

[12] L. Hoo, B. Halder, J. Tellado, and J. Cioffi, "Multiuser Transmit Optimization for Multicarrier Broadcast Channels: Asymptotic FDMA Capacity Region and Algorithms," in *IEEE Trans. on Communications*, vol. 52, no. 6, pp. 922-930, June 2004.

[13] J. Huang, V. Subramanian, R. Agrawal, and R. Berry, "Downlink Scheduling and Resource Allocation for OFDM Systems," *IEEE Trans. on Wireless Commun., Accepted, 2008.*

[14] D. Kivanc, G. Li, and H. Liu, "Computationally efficient bandwidth allocation and power control for OFDMA," in *IEEE Trans. Wireless Commun.*, vol. 2, no. 6, pp. 1150-1158, Nov. 2003.

[15] Seoshin Kwack, Hanbyeol Seo and Byeong Gi Lee, "Suitability-Based Subcarrier Allocation for Multicast Services Employing Layered Video Coding in Wireless OFDM Systems", *IEEE 66th Vehicular Technology Conference, VTC-2007 Fall*, pp. 1752 - 1756, Sept. 30 2007-Oct. 3 2007.

[16] H. Kushner and P. Whiting, "Asymptotic properties of proportional-fair sharing algorithms," in *Proc. 40th Annual Allerton Conference on Communication, Control, and Computing*, Oct. 2002.

[17] "IEEE 802.16e-2005 and IEEE Std 802.16-2004/Cor1-2005," `http://www.ieee802.org/16/`.

[18] R. Jain, D. Chiu and W. Hawe, "A Quantitative Measure of Fairness and Discrimination for Resource Allocation in Shared Systems." DEC Research Report TR-301, 1984.

[19] J. Jang and K. B. Lee, "Transmit Power Adaptation for Multiuser OFDM System," in *IEEE Journal on Selected Areas in Communications*, vol. 21, no. 2, pp. 171-178, Feb. 2003.

[20] H. Jin, R. Laroia, and T. Richardson, "Superposition by position," preprint, 2006.

[21] *JSVM 8 Reference Software*, JVT-Q203, May 2007.

[22] J. Lee, H. Lou and D. Toumpakaris, "Analysis of Phase Noise Effects on Time-Direction Differential OFDM Receivers," *IEEE GLOBECOM*, 2005

[23] W. Li, "Overview of fine granularity scalability in MPEG-4 video standard," *IEEE Transactions on Circuits and Systems for Video Technology*, vol. 11, no. 3, pp. 301 -317, March 2001.

[24] G. Liebl, T. Schierl, T. Wiegand and T. Stockhammer, "Advanced Wireless Multiuser Video Streaming Using the Scalable Video Coding Extensions of H.264/MPEG4-AVC." ICME, 2006

[25] J. Lou, H. Cai, and J. Li, "A Real-Time Interactive Multi-View Video System," *proc. of the 13th annual ACM international conference on Multimedia*, Singapore, 2005.

[26] P. Pahalawatta, R. Berry, T. Pappas, and A. Katsaggelos, "Content-Aware Resource Allocation and Packet Scheduling for Video Transmission over Wireless Networks," *IEEE J. Select. Areas Commun.*, vol. 25, no. 4, pp. 749–759, 2007.

[27] P. Pahalawatta, T. N. Pappas, R. Berry, T. Pappas, and A. Katsaggelos, "Content-Aware Resource Allocation for Scalable Video Transmission on Multiple Users over A Wireless Network," *IEEE ICASSP'07*, Honolulu, USA, Apr. 2007.

[28] T. Schierl, T. Stockhammer and T. Wiegand, "Mobile Video Transmission using Scalable Video Coding (SVC)," *IEEE Trans. on Circuits and Systems for Video Technology, Special issue on Scalable Video Coding*, June 2007.

[29] H. Schwarz, D. Marpe, and T. Wiegand, "Overview of the scalable H.264/MPEG4-AVC extension," in *Proc. IEEE International Conference on Image Processing (ICIP'06)*, Atlanta, GA, USA, Oct. 2006.

[30] A. L. Stolyar, "On the asymptotic optimality of the gradient scheduling algorithm for multiuser throughput allocation," Operations Research, vol. 53, No. 1, pp. 12–25, 2005.

[31] G. M. Su, Z. Han, M. Wu, and K. J.R. Liu, "A Scalable Multiuser Framework for Video over OFDM Networks: Fairness and Efficiency," *IEEE Trans. on Circuits and Systems for Video Technology*, vol. 16, no. 10, pp. 1217–1231, 2006.

[32] M. Van der Schaar, Y. Andreopoulos, and Z. Hu, "Optimized Scalable Video Streaming over IEEE 802.11 a/e HCCA Wireless Networks under Delay Constraints," *IEEE Transactions on Mobile Computing*, vol. 5, pp. 755-768, June 2006.

[33] T. Wiegand,G. J. Sullivan, G. Bjontegaard, and A. Luthra, "Overview of the H.264/AVC Video Coding Standard," *IEEE Trans. on Circuits and Systems for Video Technology*, vol. 13, no. 7, July 2006.

[34] "Orthogonal frequency-division multiplexing," Wikipedia, http://en.wikipedia.org/w/index.php?title=Orthogonal_frequency-division_multiplexing&oldid=153352313.

[35] C. Y. Wong, R. S. Cheng, K. B. Letaief and R. D. Murch, "Multiuser OFDM with Adaptive Subcarrier, Bit and Power Allocation," in *IEEE Journal on Selected Areas in Communications*, vol. 17, no. 10, Oct. 1999.

[36] J. Xu, X. Shen, J. W. Mark, and J, Cai, "Quasi-Optimal Channel Assignment for Real-Time Video in OFDM Wireless Systems," *Wireless Communications, IEEE Transactions on*, Volume 7, Issue 4, pp. 1417 - 1427, April 2008.

[37] Y. Yi and M. Chiang, "Stochastic network utility maximization: A tribute to Kelly's paper published in this journal a decade ago," *European Transactions on Telecommunications*, vol. 19, no. 4, pp. 421-442, June 2008.

[38] H. Yin and H. Liu, "An Efficient Multiuser Loading Algorithm for OFDM-based Broadband Wireless Systems," in *Proc. of IEEE Globecom*, pp. 103-107, Nov. 2000.

[39] W. Yu and R. Lui, "Dual methods for nonconvex spectrum optimization of multicarrier systems," *IEEE Transactions on Communications*, vol. 54, no. 7, pp. 1310–1322, July 2006.

[40] Y. J. Zhang and K. B. Letaief, "Adaptive Resource Allocation and Scheduling for Multiuser Packet-based OFDM Networks," in *Proc. of IEEE ICC*, pp. 2949-2953, June 2004.

[41] Y. J. Zhang and K. B. Letaief, "Multiuser Adaptive Subcarrier-and-Bit Allocation With Adaptive Cell Selection for OFDM Systems," in *IEEE Transactions on Wireless Communications*, vol. 3, no. 5, Sept. 2004.

11

# A Hybrid Error Concealment Technique for H.264/AVC Based on Boundary Distortion Estimation

Shinfeng D. Lin, Chih-Cheng Wang, Chih-Yao Chuang and Kuan-Ru Fu
*Department of Computer Science and Information Engineering National Dong Hwa University, Hualien, Taiwan 974*

## 1. Introduction

Video compression technologies have been extensively studied in recent years. The basic concept of video compression is to reduce the amount of bits for video representation by exploiting spatial and temporal correlations in image sequences. In recent years, H.264/AVC (Advanced Video Coding) is the state-of-the-art video coding standard established by ITU-T Video Coding Experts Group and ISO/IEC Moving Pictures Experts Group. H.264/AVC provides a better compression efficiency and visual quality than prior standards, owing to it adopts some unique techniques to reduce the redundant information, such as multiple reference frames, variable block size, quarter-sample-accurate motion compensation, etc. In H.264/AVC encoder, integer DCT procedure transforms residual data into the frequency domain. Further through quantization will generate many continuous zero coefficients. Two excellent entropy coding schemes can reduce coding redundancy: context-adaptive variable length coding (CAVLC) (Bjontegarrd and Lillevold, 2002) and context-adaptive binary arithmetic coding (CABAC) (Marpe et al., 2003). Therefore, H.264/AVC has higher compression ratio than prior standards and is more appropriate to limited transmission channel. However, this highly compressed video bit stream is very fragile over transmission environments.

In the error-prone transmission channel, packet loss of the highly compressed video bit stream will cause the serious distortion. The distortion will propagate to its successive frames. This is because video coding standards utilize complex predictions to enhance the coding efficiency, especially as H.264/AVC. Thus, how to recover the lost video data in the decoder is critically essential. Since erroneous data would not only make seriously degrade in the current frame but also propagate to the following frames. For solving above-mentioned problems, the error resilience and the error concealment techniques have been proposed in many literatures.

The error resilience is a mechanism in the encoder for resisting packet loss. These preventative mechanisms are designed to improve the robustness of bit streams in noisy networks. On the other hand, the error concealment is an effective mechanism in the decoder. It applies to concealing corrupted regions by referencing previous decoded data. As a video sequence usually has strong spatial and temporal correlation, the corrupted

macro-blocks (MBs) can be approximated from the information of the neighbouring MBs in spatial or temporal domain.
Temporal error concealment (TEC) approaches usually employ the dependence of continuous frames to estimate the lost motion vectors (MVs). Further corrupted MBs can be replaced with the corresponding MBs in reference frames. Corresponding MBs are judged by estimated MVs, obtained by boundary matching algorithms (BMA) (Lam et al., 1993). Spatial error concealment (SEC) approaches adopt neighbouring correct data in the current frame to restore the lost data. One of the remarkable SECs is bilinear interpolation (BI). Bilinear interpolation (BI) calculates weighted average pixel values from boundary pixels. Some SECs interpolate the lost pixels according to the estimated edge directions, such as directional interpolation (DI) mode, multi-directional interpolation (MDI) (Kwok and Sun, 1993) mode and selective directional interpolation (SDI) (Kung et al., 2006) mode.
This article proposes a hybrid error concealment technique which consists of both the proposed temporal and the proposed spatial error concealment approaches. If TEC approach is not appropriate for the corrupted MB, SEC approach will further be adopted. Simulation results show that the recovery performance could be enhanced by the proposed hybrid error concealment technique, even by the proposed temporal error concealment approach.

## 2. The proposed hybrid error concealment in H.264/AVC

The proposed hybrid error concealment technique is implemented in H.264/AVC decoder. It could make trade-off not only between TEC and SEC approaches but also between different error concealment schemes. The flowchart of the proposed technique is shown in Figure 1. In general, the recovery performance of TEC is better than SEC. However, SEC is better than TEC in some circumstances, such as scene-change frames or high motion regions. Therefore, while error occurs, the proposed technique will initially adopt the proposed TEC approach. If temporal information is unobtainable or inappropriate for restoring the corrupted data, the proposed technique will further switch to utilize the SEC approach according to the measure of temporal activity, $T_{MSE}$, and spatial activity, $S_{Var}$. The proposed SEC approach (Wang et al., 2010), adaptively integrating some interpolation schemes, will restore the corrupted data. Therefore, the proposed hybrid error concealment technique could enhance the recovery performance especially in scene-change frames and high motion regions. In other words, the recovery performance of the proposed TEC approach could be enhanced by adaptively utilizing the proposed SEC approach (Wang et al., 2010).
The switching mechanism in the proposed hybrid error concealment is based on temporal activity, $T_{MSE}$. While the temporal activity is greater than the spatial activity, $S_{Var}$, and a pre-determined threshold, the proposed SEC approach will further be adopted. $T_{MSE}$ and $S_{Var}$ are calculated by the Equation (1) and (2), respectively.

$$T_{MSE} = \frac{\sum (x_i - x_i')^2}{N} \tag{1}$$

$$S_{Var} = \frac{\sum (x_i - \mu)^2}{N} \tag{2}$$

where $x_i$ and $x_i'$ denote boundary pixel values around the corrupted MB in current frame and boundary pixel values around the replacement MB in reference frame, respectively. μ is the mean value of boundary pixel values around the corrupted MB.

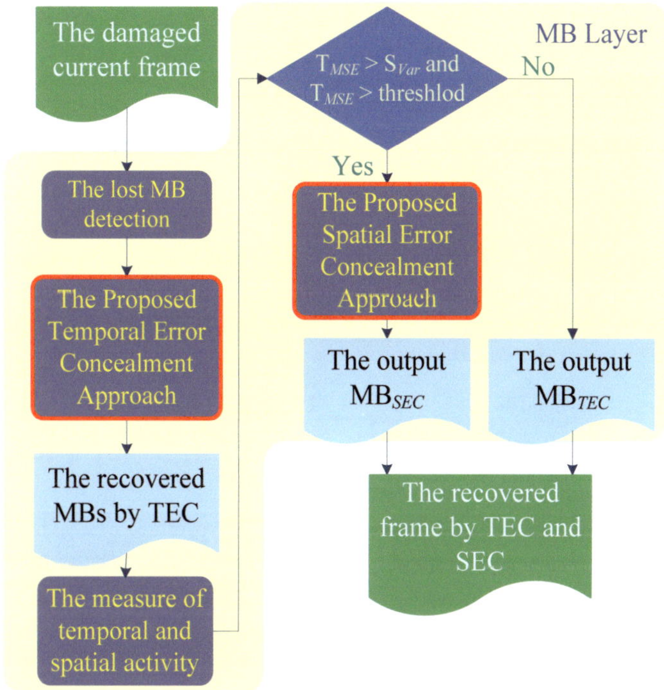


Fig. 1. The flowchart of the proposed hybrid error concealment technique

In the temporal domain, the proposed TEC approach determines an optimal result to restore the corrupted MB according to the internal boundary distortion estimation. This optimal result can be determined from one of the following two restored candidate MBs. One candidate is obtained by adopting mean absolute difference (MAD) of external boundary pixels to search for the most similar MB. The other is obtained by adaptively integrating the above-mentioned MB's data and an enhanced data with the proposed texture-based selective calibration. Inspired by bi-linearity interpolation filter (BIF) (Cui et al., 2009), this enhanced data is measured by the proposed estimated boundary residuals. In the spatial domain, the proposed SEC approach determines an integrated method to optimize recovery performance. The determination is based on a unique measure, the proposed external boundary distortion estimation. One of the integrated methods combines results of selective directional interpolation (SDI) (Yi et al., 2009) and bilinear interpolation (BI) with the adaptive weight. The other integrates results of multi-directional interpolation (MDI) (Zhan and Zhu, 2009) and BI with the adaptive weight. The details of the proposed TEC and SEC approaches will be briefly described in the following sub-sections.

### 2.1 The proposed temporal error concealment approach

The proposed temporal error concealment approach could find out the optimal restored data for concealment. Its flowchart is shown in Figure 2. First, the similar MB is estimated by a conventional temporal method to replace the corrupted MB. Secondly, the enhanced MB is calculated by appending enhanced residuals to the replaced MB. Then the proposed temporal adaptive weight-based switching (TAWS) algorithm adaptively integrates above two estimated data into the integrated MB. Finally, the proposed texture-based selective calibration (TSC) algorithm will find out the most appropriate restored data for corrupted MBs based on boundary distortion estimation. These exhaustive steps are described in the following sub-sections.

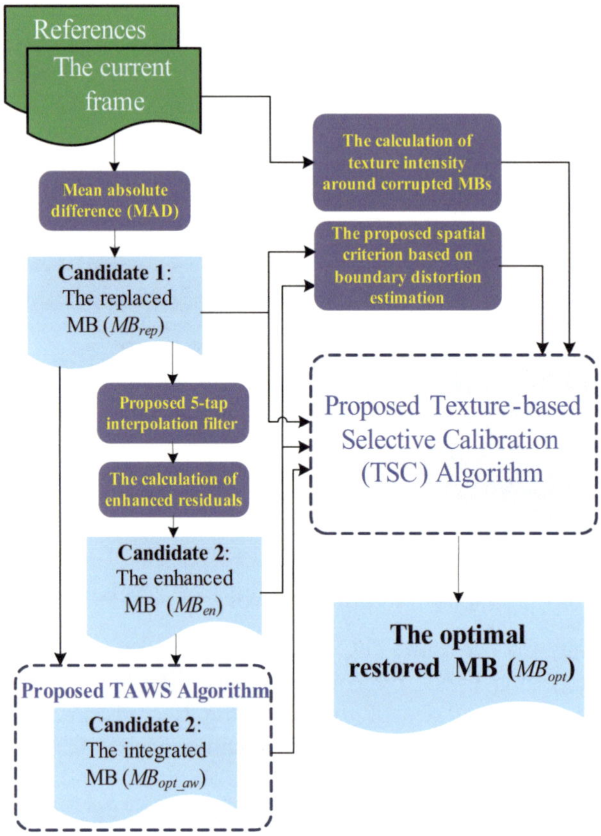


Fig. 2. The flowchart of the proposed temporal error concealment approach

### 2.1.1 Searching for the most similar MB by mean absolute difference

The most similar MB for corrupted MB is estimated in the first step. Like the restoring component of AECOD (Qian et al., 2009), the mean absolute difference (MAD) of external boundary pixels is adopted to search for the most similar MB. Then the corrupted MB is replaced with the most similar MB, namely replaced MB ($MB_{rep}$). If certain boundary of the corrupted MB is not available, the corresponding coefficient is set to be 0.

### 2.1.2 Calculation of boundary residuals for generating enhanced macro-blocks

This step utilizes boundary residuals to perform the proposed 5-tap interpolation filter in order to enhance the recovery performance. Firstly, boundary residuals are obtained by subtracting the boundary pixels around corrupted MB from the boundary pixels around the most similar MB in the previous frame. These are calculated by Equation (3), where *BR*, *CBP*, and *RBP* denote the boundary residual, the boundary pixels of the current frame and the boundary pixels of the reference frame, respectively.

$$MB_{BR}(x,y,n) = MB_{CBP}(x,y,n) - MB_{RBP}(x,y,n-1) \tag{3}$$

Secondly, inspired by (Zhan and Zhu, 2009), enhanced residuals for the replaced MB are estimated. The improved 5-tap filter is developed to interpolate the enhanced residuals. Its equations are expressed as Equation (4) and (5),

$$er_i = \frac{\sum_{n=0}^{4} x_n y_n}{\sum_{n=0}^{4} x_n}, \quad \text{where} \begin{cases} \text{for general cases} \\ \quad (x_n, y_n) = ([1,3,1],\ [BR_{c1}, BR_{c2}, BR_{c3}]) \\ \text{for boundary conditions} \\ \quad (x_n, y_n) = ([1,3,6,3,1],\ [BR_1, BR_2, BR_3, BR_4, BR_5]) \end{cases} \tag{4}$$

$$er_{c2} = \frac{[BR_{c3} + BR_{c4} + er_{c1} + er_{c3}]}{4}, \quad \text{four corner points only} \tag{5}$$

and its corresponding figure is shown in Figure 3. Then, the estimated residuals will be appended to the replaced MB. In the beginning, the proposed interpolation filter estimates the enhanced residual of the outermost loop by Equation (4), except for the four corner points. Next, the enhanced residual of corner point is calculated by adopting Equation (5) to average the four neighbouring values, where $BR_{c3}$, $BR_{c4}$, $er_{c1}$ and $er_{c3}$ are shown in Figure 3(a).

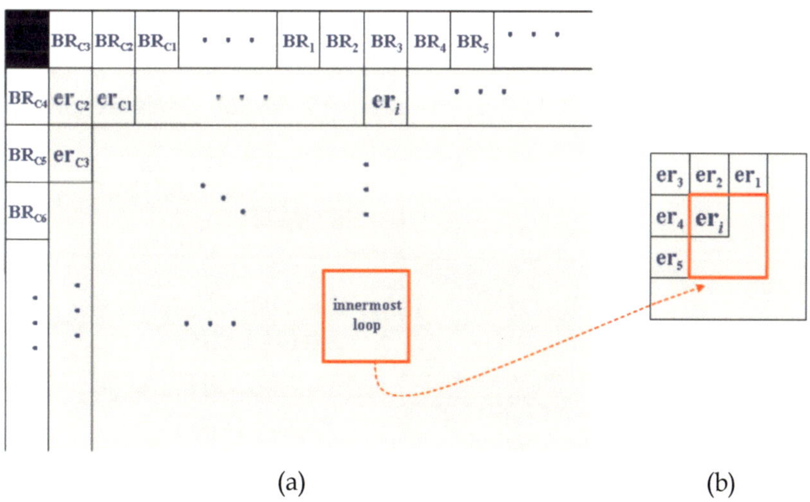


Fig. 3. The proposed 5-tap interpolation filter (a) The filter in the outer loop of the replaced MB; (b) The filter in the innermost loop of the replaced MB.

Similarly, enhanced residuals of the second-outer loop are interpolated by adopting enhanced residuals of the first-outer loop. The filter can estimate enhanced residuals for the

replaced MB sequentially from the outermost loop to inner loops. Then, enhanced residuals of the innermost loop are calculated by averaging the partially five surrounding values, such as $er_1$, $er_2$, $er_3$, $er_4$ and $er_5$ in Figure 3(b). Therefore, 256 enhanced residuals can be estimated by above-mentioned procedures.
Finally, the estimated residuals are appended to the enhanced MB. The appended data is the enhanced MB, $MB_{en}$.

### 2.1.3 The proposed boundary distortion estimation

This step calculates the standard deviation and the proposed boundary distortion estimation for two following sub-sections. The standard deviation, σ, of correctly received 4-pixels wide neighbouring boundary pixels is calculated to represent the texture intensity of corrupted MB. Its equations are shown as Equation (6) and Equation (7).

$$\sigma = \sqrt{\frac{1}{N \times M - 1} \sum_{i=1}^{N} \sum_{j=1}^{M} \left( P(i,j) - \mu \right)^2} \tag{6}$$

$$\mu = \frac{1}{N \times M} \sum_{i=1}^{N} \sum_{j=1}^{M} P(i,j) \tag{7}$$

In Equation (6) and Equation (7), $P(i, j)$ and $\mu$ denote the pixel value of correctly received neighbouring boundary region and the mean value of boundary pixels, respectively. $N \times M$ denotes the amount of all boundary pixels.
The proposed boundary distortion estimation is estimated from two values, the replaced MB and enhanced MB. It is illustrated in Figure 4 and its equation is expressed as

$$BD_n = \sum_{i=1}^{64} \left| EB(i) - IB(i) \right| \tag{8}$$

In Equation (8), $BD_n$, $EB(i)$ and $IB(i)$, respectively, denote the boundary distortion value of the replaced MB or enhanced MB ($MB_n$), the external boundary pixels around $MB_n$ and the internal boundary pixels of $MB_n$.

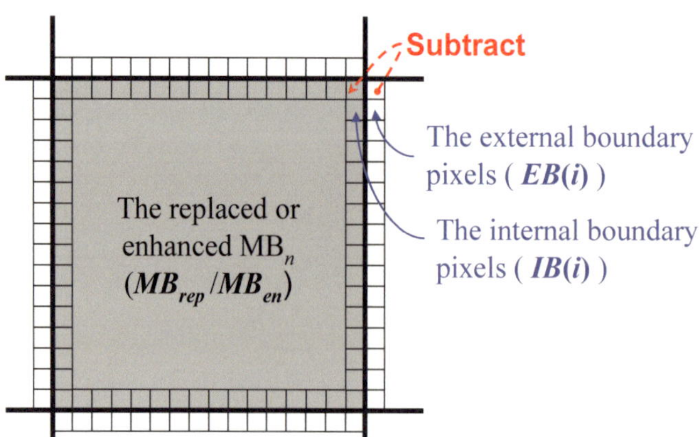


Fig. 4. The proposed boundary distortion estimation

### 2.1.4 Applying the temporal adaptive weight-based switching algorithm

The proposed temporal adaptive weight-based switching algorithm (TAWS) is adopted to determine a weight, ω, and calculating the optimal integrated MB, $MB_{opt\_aw}$, for the last step. The optimal integrated MB is calculated by adaptively integrating the replaced MB, $MB_{rep}$, and enhanced MB, $MB_{en}$, with the adaptive weight. This algorithm is described as follows:

$\omega = 1$
for (i = 1; i < 10; i++)
{
$MB_{aw}(i) = \omega \times MB_{rep} + (1 - \omega) \times MB_{en}$
$\omega = \omega - 0.125$
}
$MB_{opt\_aw} = \textbf{MinBD(} MB_{aw}(i) \textbf{)}$

In above algorithm, $MB_{aw}$ is the integrated MB with the temporal adaptive weight-based switching algorithm. The function **MinBD( )** is utilized to find the optimal integrated MB, $MB_{opt\_aw}$, with minimal boundary distortion.

### 2.1.5 Applying the texture-based selective calibration algorithm

In the last step of the proposed temporal error concealment technique, the texture-based selective calibration algorithm (TSC) is proposed to determine the optimal restored MB, $MB_{opt}$. The determination is based on many criteria, such as boundary distortions and standard deviation, σ. The proposed TSC algorithm is described as follows:

Set initial thresholds ($SD_{up} = 100$; $SD_{low} = 75$; $BD_{th} = 1$)
for ($i = 0$; $i < 4$; $i$++)
{
if ($i - 0$)
if ($\sigma > SD_{low}$)
if ($BD_{rep} > BD_{en}$ & $|BD_{rep} - BD_{en}| > BD_{th}$)
$\mathbf{MB_{opt} = 0.5 \times MB_{rep} + 0.5 \times MB_{en}}$
else
$\mathbf{MB_{opt} = MB_{rep}}$
else
if ($\sigma > SD_{low}$ & $\sigma < SD_{up}$)
if ($BD_{rep} > BD_{en}$ & $|BD_{rep} - BD_{en}| > BD_{th}$)
$\mathbf{MB_{opt} = MB_{opt\_aw}}$
else
$\mathbf{MB_{opt} = MB_{rep}}$
$SD_{up} = SD_{up} - 25$
$SD_{low} = SD_{low} - 25$
$BD_{th} = BD_{th} + 2$
}

In the above algorithm, the standard deviation is normalized form 0 to 100 firstly. $SD_{up}$ and $SD_{low}$ are the dynamic upper-bound and dynamic lower-bound of the standard deviation, respectively. They could determine four intervals of standard deviation to represent different texture intensity: high, medium-high, medium-low and low texture. The threshold,

BDth, is utilized to determine the magnitude of boundary distortion. It is calculated by $BD_{rep}$ and $BD_{en}$, the boundary distortion of the replaced MB, $MB_{rep}$, and the enhanced MB, $MB_{en}$, respectively. $SD_{up}$ and $SD_{low}$ decrease 25 and $BD_{th}$ increases 2 after each iteration. In other words, the interval with higher texture corresponds to smaller threshold for boundary distortion, $BD_{th}$. In our observations, the optimal restored MB is generally the replaced MB. As to the interval with higher texture, it will be obtained by averaging $MB_r$ and $MB_e$. Therefore, this proposed TSC algorithm could optimize the recovery performance for damaged MBs by many above-mentioned criteria.

### 2.2 The proposed spatial error concealment approach

The proposed spatial error concealment approach is based on adaptive weight-based switching directional interpolation, namely AWSDI (Wang et al., 2010). It utilizes a spatial adaptive weight-based switching algorithm (SAWS) to adaptively switch two integrated modes in order to optimize recovery performance. This approach adopts a unique spatial evaluation criterion, judged by boundary distortion estimation. One of the integrated modes combines SDI (Kung et al., 2006) and BI with the adaptive weight. The other integrates MDI and BI with the adaptive weight. Flowchart of the proposed spatial error concealment is shown in Figure 5. The steps of the proposed spatial error concealment are addressed in the following sub-sections.

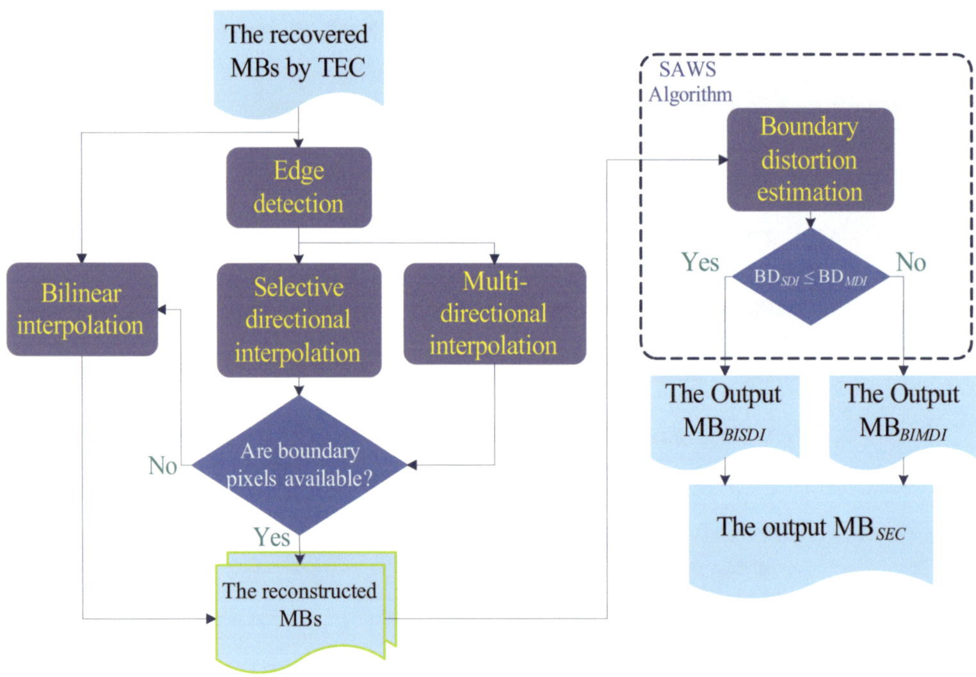


Fig. 5. Flowchart of the proposed spatial error concealment approach

#### 2.2.1 Determining the dominant edge points by edge detection

Firstly, the edges of boundary regions around a corrupted MB are detected. Then, estimated edges would be refined according to the detected edges. In spatial error concealment approaches, directional interpolation algorithms recover the corrupted MB by interpolating lost pixels along estimated edge directions. The estimated edge directions of the corrupted MB are corresponding to detected edges in boundary regions due to spatial dependency. Therefore, the proposed spatial error concealment approach adopts Sobel gradient filter with 4-pixel wide boundary regions. Then the dominant edge points, $P_{edge}(i, j)$, are determined for the following directional interpolations. The determination is expressed as

$$P_{edge}(i,j) = \begin{cases} P(i,j), & G(i,j) \geq \max(G(i,j))/2 \\ 0, & G(i,j) < \max(G(i,j))/2 \end{cases} \tag{9}$$

Equation (9) means that if the gradient magnitude $G(i, j)$ of the pixel $P(i, j)$ is greater than or equal to one-half of the maximum magnitude, the pixel will be determined as the dominant edge point. The maximum magnitude, $\max(G(i,j))$, denotes the maximum gradient magnitude of all the boundary pixels.

### 2.2.2 Integration of three interpolation modes

In this step, the proposed technique integrates pre-recovery results of three interpolation modes (BI, SDI and MDI) with an adaptive weight, w. The weight will be determined in the last step. Each corrupted macro-block has to be recovered by BI, SDI and MDI initially. Then three pre-recovery results, $MB_{BI}$, $MB_{SDI}$ and $MB_{MDI}$, are integrated into two results, $MB_{BISDI}$ and $MB_{BIMDI}$, with an adaptive weight w, respectively. In addition, the main difference between our integration and recent literatures (Kung et al., 2006; Zhan and Zhu, 2009) is that other methods adopted fixed weight to integrate or switch pre-recovery results. Conversely, the proposed integrated results are generated with an adaptive weight, which will be determined by the evaluation criterion.

The main reason of above-mentioned integrations is that SDI and MDI could not restore well in some cases, such as the smooth MB, too complex texture MB. Conversely, BI could not restore well in the slant directions texture MB. Therefore, it is essential to adaptively integrate various interpolation modes. These two integrated results will be applied to enhancing the recovery performance.

### 2.2.3 Calculation for the proposed spatial evaluation criterion

This step calculates the boundary distortion for the last step. The last step will select the best integrated result with minimal boundary distortion for one corrupted macro-block. By subtracting the correctly received boundary from pseudo-recovered boundary as shown in Figure 6, the boundary distortion is calculated. The pseudo-recovered boundary is generated as the following.

Firstly, the first-loop external boundary is assumed to be lost. Then, the second-loop external boundary is utilized to restore the first-loop external boundary. The recovered first-loop external boundary is the pseudo-recovered boundary. In this process, the recovery method is the same as the integrated macro-block, $MB_{BISDI}$ or $MB_{BIMDI}$. It is worth pointing that the criterion is based on the similarity between original external boundary and pseudo-recovered boundary. This is because if the pseudo-recovered boundary using certain integrated mode is more similar with original boundary, this integrated mode is more adequate to the corrupted macro-block.

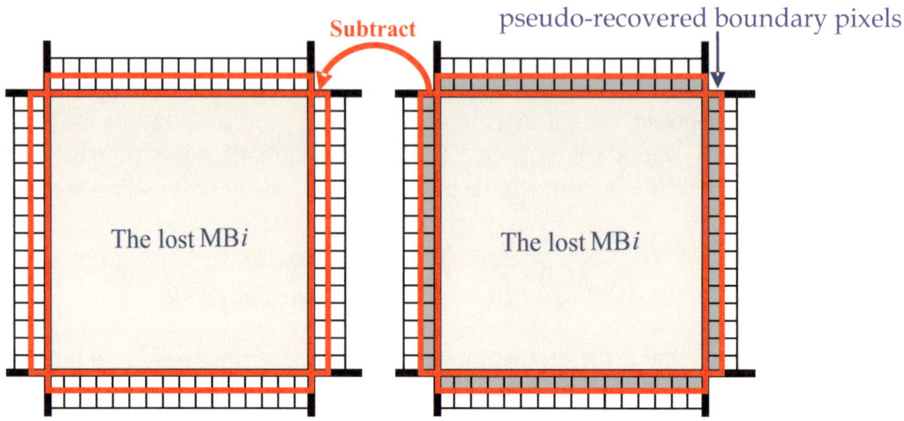


Fig. 6. The proposed evaluation criterion based on boundary distortion estimation

#### 2.2.4 Applying the spatial adaptive weight-based switching algorithm

In the last step, the proposed spatial error concealment adopts the spatial adaptive weight-based switching (SAWS) algorithm to determine the optimal recovered MB, $MB_{opt}$. The determination is based on boundary distortion estimation calculated by Step 3. It is defined as the following algorithm:

$\omega = 1$
For ($i = 1; i < 10; i{+}{+}$)
{
$MB_{BISDI}(i) = \omega \cdot MB_{BI} + (1 - \omega) \cdot MB_{SDI}$
$MB_{BIMDI}(i) = \omega \cdot MB_{BI} + (1 - \omega) \cdot MB_{MDI}$
$\omega = \omega - 0.125$
}
$MB_{opt}$ = **MinBD( MinBD(** $MB_{BISDI}(i)$ **), MinBD(** $MB_{BIMDI}(i)$ **) )**

$MB_{BISDI}$ and $MB_{BIMDI}$ are the integrated results obtained by section 2.2.2. In this algorithm, the interval of each adaptive weight is 0.125. The most adequate weight will be found out by the function **MinBD( )**, utilized to select the optimal recovered macro-block with minimal boundary distortion. Therefore, the spatial adaptive weight-based switching algorithm could optimize the recovery performance of corrupted macro-blocks.

## 3. Simulation results

The proposed hybrid error concealment technique is implemented in the decoder of H.264/AVC Reference Software Joint Model 16.2 (JM 16.2). Three benchmark sequences, such as *carphone*, *Stefan* and *foreman* are employed in our simulations. These sequences are encoded by the H.264/AVC standard. The frame size is both at QCIF (176×144) and CIF (352×288) resolution, and the frame rate is 30 fps. The period of I frame reset is 15 and the number of reference frames is 1. A constant quantization parameter (QP) of 28 is maintained for all frames and the slice type is set to be dispersed FMO. The packets are randomly selected and dropped according to the predefined packet loss rate (PLR). The PLR is set to be 5%, 10% and 15%. Table 1 lists the comparison of the proposed temporal error concealment approach and the proposed hybrid error concealment technique with JM 16.2. And the comparisons of subjective quality are shown in Figures 7~9.

The performance of the proposed hybrid error concealment technique is impressive. This is because the proposed technique not only adaptively switches TEC approach to SEC approach but also enhances each approach. The proposed TEC approach improves the BIF and adaptively integrates BIF with a conventional scheme, using MAD criterion. In cases of scene-change frames or high motion regions, the performance of the proposed TEC approach may be not good enough. Then the proposed SEC approach will further be adopted. It adaptively combines several interpolation modes to two integrated methods. Finally, the unique evaluation criterion, based on external boundary distortion estimation, is utilized to measure out the best integrated method. Thus, the proposed hybrid error concealment technique has excellent performance.

| Sequence | | PLR (%) | JM 16.2 | Proposed TEC | Proposed HEC |
|---|---|---|---|---|---|
| QCIF | *carphone* | 5 | 32.53 | 34.52 | **34.64** |
| | | 10 | 30.98 | 32.35 | **32.44** |
| | | 15 | 28.96 | 30.70 | **30.78** |
| | *Stefan* | 5 | 29.15 | 29.34 | **29.53** |
| | | 10 | 26.12 | 26.34 | **26.47** |
| | | 15 | 23.97 | 23.99 | **24.20** |
| | *foreman* | 5 | 31.86 | 32.63 | **32.93** |
| | | 10 | 28.78 | 29.46 | **29.56** |
| | | 15 | 26.39 | 26.94 | **27.28** |
| CIF | *carphone* | 5 | 33.51 | 35.37 | **35.37** |
| | | 10 | 31.50 | 32.93 | **32.93** |
| | | 15 | 29.76 | 31.10 | **31.19** |
| | *Stefan* | 5 | 31.02 | 31.22 | **31.38** |
| | | 10 | 27.58 | 27.36 | **27.56** |
| | | 15 | 25.38 | 24.92 | **25.20** |
| | *foreman* | 5 | 32.84 | 33.75 | **34.13** |
| | | 10 | 29.69 | 30.77 | **30.94** |
| | | 15 | 27.30 | 28.15 | **28.35** |

Table 1. Comparison of the proposed hybrid error concealment technique with JM

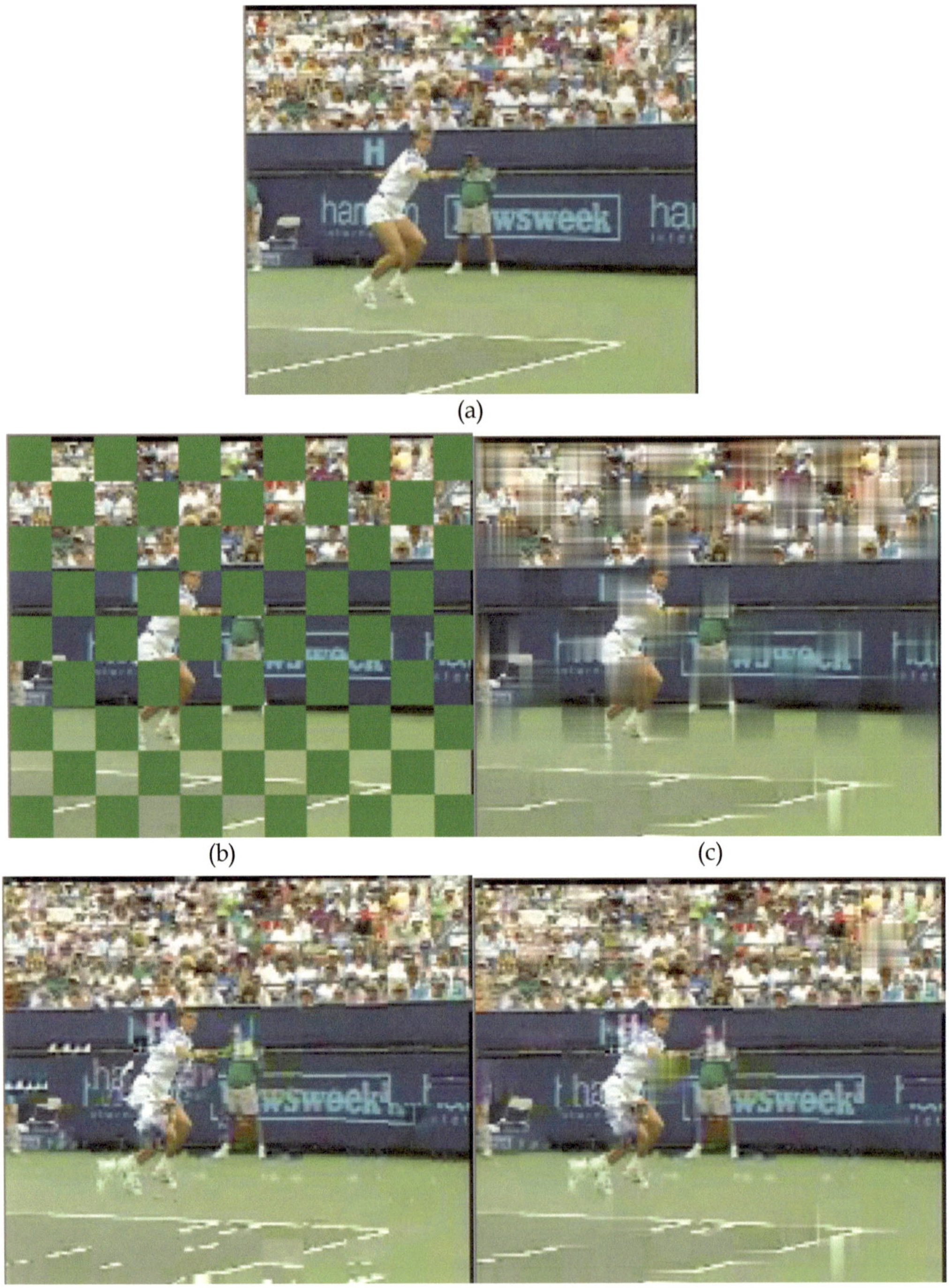

(a)

(b) (c)

(d) (e)

Fig. 7. Recovery performance for the 190th frame of *Stefan* (QCIF, GOP=10) (a) The error-free frame; (b)The corrupted frame; (c)JM (21.7594 dB); (d)Proposed TEC (20.9881 dB); (e) Proposed HEC (22.1987 dB)

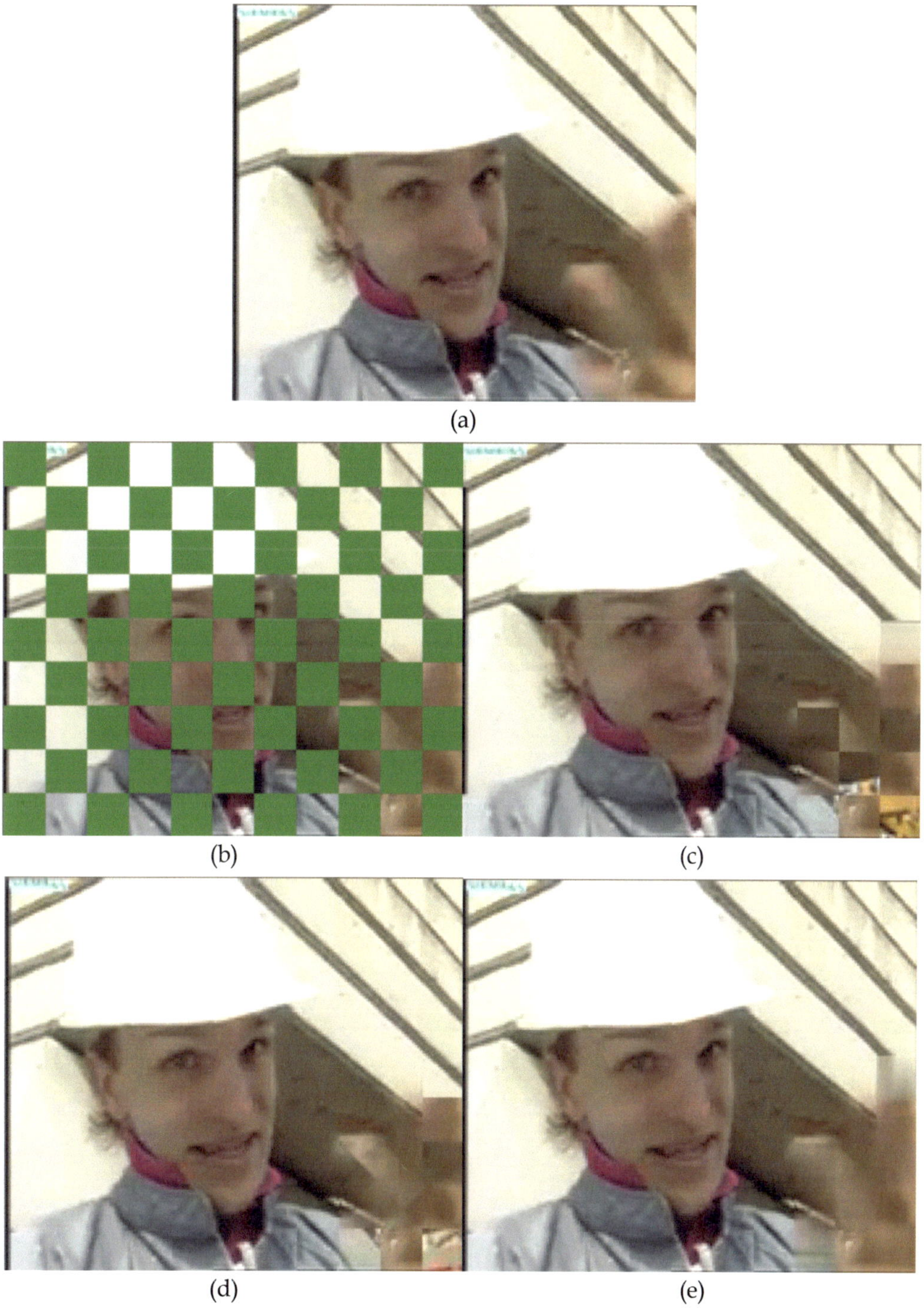

Fig. 8. Recovery performance for the 152th frame of *foreman* (QCIF, GOP=10) (a) The error-free frame; (b)The corrupted frame; (c)JM (26.7743 dB); (d) Proposed TEC (28.9247 dB); (e) Proposed HEC (30.3790 dB)

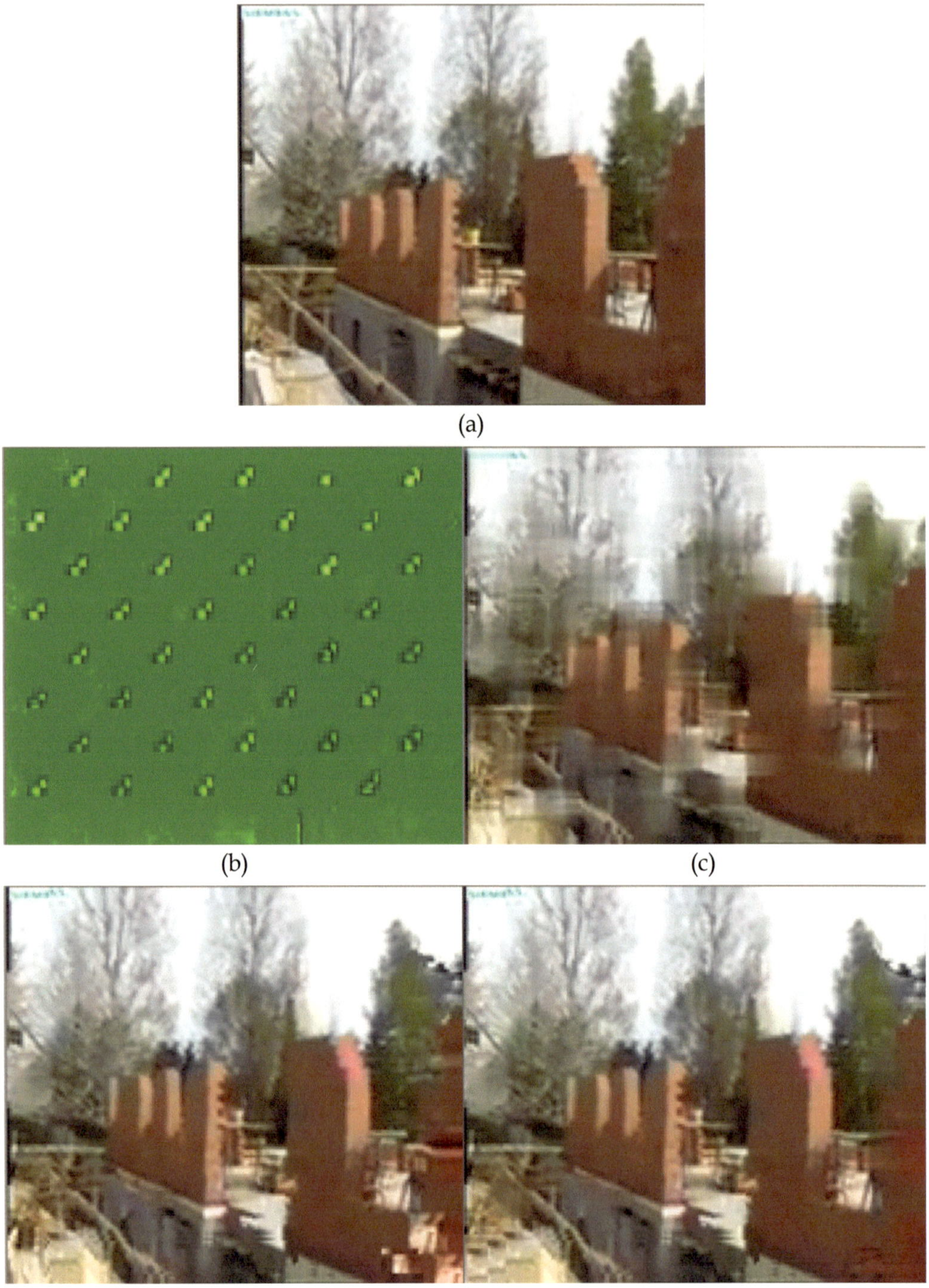

Fig. 9. Recovery performance for the 225 th frame of *foreman* (QCIF, GOP=10) (a) The error-free frame; (b)The corrupted frame; (c)JM (23.1123 dB); (d) Proposed TEC (21.6732 dB); (e) Proposed HEC (23.4388 dB)

## 4. Conclusion

In this article, a hybrid error concealment technique in H.264/AVC decoder has been proposed. It could effectively restore the corrupted data by adaptively switching temporal error concealment approach to spatial error concealment approach. The hybrid error concealment technique performs a temporal error concealment approach initially. If the performance is not good enough, especially in scene-change frames or high motion regions, the spatial error concealment approach is employed. Both temporal and spatial error concealment approaches adopt the proposed temporal or spatial adaptive weight-based switching algorithm to optimize the performance of each integrated macro-block. Then the boundary distortion estimation is utilized to determine the best integrated method for a corrupted macro-block. Simulation results show that the proposed hybrid error concealment technique performs excellent gains of up to 2 dB compared to that of the Joint Model (JM) decoder for a wide range of benchmark sequences.

## 5. References


Bjontegarrd, G. & Lillevold, K. (2002) Context-adaptive VLC Coding of Coefficients, JVT document JVT-C028, Firefax, Virginia, USA, 2002.

Marpe, D. ; Schwarz, H. & Wiegand, T. (2003) Context-based adaptive binary arithmetic coding in the H.264/AVC video compression standard, IEEE Transactions on Circuits and Systems for Video Technology., vol. 13, no. 7, Jul. 2003, pp. 620–636.

Lam, W.-M.; Reibman, A. R.; & Liu, B. (1993) Recovery of lost or erroneously received motion vectors, *IEEE International Conference on Acoustics, Speech, and Signal Processing*, vol. 5, Apr. 1993, pp. 417-420.

Kwok, W. & Sun, H. (1993) Multi-Directional Interpolation for Spatial Error Concealment, *IEEE Transactions on Consumer Electron*, vol. 39, Aug. 1993, pp. 455-460.

Wiegand, T.; Sullivan, G.-J.; Bjontegaard, G. & Luthra, A. (2003) Overview of the H.264 AVC Video Coding Standard, *IEEE Transactions on Circuits and Systems for Video Technology*, vol. 13, no. 7, pp. 560-576, July 2003.

Kung, W.-Y.; Kim, C.-S. & Kuo, C.-C. J. (2006). Spatial and Temporal Error Concealment Techniques for Video Transmission Over Noisy Channels, *IEEE Transactions on Circuits and Systems for Video Technology*, vol. 16, no. 7, Jul. 2006, pp. 789-803.

Wang, C.-C.; Chuang, C.-Y. & Lin, S. D. (2010) An Integrated Spatial Error Concealment Technique for H.264/AVC Based-on Boundary Distortion Estimation, *Fifth International Conference on Innovative Computing, Information and Control*, Dec. 2010, pp. 1-4.

Chen, S. & Leung, H. (2009) A Temporal Approach for Improving Intra-Frame Concealment Performance in H.264/AVC, *IEEE Transactions on Circuits and Systems for Video Technology*, vol. 19, no. 3, Mar. 2009, pp. 422-426.

Cui, Y.; Deng, Z. & Ren, W. (2009) Novel Temporal Error Concealment Algorithm Based on Residue Restoration, *IEEE International Conference on Wireless Communications, Networking and Mobile Computing*, Sep. 2009, pp. 1-4.

Zhan, X. & Zhu, X. (2009) Refined Spatial Error Concealment with Directional Entropy, *IEEE International Conference on Wireless Communications*, Networking and Mobile Computing, Sep. 2009, pp. 1-4.

Qian, X.; Liu, G. & Wang, H. (2009) Recovering Connected Error Region Based on Adaptive Error Concealment Order Determination, *IEEE Transactions on Multimedia*, vol. 11, no. 4, Apr. 2009, pp. 683-695.

Yi, J.-W.; Cheng, E. & Yuan, F. (2009) An Improved Spatial Error Concealment Algorithm Based on H.264, *IEEE International Symposium on Intelligent Information Technology Application*, vol. 3, Nov. 2009, pp. 455-458.

# 12

# FEC Recovery Performance for Video Streaming Services Based on H.264/SVC

Kenji Kirihara, Hiroyuki Masuyama, Shoji Kasahara and Yutaka Takahashi
*Kyoto University*
*Japan*

## 1. Introduction

With the recent advancement of video coding techniques and wide spread use of broadband networks, video streaming services over the Internet have attracted considerable attention. The recent video streaming services cover multimedia messaging, video telephony, video conferencing, standard and high-definition TV broadcasting, and those services are provided over wired/wireless networks (Schwarz et al. 2007). The Internet, however, is a best-effort network, and hence the quality of service (QoS) for video streaming is not strictly guaranteed due to packet loss and/or delay. The varying connection quality of the Internet has accelerated the development of adaptive mechanisms of video coding technologies.

MPEG and H.26x are video coding standards which have been widely deployed. MPEG4's latest video codec is Part 10 or the advanced video codec (AVC), which is also identically standardized as ITU H.264 (Marpe et al. 2006). The fundamental coding mechanism of H.264/AVC consists of a Video Coding Layer (VCL) and a Network Abstraction Layer (NAL). The VCL generates a coded representation of a source content, and the resulting data is formatted with header information by the NAL. Pictures are partitioned into small coding units called macroblocks, which organized by the following three slices:

- I-slice: intra-picture predictive coding based on spatial prediction from neighboring regions.
- P-slice: intra-picture predictive coding and inter-picture predictive coding.
- B-slice: intra-picture predictive coding, inter-picture predictive coding, and inter-picture bi-predictive coding.

With these three types of slices, H.264/AVC succeeds in providing largely increased flexibility and adaptability in comparison with previous standards such as H.261, MPEG-1 Video, H.262, MPEG2 Video, H.263, and MPEG-4 Visual. The latest standardization effort addressing scalability is the extension of H.264/AVC called scalable video coding (SVC) (Schwarz et al. 2007; Wien et al. 2007). In 2007, the SVC scalability extension has been added to the H.264/AVC standard. In this paper, this extended version of H.264/AVC is referred to as H.264/SVC.

In (Van der Auwera et al. 2008a; Van der Auwera et al. 2008b), the fundamental traffic characteristics of H.264/AVC were extensively studied. It was reported that the bit rate variability for H.264/AVC is significantly higher than that for the MPEG-4 Part 2 encoder, particularly in the low to medium quality range. This large variability of H.264/AVC may

cause heavily bursty nature of packet traffic over the Internet. It is also expected that this bursty nature emerges even for the streaming services based on H.264/SVC.
Now consider H.264/SVC-based streaming services over the network consisting of optical backbone networks and low-speed access networks. Note that in this network, backbone edge routers are likely to be the bottleneck of the packet flows of H.264/SVC-based streaming services. It was reported in (Van der Auwera et al. 2008a) that the coefficient of variation (CoV) of the frame size increases as the video quality increases, indicating that the video traffic becomes more variable. Therefore, it is important to investigate the impact of the variability of the frame size on video quality.
In terms of the resilience to packet loss due to network congestion, there are two basic techniques for packet-loss recovery: Automatic Repeat reQuest (ARQ) and Forward Error Correction (FEC). ARQ is an acknowledgement-based error recovery technique, in which lost data packets are retransmitted by the sender host. However, this retransmission mechanism is activated by receiving duplicate acknowledgement (ACK) packets or timer time-out, causing a large end-to-end delay. This large delay is not suitable for real-time applications such as video streaming and web conference.
On the other hand, FEC is a well-known coding-based error recovery scheme (Carle & Biersack 1997; Perkins et al. 1998). FEC is a one-way recovery technique based on open-loop error control, and hence FEC is suitable for real-time applications. In FEC, redundant data is generated from original data, and both original and redundant data are transmitted to the receiver host. If the amount of lost data is less than or equal to a prespecified threshold, the lost data can be reconstructed on the receiver host. In this paper, we consider a packet-level FEC scheme (Shacham & Pckenney 1990). Because FEC needs no retransmission, it is suitable for real-time applications with stringent delay constraint such as video streaming. However, FEC does not work well against packet burst loss because the amount of redundant data has to be pre-determined with the estimate of the packet loss probability.
In this paper, focusing on the bottleneck router, we consider variable frame size's impact on frame loss. It is assumed that the number of packets in a frame is variable and that the interval of sending packets is constant on the transport layer. We model the bottleneck router as a single-server queueing system with two independent input processes: a general renewal input process for video streaming packets and a Poisson arrival process for background traffic multiplexed at the bottleneck router. Taking into account the variable nature of the number of packets in a frame, we derive the data-loss ratio of main traffic. In numerical examples, we investigate how the variability of the frame size affects the data-loss ratio. FEC recovery performance is also studied.
The rest of this paper is organized as follows. Section 2 shows related work, and in Section 3, we describe our analysis model, deriving the performance measure. Section 4 presents some numerical examples, and Section 5 concludes the paper.

## 2. Related work

H.264/AVC and its extension to the scalable video coding have been aggressively and extensively studied. The history of H.264/AVC and recent advancement toward SVC are well surveyed in (Schwarz et al. 2007).
It is well known that the traffic characteristics of encoded video have a significant impact on network transport. Its characteristics have been extensively studied in the literature. In particular, the authors in (Van der Auwera et al. 2008a; Van der Auwera et al. 2008b) compared H.264/AVC and MPEG4 Part 2 using two performance measures: the peak

signal-to-noise ratio (PSNR) and CoV of the frame size. They claimed that H.264/AVC codec can save the average bit rate more largely than MPEG4 Part 2 codec, and that the variability of H.264/AVC video traffic is higher than that MPEG4 Part 2 video traffic. They also examined how the frame-size smoothing is effective in mitigating the bit rate variability.

In general, video traffic exhibits a long-term correlation nature, which is hardly modeled with traditional Markovian arriving processes. In (Kempken et al. 2008), the authors considered discrete-time semi-Markov models of H.264/AVC video traffic. Focusing on the short term autocorrelation and the preservation of the mean value of the distribution of the size of group of pictures (GoP), the parameters of a discrete-time batch Markovian arrival process are optimized by simulated annealing approach.

In (Avramova et al. 2008), the tail probability of the queue length of a bottleneck router was studied with the effective bandwidth approach and trace-driven simulation experiments. In the effective bandwidth approach, the tail probability of the queue length can be well approximated when the number of input sources is large. The authors derived two estimates of the tail probability from two arrival processes: one is based on a fractional Brownian motion and the other a Markov-modulated fluid one. Those estimates were compared to trace-driven simulation.

In this paper, we focus on the multiplexing nature of the bottleneck router. In terms of this modeling point of view, the authors in (Muraoka et al. 2007) focused on the bottleneck edge router, evaluating the packet recovery performance of FEC for a single-server queueing system with finite buffer fed by two input processes: one is a general renewal input process, and the other is Poisson arrival process. Assuming that the packet size is exponentially distributed, the packet- and block-level loss probabilities were analyzed. In (Muraoka et al. 2009), the authors extended the model in (Muraoka et al. 2007) to a GI+M/SM/1/K queue in which the packet transfer time is governed by a two-state Markovian service process, investigating the recovery performance of FEC over wired-wireless networks. Note that in (Muraoka et al. 2007; Muraoka et al. 2009), the frame size is assumed to be constant. In this paper, we consider the case in which the frame size is variable.

## 3. Model and analysis

### 3.1 Variable frame size

We consider H.264/SVC-based streaming service. Each video frame contains original data packets and FEC redundant data packets, where the latter ones are generated from the former ones. The original data packets of a video frame is retrieved if the number of loss packets is less than or equal to that of the FEC redundant data packets. Otherwise the frame is lost. In what follows, we assume that the first packet of a video frame arrives to the bottleneck router at time $T_1 > 0$. The video frame is called "frame 1" hereafter. The subsequent video frames is called "frame 2", "frame 3", "frame 4" and so on. Let $D_k$ $(k = 1, 2, \dots)$ denote the number of the original data packets in frame $k$. We assume that $D_k$'s are independently and identically distributed (i.i.d.) with a probability mass function $d(n)$ $(n = 1, 2, \dots)$. We also assume that the number of FEC packets in frame $k$ is equal to $\lceil \gamma D_k \rceil$, where $\gamma \geq 0$ denotes the redundancy. Thus the total number of packets in frame $k$ is equal to $D_k + \lceil \gamma D_k \rceil$.

### 3.2 Model

We model the bottleneck router as a single-server queueing system with a buffer of capacity $K$, which is fed by two independent input processes. The one is a Poisson flow of packets in background traffic, whose arrival rate is equal to $\lambda$. The other is a renewal packet flow of video frames from a streaming server, which is called main traffic. Let $T_m$'s ($m = 2, 3, \ldots$) denote arrival epochs of main-traffic packets after the arrival of the first packet of frame 1 at time $T_1$, where $0 < T_1 < T_2 < T_3 < \cdots$. Note here that the first packet of frame $k$ ($k = 1, 2, \ldots$) arrives at time $T_{m_k}$, where $m_k = \sum_{i=1}^{k-1}(D_i + \lceil \gamma D_i \rceil) + 1$. The interarrival times of packets in main traffic are i.i.d. with a general distribution $G(x)$ ($x \geq 0$), i.e., for each $m = 1, 2, \ldots,$ $\Pr[\tau_m \leq x] = G(x)$ ($x \geq 0$), where $\tau_m = T_{m+1} - T_m$. The service times of packets in both main and background traffic are i.i.d. according to an exponential distribution with mean $1/\mu$. Consequently, we have a GI+M/M/1/$K$ queueing system for the bottleneck router.

### 3.3 Stationary distribution of packets in the bottleneck router

This subsection considers the stationary queue length distribution immediately before an arrival from main traffic in the GI+M/M/1/$K$ queueing system, which is described in the previous subsection. Recall that packets in main traffic arrive at times $T_m$'s ($m = 1, 2, \ldots$). Let $L_m^-$ ($m = 1, 2, \ldots$) denote the total number of packets in the system immediately before time $T_m$. Note that during the interval $(T_m, T_{m+1})$, the behavior of the GI+M/M/1/$K$ queue is stochastically equivalent to that of the M/M/1/$K$ queue with arrival rate $\lambda$ and service rate $\mu$. Thus $\{L_m^-; m = 1, 2, \ldots\}$ is a Markov chain whose transition probability matrix $\mathbf{\Pi}$ is given by

$$\mathbf{\Pi} = \mathbf{\Lambda} \int_0^\infty \exp(\boldsymbol{Q}x) \mathrm{d}G(x), \tag{1}$$

where $\mathbf{\Lambda}$ and $\boldsymbol{Q}$ denote $(K+1) \times (K+1)$ matrices that are given by

$$\mathbf{\Lambda} = \begin{pmatrix} 0 & 1 & 0 & \ldots & 0 & 0 \\ 0 & 0 & 1 & \ddots & 0 & 0 \\ \vdots & \vdots & \ddots & \ddots & \vdots & \vdots \\ 0 & 0 & 0 & \ddots & 1 & 0 \\ 0 & 0 & 0 & \ldots & 0 & 1 \\ 0 & 0 & 0 & \ldots & 0 & 1 \end{pmatrix}, \tag{2}$$

$$\boldsymbol{Q} = \begin{pmatrix} -\lambda & \lambda & 0 & \ldots & 0 & 0 \\ \mu & -(\lambda+\mu) & \lambda & \ddots & \vdots & \vdots \\ 0 & \mu & -(\lambda+\mu) & \ddots & 0 & 0 \\ 0 & 0 & \mu & \ddots & \lambda & 0 \\ \vdots & \vdots & \ddots & \ddots & -(\lambda+\mu) & \lambda \\ 0 & 0 & 0 & \ddots & \mu & -\mu \end{pmatrix}.$$

Note here that $\mathbf{\Pi}$ is aperiodic. Let $\boldsymbol{\pi}$ denote a $1 \times (K+1)$ probability vector whose $j$th ($j = 0, 1, \ldots, K$) element $\pi_j$ represents $\lim_{m \to \infty} \Pr[L_m^- = j]$. We then have

$$\boldsymbol{\pi}\mathbf{\Pi} = \boldsymbol{\pi}, \qquad \boldsymbol{\pi}\boldsymbol{e} = 1,$$

where $\boldsymbol{e}$ denotes a column vector of ones with appropriate dimension.

### 3.4 Derivation of data-loss ratio

This subsection derives the long-term ratio $P_{data}$ of the number of unretrieved data packets to that of all the original data packets. Let $N(t)$ $(t \geq 0)$ denote the total number of video frames arriving to the system in the time interval $(0, t]$. Without loss of generality, we assume $N(0) = 0$. Let $X_k$ $(k = 1, 2, \dots)$ denote the number of lost packets among frame $k$. The formal definition of $P_{data}$ is as follows:

$$P_{data} = 1 - \lim_{t \to \infty} \frac{\sum_{k=1}^{N(t)} D_k \cdot 1(X_k \leq \lceil \gamma D_k \rceil)}{\sum_{k=1}^{N(t)} D_k},$$

where $1(\chi)$ denotes the indicator function of event $\chi$. Let $Q_k^-$ $(k = 1, 2, \dots)$ denote the number of packets in the system immediate before the arrival of the first packet of frame $k$. By definition (see subsection 3.2), $Q_k^- = L_{m_k}^-$ for $k = 1, 2, \dots$. Therefore $\lim_{k \to \infty} \Pr[Q_k^- = i] = \lim_{m \to \infty} \Pr[L_m^- = i] = \pi_i$ for all $i = 0, 1, \dots, K$. Note here that $\{(D_k, Q_k^-); k = 1, 2, \dots\}$ is a Markov renewal process because $\{D_k; k = 1, 2, \dots\}$ is a sequence of i.i.d. random variables and independent of a Markov chain $\{Q_k^-; k = 1, 2, \dots\}$. Note also that each $D_k \cdot 1(X_k \leq \lceil \gamma D_k \rceil)$ can be regarded as *reward* depending on $D_k$ and $Q_k^-$. It then follows from the Markov renewal reward theorem (Wolf 1989) that

$$P_{data} = 1 - \frac{\mathrm{E}_\pi[D_1 \cdot 1(X_1 \leq \lceil \gamma D_1 \rceil)]}{\mathrm{E}[D_1]}, \tag{3}$$

where $\mathrm{E}_\pi[\,\cdot\,] = \sum_{i=0}^{K} \pi_i \mathrm{E}[\,\cdot \mid Q_1^- = i]$. From (3) and $Q_1^- = L_1^-$, we have

$$\begin{aligned} P_{data} &= 1 - \frac{\sum_{i=0}^{K} \pi_i \sum_{n=1}^{\infty} n d(n) \Pr[X_1 \leq \lceil \gamma n \rceil \mid D_1 = n, L_1^- = i]}{\sum_{n=1}^{\infty} n d(n)} \\ &= 1 - \frac{\sum_{n=1}^{\infty} n d(n) \cdot \sum_{i=0}^{K} \pi_i q(\lceil \gamma n \rceil; n, i)}{\sum_{n=1}^{\infty} n d(n)}, \end{aligned} \tag{4}$$

where $q(\nu; n, i)$ $(\nu = 0, 1, \dots, n, n = 1, 2, \dots, i = 0, 1, \dots, K)$ denotes

$$q(\nu; n, i) = \Pr[X_1 \leq \nu \mid D_1 = n, L_1^- = i]. \tag{5}$$

We can readily compute $\sum_{i=0}^{K} \pi_i q(\lceil \gamma n \rceil; n, i)$ by the recursion given in subsection 3.2 of (Muraoka et al. 2007), because $\sum_{i=0}^{K} \pi_i q(\lceil \gamma n \rceil; n, i)$ is equivalent to $\sum_{k=0}^{\lceil \gamma n \rceil} \boldsymbol{p}_{n+\lceil \gamma n \rceil}(k)\boldsymbol{e}$ therein.

## 4. Numerical examples

In this section, we evaluate the impact of the variable frame size using the data-loss ratio derived in the previous section. The transmission rate of video streaming service is set to 20 Mbps, and the output transmission speed of the bottleneck router is 100 Mbps. We consider two system capacity cases: $K$ = 10 and 100. It is assumed that the video-frame rate is 30 [frame/s], and that the packet size is constant and equal to 500 bytes. Then, the service rate of a packet at the bottleneck router is $\mu = 2.5 \times 10^4$ [packet/s].

We assume that the packet interarrival time of main traffic is constant. Let $D_{\min}$ $(D_{\max})$ denote the minimum (maximum) value of the frame size. In terms of $d(n)$, we consider the following uniform distribution.

$$d(n) = \begin{cases} 1/(D_{\max} - D_{\min} + 1), & D_{\min} \leq n \leq D_{\max}, \\ 0, & 0 \leq n < D_{\min}, n > D_{\max}. \end{cases}$$

| Type | Main traffic | $\bar{M}$ | $D_{\min}$ | $D_{\max}$ | CoV |
|---|---|---|---|---|---|
| I | 20 Mbps | 167 | 151 | 183 | 0.0570 |
| II | 20 Mbps | 167 | 39 | 295 | 0.442 |

Table 1. Basic parameters for uniform distribution.

| Name | Original filename | Date/Cpat.on | Duration |
|---|---|---|---|
| Leipzig-II | 20030221-121359-0.g2 | February 21 12:13:59 2003 | 164min |
| Leipzig-II | 20030222-150000-0.g2 | February 22 15:00:00 2003 | 360min |

Table 2. General information about the trace used for simulation experiments.

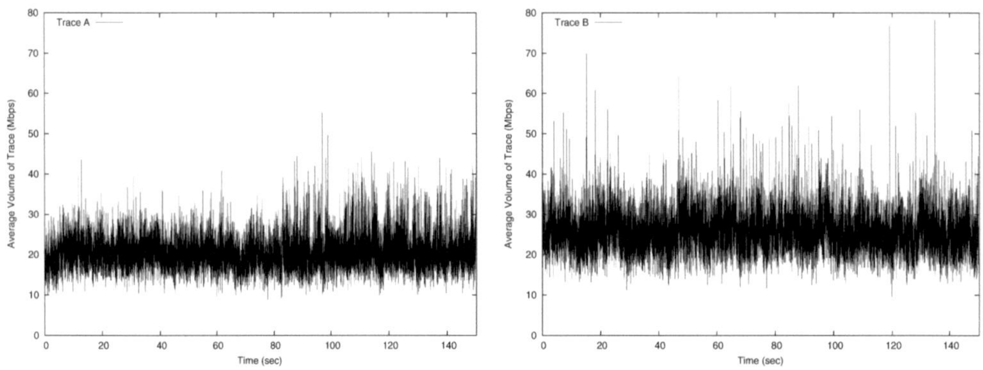


Fig. 1. The average bit rate of trace data.

The basic parameter set is shown in Table 1. In the following, we denote CoV as the coefficient of variation of the frame size. Let $\bar{M}(\gamma)$ denote the average of the number of packets in a frame, which is given by

$$\bar{M}(\gamma) = \sum_{n=1}^{\infty}(n + \lceil \gamma n \rceil)d(n).$$

When the video transmission rate is 20 Mbps, the mean number of original data packets in a frame is $\bar{M}(0) = 167$.

We validate the analytical model by simulation experiments driven by traces of the NLANR repository (PMA). The trace data was used for the inter-arrival times of background traffic, and the other settings are the same as the analysis. Table 2 shows the details of the trace data used for simulation experiments in this paper. The subset of each trace data was used for the simulation experiment. In the following, we call the trace data from 20030222-150000-0.g2 (resp. 20030221-121359-0.g2) is called Trace A (resp. Trace B). Each trace was used for the inter-arrival times of packets in background traffic.

Figure 1 shows the average bit rate of the trace data. Note that Trace B represents the trace data whose volume varies greatly. Figure 2 illustrates the histogram of the trace data. The left-hand (resp. right-hand) figure in Fig. 2 shows the histogram of Trace A (resp. Trace B). When the packet size is 500 bytes, the volume of Trace A (resp. Trace B) is equal to 20.3 Mbps (resp. 25.5 Mbps) and the corresponding arrival rate $\lambda$ is $5.09 \times 10^3$ (resp. $6.37 \times 10^3$) [packet/s]. The average of the packet inter-arrival times for Trace A (resp. Trace B) is $1.97 \times 10^{-1}$ (resp. $1.56 \times 10^{-1}$). The variance of the packet inter-arrival times for Trace A (resp. Trace B) is $4.56 \times 10^{-2}$ (resp. $3.11 \times 10^{-2}$). The resulting CoV of the packet inter-arrival times for Trace A (resp. Trace B) is 1.08 (resp. 1.13).

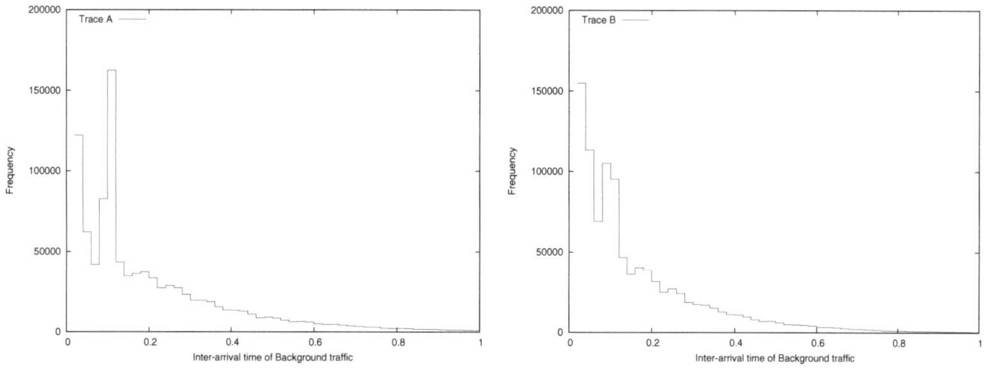


Fig. 2. Histogram of trace data.

### 4.1 Impact of system capacity

In this subsection, we investigate how the system capacity affects the data-loss ratio. In the following figures, analytical results are shown with lines, compared with simulation results represented by dots with 95% confidence intervals.

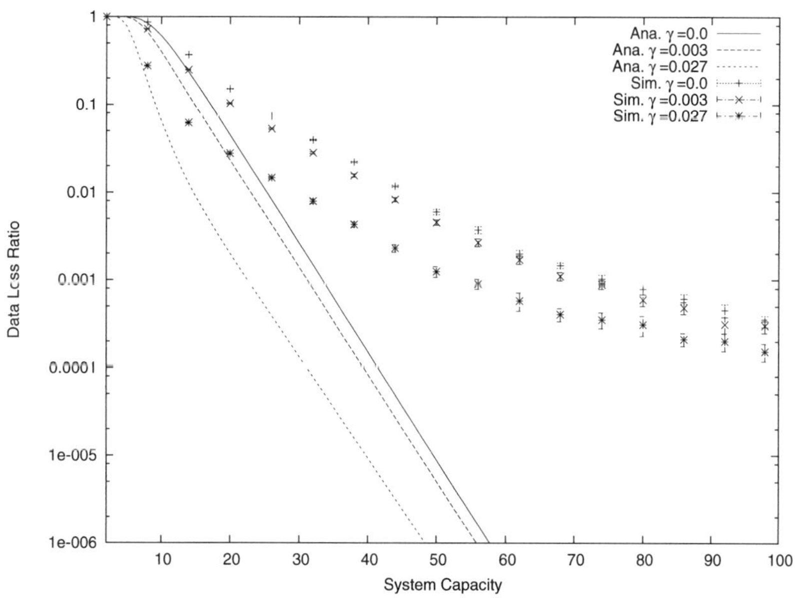


Fig. 3. System capacity vs. data-loss ratio. (The transmission rate 50 Mbps, main traffic 20 Mbps, Trace A, Type I)

Figure 3 (4) shows the data-loss ratio against the system capacity $K$ when the frame size distribution is Type I (II). We calculated the data-loss ratio for $\gamma = 0$, 0.003 and 0.027. Note that the corresponding value of $\bar{M}(\gamma)$ is $\bar{M}(0) = 167$, $\bar{M}(0.003) = 168$ and $\bar{M}(0.027) = 172$. Here, the transmission rate of the bottleneck router is 50 Mbps, and the packet arrival rate of background traffic is $5.09 \times 10^3$ [packet/s], the mean packet arrival rate of Trace A.

In Figure 3, for each $\gamma$, simulation results are greater than analytical results. In addition, the discrepancy between analysis and simulation is large even for a small $K$. This is because the packet interarrival times of the trace data used for background traffic in simulation are more

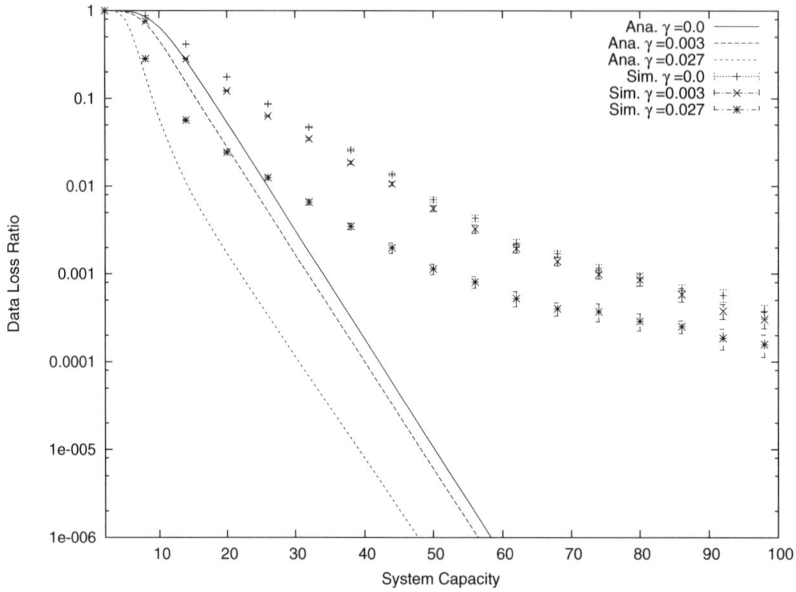


Fig. 4. System capacity vs. data-loss ratio. (The transmission rate 50 Mbps, main traffic 20 Mbps, Trace A, Type II)

correlated than the Poisson process assumed for the analytical model. We also observe that the data-loss ratio decreases with the increase in $K$, as expected. The data-loss ratio is decreased by FEC, however, increasing the system capacity is more effective than FEC.

Comparing Figures 3 and 4, we observe that when CoV is large, the data-loss ratio for a large FEC redundancy is slightly smaller than that for a small FEC redundancy. This implies that FEC is effective for the video transmission in which the video frame size has a large variability.

Figure 5 (6) shows the data-loss ratio against the system capacity $K$ when the frame size distribution is Type I (II). Most of the parameters are the same as Figure 3 (4), except that the packet arrival rate of background traffic is $6.37 \times 10^3$ [packet/s], the mean packet arrival rate of Trace B. Note that the CoV of the packet inter-arrival times for Trace B is larger than that for Trace A. From Figures 5 and 6, we observe the same tendencies as Figures 3 and 4. From these results, we can claim that the analysis is useful in a qualitative sense to investigate the effect of the variability of the frame size on the data-loss ratio.

#### 4.2 Impact of variable frame size

In this subsection, we investigate how the variable frame size affects the data-loss ratio. It is supposed that the transmission rate of the bottleneck router is 50 Mbps (100 Mbps). Thus the packet service rate of the bottleneck router is $\mu = 1,25 \times 10^4$ ($2.5 \times 10^4$) [packet/s].

Figures 7 and 8 illustrate the data-loss ratio against the CoV of the frame size in case of the $K$=10 and 40. In each K, we calculated the data loss ratio for $\gamma = 0, 0.003$ and 0.027. Note that the corresponding value of $\bar{M}(\gamma)$ is $\bar{M}(0) = 167$, $\bar{M}(0.003) = 168$ and $\bar{M}(0.027) = 172$. In order to change the value of CoV, we decrement (increment) $D_{\text{min}}$ ($D_{\text{max}}$) by one, keeping the mean frame size constant.

In Figure 7, the data-loss ratio grows monotonically with the increase in CoV in cases of $\gamma$=0 and 0.003. This is simply due to a small FEC redundancy. On the other hand, the data-loss ratio gradually decreases when the redundancy $\gamma$ is 0.027. In Figure 8, we observe similar

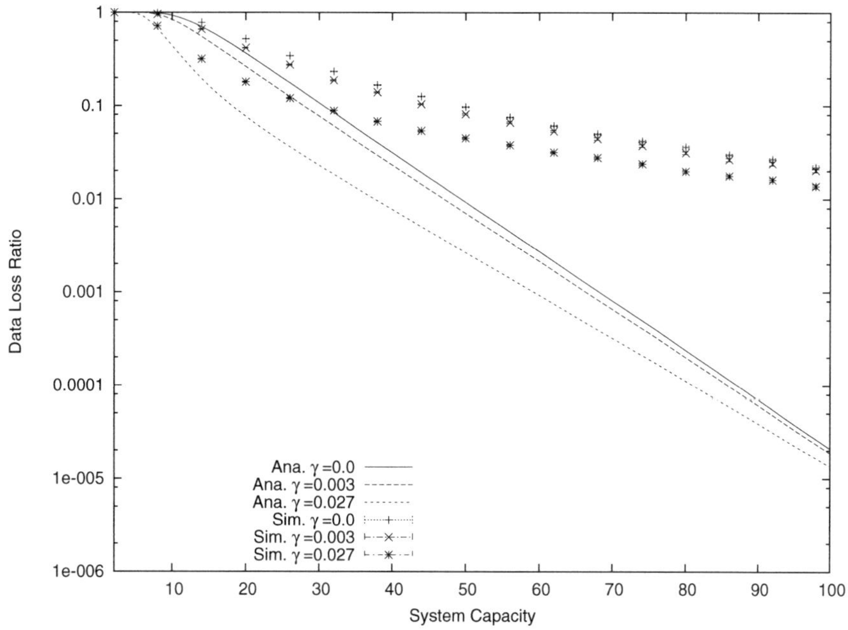


Fig. 5. System capacity vs. data-loss ratio. (The transmission rate 50 Mbps, main traffic 20 Mbps, Trace B, Type I)

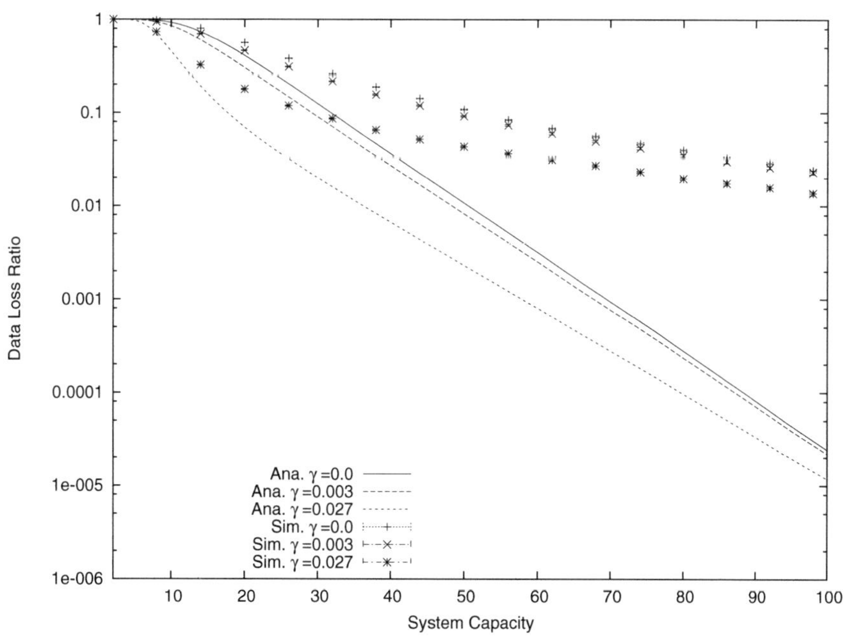


Fig. 6. System capacity vs. data-loss ratio. (The transmission rate 50 Mbps, main traffic 20 Mbps, Trace B, Type II)

characteristics as Figure 7. Note that the data-loss ratio in Figure 8 is smaller than that in Figure 7 and the impact of the variable frame size is small.
Figures 9 and 10 illustrate the data-loss ratio against the frame size in cases of $K$ =10 and 20. Here, the transmission rate of the bottleneck router is 100 Mbps. In Figure 9, when $\gamma$=0 and 0.003, the data-loss ratio gradually grows with the increase in CoV, so the tendency is similar to the case where the transmission rate of the bottleneck router is 50 Mbps. In case of $\gamma$=0.027, on the other hand, the data-loss ratio increases step by step when the CoV increases. The data-loss ratio of a large CoV is about 400 times larger than that of a small CoV. In other words, when the FEC redundancy increases, the data-loss ratio becomes small but is significantly affected by CoV. In Figure 10, we observe the same characteristics as Figure 9. Note that the data-loss ratio is more improved for the system with a large capacity.

### 4.3 Impact of background traffic

In this subsection, we investigate how the data-loss ratio is affected by the volume of background traffic. Figure 11 represents the data-loss ratio against the volume of background traffic in cases of $K$ = 10 and 100. In terms of $d(n)$, we consider Types I and II. The FEC redundancy $\gamma$ is set to 0 and 0.027. It is observed that the data-loss ratio grows with the increase in the volume of background traffic, as expected. When $K$ is small, FEC is effective in decreasing the data-loss ratio. However, the data-loss ratio for a large FEC redundancy is significantly affected by CoV. When $K$ is large, on the other hand, the data-loss ratio is significantly improved. This implies that increasing the buffer size is more effective than FEC for a bottleneck router in congestion.

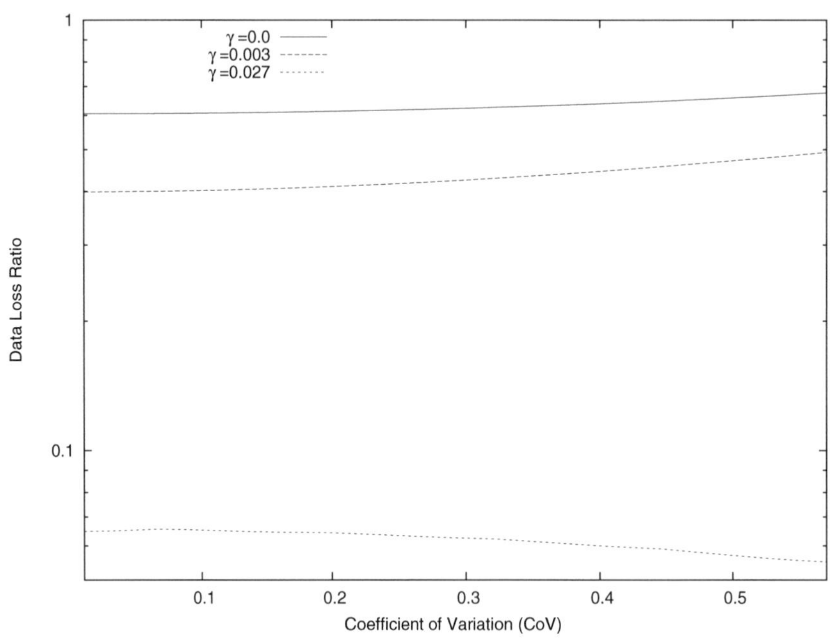


Fig. 7. CoV vs. the data-loss ratio. (The transmission rate 50 Mbps, background traffic 20.3 Mbps, $K$ = 10)

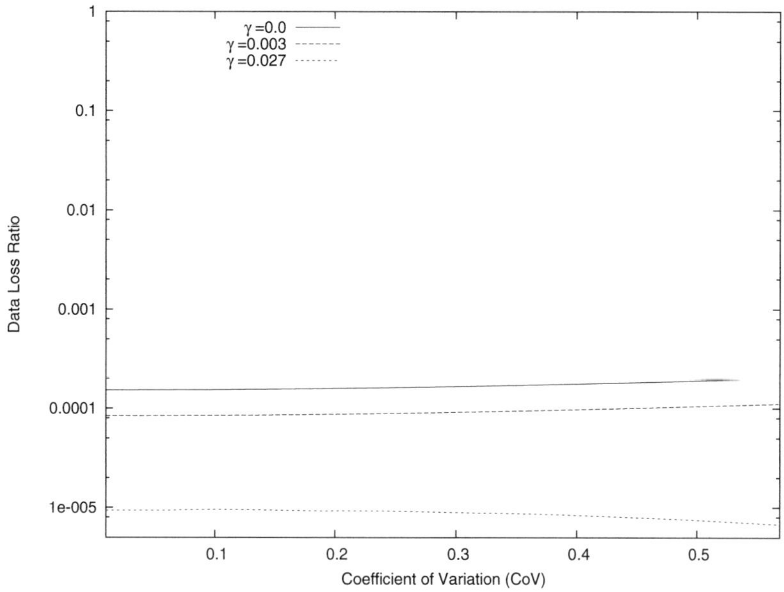


Fig. 8. CoV vs. the data-loss ratio. (The transmission rate 50 Mbps, background traffic 20.3 Mbps, $K - 40$)

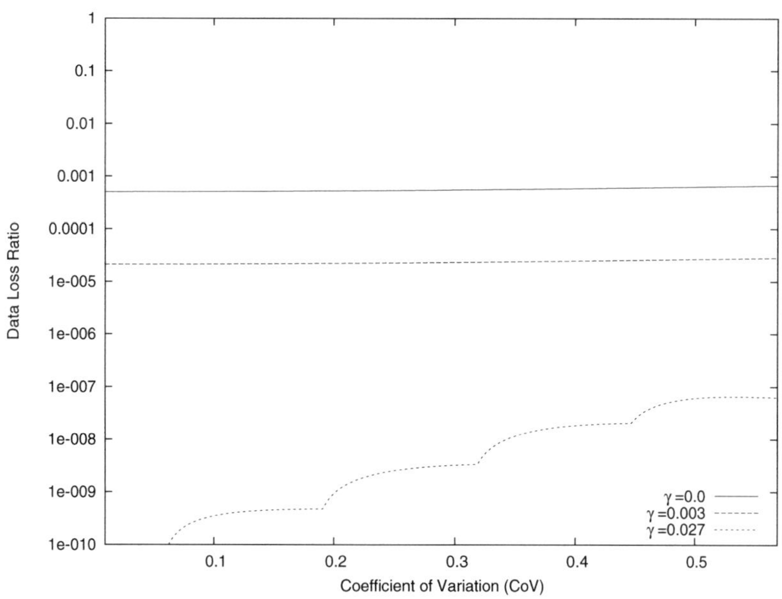


Fig. 9. CoV vs. the data-loss ratio. (The transmission rate 100 Mbps, background traffic 20.3 Mbps, $K = 10$)

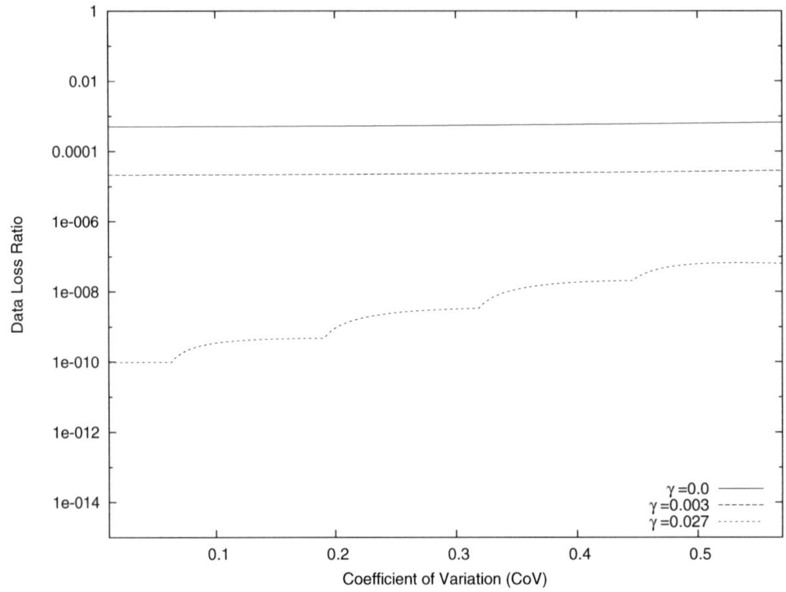


Fig. 10. CoV vs. the data-loss ratio. (The transmission rate 100 Mbps, background traffic 20.3 Mbps, $K = 20$)

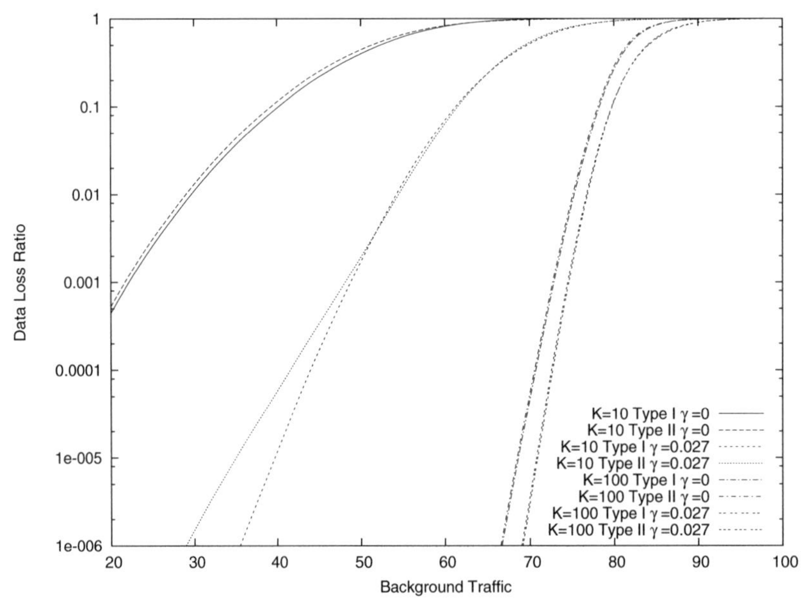


Fig. 11. Background traffic vs. the data-loss ratio.

## 5. Conclusions

In this paper, focusing on the bottleneck router, we considered the impact of the frame-size variability on frame loss. We modeled the bottleneck router as a single-server queueing system with two independent input processes: a general renewal input process and a Poisson arrival process, deriving the data-loss ratio of main traffic. The analysis was validated in a qualitative sense by trace-driven simulation. Numerical examples showed the data-loss ratio is not significantly affected by the variability of the frame size. It was also claimed that increasing the buffer size is more effective than FEC for a bottleneck router in congestion.

## 6. References


[Avramova et al. 2008] Avramova, Z., De Vleeschauwer, D., Laevens, K., Wittevrongel, S. & Bruneel, H. (2008). Modelling H.264/AVC VBR video traffic: comparison of a Markov and a self-similar source model, *Telecommunication Systems*, 39 (2): 91-102.

[Carle & Biersack 1997] Carle, G. & Biersack, E. W. (1997). Survey on error recovery techniques for IP-based audio-visual multicast applications, *IEEE Network Magazine*, 11 (6): 24–36.

[Kempken et al. 2008] Kempken, S., Hasslinger, G. & Luther, W. (2008). Parameter estimation and optimization techniques for discrete-time semi-Markov models of H.264/AVC video traffic, *Telecommunication Systems* 39 (2): 77–90.

[Marpe et al. 2006] Marpe, D., Wiegand, T. & Sullivan, G. (2006). The H.264/MPEG4 advanced video coding standard and its applications, *IEEE Communications Magazine*, 44 (8): 134–143.

[Muraoka et al. 2007] Muraoka, S., Masuyama, H., Kasahara, S. & Takahashi, Y. (2007). Performance analysis of FEC recovery using finite-buffer queueing system with general renewal and Poisson inputs, *Proceedings of Managing Traffic Performance in Converged Networks*, LNCS4516, Springer, 707–718.

[Muraoka et al. 2009] Muraoka, S., Masuyama, H., Kasahara, S. & Takahashi, Y. (2009). FEC recovery performance for video streaming services over wired-wireless networks, *Performance Evaluation*, 66 (6): 327–342.

[Perkins et al. 1998] Perkins, C., Hodson, O. and Hardman, V. (1998). A survey of packet loss recovery techniques for streaming audio, *IEEE Network Magazine*, 12 (5): 40–48.

[Schwarz et al. 2007] Schwarz, H., Marpe, D. & Wiegand, T. (2007). Overview of the scalable video coding extension of the H.264/AVC standard, *IEEE Transactions on Circuits and Systems for Video Technology* 17 (9): 1103–1120.

[Shacham & Pckenney 1990] Shacham, N. & Pckenney, P. (1990). Packet recovery in high-speed networks using coding and buffer management," *Proceedings of IEEE INFOCOM* 1: 124–131.

[Van der Auwera et al. 2008a] Van der Auwera, G., David, P. T. & Reisslein, M. (2008). Traffic and quality characterization of single-layer video streams encoded with the H.264/MPEG-4 advanced video coding standard and scalable video coding extension, *IEEE Transactions on Broadcasting* 54 (3): 698–718.

[Van der Auwera et al. 2008b] Van der Auwera, G., David, P. T. & Reisslein, M. (2008). Traffic characteristics of H.264/AVC variable bit rate video, *IEEE Communications Magazine* 46 (11): 164–174.

[Wien et al. 2007] Wien, M., Schwarz, H. & Oelbaum, T. (2007). Performance analysis of SVC, *IEEE Transactions on Circuits and Systems for Video Technology* 17 (9): 1194–1203.

[Wolf 1989] Wolff, R. W. (1989). *Stochastic modeling and the theory of queues*, Prentice-Hall.
[PMA] Passive Measurement and Analysis (PMA). URL: http://pma.nlanr.net /Special/leip2.html

# 13

# Line-based Intra Coding for High Quality Video Using H.264/AVC

Jung-Ah Choi and Yo-Sung Ho
*Gwangju Institute of Science and Technology (GIST)*
*Republic of Korea*

## 1. Introduction

H.264/AVC is currently one of the most commonly used video coding standards. The compression efficiency of H.264/AVC is higher than any other previous video coding standards, as it includes more sophisticated coding techniques, such as intra prediction, variable block size motion estimation, rate-distortion optimized mode decision, and entropy coding (Luthra *et al.*, 2003; Sullivan & Wiegand, 2005; Wiegand *et al.*, 2003).

Intra prediction is an important technique in image and video coding to reduce the spatial redundancy between spatially adjacent blocks. Unlike previous coding standards such as H.263+ and MPEG-4 Part-2, in which intra predictions were performed in the transform domain, the intra prediction of H.264/AVC is completely defined in the pixel domain by referring to neighboring samples of coded blocks (Sullivan *et al.*, 2004; Sullivan *et al.*, 2004).

Recently, many intra prediction approaches have been proposed. To capture the local information of neighboring reconstructed samples more accurately, 34 prediction modes are employed in angular intra prediction for the Intra_8×8 mode (Ugur *et al.*, 2010), and arbitrary directional intra (ADI) for the Intra_16×16 mode (McCann *et al.*, 2010). In order to combine two types of the H.264/AVC intra prediction modes, bidirectional intra prediction (BIP) is proposed (Matsuo *et al.*, 2007).

In some cases, the image blocks have repeated patterns instead of distinctive direction information. In this case, utilizing the global information in place of the spatial neighboring samples will bring better coding efficiency. Related works include intra displacement compensation (IDC) (Yu & Chrysafis, 2002) and template matching (TM). IDC uses an intra-displacement vector per block partition to get the reference samples. In TM, they choose to match the templates which have already been reconstructed. Further enhancements using the TM scheme are matching using a single template (Tan *et al.*, 2006), backward-adaptive texture synthesis (Wei & Levoy, 2000), multiple candidates (Tan *et al.*, 2007), priority-guided template matching (Guo *et al.*, 2008), and locally adaptive illumination compensation (Zheng *et al.*, 2008).

Although these approaches improve the coding performance, they still suffer from the limitation of the block-based structure. In the block-based structure, it is difficult to predict the samples far from the reconstructed block boundaries. Thus, a new intra prediction method, line-based intra prediction (Sohn & Han, 2007; Peng *et al.*, 2010) is suggested. Until now, line-based coding seems to overcome the shortcomings of block-based prediction, because each line within the current block shares an equal processing and is predicted and transformed as a basic unit. Since the basic prediction unit is smaller than the case of block-based prediction, the amount of the residual data is reduced so that entire coding efficiency is improved. However, these works require modifying syntax elements of H.264/AVC and overhead bits for prediction modes should be delivered to the decoder side. Also, it is not easy to implement in the current H.264/AVC standard.

In this chapter, we have tried to design the implicit line-based prediction for high bit-rate compression. In our observation, high-definition (HD) contents are likely to have complex patterns - a lot of homogeneous texture patterns with variations such as gradation. However, Intra_16×16 has only four simple prediction directions. In H.264/AVC Intra_16×16 prediction, 256 pixels within the current block are predicted from maximum 33 neighboring pixels. Thus, its prediction accuracy is not enough to be selected as the best mode. As a result, Intra_4×4 or Intra_8×8 is determined as the best mode for most macroblocks.

To improve the prediction accuracy of the Intra_16×16 mode and take full advantage of the line-based structure, we implicitly implement line-based coding to directional prediction modes of the Intra_16×16 mode such as vertical and horizontal mode. In terms of syntax elements that are transmitted to the decoder, the Intra_4×4 mode requires more bits to represent the mode information than the Intra_16×16 mode. As such, with the proposed method, the entire number of coding bits will be efficiently reduced. Note that the proposed method does not require any modification of syntax element in H.264/AVC, so it can be easily applied to the current standard.

## 2. Overview of intra prediction methods in H.264/AVC

Intra prediction requires data from only within the current picture. Unlike the previous video coding standards such as H.263+ and MPEG-4 Visual, intra prediction in H.264/AVC is always conducted in the spatial domain, by referring to neighboring pixels of the current block. Moreover, to better capture the local properties of video signal, H.264/AVC employs flexible macroblock partition modes: Intra_4×4, Intra_8×8, and Intra_16×16. For predicting the luminance component, nine prediction modes are employed in both Intra_4×4 and Intra_8×8 modes, and four prediction modes are utilized for Intra_16×16. The details of the prediction process are shown in following subsections.

The efficiency of each partition mode is first evaluated by the encoder using the Lagrangian cost function, defined as

$$J = D + \lambda_{MODE} \times R \qquad \textit{where}\, MODE \in \{\text{Intra\_4}\times 4, \text{Intra\_16}\times 16\} \tag{1}$$

where the distortion term is the absolute difference between the original and reconstructed signals, the rate term represents the amount of actual bits produced by H.264/AVC entropy coding, and $\lambda_{MODE}$ is the Lagrangian constant, which depends on the quantization level. After this, the best mode which optimizes the cost function will then be selected for the actual coding. After intra prediction, the difference between estimated and real sample values, called residual data is coded and transmitted.

### 2.1 Overview of Intra_4x4 prediction

In Intra_4×4 mode, each 4×4 luma block is predicted from spatially neighboring pixels. The 16 pixels within the 4×4 block are predicted using position-specific linear combinations of previously-decoded pixels from adjacent blocks. The encoder can either select DC prediction or one of eight directional prediction types, as illustrated on Fig. 1. The directional modes are designed to model object edges at various angles.

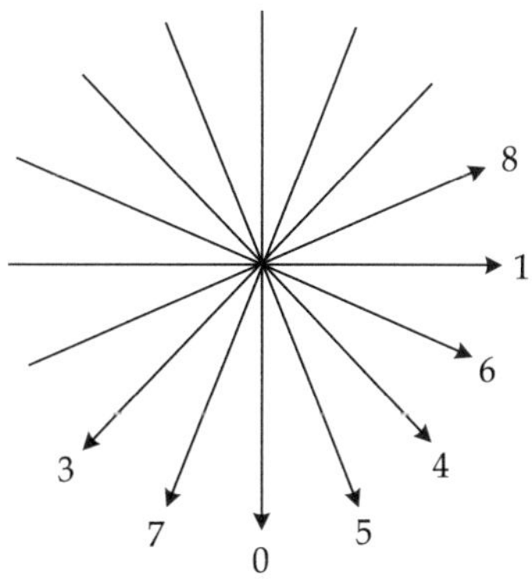


| Mode number | Name of prediction mode |
|---|---|
| 0 | Vertical |
| 1 | Horizontal |
| 2 | DC |
| 3 | Diagonal Down-Left |
| 4 | Diagonal Down-Right |
| 5 | Vertical-Right |
| 6 | Horizontal-Down |
| 7 | Vertical-Left |
| 8 | Horizontal-Up |

Fig. 1. Nine prediction directions of Intra_4×4 mode.

### 2.2 Overview of Intra_8x8 prediction

For high quality video, Intra_8×8 prediction is introduced in H.264/AVC high profile by extending the concepts of Intra_4×4 mode. Prediction directions of Intra_8×8 mode are same with those of Intra_4×4 mode, except the size of block. Each Intra_8×8 prediction generates 64 predicted pixel values within the 8×8 block using some or all of the upper and left-hand neighboring pixels.

### 2.3 Overview of Intra_16x16 prediction

The Intra_16×16 prediction mode is selected in relatively homogeneous area. Four prediction modes are supported, as shown in Fig. 2. The 256 pixel values within the macroblock are generated from some or all of the upper and left-hand neighboring pixels. These modes are specified similar to modes in Intra_4×4 predictions except the plane prediction.

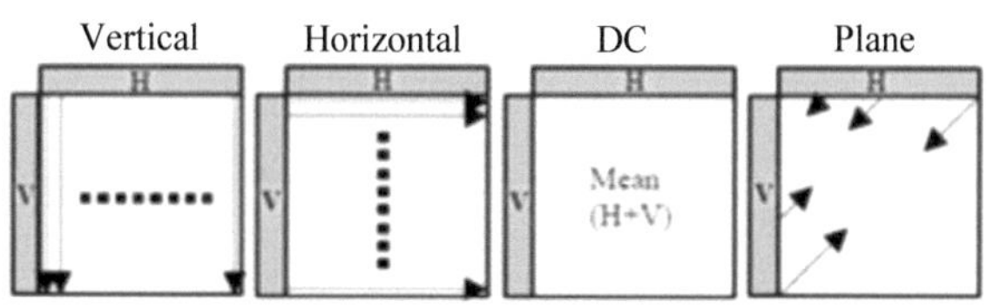


| Mode number | Name of prediction mode |
|---|---|
| 0 | Vertical |
| 1 | Horizontal |
| 2 | DC |
| 3 | Plane |

Fig. 2. Four prediction mode directions for Intra_16×16.

Although the intra prediction in H.264/AVC shows lower complexity and good coding efficiency, there is still room for further improvement. The correlation between two samples is inversely relative to the distance between them. Therefore, samples at each position within one block should be predicted closer reference pixels.

## 3. Analysis of characteristics of high quality video coding for HD contents

In high resolution video service, the quality of reconstructed video is important. Figure 3 shows the decoded video of the high definition (HD) contents, *BQTerrace* using various quantization parameters (QP) from 24 to 32. Over 28, we can observe that the complex texture region within the white circle is abruptly corrupted.

Fig. 3. Decoded quality comparison (left: QP=24, middle: QP=28, right: QP=32).

Since an intra-coded frame can be used as a reference frame of inter frames, the quality is more important than any others. Thus, we determine that the suitable QP for high quality video coding is below 28. In this research, we set QP from 16 to 28 (high bitrate compression). Using this range of QP, we can encode the high resolution video without noticeable quality degradation.

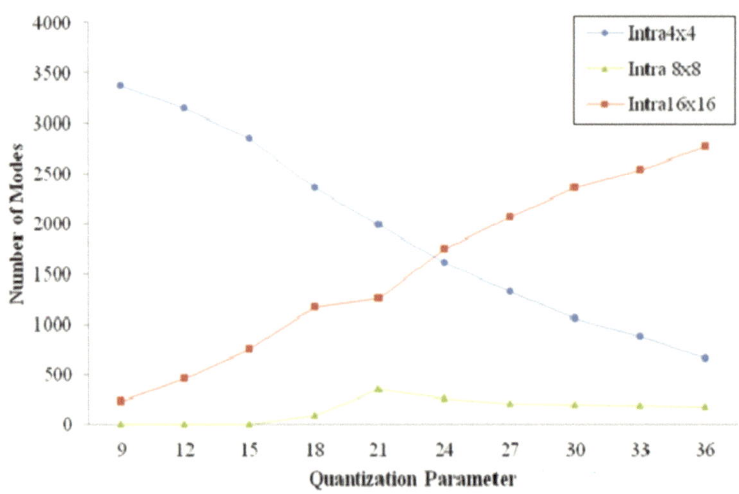


Fig. 4. Selected best mode distribution for various quantization parameters.

We checked the selected best mode distribution for various QPs, as shown in Fig. 4. In low bitrate, the number of Intra_16×16 modes is larger than the number of Intra_4×4 modes. In high bitrate, the number of Intra_16×16 modes is smaller. This result indicates that the prediction accuracy of Intra_16×16 mode is not sufficient for selection as the best mode in high bitrate compression. From this observation, we can know that the performance of H.264/AVC Intra_16×16 prediction in high bitrate compression should be improved.

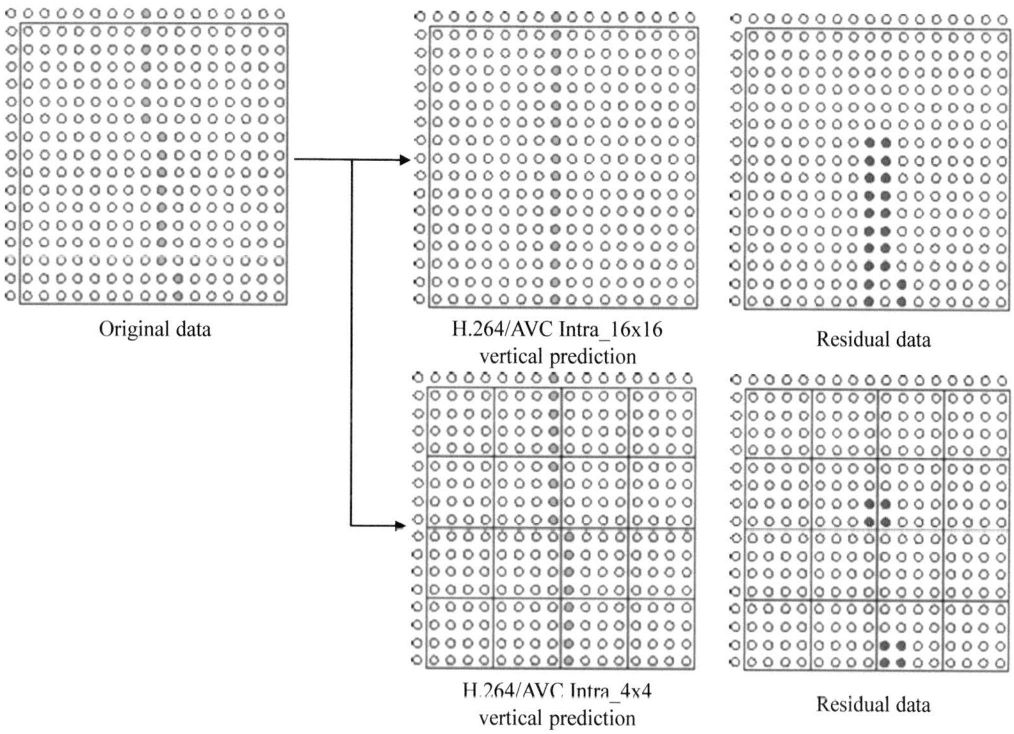


Fig. 5. Prediction result comparison between the Intra_16×16 and Intra_4×4 modes.

High resolution video generally has many complex patterns due to its substantially higher resolution. Figure 5 shows the prediction results of Intra_16×16 and Intra_4×4 modes, when we try to predict the left-hand block. Red circle in Fig. 5 stands for remaining pixels that are not removed by prediction, i.e. residual data. We can know that the amount of residual data after Intra_4×4 prediction is smaller than that after Intra_16×16 prediction. Simple directional prediction of Intra_16×16 cannot cover this kind of block. In this reason, Intra_4×4 mode is frequently selected as the best mode. Especially, in high bitrate, the correlation between reference pixels and current pixels is kept, because the noise of quantization and the smoothing effect of deblocking filter in high bitrate are smaller than that in low bitrate.

## 4. Implicit line-based intra prediction

In this section, we introduce an implicit line-based intra coding method (Choi *et al.*, 2010). In the conventional intra prediction of H.264/AVC, the Intra_16×16 mode is selected as the best mode in the homogeneous region. However, since the prediction unit is 16×16 block, pixels located further provide poor prediction performance in the vertical and horizontal modes. Thus, when the input sequence has a homogeneous texture pattern with variations such as gradation, the Intra_16×16 mode in H.264/AVC cannot yield sufficient prediction accuracy. It results in the increase of the residual data.

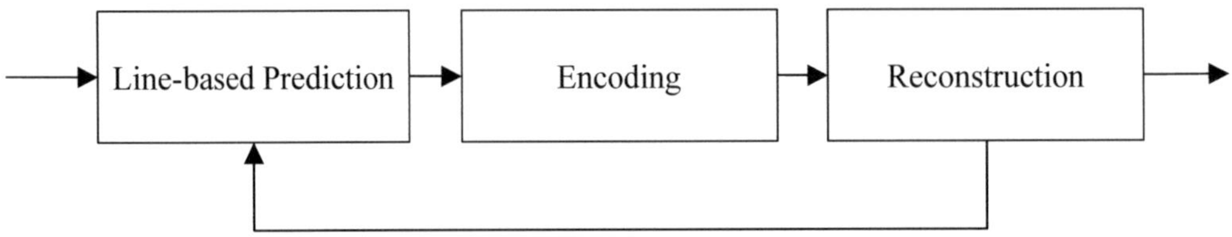


Fig. 6. Line-based prediction process.

In order to improve prediction accuracy of the Intra_16×16 mode, we propose a more efficient line-based intra prediction method in H.264/AVC by modifying the relevant coding procedure of the Intra_16×16 mode. The entire coding procedure of the proposed line-based intra prediction is shown in Fig. 6. The proposed method can be summarized in the following steps:

**Step 1.** Prediction of the first line of pixels (LOP).
**Step 2.** Transformation and quantization of the residual LOP (Encoding).
**Step 3.** Inverse quantization and inverse transformation (Reconstruction).
**Step 4.** Encoding next LOP using the reconstructed LOP.

Further details of the proposed coding method are described in the following subsections.

### 4.1 Prediction of the first LOP

To take full advantage of the correlation between pixels, we perform a line-based prediction instead of the traditional block-based prediction. Note also that in the proposed method we do not predict the entire macroblock in one operation. Figures 7(a) and 7(b) show the proposed line-based prediction procedures for the vertical and horizontal modes, respectively.

For the vertical mode, we define 1×16 pixels as the LOP. Then, we make prediction values for this LOP by copying neighboring pixels in the upper macroblock, as shown in Fig. 7 (a). The prediction equation of the vertical mode is given by

$$pred(x,0) = p(x,-1), \quad x \in \{0,1,2,\cdots 15\} \tag{2}$$

where $pred(\cdot)$ and $p(x, -1)$ represent predicted values and neighboring pixel values of previously coded upper macroblock. After this prediction, the predicted LOP is subtracted from the corresponding LOP of the original block to produce residual data; only the residual LOP is encoded.

On the other hand, we define 16×1 pixels as the LOP for the horizontal mode, then make prediction values for this LOP using

$$pred(0,y) = p(-1,y), \quad y \in \{0,1,2,\cdots 15\}. \tag{3}$$

The predicted LOP is subsequently subtracted from the corresponding LOP of the original block to produce residual LOP.

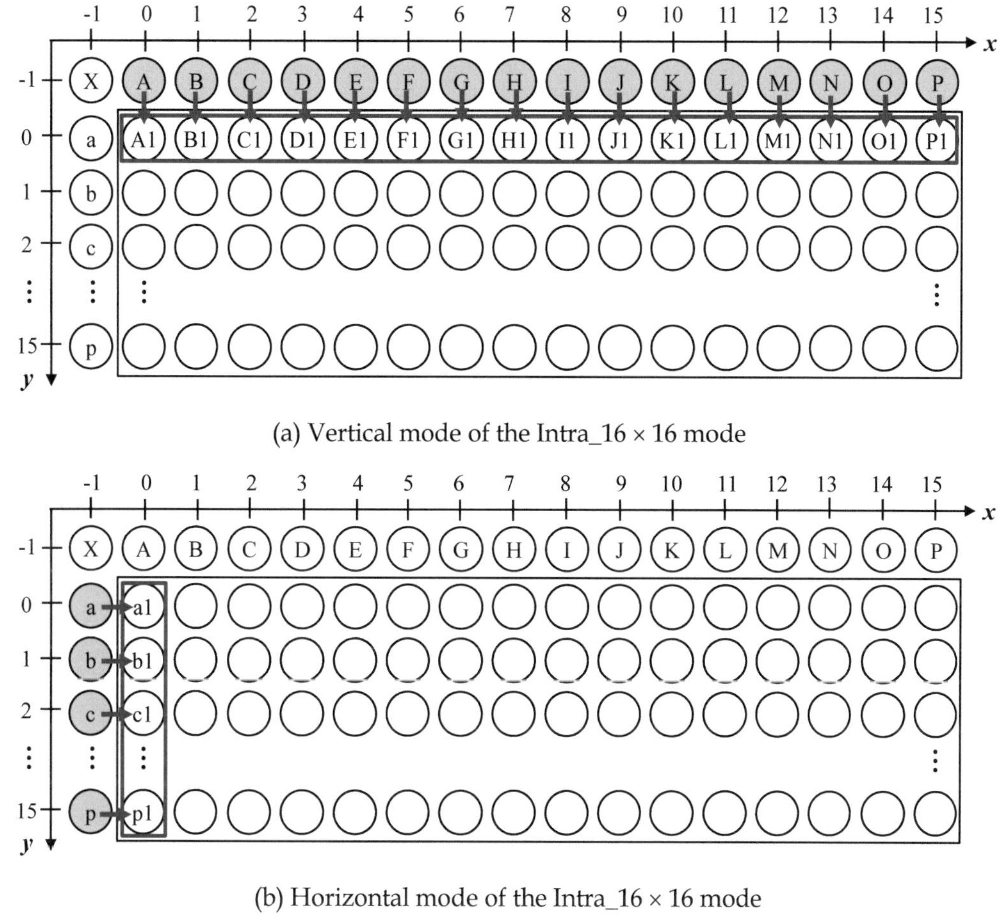


Fig. 7. Prediction method for the first LOP.

### 4.2 Transformation and quantization of residual LOP

After prediction of the first LOP, the residual LOP is transformed and quantized to give a set of quantized transform coefficients. In recent research works, line-based prediction with one dimensional (1D) transform has been introduced (Chen & Han, 2009; Sohn & Han, 2007). Their Intra_4×4 prediction method is cooperated with 1D transform. However, in the case of Intra_16×16 block, coding performance is not guaranteed because the residual signal after line-based prediction is quite random and there is not so much dependency in 1D signal. Thus, the 4×4 integer discrete cosine transform (DCT) and the quantization of the conventional H.264/AVC are used. There could be a potential work for finding the best rearrangement pattern for residual 1D data.

Prior to the transformation, the residual LOP should be rearranged to construct the 4×4 block, X. Note that an accurate prediction reduces the quantity of residual data to be coded. As the residual data decreases, its correlation is subject to a substantial decrease; thus, since line-based prediction gives more accurate prediction results than the conventional prediction, the correlation of its residual data becomes lower. To construct the 4×4 block to be used for the transformation and quantization, we rearrange the residual LOP in raster order, as shown in Fig. 8. For this low-correlated signal, there is no rearrangement method that can provide an even better coding efficiency than the raster scan, which we have confirmed by performing extensive experiments using various rearrangement methods, including zigzag order.

| | | | | | | | | | | | | | | | |
|---|---|---|---|---|---|---|---|---|---|---|---|---|---|---|---|
| 1 | 2 | 3 | 4 | 5 | 6 | 7 | 8 | 9 | 10 | 11 | 12 | 13 | 14 | 15 | 16 |

| | | | |
|---|---|---|---|
| 1 | 2 | 3 | 4 |
| 5 | 6 | 7 | 8 |
| 9 | 10 | 11 | 12 |
| 13 | 14 | 15 | 16 |

Fig. 8. Rearrangement of residual LOP for transformation.

The transformation operates on the 4×4 rearranged block of the residual data, with the procedure of the 4×4 forward transform being as follows:

$$Y = \begin{bmatrix} 1 & 1 & 1 & 1 \\ 2 & 1 & -1 & -2 \\ 1 & -1 & -1 & 1 \\ 1 & -2 & 2 & -1 \end{bmatrix} [X] \begin{bmatrix} 1 & 2 & 1 & 1 \\ 1 & 1 & -1 & -2 \\ 1 & -1 & -1 & 2 \\ 1 & -2 & 1 & -1 \end{bmatrix} \tag{4}$$

where X is the reordered residual LOP and Y represents the transformed coefficients. After performing the forward transform, the quantization of transformed coefficients is given by

$$Z_{(i,j)} = sign(W_{(i,j)}) \cdot (\left|W_{(i,j)}\right| \cdot MF_{(i,j)} + f) >> (15 + Q_D) \tag{5}$$

where $MF(i,j)$ represents the multiplication factor and $f$ controls the dead zone. In the reference model software, $f$ is $2^{(15+Q_D)}/3$. In addition, the symbol >> indicates a binary shift right, $sign(\cdot)$ represents the sign function, and $Q_D$ represents the greatest integer smaller than or equal to QP/6.

### 4.3 Inverse quantization and inverse transformation

The encoder immediately reconstructs the inverse transformed and inverse quantized block of the residual LOP to provide reference data for further predictions of the next LOPs. First, the inverse quantization is performed as follows:

$$Y'_{(i,j)} = (Z_{(i,j)} \cdot SF_{(i,j)}) << Q_D \tag{6}$$

where $SF_{(i,j)}$ is the scaling factor. The following equation represents the inverse transform.

$$X' = \begin{bmatrix} 1 & 1 & 1 & 1/2 \\ 1 & 1/2 & -1 & -1 \\ 1 & -1/2 & -1 & 1 \\ 1 & -1 & 1 & -1/2 \end{bmatrix} [Y'] \begin{bmatrix} 1 & 1 & 1 & 1 \\ 1 & 1/2 & -1/2 & -1 \\ 1 & -1 & -1 & 1 \\ 1/2 & -1 & 1 & -1/2 \end{bmatrix} \quad (7)$$

The differential block X′ is produced; note that X′ is not same as X because of the quantization error. Then, X′ is rearranged from a 4×4 block to a line, as shown in Fig. 9. We add the predicted LOP to X′ to create the reconstructed LOP, which is then used as reference data for predicting the next LOP.

| | | | |
|---|---|---|---|
| 1 | 2 | 3 | 4 |
| 5 | 6 | 7 | 8 |
| 9 | 10 | 11 | 12 |
| 13 | 14 | 15 | 16 |

↓

| | | | | | | | | | | | | | | | |
|---|---|---|---|---|---|---|---|---|---|---|---|---|---|---|---|
| 1 | 2 | 3 | 4 | 5 | 6 | 7 | 8 | 9 | 10 | 11 | 12 | 13 | 14 | 15 | 16 |

Fig. 9. Rearrangement of the reconstructed block for further prediction.

### 4.4 Further prediction using reconstructed LOP

Using the reconstructed LOP, the next LOP is predicted, as shown in Fig. 10. Figures 10(a) and 10(b) show the prediction process of the vertical and horizontal modes, respectively; this process is repeated until the last LOP within the current macroblock.

The equation for further predictions of the vertical mode is

$$pred(x,y) = r(x,y-1), \quad x \in \{0,1,2,\cdots 15\}, \; y \in \{1,2,\cdots 15\} \quad (8)$$

where r(x, y-1) indicates the reconstructed pixels and y is the line index that represents the position of the current line within the macroblock, which varies from 1 to 15.

Predictions of the horizontal mode are performed using a similar method. Equation (9) shows the prediction equation for the horizontal mode, with the only change being the prediction direction. Unlike the vertical mode, x is the line index that represents the position of the current line, and it varies from 1 to 15.

$$pred(x,y) = r(x-1,y), \quad x \in \{1,2,\cdots 15\}, \; y \in \{0,1,2,\cdots 15\}. \quad (9)$$

The coded block pattern (cbp) signals as to whether there are coefficients in the transform block or not. In the conventional H.264/AVC, one cbp is calculated for each macroblock in the intra 16×16 mode. Thus, we should change the calculation procedure for cbp in the proposed algorithm. Since the prediction unit of the proposed intra 16×16 coding is in terms of LOP, we can compute the cbp for each LOP. The cbp for the macroblock is then calculated from the cumulative value of cbp for each LOP.

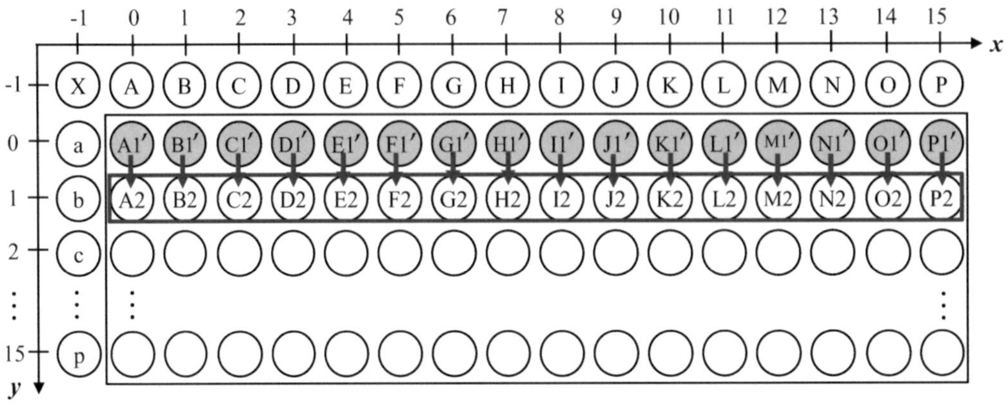


(a) Vertical mode of the Intra_16×16 mode

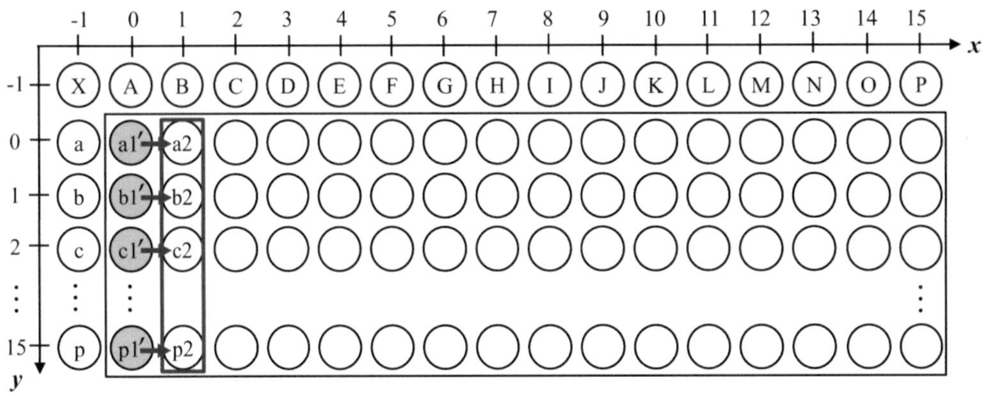


(b) Horizontal mode of the Intra_16×16 mode

Fig. 10. Further prediction using the reconstructed LOP.

Figure 11 shows the improvement of the prediction accuracy by the proposed method. The left-hand original data is same with that in Fig. 5. Using the proposed method, we can predict the original data well and the amount of the residual data is significantly reduced. Moreover, by comparing Fig. 5 and Fig. 11, we can confirm that the prediction performance of the proposed method is better than that of the Intra_4×4 mode.

## 5. Experimental results and analysis

In order to verify the efficiency of this method, we performed experiments on *Bigships* (1280x720), *Jets* (1280x720), *ShuttleStart* (1280x720), *BasketballDrive* (1920x1080), *Cactus* (1920x1080), *BQTerrace* (1920x1080) with YUV 4:2:0 in 8 bits per pixel format. The proposed method is implemented in the H.264/AVC reference software version JM 12.2(Fraunhofer Institute for Telecommunications Heinrich Hertz Institute, 2011).

Implementation of the proposed method was achieved by replacing the conventional Intra_16×16 vertical and horizontal modes. All the tested sequences are intra only coded and have various frame rates. The detailed encoding parameters for the experiment are summarized in Table 1.

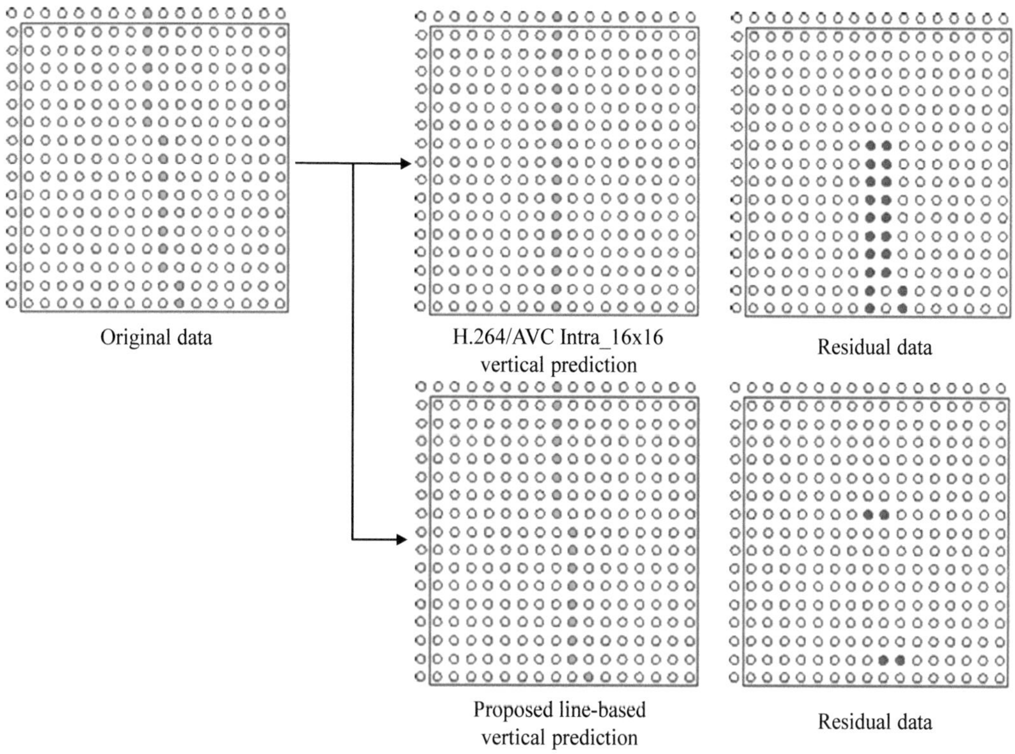


Fig. 11. Prediction result comparison between the conventional Intra_16×16 and proposed line-based Intra_16×16 predictions.

| Parameter | Value |
|---|---|
| *ProfileIDC* | 100 (High) |
| *IntraPeriod* | 1 (only intra coding) |
| *QPISlice* | 16, 20, 24, 28 |
| *Transform8x8Mode* | 1 |
| *SymbolMode* | 1 |

Table 1. Encoding parameters

In order to verify the efficiency of our proposed method, we compare coding result of the proposed method with that of H.264/AVC. The results for several test sequences are shown in Table 2. Here, the Bjøntegaard delta peak signal-to-noise ratio (dB) and the Bjøntegaard delta bitrate (%) are used to evaluate performance of the proposed algorithm(Bjontegaard, 2008). In the experiment, we used all intra prediction modes (Intra_16×16, Intra_8×8, and Intra_4×4 modes) by turning on the *Transform8x8Mode* option. We confirmed that the proposed method provides average bit savings of 6.42% for 720p and 1080p HD resolution sequences, compared to the conventional H.264/AVC FRExt high profile.

| Sequence | QP | H.264/AVC | | Proposed Algorithm | | Bjøntegaard Delta | |
|---|---|---|---|---|---|---|---|
| | | PSNR (dB) | Bitrate (Kbps) | PSNR (dB) | Bitrate (Kbps) | BDPSNR (dB) | BDRATE (%) |
| *Bigships* (HD, 1280×720) First frame | 16 | 47.08 | 61143.12 | 46.00 | 51110.40 | 0.31 | -4.74 |
| | 20 | 43.47 | 40422.96 | 42.62 | 33569.76 | | |
| | 24 | 40.54 | 25798.08 | 40.01 | 23119.68 | | |
| | 28 | 37.76 | 16042.80 | 37.46 | 15061.68 | | |
| *Jets* (HD, 1280×720) First frame | 16 | 46.45 | 32622.48 | 45.99 | 23141.04 | 0.20 | -7.57 |
| | 20 | 43.67 | 16313.04 | 43.37 | 13814.40 | | |
| | 24 | 42.00 | 8712.00 | 41.82 | 8208.72 | | |
| | 28 | 40.45 | 5236.56 | 40.25 | 4983.12 | | |
| *ShuttleStart* (HD, 1280×720) First frame | 16 | 48.58 | 19584.24 | 48.04 | 16558.56 | 0.09 | -2.55 |
| | 20 | 46.13 | 11039.04 | 45.77 | 9649.68 | | |
| | 24 | 44.14 | 6380.64 | 43.89 | 5915.28 | | |
| | 28 | 42.13 | 3559.20 | 41.97 | 3405.12 | | |
| *BasketballDrive* (HD, 1920×1080) First frame | 16 | 48.13 | 112107.12 | 46.42 | 76696.56 | 0.51 | -14.90 |
| | 20 | 42.83 | 59862.48 | 42.34 | 45584.40 | | |
| | 24 | 40.33 | 27544.08 | 40.16 | 25075.44 | | |
| | 28 | 38.84 | 14913.84 | 38.70 | 14117.28 | | |
| *Cactus* (HD, 1920×1080) First frame | 16 | 46.48 | 172070.88 | 45.79 | 150515.00 | 0.29 | -5.78 |
| | 20 | 42.25 | 106455.36 | 41.83 | 92064.72 | | |
| | 24 | 39.38 | 60227.52 | 39.07 | 54915.84 | | |
| | 28 | 37.36 | 34913.28 | 37.13 | 32742.72 | | |
| *BQTerrace* (HD, 1920×1080) First frame | 16 | 48.06 | 169545.12 | 47.26 | 158143.90 | 0.30 | -2.98 |
| | 20 | 44.52 | 124250.16 | 43.64 | 112598.60 | | |
| | 24 | 40.23 | 83761.44 | 39.51 | 73423.44 | | |
| | 28 | 36.90 | 53018.64 | 36.38 | 47027.52 | | |
| Average | | | | | | **0.28** | **-6.42** |

Table 2. Performance comparison between H.264/AVC and the proposed method

Figure 12 shows the rate-distortion curve of test sequences. We can find that the proposed technique achieves consistent gains for all test sequences and especially efficient in the high bitrate range. As expected, the proposed method performed much better in test sequences such as *BasketballDrive* that contain a lot of gradation patterns, as shown in Fig. 13. Table 3 shows the mode distribution change for all test sequences when we use the proposed method. In the tables, we can observe that the number of intra 16×16 modes, i.e., the best modes of some blocks changed to Intra_16×16 mode. This change implies that the proposed prediction method improves prediction accuracy of intra 16×16 coding quite well. Providing same image quality, Intra_4×4 requires more bits to represent the mode information than the Intra_16×16 mode, we can reduce the bit rate using the proposed method.

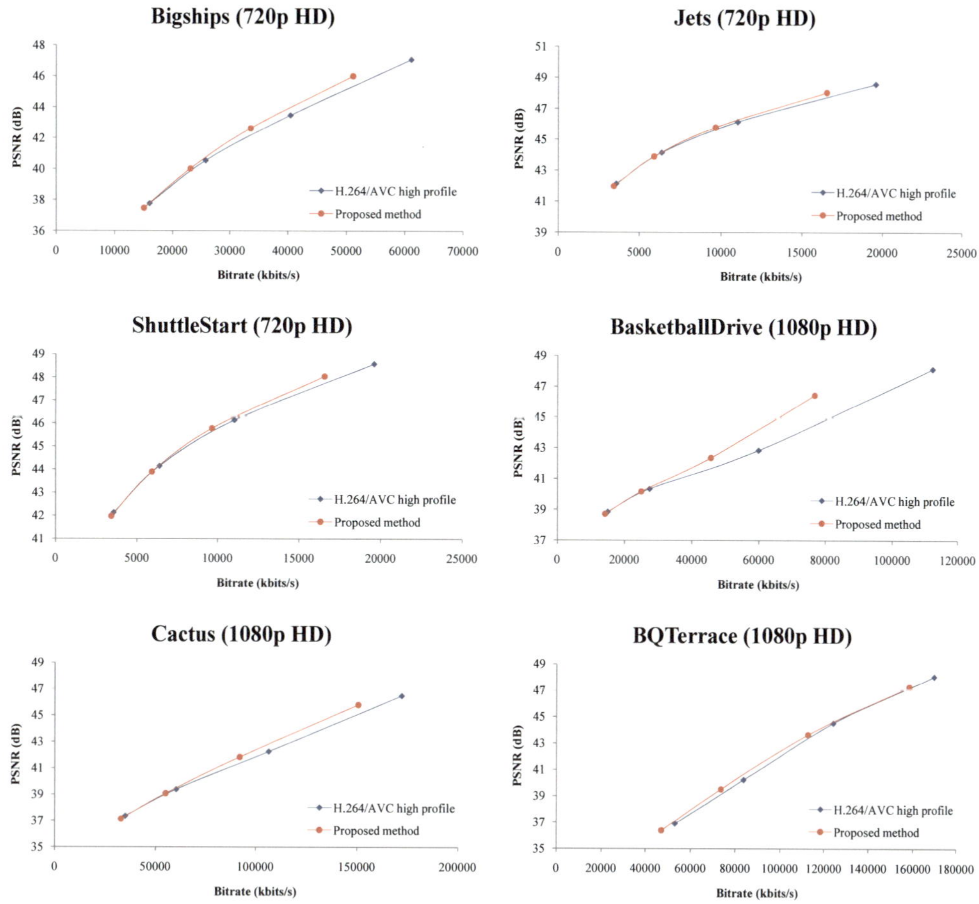


Fig. 12. Rate-distortion curve of proposed technique.

Fig. 13. *BasketballDrive* that contains a lot of complex patterns.

| Sequence | QP | H.264/AVC | | | Proposed Method | | | I16MB Increase (%) |
|---|---|---|---|---|---|---|---|---|
| | | I16MB (%) | I8MB (%) | I4MB (%) | I16MB (%) | I8MB (%) | I4MB (%) | |
| *Bigships* (HD, 1280×720) First frame | 16 | 0.1 | 96.3 | 3.5 | 33.5 | 64.1 | 2.5 | 33.3 |
| | 20 | 3.7 | 81.6 | 14.7 | 25.7 | 67.5 | 6.8 | 21.9 |
| | 24 | 15.7 | 64.7 | 19.6 | 12.7 | 69.5 | 17.8 | -3.0 |
| | 28 | 28.4 | 59.4 | 12.2 | 26.7 | 61.5 | 11.8 | -1.7 |
| *Jets* (HD, 1280×720) First frame | 16 | 5.6 | 47.3 | 47.1 | 18.4 | 42.0 | 39.6 | 12.8 |
| | 20 | 4.1 | 60.9 | 34.9 | 18.9 | 51.0 | 30.1 | 14.7 |
| | 24 | 9.4 | 59.4 | 31.2 | 14.6 | 57.9 | 27.5 | 5.2 |
| | 28 | 14.9 | 63.7 | 21.4 | 18.2 | 61.9 | 19.9 | 3.3 |
| *ShuttleStart* (HD, 1280×720) First frame | 16 | 1.4 | 76.2 | 22.4 | 7.3 | 70.0 | 22.8 | 5.8 |
| | 20 | 6.3 | 69.1 | 24.6 | 10.8 | 63.2 | 26.0 | 4.5 |
| | 24 | 15.4 | 37.7 | 46.9 | 26.2 | 34.3 | 39.5 | 10.8 |
| | 28 | 12.7 | 37.4 | 49.9 | 23.5 | 35.7 | 40.7 | 10.8 |
| *BasketballDrive* (HD, 1920×1080) First frame | 16 | 1.6 | 45.8 | 52.6 | 19.3 | 36.9 | 43.8 | 17.7 |
| | 20 | 2.4 | 51.3 | 46.3 | 17.6 | 46.7 | 35.7 | 15.1 |
| | 24 | 5.8 | 53.5 | 40.7 | 10.9 | 53.4 | 35.8 | 5.1 |
| | 28 | 9.3 | 60.7 | 30.0 | 10.3 | 60.2 | 29.5 | 1.0 |
| *Cactus* (HD, 1920×1080) First frame | 16 | 25.2 | 39.4 | 35.4 | 51.5 | 24.4 | 24.1 | 26.4 |
| | 20 | 13.9 | 61.7 | 24.4 | 21.8 | 58.3 | 19.9 | 7.8 |
| | 24 | 22.4 | 50.3 | 27.3 | 26.0 | 53.8 | 20.2 | 3.6 |
| | 28 | 32.4 | 52.4 | 15.2 | 45.2 | 40.1 | 14.7 | 12.8 |
| *BQTerrace* (HD, 1920×1080) First frame | 16 | 35.0 | 58.4 | 6.6 | 34.0 | 33.8 | 32.2 | -1.0 |
| | 20 | 45.3 | 46.9 | 7.9 | 45.6 | 46.0 | 8.4 | 0.3 |
| | 24 | 58.6 | 31.4 | 10.0 | 59.8 | 31.3 | 8.9 | 1.2 |
| | 28 | 65.5 | 29.5 | 5.0 | 63.8 | 30.6 | 5.6 | -1.7 |

Table 3. Mode distribution change

## 6. Conclusion

In this chapter, we proposed an efficient line-based intra 16×16 prediction method for high bitrate compression. Considering the different characteristics of high definition (HD) contents, we modified the intra coding mechanism without any change of syntax elements of the H.264/AVC standard. Note that we break from the traditional block-based prediction method and designed a new prediction method based on line-of-pixels (LOP). As a result, we could achieve a more accurate intra 16×16 mode by reducing the distance between the reference and current pixels. Experimental results show that the proposed method provides approximately 6.42% bit savings, compared to the H.264/AVC FRExt high profile.

## 7. Acknowledgment

This research was supported by the MKE (The Ministry of Knowledge Economy), Korea, under the ITRC (Information Technology Research Center) support program supervised by the NIPA (National IT Industry Promotion Agency). (NIPA-2011-(C1090-1111-0003)).

## 8. References

Bjontegaard G. (2008). Improvements of the BD-PSNR model. *Document of ITU-T Q.6/SG16*, Berlin, Germany, July 16-18, 2008

Chen J. & Han W. (2009). Adaptive linear prediction for block-based lossy image coding. *Proceedings of International Conference on Image Processing*, ISBN 978-1-4244-5654-3, Cairo, Egypt, November 2009

Choi J. & Ho Y. (2010). Line-by-line intra 16×16 prediction for high-quality video coding. Proceedings of International Conference on Multimedia & Expo, ISBN 978-1-4244-7492-9, Singapore, July 2010

Fraunhofer Institute for Telecommunications Heinrich Hertz Institute. Joint Video Team, *H.264/AVC Reference Software Version 12.2* [Online], January 2011, Available from: http://iphome.hhi.de/shehring/tml/download/old_jm/jm12.2.zip

Guo Y., Wang Y., & Li Q. (2008). Priority-based template matching intra prediction. *Proceedings of International Conference on Multimedia and Expo*, ISBN 978-1-4244-2570-9, Hannover, Germany, June 2008

Luthra A., Sullivan G., & Wiegand T. (2003). Introduction to the special issue on the H.264/AVC video coding standard. *IEEE Transactions on Circuits and Systems for Video Technology*, Vol.13, No.7, (July 2003), pp. 557–559, ISSN 1051-8215

Matsuo S., Takamura S., Kamikura K., & Yashima Y. (2007). Weighted intra prediction. *Document of ITU-T Q.6/SG16*, Shenzhen, China, October 20, 2007

McCann K., Han W., & Kim I. (2010). Samsung's response to the call for proposals on video compression technology. *Document of Joint Collaborative Team on Video Coding of ISO/IEC JTC1/SC29/WG11 and ITU-T Q.6/SG16*, Dresden, DE, April 15-23, 2010

Peng X., Xu J., & Wu. F. (2010). Line-based image coding using adaptive prediction filters. *Proceedings of International Symposium on Circuits and Systems*, ISBN 978-1-4244-5309-2, Paris, France, May 2010

Sullivan G., McMahon T., Wiegand T., & Luthra A. (2004). Draft text of H.264/AVC fidelity range extensions amendment to ITU-T Rec. H.264|ISO/IEC 14496-10 AVC. *Document of Joint Video Team of ISO/IEC JTC1/SC29/WG11 and ITU-T Q.6/SG16*, Redmond, WA, USA, July 17-23, 2004

Sullivan G., Topiwala P., & Luthra A. (2004). The H.264/AVC advanced video coding standard: Overview and introduction to the fidelity range extensions. *Proceedings of SPIE Conference, Special Session on Advances in the New Emerging Standard: H.264/AVC*, pp. 454–474, Denver, Colorado, USA, August 2004

Sullivan G. & Wiegand T. (2005). Video compression–from concepts to the H.264/AVC standard. *Proceedings of the IEEE*, Vol.93, No.1, (January 2005), pp. 18–31, ISSN 0018-9219

Sohn Y. & Han W. (2007). One dimensional transform for H.264-based intra coding. *Proceedings of Picture Coding Symposium*, ISBN 978-989-8109-04-0, Lisboa, Portugal, November 2007

Tan T., Boon C., & Suzuki Y. (2006). Intra prediction by template matching. *Proceedings of International Conference on Image Processing,* ISBN 1-4244-0481-9, Atlanta, Georgia, USA, October 2006

Tan T., Boon C., & Suzuki Y. (2007). Intra prediction by averaged template matching predictors. *Proceedings of Consumer Communications and Networking Conference,* ISBN 1-4244-0667-6, Las Vegas, Nevada, USA, January 2007

Ugur K., Andersson K., & Fuldseth A. (2010). Description of video coding technology proposal by Tandberg, Nokia, Ericsson. *Document of Joint Collaborative Team on Video Coding of ISO/IEC JTC1/SC29/WG11 and ITU-T Q.6/SG16,* Dresden, DE, April 15-23, 2010

Wei L. & Levoy M. (2000). Fast texture synthesis using tree-structured vector quantization. *Proceedings of SIGGRAPH,* ISBN 978-020-1485-64-6, New Orleans, Louisiana, USA, July 2000

Wiegand T., Sullivan G., Bjøntegaard G., & Luthra A. (2003). Overview of the H.264/AVC video coding standard. *IEEE Transactions on Circuits and Systems for Video Technology,* Vol.13, Vo.7, (July 2003), pp. 560–576, ISSN 1051-8215

Yu S. & Chrysafis C. (2002). New intra prediction using intra-macroblock motion compensation. *Document of Joint Collaborative Team on Video Coding of ISO/IEC JTC1/SC29/WG11 and ITU-T Q.6/SG16,* Fairfax, VA, USA, May 4-11, 2002

Zheng Y. Yin P., Escoda O., Li X., & Gomila C. (2008). Intra prediction using template matching with adaptive illumination compensation. *Proceedings of International Conference on Image Processing,* ISBN 978-4244-1764-3, San Diego, California, USA, October 2008

# 14

# Swarm Intelligence in Wavelet Based Video Coding

M. Thamarai and R. Shanmugalakshmi
*Karpagam college of Engineering, Government college of Technology, Coimbatore, India*

## 1. Introduction

Video compression plays an important role in modern multimedia applications such as video streaming, video telephony, video conferencing, etc., A lot of compression algorithms those have been developed are not sufficient for the multimedia applications. In general video coding techniques are classified into two. Discrete Cosine transform (Block based) technique, which is used in the standard compression algorithms such as H.261, H.262, H.264 and wavelet transform based technique. Motion compensated wavelet transform based video coding algorithms are going to be taken as one of the standard compression techniques, since multi resolution capability of the wavelets improves the quality of the signal than that of the DCT based one.

### 1.1 Necessity of video compression and standards

A low bit rate video coding (bit rate less than 64 kbs) needs high compression ratio (above 150). In high compression ratio video coding, block based coders introduce blocking artifact and ringing effect (Due to Gibbs phenomena) in the reconstructed signal. High compression image coding has triggered strong interests in recent years. In this type of coding, visible distortions of the original image are accepted in order to obtain very high compression factors. High compression image coders can be split into three distinct groups. The first group is called waveform coding and consists of transform and subband coding. The second group called second generation techniques, consisting of techniques attempting to describe an image in terms of visually meaningful primitives (contour and texture, for example). The third group is based on the fractal theory.

An uncompressed video sequence for very low bit rate applications typically requires a bit stream of up to 10 Mbit/s. In order to achieve very low data rates, compression ratios of about 1000 : 1 are required to meet the needs of the large public. Intensive research has been performed in the last decade to attain this objective [Touradjebrahimi et. al, 1995]. Variations of the recommendation H.261 for very low bit rate applications have been defined as simulation models. For these simulation models, severe blocking artifacts occur at very low data rates.

Wavelet based video coding is developing a new area in video coding for last two decades. Because of the multi resolution property, wavelet tool is suitable for image enhancement and compression. Rather than a complete transformation into the frequency domain, as in DCT or FFT (Fast Fourier Transform), the wavelet transform produces coefficient values which represent both time and frequency information. The hybrid spatial-frequency representation of the wavelet coefficients allows for analysis based on both spatial position and spatial frequency content. While most wavelet-based compression techniques employ the traditional critically sampled discrete wavelet transform (DWT), alternative wavelet transforms have recently been proposed. Specifically, the complex dual-tree discrete wavelet transform (DTCWT) has undergone investigation in 3D video-coding systems [B. Wang, et. al, 2004].

### 1.2 Particle swarm optimization

Particle Swarm Optimization (PSO) is global optimization technique based on swarm intelligence. It simulates the behavior of bird flocking [Kennedy et. al, 1995]. It is widely accepted and focused by researchers due to its profound intelligence and simple algorithm structure. Currently PSO has been implemented in a wide range of research areas such as functional optimization, pattern recognition, neural network training and fuzzy system control etc., and is successful. In PSO, each potential solution is considered as one particle. The system is initialized with a population of random solutions (particles)and searches for optima (global best particle), according to some fitness function, by updating particles over generations; that is, particles "fly" through the N-dimensional problem search space to find the best solution by following the current better-performing particle. When compared to Genetic Algorithm, PSO has very few parameters to adjust and easy to implement. The variants of PSO's such as Binary PSO, Hybrid PSO, Adaptive PSO and Dissipative PSO are used in various image processing applications.

Recently PSO has been extended to deal with multiple objective optimization problems [K. U. Parsopoulos et. al, 2002]. In the past few years many research works have been focused on modifying PSO to handle multiple objective optimization problems known as multi objective particle swarm optimizer MOPSO. The fixed population size MOPSO and variable population size PSO (Dynamic PSO) are used throughout the evolution process to explore the search space to discover the non dominated individuals (particles). Most of the real life problems are multi objective nature.

Multi objective optimization using PSO has been used in Digital image processing like image segmentation, data clustering etc. Here Video compression also viewed as a muliobjective one. The constraints are Means Square Error (MSE), Computation Time, and Computation complexity and compression ratio. In this chapter the only three constrains (Means Square Error (MSE), Computation Time and compression ratio) are considered for the PSO based optimization. All the three are minimization functions. The fixed population size MOPSO is used throughout the evolution process to explore the search space to discover the non dominated individuals (particles).

First the image is decomposed into subband using the Dual tree wavelet transform and the subband coefficients are minimized using noise shaping method. After that the MOPSO algorithm is used to select the optimum subband which provides less mean square error and desired bit rate. In this MOPSO weighted average approach is used. The constraints total weight age is one. The obtained results are compared with the standard algorithms.

## 2. Shortcomings in the conventional discrete wavelet transform

Theoretically-sampled form of the wavelet transform (Discrete Wavelet transform DWT) provides the most compact representation; DWT has the following advantages:

- Multi-scale signal processing technique (Both frequency and time resolution).
- DWT transform itself introduces compression.
- Straightforward computation technique.

However, it has several limitations as explained below. It lacks the shift-invariance property and in Image processing applications it has poor resolution in distinguishing the orientations of the object and in multiple dimensions it does a poor job of distinguishing orientations, which is important in image processing. The four drawbacks of DWT are as follows [Ivan. W. Selesnick et. al, 2005].

- wavelet coefficients are oscillatory in nature.
- Since wavelets are band pass filters the wavelet coefficients tend to oscillate between positive and negative singularities as shown in fig. 1 This considerably complicates the singularity extraction and modeling and feature extraction. Shift variant

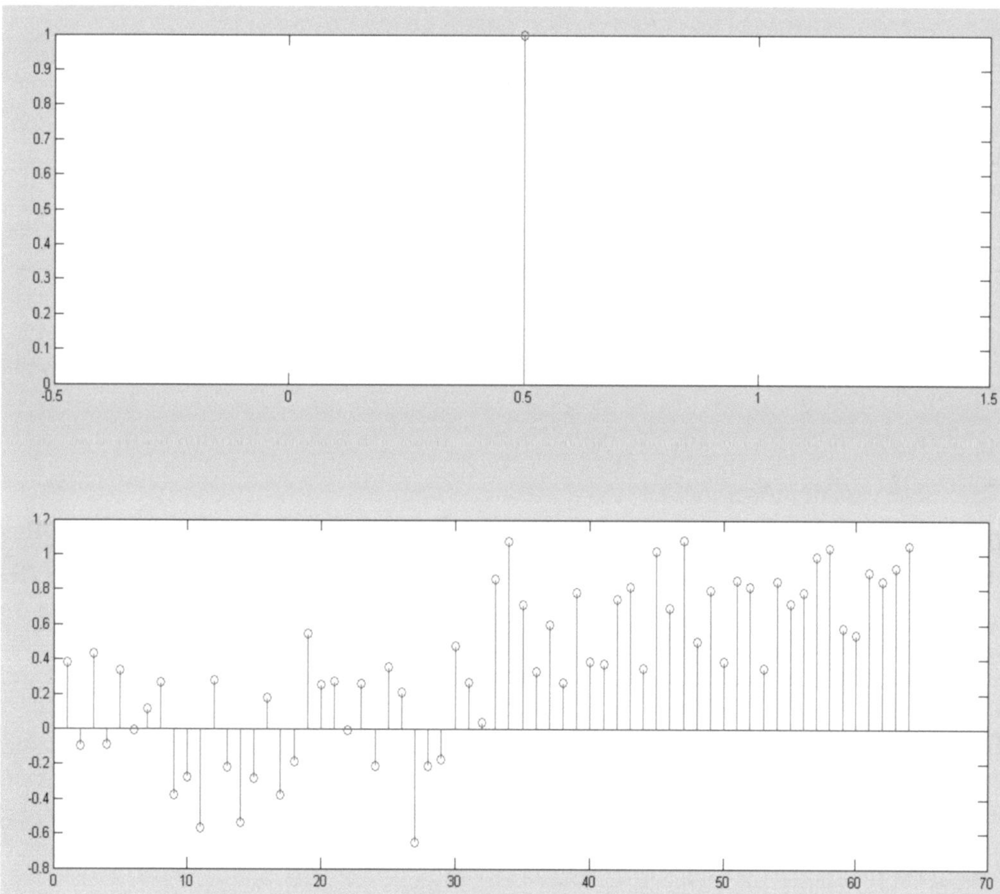


Fig. 1. Oscillatory nature of DWT Coefficients for the signal x(n-0.5)

A small shift of the signal greatly perturbs the wavelet coefficient oscillation pattern around singularities (see Figure 2). Shift variance also complicates wavelet-domain processing; algorithms must be made capable of coping with the wide range of possible wavelet coefficient patterns caused by shifted singularities.

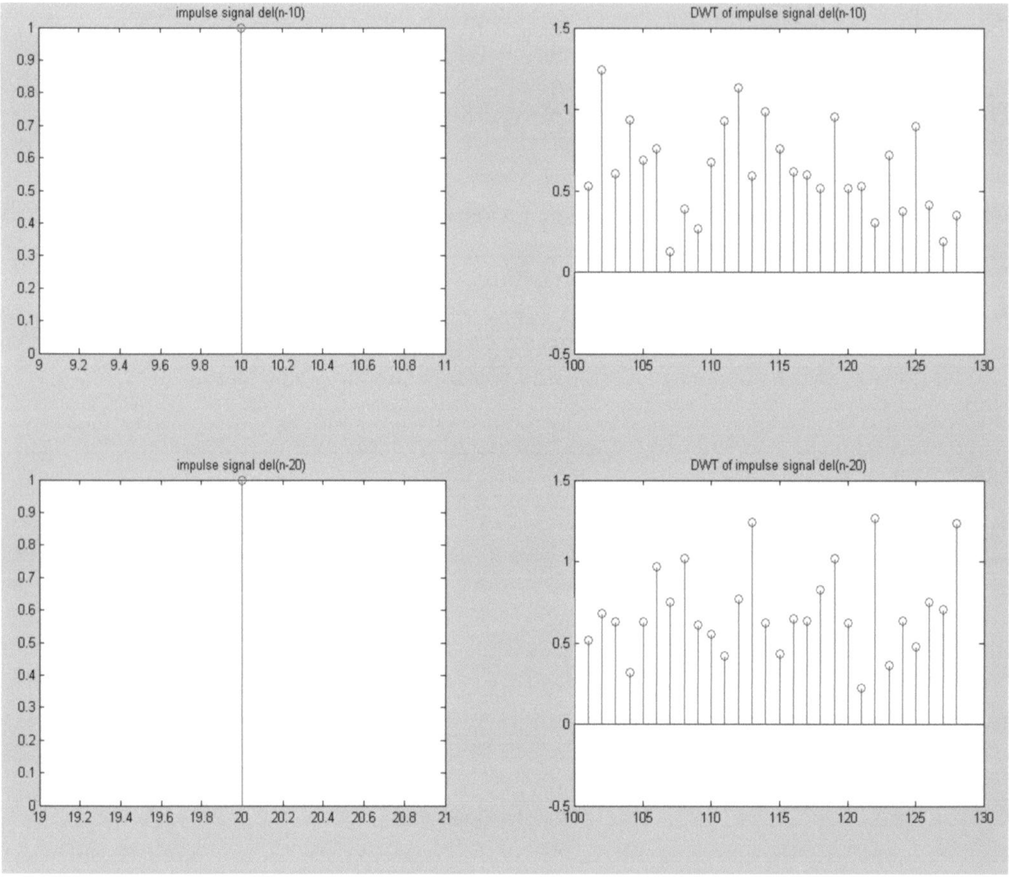


Fig. 2. Shift variant property of DWT

This can be explained with the help of the unit step signal x(n). The x(n) and its shifted version x(n-3) are subjected to DWT and DT CWT decomposition at a level of 3. The spectrum of DWT δ(n-10) is different from the δ(n-20). These two signals are shown in figure 2. Therefore small shift in the input signal results the variation of the DWT coefficients. DWT coefficient values varies based on shifting than DT CWT.

- Aliasing:

The wavelet coefficients of a signal are computed iteratively with the help of sub band decomposition using low pass and high pass filters. These filters are non ideal and results in substantial aliasing. The inverse DWT cancels this aliasing, only if the wavelet and scaling coefficients are not changed. Any wavelet coefficient processing (thresholding, filtering, and quantization) upsets the delicate balance between the forward and inverse transforms, leading to artifacts in the reconstructed signal.

- Lack of directionality:

The multidimensional wavelets produce a check board pattern, and is oriented in several directions. This lack of directional selectivity greatly complicates modeling and processing of geometric image features like ridges and edges.

2D wavelet transform is formed by three wavelets.

## 3. Dual tree discrete wavelet transform (DTDWT)

It is an expansive type of transform. An expansive type transform is one which converts M number of samples into N coefficients (N>M). According to its name it uses two critically sampled DWTs in parallel for signal decomposition and reconstruction.

### 3.1 Properties

1. The coefficients of dualtree wavelet transform (1-D) are positive. The dualtree wavelet coefficients of signal x(n-0.5) is shown in figure 3 and are non oscillatory nature.
2. Shift invariant property [Ivan. W. Selesnick et. al, 2005]. The DTDWT of $x(n) = \delta(n-60)$ and $x(n) = \delta(n-70)$ are shown in figure 4. The wavelet coefficients of both cases are more or less equal and thus the transform satisfies the shift invariant property.

Directional property: The basis function of dual tree discrete wavelet transform is oriented at a certain direction as +75, -75, +45, -45, +15 and -15. Because of this, check board problems are not present in Dual tree wavelet transforms and no need to estimate motion vectors in a video sequence. Since the transform has multi directional kernels, motion estimation and compensation is a tedious process in the conventional video coding standards. But in the case of DWT, HH band mixes the directions of +45 and -45 together, resulting in check board pattern. The kernels of DWT and Dual tree DWT are shown in figure 5, figure 6 and figure 7.

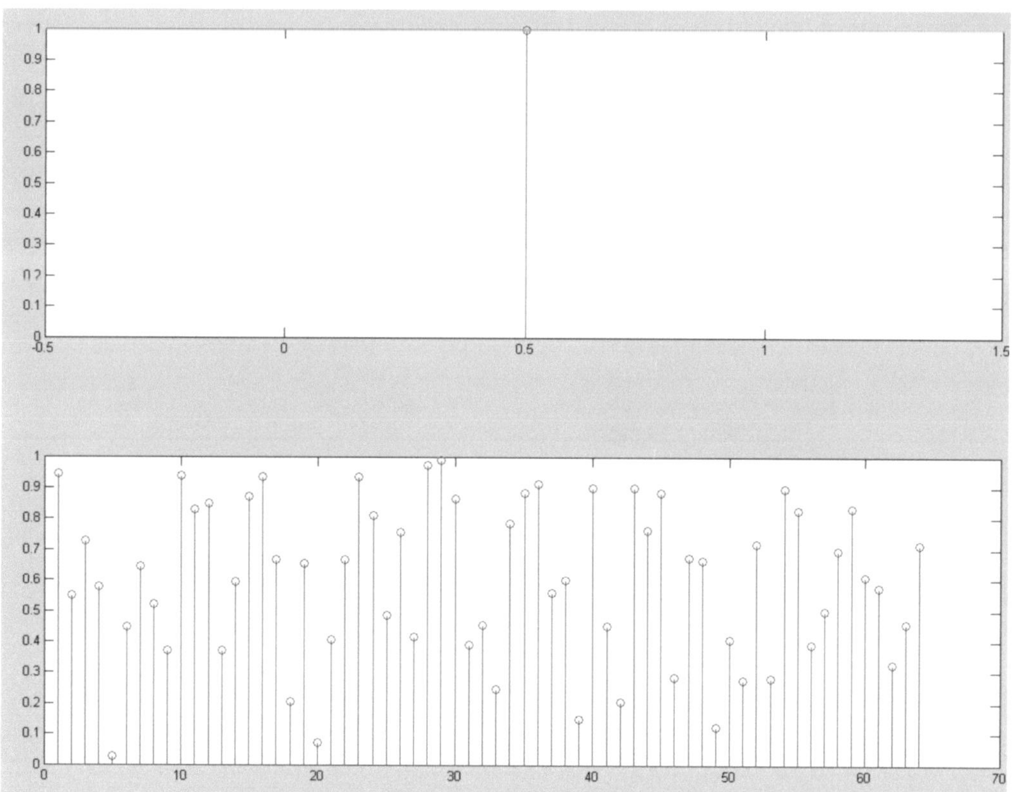


Fig. 3. Signal x(n-0.5) and its dtdwt spectrum

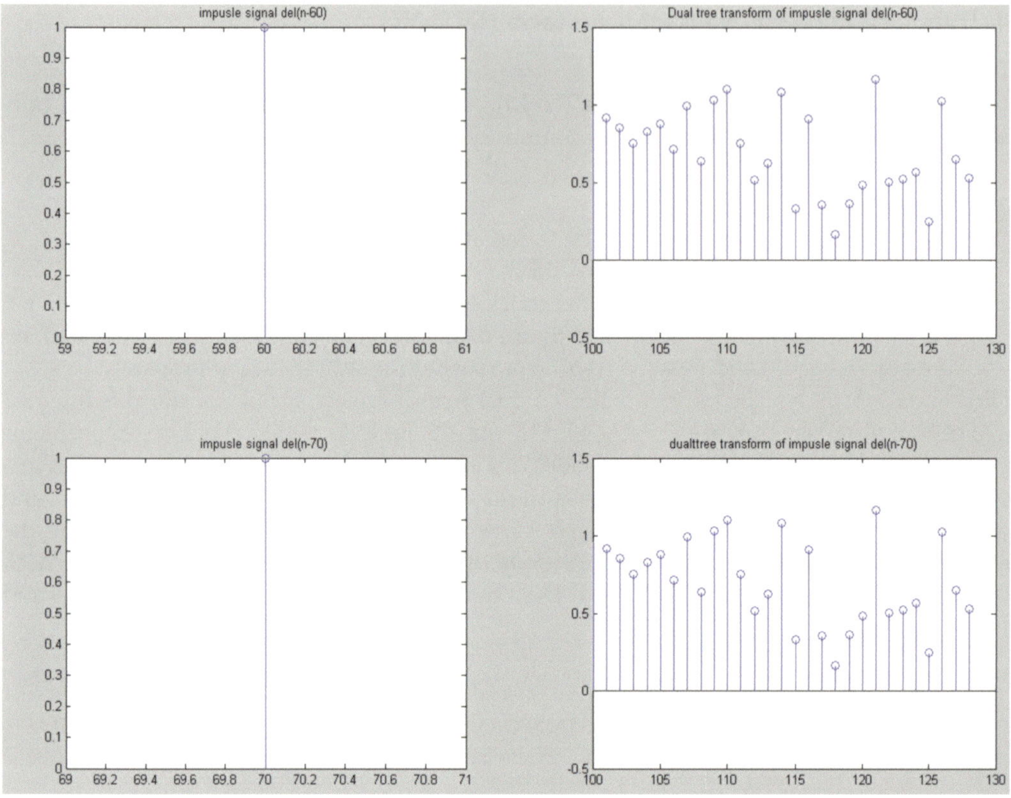


Fig. 4. The two impulse signals x(n) = δ(n − 60) and *x(n)* = *δ(n* − 70*)* and their dual-tree complex discrete wavelet transform coefficients

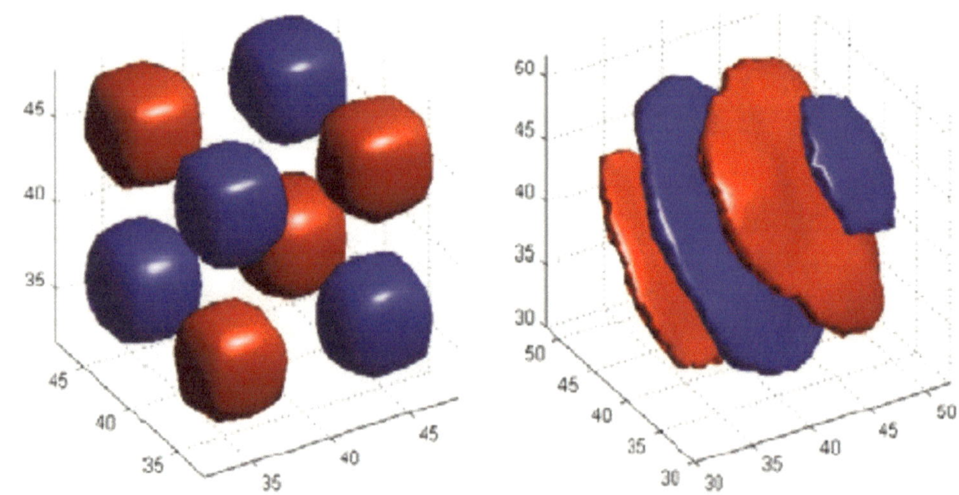

Fig. 5. Kernels of DWT and dual tree DWT

2D dual tree wavelet transform uses six wavelets. The spatial and frequency domain representation of these six wavelets are shown in fig. 7. In both domains the check board problem is not there. Figure 8 represents the high compact representation property of 2D DTDWT [Ivan. w. Selesnick 2003].

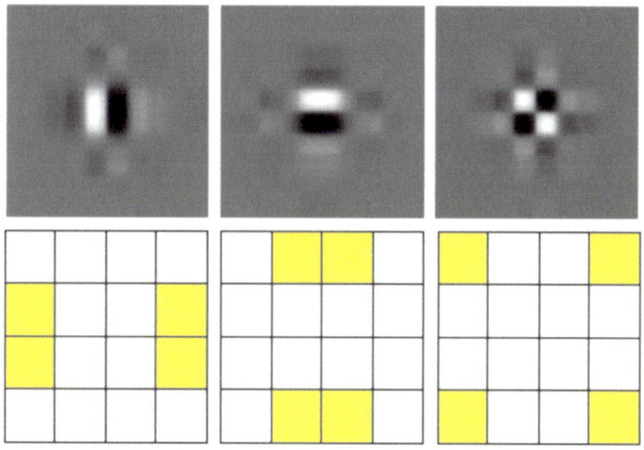

Fig. 6. Three different wavelets. Top row - discrete wavelet transforms in spatial domain. Bottom row - corresponding dwt in frequency domain

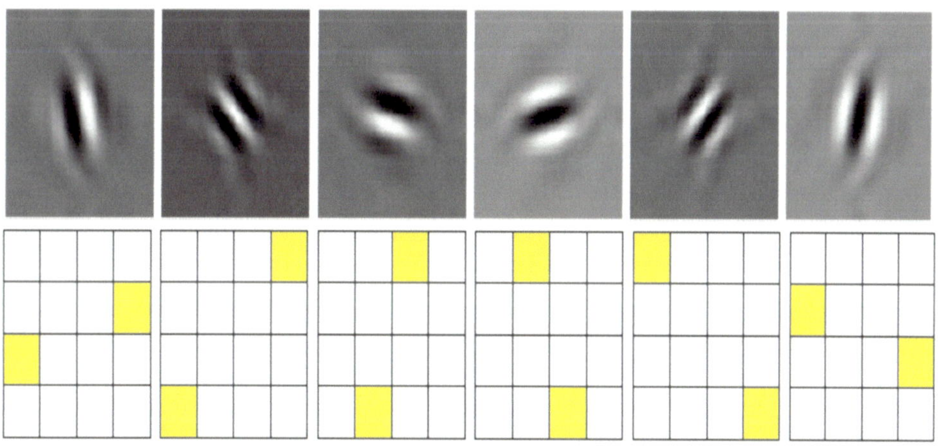

Fig. 7. Top row shows the 2D Dual tree wavelet transform in spatial domain and bottom row shows the same in frequency domain.

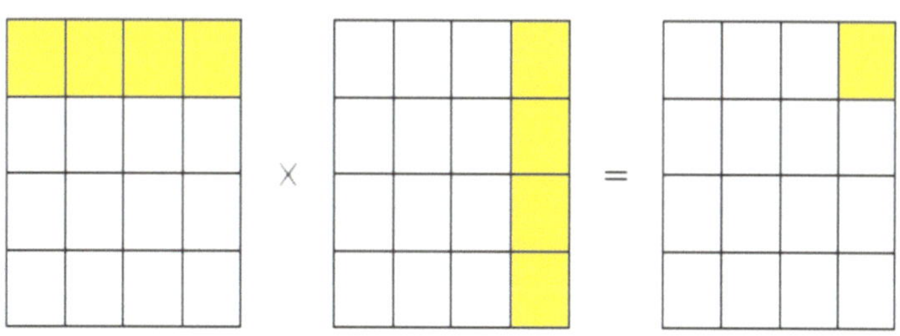

Fig. 8. Compact representation of DTDWT

### 3.2 Filter bank of dualtree discrete wavelet transform

According to its name the 1 D Dual tree wavelet transform uses two wavelet trees. The input signal is applied to the two trees and it is decomposed into four subband. h0(n), h1(n) and g0(n), g1(n) are the low pass and high pass filters of the two wavelet trees respectively. The three level decomposition of the transform results in 8 subbands as shown in figure 9.
Similarly the synthesis filter bank of 1-D dual tree wavelet transform contains two synthesis wavelet filter banks as shown in figure 10.

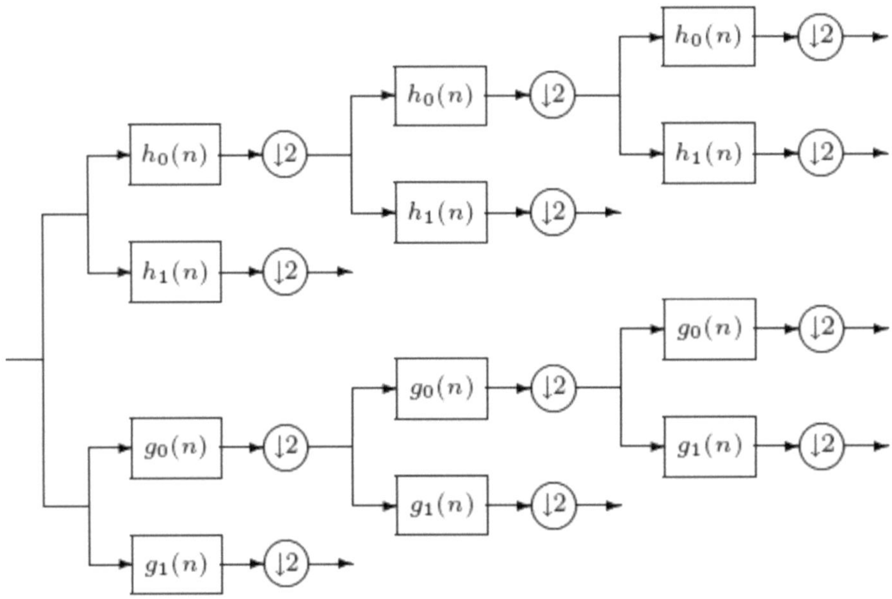


Fig. 9. Analysis filter bank of 1-D dualtree wavelet transform

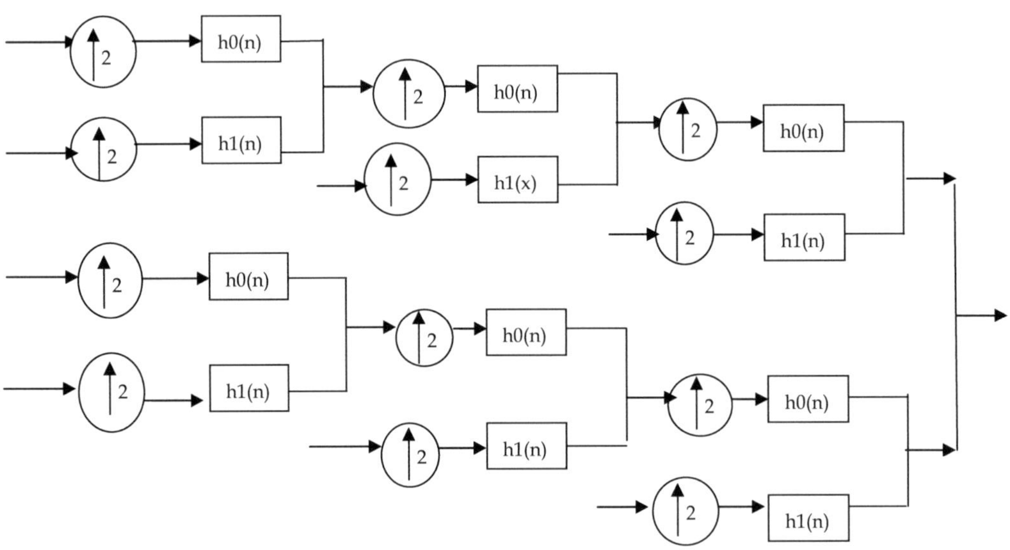


Fig. 10. Synthesis filter bank of 1-D dual tree wavelet transform

### 3.3 3-D Dual tree wavelet transform

The 3-D wavelet transform is obtained as a combination of four wavelets.
The one dimensional complex wavelet transform is given by

$$\Psi(x) = \Psi h\,(x) + j\Psi g(x) \tag{1}$$

2D dual tree complex wavelet function

$$\begin{aligned}\Psi(x,y) &= (\Psi h\,(x)+j\Psi g(x))+\,(\Psi h(y)+j\Psi g(y)) \\ &= (\Psi h\,(x)\Psi h(y))-\,(\Psi g(x)\Psi g(y))+j(\Psi g(x)\Psi h(y))+(\Psi h(x)\Psi g(y))\end{aligned} \tag{2}$$

Real part of

$$\Psi(x,y) = (\Psi h\,(x)\Psi h(y)) - (\Psi g(x)\Psi g(y)) \tag{3}$$

The 3-D separable dual tree wavelet transform is obtained as follows [Ivan. w. Selesnick et. al, 2003].
The three dimensional complex wavelet is defined as

$$\Psi(x,y,z) = (\Psi h\,(x) + j\Psi g(x))\,(\Psi h(y) + j\Psi g(y))\,(\Psi h(z) + j\Psi g(z)) \tag{4}$$

Real part

$$[\Psi(x,y,z)] = \Psi_1(x,y,z) - \Psi_2(x,y,z) - \Psi_3(x,y,z) - \Psi_4(x,y,z) \tag{5}$$

So it is necessary to take four separable transforms instead of three in the case of 2-D transform.
3-D separable wavelet transform is obtained by the orthonormal combination matrix of four three dimensional wavelet transforms as in equation (6)

$$\left.\begin{aligned}\Psi a(x,y,z) &= 0.5\,[\Psi_1(x,y,z)-\Psi_2(x,y,z)-\Psi_3(x,y,z)-\Psi_4(x,y,z)] \\ \Psi b(x,y,z) &= 0.5\,[\Psi_1(x,y,z)-\Psi_2(x,y,z)+\Psi_3(x,y,z)+\Psi_4(x,y,z)] \\ \Psi c(x,y,z) &= 0.5\,[\Psi_1(x,y,z)-\Psi_2(x,y,z)+\Psi_3(x,y,z)-\Psi_4(x,y,z)] \\ \Psi d(x,y,z) &= 0.5\,[\Psi_1(x,y,z)+\Psi_2(x,y,z)+\Psi_3(x,y,z)-\Psi_4(x,y,z)]\end{aligned}\right\} \tag{6}$$

where $\psi_1$, $\psi_2$, $\psi_3$, $\psi_4$ are real 3-D wavelets defined in [Ivan. w. Selesnick, et. al, 2003].
By applying this combination matrix to each sub band, the 3-D oriented dual-tree wavelet transform is obtained. The low subbands $\psi_1$, $\psi_2$, $\psi_3$, $\psi_4$ are always positive (because they are low-pass filtered values of the original image pixels), $\psi_a$ is always negative and other three low subbands are all positive. This property of low sub bands can be used to code the sign information of low sub bands very efficiently.
However, [Wang's et. al, 2004] investigation has shown that after noise shaping, 3-D DTDWT needs fewer coefficients than 3-D DWT to achieve the same video quality for all sequences. This result is encouraging and has prompted to explore the use of this transform for video coding.
The one level decomposition of such a filter is shown in figure 11.

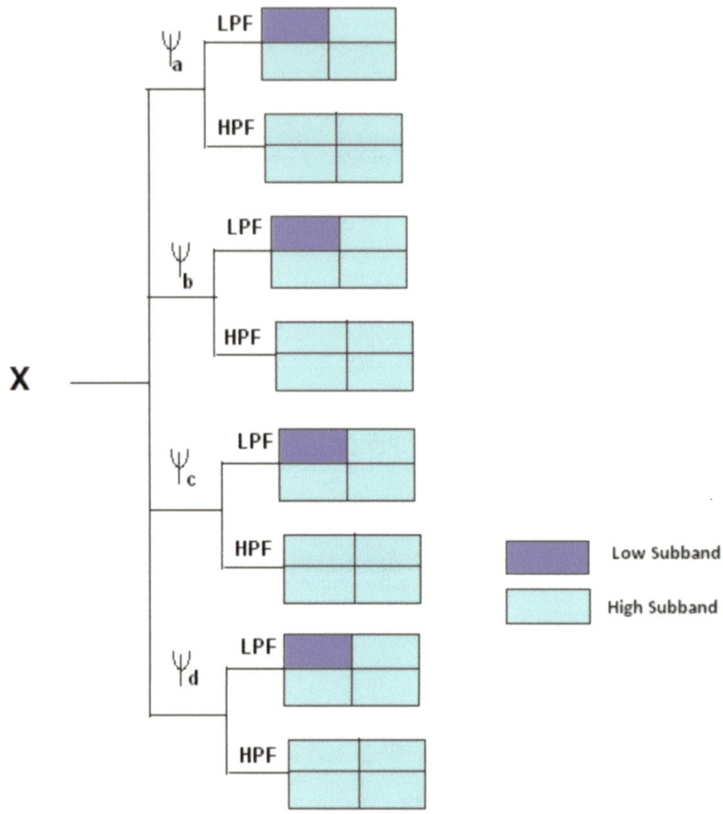


Fig. 11. The 3D Dual tree wavelet transform filter bank with one level decomposition of input signal x

Being an expansive type transform, the number of significant coefficients are identified by noise shaping algorithm [T. H. Reeves et. al, 2002]. In this algorithm, the coefficients are obtained by running the projection algorithm with a preset initial threshold and gradually reducing it until the number of coefficients reach N,a target number. In each iteration the error coefficients are multiplied by a positive real number K and added back to the previously chosen large coefficients to compensate for the loss of small coefficients due to thresholding. This algorithm is applied for video signals and its performance is verified [ Beibei Wang et.al,2004].

The DTDWT is an over complete transform with limited redundancy ($2^m$:1 for m dimensional signals) Thus for 3D DTCWT the redundancy becomes 8:1 However the real DT DWT reduces the redundancy as 4:1 but with the same motion selectivity. [Beibei Wang et al 2004] proved that without motion compensation (conventional method) the DTDWT performs video coding in a better way.

## 4. Particle swarm optimization and Multi objective PSO

In PSO algorithm, each individual is called a particle and is subjected to movement in a multidimensional search space to find the best solution. Particles have their own memory, so they retain the part of their previous states. Each particle's movement from initial value to next position during iteration period is based on their initial velocity and two randomly weighted influences such as Individuality and Sociality

Individuality is the ability to retain the particle's best position and Sociality is the ability to move towards the neighborhood's best previous position. The velocity and position of the particles are updated as follows

$$V_{id}(t+1) = w \times v_{id}(t) + c_1 \times rand_1(.) \times (p_{id} - x_{id}) + c_2 \times rand_2(.) \times (p_{gd} - x_{id}) \quad (7)$$

$$x_{id}(t+1) = x_{id}(t) + v_{id}(t+1), \quad 1 \le i \le N, \quad 1 \le d \le D \quad (8)$$

where, N is the number of particles and D is the dimensionality; $Vi = (v_{i1}, v_{i2},\dots, v_{iD})$, $v_{id} \in [-v_{max}, v_{max}]$ is the velocity vector of particle i, which decides the particle's displacement in each iteration. Similarly, $Xi = (x_{i1}, x_{i2}, \dots , x_{iD})$, $x_{id} \in [-x_{max}, x_{max}]$ is the position vector of particle i which is a potential solution in the solution space. The quality of the solution is measured by a fitness function; w is the inertia weight which decreases linearly during a run; $c_1$, $c_2$ are both positive constants, called the acceleration factors which are generally set to 2.0; $rand_1(.)$ and $rand_2(.)$ are two independent random number distributed uniformly over the range [0, 1]; and $p_g$, $p_i$ are the best solutions discovered so far by the group and itself respectively.

In the t + 1 time iteration, particle i uses $p_g$ and $p_i$ as the heuristic information to update its own velocity and position. The first term in the above equation represents diversification, while the second and third intensification. The second and third terms should be understood as the trustworthiness towards itself and the entire social system respectively. Therefore, a balance between the diversification and intensification is achieved based on which the optimization progress is possible

### 4.1 Simple PSO algorithm

1. Initialize particles of population size N
2. Find the fitness value of each particle using the defined fitness function
3. Update the velocity and position of each particle according to equations
4. Check the stopping criteria. If it is reached then stop. Otherwise go to step 2

#### 4.1.1 Stopping criteria

There are two types of stopping criteria used.

1. Maximum number of iterations: In certain problems after certain number of maximum iteration there is much more change in the particles position and velocity. After reaching this condition the algorithm stops.
2. Minimum inertia weight: The inertia weight w is reduced from iteration to iteration as follows

$$\left( wmax\text{-}\frac{wmax\text{-}wmin}{Itermax} \right) Iter \quad (9)$$

Where Itermax-maximum iteration number and Iter-current iteration

For minimization problems, we specify a very small threshold ε, and if the change of $p_g$ during t times of 4 iteration is smaller than the threshold, we consider the group's best value very near to the global optimum, thus the matching procedure stops.

### 4.2 Multi objective PSO

Most of the problems in the real world are multi objective in nature. And they have multiple optimum solutions for different objectives. Initially most proposed of the PSO methods deal with single solution. Some problems may have more than one global optimum or both global and local optima need to be located. Therefore some variants have been developed to deal with particular problem with multiple solutions. Niching algorithms have been proposed to deal with particular problem with multiple solutions. Multi objective optimization with particle swarms, called MOPSO is developed to solve the problems those require simultaneous optimization of number of objectives. Many PSO algorithms have been developed under dynamic environments rather than static environment.
The general multi objective optimization problems can be defined in the following format.
Optimize

$$f(\bar{x}) = \left[f1(\bar{x}), f2(\bar{x}) \ldots fn(\bar{x})\right] \text{ where } \bar{x}=(x1,x2,\ldots\ldots Xn)\varepsilon \bar{R}n \quad (10)$$

which satisfies the m inequality constrains $gj(\bar{x}) \leq 0$ for j=1,2 .... m and p equality constraints $hj(\bar{x}) = 0$ for j=1,2, .... P the constraints gi(x) and hj(x) define the feasible region $\Omega$ and any point in the $\Omega$ defines a feasible solution.
For multi objective optimization problems, objective functions may be optimized separately from each other and of the best solution can be found for each objective dimension. However suitable solutions for all the functions can seldom be found. This is because most of the objective functions are in conflict with each other.
The family of solutions of a multi objective optimization problem is composed of all those potential solutions such that the components of the corresponding objective vectors cannot be improved simultaneously. These types of solutions are known as pereto optimal solutions. The population size of MOPSO is larger than the traditional PSO, in order to cover more pereto optimal solutions.
In order to handle multiple objectives, PSO must be modified before being applied to MO problems. In most approaches [Xiaohui et. al, 2003] the major modifications of the PSO algorithms are the selection process of gbest and pbest. In [Cello cello et al, 2004] the paper developed a grid based gbest selection process and also employed a second population to store the non dominated solutions. From the second population, using roulette wheel selection, they selected the gbest randomly. The pbest is selected according to the pareto dominace.
[Parsopoulos et al 2002] used different population for different objectives. It is called vector evaluated particle swarm, n no.of swarms are used to solve n objectives. In their algorithm, when one swarm updates the velocities of the particle the other swarm is used to find the best particle to follow. In another method [Fields et. al, 2002] a new data structure is proposed to cope with the shortcomings of using constant size population. Ans also [Xiaohui et. al, 2003] proposed a method called dynamic neighborhood PSO. In [Xiaohui et al 2003], multiobjectives are divided into two groups F1 and F2. F1 is the neighborhood objective and F2 is the optimization objective. Based on the distance measured, the nearest m particles are grouped as the neighbors of F1 and remaining are assumed as the neighbors of F2. From the grouped neighborhood around F1 the nbest(gbest) is selected. Pbest is the position in a particles history. Whenever the current solution dominates the pbest,only then the pbest is updated.

Evolutionary optimization techniques play an important role in image processing such as Image compression, clustering and object tracking etc., but there has not been much in video coding. In this work we explore the possibility of applying multi objective optimization algorithm to improve the performance of compression algorithm in order to support multimedia applications especially for video. To formulate the mathematical equation to the problem, we consider functions related to the compression rate, computation time and number of frames.
The objective functions describing the MOPSO system for video coding can be represented in figure 12.

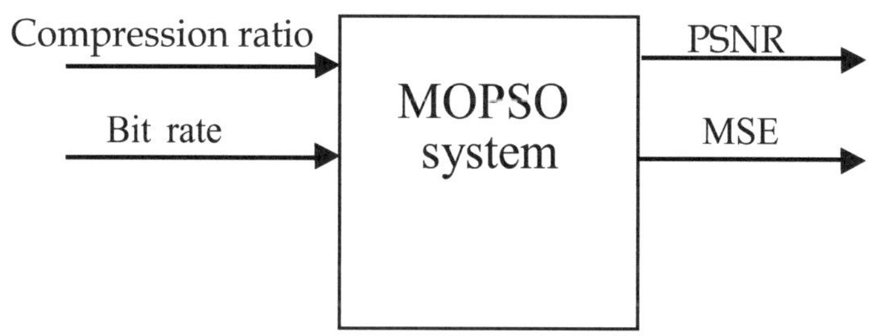


Fig. 12. MOPSO system for video coding

In this MOPSO two swarms are assigned for two objective functions. The objective functions taken are shown in figure 12. The compression ratio and bit rate are considered here as constraints. According to the given constraints the PSNR and MSE are measured.

## 5. Video coding with Multi objective PSO

The proposed video coder block diagram is shown in figure 13. The input video sequence at the frame rate of 10 frames per second is decomposed (3- levels) using dual tree discrete wavelet transform. There are two sets of filters are used. At level 1, 13-19 near orthogonal filters and at levels ≥ 2, 14 tap Qshift filters are used. The number of significant coefficients is obtained using noise shaping algorithm. Here the initial preset threshold value is set as 220 and is reduced until the number of coefficients reach 40. The energy compensation parameter K is set as 1.8 for better performance. The selected 40 coefficients are considered as particles. These particles are subjected to the MOPSO algorithm. Here fixed population size of 40 is used. The non dominated solutions (individual particles) are selected according to constrains of compression ratio and bit rate.
The conventional linear aggregating function is used to select the global best solution. Here the 40 swarms are simultaneously searched for their individual objective function. The aggregate multi objective function is calculated as follows.
$F(x) = \Sigma w_i k_i$ $w_i$ -non negative weights Here $w_1 = 0.6$ and $w_2 = 0.4$ The summation of wi is equals to one.
F1(x) = Means square error
F2(x) = computation complexity
Two video sequences foreman and rhinos are tested and their PSNR values of different compression ratios are given in the table 1.

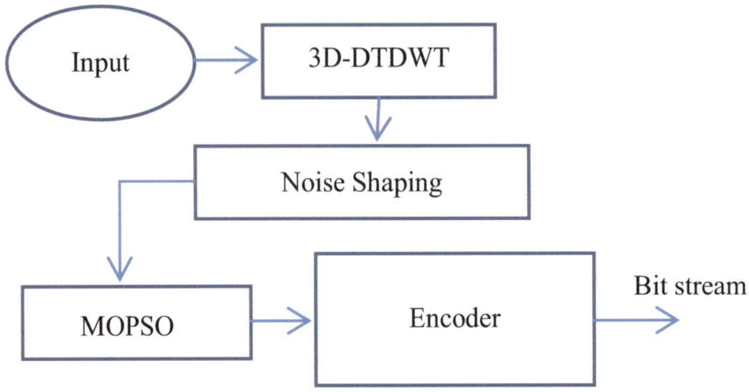


Fig. 13. The block diagram of the proposed system

### 5.1 Modification in the coder blocks (MOPSO)

In our improved PSO, the new positions are calculated by performing single-point crossover operation with the existing position as performed in GA. This operation avoids the local minima and leads to find the optimum blocks with minimum computational complexity.
where the size of a frame is N × N. The motion estimate quality between the original $I_{ogn}$ and the constructed video sequences $I_{cont}$ is measured in PSNR which is defined as:

$$\mathrm{PSNR} = 10 \log_{10} \frac{I_{max}^2}{\sigma_e^2} \tag{9}$$

$$\sigma_e^2 = \mathrm{MSE} = \frac{1}{N} \sum_{k=0}^{K} \sum_{i=0}^{N} \sum_{j=0}^{N} \left( I_{ogn}(i,j,k) - I_{cmp}(i,j,k) \right)^2 \tag{10}$$

where K is the number of frames in the video sequence and $I_{max}$ is the maximum gray level value in the frame.
In standard PSO, at each iteration a best position is chosen from the particles known as 'Xpbest'. This best solution is compared with the best solution so far (Xgbest). If current is the best then the global best is interchanged with Xpbest, otherwise the procedure is continued with previous best. In this case, the particles are independent of each other, they are not sharing the information about their travel. This leads to local minimum and may be taking long time for convergence. In our proposed method, we are choosing 'n' number of best solutions at each iteration. The value should satisfy the condition: $1 < n < N/2$, where N = total number of particles.
And these 'n' best solutions are compared with previous best solutions. Finally 'n' best solutions are chosen globally. And with these 'n' best solutions are matted with each other at random to fill the population size. Here, we are performing single-point crossover operation to perform matting. For example, if n = 3, and the population size is 5, consider the following 3 best solutions.

1 0 1 0 0 1 0 1 0 1 0 1 0
1 0 0 0 0 1 1 1 0 0 0 1 1
1 0 1 0 0 1 0 1 1 1 0 0 1

With these 3 best solutions, to fill the population we need 2 more series that can be generated by performing single point crossover between 2 & 3 as given below.

| | |
|---|---|
| ($2^{nd}$ best) | 1 0 0 0 0 1 1 1 0 0 0 1 1 |
| ($3^{rd}$ best) | 1 0 1 0 0 1 0 1 1 1 0 0 1 |
| (Crossover at $5^{th}$ bit) | |
| ($4^{th}$ solution) | 1 0 1 0 0 1 0 1 0 0 0 1 1 |
| ($5^{th}$ solution) | 1 0 0 0 0 1 1 1 1 1 0 0 1 |

And we have introduced a parameter called Velocity Rate (VR) to control the updation of velocity based on the performance history of the particles. Initially all particles are assigned 1 as velocity rate. At each iteration, based on the fitness value the VR is either increased or decreased by 0.1 for each particle. If VR value of the particle which gives the optimum value will be increased to 0.5, and the updated velocity is multiplied with VR. The equation (1) is modified as

$$V_{id}(t+1) = w \times v_{id}(t) + c_1 \times rand_1(.) \times (p_{id} - x_{id}) + c_2 \times rand_2(.) \times (p_{gd} - x_{id}) + VR \quad (11)$$

And we are introducing one more parameter in our modified PSO, which is the direction (angle) of the particles. Here we have eight different directions, 0°, 45°, 90°, 135°, 180°, 225°, 270°, and 315°, from these the particles can choose any one direction at random to select the optimum value, but the condition is that, all the particles have to move in the same direction. With these novel parameters, the PSO can avoid premature convergence.

Algorithm:

**Step 1.** Generate initial population of Swarm (Xi) and Velocity (Vi).
**Step 2.** Each swarm represents subset of blocks.
**Step 3.** Calculate the fitness value of each swarm.
**Step 4.** Calculate 'n' number of Xgbest for each particle.
**Step 5.** Change the position and velocity of each particle based on crossover operator and modify velocity rate.
**Step 6.** Again calculate the fitness value of each swarm.
**Step 7.** Find out 'n' number of Xpbest for each particle.
**Step 8.** Evaluate the objective function(Weighted average g approach)
**Step 9.** Compare Xgbest and XPbest, hold best as Xgbest.
**Step 10.** Repeat steps from 3 to 9 until the stopping criteria

The algorithm for the general MOPSO system:

**Step 1.** MOPSO()
**Step 2.** Iinitialize swarms()
**Step 3.** Iteration=1
**Step 4.** White iteration<maximum iteration do
**Step 5.** Fitness function evaluation
**Step 6.** Update position and velocity
**Step 7.** Calculate objective vector
**Step 8.** Update non dominant set()
**Step 9.** Iter=iter+1
**Step 10.** End while

| Video Sequences | Foreman | | | Rhinos | | |
|---|---|---|---|---|---|---|
| Compression Ratio | 1:4 | 1:3 | 1:2 | 1:4 | 1:3 | 1:2 |
| Bit-rate(kbps) | 730 | 1000 | 1424 | 730 | 1000 | 1424 |
| DTDWT | 31.79 | 32.45 | 34.51 | 26.95 | 29.62 | 31.15 |
| DTDWT+PSO | 33.90 | 34.90 | 35.90 | 28.66 | 33.11 | 34.97 |
| DTDWT+MOPSO | 34.01 | 37.43 | 40.45 | 29.11 | 33.94 | 35.98 |
| 3D-SPIHT | 29.32 | 31.47 | 33.86 | 26.42 | 27.29 | 30.93 |

Table 1. Average PSNR comparison at different bit rates and compression ratios.

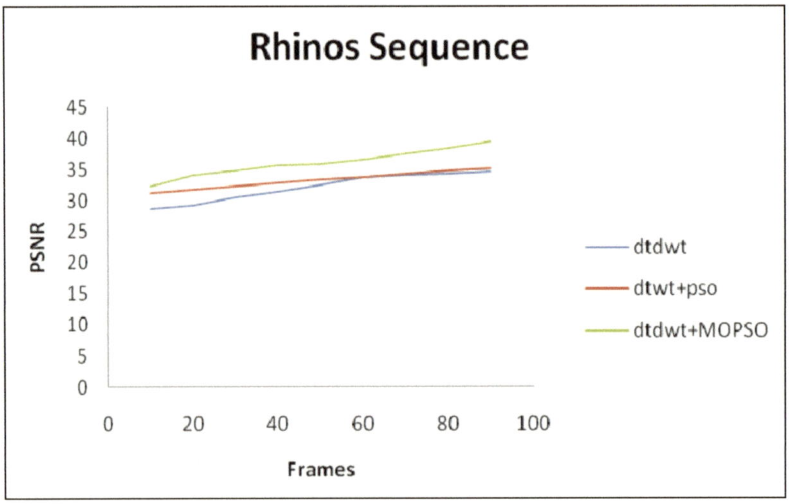


Fig. 14. Performance analysis of Rhinos Sequence.

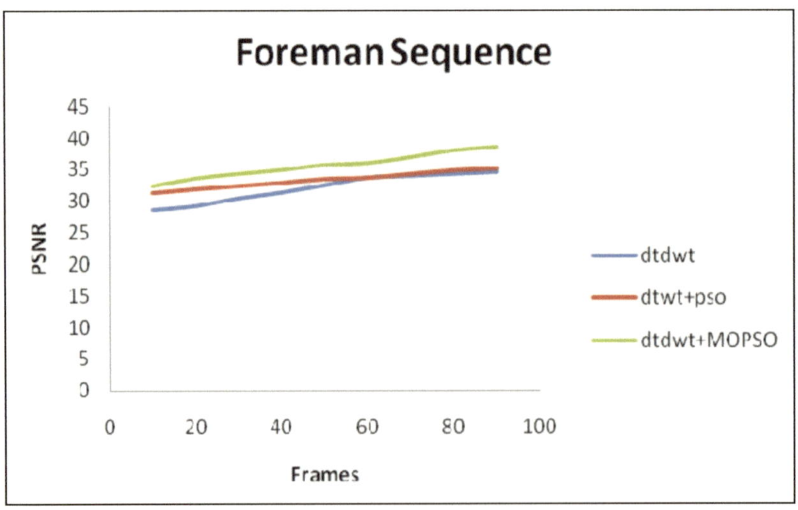


Fig. 15. Performance analysis of Foreman Sequence.

Two video sequences "Foreman" and "Rhinos" are used for testing. Both sequences have 80 frames with a frame rate of 30 fps. Table 1 lists the average PSNR of the two sequences at different bit rates. For a video sequence which has many edges and motions, such like "Foreman", DTDWT+PSO outperforms 3-D SPIHT more than 4 dB. For sequence "Rhinos", DTDWT+PSO offers around 2 dB better PSNR results. Whereas our proposed codec DTDWT+MOPSO outperforms better than DTDWT, 3-D SPIHT with more than 3 dB for both the sequences. Subjectively, DTDWT+MOPSO has better performance than the existing and has the redundancy caused by symmetric extension, the coding results are very promising. Figures 14 and 15 show the performance of the system(PSNR value) with increasing number of frames. The proposed system provides constant PSNR with increasing number of frames.

## 6. Conclusion

The excellent directional and shift invariant property of Dual tree discrete wavelet transform is used for video coding without motion estimation and compensation. The optimum subband coefficients are selected using multi objective pso with the objective factors of compression ratio and bit rate. The n best solutions particles are selected by means of modification in the velocity rate and incorporating the directional properties of the subbands of DT DWT and crossover among the best solutions. In the multi objective PSO, the pareto optimal solutions are selected based on the constraints and weighted average approach. The performance of the proposed method is measured in terms of PSNR. The PSNR value of this combination(DTDWT+MOPSO) is better when compared to the other methods. In future, by analyzing the inter and intra correlations among the subbands of DTDWT and also by adding the constraints of minimum computation complexity and computation time in the MOPSO, the system performance can be improved.

## 7. References

Touradjebrahimi, Emmanuel Reusens and Wei Li (1995) *New trends in very low bit rate video coding*" Proceedings of the IEEE

B. Wang, Y. Wang, I. Selesnick, and A. Vetro, (2004) *An investigation of 3D dual-tree wavelet transform for video coding,* in Proceedings of the International Conference on Image Processing, vol. 2, Singapore, pp. 1317–1320.

Kennedy, J., Eberhart, R. C(1995) *Particle swarm optimization,* in IEEE International Conference on Neural Networks, pp. 1942-1948.

K. U. Parsopoulos, M. N. Varahatis (2002), *Particle swarm optimization method in multi objective problems,* Proceedings of the 2002 ACM Symposium on applied Computing Madrid, Spain,ACM Press pp. 603-607

Ivan. w. Selesnick, Richard Baraniuk, Nick G. Kingsbury (November 2005) *The Dualtree Complex Wavelet transform- A coherent framework for multiscale signal and image processing,* IEEE Signal processing Magazine pp. 123 - 151

Ivan. w. Selesnick, Ke. Yong Li (August 2003) *Video denoising using 2D and 3D Complex dualtree wavelet ransform, Proceedings, Wavelet applications in signal and image processing* X SPIE 5207.

Beibei Wang, Yao Wang, Ivan Selesnick & Anthony Vetro (December 2004) *Video coding without motion compensation using a 3 D Dualtree wavelet transform, Mitsubishi Electric Research Laboratories Inc., 2004*

T. H. Reeves and N. G. Kingsbury (September 2002), *Over complete image coding using iterative projection-based noise shaping,* Signal Processing Group University of Cambridge U.K.ICIP 02, Rochester, New York,

Xiaohui Hu Russell C.Eberhart & Yuhui Shi (2003), *Particle Swarm with extended memory for multi objective optimization,* Prudue University, Indianapp. 193-197. IEEE Proceedings.

C. A. Cello, G. T. Pulido & M. S. Leehuga (2004), *Handling multi objective with particle swarm optimization,* IEEE evolutionary computing 2004

Fieldsend & J. E. Singh (2002) *A multi objective algorithm based upon particle swarm optimization, an efficient data structure and Turbulance,* Proceedings of the 2002 U.K. workshop on computational Intelligence, Birminham U.K. pp. 37-44.

# Part 4

# Advanced Implementations of Video Coding Systems

# Variable Bit-Depth Processor for 8×8 Transform and Quantization Coding in H.264/AVC

Gustavo A. Ruiz and Juan A. Michell
*Department of Electronics and Computers, University of Cantabria*
*Spain*

## 1. Introduction

The H.264/AVC (Advanced Video Codec) is the latest standard for video coding established by the Joint Video Team ITU-T VCEG and ISO/IEC MPEG (Wiegand et al., 2003) (Sühring, 2010) (Links, 2010). This standard has many innovations, such as hybrid prediction/transform coding of intra frames and integer transforms (Richardson, 2004). Fig. 1 presents a simplified block diagram of the H.264/AVC encoder with the following main blocks: motion estimation (ME), motion compensation (MC), intra prediction, forward transform (FT), forward quantization (FQ), inverse quantization or re-scaling (IQ), inverse transform (IT), entropy coding and de-blocking filter, among others. Initially, most of the work done on H.264 was oriented toward its software implementation. However, in recent years the contributions to the hardware implementation of H.264 have increased greatly, enabling the implementation of fast architectures for real-time video applications (Lin et al., 2008) (Finchelstein et al., 2009) (Liu et al., 2009).

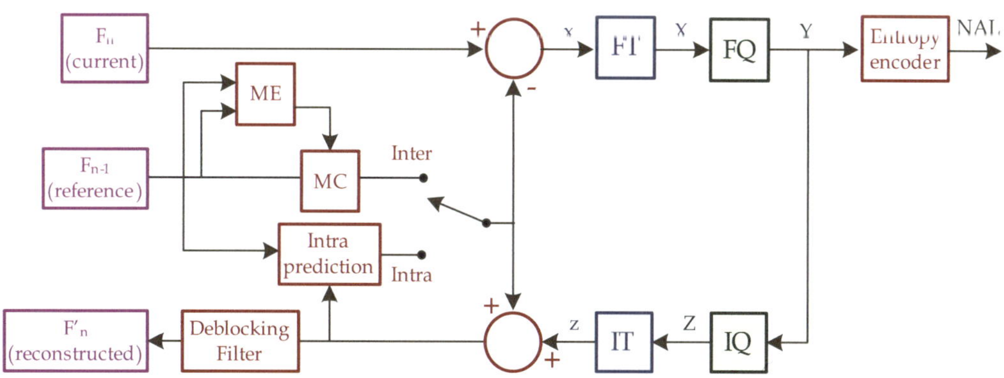


Fig. 1. Diagram of the H.264/AVC encoder.

The initial version of H.264/AVC used a transform hierarchy based on three transforms that are computed in integer arithmetic, two of size 4×4 and one of 2x2. In July 2004, the first amendment to the H.264 standard was presented, named Fidelity Range Extensions (FRExt) (JVT, 2004), in which a new set of tools was specified to increase the high-fidelity video encoding efficiency, focusing on professional applications and high-definition videos. One of the most significant differences between the H.264 FRExt codification and the non-FRExt one is the use of an 8×8 integer transform (Gordon, 2004), which is an integer approximation of the 8×8 2-D Discrete Cosine Transform (DCT), as well as the original 4×4 and 2×2 transforms. The H.264 FRExt enables high quality video by supporting varied chroma sub-sampling formats –4:2:0, 4:2:2 and 4:4:4– with greater color bit-depth ranging from 8-bit up to 14-bit and resolution ranging from QCIF (176x144) to Full HD (1920x1080), both in progressive and interlaced scanning. There are several AVC/H.264 profiles to encode pixels with a bit depth greater than 8 bits: High 10 Profile (8 bits up to 10 bits), high 4:2:2 profile (8 bits up to 10 bits), high 4:4:4 predictive profile (8 bits up to 14 bits), high 10 intra profile (8 bits up to 10 bits), high 4:2:2 intra profile (8 bits up to 10 bits), high 4:4:4 intra profile (8 bits up to 14 bits) and CAVLC 4:4:4 intra profile (8 bits up to 14 bits). Increasing bit depth provides improved accuracy in the compression scheme as well as in motion compensation, in intra prediction and in-loop filtering (Gish, 2002) (Gish, 2003) (Lavier, 2009). Indeed, extensive experimentation proves that the coding efficiency with the largest bit-depth is higher on videos that contain shallow textures and low noise, and perceivable gains exist in the reduction of three kinds of artifacts: contouring, banding and mosquito noise. Currently, bit-depth is especially focused on video quality (Sims et al., 2005). The coding efficiency can be improved by increasing the internal bit depth in relation to the external bit depth used in the video codec (Chujoh & Noda, 2007a, 2007b). Moreover, bit-depth scalability is potentially useful considering that for the foreseeable future, conventional 8-bit and high-bit digital imaging systems will exist simultaneously in the market, providing multiple representations of different bit-depths for the same visual content (Chujoh & Noda, 2006) (Gao & Wu, 2006) (Gao et al., 2010). Other applications of bit-depth are the bit-depth transform of the characteristics for high bit-depth images to maximize the encoding efficiency (Ito et al., 2010), the novel bit-depth expansion method used to remove the contouring effects in smooth regions when mapping low-color bit-depth image to high-color bit-depth (Chen et al., 2009) or the three bit-depth scalable coding architectures compatible with H.264 (Chiang at al., 2009).

This chapter presents a variable bit-depth processor with pipeline architecture for real-time implementation of the complete process for the 8×8 transform and quantization coding in the H.264/AVC. The processor manages different bit-depths - 8 bits up to 14 bits - and quantization parameters (QP) fulfilling the requirements of H.264/AVC. Hardware solutions to reduce its complexity, combined with an efficient implementation, provide a high-speed, high-throughput circuit at a low cost in area. A prototype of the processor, which has been synthesized in a 130nm HCMOS technology, uses 26.5k gates and achieves a maximum speed of 330 MHz with a throughput of 2640 Mpixels/s; this throughput is enough to reach a processing capacity for 1080HD (1920×1088@30fps) real-time video streams.

The remainder of this chapter is organized as follows. Sections 2 and 3 describe the 8×8 transform and quantization in H.264/AVC, providing the necessary mathematical background with special emphasis on describing the effect of the bit-depth in quantization and rescaling expressions. The 8×8 transform provides excellent compression performance in high-resolution video streams with a level of complexity only slightly higher than the 4×4 transform. Its implementation can also be done in terms of additions and shifts and no multiplications are necessary, despite the fact that the coefficients are not powers of 2 in all cases. Quantization and rescaling enable the encoder to control the trade-off between bit-rate and quality. H.264 assumes a bit-depth-dependent scalar quantizer without division and/or floating arithmetic based on post and pre-scaling matrices. Section 4 describes the proposed architecture for implementing the configurable process of transform and quantization for an 8×8 luma block capable of operating with different bit-depths (8 bits up to 14 bits). This section includes a description of the main modules: 1D configurable forward and inverse transform, 8×8 transpose register and the optimized arithmetic circuit needed to perform the computation of bit-depth-dependent quantization and rescaling in a unified structure. A review of the state-of-the-art of the previous implementations and references is also included. However, most hardware implementations only operate in 8 bits and further bit-depths have not been taken into account. Section 5 shows the characteristics and the performance of the proposed processor as well as comparisons with other published and related implementations. These comparisons are made in terms of area, speed and power.

## 2. 8×8 Transform in the H.264/AVC

The FRExt amendment to H.264 proposes a scheme based on an 8×8 integer approximation of DCT transform to be added to the existing 4×4 transform in order to improve high-definition video compression (Gordon & Wiegand, 2004). This transform provides excellent compression performance in high-resolution video streams with a level of complexity only slightly higher than the 4×4 transform even though the coefficients are not powers of 2 in all the cases. However, it's implemented using additions and shifts and no multiplications are necessary. Moreover it uses integer arithmetic which eliminates the mismatch issues between the encoder and the decoder.

The forward 8×8 integer transform is applied to each block in the residual luminance component (**x**) of the input video stream as follows

$$X = T \cdot x \cdot T^{t} \tag{1}$$

where **T** is a matrix of dimension 8×8 which represents the transform kernel defined as

$$T = \frac{1}{8} \cdot \begin{bmatrix} 8 & 8 & 8 & 8 & 8 & 8 & 8 & 8 \\ 12 & 10 & 6 & 3 & -3 & -6 & -10 & -12 \\ 8 & 4 & -4 & -8 & -8 & -4 & 4 & 8 \\ 10 & -3 & -12 & -6 & 6 & 12 & 3 & -10 \\ 8 & -8 & -8 & 8 & 8 & -8 & -8 & 8 \\ 6 & -12 & 3 & 10 & -10 & -3 & 12 & -6 \\ 4 & -8 & 8 & -4 & -4 & 8 & -8 & 4 \\ 3 & -6 & 10 & -12 & 12 & -10 & 6 & -3 \end{bmatrix} \tag{2}$$

In the JM reference software (Sühring, 2010), the property of separability of this 8×8 transform is used to implement equation (1) in a separable way as a 1D horizontal (Eq. (3)) transform followed by a 1D vertical (Eq. (4)) transform according to the following equations

$$p = \left( \left( \left( x \cdot T_1^{t} \right) \cdot T_2^{t} \right) \cdot T_3^{t} \right) \tag{3}$$

$$X^{t} = \left( \left( \left( p^{t} \cdot T_1^{t} \right) \cdot T_2^{t} \right) \cdot T_3^{t} \right) \tag{4}$$

Equations (3) and (4) are obtained from the decomposition of **T** as a sparse matrix product of matrices $\mathbf{T}_1$, $\mathbf{T}_2$ and $\mathbf{T}_3$ defined as

$$T_1 = \begin{bmatrix} 1 & 0 & 0 & 0 & 0 & 0 & 0 & 1 \\ 0 & 1 & 0 & 0 & 0 & 0 & 1 & 0 \\ 0 & 0 & 1 & 0 & 0 & 1 & 0 & 0 \\ 0 & 0 & 0 & 1 & 1 & 0 & 0 & 0 \\ 1 & 0 & 0 & 0 & 0 & 0 & 0 & -1 \\ 0 & 1 & 0 & 0 & 0 & 0 & -1 & 0 \\ 0 & 0 & 1 & 0 & 0 & -1 & 0 & 0 \\ 0 & 0 & 0 & 1 & -1 & 0 & 0 & 0 \end{bmatrix} \quad (5)$$

$$T_2 = \begin{bmatrix} 1 & 0 & 0 & 1 & 0 & 0 & 0 & 0 \\ 0 & 1 & 1 & 0 & 0 & 0 & 0 & 0 \\ 1 & 0 & 0 & -1 & 0 & 0 & 0 & 0 \\ 0 & 1 & -1 & 0 & 0 & 0 & 0 & 0 \\ 0 & 0 & 0 & 0 & 3/2 & 1 & 1 & 0 \\ 0 & 0 & 0 & 0 & 1 & 0 & -3/2 & -1 \\ 0 & 0 & 0 & 0 & 1 & -3/2 & 0 & 1 \\ 0 & 0 & 0 & 0 & 0 & 1 & -1 & 3/2 \end{bmatrix} \quad (6)$$

$$T_3 = \begin{bmatrix} 1 & 1 & 0 & 0 & 0 & 0 & 0 & 0 \\ 0 & 0 & 0 & 0 & 1 & 0 & 0 & 1/4 \\ 0 & 0 & 1 & 1/2 & 0 & 0 & 0 & 0 \\ 0 & 0 & 0 & 0 & 0 & 1 & 1/4 & 0 \\ 1 & -1 & 0 & 0 & 0 & 0 & 0 & 0 \\ 0 & 0 & 0 & 0 & 0 & -1/4 & 1 & 0 \\ 0 & 0 & 1/2 & -1 & 0 & 0 & 0 & 0 \\ 0 & 0 & 0 & 0 & 1/4 & 0 & 0 & -1 \end{bmatrix} \quad (7)$$

Table 1, which it is directly extracted from the JM reference software, shows the expressions used to compute the 1D transforms involved in equations (3) and (4). In this Table, **IF** denotes the vector of input values (**IF** represents either each row of **x** in equation (3) or each column of **p** in (4)), **OF** denotes the transformed output vector (**OF** represents either each row of **p** in equation (3) or each column of **X** in (4)), and **a** and **b** are internal variables. In a 3-stage butterfly, stage 1 implements the operations involved in $\mathbf{T}_1$, stage 2 implements $\mathbf{T}_2$ and stage 3 implements $\mathbf{T}_3$. The multiplications by the coefficients 1/2, 1/4 and 3/2=1+1/2 are implemented by means of shift-right (>>) operations which cause truncation errors which are propagated through the datapath. To avoid mismatch between the encoder and decoder, the implementation of 1D transform must fulfill the operations specified in the standard. As a result, any implementation of this transform must be in compliance with the arithmetic described in Table 1 and no other alternative is possible.

| *Stage 1* – $\mathbf{T}_1$ | *Stage 2*– $\mathbf{T}_2$ | *Stage 3* – $\mathbf{T}_3$ |
|---|---|---|
| $a_0=IF_0+IF_7$ | $b_0=a_0+a_3$ | $OF_0=b_0+b_1$ |
| $a_1=IF_1+IF_6$ | $b_1=a_1+a_2$ | $OF_1=b_4+(b_7>>2)$ |
| $a_2=IF_2+IF_5$ | $b_2=a_0-a_3$ | $OF_2=b_2+(b_3>>1)$ |
| $a_3=IF_3+IF_4$ | $b_3=a_1-a_2$ | $OF_3=b_5+(b_6>>2)$ |
| $a_4=IF_0-IF_7$ | $b_4=a_5+a_6+((a_4>>1)+a_4)$ | $OF_4=b_0-b_1$ |
| $a_5=IF_1-IF_6$ | $b_5=a_4-a_7-((a_6>>1)+a_6)$ | $OF_5=b_6-(b_5>>2)$ |
| $a_6=IF_2-IF_5$ | $b_6=a_4+a_7-((a_5>>1)+a_5)$ | $OF_6=(b_2>>1)-b_3$ |
| $a_7=IF_3-IF_4$ | $b_7=a_5-a_6+((a_7>>1)+a_7)$ | $OF_7=-b_7+(b_4>>2)$ |

Table 1. Forward 1D transform algorithm extracted from the JM software reference.

The inverse 8×8 integer transform of a block of coefficients of size 8×8 (**Z**) is defined through the equation

$$z=T^{t}\cdot Z\cdot T \tag{8}$$

Likewise to the forward transform, the 8×8 inverse transform can be computed as the concatenation of a 1D horizontal inverse transform (Eq. (9)) and a 1D vertical inverse transform (Eq. (10)) through the decomposition of $T$ as a sparse matrix product of matrices $\mathbf{G}_1$, $\mathbf{G}_2$ and $\mathbf{G}_3$ giving

$$q=\left(\left(\left(Z\cdot G_1\right)\cdot G_2\right)\cdot G_3\right) \tag{9}$$

$$z^{t}=\left(\left(\left(q^{t}\cdot G_1\right)\cdot G_2\right)\cdot G_3\right) \tag{10}$$

The $\mathbf{G}_1$, $\mathbf{G}_2$ and $\mathbf{G}_3$ matrices are defined as

$$G_1=\begin{bmatrix} 1 & 0 & 0 & 0 & 1 & 0 & 0 & 0 \\ 0 & 0 & 0 & 1 & 0 & -1 & 0 & 3/2 \\ 0 & 0 & 1/2 & 0 & 0 & 0 & 1 & 0 \\ 0 & -1 & 0 & -3/2 & 0 & 0 & 0 & 1 \\ 1 & 0 & 0 & 0 & -1 & 0 & 0 & 0 \\ 0 & 1 & 0 & 0 & 0 & 3/2 & 0 & 1 \\ 0 & 0 & -1 & 0 & 0 & 0 & 3/2 & 0 \\ 0 & -3/2 & 0 & 1 & 0 & 1 & 0 & 0 \end{bmatrix} \tag{11}$$

$$G_2=\begin{bmatrix} 1 & 0 & 0 & 0 & 0 & 0 & 1 & 0 \\ 0 & 1 & 0 & 0 & 0 & 0 & 0 & -1/4 \\ 0 & 0 & 1 & 0 & -1 & 0 & 0 & 0 \\ 0 & 0 & 0 & 1 & 0 & 1/4 & 0 & 0 \\ 0 & 0 & 1 & 0 & 1 & 0 & 0 & 0 \\ 0 & 0 & 0 & 1/4 & 0 & -1 & 0 & 0 \\ 1 & 0 & 0 & 0 & 0 & 0 & -1 & 0 \\ 0 & 1/4 & 0 & 0 & 0 & 0 & 0 & 1 \end{bmatrix} \tag{12}$$

$$G_3=\begin{bmatrix}1&0&0&0&0&0&0&1\\0&0&0&1&-1&0&0&0\\0&1&0&0&0&0&1&0\\0&0&1&0&0&-1&0&0\\0&0&1&0&0&1&0&0\\0&1&0&0&0&0&-1&0\\0&0&0&1&1&0&0&0\\1&0&0&0&0&0&0&-1\end{bmatrix} \quad (13)$$

Table 2 shows the expressions for computing these 1D transforms used in the JM reference software. In a similar way to the forward 1D transform, a 3-stage butterfly structure is used where stage 1 implements the operations specified in $\mathbf{G}_1$, stage 2 in $\mathbf{G}_2$ and stage 3 in $\mathbf{G}_3$. Here, **II** denotes the vector of input values (**II** represents either each file of **Z** in equation (9) or each column of **q** in (10)), **OI** denotes the transformed output vector (**OI** represents either each file of **q** in equation (9) or each column **z** in (10)), and **ia** and **ib** are internal variables.

| *Stage 1* – $\mathbf{G}_1$ | *Stage 2*– $\mathbf{G}_2$ | *Stage 3* – $\mathbf{G}_3$ |
|---|---|---|
| $ia_0=II_0+II_4$ | $ib_0=ia_0+ia_6$ | $OI_0=ib_0+ib_7$ |
| $ia_1=-II_3+II_5-II_7-(II_7>>1)$ | $ib_1=ia_1+(ia_7>>2)$ | $OI_1=ib_2+ib_5$ |
| $ia_2=(II_2>>1)-II_6$ | $ib_2=ia_4+ia_2$ | $OI_2=ib_4+ib_3$ |
| $ia_3=II_1+II_7-II_3-(II_3>>1)$ | $ib_3=ia_3+(ia_5>>2)$ | $OI_3=ib_6+ib_1$ |
| $ia_4=II_0-II_4$ | $ib_4=ia_4-ia_2$ | $OI_4=ib_6-ib_1$ |
| $ia_5=-II_1+II_7+II_5+(II_5>>1)$ | $ib_5=(ia_3>>2)-ia_5$ | $OI_5=ib_4-ib_3$ |
| $ia_6=II_2+(II_6>>1)$ | $ib_6=ia_0-ia_6$ | $OI_6=ib_2-ib_5$ |
| $ia_7=II_3+II_5+II_1+(II_1>>1)$ | $ib_7=-(ia_1>>2)+ia_7$ | $OI_7=ib_0-ib_7$ |

Table 2. Inverse 1D transform algorithm extracted from the JM software reference.

## 3. Quantization and rescaling in the H.264/AVC

The forward quantization process in H.264/AVC FRExt is performed for the transformed coefficients (**X**) computed in equations (3) and (4) according to the following equations

$$\begin{aligned}&\left|Y_{i,j}\right|=\left(QF_{i,j}\cdot\left|X_{i,j}\right|+lev\_off\right)>>qbits\\&sign\left(Y_{i,j}\right)=sign\left(X_{i,j}\right)\end{aligned} \quad (14)$$

where

$$qbits=QP_{sc}/6+16 \quad (15)$$

In this equation, $QP_{sc}$ is the scaled quantization parameter defined as

$$QP_{sc}=QP+6\cdot(bd-8) \quad (16)$$

QP takes an integer value (from 0 to 51) and determines the level of coarseness of the quantization process enabling the encoder to control the trade-off between bit rate and

quality. The parameter bd represents the bit-depth video content, $8 \le bd \le 14$. There are lots of professional applications which require higher bit depth support such as studio application and HD application. In H.264/AVC, 7 of 11 profiles support more than 8-bit bit depth starting from High10 which supports 10-bit bit depth. High 444 Predictive and some related profiles support up to 14 bits. As can be seen in equation (16), $QP_{sc}$ depends on the quantization parameter QP as well as bd; note $QP_{sc}=QP$ for bd=8 bits. This means that $QP_{sc}$ can have a value from 0 to 51 when bd=8 and from 36 to 87 for bd=14.
The approximation factor, lev_off, used in equation (14) is defined as

$$\text{lev\_off}=\left(682\cdot \text{intra}+342\cdot \overline{\text{intra}}\right)<<\left(\text{qbits-11}\right),\quad \text{intra}\in\{0,1\} \tag{17}$$

where intra=1 is used for intra coefficient quantization and intra=0 for inter coefficient quantization.
The forward quantization matrix, **QF**, is

$$QF=\begin{bmatrix} kf_0 & kf_1 & kf_2 & kf_1 & kf_0 & kf_1 & kf_2 & kf_1 \\ kf_1 & kf_3 & kf_4 & kf_3 & kf_1 & kf_3 & kf_4 & kf_3 \\ kf_2 & kf_4 & kf_5 & kf_4 & kf_2 & kf_4 & kf_5 & kf_4 \\ kf_1 & kf_3 & kf_4 & kf_3 & kf_1 & kf_3 & kf_4 & kf_3 \\ kf_0 & kf_1 & kf_2 & kf_1 & kf_0 & kf_1 & kf_2 & kf_1 \\ kf_1 & kf_3 & kf_4 & kf_3 & kf_1 & kf_3 & kf_4 & kf_3 \\ kf_2 & kf_4 & kf_5 & kf_4 & kf_2 & kf_4 & kf_5 & kf_4 \\ kf_1 & kf_3 & kf_4 & kf_3 & kf_1 & kf_3 & kf_4 & kf_3 \end{bmatrix} \tag{18}$$

whose elements are obtained by evaluating the expression

$$kf_m = MF\left(\text{mod}(QP_{sc},6), m\right)\quad,\quad \forall m\in\{0,1,2,3,4,5\} \tag{19}$$

In this equation, **MF** is the multiplication factor matrix of dimension 6×6, and the term mod($QP_{sc}$, 6) and m denote the row and column indices respectively. **MF** is specified as

$$MF=\begin{bmatrix} 13107 & 12222 & 11428 & 16777 & 15481 & 20972 \\ 11916 & 11058 & 14980 & 10826 & 14290 & 19174 \\ 10082 & 9675 & 12710 & 8943 & 11985 & 15978 \\ 9362 & 8931 & 11984 & 8228 & 11259 & 14913 \\ 8192 & 7740 & 10486 & 7346 & 9777 & 13159 \\ 7282 & 6830 & 9118 & 6428 & 8640 & 11570 \end{bmatrix} \tag{20}$$

The inverse quantization or rescaling "re-scales" the quantized transform coefficients (**Y**) coefficients computed in (14). The rescaling process, which is different to that used in the 4×4 transform (Malvar et al., 2006), is defined by the following equation directly extracted from the JM reference software as

$$Z_{i,j}=\left(\left(\left(QI_{i,j}<<4\right)\cdot Y_{i,j}\right)<<\left(QP_{sc}/6\right)+1<<5\right)>>6 \tag{21}$$

where **QI** is the rescaling matrix defined as

$$QI=\begin{bmatrix} ki_0 & ki_1 & ki_2 & ki_1 & ki_0 & ki_1 & ki_2 & ki_1 \\ ki_1 & ki_3 & ki_4 & ki_3 & ki_1 & ki_3 & ki_4 & ki_3 \\ ki_2 & ki_4 & ki_5 & ki_4 & ki_2 & ki_4 & ki_5 & ki_4 \\ ki_1 & ki_3 & ki_4 & ki_3 & ki_1 & ki_3 & ki_4 & ki_3 \\ ki_0 & ki_1 & ki_2 & ki_1 & ki_0 & ki_1 & ki_2 & ki_1 \\ ki_1 & ki_3 & ki_4 & ki_3 & ki_1 & ki_3 & ki_4 & ki_3 \\ ki_2 & ki_4 & ki_5 & ki_4 & ki_2 & ki_4 & ki_5 & ki_4 \\ ki_1 & ki_3 & ki_4 & ki_3 & ki_1 & ki_3 & ki_4 & ki_3 \end{bmatrix} \tag{22}$$

whose elements are obtained by evaluating the expression

$$ki_m = MI\left(\text{mod}(QP_{sc},6), m\right), \quad \forall m \in \{0, 1, 2, 3, 4, 5\} \tag{23}$$

Here, **MI** is the rescaling factor matrix specified as

$$MI=\begin{bmatrix} 20 & 19 & 25 & 18 & 24 & 32 \\ 22 & 21 & 28 & 19 & 26 & 35 \\ 26 & 24 & 33 & 23 & 31 & 42 \\ 28 & 26 & 35 & 25 & 33 & 45 \\ 32 & 30 & 40 & 28 & 38 & 51 \\ 36 & 34 & 46 & 32 & 43 & 58 \end{bmatrix} \tag{24}$$

## 4. Variable bit-depth processor for the 8×8 transform and quantization

Fig. 2 shows the block diagram of the proposed variable bit-depth processor for real-time implementation of the complete process for the 8×8 transform and quantization coding in the H.264/AVC. This processor includes the following main modules: configurable forward and inverse 1D integer transform, bit-depth dependent quantization and rescaling module, and transpose register memory. This architecture, which fulfils the requirements of H.264/AVC FRExt, has been conceived to operate with different bit-depth (bd) – 8 bits up to 14 bits with the aim of achieving a high performance with a reduced hardware complexity implementation. In order to provide an efficient processor, hardware solutions have been developed for the different circuit modules. The 8×8 forward and inverse transforms are calculated using the separability property simplifying its architecture to a single configurable 1D forward (FT)/inverse (IT) transform processor and a transpose register array. Forward quantization (FQ) and rescaling (IQ) operations are computed in the same circuit for the different bit-depth requirements. Here, new expressions are proposed allowing efficient hardware implementation by avoiding the sign conversion and minimizing the arithmetic operations involved. Furthermore, an exhaustive analysis in the dynamic range of the datapath was performed to fix the optimum bus widths with the aim of reducing the size of the circuit while avoiding overflow. Finally, the critical paths of the various computing units have been carefully analyzed and balanced using a pipeline scheme in order to maximize the operation frequency without introducing an excessive latency.

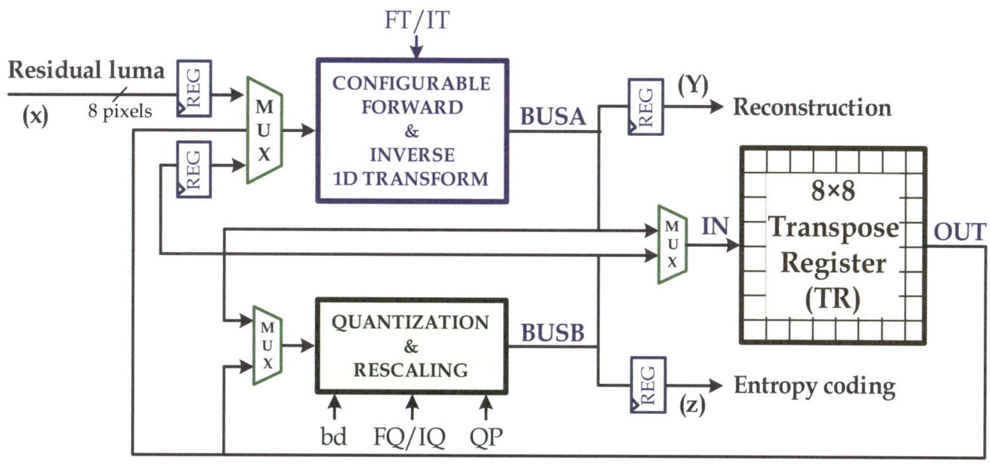


Fig. 2. Block diagram of the variable bit-depth processor.

This circuit processes 8 input data in parallel, starting by reading the residual luminance component (**x**) row by row until the entire 8×8 input block is read. The forward 1D transform module generates the intermediate coefficients **p** to be stored in the transpose register row-wise. After 8 clock cycles, these coefficients are read column-wise and processed again in the 1D transform module. Then, the resulting **X** coefficients are quantized column by column in parallel in the quantization and rescaling module and stored in the transpose register column-wise. On finishing this operation, the quantized coefficients (**Y**) are rescaled row by row and the results (**Z**) are sent to inverse 1D transform whose output data (**q**) are stored in the transpose register row-wise. Finally, the coefficients **q** are fetched to the transpose register column-wise to be processed in the inverse 1D transform to obtain the recovered residual luminance (**z**).

### 4.1 Forward and Inverse 8×8 transform

The 8×8 transform proposed in FRExt for addition to the JVT specification in the H.264/AVC is based on the fact that at SD resolutions and above, the use of block sizes smaller than 8×8 is limited. One of the first papers (Amer et al., 2005) related to this matter was the FPGA pipelined implementation of a simplified 8×8 transform and quantization. Another FPGA implementation of an algebraic integer quantization approach to computing the 8×8 TRANSFROM was presented in (Wahid et al., 2006). (Silva et al., 2007) proposed high-throughput architecture of the forward 8×8 transform to encode high-definition videos in real time with a latency of 5 clock cycles to process 1D transform. This architecture was synthesized in FPGA with a minimum period of 8.13ns and in a TSMC 0.35μm CMOS standard cell technology leading to a period of 8.05ns. Recently, (Park & Ogunfunmi, 2009) presented a reduced and parallel FPGA implementation of an 8×8 integer transform, quantization and scaling for H.264. Here, each pixel is processed one by one on a simplified pipelined architecture without multiplication.

In the adaptive block-size transform of the FRExt, different kinds of transforms are required: 8×8 forward/inverse transform, 4×4 forward/inverse transform, 4×4 forward/inverse Hadamard transform and 2×2 forward/inverse Hadamard transform. In order to reduce hardware, diverse configurable data-path architectures to support all of these transforms in a unified scheme have been proposed. Other examples of this kind of architectures include; the multi-transform processor where the quantization is performed at the pace demanded by the entropy coder in (Bruguera & Osorio, 2006), the low hardware cost suitable for VLSI implementations in (Fan, 2006), the reduced hardware and high latency in (Chao et al., 2007), the high-performance architecture for high-definition applications in ( Ma & et. al, 2007), the IP design to be implemented on an ASIP-controlled SoC platform in (Ngo et al., 2008), the high-performance, low-power unified transform architecture in (Choi et al., 2008), the highly parallel joint circuit architecture in (Li et al., 2008), and the fast, high-throughput and cost-effective implementation in (Hwangbo & Kyung, 2010).

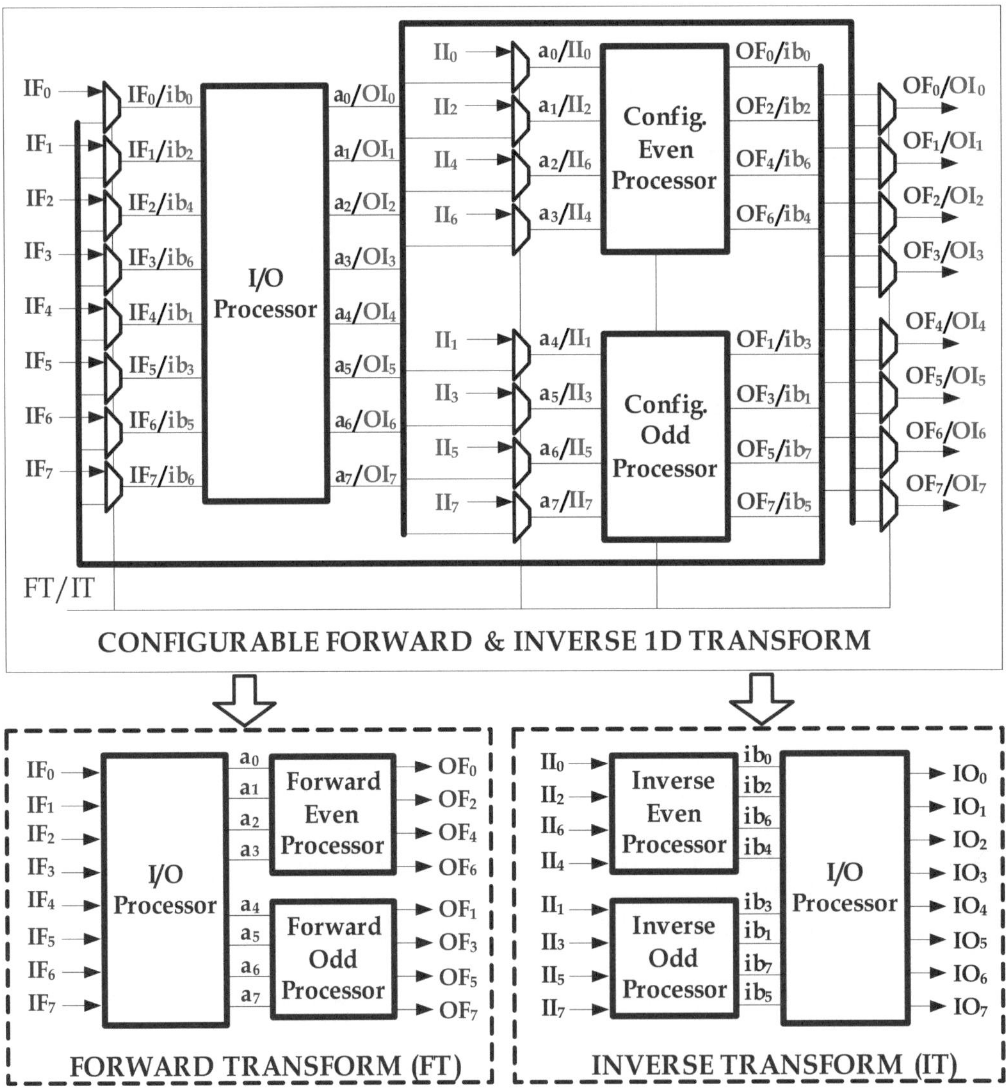


Fig. 3. Block diagram of the forward/inverse transform. The equivalent scheme is also shown for the forward transform (bottom-left) and inverse transform (bottom-right).

Initially, the specifications of H.264 adopted an integer approximation of 4×4, but when transforms are larger, significant compression performance gains have been reported for High-Definition (HD) resolutions. Thus, a new integer transform of 8×8 was proposed in the Fidelity Range Extensions (FRExt) to be added to the previously existing specifications, which were verified in SD resolutions. In fact, the use of block sizes 8x8 and bigger is dominant. Following this assumption, we proposed architecture for computing the 8×8 forward/inverse transform based on a configurable high-throughput 1D processor which has been conceived to implement the arithmetic operations described in Table 1 and Table 2 aiming to fulfill two objectives. First, to avoid mismatches between the encoder and decoder there is no possible alternative in the implementation of the operations other than those specified in these tables, which are directly extracted from the JM reference software. Second, these equations share compatible arithmetic which leads to hardware reduction if a configurable data-path is used. To comply with these prerequisites, arithmetic operations presented in Tables I and II can be implemented in terms of a three-processor architecture that fulfils the requirements of H.264. These processors, as is shown in Fig. 3, are named I/O, even and odd. The operation mode, forward (FT) and inverse (IT), is arranged by multiplexers which select the inputs and modify the inner arithmetic operations of each processor. The schematic at the bottom left in Fig. 3 represents the equivalent scheme for computing the forward 1D transform. In this configuration, the eight elements of **IF** are input to the I/O processor and their outputs run in parallel into the even and odd processors to generate the output **OF**. In the first 1D transform, the input **IF** takes each row of **x** and generates each row of **p** at the output **OF** according to equation (3), and in the second one, each column of **p** is processed to generate each column of **X** according to equation (4). In contrast, the schematic at the bottom left shows the equivalent scheme for the inverse 1D transform. The input data **II** are connected to the even and odd processors while the output data **OI** are generated in the I/O processor. In this configuration, the first inverse 1D transform processes each row of **Z**, generating each column of **q** at the output **OI** according to equation (9), and the second one **q** is read column by column generating each row of **z** according to equation (10).

Fig. 4 shows the data-path of the processors I/O, even and odd. The I/O processor implements the arithmetic operations involved in $\mathbf{T_1}$ (Stage 1 in Table 1) and in $\mathbf{G_3}$ (Stage 3 in Table 2). It is exclusively made up of adders and subtractors where the inputs are properly arranged depending on the operation mode: forward or inverse. Nonetheless, the operations of $\mathbf{T_2}$, $\mathbf{G_2}$, $\mathbf{T_3}$ and $\mathbf{G_1}$ are split up into two processors (even and odd) aiming for the maximum compatibility. As a result, the arithmetic of the even processor varies depending on the operation mode as

$$\begin{matrix}Forward\\Even\\Processor\end{matrix}\begin{cases}OF_0 = a_0 + a_3 + a_1 + a_2\\OF_2 = a_0 - a_3 + ((a_1 - a_2) >> 1)\\OF_4 = a_0 + a_3 - (a_1 + a_2)\\OF_6 = ((a_0 - a_3) >> 1) - (a_1 - a_2)\end{cases}\qquad\begin{matrix}Inverse\\Even\\Processor\end{matrix}\begin{cases}ib_0 = II_0 + II_4 + II_2 - (II_6 >> 1)\\ib_2 = II_0 - II_4 + (II_2 >> 1) - II_6\\ib_4 = II_0 - II_4 - (II_2 >> 1) + II_6\\ib_6 = II_0 + II_4 - II_2 + (II_6 >> 1)\end{cases}\qquad(25)$$

This means that this processor is configurable by means of multiplexers used to modify the data path according to the operation mode. In a similar way, the odd processor implements the following equations

$$\begin{matrix}Forward\\Odd\\Processor\end{matrix}\begin{cases}b_4 = a_5 + a_6 + ((a_4 >> 1) + a_4); & OF_1 = b_4 + (b_7 >> 2)\\ b_5 = a_4 - a_7 - ((a_6 >> 1) + a_6); & OF_3 = b_5 + (b_6 >> 2)\\ b_6 = a_4 + a_7 - ((a_5 >> 1) + a_5); & OF_5 = b_6 - (b_5 >> 2)\\ b_7 = a_5 - a_6 + ((a_7 >> 1) + a_7); & OF_7 = -b_7 + (b_4 >> 2)\end{cases} \quad (26)$$

$$\begin{matrix}Inverse\\Odd\\Processor\end{matrix}\begin{cases}ia_1 = II_5 - II_3 - ((II_7 >> 1) + II_7); & ib_1 = ia_1 + (ia_7 >> 2)\\ ia_3 = II_1 + II_7 - ((II_3 >> 1) + II_3); & ib_3 = ia_3 + (ia_5 >> 2)\\ ia_5 = II_7 - II_1 + ((II_5 >> 1) + II_5); & ib_5 = -ia_5 + (ia_3 >> 2)\\ ia_7 = II_3 + II_5 + ((II_1 >> 1) + II_1); & ib_7 = ia_7 - (ia_1 >> 2)\end{cases} \quad (27)$$

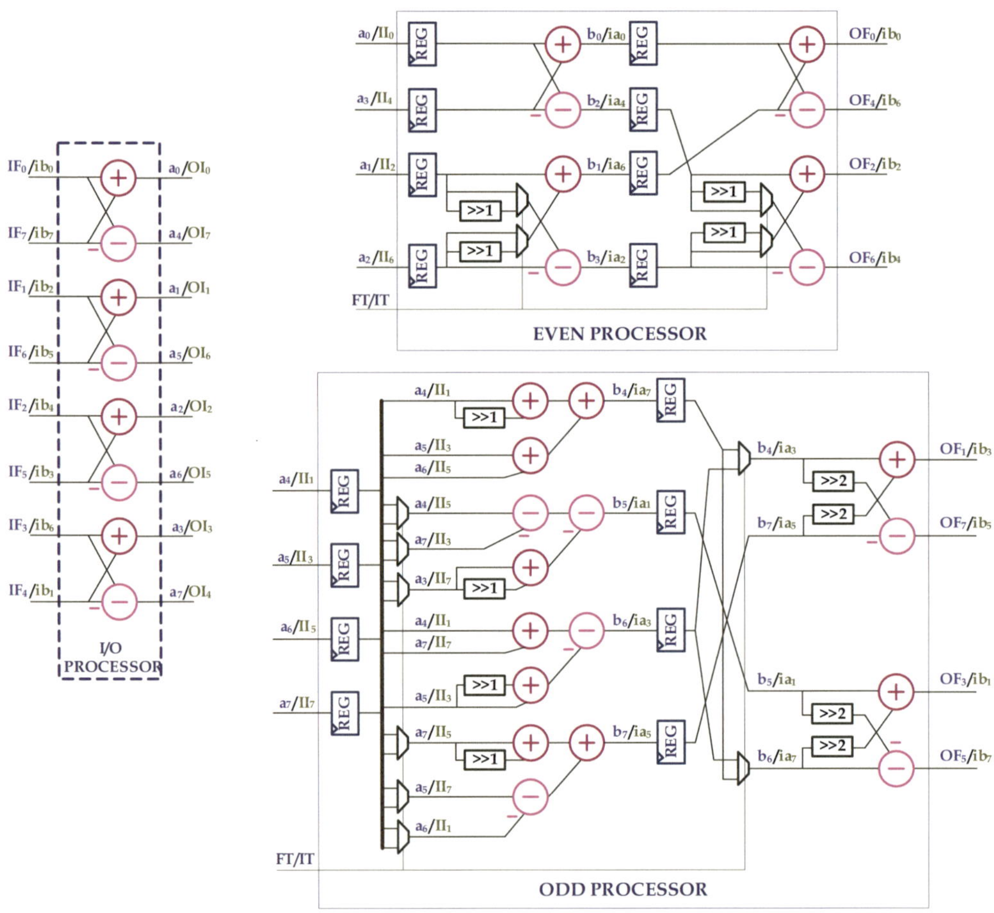


Fig. 4. Schematic of the processors shown in Fig. 3.

The entire circuit to work out the 1D transform takes a total of 32 additions/subtractions and 10 right-shifts that are built by means of data-bus wiring (no additional hardware is necessary). To prevent overflow in the computing of the transform, we consider the biggest bit-depth of 14 bits for each luminance sample; this means an unsigned integer number from 0 to 16383. However, this processor operates with the residual luminance whose value is ±16383, 15 bits being necessary for its representation. If k represents the input bus width, then k=15 bits for the first forward 1D transform and k=18 for the second one. The intermediate data $a_{0\ \mathrm{to}\ 7}$ must be of k+1 bits, $b_{0\ \mathrm{to}\ 3}$ of k+2, $b_{4\ \mathrm{to}\ 7}$ of k+3, and, finally, the output data of k+3. The range of the coefficients is ±16383·8=±131064 (18 bit) for the first 1D transform, and ±131064·8=±1048512 (21 bit) for the second one. However, the quantization and scaling process increases the data-path by 1 bit, giving input data of 22 bits before calculating the inverse 8×8 transform, this bit width being what limits the data-path of the whole transform module to prevent overflow. This means that all arithmetic in the forward and inverse 1D transform module is performed in 22 bits and the latency is 2 clock cycles.

### 4.2 Transpose register array

The transpose memory stores 8×8 data and allows simultaneous read and write operations while doing matrix transposition. To achieve this, the 8 input data are read out of the buffer column-wise if the previous intermediate data were written into the buffer row-wise, and vice versa. The transpose buffer based on D-type flip-flops (DFF) (Zhang & Meng, 2009) has been chosen as it is more suitable for pipeline architectures, unlike other proposed architectures based on RAM memories. Indeed, solutions based on a single RAM (Do & Le, 2010) lead to high latency, while those based on duplication of the RAMs (one for processing columns and the other for rows) have a high area cost (Ruiz & Michell, 1998), and those based on bank of SRAMs have a high cost in area (Bojnordi et al., 2006) or in alignment modules (Li et al., 2008).

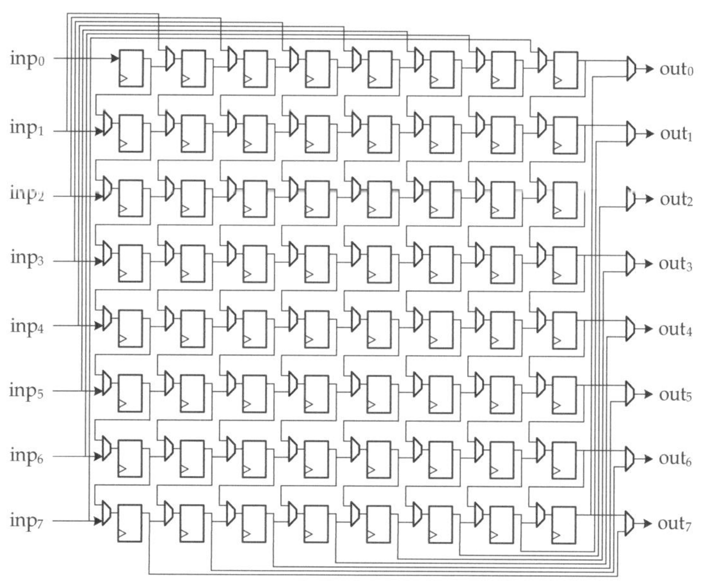


Fig. 5. 8×8 transpose register array.

Fig. 5 shows the schematic of an 8×8 transpose register array of 22 bits each element whose basic cell is a FFD and a multiplexer. Each FFD of the array is interconnected via 2:1 multiplexers forming 8 shift-registers of length 8 either in the horizontal direction (columns) or in the vertical direction (rows). A selection signal controls the direction of shift in the registers. The loading and shifting mode in the buffer alternates each time a new block of input data is processed: the even (odd) 8×8 block is stored by columns (rows) in the buffer. As a result, the transpose buffer has a parallel input/output structure and the data are transposed on the fly supporting a continuous data flow with the smallest possible size and minimal latency (8 clock cycles).

### 4.3 Quantization and rescaling

H.264 assumes a scalar quantizer avoiding division and/or floating point arithmetic. Most of the proposed quantization and rescaling hardware solutions attempt to directly implement the expressions defined in the standard, but only a few facilitate its implementation. Moreover, all of them work in 8-bit bit-depth and further bits are not considered. (Amer et al., 2005) presented a simple forward quantizer FPGA design to be run on a Digital Signal Processor. (Wahid et al., 2006) proposed an Algebraic Integer Quantization to reduce the complexity of the quantization and rescaling parameters required for the H.264. The architecture described by (Bruguera and Osorio, 2006) is based on a prediction scheme that allows parallel quantization by detecting zero coefficients to facilitate the entropy encoding. In (Chunganet al., 2007), the multiplier and RAM/ROM were removed by using a 16 parallel shift-adder scheme. An inverse quantizer based on 6-stage pipelined dual issue VLIW-SIMD architecture was proposed in (Lee, J.J. et al., 2008). (Pastuszak, 2008) presented an architecture in a FPGA capable of processing up to 32 coefficients per clock cycle. (Lee & Cho, 2008) proposed a scheme to be applied in several video compression standards such as JPEG, MPEG-1/2/4, H.264 and VC-1 where only one multiplier is used to minimize circuit size. A simplification of the quantization process to reduce overhead logic by removing absolute values leads to a decrease of around 20% in power consumption (Owaida et al., 2009). Another simplification consists of replacing the multiplier with adders and shifters to reduce hardware (Park & Ogunfunmi, 2009). An inverse quantization that adopts three kinds of inverse quantizers based on prediction modes and coefficients used in a H.264/AVC decoder was presented in (Chao et al., 2009). (Husemann et al., 2010) proposed a four forward parallel quantizer architecture implemented in a commercial FPGA board.

We propose a single circuit to compute the forward quantization and rescaling for different bit-depth requirements. In both procedures, multiplication, addition and shifting operations are involved and a configurable architecture enables the same module to perform all the specific operations in order to save hardware. The forward quantization (FQ) operates, cycle by cycle, on the coefficients of each column of the forward 8×8 transform (**X**) and the quantized coefficients (**Y**) are generated according to what is established in equation (14). In this equation, the modulus operation is necessary because the arithmetic operation "$>>$qbits" performs an integer division with truncation of the result toward zero which causes errors for $X_{i,j}<0$. For example, the integer –3 in a 4-bit two's-complement representation is 1101. The operation $-3>>2$ should be 0, but $1101>>2$ gives –1. To resolve this error, $1<<n-1$ must be added to the negative number, where n is the number of right shifts. Thus, $(1101+1<<2-1)>>2$ is 0. Applying this procedure, the absolute value of $|X_{i,j}|$ can be eliminated from equation (14) by assigning lev_off the same sign as $X_{i,j}$. To do this, a term $1<<qbits-1$ must be added when $X_{i,j}<0$. Then, equation (14) can be directly implemented as follows

$$Y_{i,j}=\left(QF_{i,j}\cdot X_{i,j}+lev\right)>>qbits \qquad (28)$$

where

$$lev = \begin{cases} lev\_off(+) = lev\_off, & for\ X_{i,j} > 0 \\ lev\_off(-) = 1 << qbits - 1 - lev\_off, & for\ X_{i,j} < 0 \end{cases} \tag{29}$$

Therefore, $|X_{i,j}|$ and a subsequent sign conversion should not be necessary in equation (28) which leads to a more efficient hardware implementation than that directly proposed from equation (14). The design to implement equation (28) must be able to manage up to 14-bit depth, that is bd=14. In this case, equation (16) shows that $QP_{sc}$ varies from 36 to 87 as QP does from 0 to 51, and qbits from 22 to 30 according to equation (15). From equations (17) and (29), lev_off(+) for intra mode varies from 1396736 to 357564416, lev_off(−) for intra mode from 2797567 to 716177407, lev_off(+) for inter mode from 700416 to 179306496 and lev_off(−) for inter mode from 3493887 to 894435327. These bounds fix the lev's bit width to 30 bits. Table 3 depicts the definition of lev according to the sign of $X_{i,j}$ and whether intra is 0 or 1, which can be easily implemented by using basic logic and shift operations.

| | | lev | Binary representation | | |
|---|---|---|---|---|---|
| intra=1 | $X_{i,j} \geq 0$ | 682<<(5+QPsc/6) | 0…0…0 | 0101010101 | 0…0…0 |
| | $X_{i,j} < 0$ | -682<<(5+QPsc/6)+(1<<qbits)-1 | 0…0…0 | 1010101010 | 1…1…1 |
| intra=0 | $X_{i,j} \geq 0$ | 342<<(5+QPsc/6) | 0…0…0 | 0010101011 | 0…0…0 |
| | $X_{i,j} < 0$ | -342<<(5+QPsc/6)+(1<<qbits)-1 | 0…0…0 | 1101010100 | 1…1…1 |
| | | | Sign extension | 10 | 6+QPsc/6 |
| | | | 30 | | |

Table 3. Definition of lev.

The inverse quantization (IQ) or rescaling specified in (21) can be simplified if this equation is rewritten as follows

$$Z_{i,j} = \left(\left(QI_{i,j} \cdot Y_{i,j}\right) << \left(QP_{sc}/6\right) + 2\right) >> 2 \tag{30}$$

Equations (28) and (30) are hardware compatible as they share the same basic arithmetic operations. Fig. 6.a shows the block diagram of the quantizer and rescaling module that is capable of processing 8 coefficients in parallel. It is composed of a control circuit and an 8-way data-path based on a configurable arithmetic unit. The control circuit generates the intermediate parameters needed for the forward quantization or rescaling mode, all of these are obtained from the scaled compression factor ($QP_{sc}$), the intra value (intra), the operation mode (FQ/IQ) and the operation synchronization (init). These parameters are: lev(+) and lev(−), $\{k_n, k_o, k_p\}$, qbits and qpper defined as

$$qpper = QP_{sc}/6 \tag{31}$$

The three coefficients $\{k_n, k_o, k_p\}$ represent either the quantization multiplication factors $kf_m \in QF_{i,j}$ specified in equations (18), (19) and (20) or the rescaling multiplication factors $ki_m \in QI_{i,j}$ defined in equations (22), (23) and (24). The indexes {n,o,p} take some of these possible values {0, 1, 2}, {1, 3, 4} or {2, 4, 5}. Only three coefficients need to be generated for the 8 arithmetic units because each row or column of the matrix **QF** in (18) or the matrix **QI** in (22) is composed of three different coefficients. All coefficients are read in a look-up table depending on the operation mode and the value of $QP_{sc}$.

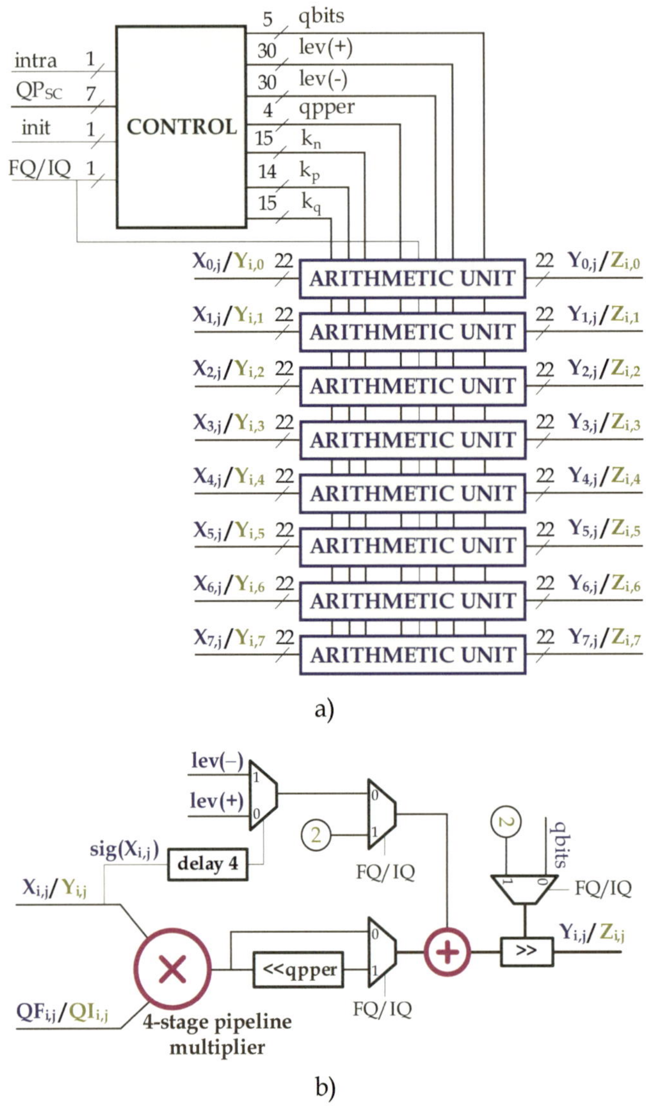


Fig. 6. Configurable forward quantizer and scaling module: a) Block diagram, and b) Schematic of the arithmetic unit.

Fig. 6.b shows a more detailed description of the configurable arithmetic unit. The main arithmetic elements are a multiplier and a adder, and multiplexers and additional logic are used to configure the implementation of equations (28) and (30). The multiplier has a high area cost and delay, so some papers (Michael & Hsu, 2008) (Zhang and et al., 2009) have proposed replacing it with a reduced number of shifts and additions by modifying the **QF** factors to be more suitable for hardware optimization. However, they introduce an error between the quantization and the inverse quantization which leads to a reduction of the rate-distortion performance. In order to avoid mismatching between encoder and decoder, in our approach an implementation of the whole multiplier is selected, with a pipeline strategy to increase its speed. After an exhaustive analysis, a Wallace-tree 4-stage pipeline multiplier was demonstrated to be the optimal solution to balance the critical path of the multiplier with the critical path of the rest of circuit. In the FQ mode, first the inputs $X_{i,j}$ and $QF_{i,j}$ are multiplied. A multiplexer selects the factor lev(+) or lev(−) to be added to the output of the multiplier depending on the sign of $X_{i,j}$. Here, a delay of 4 clock cycles in the signal of sign($X_{i,j}$) is introduced to compensate for the delay in the multiplier. At the output of the adder, a qbit shift-right (>>) operation is performed to obtain the quantized coefficient $Y_{i,j}$. In the IQ mode, the inputs $Y_{i,j}$ and $QI_{i,j}$ are multiplied. A constant 2 is added to the result and the last >>2 operation generates the scaled coefficients $Z_{i,j}$.

## 5. ASIC implementation and comparisons

A prototype of the proposed bit-depth processor has been designed and verified using different abstraction levels. Fig. 7 presents the simulation environment used to verify the functional behavior of the proposed architecture by comparing the data processed with those provided by the JM reference software (Sühring, 2010) for different data blocks of input residual luminance. The results of the diverse comparisons performed between the simulation and the reference software indicate that there are no differences between them. Initially, the processor was designed using the CoWare® Signal Processing Worksystem (SPW), editing the block diagram with the elements of the Hardware Design System (HDS) library. The first test bench was made by simulating the design with Simulation Program Builder-Interpreted (SPB-I). The code description in Verilog-RTL was automatically generated by the Verilog RTL Link from the HDS library. A new comparison was performed at this abstraction level to guarantee the correct description of the generated code. Finally, this Verilog description was synthesized using the Synopsys design compiler under HCMOS9 STMicroelectronics 130nm standard cell technology. The resulting circuit contains 26.5k cells with an area of 625700μm² and the estimated maximum operating frequency is 330 MHz. After the logic synthesis, the PrimePowerTM tool was applied to estimate the power consumption, giving 120mW@330MHz ($V_{DD}$=1.2V). The data throughput is 2640 Mpixels per second. This characteristic enables enough processing capacity for 1080HD (1920x1088@30fps) real-time video streams.

With the proposed architecture, each 8×8 block input data is processed with a latency of 44 clock cycles according to the time scheduling described in Fig. 8. BUSA indicates the output of the transform module, BUSB the output of quantization and scaling module, and IN and OUT are the input and output of the transpose register (TR); all these signals are depicted in Fig. 2. On inputting luma (**x**), it takes 3 clock cycles to generate the coefficients (**p**) and the output coefficients (**X**) are obtained from the 13th clock. These coefficients go to the quantization module and the "quantized" coefficients (**Y**), which are generated from the 18th clock cycle, are stored in the transpose register. In the rescaling process, the data **Y** are read in transpose order to compute the "rescaled" coefficients **Z** from the 31st clock cycle. On processing these coefficients in the 1D transform module, the intermediate data **q** are obtained in the 34st clock cycle. Finally, the recovered residual luminance (**z**) is ready to be processed from the 44th clock cycle and the next luma block can be input in the 49th clock cycle.

For comparison purposes, Table 4 shows the characteristics and the performances of previously published ASIC implementations, although some of them only implement parts

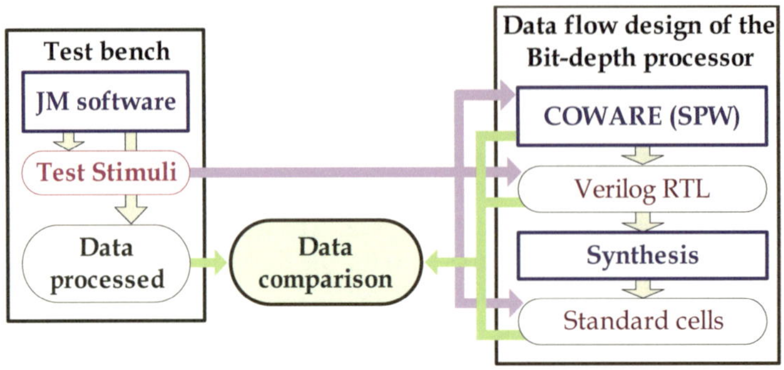


Fig. 7. Block diagram for functional verification of the proposed bit-depth processor.

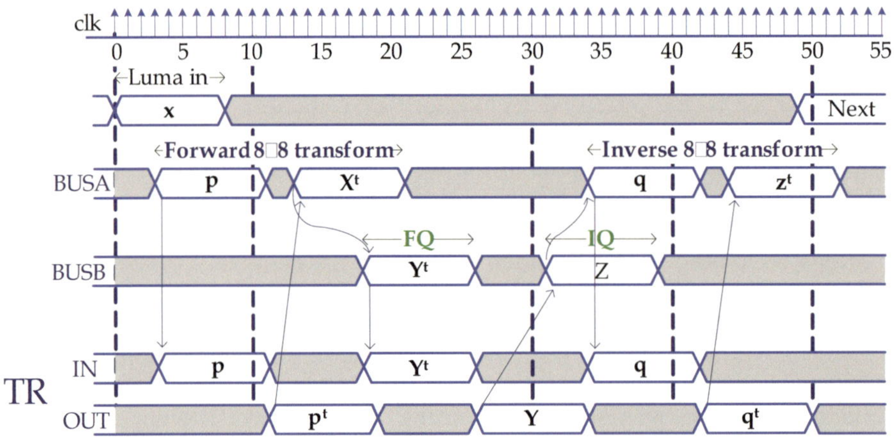


Fig. 8. Time scheduling.

of the H.264/AVC transform coding process. In (Fan, 2006), a cost effective architecture for fast (1-D) 4×4 and 8×8 forward/inverse transform was derived through the Kronecker and direct sum operations. The configurable architecture presented in (Li et al., 2008) supports the six kinds of 4×4 transforms required in the adaptive block-size transform of H.264 in order to more efficiently reuse the data-path; in this architecture, one 8×8 transform can be finished within 16 clock cycles. Based on this reusability property, another unified 4×4 and 8×8 transform architecture is proposed in (Choi at al., 2008). To increase its throughput, 4 units operate in parallel and only 5 clock cycles are needed to perform an 8×8 transform. The low power consumption is because the circuit works at quite low speed (27MHz). A pipeline 8×8 2D forward transform architecture is proposed which is capable of consuming and producing one sample per clock cycle in (Silva et al., 2007). It uses two 1-D transform processors and transpose RAM with a latency of 144 clock cycles. The high-throughput and cost-effective implementation of six different integer transforms is proposed in (Hwangbo & Kyung, 2010). This implementation maximizes the shared hardware and it is able to process 64 input pixels in a two-stage pipelined architecture to compute the direct 8×8 transform or two 4×4 transforms in parallel. Another flexible architecture is presented in (Chao at al., 2007), which is suitable for a H.264 high profile decoder capable of processing a macroblock in 95 clock cycles with the 8×8 inverse transform or only 54 clock cycles without it. The architecture described in (Lee & Cho, 2008) performs the forward 4×4 and 8×8 transform

| Ref. | Transform | | FQ | bd | Techn. | Area | Speed | Throughput | Power |
|---|---|---|---|---|---|---|---|---|---|
| | Type | Size | IQ | | (μm) | (gates) | (MHz) | (Mpixel/s) | |
| (Fan, 2006) | FWD<br>INV | (1-D)<br>4, 8 | no<br>no | 8 | TSMC<br>0.18 | 6.5k | 125 | 1000 | 2.5mW<br>@62.5MHz |
| (Li et al., 2008) | FWD<br>INV | 4×4<br>8×8 | no<br>no | 8 | UMC<br>0.18 | 13.6k+<br>RAM | 200 | 800 | N/A |
| (Choi at al., 2008) | FWD | 4×4<br>8×8 | no<br>no | 8 | AMS<br>0.35 | 27k | 27 | 346 | 9.78mW<br>@27MHz |
| (Silva et al., 2007) | FWD | 8×8 | no<br>no | 8 | TSMC<br>0.35 | 33.9k | 125 | 124 | N/A |
| (Chao at al., 2007) | INV | 4×4<br>8×8 | no<br>no | 8 | TSMC<br>0.18 | 18.5k | 125 | 860 | N/A |
| (Huang et al., 2008) | FWD<br>INV | 4×4<br>8×8 | no<br>no | 8 | UMC<br>0.18 | 39.8k<br>(NAND2) | 200 | 400 | 38.7mW<br>@50MHz |
| (Hwangbo & Kyung, 2010) | FWD<br>INV | 4×4<br>8×8 | no<br>no | 8 | UMC<br>0.18 | 63.6k | 200 | 3200<br>6400 | 86.9mW<br>@200MHz |
| (Lee & Cho, 2008) | FWD | 4×4<br>8×8 | yes<br>no | 8 | 0.18 | 36.6k+<br>RAM | 103 | 412 | N/A |
| Pastuszak, 2008) | FWD<br>INV | 4×4<br>8×8 | yes<br>yes | 8 | 0.35<br>0.18 | 229k<br>320k | 79<br>76 | 2528<br>2432 | N/A |
| (Bruguera et al., 2006) | FWD<br>INV | 4×4<br>8×8 | yes<br>yes | 8 | AMS<br>0.35 | 23.8k | 67 | 266 | N/A |
| (Michell et al., 2011) | FWD<br>INV | 8×8 | yes | 8 | STM<br>0.13 | 29.3k | 330 | 2640 | 147mW<br>@330MHz |
| Ours | FWD<br>INV | 8×8 | yes<br>yes | 8 to<br>14 | STM<br>0.13 | 26.5k | 330 | 2640 | 120mW<br>@330MHz |

Table 4. Comparison with other architectures for ASIC implementation.

and quantization for unified standard video CODEC (JPEG, MPEG-1/2/4, H.264 and VC-1). A high-throughput architecture which integrates forward transform, quantization, scaling, inverse transform and the sample reconstruction is presented in (Pastuszak, 2008). It uses reconfigurable 4×4 and 8×8 transform architecture and is able to process 32 samples/coefficients per clock cycle. The 8×8 transform is performed in only 2 clock cycles by processing a whole block of 64 input samples through a scheme based on eight 1-D transforms operating in parallel. The quantization and rescaling operate on 32 coefficients in each clock cycle. Although this architecture has low latency, the cost in area is 10 times more than in other proposed designs. In a similar way to (Li et al., 2008), a single data-path for implementing 4×4 and 8×8 forward and inverse transform as well as Hadamard transform is presented in (Bruguera et al., 2006). However, the quantization and rescaling are computed using only one multiplier each and they are performed at the pace demanded by the entropy coder.

In a previous work (Michell et al., 2011), we described a parallel architecture capable of processing 8×8 blocks without interruption with a bit-depth fixed to 8 bit. The latency of 38 clock cycles is achieved by implementing in a pipeline scheme each module used in the transform coding. Indeed, the procesor presented here uses a configurable architecture based on the reusing of different variable bit-depth modules to reduce hardware and power, all of this with a latency of 44 clock clycles. It has been designed attempting to achieve the maximum throughput at the highest possible speed. To achieve these goals, the pipeline stages have been balanced during the synthesis to maintain the critical path equivalent to 2 adders as a limit, independently of the technology used. Other challenges were the hardware-efficient modifications in the quantization and rescaling module to reduce the arithmetic complexity combined with balanced pipelined multipliers, as it is the more complex arithmetic component, to attain the high performance parameters. According to the results shown in Table 4, our design is the fastest. Its high throughput it is only surpassed by that in (Hwangbo & Kyung, 2010), which processes 16 and 32 input samples in comparison with 8 in our design, but that scheme has a large area cost despite the fact that it only implements the direct transform without quantization and rescaling. The design proposed in (Bruguera et al., 2006) has fewer gates than ours but the quite low speed (67MHz) reduces the throughput to 266Mpixels/s. By observing the differences in the speed and throughput achieved by our processor, we can conclude that these differences cannot only be attributed to the technology used, but are a consequence of the hardware modifications introduced in our design.

## 6. Conclusions

In July 2004, a new amendment called Fidelity Range Extensions (FRExt) was added to the H.264/AVC as a standardization initiative motivated by the rapidly growing demands focusing on professional applications and high-definition videos. Improvements present in FRExt include a new 8x8 integer transform, the variety of chroma sub-sampling formats and a greater colour bit-depth ranging from 8-bit up to 14-bit. Increasing bit depth provides improved accuracy in the coding efficiency with a reduction of noise and artifacts. Indeed, bit-depth scalability is potentially useful as, in a foreseeable future where different bit-depths will simultaneously coexist in the market, it provides multiple representations of different bit-depths for the same visual content.

This chapter presents a variable bit-depth processor with pipeline architecture for real-time implementation of the complete process for the 8×8 transform and quantization coding in the H.264/AVC. This architecture has been conceived with the aim of achieving a high operation frequency and high throughput without increasing the hardware complexity. Initially, the mathematical expressions of the 8×8 transform and quantization used in the standard H.264/AVC are presented to facilitate the readers' understanding of this matter. A review of the state-of-the-art of the previous implementations and references is also included; here, special emphasis is given to describing the effect of the bit-depth in quantization and rescaling formulas. However, most hardware implementations only operate in 8 bits and further bit-depths have not been taken into account. In order to achieve an efficient implementation of the processor, hardware solutions have been developed for the different circuit modules. A configurable forward and inverse 1D processor and a transpose register array enable an efficient hardware computation of the 8x8 transform. Forward quantization and rescaling operations are computed in the same circuit for different bit-depth requirements and new expressions are included enabling efficient hardware implementation by minimizing the arithmetic operations involved. Finally, the critical paths of the distinct computing units have been carefully analyzed and balanced using a pipeline scheme in order to maximize the operation frequency without introducing an excessive latency. A prototype with the proposed architecture has been synthesized in a 130nm HCMOS technology process which achieves a maximum speed of 330 MHz. The throughput of 2640 Mpixels/s allows real-time video streams of 1080HD (1920×1088@30fps) to be processed.

## 7. Acknowledgment

We wish to acknowledge the financial help of the Spanish Ministry of Education and Science through TEC2006-12438/TCM received to support this work.

## 8. References

Amer, W.; Badawy, G. & Jullien, G. (2005). A high-performance hardware implementation of the H.264 simplified 8×8 transformation and quantization. *IEEE International Conference on Acoustics, Speech, and Signal Processing*, Vol.2, pp. II-1137 - II-1140, (March 2005), doi: 10.1109/ICASSP.2005.1415610, ISBN: 0-7803-8874-7

Bojnordi, M.N.; Sedaghati-Mokhtari, N.; Fatemi, O. & Hashemi, M.R. (2006). An efficient self-transposing memory structure for 32-bit video processors. *IEEE Asia Pacific Conference on Circuits and Systems (APCCAS)*, pp. 1438–1441, doi: 10.1109/APCCAS.2006.342472, ISBN: 1-4244-0387-1

Bruguera, J.D. & Osorio, R.R. (2006). A unified architecture for H.264 multiple block-size DCT with fast and low cost quantization. *Proceedings of the 9th EUROMICRO Conference on Digital System Design*, pp. 407-414, (October 2006), doi: 10.1109/DSD.2006.18, ISBN: 0-7695-2609-8

Chao, T.C.; Tsai, H.H.; Lin, Y.H., Yang, J.F. & Liu, B.D. (2007). A novel design for computing of all transforms in H.264/AVC decoders. *IEEE International Conference on Multimedia and Expo*, pp. 1914-1917, (July 2007), doi: 10.1109/ICME.2007.4285050, ISBN: 1-4244-1016-9

Chao, Y.C.; Wei, S.T.; Liu, B.D. & J.F. Yang, J.F. (2009). Combined CAVLC decoder, inverse quantizer, and transform kernel in compact H.264/AVC decoder. IEEE Transactions on Circuits and Systems for Video Technology, Vol.19, No.1, pp. 53-62, (January 2009), doi: 10.1109/TCSVT.2008.2009251, ISSN: 1051-8215

Cheng, C.H.; Au, O.C.; Liu, C.H. & Yip, K.Y. (2009). *IEEE International Symposium on Circuits and Systems (ISCAS 2009)*, pp. 944-947, doi: 10.1109/ISCAS.2009.5117913, ISBN: 978-1-4244-3827-3

Chiang, J.C. & Kuo, W. T. (2009). Bit-depth scalable video coding using inter-layer prediction from high bit-depth layer. *IEEE International Conference on Acoustics, Speech and Signal Processing (ICASSP 2009)*, pp. 649-652, doi: 10.1109/ICASSP.2009.4959667, ISBN: 978-1-4244-2353-8

Choi, W.; Park, J. & Lee, S. (2008). A high-performance & low-power unified 4×4 / 8×8 transform architecture for the H.264/AVC Codec. *23rd International Conference Image and Vision Computing*, pp. 1-6, (November 2008), doi: 10.1109/IVCNZ.2008.4762099, ISBN: 9781424437801

Chujoh, T. & Noda, R. (2007a). Internal bit depth increase for coding efficiency. *Joint Video Team*, Doc. VCEG-AE13.doc. Available from http://wftp3.itu.int/av-arch/video-site/0701_Mar/VCEG-AE13.zip

Chujoh, T. & Noda, R. (2007b). Internal bit depth increase except frame memory. *Joint Video Team*, Doc. VCEG-AF07.doc. Available from http://wftp3.itu.int/av-arch/video-site/0704_San/VCEG-AF07.zip

Chungan, P.; Dunshan, Y.; Xixin, C. & Shimin, S. (2007). A new high throughput VLSI architecture for H.264 transform and quantization. *7th International Conference on ASIC (ASICON '07)*, pp.950-953, (October 2007), doi: 10.1109/ICASIC.2007.4415789, ISBN: 978-1-4244-1132-0

Do, T.T.T. & Le, T.M. (2010). High throughput area-efficient SoC-based forward/inverse integer transforms for H.264/AVC. *IEEE International Symposium on Circuits and Systems (ISCAS)*, pp. 4113–4116, doi: 10.1109/ISCAS.2010.5537614, ISBN: 978-1-4244-5308-5

Fan, C.P. (2006). Cost-effective hardware sharing architectures of fast 8×8 and 4×4 integer transforms for H.264/AVC. *IEEE Asia Pacific Conference on Circuits and Systems (APCCAS)*, pp. 776–779, (December 2006), doi: 10.1109/APCCAS.2006.342136, ISBN: 1-4244-0387-1

Finchelstein, D.F.; Sze, V. & Chandrakasan, A.P. (2009). Multicore Processing and Efficient On-Chip Caching for H.264 and Future Video Decoders. *IEEE Transactions on Circuits and Systems for Video Technology*, Vol.19, No. 11, pp. 1704-1713, doi: 10.1109/TCSVT.2009.2031459, ISSN: 1051-8215

Gao, Y. & Wu, Y. (2006). Applications and requirements for color bit depth scalability. Joint Video Team, Doc. JVT-U049.doc. Available from http://wftp3.itu.int/av-arch/jvt-site/2006_10_Hangzhou/JVT-U049.zip

Gao, Y.; Wu, Y. & Chen, Y. (2009). H.264/Advanced Video Coding (AVC) backward-compatible bit-depth scalable coding. *IEEE Transactions on Circuits and Systems for Video Technology*, Vol.19, No.4, (April 2009), pp. 500-510, doi: 10.1109/TCSVT.2009.2014018, ISSN: 1051-8215

Gish, W. (2002). 10-bit and 12-bit sample depth. *Joint Video Team*, Doc. JVT-E048r2.doc. Available from http://wftp3.itu.int/av-arch/jvt-site/2002_10_Geneva/JVT-E048r2.doc

Gish, W. (2003). Extended sample depth: Implementation and characterization. *Joint Video Team*, Doc. JVT-H0.16.doc. Available from http://wftp3.itu.int/av-arch/jvt-site/2003_05_Geneva/JVT-H016.doc

Gordon, S.; Marpe, D. & Wiegand, T. (2004). Simplified use of 8×8 transforms. *Joint Video Team*, Doc. JVT-K028.doc. Available from http://wftp3.itu.int/av-arch/jvt-site/2004_03_Munich/JVT-K028.doc

JVT Joint Video Team of ITU-T and ISO/IEC (2004). Draft text of H.264/AVC fidelity range extensions amendment. *Joint Video Team*, Doc. JVT-L047d9wcm.doc. Available from http://wftp3.itu.int/av-arch/jvt-site/2004_07_Redmond/JVT-L047d9wcm.zip

Huang, C.Y.; Chen, L.F. & Lai, Y.K. (2008). A high-speed 2-D transform architecture with unique kernel for multi-standard video applications. *IEEE International Symposium on Circuits and Systems*, pp. 21-24, (May 2008), doi: 10.1109/ISCAS.2008.4541344, ISBN: 978-2-84813-1

Husemann, R.; Majolo, M.; Guimaraes, V.; Susin, A.; Roesler, V. & Lima, J.V. (2010). Hardware integrated quantization solution for improvement of computational H.264 encoder module. *IEEE/IFIP VLSI System on Chip Conference (VLSI-SoC)*, pp. 316-321, doi: 10.1109/VLSISOC.2010.5642680, ISBN: 978-1-4244-6469-2

Hwangbo, W. & Kyung, C.M. (2010). A multitransform architecture for H.264/AVC high-profile coders. *IEEE Transactions on Multimedia*, Vol.12, No.3, pp. 157-167, (April 2010), doi: 10.1109/TMM.2010.2041099, ISSN: 1520-9210

Ito, T.; Bandoh, Y.; Seishi, T. & Jozawa, H. (2010). A coding method for high bit-depth images based on optimized bit-depth transform. *IEEE International Conference on Image Processing (ICIP)*, pp. 3141-3144, doi: 10.1109/ICIP.2010.5653459, ISBN: 978-1-4244-7994-8

Lee, J.J.; Park, S. & Eum, N.W. (2008). Design of application specific processor for H.264 inverse transform and quantization. *International SoC Design Conference (ISOCC '08)*, pp. II-57 - II-60, (November 2008), doi: 10.1109/SOCDC.2008.4815683, ISBN: 978-1-4244-2598-3

Lavier, P. (2009). Using 10-bit AVC/H.264 encoding with 4:2:2 for broadcast contribution. Ateme company. Confidential report. Available from http://extranet.ateme.com/download.php?file=1114

Lee, S. & Cho, K. (2008). Design of high-performance transform and quantization circuit for unified video CODEC. *IEEE Asia Pacific Conference on Circuits and Systems*, pp. 1450-1453, (November 2008), doi: 10.1109/APCCAS.2008.4746304, ISBN: 0230019544

Lee, Y.; Hong, K. & Kim, S. (2010). An adaptive image bit-depth scaling method for image displays. *IEEE Transactions on Consumer Electronics*, Vol.56, No.1, (March 2010), pp. 141-146, doi: 10.1109/ICCE.2010.5418895, ISSN: 0098-3063

Li, Y.; He, Y. & Mei, S. (2008). A highly parallel joint VLSI architecture for transforms in H.264/AVC. *Journal of Signal Processing Systems*, Vol.50, No.1, (January 2008), pp. 19–32, doi: 10.1007/s11265-007-0111-4, ISSN: 1939-8115

Lin, Y.K.; Li, D.W.; Lin, C.C.; Kuo, T.Y.; Wu, S.J.; Tai, W.C.; Chang, W.C. and Chang, T.S. (2008). A 242mW 10mm2 1080p H.264/AVC High-Profile Encoder Chip. *IEEE International Solid-State Circuits Conference (ISSCC 2008)*, pp. 314-316, doi: 10.1109/ISSCC.2008.4523183, ISBN: 978-1-4244-2010-0

(Links, 2010). Interesting webpage including links to further resources on H.264 and video compression. Available from http://www.vcodex.com/links.html

Liu, Z.; Song, Y.; Shao, M.; Li, S.; Li, L.; Ishiwata, S.; Nakagawa, M.; Goto, S. & Ikenaga, T. (2009). HDTV 1080p H.264/AVC encoder chip design and performance analysis. *IEEE Journal of Solid-State Circuits*, Vol.44, No.2, pp. 594-608, (February 2009), doi: 10.1109/JSSC.2008.2010797, ISSN: 0018-9200

Ma, Y.; Song, Y.; Ikenaga, T. & Goto, S. (2007). A high throughput multiple transform architecture for H.264/AVC fidelity range extensions. *Journal of Semiconductor Technology and Science*, Vol.7, No.4, pp. 247-253, (December 2007), ISSN: 1598-1657

Malvar, H.S.; Hallapuro, A.; Karczewicz, M. & Kerofsky, L. (2003). Low-complexity transform and quantization in H.264/AVC. *IEEE Transactions on Circuits and Systems for Video Technology*, Vol.13, No.7, (July 2003), pp. 598-603, doi: 10.1109/TCSVT.2003.814964, ISSN: 1051-8215

Marpe, D.; Wiegand, T. & Gordon, S. (2005). H.264/MPEG4-AVC fidelity range extensions: Tools, profiles, performance, and application areas. *IEEE Int. Conf. Image Processing*, pp. 593-596, (Sept. 2005), doi: 10.1109/ICIP.2005.1529820, ISBN: 0-7803-9134-9

Michael, M.N. & Hsu, K.W. (2008). A low-power design of quantization for H.264 video coding standard. IEEE International SOC Conference, pp. 201-204, (September 2008), doi: 10.1109/SOCC.2008.4641511, ISBN: 978-1-4244-2596-9

Michell, J.M.; J.M. Solana, J.M. & Ruiz, G.A. (2011). A high-throughput ASIC processor for 8×8 transform coding in H.264/AVC. *Signal Processing: Image Communication*, (in press), doi: 10.1016/j.image.2011.01.001, ISSN: 0923-5965

Ngo, N.T., Do. T.T.T., Le, T.M., Kadam, Y.S. & Bermak, A. (2008). ASIP-controlled inverse integer transform for H.264/AVC compression. *IEEE/IFIP International Symposium on Rapid System Prototyping*, pp. 158-164, (June 2008), doi: 10.1109/RSP.2008.34, ISBN: 978-0-7695-3180-9

Owaida, M.; Koziri, M.; Katsavounidis, I. & Stamoulis, G. (2009) A high performance and low power hardware architecture for the transform & quantization stages in H.264. *IEEE International Conference on Multimedia and Expo (ICME 2009)*, pp. 1102-1105, doi: 10.1109/ICME.2009.5202691, ISBN 978-1-4244-4291-1

Park, J.S. & Ogunfunmi, T. (2009). A new hardware implementation of the H.264 8×8 transform and quantization. *IEEE International Conference on Acoustics, Speech and Signal Processing (ICASSP)*, pp. 585-588, doi: 10.1109/ICASSP.2009.4959651, ISBN: 978-1-4244-2354-5, ISSN: 1520-6149

Pastuszak, G. (2008). Transforms and quantization in the high-throughput H.264/AVC encoder based on advanced mode selection. *IEEE Computer Society Annual Symposium on VLSI*, pp. 203-208, (April 2008), doi: 10.1109/ISVLSI.2008.13, ISBN 0-7695-2533-4

Richardson, I.E.G. (2004). H.264 and MPEG-4 Video Compression. John Wiley & Sons (Ed), ISBN: 0-470-84837-5

Ruiz, G.A. & Michell, J.A. (1998). Memory Efficient Programmable Processor Chip for Inverse Haar Transform. *IEEE Transactions on Signal Processing*, Vol.46, No.1, (January 1998), pp 263–268, doi: 10.1109/78.651233, ISSN: 1053-587X

Silva, T.L.; Diniz, C.M.; Vortmann, J.A.; Agostini, L.V.; Susin, A.A. & Bampi, S. (2007). A pipelined 8×8 2-D forward DCT hardware architecture for H.264/AVC high profile encoder. *Proceedings of the 2nd Pacific Conference on Advances in Image and Video Technology*, pp. 5-15, doi: 10.1007/978-3-540-77129-6_5, ISBN: 3-540-77128-X 978-3-540-77128-9

Sims, S.R.F; Mills, J.A. & Topiwala, P.N. (2005). Evaluation of video compression for 8-bit and 12-bit IR data with H.264 fidelity range extensions. *Proc. SPIE the International Society for Optical Engineering*, Vol.5807, pp. 329-340, doi: 10.1117/12.603853, ISBN: 9780819457929

Sühring, K. (2010). H.264/AVC Software Coordination. Fraunhofer Institute for Telecommunications, Heinrich Hertz Institute, Image Processing Research Department, Berlin, Germany. Available from http://iphome.hhi.de/suehring/tml

Wahid, K.; Dimitrov, V. & Jullien, G. (2006). New Encoding of 8×8 DCT to make H.264 lossless. *IEEE Asia Pacific Conference on Circuits and Systems (APCCAS)*, pp. 780-783, doi: 10.1109/APCCAS.2006.342137, ISBN: 0470847549

Wiegand, T.; Sullivan, G.J.; Bjontegaard, G. & Luthra, A. (2003). Overview of the H.264/AVC video coding standard. *IEEE Transactions on Circuits and Systems for Video Technology*, Vol.13, No.7, (July 2003), pp. 560-576, doi: 10.1109/ICIP.2005.1529820, ISSN: 1051-8215

Zhang, Q. & Meng, N. (2009). A low area pipelined 2-D DCT architecture for JPEG encoder. *IEEE International Midwest Symposium on Circuits and Systems (MWSCAS)*, (August 2009), pp. 747-750, doi: 10.1109/MWSCAS.2009.5235989, ISSN: 1548-3746

Zhang, Y.; Jiang, G. & Yu, M. (2009). Low-complexity quantization for H.264/AVC. *Journal of Real-Time Image Processing*, Vol.4, No.1, pp. 3-12, doi: 10.1007/s11554-008-0098-5, doi: 10.1007/s11554-008-0098-5, ISSN: 1861-8200

# 16

# MJPEG2000 Performances Improvement by Markov Models

Khalil Hachicha, David Faura, Olivier Romain and Patrick Garda
*LIP6-CNRS, Université Pierre et Marie Curie 4 Place Jussieu, Paris France*

## 1. Introduction

When the noise dramatically increases, the similarity between successive images is reduced, causing an increase in residue and involving the presence of more indistinguishable, non-zero coefficients. The prediction becomes less accurate and the bitrate rapidly increases. As consequence, more bandwidth is required to transmit a video sequence and pictures quality are affected. To solve this problem, we explored different motion analysis techniques. The analysis of motion is approached mathematically through the extraction of motion information from a sequence of images by means of specific data processing algorithms. Many algorithms of detection, estimation and interpretation of motion were developed with various parameters models. We reworked and developed a Markov model using the potential functions foreseen by the motion detection combining the spatial and the temporal information[1][2]. This algorithm allow a robust moving pixel segmentation and reduces the variation of the luminance that results more often from noise rather than motion. In [3], we explored the impact of adding the Markov technique to MJPEG2000 video codecs. In this work we propose to improve the MMJPEG2000 video codec by adding a new techniques allowing to improve the quality of the decoded sequence. The paper consists of 5 sections devoted to the following topics : First, we provide an explanation of the basis and contribution of the Markov model. Next, we explain the steps followed to embed the Markov algorithm in the MJPEG2000. We evaluate the new techniques and we assess theirs true performance with regard to different video types. We also estimate the different gains in bitrate and the resulting image quality. Next, we explore the possibility to embed the Markov technique on embedded platefroms as Stratix FPGA.

## 2. Motion detection algorithm based on Markov Model

The purpose of this technique is to localize moving and static areas in a dynamic scene. Then we attribute to each site $s(x,y)$ one of the two labels : 1 if $s$ belongs to a moving area and 0 if $s$ belongs to the static background. The most probable configuration is done by using the Maximum A Posteriori criterion (MAP).

### 2.1 Notations

| Symbols | Explanations |
|---|---|
| s | Site, imply also pixel with (x,y) coordinates. |
| $O_{t+1} = \{O_{t+1}(s), s \in E\}$ | The absolute value of the frame of difference. |
| $I_{t+1} = \{I_{t+1}(s), s \in E\}$ | The current frame. |
| $O_{t+1}(s)$ | Indicates one site in the $O_{t+1}$frame. |
| E | The set of the frame sites. |
| r,rp,rf | Neighbours (r: spatial, rp and rf : temporal, past and future) |
| $\psi$ | Modeling the observation. |
| b | White noise with a variance of $\sigma^2$ |
| Um | The energy associated with the model. |
| Us | Spatial energy. |
| Ut | Temporal energy. |
| $Vs$ | Potential function associated with each spatial clique |
| Vt | Potential function associated with each temporal clique |
| $Vp$ | Potential function associated with the past temporal clique |
| Vf | Potential function associated with the future temporal clique |

Table 1. Notations

### 2.2 Algorithm Principle

It is composed of two distinct steps (Fig. 1):

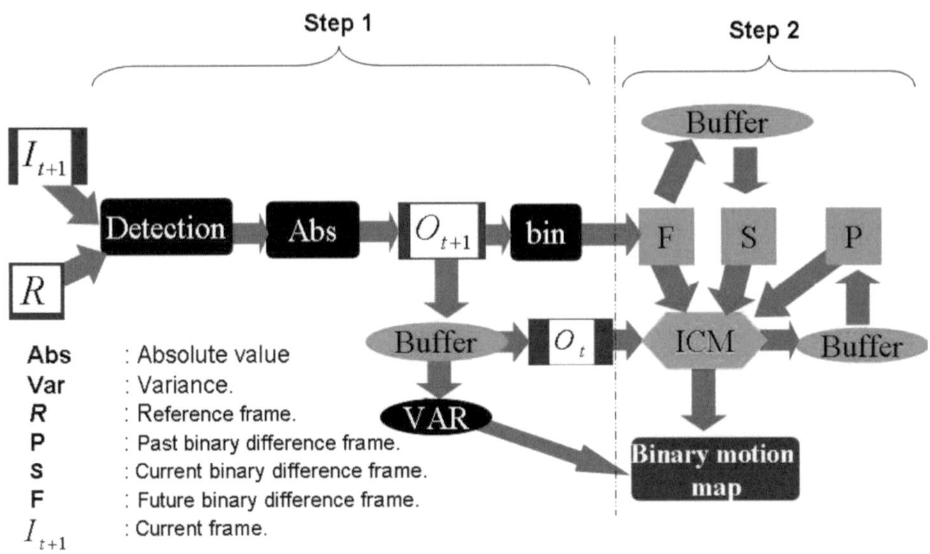


Fig. 1. Generation of the binary map

1. we compute the absolute value of the difference matrix between the current frame $I_{t+1}$ and the reference frame R, we binarize the $O_{t+1}$ matrix by setting a threshold $\theta$, and we

determine the variance of the $O_{t+1}$ matrix.

$$O_{t+1} = |I_{t+1} - R| \qquad (1)$$

2. For each image site, we calculate the local energy relative to both the immobile and the mobile state. After, we allocate the state which minimizes the energy to the site being treated. Leaving the Iterated Conditional Mode algorithm, we achieve an image of minimal energy which represents the binary motion map. The scheme of the complete algorithm is given in Fig. 1. We note that D(t) represents the frame of difference, S the actual binary frame to code and P the past binary frame.

### 2.3 Energy calculation

The energy expression is the sum of two terms :

- *The energy associated with the data (Ud) (2):*

$$Ud(s) = \frac{1}{2\sigma^2}(O_{t+1}(s) - \psi(s))^2 \begin{cases} \psi(s) = 0, \; if \; s = 0 \\ \psi(s) = \alpha, \; if \; s = 1 \end{cases} \quad (2)$$

$$O_{t+1}(s) = \psi(s) + b \quad (3)$$

- *The energy associated with the model Um (4):* It is a regularisation term. Its expression is given by the some of the spatial energy Us and the temporal energy Ut:

$$Um(s) = Us(s) + Ut(s, rp, rf) \qquad (4)$$

- The energy associated with the model consists of the spatial energy (5) that is supposed to model the consistency and the compactness of a moving object and the temporal energy (6) which represents the variation of the intensity function when the frame changes.

$$Us(s) - \sum_{s} Vs(s) \begin{cases} Vs(s) = -\beta_s, \; if \; s = r \\ Vs(s) = +\beta_s, \; if \; s \neq r \end{cases} \quad (5)$$

$Vs$ is an elementary potential function associated with each spatial clique. The positive parameter $\beta_s$ is defined for spatial cliques.

$$Ut(s, rp, rf) = Vp(s, rp) + Vf(s, rf) \; (6)$$

$$\begin{cases} Vp = -\beta_p, \; if \; s = rp \\ Vp = +\beta_p, \; if \; s \neq rp \end{cases} \begin{cases} Vf = -\beta_f, \; if \; s = rf \\ Vf = +\beta_f, \; if \; s \neq rf \end{cases}$$

$Vp$ and $Vf$ are two potential functions associated respectively with the past and future temporal cliques. The parameters $\beta_p$ and $\beta_f$ are defined for temporal cliques.

### 2.4 Parameters setting

The different parameters values which were tested and used in previous work are given in Table 2.

The setting of the parameters value is based on empirical observations: good agreement between contours of masks and actual moving objects, contextual homogeneity of detected masks and insensitivity to acquisition noise[6][7].

| Parameters | Parameter values |
|---|---|
| $\beta_p$ | 10 |
| $\beta_s$ | 20 |
| $\beta_f$ | 30 |
| $\alpha$ | 15 |
| $\theta$ | 7 |

Table 2. Parameters values

### 2.5 Experimental results

Some of our results can be visualized below (Fig. 2). In the first image, we find simple motion detection by a difference between two consecutives frames. The second represents the binary motion map created from the frame of differences. The multiplication by the mask allows only the conservation of the variation of luminance which reflects the motion.

Fig. 2. Markov tests results

## 3. Markov algorithm Integration on MJPEG2000 video codec

The JPEG2000 standard is based on two principles: the wavelet transform and EBCOT (Embedded Block Coding With Optimized Truncation). It has better performance in terms of quality/bitrate than the JPEG standard and has more features than other coding standards for still images [8] [9][10]. The compression algorithm considers each component of the image as divided into rectangular tiles treated independently. The first step is the subtraction of an offset coefficient for each tile (DC shift). After that, a lossless color transform RCT (Reversible Color Transform) or ICT (Irreversible Color Transform) is performed. A quantization is achived after selecting the compression mode. The value of this quantization can be modified by using a region of interest (ROI, Region Of Interest). It is a region of the encoded image compressed with higher accuracy at the expense of other areas of the image that are compressed to a lower rate and then degraded [11][12]. The tiles are then broken down into blocks. Coding blocks is done bit-plane by bit plane by an adaptive arithmetic coder (MQ-coder). At the end of the coding, if the output target is not reached, a post-compression algorithm used to truncate the compressed stream. Finally, this flow is encapsulated and organized in one of five modes of data provided by the standard. The video stream MJPEG2000 is a juxtaposition of images compressed by JPEG2000 algorithm. Despite its performance in terms of quality/speed, several authors worked on image stream improving. Two approaches are possible: The first is described in [13] for video monitoring applications.

The image stream is divided into reference image and images containing objects from the regions of interest. The reference images are updated (using a cutting area) by an adaptive Gaussian method [14]. The ROI [15] is obtained dynamically by detecting areas of movement and is encoded by the method "maxshift". It should be noted that in [15], the standard color transform is modified by a logarithmic color transform called LUX, which improves the color rendering of images. A similar approach is presented in [16] where the ROI and the background image are obtained using an algorithm based on Gaussian statistics. We present in [3] a different approach. Indeed, the image stream is separated into reference images and images obtained by masking differences with a bitmap of the movement. This method derives from Frantz Lohier [17] who demonstarted that the masking technique coupled with an encoder MJPEG greatly improves the performance of the encoder. In [18], the technique has been used with an encoder based on wavelets [19], demonstrating the feasibility of extending the technique. Table 3 summarizes the results of the community in this area.

| Method | improvement | References |
|---|---|---|
| artefacts filtring | PSNR + 0.2 à 0.5 dB | [20] |
| psycho ponderation | PSNR + 0.2 à 0.5 dB | [21] |
| motion detecting | bit rate - 10 % | [22] |
| Post-compression | Speed/memory | [23] |

Table 3. state of the art

The methods described in this section are primarily based on the determination of the ROI, the application of the weighting psycho-visual coefficients and the improvement of the wavelet truncation points of the compressed stream. Despite the improvements they make, they remain small compared to the use of methods that alter the flow of images and in particular the differential method (Table 4). We propose in this paper an approach based on the differential method coupled with Markov algorithms to significantly improve MJPEG2000 performances.

| Methods | Improvements | Authors |
|---|---|---|
| ROI JPEG2000 | 1 CIF/s G3M. CIF à 660 kbps, PSNR + 4 dB | [25] |
| differential masking | decreasing the bitrate from 15% to 35% | [18] |

Table 4. Quality-bitrate improvement

### 3.1 Impact of the number of iterations

Respecting the fact that the real-time constraints of digital systems is not compatible with the expectation of convergence of the regularization algorithm, a small number of iterations is used to solve this problem. Its influence on the quality of the images were assessed by measuring the PSNR of the reconstructed images and the entropy of images of differences. Figure 3 shows the impact of the use of 1, 2, 3 and 4 iterations on PSNR. We note that using a single iteration of ICM for the regularization of the binary map degrade the performance of masking. Therefore we chose a single iteration.

### 3.2 Thresholding

The quality of the final bitmap depends on the result of thresholding. The background noise corresponds to the sites where there is no motion and where the intensity variations is due to the noise of the acquisition system. For further developments, we consider the distributions of

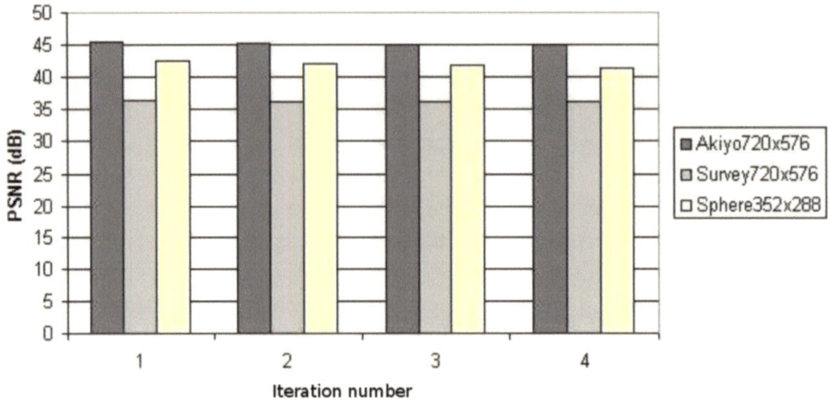


Fig. 3. Iteration impact on PSNR

moving objects and background noise are Gaussian. The analysis of the intensity distribution of pixels in the image is one of the methods allowing the separation of classes. Several methods using histogram thresholding are presented and discussed in [24]. In this section, an adaptive thresholding method based on the histogram of the image observations is proposed. It has low complexity and meet our needs. The conditions of the good working of our algorithm are as follow [25] :

- Fixed camera.
- Illumination changes slowly and gradually.
- The noise is additive Gaussian, uncorrelated, has a low intensity compared to the signal.

Under these assumptions:

- The pixels belonging to moving objects occupy a small portion of the image.

With these assumptions, the difference image contains a large population of pixels close to zero. Figure 4 is an example of image histogram differences of a sequence of video monitoring. An histogram that respects these assumptions can be represented as a bimodal curve. The first lobe is the background (to eliminate). it has a height much greater than the second and a large population of low intensity, close to zero. The second lobe represents the moving objects. Figure 5 illustrates the proposed method.
Based on our method [26] corresponding to a graphical analysis of the histogram to extract the first lobe, we offer an estimation of the mean $\mu$ and the standard deviation of background $\sigma_b$ from the histogram of the image. The first lobe of the histogram is based on the intensity of x expressed as follows:

$$B(x) = \frac{1}{\sigma_{b\sqrt{2\pi}}} \exp^{-\frac{1}{2}(\frac{x-\mu}{\sigma_b})^2} \tag{1}$$

In the circumstances described above, the average value is the maximum H of the Gaussian and is close to zero. H also corresponds to the maximum of the histogram of the image. If $x = \mu$ , we get :

$$B(\mu) = \frac{1}{\sigma_{b\sqrt{2\pi}}} = max(B(x)) = H \tag{2}$$

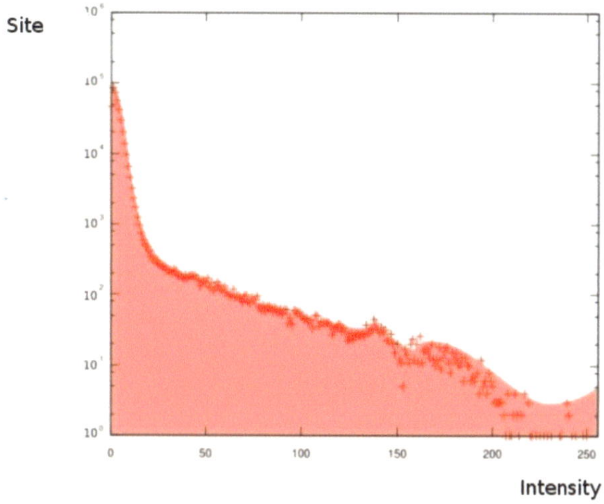


Fig. 4. image histogram

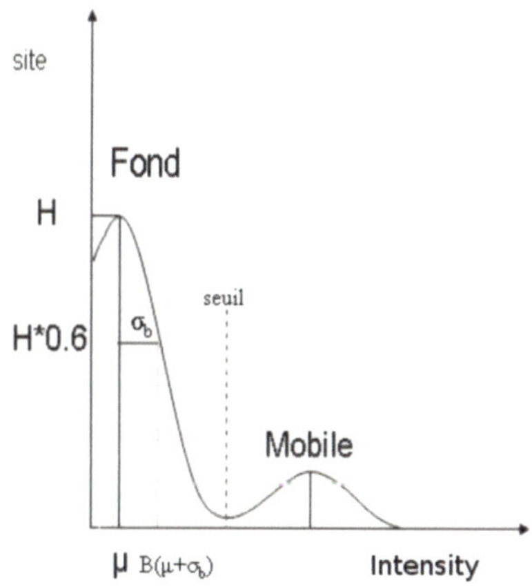


Fig. 5. Gaussian model

we obtain a relationship between the position of the Gaussian and the maximum value H.

$$B(x) = H \centerdot \exp^{-\frac{1}{2}(\frac{x-\mu}{\sigma_b})^2} \tag{3}$$

To get an estimate of the standard deviation, we simply compute $x = \mu + \sigma_b$, then:

$$B(\mu + \sigma_b) = H \centerdot \exp^{\frac{1}{2}} \simeq H \centerdot 0.6 \tag{4}$$

So there is a relationship between standard deviation and the maximum height. If we place ourselves at a height equal to the Gaussian $P(x) = H \times 0.6$, the corresponding value of x gives a direct estimate of $\mu + \sigma_b$. The mean $\mu$ and standard deviation $\sigma_b$ can be obtained by a sequential scan of the histogram. The value of standard deviation is approximated by standing at a height of $H \times 0.5$. Right shifting the bits of the Gaussian height value gives a good estimate of the standard deviation: $1.1774 * \sigma b$, we define the threshold of binarization as follow :

$$seuil = \mu + k.\sigma_b \tag{5}$$

The parameter k adjusts the rate of the gaussian background elimination. Figure 6 shows the variation of the automatic threshold value according to k.

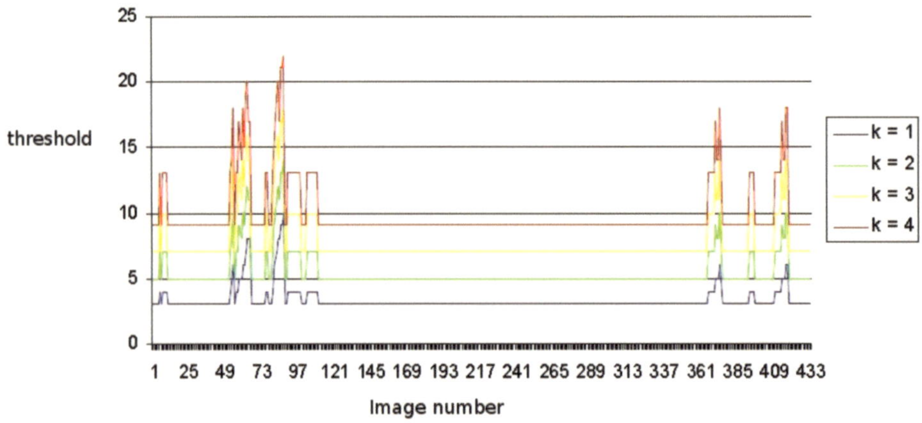


Fig. 6. Thereshold according to k parameter, Akyio séquence

### 3.3 Reference frames update

In the literature, there are several strategies to update the reference image [27] [28]. Methods related to motion detection zones will update the reference image for each new image if there is a change in the reference image. This approach provides an accurate motion detection but, at the same time, inscreases the number of transmitted reference frames. To refresh the reference image, we used an indexing video technique. The purpuse is to classify the transition effects in a video sequences [29] [30]. Transition effects are abrupt changes of context and gradual changes. We must define two thresholds, $\tau_1$, the high threshold and $\tau_2$ the low threshold, $\tau_1 >> \tau_2$, and compare $\tau$ percentage of pixels affected by motion. $\tau$ is obtained as follows : P(x,y) is the pixel value of the binary map of moving E(t) at position (x, y), l and c being respectively the number of line and column of the image then:

$$\tau = \frac{\sum_{x=0}^{l-1} \sum_{y=0}^{c-1} P(x,y)}{l \times c} \times 100 \tag{6}$$

In our approach, $\tau_1$ and $\tau_2$ are chosen empirically to values equal to 10% and 40%. We have considered three configurations (Table 5) :

### 3.4 Masking operation

The masking operation is needed to regulate and eliminate the impulse noise. This operation plays a gatekeeper role and only the intensity variations that are relevant will be retained while others will be forced to zero. The masking operation is obtained by performing a binary AND between the bitmap of motion E (t) and the absolute difference image O (t). At the same

| | $\tau$ | Motion | Action |
|---|---|---|---|
| 1) | $\tau > \tau_1$ | high | We send immediatly a reference frame |
| 2) | $\tau_1 > \tau > \tau 2$ | intermediate | If 12 successive frame, update the reference frame. |
| 3) | $\tau < \tau_2$ | low | There is no need to update the reference image. |

Table 5. Reference frames update

time, a dynamic shift is made so that the masked difference image D * t has the same dynamics as the original image. The value $d_t(s)$ of the difference is masked:

$$d_t(s) = 128 + (1 - 2 * sig_t(s) * \left(\frac{e_t(s).o_t(s)}{2}\right)) \quad (7)$$

This forces to zero the pixels which are not detected as motion pixels.

## 4. Évaluation de l'algorithme

The test database consists of 14 video sequences with very different contexts with a number of images ranging from 100 to 1500. We present two sequences: Akyio and Survey in QCIF format. We performed a software version of the algorithm for masking images of difference. We chose two methods to assess quality:

- The PSNR (Peak Signal to Noise Ratio). It gives a statistical measure of damages.
- Estimation with a perceptual quality metric (double stimulus method) : We compare the original sequence to decompressed sequences. The observer must then assign a rating to the degraded image using a predefined scale. But these tests have the disadvantage of being expensive and time consuming. The perceptual metric represent an alternative to subjective tests. They exploit the HVS characteristics to improve the correlation between the notes that they provide and those given by a set of observers [31]. The perceptual evaluation is performed with the software VQM (Video Quality Metric).

### 4.1 MJPEG2000 and MMJPEG2000 comparison

The compression system we used to perform our tests consists of three separate modules. The first of these modules is the difference image generator. The used encoder is Kakadu [32]. It follows the standard JPEG2000. We used 4 levels of wavelet decomposition and the "-no_weights" option is enabled. The last module is a module to concatenate the compressed stream and to add the Motion JPEG2000 headers [33]. We notice that we created sequences with reference frames compression ratios equal to 16 and 6 values for difference frames, ranging from 32 to 256.

#### 4.1.1 statistical comparaison

Figure 7 shows the evolution of the PSNR (sequence Survey). It enables a statistical comparison between MMJPEG200 and MJPEG2000. We notice that the MMJPEG2000 video codecs improves the quality compared to a classic MJPEG2000 video codec. The gain varies between 4 dB and 10 dB.

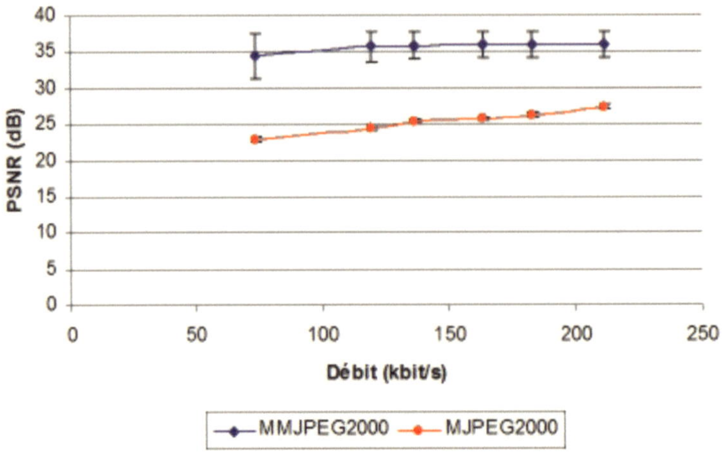


Fig. 7. MMJPEG2000 vs MJPEG2000 : Survey sequence

#### 4.1.2 Comparison with an objective perceptual quality metric

Figure 8 shows the evolution of MOS sequence Survey. It allows a fair comparison between MMJPEG200 MJPEG2000 by estimating the perceived quality. We notice a big improvement except for the low compression ratio.

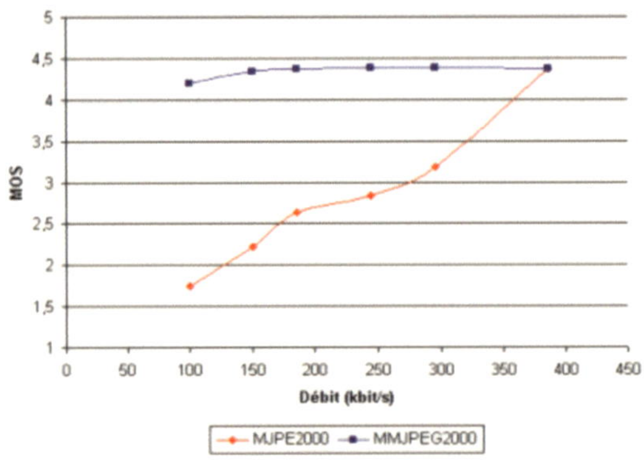


Fig. 8. Perceptual metric quality, Akiyo sequence

#### 4.1.3 Visual comparison

Figure 9 shows part of the sequence Survey. It allows to compare the visual quality of compressed sequence by MJPEG2000, Markov-MJPEG2000 and the original sequence. The sequences are compressed to obtain a rate of 120 kbit/s for the sequence Survey.

## 5. Implementation on the Stratix FPGA platforme

The design of the Markov motion detection algorithm was done under QuartusII. VHDL language was used for the system description and the synthesis process was oriented for maximum speed. In the conception, we split the algorithm into three functional blocks.

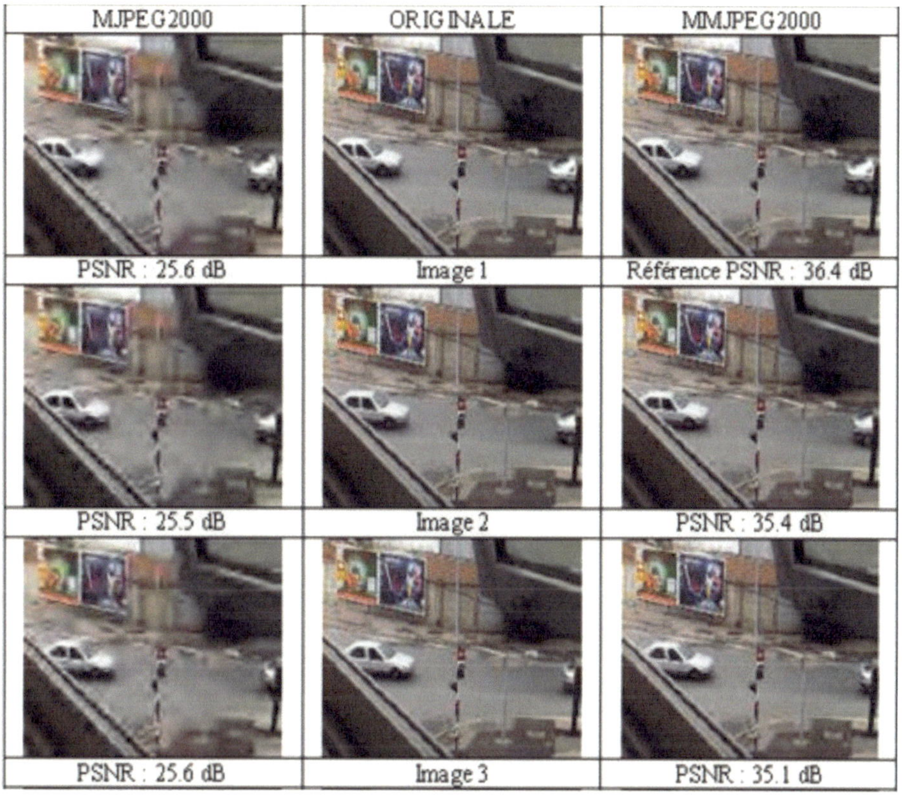


Fig. 9. Comparaison visuelle : séquence survey

The first one is the data controller allowing to grab and store the data to the memory. The next functional block performs the binarization function. The last achieves the energy minimization. In the following, we give more details about the threshold module and the energy minimization module.

#### 5.0.4 *The Threshold module*

The threshold module gives the binary data to the energy minimization module. To perform this task, the differences between matching blocks and the variance must be computed. We note that the difference is obtained by the subtraction between the reference block and the actual block to code. The results are stored in a dedicated memory and the standard deviation calculation is performed at the same time (Figure 10). When the processing is finished, a flag is set indicating to the controller to start the data thresholding. It consists in comparing the pixel differences to a fixed threshold $\theta$.

#### 5.0.5 *The Energy minimization module*

The energy minimization module gets the needed pixel from the thresholding module and decides if the pixel is moving or not. It is composed of four sub-modules (Figure 11).
The line buffer sub-module allow to store the pixel neighbors. In our algorithm, we need 3 lines and the newest line overwrites the oldest one. ( L0 is the current line, L-1 the oldest) (Fig

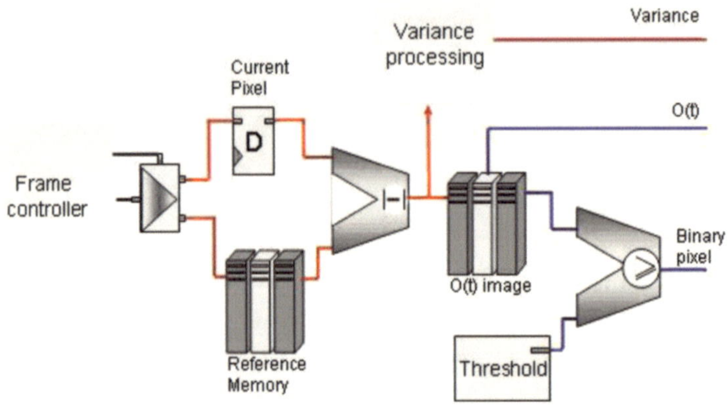


Fig. 10. Threshold module

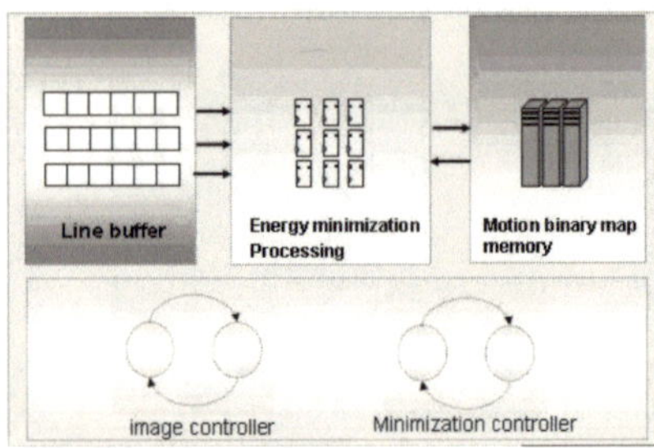


Fig. 11. Energy minimization module

12). We note that the size of the lines depends on the number of columns in the frame. Thus for a bloc size (M x N), we need 3 lines of N columns.

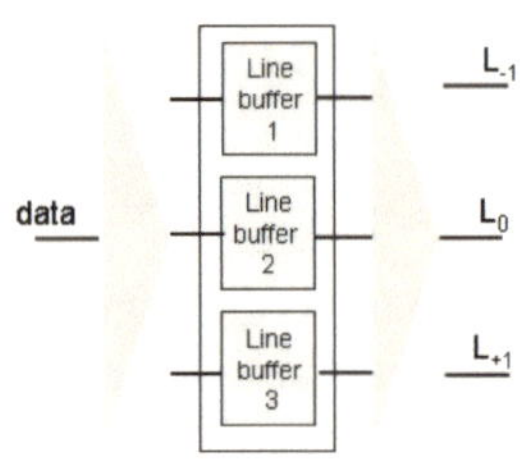


Fig. 12. Line buffer

The minimization is achieved line by line, left to right. We created 9 registers for the spatial neighbors and one register for the temporal. At each clock cycle, the neighborhood is updated with 3 new pixels from the 3 line buffers. Each data moves by one position, so the oldest values are discarded (Fig. 18). To compute the spatio-temporal energy, we compute the energy corresponding to the state of the binary current pixel, the surrounding spatial and temporal pixels. This value is stored in a model energy Look-Up Table. The model energy, the variance and the current observation value are used to process the energy minimization (Fig. 13).

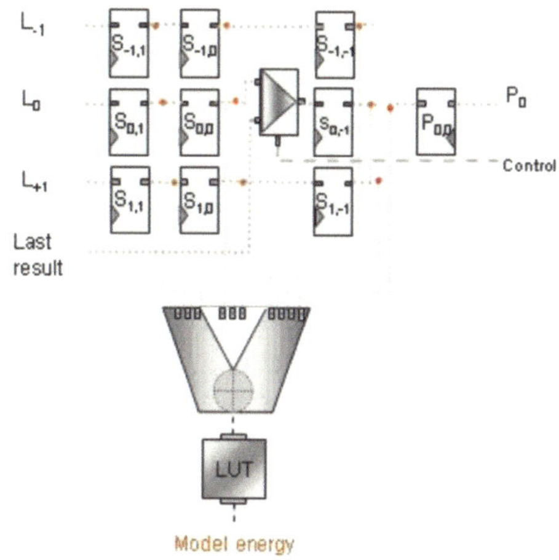


Fig. 13. Model energy processing

#### 5.0.6 Experimental setup and results

The experimental board is composed principally of an Altera Stratix FPGA paltform. We added to the FPGA two daughter boards :

- A video daughter board connected to the digital CMOS camera[34].
- A Lancelot daughter board allowing to display the created mask and the video input[35].

The stratix M-RAM is used to store the binary motion map and the current frame. By this way, both frames can be displayed on a VGA screen (Fig 14).

Fig. 14. Motion detection experimental prototype

The system process 3200 macroblock per second (312 us/Macroblock). The maximum IC frequency is 75 MHz. The motion detection IC takes only 4.6% of the total FPGA logic elements. This result allows us to implement more functionality in the FPGA such as the other parts of the H264 or MJPEG2000 video codecs. We used 13 embedded multipliers in our design. The majority are used to compute the variance. Without the embedded Stratix multipliers, we note that the number of used Logic Elements grows by a factor of three and the maximum working frequency fall down to 50 MHZ.

## 6. Conclusion

Within this framework, we have been interested in the discovery of new methodologies allowing the reduction of the bitrate for noisy sequences while maintaining adequate quality of the rebuilt sequences. Particularly, we have demonstrated that the addition of the Markov algorithm presents an effective solution in reducing the noise contained in the video sequences. We showed that the new Markov/MJPEG2000 video codec improve significantly the performances achived by a classic MJPEG2000 video codec while keeping a standard bitstream. We have also been interested in evaluating Markovian technique under a PC platform and on embedded architectures intended for the multi-media applications. The complete implementation of the Markov algorithm carried out exclusively on a stratix FPGA, demonstrated the possibility of using this technique on embedded architecture.

## 7. References

[1] J.Zhang, Mean field theory in EM procedures for MRFs, IEEE Trans.Signal Processing, vol. 40, pp. 2570-2583, October 1992.

[2] Khalil Hachicha, Patrick Garda: Noise-robustness improvement of the H.264 video coder. J. Electronic Imaging 17(3): 033019 (2008)

[3] David Faura, Olivier Romain, Patrick Garda: MMJPEG2000: A Video Compression Scheme Based on JPEG2000. ICIP 2006: 3145-3148

[4] F.Luthon, A.Caplier, M.Liévin, Spatiotemporal approach to video segmentation : Application to motion detection and lip segmentation, Signal Processing, 76(1) : 61-80, July 1999.

[5] C.Dumontier, F.Luthon, J-P.Charras, Real-time DSP implementation for MRF-based video motion detection, IEEE Transactions on Image Processing, Volume 8, Issue 10, Oct. 1999 Page(s) : 1341-1347.

[6] A.Caplier, F.Luthon and C.Dumontier, Real-time implementations of an MRF-based motion detection algorithm. Real time Imaging, 4: 41-54, 1998.

[7] F.Lohier, P.Garda, L.Lacassagne Procédé et dispositif de traitement de sequences dimages avec masquage. National Patent N FR 62060 L, 3 february 2000, France. International extension pending.

[8] D.Santa-Cruz, T.Ebrahimi, "An analytical study of JPEG 2000 functionalities", ICIP'00, vol 2, pp 49-52, Septembre 2000.

[9] A.Skodras, C.Christopoulos et T.Ebrahimi, "The JPEG2000 Still Image Compression Standard", IEEE Signal Processing Magazine, vol 18, pp 36-58, September 2001.

[10] M.D.Adams, "The JPEG-2000 Still Image Compression Standard", Tech Rep N2412, ISO/IEC JTC1/SC29/WG1 , September 2001.

[11] M.M.Subedar, L.J.Karam, G.P,Abousleman, "JPEG2000-Based shape adaptive algorithm for the efficient coding of multiple region of interest", ICIP'04, vol 2, pp 1293-1296, October 2004.

[12] Z.Wang, S.Banerfee, B.L.Evans, and A.C.Bovik, "Generalized bitplane by bitplane shift method for JPEG2000 ROI coding", ICIP'02, vol 3, pp 81-84, October 2002.

[13] T.Totozafiny, O.Patrouix, F.Luthon, J.M.Coutelier, "Motion reference image JPEG2000: Road surveillance application with wireless device", Visual Communications and Image Processing, VCIP'05, Beijing, July 2005.

[14] T.Totozafiny, "Compression d'images couleur pour application à la télésurveillance routière par transmission vidéo à très bas débit", Université de Pau et des pays de l'Adour, Juillet 2007.
[15] F.Luthon, B.Beaumesnil, "Color and ROI with JPEG2000 for wireless videosurveillance", International Conference on Image Processing, 2004, vol 5, pp 3205-3208, October 2004.
[16] F.Luthon and A.Caplier, "Motion detection and segmentation in image sequences using Markov Random Field Modeling", 4th Eurographics Animation and Simulation Workshop, pp 265-275, September 1993.
[17] F.Lohier, P.Garda, L.Lacassagne, "Masked-Motion-JPEG2000: A new reduced complexity video sequence compression scheme based on a MRF-motion detection algorithm toward inter frame masking", Conf. On Signal Processing Applications and Technology, October 2000.
[18] http://www.analog.com/en/prod/0,,765 810_ADV601,00.html.
[19] P.Bourdon, B.Augereau, C.Olivier, C.Chatellier, "A PDE-based method for ringing artefact removal on greyscale and color JPEG2000 images", IEEE International Conference on Acoustics, Speech, and Signal Processing, vol 3, pp 729-732, April 2003.
[20] K.Varma, A.E.Bell, "Improving JPEG2000's perceptual performance with weights based on both constrast sensitivity and standard deviation", ICASSP'04, vol 3, pp 665-668, May 2004.
[21] J.H.Kim , S.B.Kim and C.S.Won, "Motion JPEG2000 Coding Scheme Based on Human Visual System for Digital Cinema", Springer Berlin / Heidelberg Book Advances in Image and Video Technology, vol 4319, pp 869-877, 2006.
[22] Y.M.Yeung, O.C.Au, "Efficient Rate Control for JPEG2000 Image Coding", IEEE Transactions on Circuits and Systems for Video Technology, vol 15, no 3, pp 335-344, March 2005.
[23] P.K.Sahoo, S.Soltani, A.K.C.Wong, and Y.C.Chen "A survey of thresholding techniques". Computer Vision, Graphics and Image Processing, vol 41, pp 233-260, 1988.
[24] F.Luthon, M.Lievin, F.Faux , "On the use of entropy power for threshold selection", Elsevier Science, Signal processing, vol 84, no 10, pp. 1789-1804 , 2004.
[25] P.L.Rosin, "Unimodal thresholding", ELSEVIER Pattern Recognition, vol 34, pp 2083-2096, 2001.
[26] P.Vannoorenberghe, C. Motamed, J.-G.Postaire, "Réactualisation d'une image de référence pour la détection du mouvement dans les scènes urbaines", Traitement du Signal, vol 15, no 2, pp 139-148, 1998.
[27] G.Ahanger, T.Little, "A survey of technologies for parsing and indexing digital video", Journal of visual communication and image representation, vol 7, pp 28- 43, March 1996.
[28] I.Oliveira , N.Correira, N.Guimaraes, "Image Processing Technique for Video Content Extraction", Image indexing and retrieval, pp 61-70, August 1997.
[29] ITU-R Recommendation BT.1683, "Objective perceptual video quality measurement techniques for standard definition digital broadcast television in the presence of a full reference", Recommendations of the ITU, Radiocommunication Sector, 2004.
[30] T.Tiffany et S.Hakim, " L'apport d'un bloc de segmentation d'erreur dans l'évaluation de la qualité d'images", GRETSI'01, Toulouse, 2001.
[31] M.Pinson and S.Wolf, "A new standardized method for objectively measuring video quality", IEEE Transactions on Broadcasting, vol. 50, No 3, pp. 312- 322, September 2004.

[32] D.S.Taubman, M.W.Marcellin JPEG2000, "Image Compression, Fundamentals, Standards and Practice". Boston: Kluwer Academic Publishers, 2002.
[33] OV6620 single chip CMOS CIF Color difital camera, http://www.ovt.com.
[34] Lancelot User Manual, Product Brochure, Microtronix, http://www.microtronix.com

# Part 5

## Semantic-based Video Coding

17

# What Are You Trying to Say? Format-Independent Semantic-Aware Streaming and Delivery

Joseph Thomas-Kerr[1], Ian Burnett[2] and Christian Ritz[3]
[1,3]*University of Wollongong*
[2]*Royal Melbourne Institute of Technology*
*Australia*

## 1. Introduction

> *"[Elizabeth Bennett]* ***looked at her father to entreat his interference****, lest Mary should be singing all night. He took the hint, and, when Mary had finished her second song, said aloud, 'That will do extremely well, child.* ***You have delighted us long enough.****' "* —
>
> Pride and Prejudice, 1813, Jane Austen (1813)

Users automatically associate many layers of meaning with the media content they consume, yet computers have barely begun to scrape the surface of this information. For example, consider the passage above. The subtle exchange of glances between Elizabeth and her father would be readily apparent to most human observers, but it is unlikely that a computer processing a video of the scene would be able to recognise their meaning. Furthermore, while the double-entendre in Mr Bennett's remark would be clear to most human listeners, algorithmic recoginition of this or other modes of speech are in their infancy (Paleari & Huet, 2008).

Other research communities are developing means to communicate such semantic information (whether computed or manually generated) in ways that are able to transcend the original context of the information.This work—originating from Knowledge Representation, but more popularly known as the Semantic Web—has provided languages such as the Resource Description Framework (RDF) (Beckett, 2004) and Web Ontology Language (OWL) (Dean & Schreiber, 2004) which can be used to express concepts in such a way that "this picture has many buildings" may also imply that "it is a cityscape", and "it contains man-made objects."

Recent multimedia coding formats developed by MPEG and ITU-T such as Scalable Video Coding (SVC) (ISO/IEC, 2007) and Scalable-to-Lossless Coding (SLS) (ISO/IEC, 2004a) offer the ability to dynamically adapt their bitrate to changing conditions. Current systems perform this adaptation on the basis of static channel parameters such as terminal and network capabilities (Timmerer et al., 2006) or dynamic estimation of channel capacity (Chou, 2006). There are, in fact, numerous examples of using *content semantics* to identify the best way to adapt content to dynamic conditions: Section 2 describes this in further detail. However, while others have proposed specific semantics to be used in the delivery process, there exists no generic system for connecting arbitrary semantics to the adaptation/delivery process.

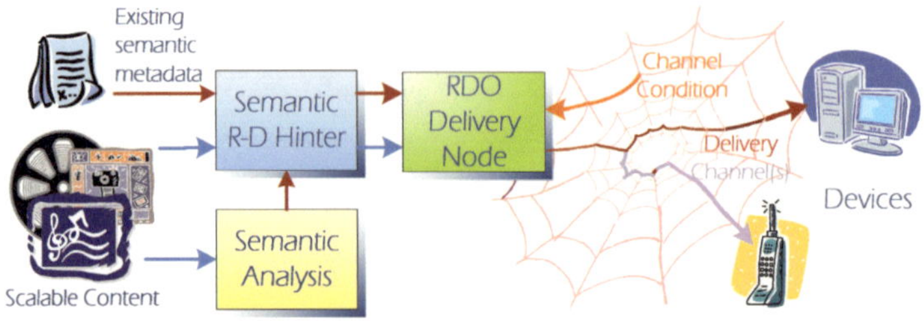


Fig. 1. A framework for semantic-aware multimedia delivery

Fig. 2. News reports have a regular structure

This chapter proposes and demonstrates just such a system, as shown in Figure 1. An overview of the system was presented in Thomas-Kerr et al. (2009); the present work greatly expands upon the complexities of its concept and design. Combining semantics and multimedia delivery in a generic fashion is, unsurprisingly, a task that draws on numerous disparate fields. When possible, sufficient detail has been provided to appreciate the background concepts, however, the reader is referred to the relevant citations for further information.

## 2. Semantics in the delivery process

A typical news report (Figure 2) provides a good example of how content semantics could be useful in multimedia delivery. News reports often have a fairly consistent structure, beginning with a studio introduction, then footage of the event (often with commentary overlaid on top of audio from the event), using subtitles if subjects are speaking in a foreign language, and sometimes concluding with further studio footage. As a report proceeds through these various stages, the relative importance of the audio and video varies. For example, in the studio introduction, virtually all of the semantic content of the presentation is carried in the audio. On a low-bandwidth (e.g. mobile) channel, reduction of the frame-rate in this region would have little impact on the transmission of the content semantics. When the report cuts to on-site footage, a much greater proportion of the semantic content is carried by the visuals, though the amount would vary from one report to another. If subtitles are overlaid on the video, virtually all of the semantic content is conveyed by the video, and bits spent on audio in this section will contribute much less to the successful delivery of the semantics.

As a second example, instead of comparing relative semantic importance along the modal dimension (as is the case above), similar comparisons could be made on the temporal axis. Here, segments of the news report would be annotated with an indication of the relative importance of the segment to the story as a whole. Users could receive a short "digest", the full story, or something in between. This approach could also work for coverage of sporting events.

Numerous other types of semantic metadata have been identified which can assist in delivery optimisation: Bertini et al. (2006), Xu et al. (2006), and Baba et al. (2004) all argue that applying the same adaptation operation to different parts of a multimedia presentation will have differing effects in the perceptual quality of the presentation as a whole.

More specifically, both Bertini et al. (2006) and Xu et al. (2006) propose adaptation on the basis of semantic classification of sporting events into categories such as Shot on Goal, Corner (for soccer), or Shot, Foul, Penalty (for Basketball), among others. User preferences are used to prioritize the categories, and this priority information is then used to guide the adaptation. That is, given a bandwidth constraint such that the full content can't be delivered, the adaptation engine reduces the bit rate of lower priority sections before those with higher priority.

The semantic metadata used in the preceding examples can be considered as very high-level, and coarse-grained. That is, it identifies relatively large segments of content, using concepts with a high level of abstraction from the digital representation of the content. In the first case, heuristic methods are proposed to automatically classify content segments, with a precision of 83% to 96% Bertini et al. (2006).

Baba et al. (2004) propose adaptation of speech signals on the basis of a much lower-level semantic concept: sound volume. They argue that regions of (relative) silence within a speech signal carry no *semantic information*, and as such may be truncated during playback. In fact, this feature of speech[1] may be used to guide adaptation, allowing regions of silence to be constrained to a zero bit rate (or as close as the scalable codec or synchronization scheme will allow) with no perceptible loss of fidelity.

Cranley & Murphy (2006) suggest further low-level semantics that may be used to optimize delivery. They use measures of the temporal and spatial complexity to trade-off frame rate with resolution for scalable codecs, to achieve a so-called Optimum Adaptation Trajectory.

The semantic-aware content delivery framework proposed in this chapter provides a way to incorporate these and other semantics into the delivery of multimedia. This is achieved in a way that is flexible enough to support the increasingly diverse range of formats, semantics, and networks that are used (or useful) for content delivery (Brightman, 2005). Before a detailed discussion of this framework, Section 3 (below) identifies a number of key features that are necessary for the framework to successfully address the challenges posed by this diversity. The proposed framework itself is then detailed in Section 4, along with an analysis of existing work that is able to fulfil some constituent parts. Section 5 describes subjective testing validating the approach, and Section 6 offers some concluding remarks.

## 3. Features

Multimedia semantics is an extremely diverse field. Similarly, multimedia delivery is categorised by an exponentially growing array of devices that access and process multimedia,

[1] or audio, although silence is less prevalent there

and an increasing number of formats in which multimedia content is encoded. Given this complexity, this section argues that sucessfully combining semantics and delivery requires a flexible approach, where the semantics and formats used are not hard-coded, but instead described declaratively as content metadata.

### 3.1 Format-independence

The present, exponential rate of growth in both multimedia devices (hardware and software) and content formats is increasing the difficulty of maintaining interoperability. To be effective in this environment, a semantic-aware delivery framework must support content that is encoded in any current, or future, format. As has been shown (Thomas-Kerr et al., 2008), for many multimedia operations, it is possible to abstract the format-specific details of any given codec into a data file (hardware and software is then format-independent). This greatly simplifies interoperability, since a new content format can be integrated into existing devices merely by dissemninating a file that describes its format-specific details. Crucially (given the exponential growth in the range and diversity of multimedia devices) no modification of hardware or software is necessary.

This argument also holds for the syntax in which semantic metadata is encoded; as discussed (Section 4.2.2 on page 12) there are many syntaxes used to encode the metadata needed for semantic-aware delivery. Further, as is the case for content formats, the framework must also cope with new metadata formats, as they are developed. In response to these observations, methods for adapting metadata syntax without requiring changes to software or hardware have been proposed (Thomas-Kerr et al., 2006) and are important to allow a semantic-aware delivery framework to be as widely applicable as possible.

### 3.2 Semantic-independence

The range of semantics that people associate with media content is effectively infinite. The examples cited in Section 2 therefore represent just a small sample of the possibilities for using semantics to guide multimedia delivery. As such, it is important that a semantic-aware delivery framework not be limited to using a small, defined set of concepts.

### 3.3 Multiple optimisation algorithms

As will be seen in Section 4.1, a considerable number of algorithms have been developed for optimising the Rate-Distortion (R-D) performance of multimedia delivery (Chakareski et al., 2004a; Chou, 2006; Cranley & Murphy, 2006; Eichhorn, 2006). These algorithms vary in their guarantees of tractability, complexity, and the range of metadata required as inputs to the process. As a result, different algorithms may be preferable in certain scenarios, and so flexibility in this regard is an important characteristic of a semantic-aware delivery framework.

### 3.4 Segmentation and association

The examples cited in Section 2 on page 2 differentiate the semantic importance of segments of content that have been segmented along numerous axes. The most straightforward is with the sporting analysis and speech sound-level concepts, where some *temporal* segments are more important than others. This is also the case in the news example, but here a distinction is also made along the *mode* axis: in some temporal segments the video has more semantic importance, in other segments it is the audio. Cranley et al. (2003) distinguish

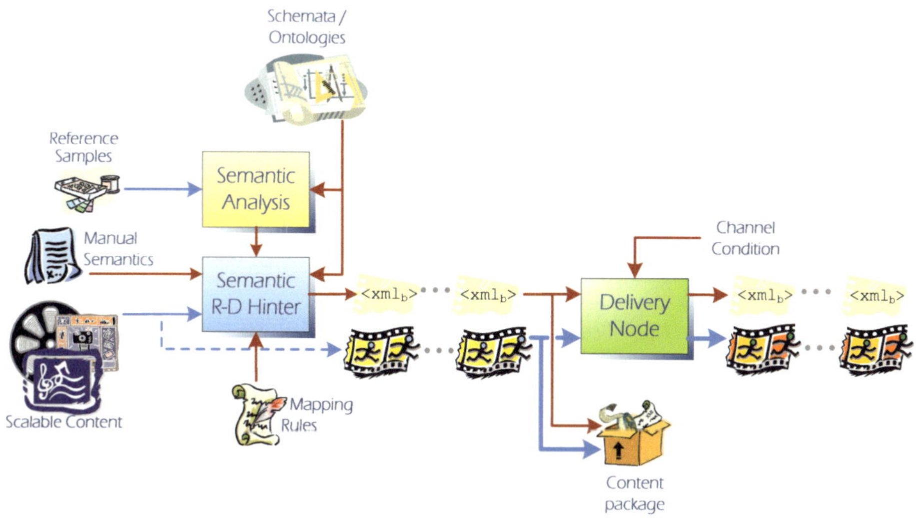


Fig. 3. An architecture for Mulimedia Delivery that incorporates content semantics

between semantic importance along the *temporal* and *spatial* axes. Although it has not been widely utilised, MPEG-4 (ISO/IEC, 2004b) generalises this concept still further by introducing other modes (text, graphics, and hybrid coding), and additionally provides the ability to arrange multiple audiovisual "objects" within a scene. In such a scenario, it may be highly advantageous to attach (time-varying) semantic importance to each of these modes and objects.

Clearly, the utility of a semantic delivery framework would depend considerably on it having the flexibility to segment content along all of these (and potentially other) dimensions. After segmentation, such a framework would need to be able to associate semantic and other metadata with these segments, in such a way that they can be input to an algorithm that makes the trade-offs described.

## 4. A framework for format-independent semantic-aware multimedia delivery

Figure 3 depicts the proposed architecture of a semantic-aware delivery framework. As proposed by Chakareski et al. (2004b), the Rate-Distortion Optimisation (RDO) process is split into two parts: generation of R-D metadata is performed offline by a *hinter*, minimising the amount of computation that must be done by the real-time *delivery node*. The present work extends this concept by proposing an architecture for the hinter that is format-independent, for the reasons outlined earlier in Section 3. Additionally, the hinter in Figure 3 provides for *Semantic Distortion* (see below, Section 4.2.2 on page 12) to be combined with the "classical" approach to distortion where decoded samples are compared to the samples that were originally encoded, using a measure such as (peak-)SNR, referred to as *Sample Distortion*.

### 4.1 Delivery node

With the static content analysis performed offline by a hinter, a delivery node (Figure 4 on the next page) is left only to decide whether and when to forward, drop or truncate (where applicable) each packet. That decision is made on the basis of some type of rate-distortion

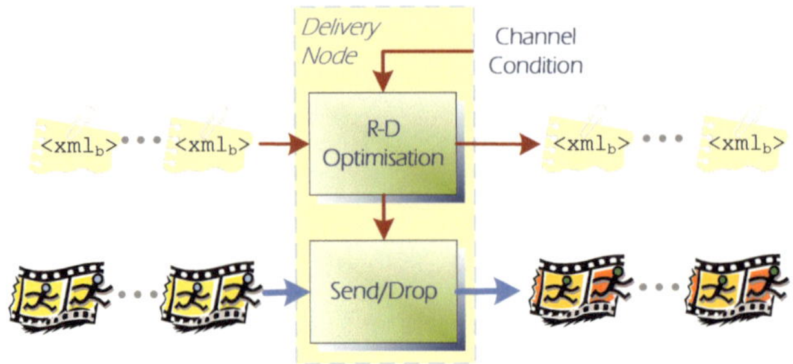


Fig. 4. A delivery node uses content hints to perform R-D optimisation

optimisation algorithm, which takes as its inputs feedback about the channel condition, and metadata from the semantic hinter. These elements are described in the following sections.

#### 4.1.1 R-D optimisation

There are a number of rate-distortion optimisation algorithms. Different algorithms perform better in particular scenarios, and so this semantic-aware framework avoids prescribing one over another. Instead, the framework allows the most suitable algorithm(s) to be implemented on any given delivery node.

Chou (2006) proposes the use of classical optimisation of R-D performance $D(R)$ by minimising the Lagrangian $D + \lambda R$ for some $\lambda$. The formulation of distortion must consider the error probability-cost functions for each unit of data, as well as the interdependencies between Data Units, since descendent packets (e.g. any motion-compensated frame, or enhancement layers in SVC) generally cannot be decoded if their ancestors are not received.

Chakareski et al. (2004a) note that although the algorithm proposed by Chou is theoretically optimal and suitable for certain applications, it comes at the cost of significant computational complexity. Consequently, Chakareski proposes a low-complexity approximation of the lagrangian optimisation problem, by ignoring interdependencies between Data Units and instead assuming that distortion from packet loss on subsequent packets is additive.

Eichhorn (2006) suggests the opposite approximation: Chakareski ignores actual dependencies; Eichhorn ignores actual distortions, and asserts that dependency alone may be sufficient. Finally, Cranley & Murphy (2006) trade temporal resolution against spatial resolution and use subjective testing to arrive at a so-called Optimum Adaptation Trajectory.

#### 4.1.2 Serialisation of hinter metadata

On the one hand, a binary syntax could be specified for hinter metadata, in order to maximise space efficiency over-the-wire[2]. However, this makes extension of the data set (as is likely inevitable as new optimisation techniques are developed) difficult to achieve without breaking existing implementations. For this and other reasons, most recent metadata uses XML rather than binary syntax, because of the ease with which it is processed and parsed, despite its inherent verbosity. As it turns out, it is possible to achieve most of the benefits of both, using the so-called Binary format for Metadata (BiM) (Niedermeier et al., 2002). BiM uses XML Schema to provide efficient binary encodings of XML data. This means that the R-D metadata can be created and processed as XML, but if it must be transmitted, BiM can achieve

[2] That is, when this metadata must be transmitted on-the-wire, which is only the case if the Delivery Node is remote from the content, for example if it is a gateway node.

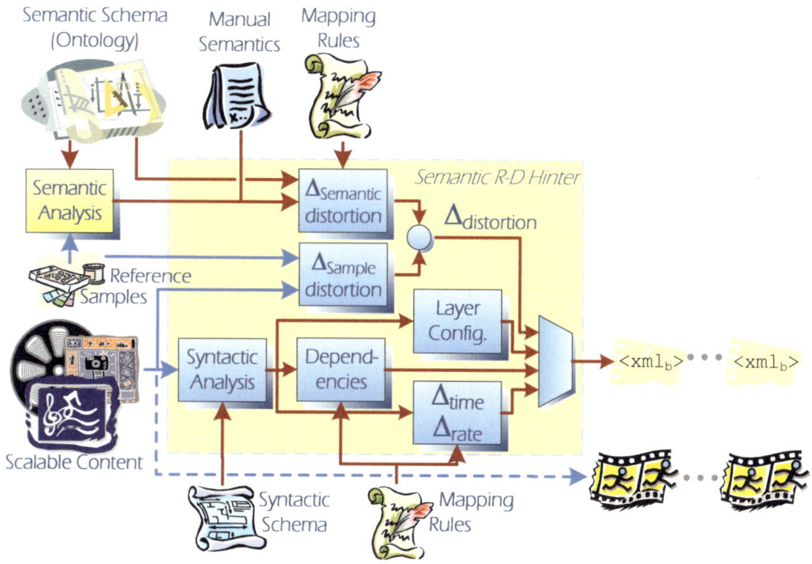


Fig. 5. The semantic hinter computes R-D metadata based on content syntax and semantics

transmission efficiencies close to those of a dedicated binary syntax. Furthermore, at the downstream node, the binary representation may be parsed directly, without decompression, avoiding any additional time complexity.

### 4.1.3 Summary

In deciding whether to forward or drop each packet as it is received, the Delivery Node utilises some sort of optimisation algorithm. Several of these were discussed above (Section 4.1.1). Depending on the algorithm chosen, different metadata is required from the R-D Hinter, although a common subset of data including $\Delta_{time}$, $\Delta_{rate}$ and segmentation is required for the forward/drop routine. Otherwise, this metadata may contain the set of distortion increments $\Delta D_l$, the Data Unit dependence graph, or Spatial Information (SI) and Temporal Information (TI) values[3]. This also points to the need for a negotiation process between the Delivery Node and the node holding the content to identify the desired optimisation algorithm based on the available metadata, although in some cases a node may be able to generate missing metadata on-the-fly (with the concordant time penalty).

If the Delivery Node is remote from the content and metadata, for example if it is a gateway node that spans two heterogeneous networks, then it may be desirable to minimise the bandwidth used by the R-D metadata, by utilising BiM (Niedermeier et al., 2002) to binarise the data. In this case, the Delivery Node would use a BiM parser that directly interprets the binarised metadata and passes the output data points directly to the RDO algorithm.

### 4.2 Semantic R-D hinter

The role of the hinter (Figure 5) is to prepare the metadata needed by the R-D Optimisation algorithm. This metadata can then be stored in a file (such as an ISO (ISO/IEC, 2005a) or Quicktime (Apple, 2001) container) for later use, or transmitted with the content to a local or remote delivery node. The hinter itself is composed by elements that analyse the semantics

[3] refer to Cranley & Murphy (2006) for a detailed discussion of these parameters.

and the syntax of the content. The former (semantic analysis) obtains the higher-level characteristics of the content which are typically not evident in the compressed domain, but must be identified from the original (reference) samples or entered manually. Section 4.2.2 on page 12 considers semantic analysis in greater detail. On the other hand, syntactic analysis (discussed in Section 4.2.1) extracts the interdependency, temporal and scalability metadata that are direct parameters of the compressed bitstream.

### 4.2.1 Syntactic analysis

Syntactic analysis is the process by which the hinter exposes the syntactical elements of multimedia that are needed by a given RDO algorithm. This occurs in two stages. First, the underlying syntactic structure of the content must be exposed so as to provide access to the internal data fields. In this work, *binary schemata* (Thomas-Kerr et al., 2007) are used to achieve this functionality. Secondly, a *mapping* must be made from the arbitrary raw data fields exposed by a schema, to the specific concepts needed for RDO.

#### Binary Schemata

Recent coding formats utilise increasingly complex multi-layer structures to encode media in ever-fewer bits. As a result, identifying the timestamp, interdependencies or even byte-boundaries of an encoded Data Unit requires significant parsing. In most systems, this parsing is performed by format-specific software or hardware, that is, the format of the codec is "hard coded" into the parser. However, because the number of coding formats is large and growing, such a hard-coded approach makes it increasingly difficult to maintain interoperability with the available coded content.
An alternative is to use a reconfigurable or generic parser for syntactic analysis, where the specific syntax of individual codecs is stored in a schema *data file*. Support for additional formats may then be added via a new file, rather than new hardware or software. While there are numerous syntax description languages (such as the common EBNF (Klint et al., 2005)), only a few of which provide sufficient expressivity to function as a schema language for a generic parser (see Thomas-Kerr, Janneck, Mattavelli, Burnett & Ritz (2007)): BSDL and XFlavor (Hong & Eleftheriadis, 2002) (and a hybrid of the two—BFlavor (Neve et al., 2006)).
Any of these languages are suitable for syntax schemata in the model. Each provides an XML "view" of binary data which can be used to construct the rules required for further analysis. In XFlavor and BFlavor there is a level of indirection between the binary schema and the XML schema, whereas in BSDL they are one and the same: a BSDL Schema is an augmented XML Schema (Thompson et al., 2004).
Lehti & Fankhauser (2004) show that the object-based structure of XML Schemata (and the XML data they describe) means that it is possible to map from XML Schema complex and simple types (which directly or indirectly represent binary structures in the case of a BSDL Schema) to OWL classes and properties (respectively).
This approach is far from elegant, because XML Schemata describe syntax whereas OWL (Dean & Schreiber, 2004) and RDF (Beckett, 2004) describe semantics, and mixing the two in this way can lead to significant ambiguity. Nonetheless, it is useful, since combining it with one of the binary schemata languages described above allows binary data to be directly integrated with OWL/RDF-based data). This means that binary content may be processed and queried as if it were RDF triples. Figure 6 on the next page depicts an example of the

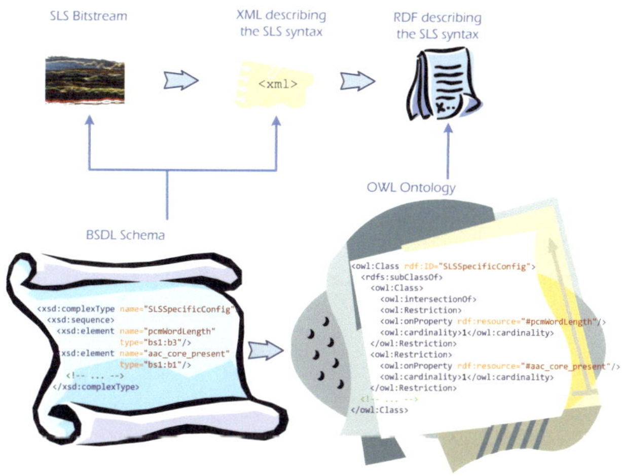


Fig. 6. A binary schema can be used to expose the structure and data of a bitstream as OWL/RDF

approach. A BSDL schema describes the binary structure of an SLS bitstream (the example shows an SLSSpecificConfig structure (ISO/IEC, 2005b)). At the same time, this BSDL schema describes the structure of an XML representation of the syntax of the binary bitstream. Lehti's technique is then used to map the BSDL/XML schema into OWL classes, and to map the XML metadata into RDF triples. This allows the binary structure of the SLS bitstream, along with the data it contains, to be reasoned on and combined with other OWL/RDF semantic metadata. [4]

## Mapping Rules

The metadata exposed by using a binary schema will be specific to the format that the schema describes (e.g. SLS, Flash, SVC). In order to use this metadata in a semantic-aware delivery framework, it is necessary to be able to map from the format-specific structures exposed by the binary schema, to the set of format-independent metadata needed by the RDO algorithm being used. The list of metadata required will vary depending on the particular RDO algorithm being used, but will generally include items such as

- segmentation of the content into Data Units;
- decoding interdependencies between Data Units; and
- temporal relations between Data Units;

One such set of mapping rules may be used to describe the extraction of RDO metadata from SLS bitstreams, while another set of mappings describe the process for Flash, and a third for H.264/SVC (as shown – Figure 7).

[4] It should also be noted that BSDL allows the bitstream to be described at whatever level is required, in order to avoid unnecessary verbosity. That is, if the reasoning to be performed requires only that the binary data be split into frames, then the BSDL Schema may be written in such a way that it emits a single XML element per frame. On the other hand, if certain fields within a frame are necessary for reasoning (such as a timestamp, sample rate, etc.) then the schema is able to expose these fields without showing the entire detail of the inside of a frame. See (Thomas-Kerr et al., 2007) for more information.

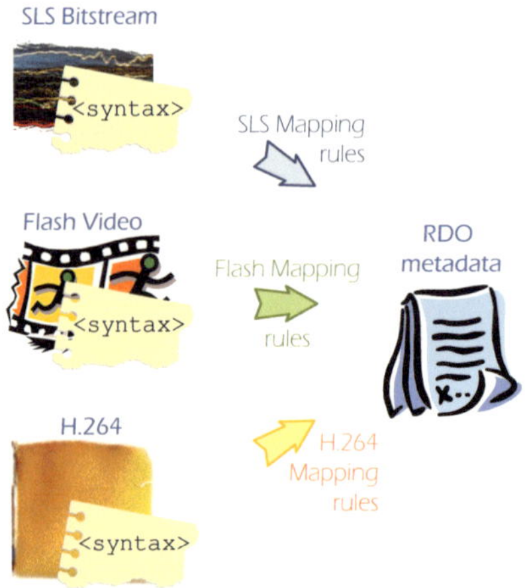


Fig. 7. Mapping rules can be used to translate from format-specific structures into the format-independent metadata needed for a semantic-aware RDO delivery framework

```
<xsd:element name="pic_parameter_set_rbsp">
  <xsd:annotation><xsd:appinfo>
    <bs2x:variable name="pps" bs2x:position="pic_parameter_set_id + 1"/>
  </xsd:appinfo></xsd:annotation>
  <xsd:complexType>
    <xsd:sequence>
      <xsd:element name="pic_parameter_set_id" type="bs1:unsignedExpGolomb"/>
      <xsd:element name="seq_parameter_set_id" type="bs1:unsignedExpGolomb"/>
      <!-- ... -->
    </xsd:sequence>
    <xsd:attribute ref="rdo:ancestors" bs0:value="for $spsID in svc:seq_parameter_set_id return $svc:sps
    [$spsID+1]/../@rdo:id"/>
  </xsd:complexType>
</xsd:element>
```

**Listing 1.** Augmented BSDL test schema exposing the ancestor Data Units of an SVC PPS

A number of options exist for expressing such rules:

➢ **In the binary domain:** A BSDL Schema may be extended so that it appends attributes to the output which correspond to the needed RDO content features (size, dependencies, etc). The advantage of this approach is that the description of how these features are extracted from the binary data is very concise. The disadvantage is that this description is embedded in the BSDL Schema and is therefore tightly coupled, limiting reusability.

Listing 1 is an example of this approach. It shows part of a BSDL schema that outputs an rdo:ancestors attribute expressing the interdependency of Data Units[5]. Thus, attribute declarations like this are one way to provide mapping rules from the format-specific binary structure of the schema, to the format-independent concepts needed for RDO (which are represented by members of the rdo namespace).

[5] The for structure used by the attribute value specification is not a loop, but rather a workaround for the fact that XPath does not have a current() function (cf. the sps variable in Listing 3).

```
<xsl:template match="pps">
  <xsl:variable name="sps"
    select="preceding::sps[seq_parameter_set_id =
                              current()/seq_parameter_set_id][1]"/>
  <xsl:copy>
    <xsl:attribute name="rdo:ancestors" select="$sps/@rdo:groupID"/>
  </xsl:copy>
</xsl:template>
```

**Listing 3.** XSLT fragment annotating pps elements with ancestor metadata

- **In the XML domain:** A second option is to describe the identification of the necessary features using XQuery (Boag et al., 2007) or an XSLT (Clark, 1999) stylesheet. This removes the tight coupling with the BSDL Schema, but is less succint, and adds an additional layer of complexity to the process. Listing 3 shows a fragment of an XSLT stylesheet that adds the same rdo:ancestors attribute to a BSDL description.
- **In the semantic domain:** Alternatively, the BSDL Schema may be directly converted to OWL classes, allowing the feature identification process to be specified using an ontological reasoning tool such as the Semantic Web Rule Language (SWRL) (Horrocks et al., 2004). One disadvantage of this approach is that RDF is inherently unordered, and so Data Unit order must be explicitly imposed using sequence numbers, timestamps or the like. Furthermore, some assertions about the order of such sequence numbers are non-monotonic (see for example Listing 4).

  Examples of mapping rules using SWRL are (the prefix svc is used for the BSDL Schema, and rdo for the RDO ontology):

  $$\text{svc:nalUnit(?x)} \rightarrow \text{rdo:dataUnit(?x)} \qquad \ldots(2)$$

  which implies that a Network Abstraction Layer (NAL) Unit is an atomic unit of data for the purposes of RDO. This deceptively simple rule is in fact making use of the inheritance properties afforded by SWRL and the semantic web, since there are no direct instances of svc:nalUnit within an svc instance, but rather it is the abstract superclass of all other top-level objects in an SVC stream. This inheritance is unavailable to an XSLT-based rule (e.g. Listing 3), where separate rules must be specified for each instance type); and Listing 4 which (almost) states that a Picture Parameter Set (PPS) has a dependency to the *most recent SPS with an ID that matches the one given in the PPS*. If multiple SPS' with the given ID are present in the bitstream prior to the PPS, then rule 4 on the next page will incorrectly match all of them. The missing constraint—"most recent"—is nonmonotonic and hence not supported by SWRL or OWL-DL[6]. Consequently, an XML-based approach has been applied to the mapping rules for syntactic parameters in the example system implemented in this work (see Section 5 on page 19). Future work on SWRL and/or other Semantic Web rule languages may provide the expressivity needed for this and other rules required for RDO parameters.

Examples of mapping rules for $\Delta_{rate}$ and $\Delta_{time}$ are given in Section 5 on page 19.

[6] The missing "most recent" constraint is specified in the XSLT example (Listing 3) by the preceeding:: axis and [1] predicate

```
svc:pps(?pps) ∧ svc:spsID(?pps,?spsID) ∧ svc:sps(?sps) ∧ svc:spsID(?sps,?spsID) ∧
svc:seqNo(?pps,?ppsSeqNo) ∧ svc:seqNo(?sps,?spsSeqNo) ∧ swrlb:lessThan(?spsSeqNo,?ppsSeqNo)
                    → rdo:dependsOn(?pps,?sps)
```

**Listing 4.** A not-quite-complete rule for specifying the interdependency between a PPS and the SPS it references

#### 4.2.2 Semantic analysis

The aim of semantic analysis is to generate metadata that can subsequently be reasoned on to compute Semantic Distortion. There are many options for generating and obtaining semantic metadata, as discussed below. Crucially, there are also several disparate widely-used methods for serialising this metadata (RDF (Beckett, 2004), XML (Bray et al., 2008), as well as numerous binary forms (ISO/IEC, 2002b; Matroska, n.d.; Nilsson, 2000)). To be able to reason on such metadata (in order to compute Semantic Distortion) it must generally be translated into a single form. There are several options for this, but for the sake of brevity, and because it is the most powerful option for semantic reasoning, this section will focus on translation of binary and XML metadata into RDF/OWL.

**Generating the desired content semantics**

The first stage of semantic analysis involves extracting the desired semantics from the content (e.g. "this scene depicts the studio anchor discussing the news story"—see Figure 9 on page 17). As described in the introduction, this remains a challenging problem, with many efforts directed toward algorithms able to expose various specific semantics for media content. This process typically uses the uncompressed samples of the original content and (partly because of the volume of this data) can be very computationally expensive (Figure 5 on page 7). While such semantic metadata may not be specifically designed for the delivery process, it can often, nonetheless, contribute to it. For either of these reasons the semantic analysis may often be performed asynchrononously to the operation of the RDO-hinter. Further, much semantic metadata is presently annotated by hand, consider Flickr/Youtube tags, or iTunes song ratings, for example.

Whether semantic metadata is the result of an (a)synchronous analysis step or manual annotation, the result is a set of metadata about the content that is expressed in some machine-processable form. Such metadata is increasingly specified using ontologies, which simplify the integration of heterogeneous data sources as well as the reuse of information for applications other than those for which it was first developed (Naphade et al., 2006). However, this is far from universal, and a great deal of existing semantic metadata is stored as XML or binary data (see, for example, (ISO/IEC, 2002b; Matroska, n.d.; Nilsson, 2000)).

**Translating XML metadata**

As discussed earlier (Section 4.2.1), it is possible to map XML-Schema-based metadata directly into the semantic domain (Lehti & Fankhauser, 2004). This may be imprecise—it is generally possible to express the same semantics using several different XML structures (e.g. element

```
time:DateTimeInterval(?dti) ^ dolce:HAPPENS-AT(?com, ?dti) ^
cyc:languageUsed(?com, cyc:EnglishLanguage) ^
swrlx:makeOWLThing(?sd,?dti) ^ swrlx:makeOWLThing(?sdq,?dti)

        →

rdo:hasDistortion(?com, ?sd) ^ rdo:SemanticDistortion(?sd) ^
dolce:HAS-QUALE(?sd, rdo:Multiplicative) ^
dolce:HAS-QUALE(?sd, ?sdq) ^ rdo:ContinuousQuale(?sdq) ^
rdo:hasMagnitude(?sdq, 2)
```

select all intervals where the language used is English

create new entities for SD

associate the new entities with each interval

see section 3.2.2

specify a magnitude of 2 for the SD of each interval where the language used is english

**Listing 5**. A SWRL rule that specifies the Semantic Distortion of English Communication

content vs attributes)[7]. An alternative proposed by Hunter is to use an upper-level ontology (Hunter, 2001), which is more robust, specifically because it involves a time-consuming manual mapping from the (implicit) semantics underlying the XML representation to a set of explicit ontological relations. Both of these approaches are feasible for a semantic-aware delivery framework.

### Translating binary metadata

There are a number of very widely used binary formats for semantic metadata: ID3 (Nilsson, 2000), EXIF (JEITA, 2002), and MPEG-4/Quicktime (Apple, 2001; ISO/IEC, 2004b) for instance. In this case, a syntactic analysis of this metadata must precede further processing of the semantics themselves. This syntactic analysis can be performed in the same manner that interdependencies and other constructs are exposed (Section 4.2.1). This will yield an XML description of the structure of the metadata, including the name and value of all of the desired metadata fields. This XML may then be mapped into the semantic domain, as above.

### Computation of Semantic Distortion

This is the second stage of semantic analysis, and is one of the central contributions of this work. *Semantic Distortion* (SD) is defined as a measure of the "SNR" between the intended semantic (meaning) of the content before it is encoded, as compared to the semantics conveyed by the content that is rendered for its recipient(s). The contribution to Semantic Distortion that this chapter is primarily concerned with is that contributed by the delivery process, however the approach may also potentially be useful for other aspects of multimedia processing.

[7] In contrast, when Section 4.2.1 discussed mapping *BSDL Schema* to an ontology, there was no such imprecision. BSDL has already restricted the expressivity of XML Schema in order to guarantee an unambiguous mapping between the binary and XML domain and back again. As a result, mapping BSDL into the semantic domain is also unambiguous.

Clearly, this notion of Semantic Distortion is highly subjective (as indeed are many of the semantics of any given piece of media content). However, even approximations of Semantic Distortion as perceived by parties on the server-side of the process possess substantial value for optimising the delivery of the content semantics, as shown in Section 5 on page 19.
Given this definition of Semantic Distortion, it is possible to define a series of rules that map from concepts expressed in semantic metadata to a quantitative measure of SD. Although the content of mapping rules for SD will differ from those of syntactic analysis (see 4.2.1 on page 8), they have the same range of options for specification: directly within a (binary) schema, in the XML domain, or in the ontological domain. In contrast to the aforementioned syntactic mappings, SD rules translate readily into SWRL, such as Listing 5[8] which states that if there is an instance of *Communicating* during a certain time interval that uses the *English Language*, then the magnitude of the Semantic Distortion for that interval is doubled[9]. This rule covers both spoken communication (in which case the SD is associated with the audio track(s)), and visual communication (e.g. subtitles; where the SD is applied to the video).

### Combination of Semantic Distortion with sample distortion

This is pivotal to the correct operation of the R-D optimisation algorithm. Chou (2006) considers Sample Distortion to be *additive*, that is, the overall distortion $D(\pi)$ is a large initial value $D_0$ less the sum of the distortion of all packets $D_l$ *received and useful* (which are computed by the product sequence):[10]

$$D(\pi) = D_0 - \sum_l \Delta D_l \prod_{l' \preceq l} (1 - \epsilon(\pi_{l'})) \quad \ldots(6)$$

However, the sample distortions used in Equation 6 are all measured according to a single algorithm, and hence have the same scaling and are directly comparable. This is not usually the case for Semantic Distortion, and is certainly not so when comparing Semantic Distortion with Sample Distortion. Instead, it is proposed that Semantic Distortion be considered to be *multiplicative*; that is, that SD represents a weighting factor that may be applied to a value of sample distortion for a packet, or group of packets. There are several motivations for this:

- First, multiplicative combination obviates the need for normalisation based on potentially unknown response curves for distortion algorithms (both sample and semantic). For example, say a Data Unit has a Sample Distortion with a magnitude of 0.3 dB, and a Semantic Distortion (based on the language of the communication) of magnitude 2. It is clear that these values cannot be combined additively without ensuring that they are first normalised to the same scale. However, while sample distortion uses objective measurements such as (P)SNR, the same cannot in general be said of

[8] where cyc: refers to the CYC upper-level ontology (Matuszek et al., 2006), time: to the OWL-Time ontology (Pan & Hobbs, 2004), dolce: to the DOLCE ontology (Gangemi et al., 2002), and rdo: to the ontology defined in 4.3 on the facing page. Note that the use of Cyc, OWL-Time, and DOLCE are not intended to be normative, they are used merely as an example of how to define mapping rules for SD.

[9] Note that the factor of 2 is in this case relatively arbitrary—yet still shown to be useful (Section 5)—see Section 6.1 on page 23 for a discussion about possible future work on methods for evaluating Semantic Distortion.

[10] where $l' \preceq l$ selects all packets $l'$ that are ancestors of $l$ as well as $l$ itself, $\pi$ is the vector of packet transmission policies, and $\epsilon$ the error/delay probability distribution for any given policy

subjective measurements of Semantic Distortion. Even though there are numerous quantitative measures (see for example ITU-T (1998)), comparison between data from different quantitative tests is challenging. Furthermore, Semantic Distortion is intended to encompass a wide range of data, as discussed (Section 2), beyond formal subjective testing. Combining disparate data sets multiplicitively avoids this need to normalise.

- Combination of several *Semantic Distortion* data-sets relating to a piece of content typically has similar issues relating to normalisation. Consider, with the above example, the addition of a second Semantic Distortion data set computed from Temporal Information (TI). The SD for the Data Unit in question has a magnitude of 0.7. Combining this datum with the others is straightforward as a scaling factor (i.e. multiplicative).
- Finally, multiplicative combination retains a known zero point. This is important if either sample or any Semantic Distortion has a magnitude of zero; in the first case, this indicates that the packet has no effect on the reconstruction of the signal; in the second, that it does not convey any semantics. Either way, these features must be transmitted to the output distortion value.

### 4.3 An Ontology for Semantic Distortion

The mapping process described in Section 4.2.2 on page 12 requires the definition of appropriate concepts to be used as the destination of the rules. These concepts fall into two categories: the formal definition of a Data Unit in so far as it pertains to R-D optimisation, and the definition of Semantic Distortion itself. These are described below in Sections 4.3.1 and 4.3.2, respectively. These definitions and their associated concepts are attached to the DOLCE (Gangemi et al., 2002) upper-level ontology, because of its precise separation of fundamental concepts[11]. Figure 8 on the following page depicts the Semantic Distortion ontology (prefixed by sd) along with its DOLCE ancestors (prefixed by dolce). Refer to (Gangemi et al., 2002) for a full treatment of DOLCE; the following description should suffice for this work.

The fundamental distinction in DOLCE is between *enduring* and *perduring* entities (Figure 8). The precise philosophical definition of these terms is complex and also somewhat controversial (Gangemi et al., 2002), but for the purpose of this chapter it will suffice to say that the former are entities that *exist* in some region of time (and possibly space), whereas the latter are events that *occur* during a region of (space-)time. Both endurants and perdurants have *qualities*, and a distinction is made between a quality (e.g. color, temperature) and its *quale*—a region defining the "value space" of a particular quality (e.g. red, 298K). This is partly inspired by the fact that an endurant individual will permanently have particular quality individuals (i.e. it will always have *a* color), but the value of those qualities may change over time. Quales belong to the class of all *abstract* concepts that are neither endurant nor perdurant.

While DOLCE includes the abstract notions of a temporal quality and a temporal region, RDO requires a more concrete conceptualisation of time in order to be able to synchronise semantic metadata with the underlying media Data Units. Furthermore, the metadata that a semantic-aware delivery framework must assimilate will have a large variety of fundamentally different representations of time:

- MPEG-7 (ISO/IEC, 2002a);
- SMPTE (of Motion Picture & Engineers, 1999);

[11] As described previously (Section 4.2.2 on page 12), the choice of DOLCE is not normative but rather a preferred embodiment

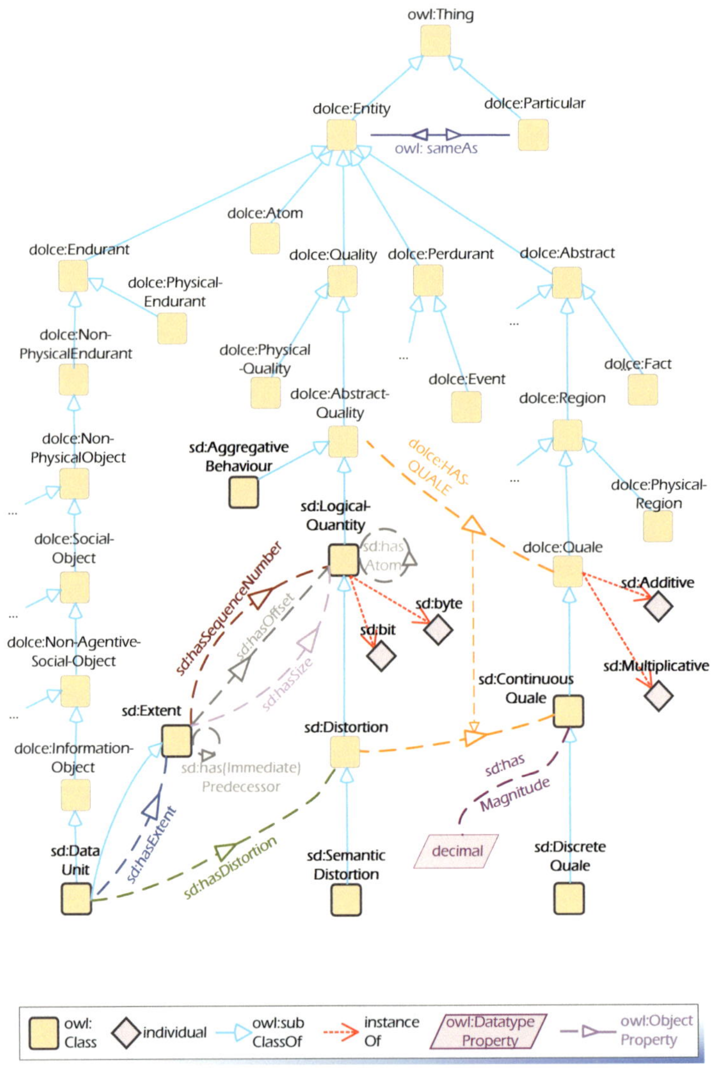


Fig. 8. An ontology for Semantic Distortion

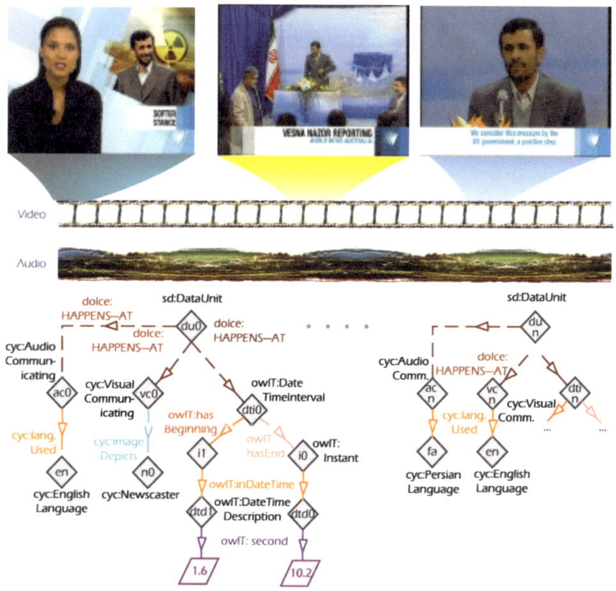


Fig. 9. Example of the semantic annotation of an Audio-Visual Clip

- ➢ XML Schema (*XML Schema Part 2: Datatypes Second Edition*, 2004);
- ➢ OWL Time (Hobbs & Pan, 2006); as well as
- ➢ the innumerable binary syntaxes used by media formats.

Each representation uses a different syntax to represent time. If these are to be reasoned on as part of semantic-aware delivery, methods are required to translate from one to another.
Throughout the proceeding discussion, the example shown in Figure 9[12] will be used to illustrate each concept. The example consists of a short Audio-Visual clip that forms part of a news article on events in the Middle-East[13]. The first part of the clip depicts a studio presenter introducing the story (the temporal interval containing this section is described by an owlT:DateTimeInterval, and the visual and aural communication features with cyc:(Visual/Audio)Communicating). Subsequently, contextual footage is shown of the subject walking to the podium while an off-screen narrator continues the story. Finally, the subject speaks in Persian with English subtitles appearing below (using similar owlT:DateTimeInterval and cyc:(Visual/Audio)Communicating instances). These features are annotated via CYC (Matuszek et al., 2006) classes and properties and then reasoned on using mapping rules (Listing 4).

#### 4.3.1 Data units

For the purposes of R-D Optimisation, Chou (2006) designates an atomic segment of data as a DataUnit, where each packet on the network may contain at most one Data Unit. Rule 2 on page 11 is an example of the use of DataUnit, showing how it enables format-independence

---

[12] Individual IDs used in Figures 9–10 are used purely to differentiate individuals from each other. The general naming scheme used for these IDs is to abbreviate the *type name* of the individual and append a number which increments from 0, 1. . . n for each type. For example, the first instance of the Owl-Time class DateTimeInterval in Figure 9 has the ID dti0.

[13] This clip was used by permission from SBS World News Australia.

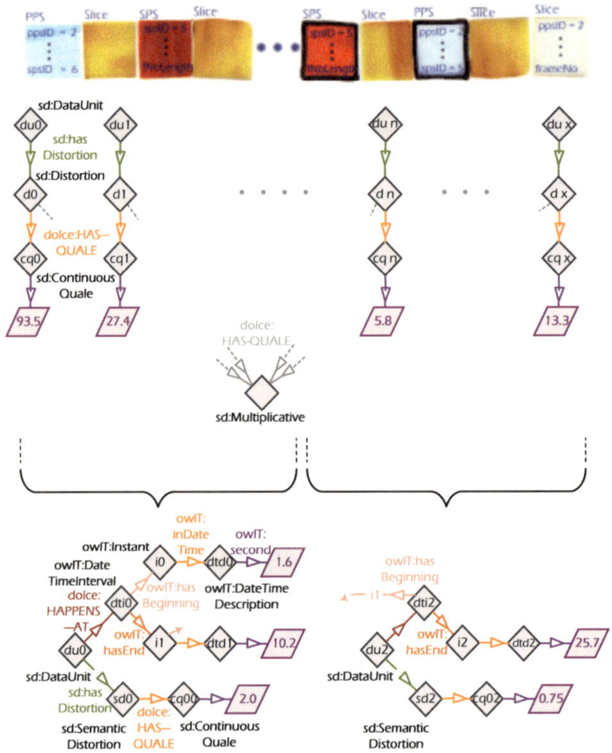


Fig. 10. Example instances of SD classes describing the distortion of a H.264/AVC bitstream

by mapping from arbitrary format-based structures to a single interface for RDO. Figure 10 depicts an example H.264/SVC bitstream, along with instances of the Semantic Distortion classes that deliniate the Data Units in the stream.

### 4.3.2 Distortion

Distortion is the other central concept in RDO. It is a type of Logical Quantity that measures "the amount by which the distortion at the receiver will decrease if the Data Unit is decoded (on time)" (Chou, 2006). Distortion has at least two distinct types: sample and semantic, which were described earlier (Section 4.2.2 on page 12). Distortion in general has a continuous value-space (continuousQuale), which in turn has a data-type property hasMagnitude. Distortion also has an hasAggregativeBehaviour property (this relation is not shown), which may be Additive or Multiplicative. It is left to the user to decide which behaviour(s) to assign.
Figure 10 shows an example of the distortion instances for a bitstream. In this example, each NAL unit in a H.264 bitstream is given a sample-based distortion according to its contribution to a scheme (for example that proposed by Chou (2006))—these are the DataUnit, Distortion and Quale individuals toward the top of the figure. In this instance, SemanticDistortion applies to more coarsely-grained Data Units. These are specified using OWL-Time intervals (by mapping from the intervals previously shown in Figure 9 on the preceding page). Each instance of Semantic Distortion intersects many Data Units in the actual media. Assigning Semantic Distortion to individual media Data Units is done by the mapping rules associated with syntactic analysis (Section 4.2.1, above).

### 4.4 Summary

In summary (refer to Figure 1 on page 2), there are three primary components to the proposed semantic-aware multimedia delivery framework:

- a *hinter*, which computes all of the content-based metadata offline;
- a *delivery node* which is left with as little work to do as possible, since the hinter has already performed much of the necessary computation. The delivery node simply forwards or drops each packet as it arrives, based on some optimisation algorithm; and
- *semantic analysis*, used to provide the hinter with metadata that can be used to compute *Semantic Distortion*.

The novelty of this work consists in tying semantic analysis and semantic metadata to the R-D hinter, as well as an architecture for this hinter so that it operates in a format-independent manner. More specifically, the work contributes:

(a) the definition of *Semantic Distortion* (SD) (Section 4.2.2 on page 12);

(b) an ontology for RDO concepts and for SD that enables it to be inferred from arbitrary semantics, and then combined with sample distortion (Section 4.3 on page 15);

(c) extension of the concept of an R-D Hinter to encompass SD (Section 4.2 on page 7);

(d) a format-independent architecture for the semantic hinter, which operates by extracting all format-specific details into declarative data (schemata and mapping rules). It is argued that this is imperative to allow the increasingly diverse range of formats and devices to interoperate (Section 4.2.1 on page 8); and

(e) a semantic-independent architecture for the hinter, again accomplished by using schemata (ontologies) and mapping rules (Section 4.2.2 on page 12);

## 5. Subjective testing

### 5.1 Methodology

Double-blind, randomised subjective testing was used to validate the hypothesis that the use of Semantic Distortion can improve multimedia delivery. The scenario used for these tests was a mobile environment—where channel characteristics are often highly variable, and handset capabilities mean that audio and video require relatively similar bandwidth. As such, the source material was encoded at 22.05kHz for the audio, and the video at QVGA resolution and 15 frames per second. Initial trials were conducted using a mobile (cellular) handset, but it was decided that this introduced a significant number of variables (e.g. the particularly small screen size, problems with controlling playback, and uncertainties about the quality of the audio rendering hardware) without lending any additional credence to the experiment per se (as opposed to conducting the trials using a notebook, but using mobile-ready content). Consequently, respondents evaluated video displayed on the screen of a Compaq nc4000 notebook (1024x768 total resolution, 12" screen), and listened through Sony MDR-V500 headphones. Respondents were free to adjust volume and viewing distance as desired, with the latter ranging from 8 to 16H (the QVGA image measured 75mm W $\times$ 58mm H). The testing was conducted according to ITU-T P.911 (ITU-T, 1998), including the conditions prescribed in Table 4[14]. Pairwise Comparison (PC) was used to evaluate the hypothesis that

[14] screen luminance, ratios & chromitacity, background illumination and noise level

```
cyc:VisualCommunicating(?vid) ∧ t:DateTimeInterval(?dti) ∧ dolce:HAPPENS−AT(?vid, ?dti) ∧
cyc:imageDepicts(?vid, cyc:StillImage)∧swrlx:makeOWLThing(?sd, ?dti)∧swrlx:makeOWLThing(?sdq, ?dti)
  →
rdo:hasDistortion(?vid, ?sd) ∧ rdo:SemanticDistortion(?sd) ∧ dolce:HAS−QUALE(?sd, rdo:Multiplicative) ∧
  dolce:HAS−QUALE(?sd, ?sdq) ∧ rdo:ContinuousQuale(?sdq) ∧ rdo:hasMagnitude(?sdq, 0.5)
```

**Listing 7.** A rule from the test data asserting that still images have a (relative) SD of 0.5

> *"use of Semantic Distortion in multimedia delivery improves the communication of the meaning/semantics of the content."*

To this end, the nineteen respondents were asked to decide which clip (A or B) "best conveys the gist of the news article to you." Respondents were not skilled in the arts of multimedia delivery, or subjective testing. An approximately equal number of each gender was chosen, and participants ranged in age from 16 to 70. Levels of familiarity with digital media varied as may be expected within the stated age range. Respondents had normal or corrected-to-normal eyesight, and normal hearing (with the exception of two participants who had mild age-related high-frequency hearing loss).

There were four clips plus an initial (hidden) training clip, all exhibiting some or all of the characteristics depicted in Figure 2 on page 2. Three were news footage, and the fourth part of an interview between an English interviewer and a Japanese interviewee, all between 25 and 45 seconds in length. The audio from each clip was encoded using Scalable to Lossless Coding (SLS) (ISO/IEC, 2005b) with an AAC base layer of 6kbps to provide a large scalable range. Scalable Video Coding (SVC) (ISO/IEC, 2007) was used for the video with 8 coarse-grained scalability (CGS) SNR (quality) layers (with LQP at 30, 34, 38, 42, 45, 48, 51, 54 for layer 0 to 7 (respectively), and $RQP = LQP + 2dB$) and 4 medium-grained SNR layers. Spatial and Temporal layers can be beneficial to semantic-aware optimisation (see, for example Cranley & Murphy (2006)) but it was decided to limit the sources of variability for the present experiment. In that regard, no attempts were made at error concealment[15], even though this would have an impact on a user's perception of a real world system employing SD.

### 5.1.1 Semantic analysis

Semantic analysis for each clip was conducted using classes from the Cyc (Matuszek et al., 2006) ontology, to provide semantics indicating the language of communication (spoken or written), among other things. The choice of Cyc for this task was purely as an example, the semantic-aware delivery framework places no constraints on specific metadata ontology(s) (as discussed in Section 3 on page 3). Mapping rules were created for these classes (Listing 4 is one of these, and Listing 7 another[16] describe how particular semantics relate to SD. Temporal regions were specified using OWL-Time (Hobbs & Pan, 2006). Again, this choice is by way of example only, other temporal schemata may equally be used. Figure 10 on page 18 depicts example SD and OWL-Time instances.

[15] except for silencing of an SLS decoder bug observed at particularly low bit rates that that led to saturation of the signal in sections where there should be silence. This bug was observed equally on both clips in a pair, and would otherwise have caused discomfort for test subjects.

[16] Full rules are available in Appendix I of Thomas-Kerr (2009)

### 5.1.2 Syntactic analysis

Syntactic analysis was conducted using a BSDL Schema for SLS and another for SVC (see Appendix I in Thomas-Kerr (2009)), then an XSLT stylesheet to map SLS & SVC fields to the necessary RDO metadata (as per Section 4.2.1 on page 8). Delivery optimisation was performed using a very simple algorithm, so as to limit (as much as possible) the testing to the Semantic Distortion concept, rather than introduce a second independent variable in a sophisticated optimisation routine. Essentially, the algorithm used was

1. Using the rules generated in Section 5.1.1, compute SD values for the entire clip;
2. Aggregate the SD values separately for audio and for video, according to the behavior specified (see Sections 4.2.2 and 4.3);
3. Segment the clip into regions so that each region has a constant SD for audio and a constant SD for video;
4. For each region
   (a) Apportion the target bandwidth between the audio and video stream according to the aggregated SD for each component;
   (b) Truncate each SLS frame so as to achieve the apportioned audio bit-rate; and
   (c) Drop SVC NALUs to most closely approximate the target video rate (while respecting the discardable flag).

Each clip was encoded to three different bit rates using this method, for a total of twelve clips, plus the hidden training clip. For each semantic-aware clip produced using this algorithm, a reference clip was created with the same average audio and video bit rates as the semantic-aware clip (by truncating the SLS and dropping SVC NALUs). This means that the semantic-aware clip devotes more of the available bandwidth to that part (in this example, audio or video) that carries more of the semantics of the content, whereas the reference sample uses the same total bandwidth, but has a static ratio between audio and video. This is illustrated in Figure 11 which shows the semantically-adapted and equivalent average rate series for the audio tracks of the high-bitrate "iran" sequence. The video tracks are not shown since the coarser granularity of the video scalability means that variance is too great to discern average trends. Nonetheless, the audio tracks clearly show how the adaptation algorithm responds to varying SD, and also that both audio tracks have the same total average rate.

### 5.2 Results

In total, 72% of the semantic-aware clips were preferred by subjects when compared to the average-rate reference clip (as shown, Figure 12), with a variance of 20.57%[17] and a 95% confidence interval of ±5.74%.

Of the twelve pairs, one very low-rate semantic-aware clip was rated as worse than its average-rate partner. It is likely that this is due to the deliberate simplicity of the adaptation algorithm. A more sophisticated algorithm would be expected to deal with such outliers more effectively. Having said this, three respondents independently remarked that they preferred one particular low-rate non-semantic-aware clip because it accorded the speaker "more respect" by making his voice clear, even though they couldn't understand it. Because

[17] variance is not considered to be particularly informative in this instance, due to the binary nature of each sample in a Parwise Comparison (the respondant picks one clip or the other). Because of this, every sample is relatively distant from the mean.

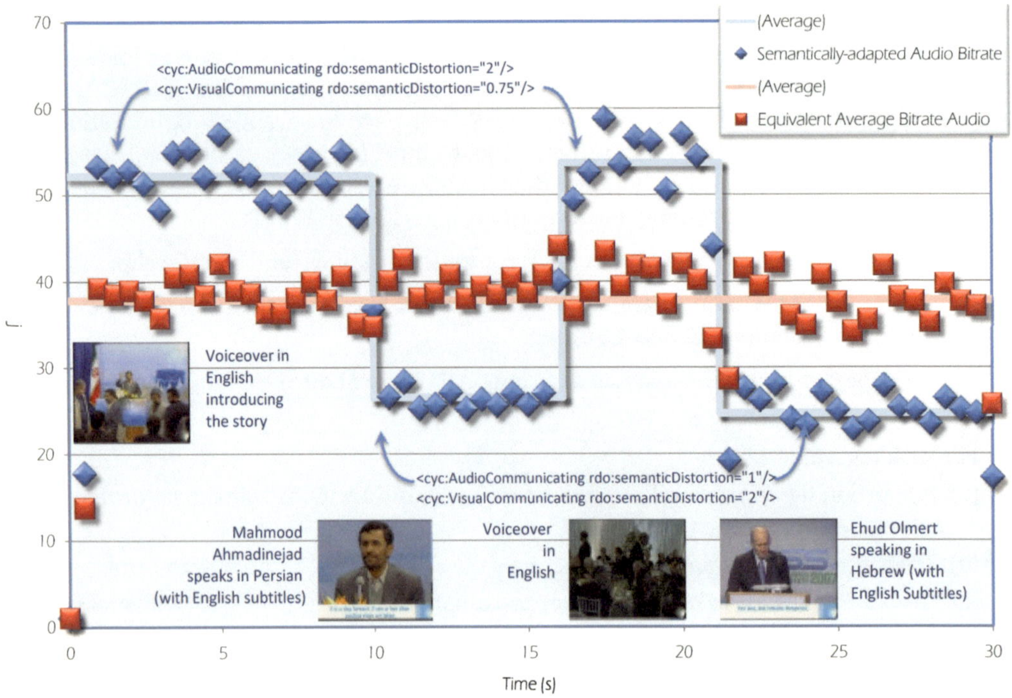


Fig. 11. Semantic adaptation apportions bandwidth according to the content *meaning*

the tests were double-blind, it is not known whether this comment corresponded to the clip in question.

Another two clips were voted as no better and no worse, and the remaining nine semantic-aware clips were preferred 84% of the time. This demonstrates that Semantic Distortion is of significant benefit in the multimedia delivery process. Moreover, the system proposed in Section 4 is effective in processing Semantic Distortion and R-D optimisation-related metadata in a way that meets the objectives identified in Section 3. In contrast, however, the result also suggests that the use of Semantic Distortion to optimise the apportionment of bandwidth between audio and video streams could possibly not be beneficial for a minority of content, at least without more sophisticated optimisation algorithms. However, while the modal trade-offs employed for these few cases fails to yield an improvement, it is quite possible that other uses of Semantic Distortion (see Section 4.1 on page 5) may give the desired results. Further investigation of this is left to future work.

## 6. Conclusion

This chapter describes a framework for incorporating semantics into the multimedia delivery process. It builds on existing work for exposing semantics in content and delivering media in a rate-distortion optimal way. In effect, this alters the conceptual end-points of the multimedia delivery chain. Instead of server-client, using semantics extends the process to (human) creator-consumer, by minimising distortion of the *intended meaning* of the content (see for example the news report in Figure 2 on page 2). At the same time, the framework provides the flexibility to incorporate new semantics, optimisation algorithms, and content formats as

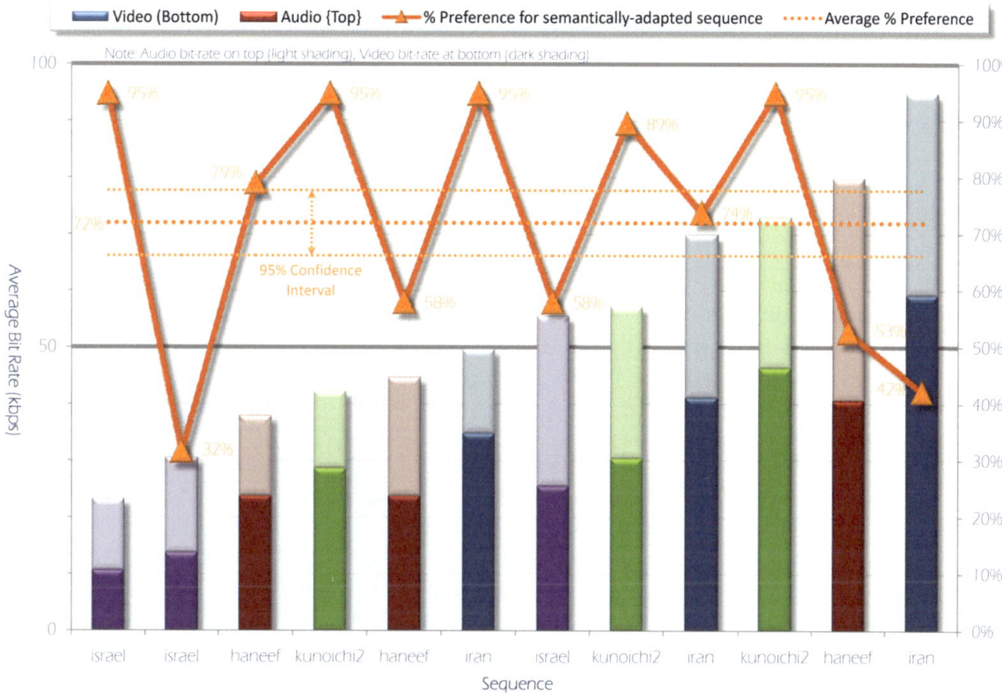


Fig. 12. Subjective testing shows a 72% preference for Semantically-aware media delivery

they become relevant. This process can operate largely without the addition of new software or hardware, since format-specific details are provided in schemata rather than hard-coded. The framework has been validated via subjective testing that asked candidates to make a pairwise comparison between a video clip that had been semantically adapted (more bandwidth devoted to that mode carrying more of the content semantics) and one adapted to an equivalent constant average bitrate. In total, 72% of the semantically adapted clips were preferred by subjects when compared to the average-rate reference clip. Of the twelve pairs, one semantically adapted clip was rated worse than its average-rate partner. Two were voted as no better and no worse, and the remaining semantically adapted clips were preferred 84% of the time.

This result demonstrates that Semantic Distortion is of significant benefit in the multimedia delivery process. Furthermore, it validates the format-independent architecture proposed in Figure 3, as well as the simple algorithm used to semantically adapt content along its modal axis, across a range of bit-rates typical of current mobile communication channels. Nevertheless, the results suggest significant scope to develop higher performance semantic adaptation algorithms. Some possibilities for this are suggested in the following chapter.

### 6.1 Future work

The present work has focused predominantly on the format-independent semantic hinter. Future work may consider more closely the design of the semantic analysis and delivery node modules (see Figure 3 on page 5). In this work, the syntax of compressed media content was described declaratively (using schemata) to enable a generic hinter to extract data for the R-D process. Semantic analysis, on the other hand, is generally conducted using raw (uncompressed) media data, however here too numerous content formats are used. Furthermore, there are a wide range of low-level semantic features (e.g. color, texture, luminance) that are extracted from the raw data in order to infer higher-level semantics. Future work could therefore investigate declarative mechanisms for (a) describing how low-level features are computed from a given content format, and (b) mapping such features to high-level semantics.

Secondly, future work should consider how to describe an R-D optimisation algorithm using declarative language. This chapter has addressed the format-independent design of the RDO metadata and send/drop module (Figure 4 on page 6). However, it has not fully addressed a generic mechanism for describing the RDO algorithm itself. Such a mechanism would allow new RDO algorithms to be installed in a diverse variety of existing delivery nodes without requiring their hardware or software to be upgraded.

## 7. References


Apple (2001). QuickTime File Fmt., `http://developer.apple.com/reference/QuickTime/`.

Austen, J. (1813). *Pride and Prejudice*, T. Egerton, Whitehall.

Baba, M. et al. (2004). Adaptive multimedia playout method based on semantic structure of media stream, *Comms. and IT, IEEE Intl. Symp. on*, pp. 269–273.

Beckett, D. (2004). RDF/XML Syntax Specification (Revised), `http://www.w3.org/TR/rdf-syntax-grammar/`.

Bertini, M. et al. (2006). Semantic adaptation of sport videos with user-centred performance analysis, *Multimedia, IEEE trans. on* 8(3): 433–443.

Boag, S. et al. (2007). XQuery 1.0: An XML Query Language, `http://www.w3.org/TR/xquery`.

Bray, T. et al. (2008). Extensible Markup Language (XML), `http://www.w3.org/TR/xml/`.

Brightman, I. (2005). The trillion dollar challenge: Principles for profitable convergence, *Technical report*, Deloitte; Technology, Media Telecommunications. Available: `http://www.deloitte.com/dtt/cda/doc/content/UK_TMT_TrillionDollarChallenge_05.pdf`.

Chakareski, J. et al. (2004a). Low-complexity rate-distortion optimized video streaming, *Image Processing, Intl. Conf. on* 3: 2055–2058.

Chakareski, J. et al. (2004b). R-D hint tracks for low-complexity RD-optimized video streaming, *Proc. IntŠl Conf. Multimedia and Exhibition* 2: 1387–1390.

Chou, P. (2006). Rate-distortion optimized streaming of packetized media, *IEEE Transactions on Multimedia* 8(2): 390–404.

Clark, J. (1999). XSL transformations (XSLT), `http://www.w3.org/TR/xslt`.

Cranley, N. & Murphy, L. (2006). *Incorporating User Perception in Adaptive Video Streaming Systems*, Idea Group, chapter 12, pp. 242–263.

Cranley, N. et al. (2003). User-perceived quality-aware adaptive delivery of MPEG-4 content, *13th Intl. workshop on Network and operating systems support for digital A/V* pp. 42–49.

Dean, M. & Schreiber, G. (2004). OWL Web Ontology Language Ref., `http://www.w3.org/TR/owl-features/`.

Eichhorn, A. (2006). Modelling dependency in multimedia streams, *Multimedia, 14th ACM intl. conf. on*, ACM Press New York, NY, USA, pp. 941–950.

Gangemi, A., Guarino, N., Masolo, C., Oltramari, A. & Schneider, L. (2002). Sweetening ontologies with DOLCE, *Lecture notes in computer science* pp. 166–181.

Hobbs, J. & Pan, F. (2006). Time ontology in owl, `http://www.w3.org/TR/owl-time/`.

Hong, D. & Eleftheriadis, A. (2002). XFlavor: bridging bits and objects in media representation, *Multimedia and Expo, IEEE Intl. Conf. on*, pp. 773–776.

Horrocks, I. et al. (2004). SWRL: A Semantic Web Rule Language Combining OWL and RuleML, `http://www.w3.org/Submission/SWRL`.

Hunter, J. (2001). Adding multimedia to the semantic web - building an MPEG-7 ontology, *Semantic Web Working Symposium (SWWS)*, pp. 261–281.

ISO/IEC (2002a). 15938-5 IT–Multimedia content description interface, MDS.

ISO/IEC (2002b). 15938 Information technology—Multimedia content description interface.

ISO/IEC (2004a). 14496-3/Amd.5 Scalable to Lossless Coding.

ISO/IEC (2004b). 14496 Coding of audio-visual objects—Part 1: Systems.

ISO/IEC (2005a). 14496-12, IT–Coding of A/V objects–Part 12: ISO base media file format.

ISO/IEC (2005b). 14496-3:2005/Amd 3, Scalable Lossless Coding.

ISO/IEC (2007). 14496-10:2005/FDAM 3 Scalable Video Coding.

ITU-T (1998). Subjective A/V Quality Assessment Methods for Multimedia Apps., Rec. P.911.

JEITA (2002). Exchangeable image file format (EXIF) for digital still cameras.

Klint, P. et al. (2005). Toward an engineering discipline for grammarware, *ACM Trans. on Software Engineering Methodologies* 14(3): 331–380.

Lehti, P. & Fankhauser, P. (2004). XML data integration with OWL: experiences challenges, *Applications the Internet, 2004. Proceedings. 2004 Int.l Symp. on* pp. 160–167.

Matroska (n.d.). Specification of the Matroska container, `http://matroska.org/technical/specs/index.html`.

Matuszek, C. et al. (2006). An Introduction to the Syntax and Content of Cyc, *Formalizing and Compiling Background Knowledge and Its Applications to Knowledge Representation and Question Answering, AIII Symp. on* pp. 44–49.

Naphade, M. et al. (2006). Large-scale concept ontology for multimedia, *IEEE MultiMedia Magazine* 13(3): 86–91.

Neve, W. et al. (2006). BFlavor: A harmonized approach to media resource adaptation, inspired by MPEG-21 BSDL XFlavor, *Signal Processing: Image Comms.* 21(10): 862–889.

Niedermeier, U. et al. (2002). An MPEG-7 tool for compression and streaming of XML data, *Multimedia and Expo, IEEE Intl. Conf. on*, pp. 521–524.

Nilsson, M. (2000). ID3 tag v2.4.0 - Main, `http://www.id3.org/id3v2.4.0-structure`.

of Motion Picture, S. & Engineers, T. (1999). SMPTE 12M-1999, Television, Audio and Film Ű Time and Control Code.

Paleari, M. & Huet, B. (2008). Toward emotion indexing of multimedia excerpts, *Content-Based Multimedia Indexing, 2008. CBMI 2008. International Workshop on*, pp. 425–432.

Pan, F. & Hobbs, J. (2004). Time in OWL-S, *Semantic Web Services, AIII Symp. on* pp. 29–36.

Thomas-Kerr, J. (2009). *Building Babel: Freeing multimedia processing and delivery from hard-coded formats*, PhD thesis, University of Wollongong.

Thomas-Kerr, J., Burnett, I. & Ritz, C. (2006). Enhancing Interoperability via Generic Multimedia Syntax Translation, *Proceedings of the Second International Conference on Automated Production of Cross Media Content for Multi-Channel Distribution* pp. 85–92.

Thomas-Kerr, J., Burnett, I. & Ritz, C. (2008). Format-Independent Rich Media Delivery Using the Bitstream Binding Language, *Multimedia, IEEE Transactions on* 10(3): 514–522.

Thomas-Kerr, J., Burnett, I. & Ritz, C. (2009). A system for intelligent delivery of multimedia based on semantics, *Communications and Information Technologies, 2009. ISCIT'09. International Symposium on*.

Thomas-Kerr, J., Janneck, J., Mattavelli, M., Burnett, I. & Ritz, C. (2007). Reconfigurable Media Coding: Self-Describing Multimedia Bitstreams, *2007 IEEE Workshop on Signal Processing Systems*, pp. 319–324.

Thomas-Kerr, J. et al. (2007). Is That a Fish in Your Ear? A Universal Metalanguage for Multimedia, *IEEE MultiMedia* 14(2): 72–77.

Thompson, H. S. et al. (2004). XML Schema Part 1: Structures, `http://www.w3.org/TR/xmlschema-1/`.

Timmerer, C. et al. (2006). Digital Item Adaptation - Coding Format Independence, *in* I. Burnett et al. (eds), *MPEG-21*, Wiley, Chichester, UK.

*XML Schema Part 2: Datatypes Second Edition* (2004). `http://www.w3.org/TR/xmlschema-2/`.

Xu, M. et al. (2006). Event on demand with MPEG-21 video adaptation system, *Multimedia, 14th ACM intl. conf. on* , pp. 921–930.

18

# User-aware Video Coding Based on Semantic Video Understanding and Enhancing

Yu-Tzu Lin[1] and Chia-Hu Chang[2]
[1]*National Chi Nan University*
[2]*National Taiwan University*
*Taiwan*

## 1. Introduction

Traditional video coding is devoted to represent the video data compactly by dealing with low-level features (e.g., color, motion, texture, etc.) of the video. However, with the insatiable demand of Internet and increased use of multimedia, the bit-rate control issues are more and more important. In order to achieve more efficient representation for coping with diverse network or devices, many researches devised scalable video coding schemes which adaptively change the bit-rate according to the available bandwidth or user requirements. However, most scalable video coding algorithms only consider low-level features of video content in frame-based format without utilizing semantic information, which lose the possibility of improving coding efficiency by employing semantic meaning of content. Therefore, it is valuable to investigate methodologies of semantic-level video coding to produce more compact and flexible coding results for various user preferences. Semantic analysis for video content will provide richer information about the content and then assist achieving higher compression rate with good visual quality. Besides the coding efficiency, various functions are required in current video services, such as manipulating, searching and interacting with semantic-level objects. To enhance the flexibility and interactivity for accessing and manipulating the video content adaptively for different users, user-aware functionalities based on semantic video analysis should be discussed. In this chapter, we will discuss the theory and practice of user-aware semantic video coding, focusing on the aspect of semantic manipulation and user adaptation of video, including the semantic analysis techniques, scalable coding, user attention model construction, and user-aware video coding, by considering requirements for different applications and giving an explanation about the methodologies for some example applications.

## 2. Semantic video coding

For instance, the background except the couple in the wedding video can be compressed with a higher rate than the area of the bride and groom because of its lower semantic importance (less interesting to humans). Many researches (Cheng et al., 2008; Bertini et al., 2006; Ng et al., 2010) investigate methodologies for analyzing the semantic meaning of the video. Within the MPEG-7 (ISO/IEC 15938) Multimedia Description Schemes specification, "event" is used in the Creation and Production description tools to describe the agents and tools involved in creation process. The semantic event is also a fundamental concept in the Semantics Description tools where it is used to describe what is happening or being depicted in the actual content of the video object, which also plays a major role in MPEG's latest initiative, MPEG-21 (ISO/IEC 21000). Since the MPEG-21 standard (Vetro, 2004) highlights the importance of semantic video coding, more and more semantic video analysis approaches were devised for various applications. Fig. 1 shows the architecture of semantic video coding. The result of semantic analysis provides information for enhancing the spatial and temporal processing and then improves the coding efficiency.

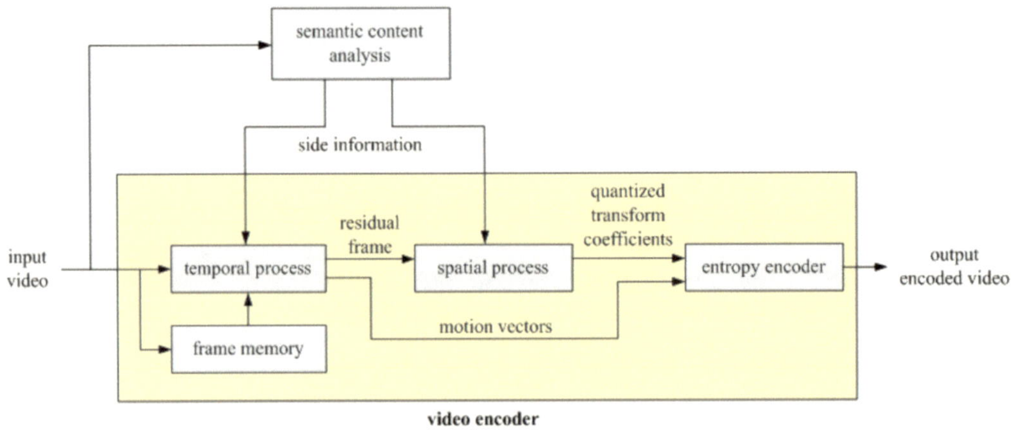


Fig. 1. The architecture of semantic video coding.

### 2.1 Object extraction and encoding

To mine semantic meaning from the video, low-level features have to be extracted at first, such as colour, texture, edge, shape, or motion features, to segment and describe objects with various descriptions, such as histogram, slope, graphs, and coefficients transformed to frequency-domain. By using the obtained low-level features of the objects, semantic rules can be applied to understand the video content by detecting meaningful events in the video. Object extraction is an essential procedure in semantic video analysis. The extracted objects are important basis for content event detection, and background except objects is the minor part of the video, which can be compressed with a higher rate while video coding. Fig. 2 (Bertini et al., 2006) shows one example of object extraction in the sports video.

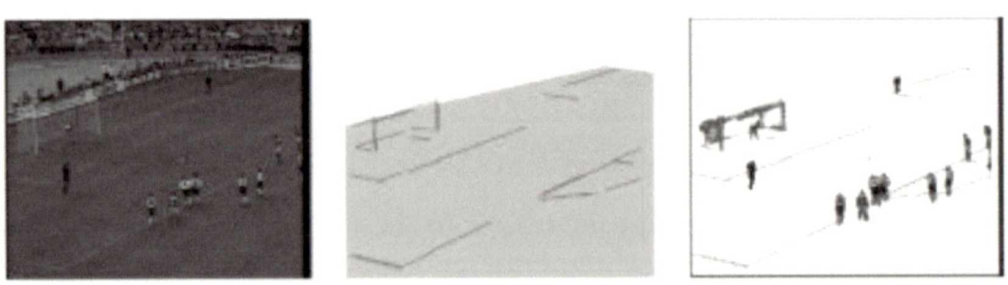

(a) (b) (c)

Fig. 2. (a) Original frame; (b) playfield shape and playfield lines; (c) soccer players' blobs and playfield lines (Bertini et al., 2006).

However, in many applications, the objects in the video can not be easily found without segmenting the frame image at first. And the stability of the object-segment extraction is important for correctly detecting events in the video content. Before object extraction, the video frame has to be firstly segmented into several segments for locating candidates of the object-segment. Unfortunately, the pixel-based segmentation results of gray-level images are usually sensitive to the changes of the image pixels. Some researches (Lin et al., 2006) proposed reliable segmentation techniques called Geometric-Invariant Segmentation which is invariant to pixel changes. Even though the object moves, different frames will have the same segmentation result, so that the object extraction would be stable. Image pixels are firstly smoothed and binarized to reduce the noise possibly introduced in the edge detection step of the proposed segmentation algorithm. Instead of binarizing the image by a hard decision method, a fuzzy binarization approach was applied. A well-known segmentation method, Fuzzy Kohonen Clustering Network (FKCN) (Bezdek et al., 1992), was often applied to segment images. The comparison is provided in Fig. 3. After segmenting the video frame, the objects can be extracted according to criteria based on domain knowledge,

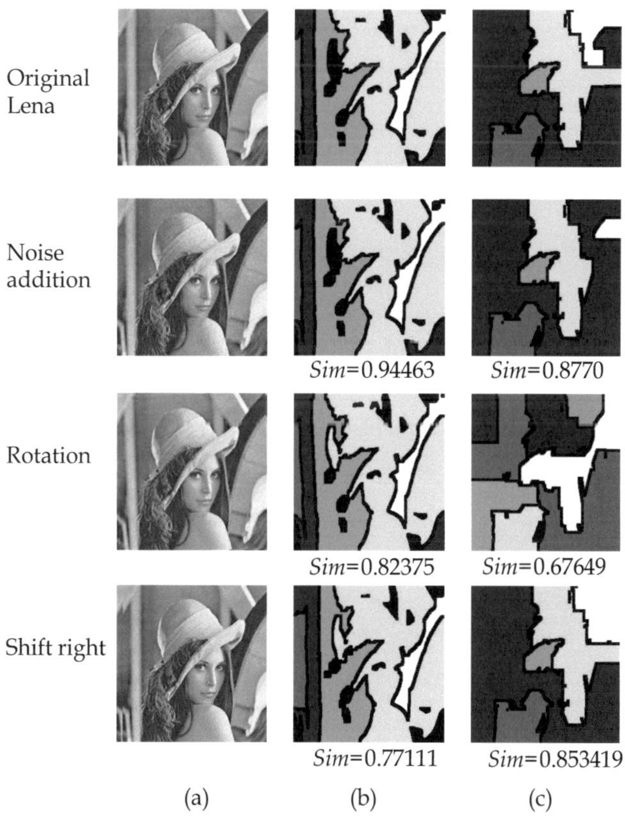


Fig. 3. The comparison between Geometric-Invariant Segmentation (GIS) and FKCN: Corresponding *Sim* values (the similarity between the segments of the manipulated image and original one) of GIS and FKCN after applying various attacks are listed below the images: (a) images manipulated by geometrical operations or signal processing, (b) the resulting images segmented by GIS, and (c) by FKCN. (Lin et al., 2006)

such as skin colour in the news video or playfield colour in the sports video. Bertini et al. (2006) segmented the playfield region from colour histogramming using grass colour information. There are many other segmentation algorithms and schemes proposed in the literature (Chen et al., 2005; Mezaris, et al., 2004; Borenstein & Ulman, 2008; Kokkinos et al., 2009).

Another type of object extraction methods is to find objects using motion features. The highlight (the atomic entities of videos at semantic level) often has specific motions in the video rather than static, so it can be detected by analyzing the motion information. Some sport analysis algorithms (Li et al., 2010) estimate the motion vector to align the background. From the global motion analyzing result of two successive frames, the background can be accurately aligned (Fig. 4). This method also can be applied in moving background sports video. The player can be detected correctly in the video of diving game. Some researches (Papadopoulos et al., 2009) derived statistical approaches to determining the motion area. The kurtosis was used to localize active and static pixels in a video sequence to measure each pixel's s activity (Fig. 5).

(a) (b) (c)

Fig. 4. Result of global motion estimation: (a) -(b) two successive video frames, and (c) the detected background (Li et al., 2010).

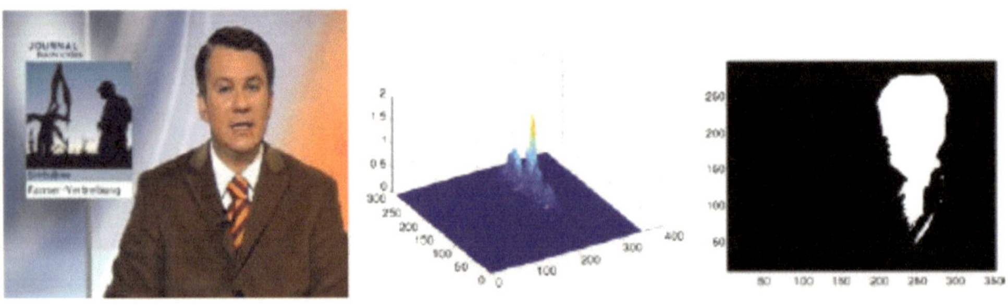

Fig. 5. One example of kurtosis field and activity area mask computation for a news video (Papadopoulos et al., 2009).

The object with higher semantic-level can be encoded by a structural description using low semantic-level objects. Xu et al. (2008) designed a hierarchical compositional model to represent the face, which makes the face representation more condensed and efficient for coding and recognition, as shown in Fig. 6. In another object-based video coding scheme (Wang et al., 2005), the high-level object is composed of the low-level shape and texture information (Fig. 7). Another semantic video coding for videophone sequences (Zhang, 1998) used an adaptive face model using the deformable template to construct a 3D wireframe for the face (Fig. 8).

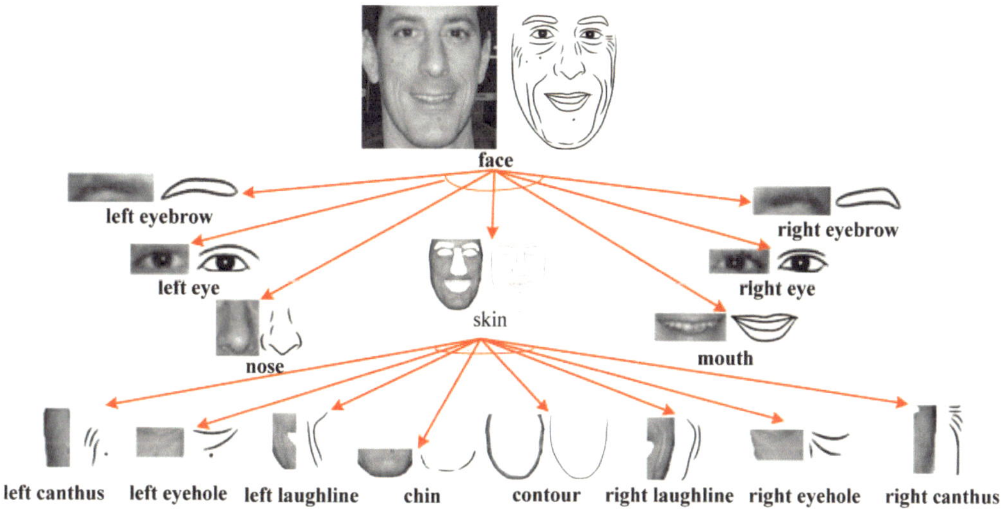


Fig. 6. The hierarchical compositional model for face representation (Xu et al., 2008).

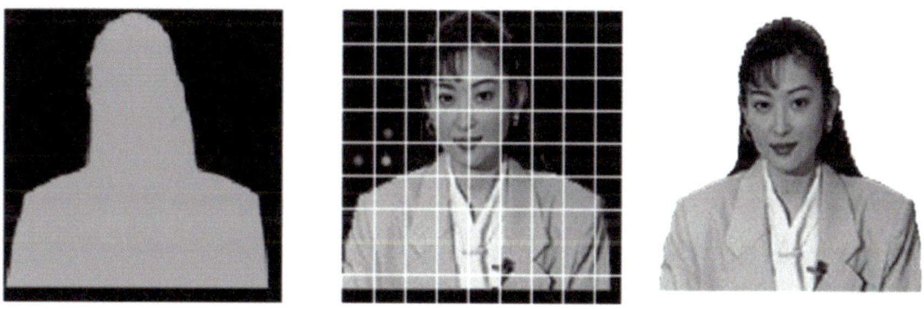

(a) (b) (c)

Fig. 7. Example of composition of shape and texture. (a) Shape. (b) Texture. (c) Composed object (Wang et al., 2005).

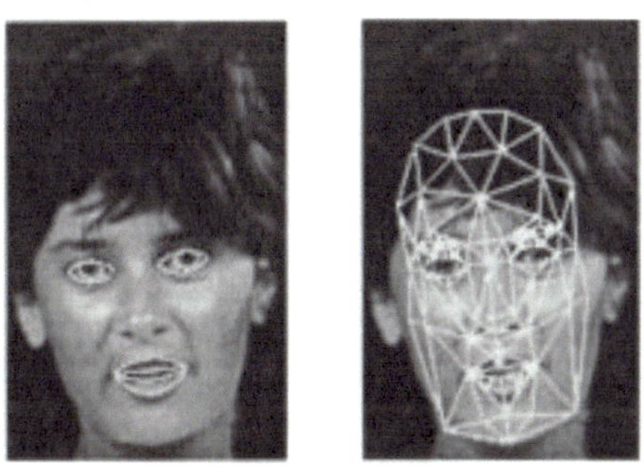

Fig. 8. The 3D wireframe of the face (Zhang, 1998).

## 2.2 Event detection and encoding

An event in the video content contains not only its spatial characteristics, but also particular features of the temporal order. Since it has even more semantic-level messages than objects, the structure of the video content should be analyzed based on more domain knowledge. A video can be represented as a multilayer structure, as illustrated in Fig. 9. Scenes, shots and frames are the units that can be found in video. A meaningful story is composed of several scenes. And a scene contains several shots which consist of the video frames that have been continuously recorded with a single camera operation. Shot change detection (Cotsaces et al., 2006; Koprinska & Carrato, 2001; Yuan et al., 2007) is to identify the shots of the video for the purpose of further video analyses and encoding.

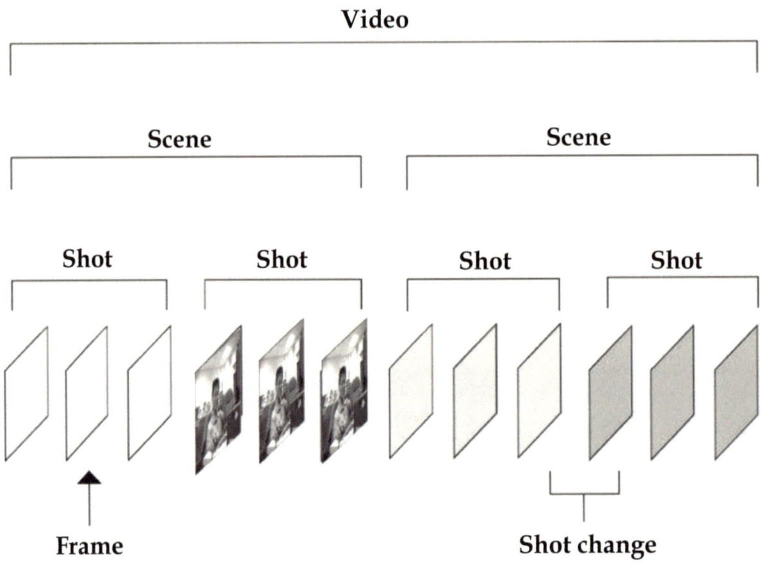


Fig. 9. The video structure.

Sports videos (Bertini et al., 2006; Li et al., 2010) were a frequently discussed application in semantic coding. Bertini et al. (2006) designed a automatic annotation scheme for soccer video based on MPEG-2 (ISO/IEC 13818), which performed event and event-object level compression by detecting camera motion, playfield zone, and players' position in the playfield (Fig. 2). And the players' position determines penalty kicks or free kicks. Further event detection for Forward launch, Shot on goal, Placed kicks, Attack action, and Counter attack are modelled with finite state machine constructed based on soccer rules.

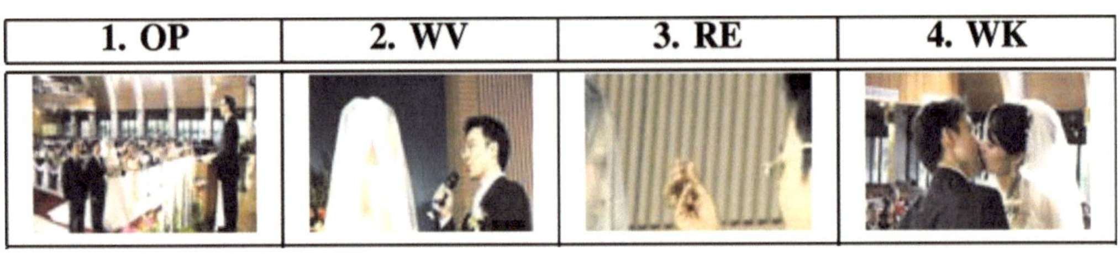


Fig. 10. One example of four successive wedding events (Cheng et al., 2008).

Besides the finite sate machine, the Hidden Markov Model (Rabiner, 1989) is another common tool for modelling the content event. Based on the observation of wedding events, including speech/music types, applause activities, picture-taking activities, and leading roles, Cheng et al. (2008) exploited an HMM framework for segmenting wedding videos, which integrates the wedding event statistical models and the event transition model. Fig. 10 illustrates one example of four successive events, in which OP, WV, RE, WK represents officiant presenting, wedding vows, ring exchange, and wedding kiss, respectively.

## 3. User-aware semantic video coding

In a heterogeneous network/device environment, the video content should be adaptively encoded to satisfy different users' requirements. However, conventional user adaptive video coding approaches transform the video into bitstreams of various formats independently of the video content. The video is represented and compressed to the adaptive transmission rate and quality by only considering the physical environment, despite of user preferences. Therefore, besides the codec aspects of transmission and presentation constraints of the user's device or transmission capacity, understanding semantic components of the video content while coding, by analyzing the video content using semantic-based temporal or spatial features, could also be a major issue to help produce more condensed and meaningful video for different transmission requirements and user preferences. In this section, we will firstly introduce scalable video coding, then explain how user-aware semantic analysis and manipulations (including construction of user attention models, ROI extraction, and enhancing the interactivity of video coding) assist in improving the coding efficiency.

### 3.1 Scalable video coding

Scalable video coding is a technique to enable the encoding standard to encode the video into a set of bitstreams with different visual quality to satisfy the needs of different terminals/channels. As defined in MPEG-2, the bitstream is encoded into a base layer and a few enhancement layers, in which the enhancement layers add spatial, temporal, and/or SNR quality to the reconstructed base layer. Later, the fine granular scalability (FGS) is developed in the MPEG-4 (ISO/IEC 14496) Visual standard, which allows a much finer scaling of bits in the enhancement layer. Based on FGS provided in the MPEG-4, (Barrau, 2002) proposed both close-loop and open-loop solutions for the FGS transcoder, which reduce the bit-rate by cutting the enhancement information at know locations.(Qian et al., 2005) combined a scalable transcoder with space time block codes (STBBC) for an orthogonal frequency division multiplexing (OFDM) system to provide robust access to the pre-encoded high quality video server from mobile wireless terminals.
Heterogeneous transcoding converts the pre-compressed bitstream into another bitstream with different format. It is particularly important for the multimedia services which pre-encode the bitstream for storage and transmission. In (Siu et al., 2007), a transcoder from MPEG-2 to H.263 is proposed to convert a B-picture to a P-picture using the information of motion compensation in the DCT domain. Since one of the major differences between MPEG-2 and H.264/AVC is that MPEG-2 uses 8-tap DCT and H.264 uses 4-tap integer (DCT-like) transform (IT), (Shen, 2004; Chen et al., 2006a) designed fast DCT-to-IT algorithms to perform the MPEG-2-to-H.264 transcoding. Since wireless channels have lower bandwidth and higher error rate than wired channels, the error resilience transcoding

over wireless channel is more important. It is particularly useful in hostile environments, such as mobile networks and the Internet. There are many strategies to provide error resilience transcoding (Vetro et al., 2005): 1. Removing the spatial/temporal redundancy can help reduce the error propagation. 2. Group the coded data into several parts according to their importance to allow the unequal protection. 3. Add error-checking bits to the bitstream for robust decoding. 4. Embed additional information into the coded stream to enable the improved error concealment. (Chen et al., 2006b) designed a content-aware intra-refresh (CAIR) transcoding to improve efficiency of the intra-refresh allocation by avoiding the error propagation in the same prediction path.

Fig. 11 illustrates a video transcoder, which provides a seamless interaction between content creation and consumption, or among different channels/terminals. The format can be characterized by the bit-rate, frame rate, coding syntax, spatial resolution, or content (as shown in Fig. 11, in which RI, FI, CI are parameters of the input video, and RO, FO, CO are those of the output video).

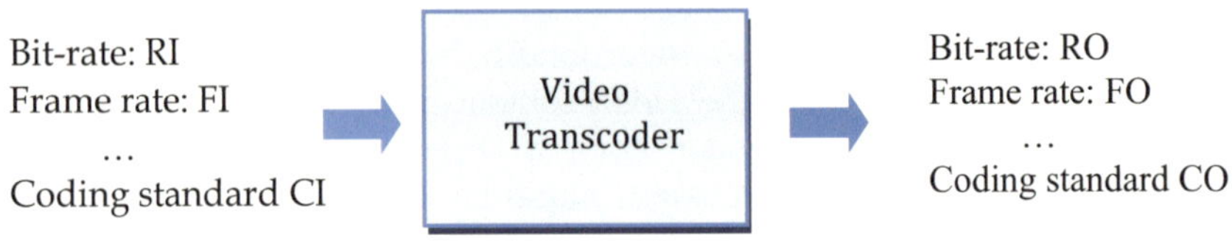


Fig. 11. The video transcoder.

Since video or image have much larger data sizes than other types of data, they have more needs for trascoding. For different applications, the requirements and techniques of the video/image trascoding are still quite different. A common requirement of transcoding is to reduce the complexity of the transcoder and the bit-rate of the data while preserving suitable content quality. It is especially an important issue for video streaming applications in both wired and wireless networks (Chen & Zakhor, 2005). To achieve a target bit-rate while maintaining consistent video/image quality and satisfying the required parameters, (e.g. bandwidth, delay, resolution, and memory constraints), there are various types of trancoding detailed as the following:

**A. Frequency domain transcoding**

Many video/image compression standards (e.g. JPEG, MPEG-2, MPEG-4, and H.264/AVC) carry out the residual coding in the DCT domain, which consists several steps: the run-length coding, quantization, and the motion compensation (MC). Consequently, many researches try to design DCT-based transcoders because the computational complexity will be much lower than in the pixel domain. (Kim et al., 2006) proposed a bit-rate adaptation method for streaming video in a QoS-based home gateway service, in which the input bitstream is partially decoded into the DCT domain first, then an adaptive motion mapping refinement and a DCT-based image downsizer are utilized to adapt the bit-rate. In (Assunco & Ghanbari, 1998), a drift-free transcoder working entirely in the frequency domain was proposed, in which a Lagrangian rate-distortion optimization was applied for bit reallocation to ensure the quality of the bitstream. Some literatures requantized the DCT coefficients to transcode the bitstream: (Werner, 1999) derived a cost function to estimate the quantizer so that the quantizer can achieve a larger SNR at the same bit-rate compared with the original quantizer used in MPEG-2. Besides, the MSE-based cost function and maximum a posteriori used in this paper need minor additional complexity. Since the time complexity issue is significant in the real-time applications, (Seo et al., 2000) found an efficient requantization by using a piecewise linearly decreasing model.

**B. Temporal resolution adaptation**

Both spatial and temporal redundancies should be considered in a video compression algorithm. Besides the MC-based transcodings, temporal redundancies can also be removed by dropping some redundant frames while preserving the temporal smoothness of coded frames. Of course, temporal resolution adaptation is also one of the bit-rate control trascoding for video. In (Shu & Chau, 2005), some video frames are skipped by considering the motion change and reduces the jerky effect caused by undesired frame skipping. (Bonuccelli et al., 2005) designed a buffer-based temporal transcoding in a real-time mobile video application. Rather than dropping frames directly, Shu & Chau (2005) proposed a frame-layer bit allocation method to assign different number of bits for different frames.

**C. Spatial resolution adaptation**

Resizing is needed to adapt the spatial resolutions to devices with different display capabilities. Moreover, with the emergence of mobile devices and the desire for users to access video originally captured in a high spatial resolution, there is also a need to reduce the resolution for transmitting to and being displayed in such devices. (Shu & Chau, 2007) designed a two-stage structure for arbitrary resizing in DCT-based transcoding, in which some constraints are derived for anti-aliasing.

Although many studies (Lei & Georganas, 2003; Warabino et al., 2000; Elsharkawy et al., 2007) have investigated methodologies to solve the problems related to transcoding in the wireless environment, the rate control and error resilience for wireless applications are still challenging problems, especially for H.264/AVC, the more efficient but complex video standard.

### 3.2 User-aware semantic video analysis

As described in Section 3.1, different coding requirements should be satisfied for heterogeneous display resolution or communication abilities, which can give temporal, spatial, and quality scalability for the encoded bit stream. However, only considering low-level codec aspects produces limited efficiency gains. Semantic-level analysis will help design more feasible and flexible coding algorithms for different users' needs. To achieve this purpose, the user-aware attention model should be constructed for different applications: For real-time road traffic monitoring, content-based scalable coding (Ho et al., 2005) can help increase the compression rate. In the wireless environment, a temporal scalability scheme with background composition (Hung & Huang, 2003) was proposed in MPEG4. And effective bit-rate control can be achieved by considering the Region of Interest (ROI) (Grois et al., 2010). As shown in Fig. 12, the ROI is used as the baselayer of H.264/AVC standard, which can provide various resolution and bit-rates for different users' needs. Table 1 presents the bit-rate savings when exploiting this method. For lecture videos, a learner-focused model can be designed to reduce the network traffic in case of the real-time streaming video (Lin et al., 2009, 2010a). Fig. 13 illustrates one example of lecture video coding, in which a lot of lecture video frames are compressed into one lecture slide with teaching focus and the temporal redundancy is reduced based on semantic-level analysis.

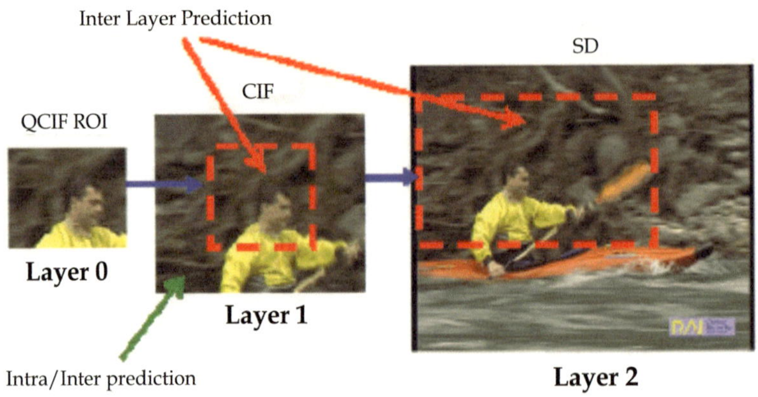


Fig. 12. Example of the ROI dynamic adjustment and scalability for mobile devices with different spatial resolution (Grois et al., 2010).

| Quantization Parameters | Four Layers (640x360, and three HD layers) | | Eight Layers (two CIF layers, three SD layers, and three HD layers) | | Bit-Rate Savings (%) |
|---|---|---|---|---|---|
| | PSRN | Bit-Rate | PSNR | Bit-Rate | |
| 32 | 34.48 | 2566.15 | 34.49 | 3237 | 20.73 |
| 34 | 33.93 | 1730.21 | 33.93 | 2359 | 26.66 |
| 36 | 33.27 | 1170.01 | 33.27 | 1759 | 33.48 |

Table 1. The bit-rate savings when using ROI adaptive scalable video coding (Grois et al., 2010).

Fig. 13. Lecture video coding: (a) the lecture video frames are compressed into (b) the lecture slide with detected teaching focuses (Lin et al., 2009).

In the following, we will introduce user-aware semantic understanding techniques for videos by extracting and analyzing user-aware visual/aural features, including the analysis of expression, gesture, emotion, motion, and event detection, for the purpose of enhancing the video coding.

Fig. 14 illustrates one example of user-aware video analysis schemes, in which the learner-focused attention model was constructed and provided for enhancing the video lecture representation (Lin et al., 2010b).

Visual analysis can be used to understand the video semantically by merely finding low-level features (color, texture, pixel histogram, etc.) or further extracting semantic-level features (gesture, expression, action, etc.) from low-level visual features, which will be introduced by providing examples in the following.

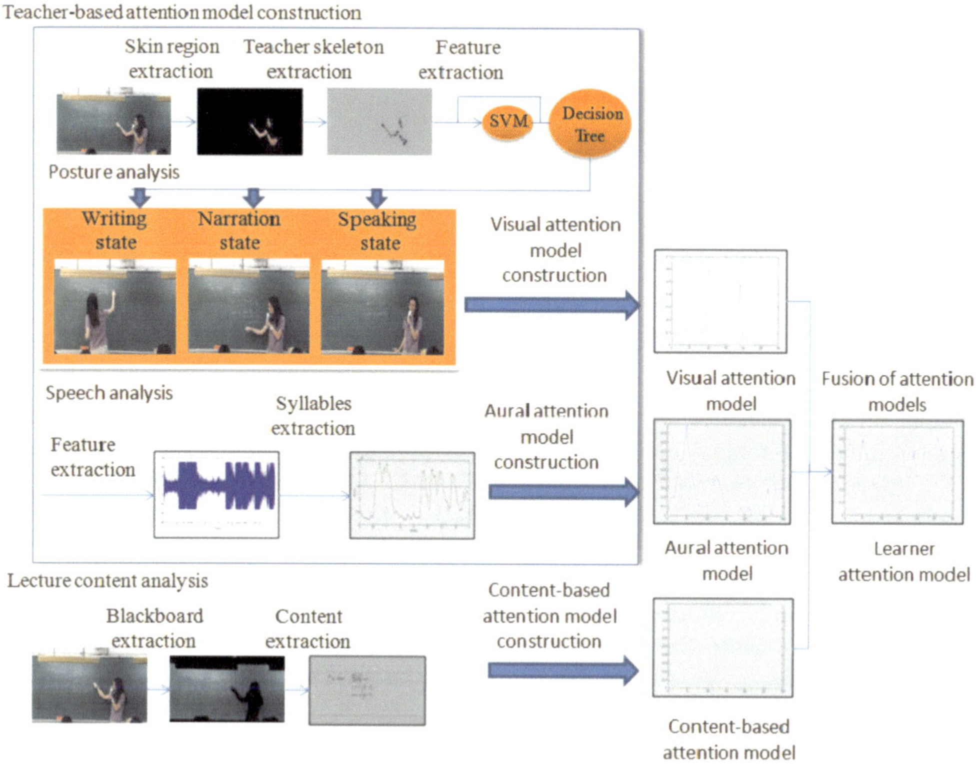


Fig. 14. One example of the user-aware video analysis scheme for constructing a learner-focused attention model. (Lin et al., Sept. 2010b)

### 3.2.1 User-aware visual analysis

Low-level features can be extracted by directed computig the visual characteristics in the spatical or frequency domain, which contains no semantic meaning for humans at first glance. In the adaptive video learning system proposed in (Lin et al., 2010b), the importance of the lecture content are decided by analyzing the extracted lecture content and also the instructor's behavior. In lecture content, color features are used to couting the chalk pixels. The blackboard region is at first obtained by extracting the regions of the blackboard colour and merging them(Fig. 15 (a)). After deciding the blackboard region, the set of chalk pixels $P_{chalk}$ can be computed as

$$P_{chalk} = \bigcup \left\{ x \middle| I(x) > I_{cp} \right\}, \tag{1}$$

where $I(x)$ is the luminance of pixel $x$ and $I_{cp}$ is the luminance threshold. Fig. 15 shows one example of lecture content extraction.

The chalk text or figures written on the blackboard by the lecturer are undoubtedly the most important part that lecturers want students to pay attention to. It is obvious that the more there is lecture content (chalk handwriting or figures), the more revealed semantics are in the lecture video. Therefore, the attention values are evaluated by extracting the lecture content on the blackboard and analyzing the content fluctuation in lecture videos.

(a) (b)

Fig. 15. Lecture content extraction: (a) the blackboard region, and (b) the extracted lecture content.

Another important low-level feature for videos is motion extracted in the pixel or compression domain. Many sophisticated motion estimation algorithms has been developed in the literature, for examples, the optical flow in (Beauchemin & Barron, 1995) and the feature tracking in (Shi & Tomasi, 1994). However, they often have high computational complexity because the operations are executed in the pixel domain and the estimated motions are accurate. In the work of (Chang et al., 2010a), accurate motion estimation is not needed, so the motion information can be directly extracted from the motion vectors of a compressed video. Since the process is done directly in the compression domain, the induced complexity is very low. Therefore, the motions in each video frame can be efficiently obtained.

As mentioned in Section 3.1.1, object extraction is an important process before deciding video events. In many user-aware applications, human detection is the major work while extracting objects. In the lecture video application, the lecturer should be detected for further analysis. In the work of Lin et al. (2009), the human area was extracted by detecting the moving object in the video frames, which was carried out by finding the eigenregions in the frames. That is, the moving objects can be distinguished from the still objects by methods of classification. The PCA (Principal Component Analysis)-based approach is used in this paper, which is detailed in the following. Three successive frames $F_{i-1}$, $F_i$, and $F_{i+1}$ are firstly transformed into a matrix $X=[F_{i-1}\ F_i\ F_{i+1}]$, then the covariance $C$ is computed as $C=X^TX$. Finally, each frame is aligned with the first two principle vectors (which are the eigenvectors of $C$ associated with the two largest eigenvalues. Thus, the area with higher values represents that with higher variances, i.e., the moving object.

After the eigenregion is extracted, the produced image (Fig. 16 (d)) is binarized and applied by morphological operators to fill and smooth the region in order to obtain a more stable mask. Fig. 16 shows one example of moving object detection, in which (a), (b), and (c) are three successive frames, (d) is the corresponding eigenregion, (e) is the binarized one, and (f) is the final mask after morphological operations.

Low-level feature can provide limited information for human perception, for example, the DCT coefficients could not be understood well by humans, even though these features play an important role in pattern recognition. Therefore, semantic understanding for videos can be improved by extracting semantic-level features like gestures, expression, actions, etc. For instance, the posture of the lecturer will generally change with the delivered lecture content or the situation in lecture presentation. For example, when teaching the math problems, the lecturer may firstly write the lecture content on the blackboard and shows their back to the

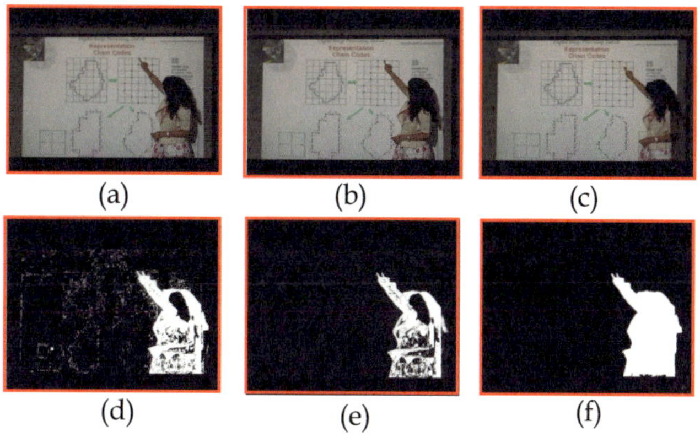


Fig. 16. Human detection: (a), (b), and (c) are successive frames, (d) Eigenregion (lighter area), (e) binarized eigenregion, and (f) the resulting mask. (Lin et al., Sept. 2010b)

students. Next, he starts to narrate the written equations and moves sideways to avoid occluding the content which students should focus their gazes on. After writing the complete lecture content, the lecturer will face the students to further explain the details. All of the lecturing statuses and postures mentioned above will repeatedly occur with alternative random order in a course presentation. Different states represent different presentation states and also different semantics. Therefore, the lecturing states can be decided according to the changes of the lecturer's posture. In (Lin et al., 2010b), the skeleton of the lecturer is extracted to represent the posture and then the lecturing states are identified by using the SVM approach. The regions of the head and hands are detected by using the skin-color features. The lecturer's skeleton is then constructed by considering the relations between the positions of head and hands.

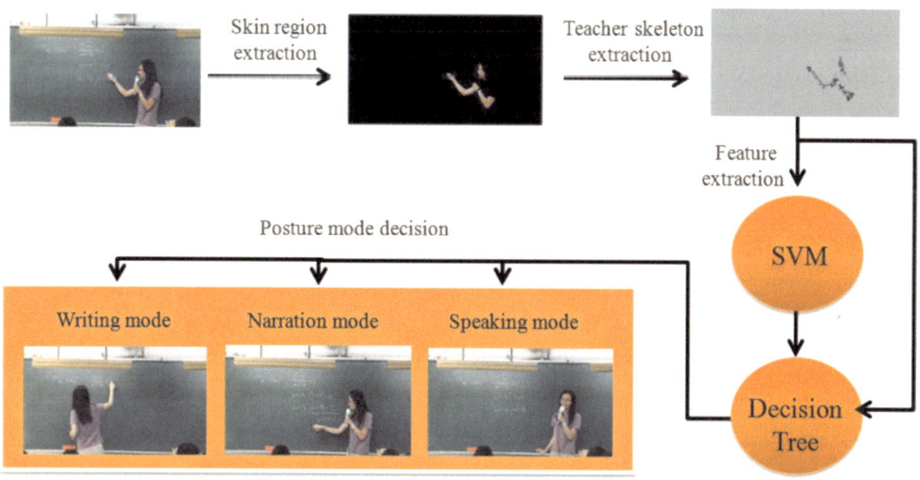


Fig. 17. Analysis of lecturer's posture.

After constructing skeletons, several features derived from the skeleton are used for posture discrimination to estimate the lecturing state (Fig. 17), including the distance between end points of the skeleton, the joint angle of the skeleton, and the orientation of the joint angle.

Then features mentioned above are used to train a SVM classifie, so that the other defined lecturing states can be identified.

### 3.2.2 User-aware aural analysis

Aural information in multimedia contents is also an important stimulus to attract viewers and should be utilized to affect the inserted virtual content. Compared to visual saliency analysis, researches on aural saliency analysis are rare. In (Ma et al., 2005), an aural attention modeling method, taking aural signal, as well as speech and music into account, was proposed to incorporate with the visual attention models for benefiting video summarization. Intuitively, a sound with loud volume or sudden change usually grabs human's attention no matter what they are looking at. If the volume of sound keeps low, even if a special sound effect or music is played, the aural stimulus will easily be ignored or be treated as the environmental noise. In other words, loudness of aural information is a primary and critical factor to influence human perception and can be used to model aural saliency. Similar to the ideas stated in (Ma et al., 2005), the sound is considered as a salient stimulus in terms of aural signal if the following situation occurs: loudness of sound at a specific time unit averages higher than the ones within a historical period which human continued listening so far, especially with peaks.

Based on the observations and assumptions, the aural saliency response $AR(T_h,T)$, is defined at a time unit $T$ and within a duration $T_h$, to quantify the salient strength of the sound. That is,

$$AR(T_h,T) = \frac{E_{avr}(T)}{\hat{E}_{avr}(T_h)} \cdot \frac{E_{peak}(T)}{\hat{E}_{peak}(T_h)}, \tag{2}$$

where $E_{avr}(T)$ and $E_{peak}(T)$ are the *average sound energy* and the *sound energy peak* in the period *T*, respectively.

After analyzing the aural saliency of the video, an *AS feature sequence* is generated which describes the aural saliency response with the range [0, 1] at each time unit *T*, as shown in Fig. 18.

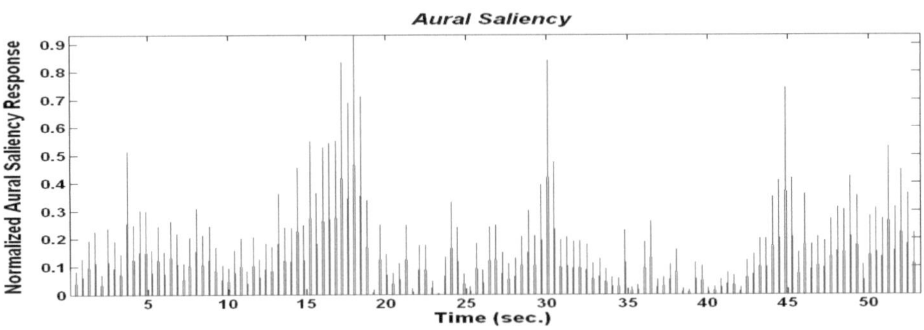


Fig. 18. The normalized aural saliency response of the audio segment.

In (Lin et al., 2010b), besides gesture and posture, making sounds or changing tones is another way that lecturers usually used to grab students' attentions while narrating the lecture content. Therefore, aural information of lecturers is an important cue to estimate the attentions for lecture videos. Since more words are spoken by lecturers within a period may imply more semantics are conveyed or delivered in such duration, the aural attention can be modeled based on the lecturer's speech speed. Generally, each Chinese character corresponds to at least one syllable, so we can analyze the syllables by extracting the envelope (Iked et al., 2005) of audio samples to estimate the lecturer's speech speed as (3).

$$W_{syllable}(t) = \begin{cases} 1 \ , \ if \ \ e(t) > C_w Max\{e(T)\} \\ 0 \ , \ otherwise \end{cases} , \tag{3}$$

where $W_{syllables}(t)$ represents whether it is a syllable ending at time t, $e(t)$ is the envelope size at time t, $T$ is a time period, and $c_w$ is a threshold.

### 3.3 ROI estimation

ROI could be considered as one of the semantic scalability in spatial dimension. The virtual content should be inserted at suitable spatial and temporal location, which is often an area attractive to humans, that is, the ROI region. While considering the human perception and viewing experience, a compelling multimedia content is usually created by artfully manipulating the salience of visual and aural stimulus. Therefore, attractive regions or objects are usually utilized to direct and grab viewers' attention and play an important role in multimedia contents. Algorithms of both patial and temporal ROI estimation will be discussed in this section.

In order to automatically identify such attractive information in visual contents, a great deal of research efforts on estimating and modeling the visual attention in human perception have proliferated for years. The systematic investigations about the relationships between the vision perceived by humans and attentions are provided in (Chun & Wolfe, 2001; Itti & Koch, 2001; Chen et al., 2003; Ma et al., 2005; Liu et al., 2007; Zhang et al., 2009). Itti et al. (2001) presented a frameworkfor a computational and neurobiological understanding of visual attention modeling. Ma et al.(2005) proposed a generic framework of user attention model by fusing several visual and aural features and applied it to video summarization. As for practical applications, numerous visual attention models were explored to adapt images (Chen et al., 2003; Liu et al., 2007) and videos (Cheng et al., 2007) for improving viewing experience on the devices with small displays. Zhang et al. (2009) proposed a distortion-weighing spatiotemporal visual attention model to extract the attention regions from the distorted videos. Instead of directly computing a bounding contour for attractive regions or objects, most approaches construct a saliency map to represent the attention strength or attractiveness of each pixel or image block in visual contents. The value of a saliency map is normalized to [0, 255] and the brighter pixel means higher salience. Several fusion methods for integrating each of the developed visual feature models have been developed and discussed in (Dymitr & Bogdans, 2000). Different fusion methods are designed for different visual attention models and applications. The goal of this module is to be able to provide a flexible mechanism to detect various ROIs as the targets, which the inserted ads can interact with, according to the users' requirements. For this purpose, Chang et al. (2009) utilize linear combinations for fusion, so that users can flexibly set each weight of corresponding feature salience maps. The ROI saliency map, which is denoted as $S_{ROI}$, is computed as

$$S_{ROI} = \sum_{i=1}^{n} w_i \times F_i , \tag{4}$$

where $F_i$ is the $i$-th feature map of that frame, and $w_i$ is the $i$-th weight of the corresponding $i$-th feature map $F_i$ with the constraints of $w_i \geq 0$, and $\sum_{i=1}^{n} w_i = 1$. The ROI can be easily derived by evaluating the center of gravity and the ranging variance on the basis of the saliency map.

A human visual system (HVS) has been introduced for finding ROIs in many researches. In (Lee et al., 2006) and (Kankanhalli & Ramakrishnan, 1998), an HVS was used to improve the quality of a watermarked image. In (Geisler & Perry, 1998), an HVS was used to skip bits without influencing the visual perceptibility of video encoding applications. It also can be applied to build the user-attentive model proposed in (Cox et al., 1997) for deciding the ROI. In (Lin et al., 2010b), the user-attentive model is constructed based on the graylevel and texture features of the image. Regions with mid-gray levels will have a high score for selection because regions with very high or low gray levels are less noticeable to human beings. In addition, the strongly textured segments will have low scores. The distances to the image center are also considered because human beings often focus on the area near the center of an image.

Besides the spatial ROIs, temporal ROIs should also be considered for removing temporal redundancy. The temporal ROI is the video clip which is attractive to humans. The curve derived from the user attention model can be used to determine the temporal ROIs, which have higher values of user attention function.

### 3.4 Interactivity of video coding

Some video coding standards, such as the MPEG-4, allow developing algorithms of audio-visual coding for not only high compression, but also interactivity and universal accessibility of the video content. In addition to the traditional "frame"-based functionalities of the MPEG-1 and MPEG-2 standards, the MPEG-4 video coding algorithm will also support access and manipulation of "objects" within video scenes. The "content-based" video functionality is to encode the sequence in a way that will allow the separate decoding and reconstruction of the objects using the concept of Visual Objects (VOs), and to allow the manipulation of the original scene by simple operations on the bit stream. The properties of objects are described in the bit stream of each object layer. As illustrated in Fig. 19, a video scene can be encoded into several Visual Object Planes (VOPs), wich can be manipulated by simple operations.

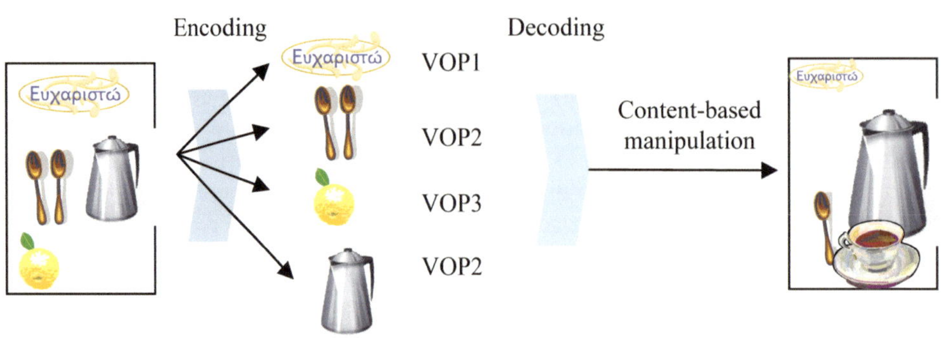


Fig. 19. Composition and manipulation of MPEG-4 videos.

To enhance the interactivity of the video content for user adaptive applications, Chang et al. (2010a, 2010b) presented an interactive virtual content insertion architecture which can insert virtual contents into videos with evolved animations according to predefined behaviors emulating the characteristics of evolutionary biology. The videos are considered not only as carriers of message conveyed by the virtual content but also the environment in which the lifelike virtual contents live. Thus, the inserted virtual content will be affected by the videos to trigger a series of artificial evolutions and evolve its appearances and behaviors while interacting with video contents. By inserting virtual contents into videos through the system, additional entertaining storylines can be easily created and the videos will be turned into visually appealing ones. The above mentioned concept is illustrated in Fig. 20.

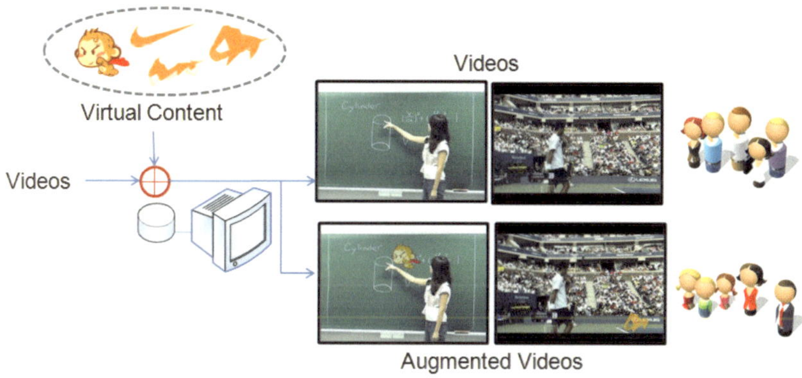


Fig. 20. The augmented videos can be served by using techniques in interactive virtual content insertion to enrich the original videos.

Fig. 21. Snapshots of sample results of the virtual learning e-Partner. The e-Partner can evolve according to the lecturer's teaching behavior in the lecture video and assist in pointing out or enhancing the important lecture content.

In (Chang et al., 2010b), a virtual learning e-partner scheme was presented. The e-partner is assigned the ability to seek for the salient object, which is detected by finding the ROIs based on the algorithms described in Section 3.3, and is simulated to obtain the color and

texture by absorbing the energy of the salient object. At last, the e-partner owns the ability to dance with the music or show the astonished expression while perceiving loud sound. Besides, the e-partner would interact with the moving salient object in an intelligent manner. The e-partner would either tend to imitate the behavior of the moving salient object, or moves to the salient object for further interactions. With the extracted feature space of the lecture videos and the behavior modeling of the e-partner, the proposed system automatically generates impressive animations with an evolution way on a virtual layer. Finally, the virtual layer, in which the e-partner is animated on, is integrated with the video layer. Fig. 21 shows sample results of the virtual learning e-partner, in which the e-partner can evolve according to the lecturer's teaching behavior in the lecture video and assist in pointing out or enhancing the important part of lecture content.
To support the interactivity of video coding, many researches (Naman & Taubman, 2007; Ng et al., 2010; Wang et al., 2005; Tran et al., 2004) propsed content-based scalable coding schemes, most of which applied the concept of VOPs of MPEG-4. Fig. 22 shows a generic architecture of semantic scalable video coding based on the multilayer structure.

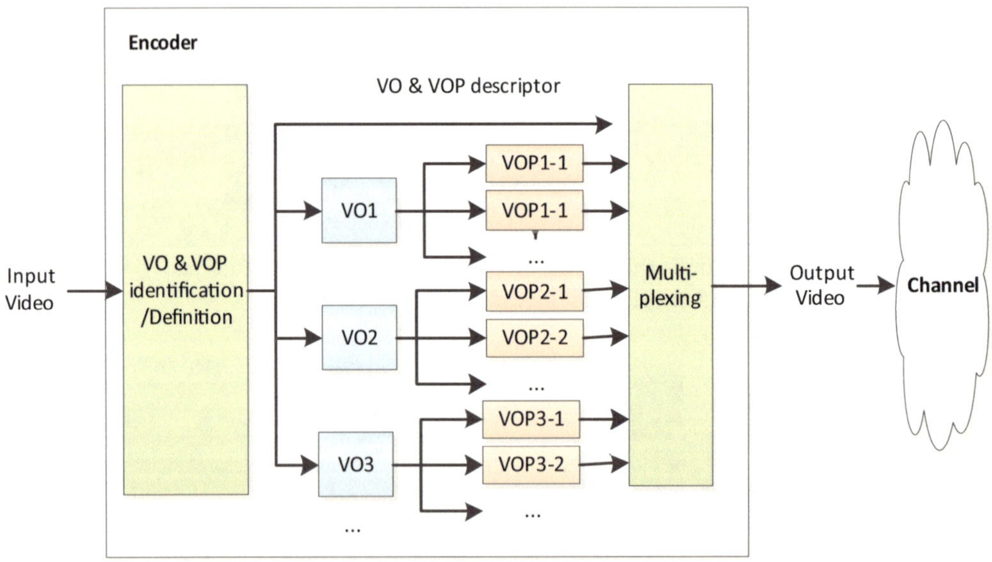


Fig. 22. The architechre of object-based scalable video coding.

## 5. Conclusion

With the rapid development of information technology, access to internet service and use of multimedia has been increasing in recent years. Since the network bandwidth is limited, it is important to investigate approaches to control the bit-rate adaptively for various requirements of different transmission capacity, devices, or user preferences. Moreover, in order to increase the flexitility and interactivitly for accessing and manipulating the video content, semantic-level analysis should be considered to achieve user-aware functionalities. In this chapter, we have introduced theory and practice of user-aware semantic video coding., includng concepts and techniques of salable video coding, transcoding, semantic analysis, and semantic coding. In addition, related methods for user adaptive video coding, containing ROI estimation, virtual content insertion, and object-based video coding, are also discussed.

## 6. Acknowledgement

This work was partially supported by the National Science Council and the Ministry of Education of China under contact no. NSC 99-2511-S-260-001-MY2.

## 7. References

Assuncao, P. A. A. & Ghanbari, M. (Dec. 1998). A Frequency-domain Video Transcoder for Dynamic Bitrate Reduction of MPEG-2 Bit Streams, *IEEE Trans. Circuits Syst. Video Technol.*, Vol. 8, No. 8, pp. 953-967.

Barrau, E. (2002). MPEG Video Transcoding to A Fine-granular Scalable Format, *IEEE ICIP*, pp. I717-720,.

Beauchemin, S. S. & Barron, J. L. (1995). The computation of optical flow, *ACM Computing Surveys*, pp. 433-467.

Bertini, M.; Cucchiara, R. ; Del Bimbo, A. & Prati, A. (June 2006). Semantic Adaptation of Sports Video with User-centred Performance Analysis, *IEEE Transactions on Multimedia,* Vol. 8, No. 3, pp. 433-443.

Bezdek, J. C. ; Tsao, E. C.-L. ; & Pal, N. R. (1992). Fuzzy Kohonen Clustering Networks, *IEEE ICFS 1992*, pp.1035–1043, 1992.

Bonuccelli, M. A.; Lonetti, F. & Martelli, F. (2005). Temporal Transcoding for Mobile Video Communication, *IEEE Proc. Mobile and Ubiquitous Systems: Networking and Services.*

Borenstein, E. & Ullman, S. (December 2008). Combined Top-Down/Bottom-Up Segmentation, *IEEE Transactions on Pattern Analysis and Machine Intelligence*, Vol. 30, No. 12, pp. 2109-2125.

Chang, C. H.; Chiang, M. C. & Wu, J. L. (2009). Evolving virtual contents with interactions in videos, *Proceedings of the ACM International Workshop on Interactive Multimedia for Consumer Electronics (IMCE)*, pp. 97-104.

Chang, C. H.; Hsieh, K. Y.; Chiang, M. C. & Wu, J. L. (Oct. 2010a). Virtual spotlighted advertising for tennis videos, *Journal of Visual Communication and Image Representation (JVCIR)*, Vol. 21, No. 7, pp. 595-612.

Chang, C. H.; Lin, Y. T. & Wu, J. L. (April 2010b). Adaptive video learning by the interactive e-partner, *Proceedings of the 3rd IEEE International Conference on Digital Game and Intelligent Toy Enhanced Learning (DIGITEL'10)*, Kaohsiung, Taiwan, pp. 207-209.

Chen, G.; Lin, S. & Zhang, Y. (2006a). A Fast Coefficients Convertion Method for the Transform Domain MPEG-2 to H.264 Transcoding, *International Conference on Digital Telecommunications (ICDT'06).*

Chen, C. M.; Chen, Y. C. & Lin, C. W. (2006b). Error-Resilience Transcoding Using Content-Aware Intra-Refresh Based on Profit Tracing, *IEEE ISCAS*, pp.5283-5286.

Chen, J.; Pappas, T. N.; Mojsilović A. & Rogowitz, B. E. (October 2005). Adaptive perceptual color-texture image segmentation, *IEEE Transactions on Image Process*, Vol. 14, No. 10, pp.1524-1536.

Chen, L.; Xie, X.; Fan, X.; Ma, X.; Zhang, H. & Zhou, H. (October 2003). A visual attention model for adapting images on small displays, Multimedia Systems, Vol. 9, No. 4, pp. 353-364.

Chen, M. H. & Zakhor, A. (2005). Rate Control for Streaming Video over Wireless, *IEEE Wireless Communications*, Vol. 12, No. 4.

Cheng, W. H.; Chuang, Y. Y .; Lin, Y. T.; Hsieh, C. C.; Fang, S. Y.; Chen, B. Y. & Wu, J. L. (November 2008). Semantic Analysis for Automatic Event Recognition and Segmentation of Wedding Ceremony Videos, *IEEE Transactions on Circuits and Systems for Video Technology*, Vol. 18, No. 11, pp. 1639-1650.

Cheng, W. H.; Wang, C. H. & Wu, J. L. (2007). Video adaptation for small display based on content recomposition, *IEEE Transactions on Circuits and Systems for Video Technology*, vol. 17, no. 1, pp. 43-58.

Chun, M. M. & Wolfe, J. M. (2001). *Visual attention in Blackwell handbook of perception*, USA: Wiley-Blackwell, Ch. 9, pp. 272-310.

Cotsaces, C. ; Nikolaidis, N. & Pitas, I. (2006). Video Shot Detection and Condensed Representation a review, *IEEE Signal Processing Magazine*, Vol. 23, No. 2, pp. 28-37.

Cox, I.; Kilian, J.; Leighton, F. & Shamoon, T. (Dec. 1997). Secure Spectrum Watermarking for Multimedia, IEEE Trans. on Image Processing, Vol. 6, No. 12, pp. 1673-1687.

Dymitr, R. & Bogdan, G. (2000). An overview of classifier fusion methods, Computing and Information Systems, Vol. 7, No. 1, pp. 1-10.

Elsharkawy, M. I.; Aly, & Elemandy, H. (2007). Secure Scalable Video Transcoding over Wireless Network, *IEEE Intelligent Computer Communication and Processing*, pp.287-292.

Geisler, W. S. & Perry, J. S. (1998). A Real-Time Foveated Multiresolution System for Low-Bandwidth Video Communication, *SPIE proceedings: Human Vision and Electronic Imaging* (*VCIP'98*), pp.294-305.

Grois, D.; Kaminsky, E. & Hadar, O. (Oct. 2010). ROI Adaptive Scalable Video Coding for Limited Bandwidth Wireless Networks, *IFIP Wireless Days*.

Ho, W. K.-H.; Cheuk, W.-K. & Lun, D. P.-K. (August 2005). Content-based Scalable H.263 Video Coding for Road Traffic Monitoring, *IEEE transaction on multimedia*, Vol. 7, No. 4, pp. 615-623.

Hung, B. G. & Huang, C. L. (December 2003). Content-Based FGS Coding Mode Determination for Video Streaming Over Wireless Networks, *IEEE Journal on Selected Areas in Communications*, Vol.21, No. 10, pp. 1595-1603.

Ikeda, O. (2005). Estimation of speaking speed for faster face detection in video-footage, *Proceedings of the International Conference on Multimedia and Expo.*, pp. 442-445.

Itti, L. & Koch, C. (March 2001). Computational modelling of visual attention, *Nature reviews*, Neuroscience, Vol. 2, No. 3, pp. 194-203.

Kankanhalli, M. S. & Ramakrishnan, K. R. (1998). Content Based Watermarking of Images, *ACM Multimedia'98*, pp.61-70.

Kim, J. W.; Kwon, G. R.; Kim, N. H.; Morales, A. & Ko, S. J. (Feb. 2006). Efficient Video Transcoding Technique for QoS-Based Home Gateway Service, *IEEE Trans. Consumer Electronics*, Vol. 52, No. 1, pp. 129-137.

Kokkinos, I.; Evangelopoulos, G. & Maragos, P. (January 2009). Texture analysis and segmentation using modulation features, generative models, and weighted curve evolution, *IEEE Transactions on Pattern Analysis and Machine Intelligence* (*T-PAMI*), Vol. 31, No. 1, pp. 142-157.

Koprinska, I. & Carrato, S. (2001). Temporal Video Segmentation: A Survey, *Signal Processing: Image Communication*, Vol. 16, pp. 477-500.

Lee, Y. H.; Kim, H. & Lee, H. K. (March 2006). Robust image watermarking using local invariant features, Optical Engineering, SPIE 2006,Vol. 45, No. 3.

Lei, Z. & Georganas, N. D. (2003). Video Transcoding Gateway for Wireless Video Access, *IEEE CCGEI*, pp.1775-1778.

Li, H.; Tang, J. ; Wu, S.; Zhang, Y. & Lin, S. (Mar. 2010). Automatic detection and analysis of player action in moving background sports video sequences, *IEEE Transactions on Circuits and Systems for Video Technology*, Vol. 20, No. 3, pp.351-364.

Lin, Y. T. ; Wu, J. L. & Kao, Y. F. (March 2006). Geometric-invariant image watermarking by object-oriented embedding, *International Journal of Computer Science and Network Security*, Vol. 6, No. 3A, pp. 169-180.

Lin, Y. T.; Yen, B. J.; Chang, C. C.; Yang, H. F. & Lee, G. C. (Dec. 2009). Indexing and teaching focus mining of lecture videos, *Proceedings of 11th IEEE International Symposium on Multimedia* (*ISM'09*), San Diego, California, USA, pp. 681-686.

Lin, Y. T.; Yen, B. J.; Chang, C. C.; Yang, H. F.; Lee, G. C. & Lin, Y. C. (2010a). Content-based indexing and teaching focus mining for lecture videos, *Interactive Technology and Smart Education*, Vol. 7, No. 3, pp.131-153.

Lin, Y. T.; Tsai, H. Y.; Chang, C. H. & Lee, G. C. (Sept. 2010b). Learning-focused structuring for blackboard lecture videos, *Proceedings of the 4th IEEE International Conference on Semantic Computing* (*ICSC'10*), Carnegie Mellon University, Pittsburgh, PA, USA.

Liu, H.; Jiang, S.; Huang, Q.; Xu, C. & Gao, W. (2007). Region-based visual attention analysis with its application in image browsing on small displays, *Proceedings of the 15th International Conference on Multimedia* (*MULTIMEDIA*), pp. 305-308.

Ma, Y.; Hua, X.; Lu, L. & Zhang, H. (2005). A generic framework of user attention model and its application in video summarization, *IEEE Transactions on Multimedia* (*T-MM*), vol. 7, no. 5, pp. 907-919.

Mezaris, V. ; Kompatsiaris, I. & Strintzis, M. G. (June 2004). Video object segmentation using Bayes-based temporal tracking and trajectory-based region merging, *IEEE Transactions on Circuits and Systems for Video Technology* (*T-CSVT*), Vol. 14, No. 6, pp. 782-795.

Naman, A. T. & Taubman, D. (Jan. 2007). JPEG2000-Based Scalable Interactive Video (JSIV), *IEEE Transactions on Image Processing*, Vol. 6, No. 1, pp. 1-16.

Ng, K. T.; Shing, Q. W.; Chan, C. & Shum, H. Y. (April 2010). Object-Based Coding for Plenoptic Videos, *IEEE Transactions on Circuits and Systems for Video Technology*, Vol. 20, No. 4, pp. 548-562.

Papadopoulos, G. H.; Briassouli, A.; Mezaris, V.; Kompatsiaris, I. & Strintzis, M. G. (Oct. 2009). Statistical motion information extraction and representation for semantic video analysis, *IEEE Transactions on Circuits and Systems for Video Technology*, Vol. 19, No. 10, pp.1513-1528.

Qian, T.; Sun, J.; Xie, R.; Su, P.; Wang, J.& Yang, X. (2005). Scalable Transcoding for Video Transmission over Space-time OFDM Systems," *IEEE SIPS*.

Rabiner, L. R. (February 1989). A tutorial on hidden Markov models and selected applications in speech recognition, *Proceedings of the IEEE*, Vol. 77, No. 2, pp. 257-285.

Seo, K. D.; Lee, S. H.; Kim, J. K. & Koh, J. S. (Nov. 2000). Rate Control Algorithm for Fast Bit-rate Conversion Transcoding, *IEEE Trans. Consumer Electronics*, Vol. 46, No. 4.

Shen, B. (2004). From 8-Tap DCT to 4-Tap Integer-Transform for MPEG to H.264/AVC Transcoding, *IEEE ICIP*.

Shi, J. & Tomasi, C. (1994). Good features to track, *Proceedings of the IEEE Conference on Computer Vision and Pattern Recognition* (*CVPR*), pp. 539-600.

Shu, H. & Chau, L.P. (Feb. 2007). A Resizing Algorithm with Two-stage Realization for DCT-based Transcoding, *IEEE Trans. Circuits and Systems for Video Technology*, Vol. 17, No. 2, pp. 248-253.

Shu, H. & Chau, L.P. (May 2005). Frame-skipping Transcoding with Motion Change H. Shu and L.P. Chau. "Frame Layer Bit Allocation for Video Transcoding, *IEEE International Symposium on Circuits and Systems*, ISCAS2005, Kobe, Japan.

Siu, W.C.; Chan, Y.L. & Fung, K.T. (Oct. 2007). On Transcoding a B-Frame to a P-Frame in the Compressed Domain, *IEEE Trans. Multimedia*, Vol. 9, No. 6, pp. 1093-1101.

Tran. S. M.; Lajos, K.; Balazs, E.; Fazekas, K. & Csaba S. (June 2004). A Survey on The Interactivity Feature of MPEG-4, *46th International Symposium Electronics in Marine*, Zadar, Croatia, pp. 30-38.

Vetro, A. (Jan.-Mar. 2004). MPEG-21 digital item adaptation: enabling universal multimedia access, *IEEE Multimedia*, Vol. 11, No. 1, pp. 84 - 87.

Vetro, A.; Xin, J. & Sun, H. (Aug. 2005). Error Resilience Video Transcoding for Wireless Communications, *IEEE Wireless Communications*, pp. 14-21.

Wang , H.; Schuster, G. M. & Katsaggelos, A. K. (2005). Rate-Distortion Optimal Bit Allocation for Object-Based Video Coding, IEEE Trans. Circuits and System for Video Technology, Vol. 15, No. 9, pp. 1113-1123.

Warabino, T.; Ota, S.; Morikawa, D. & Ohashi, M. (Oct. 2000). Video Transcoding Proxy for 3Gwireless Mobile Internet Access, *IEEE Communication Magazine*, pp. 66-71.

Werner, O. (Feb. 1999). Requantization for Transcoding of MPEG-2 Intrframes, IEEE Trans. Image Processing, Vol. 8, No. 2, pp. 179-191.

Xu, Z.; Chen, H.; Zhu, S. C. & Luo, J. (June 2008). A Hierarchical Compositional Model for Face Representation and Sketching, *IEEE Transactions on Pattern Analysis and Machine Intelligence*, Vol. 30, No. 6, pp. 955-969.

Yuan, J. ; Wang, H. ; Xiao, L. ; Zheng, W.; Lin, J., Li, F. & Zhang, B. (2007). A Formal Study of Shot Boundary Detection, *IEEE Trans. on Circuits and Systems for Video Technology*, Vol. 17, No. 2, pp.168-186.

Zhang, H.; Tian, X. & Chen, Y. (2009). A distortion-weighing spatiotemporal visual attention model for video analysis, *Proceedings of the International Congress on Image and Signal Processing*, pp.1-4.

Zhang, L. (Oct. 1998). Automatic adaptation of a face model using action units for semantic coding of videophone sequences, *IEEE Transactions on Circuits and Systems for Video Technology*, Vol. 8, No. 6, pp. 781-795.